CORPUS RUBENIANUM
LUDWIG BURCHARD

PART XXII (2)
ARCHITECTURE AND SCULPTURE

RUBENS'S HOUSE

IN TWO VOLUMES

I · TEXT

II · APPENDICES & ILLUSTRATIONS

CORPUS RUBENIANUM
LUDWIG BURCHARD

AN ILLUSTRATED CATALOGUE RAISONNÉ
OF THE WORK OF PETER PAUL RUBENS
BASED ON THE MATERIAL ASSEMBLED
BY LUDWIG BURCHARD (1886–1960)
IN TWENTY-NINE PARTS

SPONSORED BY THE CITY OF ANTWERP AND THE RUBENIANUM FUND
AND EDITED BY THE CENTRUM RUBENIANUM

Editorial Board
N. BÜTTNER – F. HEALY – K. JONCKHEERE – G. MARTIN
E. MCGRATH – L. NIJKAMP – N. DE POORTER – B. SCHEPERS
I. VAN TICHELEN – B. VANOPPEN – H. VLIEGHE – J. WOOD

Research Staff
B. SCHEPERS – B. VANOPPEN – I. VAN TICHELEN

UNDER THE PATRONAGE OF HSH PRINCE HANS-ADAM II VON UND ZU LIECHTENSTEIN
AND THE INTERNATIONAL UNION OF ACADEMIES (UAI)

RUBENS

ARCHITECTURE AND SCULPTURE

RUBENS'S HOUSE

BY
NORA DE POORTER AND FRANS BAUDOUIN

VOLUME ONE
TEXT

HARVEY MILLER PUBLISHERS

HARVEY MILLER PUBLISHERS
An Imprint of Brepols Publishers
London / Turnhout

Translated from the Dutch by Jantien Black
and
Lee Preedy (Chapters V–VIII)

Edited by Arnout Balis, Brecht Vanoppen, Isabelle Van Tichelen, Marieke D'Hooghe, Joannes van den Maagdenberg and Valerie Herremans (Images)
© 2022 Centrum Rubenianum

British Library Cataloguing in Publication Data
A catalogue record for this book is available from the British Library
ISBN (set) 978-1-912554-64-5
ISBN (volume 1) 978-1-912554-90-4
ISBN (volume 2) 978-1-912554-91-1
D/2022/0095/133

All rights reserved.
No part of this publication may be reproduced,
stored in a retrieval system, or transmitted in any form by
any means, electronic, mechanical, photocopying, recording, or
otherwise, without the prior permission of Harvey Miller Publishers.

Printed in the EU on acid-free paper.

CONTENTS

VOLUME ONE

Introduction   13-21

Chapter I: A Historical Sketch of the Property on the Wapper:
From *Raamveld* to Rubens's House
    A. The Raamhof and Bleaching Field on the Wapper   23
    B. The Thys Family and the Sale of the Parcel to Rubens   31
    C. The Houses on the Parcel on the Wapper and the
       Composition of the Purchased '*Huysinge*'   40
    D. Subsequent Extension of the Property: The Purchase of a
       Group of Houses Adjacent to Rubens's Plot   45

Chapter II: Eye Witnesses to the House:
Written and Pictorial References   49
    A. The House in the Time of Rubens and his Family: History
       and Written Sources (1611–1648)   49
    B. The House in the Time of Rubens and his Family:
       Contemporary Depictions (up to c. 1645)   58
    C. Later Residents: the Cavendishes, the Van Eyckes and Hillewerve   66
    D. Aftermath (1695–1947): Residents after Hendrik Hillewerve;
       Mols's Drawing, Destruction, Nostalgia and Reconstruction   75

Chapter III: The House in the Time of Hendrik Hillewerve:
A Closer Look at Jacob Harrewijn's Prints
    A. The Art-loving Canon   87
    B. The Two Prints by Jacob Harrewijn: General Remarks   89
    C. The Subjects of the Two Prints: A Closer Look   93
    D. The Components of the Property   97
    E. Information on the Interior of the House in the Time of Hillewerve   110
    F. The Courtyard in the Time of Hillewerve   113

Chapter IV: Construction and Remodelling:
Evidence for a Chronology
    A. Scope of Construction and Remodelling: The Timing   117
    B. Location of the Workshop: First Commissions in Antwerp
       (1609–c. 1617)   128

CONTENTS

Chapter V: The Exterior of the Studio Wing or 'Italian' Wing ... 137
    A. General Plan and Roofing of the 'Italian' or Studio Wing ... 138
    B. The North Façade ... 139
    C. The Italianate East Façade Next to the Entrance
       (Facing the Courtyard) ... 151
    D. The East Façade on the Garden Side ... 152
    E. The West or Street Façade ... 156
    F. The Problematic South Façade: the South Side of the Workshop ... 158
    G. The Idealised Street and South Façades: the House in the
       Background of *Hélène Fourment au Carrosse* ... 159
    H. The Italianate Character of the Studio Wing ... 161

Chapter VI: The 'Italian' Wing: The Wall Paintings
    A. Painted or 'Real': A Problematic Matter ... 167
    B. Technique, Execution and Date ... 173
    C. In *Trompe-l'oeil*: A Frieze of Bas-Reliefs and a Painting on Canvas ... 175
    D. The Short East-Facing Wall in the Courtyard: a Combination
       of *Trompe-l'oeil* and Reality ... 182
    E. Painted Façades in Italy and Elsewhere ... 189
    F. Painted Interiors ... 199

Chapter VII: The Interior of the 'Italian Wing' / the 'Schilderhuis' ... 201
    A. The West Side of the Studio Wing ... 201
    B. The Large Workshop on the Ground Floor ... 204
    C. The Upstairs Studio (or So-called 'Pupils' Studio') ... 211
    D. The Two Workshops: Purpose and Names ... 219
    E. Communication Between the Two Workshops: A Windlass? ... 222
    F. Not Located: 'Elegantissimum Museum',
       'Cantoor' and 'Studiolo Secreto' (Private Studio or Study?) ... 225

Chapter VIII: The East or Garden Wing with the 'Antiquarium'
(The Roman Pantheon): The Circular Structures ... 229
    A. An Art Gallery and a Bedroom (?) ... 230
    B. The 'Antiquarium' or 'Pantheon' (also Called 'The Museum') ... 232
    C. Rubens's Two Domed Rooms: Inspiration and Imitation ... 244

Chapter IX: The Portico ... 249
    A. The Portico in its Present State ... 250
    B. Depictions of the Portico and Related Architecture
       (1611–1621) and Pointers Towards Dating ... 268

C. Lost Elements of the Portico not Reconstructed: The Two-Headed Eagle, the Sphere and the Busts	274
D. The Two Statues on Top of the Portico: Lost and Reconstructed	278
E. The Portico in the Context of Italian Examples and Architectural Theory	285

Chapter X: The Garden Pavilion — 295
A. The Pavilion in its Present State	296
B. Depictions of Rubens's Garden Pavilion and Variants	299
C. Sculpture in the Garden Pavilion	308
D. The *Serliana*	316

Chapter XI: Sculpture and Sculptors
A. Sculptural Decoration	321
B. The Sculptors	325

Catalogue Raisonné
A. The Façades of the South Wing (Studio): Nos 1–19a

No. 1. Four Busts in Niches, Including a Faun: Sculptures	339
No. 2. Bust in a Niche with a Scallop, Flanked by Cornucopias: Sculpture or Mural Painting	340
No. 3. Four Unidentified Herm Busts: Sculpture or Mural Painting	341
No. 4. Six Herms: Mural Painting or Relief	342
No. 5. Hermes Belvedere: Mural Painting or Relief	343
No. 6. Flora Farnese: Mural Painting or Relief	344
No. 7. Window Surround: Architecture	345
No. 8. A Chariot Race (The Lowering of the Cloth): Mural Painting	347
No. 9. The Triumph of Apollo: Mural Painting	348
No. 10. The Sacrifice of an Ox: Mural Painting	350
No. 11. The Sacrifice of Iphigenia: Mural Painting	355
No. 12. Alexander with the Thunderbolt: Mural Painting	359
No. 13. The Calumny of Apelles: Mural Painting	362
No. 14. Zeuxis and the Maidens of Croton: Mural Painting	370
No. 15. The Drunken Hercules: Mural Painting	373
No. 16. Youthful Hero with a Lance and Chariot: Mural Painting	375
No. 17. Loggia with a Figure and Animals: Mural Painting	376
No. 18. Andromeda Liberated by Perseus: Mural Painting	377
No. 19. Staircase: Joinery	387

CONTENTS

- B. Interior: Nos 20–23
  - No. 20. The 'Antiquarium': Architecture — 389
  - No. 21. The Cupola of the 'Antiquarium': Architecture — 391
  - No. 22. The North Wall of the 'Antiquarium': Architecture — 392
  - No. 23. Head of Hercules under a Scallop and Garlands: Sculpture / Architectural Sculpture — 393
- C. Portico: Nos 24–33
  - No. 24. Portico: Architecture — 395
  - No. 25. Keystone with the Head of Medusa and a Thunderbolt: Architectural-Sculptural Element — 398
  - No. 26. Dolphins: Relief — 400
  - No. 27. Pediment with a Niche, Flanked by Two Eagles Holding a Fruit Garland: Relief — 401
  - No. 28. Ram's Heads Ending in a Volute and a Snake's Head: Relief — 402
  - No. 29. *Bucrania*: Sculpture / High Relief — 404
  - No. 30. Male Satyr Facing Right: Relief — 405
  - No. 31. Female Satyr Seen from Behind, Facing Left: Relief — 405
  - No. 32. Male Satyr Facing Left: Relief — 407
  - No. 33. Female Satyr Facing Left: Relief — 407
- D. Garden Pavilion and Garden: Nos 34–41
  - No. 34. Garden Pavilion: Architecture — 408
  - No. 35. Caryatids Left and Right (Sphinxes?): Sculptures — 409
  - No. 36. Youth with a Cornucopia (Genius Loci?): Statue — 410
  - No. 37. Venus (and Cupid): Statue — 414
  - No. 38. Bacchus: Statue — 417
  - No. 39. Bust of Hercules: sculpture — 420
  - No. 40. Hercules: Statue — 421
  - No. 41. Fountain with a Putto (Cupid) on a Dolphin: Sculpture — 425
- E. Rejected Attributions: Nos R1–R4
  - No. R1. Statue of Pictura (?): Statue Known as Mercury — 428
  - No. R2. Minerva: Statue — 430
  - No. R3. Bundle of Attributes: Painted or Relief — 431
  - No. R4. Ceres: Statue — 432

VOLUME TWO

Appendices
    I: Documents   5
    II: Timeline   32
    III: Images of Rubens's House: Fact and Fiction   42

List of Text Illustrations   71

List of Figures   75

Figures   83

Bibliography
    Literature   201
    Exhibitions   226

Explanations   227

Indexes
    I: Collections   229
    II: Subjects   231
    III: Other Works by Rubens Mentioned in the Text   236
    IV: Names and Places   242

Sources of Photographs   267

The scholarly opinions expressed in this publication are based upon physical inspection of the works when possible, current research, and circumstances known to the author(s) at this time. The published text is not a warranty of any kind of the authenticity, condition, or provenance of works treated or of the comprehensiveness of the artist's oeuvre. It should not be relied upon by any person, including but not limited to owners or others, for any purpose, including but not limited to bringing legal action or inquiry. Neither the Centrum Rubenianum, its publisher Brepols, nor any of its directors, board members, editors, authors, researchers, advisors, contractors, employees, or representatives shall have any liability whatsoever toward anyone as a result of the assertions made in the volume.
The Centrum Rubenianum and/or its authors may revise its opinions and assertions at a future date for reasons that may include, but are not limited to, new scholarship or discoveries arising or inspections taking place after the date of publication. Readers having new information about the content presented in this volume may make inquiry to the Centrum Rubenianum board. The Centrum Rubenianum will respond, at its absolute discretion, to those with sufficient basis for inquiry.

Introduction

The house that Rubens built a few years after his return from Italy, and where he lived till the end of his life, was essentially lost in the course of the substantial alterations carried out over the years. When it came to be reconstructed in 1939–1946 a great many unresolved questions had to be tackled, though eventually the difficult project was concluded successfully, even if the result in many ways departs from what is historically correct.

Undoubtedly the house, which included not only the family's living quarters and Rubens's much-admired collection, but also, and famously, contained his workshop or studio, was built or adapted to the master's own ideas. So, although almost nothing survives of Rubens's designs, the house must be considered part of Rubens's oeuvre, and cannot be omitted from the *Corpus Rubenianum Ludwig Burchard* (hereafter *CRLB*).

The present book is the result of a quest to establish as much as can be learned about the original appearance of this unique building, and about the uses and functions of its various rooms. It gathers together and analyses the architectural elements that have been preserved, the relevant archaeological information and all written and visual sources.

Part XXII and its sub-parts: a long history

Like many other volumes of the *CRLB* the present book has a history going back decades. Perhaps it even has the longest history of all: already in the 1960s Frans Baudouin, then director of the *CRLB* project (together with Roger-A. d'Hulst) decided to take on the wide-ranging Part XXII that deals with Rubens's involvement in architecture and sculpture ('Palazzi di Genova', 'Rubens's House', 'Jesuit Church', 'Architectural Sculpture' and 'Sculpture and Design for Decorative Arts'). Frans Baudouin was certainly the right person for the task. Not only did the subject fit in with his interests and studies in the fields of architecture and sculpture, but he was for 31 years (1950–1981) the director of the Rubens House, the restored and reconstructed house of the master, one of the five topics of Part XXII.

However, combining a busy professional career with the writing this *CRLB* Part did not prove to be feasible. Although Baudouin undertook many studies, published articles and gave lectures related to the themes of his *CRLB* volume over the next years, this initial plan could not be carried out within a reasonable timescale. It was necessary to abandon the idea that the entire range of complex material that made up Part XXII would be dealt with by a single author.

INTRODUCTION

The first sub-part that was re-assigned and entrusted to another author dealt with a 'special case': the drawings and engravings representing Genoese Palazzi, which were published under the auspices of Rubens in 1622, but were not designed by him. This sub-part, written by Herbert W. Roth, appeared in 2002 as XXII.1 with the title *Palazzi di Genova: Architectural Drawings and Engravings*.

This left Frans Baudouin with an enormous and difficult task: four of the five sub-parts (see above). He still saw these themes as a whole and wrote an essay as a first chapter to the intended book, in which he examined the phenomenon of the painter-architect, under the title *Peter Paul Rubens and the Notion 'Painter-Architect'*. This text he presented as a lecture at a symposium about the reception of Rubens's *Palazzi di Genova*, organised in Antwerp on the initiative of Piet Lombaerde, in 2001; it was published a year later in the conference proceedings (Baudouin, *Painter-Architect*, 2002). Given its intention and scope, this essay has not been taken over for any of the sub-parts of the CRLB.

It had never been planned that I would be the co-author of the present book, but fate decided otherwise. When Frans Baudouin died unexpectedly on 1 January 2005, the manuscript and his notes remained in his room at the Rubenianum – the room to which he came almost daily to work on his CRLB volume after his retirement. As Director of the Rubenianum and member of the Editorial Board of the CRLB, I thereupon took charge of the unfinished material. This consisted of fifteen very detailed essays. More or less finished were the chapters that Frans Baudouin had foreseen for sub-parts (2) and (3), i.e. Rubens's House and the Jesuit Church. Sub-part (4), on 'architectural sculpture', was only partly written with a half-finished overview of Rubens's designs for altar frames. The last sub-part (Sculpture) was entirely missing. And, of course, not only was the manuscript unfinished, but there had been no opportunity for any instruction or comment about its completion.

I then decided that I would take on, as editor, the sections on the two buildings in Antwerp, Rubens's House and the Jesuit Church. This plan turned out to be overambitious, and was again altered: fortunately, Ria Fabri and Piet Lombaerde were prepared to join forces and take over the section on the church. In greatly modified form, adapted to their own insights – including an investigation of the roles of Franciscus Aguilonius and Pieter Huyssens – the book was published in 2018 as Part XXII.3 under the title *The Jesuit Church of Antwerp*.

Solutions could also be found for the last two sub-parts (4 and 5). *Architectural Sculpture*, with as subject Rubens's designs for altars and sepulchral monuments, for which Frans Baudouin had produced only a few chapters, could be entrusted to Valerie Herremans, whose doctoral research had been devoted to Southern Netherlandish altar architecture (1585–1685); it

INTRODUCTION

was to appear, completely recast and rewritten, in 2019 as Part XXII.4. The final volume (*Sculpture*), taken on by Ben van Beneden, still awaits completion.

Sub-part 2: Rubens's House

It soon became clear that the Baudouin manuscript containing the chapters on Rubens's house was not only unfinished but insufficient in other ways. The manuscript consisted of six extensive essays, each with the character of an advanced 'first draft' rather than a fully finished text. Here and there were blank passages (marked 'to be completed'). The many footnotes were sometimes not filled in and, as far as the references to literature were concerned, often indicated by rather cryptic abbreviations. Above all, and crucially, there was no indication of a catalogue. In short, the manuscript was nowhere near a usable text for publication in the *CRLB*, and editorial work alone would certainly not have sufficed to remedy the situation.

Accordingly, I have not only supplemented the text as bequeathed by Frans Baudouin with a catalogue that corresponds as far as possible to the usual format of the *CRLB* (see below). I have also modified the texts of the chapters, restructuring them fundamentally and making extensive additions. Nevertheless, a considerable part of the text is still based on the wealth of data collected by Baudouin, on his observations and on his knowledge of architectural history. Many passages from Baudouin's text were retained (adapted and sometimes slightly altered or corrected as required), so that, in contrast to the situation with sub-parts 3 and 4, it was appropriate to retain his name as an author.

One of the circumstances that necessitated revision to the chapters was the fact that a great deal of new information on the house that has come to light since 2005 had to be added to and integrated in the existing texts. It also meant that many passages had to be rewritten when quite a number of hypotheses or conclusions about the house or its decoration proved no longer tenable. The subject-matter was reorganised in such a way that the original six chapters were expanded to eleven.

As regards the visual sources, the image of the garden pavilion in the Berlin double portrait (Fig. 22) had not been considered, as well as the *View of the Courtyard of Rubens's House* in Aylesbury (Fig. 16) that was brought to attention only in 2009; in addition, an archival source, in the form of a statement by Rubens himself about the making of the roof of his house had been discovered (Appendix I.14).

In terms of publications, important new material had also to be added. Apart from the older literature that appeared before or on the occasion of the restoration (the contributions by Max Rooses, Arie Delen, Paul Buschman, Frederik Clijmans and Floris Prims), the most important publications that Baudouin had included in his text were the article by Elizabeth McGrath on the frieze scenes (McGrath, *Rubens's House*, 1976–1978), the richly documented book on the houses of Rubens and Jordaens by Rutger Tijs (Tijs, *Rubens and Jordaens*, 1984), and the studies by Jeffrey Muller on the 'antiquarium' (Muller, *Rubens's Museum*, 1977), and on the collection that Rubens installed in his house (Muller, *Collector*, 1989).

In the course of the last few decades, however, this literature has been considerably supplemented. In an exhibition held in the Rubens House in 2011, *Palazzo Rubens, The Master as Architect*, Barbara Uppenkamp and Ben van Beneden focused on the Italian sources for the house, and the symbolism that can be detected in the architectural and decorative elements. Ulrich Heinen provided additional data on one of the frieze scenes (Heinen, *Immolatio Boum*, 2010).

In recent decades too, there has been renewed interest in the history of the house and its restoration, which resulted in articles by Thomas Van Driessche, and two important unpublished studies: the excellent work by Annika Devroe (Devroe, *Rubens' House*, 2008) and later the further extended report by Petra Maclot (Maclot, *Rubenssite*, 2016), describing the house in its surroundings, the so-called Rubens Site (Kolveniershof, Rubenianum and Rubenshuis). In addition, following the restoration of the portico and the garden pavilion (completed in 2019), several articles have been written, by Lode De Clercq among others, about the archaeological and material-technical aspects of these important survivals from the building.

The Chapters

It is perhaps not superfluous to give a 'road map' of the eleven chapters, to help readers find their bearings in this very extensive subject-matter.

Chapter I provides a historical sketch of the property on the Wapper, a plot of land in the centre of Antwerp, up to the point of its purchase by Rubens in 1610; this resolves, among other things, the question of why the artist chose this plot of land in the first place. The two extensive contracts that were drawn up at the time of the sale have been preserved and are reviewed in close detail.

Chapter II deals with the sources that teach us something about the vanished house, both the written evidence and the images made in Rubens's time and in later centuries. It examines what we learn from the eyewitnesses: family members, visitors to the house, colleagues and clients, and, more extensively,

INTRODUCTION

from the later occupants of the house. This information is, however, sparse and fragmentary. Apart from two (more or less realistic) depictions by Rubens himself in his paintings, the most important visual sources are the drawings by Willem Panneels (1620s), the two prints by Jacob Harrewijn that Hendrik Hillewerve had made (1684 and 1692), and the plan drawn by François Mols (1770s). The chapter also briefly touches on the role the house played in the romantic imagination of the nineteenth century, before concluding with a few words devoted to the restoration and reconstruction.

It is from the time of one of the house's later residents, Canon Hendrik Hillewerve, that the two crucial visual documents date, to which Chapter III is entirely devoted: the prints executed in 1684 and 1692 by Jacob Harrewijn after drawings by Jacques van Croes. When studied critically, these almost incredibly detailed prints, of which countless details are reproduced in the book, allow us to arrive at a more or less accurate picture of the splendour of Rubens's home, and the different components of the property.

Chapter IV brings together all the relevant information to answer two questions relating to chronological data on the genesis of the house. The first concerns the building or rebuilding work that Rubens undertook: what did it consist of, and especially what can we learn about the dating and order in which the various components were created? A second topic is that of where Rubens may have had his studio before the new one on the Wapper was finished, and when he started using this new studio.

Chapters V to VII deal with the 'Italian' wing or south wing in which the studios were housed. Chapter V gives a detailed description of the exterior of that wing with its Italian-inspired elements, while the following chapter examines an important aspect of it: the mural paintings. Considered here is the phenomenon of *trompe-l'oeil* used by Rubens in his façades in several ways. Painted and not 'real' are a part of the architectural and decorative details, a frieze with panels related to Roman reliefs and Greek painting, a loggia and a canvas with *Andromeda Liberated by Perseus*. Finally, a word is said about the tradition of painted façades in Italian cities and elsewhere.

With Chapter VII we turn to what is known about the interior of the wing that housed the studio, or rather the studios, one on the ground floor and one above it. Attention is paid to the elements in the architecture that are related to Rubens's studio practice: the dimensions required to allow for the production of works of very large format, and the way in which Rubens planned the incidence of daylight in the workspaces (zenithal light in the upper studio, and probably on the ground floor, very unusually, also light from the sunny south side). Two problematic issues relating to the connection between the two studios had to remain unanswered: the location of the upper flights of the staircase, and the possible use of a windlass still present in the attic. Finally, this

INTRODUCTION

chapter also investigates a number of rooms mentioned in the written sources, including the 'cantoor' and 'studiolo secreto', the location of which cannot be determined.

Chapter VIII is devoted to a special construction housed in the east or garden façade: the so-called 'antiquarium', where Rubens displayed his collection of antique sculpture. As evidenced by both written and pictorial sources, this room was semicircular and had a dome with an *oculus,* inspired by the Roman Pantheon.

Two parts of the house that deserve special attention are the portico between the courtyard and the garden and the garden pavilion with its statues. These authentic and still preserved constructions are described in detail in Chapter IX and Chapter X respectively. The dating and history, the sources of inspiration and the iconographic interpretations of the details are discussed.

Finally, the question remains as to who might have assisted Rubens with the sculpted decoration of his house. Very little can be determined with certainty. Chapter XI gives a brief overview of the sculptors who worked in Rubens's immediate circle and who may have had a contribution. Most attention is paid to Hans van Mildert, Lucas Faydherbe and Artus Quellinus I.

The Catalogue

It is necessary to give a word of explanation about the Catalogue, which differs in some respects from what is usual in the *CRLB*. The material to be treated consists of a house, or rather a complex of wings and other parts, most of which have disappeared; only the portico and the garden pavilion with three statues have been preserved. All the rest is known only from seventeenth-century visual material.

It has already been mentioned that Frans Baudouin did not include a catalogue in his manuscript. It can be added that in Ludwig Burchard's files too, no information at all was available to provide help in the compilation of a catalogue.

Of course, the catalogue is not intended to provide an overview of all parts of the house, but rather of those parts or details that can be assumed to have been designed by Rubens. Of Rubens's designs themselves – drawings or oil sketches? – almost nothing survives. There are only two drawings that can be associated with the frieze with scenes under the upper windows of the studio façades (Nos 10a, 13a), and two very vague chalk drawings with architectural details (Nos 7a, 13b). This means that the artist's own work could not be taken as a guide for the compilation of the catalogue, as was possible for the other volume that deals with a building: XXII.3 (*The Jesuit Church*).

Only certain catalogue numbers in the present book correspond more or less to typical entries for the *CRLB*, with 'independent' and clearly defined items. such as paintings, drawings, tapestries or sculptures. The rectangular scenes with historical subjects that decorated the façades fit into this system, as well as a number of statues and busts that have been partially preserved.

A separate solution was found for the architectural components that are discussed in detail within the relevant chapter: the 'antiquarium', the portico and the garden pavilion. In addition to these references in the chapters (VIII, IX and X), they are each given a summary entry in the catalogue with the technical data, the literature, the visual sources and also a list of variants inspired by them (Nos 20, 24 and 34).

For the rest, there is no obvious system, and I decided to use a somewhat artificial (and arbitrary) starting point for some ten catalogue numbers. These describe decorative details that are part of the portico and the garden pavilion, or could be seen in images of the lost façades. The architectural components such as pediments, *serlianas*, quoins, and certain types of arches were not chosen, nor were decorative elements such as garlands, vases, and braziers – these components are discussed in the various chapters. It seemed more interesting to choose a different starting point for a selection of details. A separate number in the catalogue was given to the details representing a living creature, human or animal (or part thereof). In this way, more could be said, with references to Rubens's oeuvre, about the herms, caryatids, satyrs, rams, eagles, dolphins, and *bucrania*, as well as the head of Medusa.

The usual rubrics of the *CRLB* catalogue are not all very well adapted to the subject matter of the present book. Because so much is known only from illustrations – especially from the two Harrewijn prints, and to a lesser extent from the Aylesbury painting – reference had to be made to these sources. These images, however, do not fully correspond to what in the *CRLB* are called 'copies', and a new rubric was introduced: 'Visual Source(s)', which thus – except, of course, in the case of elements still extant – indicates what the description in the entry is based on. The heading 'Copy' was retained but, then, only for the 'real' contemporary copies (a chalk drawing by Anthony Van Dyck, and the drawings by Willem Panneels), and in addition for yet another unusual feature: the plaster casts, old as well as modern, made of a number of sculptural items.

Moreover, two of the usual rubrics of the catalogue proved difficult to accommodate. First, as far as dating is concerned, for all the catalogue entries, without exception, only an approximate date could be given. More information can be found in the chapters where the issue is discussed, and this comment is not repeated in the catalogue. Then there is the question of material and dimensions. As to the former, in a number of cases we are in the dark because it is not always possible to tell whether a lost decorative detail was solid or painted. The approximate dimensions given for the details of the lost façades are the result of calculations I have made, combining the information in the Harrewijn prints with the reconstructed façades (which have exactly the same dimensions as the original ones).

The Appendices

As explained above, essential to understanding the structure and the special features of the present book, is the fact that a large part of Rubens's house has been preserved only partially. An important aspect of this study is therefore a search for the appearance of the lost parts of the house. But along with the appearance, the function of the many rooms, domestic and professional, is an intriguing question. The lack of 'solid ground' in this respect explains why, more than in other *CRLB* volumes, the emphasis is placed on the available source material. Rather than mentioning these sources, both written and visual, in the footnotes, scattered over the various chapters, I have brought them together systematically and listed them in the Appendices.

All written sources that tell us something about the house, both archival and literary texts, can be found in the extensive 'Documents' section (as Appendix I). The full text is given or an excerpt, depending on the relative importance. In a number of cases, a translation has been added to the text. These documents are ordered by the date or presumed date of the document itself, which does not always coincide with the date of the fact relevant to the house. The best-known example of this is Otto Sperling's account of the visit he made to Rubens's house in 1621, written up many decades later. To counter this problem, and at the same time to place the documentation in a broader chronological framework, I have added a 'Timeline' as Appendix II, which also provides other information relevant to the house and its occupants, now of course in an entirely chronological order.

Finally, Appendix III, entitled 'Images of Rubens's house: fantasy and reality', contains information about the visual sources – both the 'realistic' and the more imaginative ones. It lists paintings, prints, a few drawings and a selection of early photographs, each illustrated, and with technical data and the essential literature.

Acknowledgements

My thanks go in the first place to my colleagues at the Rubenianum for their help in so many different ways, and for their encouragement over all these years: Inez Bricteux, Lieneke Nijkamp, Martine van de Poel, Ute Staes, Marc Vandenven, the late Carl van de Velde, Nelly Verreydt, Hans Vlieghe and Bert Watteeuw; to Simon Zakowski, who, with great care, converted Frans Baudouin's handwritten chapters into a digital text; and, of course, to Viviane Verbraeken, for her help in tracking down in the Rubenianum the information needed for the completion of the bibliographic references.

I am much indebted to numerous colleagues there and elsewhere who provided information: Peter Black, Helena Bussers, Nils Büttner, Fiona Healy, Nico van Hout, Dirk Imhof, Koenraad Jonckheere, Krista de Jonge, the late Jeanine De Landtsheer, Hannelore Magnus, Madeleine Manderyck, Ingrid Moortgat, Bert Schepers, Joris Snaet, Alfons Tijs, Clara Vanderhenst and Christopher White. A word of special thanks goes to Elizabeth McGrath, for help in various ways; to Lode De Clercq, who researched the material of the plaster busts and shared his information on the statues; and to Martine Maris, who provided information on the objects as well as the documents in the collection and the archive of the Rubenshuis. Most encouraging were Ria Fabri and Piet Lombaerde, with their kind support, friendly conversations and advice on countless 'architectural' questions.

It goes without saying that this list of acknowledgements is incomplete, as I do not know the colleagues who were of assistance to the late Frans Baudouin during the many years he worked on his manuscript.

It has been a pleasure to work with Jantien Black and Lee Preedy, patient and conscientious translators as well as interested and attentive readers.

I owe a great debt to our deeply regretted colleague Arnout Balis for sharing his exhaustive knowledge of Rubensian matters, for reading the manuscript thoroughly, and improving it with many creative suggestions. One could not wish for a better *CRLB* editor.

Last, but not least, I would like to express my gratitude to the five colleagues who took on the final editorial tasks of this 'difficult' book with its intricate structure. Listed in chronological order, I thank: Marieke D'Hooghe, who was my first reader, and implemented the *CRLB* rules in the chapters; Brecht Vanoppen, who made many helpful suggestions for the text, as well as taking on the task of tracing and ordering the illustrations, and designing a well-considered layout for the illustrations/plates; Isabelle Van Tichelen, who devoted great care and a lot of energy to the final editing; and Valerie Herremans, who made additions to the layout and tracked down missing illustrations. They were assisted by Joannes van den Maagdenberg (for the Documents) and Helena Bussers (with proofreading).

Nora De Poorter

Chapter I
A Historical Sketch of the Property on the Wapper: From *Raamveld* to Rubens's House

A. The Raamhof and Bleaching Field on the Wapper

On 3 October 1609 Peter Paul Rubens married Isabella Brant (1591–1626). He was 32 years old and it was less than one year since he had returned from Italy. The couple temporarily moved in with Isabella's parents, the lawyer and municipal secretary Jan Brant and Clara de Moy, in their spacious house on the Sint-Michielsstraat (now Kloosterstraat), opposite St Michael's Abbey.[1] In his short *Vita Petri Pauli Rubenii*, Rubens's nephew Philip writes that he stayed there for several years ('aliquot annos'; see Appendix I.26). This is confirmed by the funeral roll of Jan Moretus I, who died on 22 September 1610: the guest list names 'Peeter Rubbens, painter', living in the Sint-Michielsstraat, with his name immediately following that of his father-in-law.[2]

Meanwhile Rubens was no doubt on the lookout for a property that would provide a suitable home for his family and large enough to accommodate a workshop where he could paint very large panels and canvases. He settled on a sizeable, mainly unbuilt parcel of land. It was then a bleaching green, but it had for a long time before been a yard used in the manufacture of woollen cloth (a *raamveld* or *raamhof*); it was at that time filled with wooden frames used in the process of stretching the material. Hence the property is referred to in documents as a 'bleekveld' (bleaching field), as well as by its earlier function of 'raemhoff'.[3]

---

1. The house corresponded with the plot presently occupied by the properties at nos 45–47 (Prims, *Kloosterstraat*, 1927, pp. 216–219). The remains were pulled down in 1977; for photographs of the site before this date, see F. Baudouin, in d'Hulst et al., *Kruisoprichting*, 1992, p. 48, fig. 24; see also Chapter IV, p. 131, n. 47.
2. Antwerp, Museum Plantin-Moretus, Plantin-Moretus Archief, inv. no. 1178, *Begrafenisrollen en Uitnoodigingen*, no. 2; Rooses, *Rubens*, 1904, p. 118. The literal interpretation of Philip Rubens's phrase: 'In contubernio soceri' as 'in his parents-in-law's house' has not been questioned, except by Pieter Génard, who was convinced that Rubens did not reside with his parents-in-law, but lived on the other side of the street, in the house where his mother had died (Génard, *Rubens*, 1877, pp. 323, 464, n. 1). For this house, see p. 26, n. 18; Chapter IV, p. 219.
3. It should be noted that in Antwerp (and in other cities) the wooden frames, rather than being used for bleaching linen – a persistent misunderstanding – were needed in the preparation of woollen cloth; they were used to reshape, stretch and dry lengths of woven cloth which had shrunk unevenly in the process of fulling and dyeing (see Bedeer – Janssens, *Steden in beeld*, 1993, pp. 53, 83, n. 65; Voet et al., *Antwerpen*, 1978, p. 108, fig. 47; and esp. Thijs, *Raemvelt*, 1993, pp. 301–309). It is true that the same area was used to bleach linen, which was spread out on the empty ground between the frames.

CHAPTER I - A HISTORICAL SKETCH OF THE PROPERTY ON THE WAPPER

A few cartographic sources – to which we will return later – give a general idea of the property's appearance in the sixteenth and early seventeenth century. One of the oldest, and certainly the most detailed, is the famous panoramic view of Antwerp from the east, by Virgilius Bononiensis (Fig. 1). Although dated 1565, it shows the layout of the 1550s.[4] Half a century later, when Rubens returned from Italy, the buildings on the plot would probably not have changed very much. For a proper understanding of the description that follows, it is also useful to refer to the nineteenth-century survey by François Antoine Losson (Fig. 2).[5] Although the gaps between houses have been to an extent filled in, this plan of 1846, seen from the west, shows the correct positions and relative sizes of the plots, which still correspond closely to the layout as it was in the sixteenth and seventeenth centuries. It thus shows the exact location of the parcels discussed in this chapter.

To the west, the property fronted a broad street called the Wapper, through the centre of which ran a narrow conduit carrying fresh water from the Herentals canal. On the street there was a mechanism for dipping vessels to collect water, a contraption known as the Wip or Wipper, but most often the Wapper. This name was given to the street as a whole, and so houses here are recorded in sixteenth- and seventeenth-century sale contracts and other documents as located 'in the Wapper' or 'on the Wapper'. Occasionally it is also referred to as the Vaartstraat (a *vaart* is a canal).[6] It is a misconception that the plot or house purchased by Rubens was referred to for convenience as 'De Wapper', as was assumed by those drawing up the Amsterdam sale contract of 1610, something often repeated in the literature on Rubens from Abraham Bredius (1855–1946) onwards.[7] At least, no house names for Rubens's plot have been found in the Antwerp archives before its mention as 'the house of Rubens'.[8]

The entire east side of the property was bounded by the shooting range of the Guild of the Arquebusiers, known as the Kolveniershof, a long, narrow strip of land on the Kolveniersstraat used for target practice.[9] To the south, the

4. For this unique city view, see below, pp. 40–41, n. 75.
5. On this map, see below Chapter II, pp. 78–80, n. 91.
6. Thys, *Historiek*, 1893, p. 418; Vande Weghe, *Antwerpse straatnamen*, 1977, p. 402.
7. '… in allen schijne 't voorsz. huys genaemt de Wapper' ('…in all probability the aforementioned house called the Wapper') (Appendix I.1: [2]); 'De oorspronkelijke woning waarnaast de meester zijn huis bouwde heette zelf "De Wapper"' ('The original dwelling, next to which the master built his house was itself called "The Wapper"') (Bredius, *Rubens-document*, 1912, p. 215); the house is incorrectly referred to as 'De Wapper' by Heijnen, *Familie Thys(ius)*, 1984, p. 113; Gelderblom, *Kooplieden*, 2000, p. 143; Montias, *Promise*, 2001, pp. 96–98; id., *Art at Auction*, 2002, pp. 153–155; Logan, *Rubens as a Teacher*, 2006, pp. 247–248, 259.
8. For another house, on the corner of the Wapper and the Hopland, which was apparently sometimes called 'De Wapper', see Devroe, *Rubens' huis*, 2008, I, p. 52; on the question of 'De Wapper' as a house name, see also Maclot, *Rubenssite*, 2016, pp. 42, 47.
9. On the arquebusiers ('kolveniers'), who were Rubens's rear neighbours and commissioned him to paint the famous *Triptych of the Descent from the Cross* for their altar in the Cathedral of Our Lady, see for example De Poorter, *Kolveniers*, 1988, pp. 203–252; for the wall between Rubens's house and the Kolveniershof see Chapter IV, pp. 123–124; on *The Descent from the Cross*, see Chapter IV, pp. 124, 130–132.

parcel adjoined the Hopland, then generally known as Lammekensraem(e), with the exception of a group of houses which had been split from the original plot of land. To the north it was bordered by several large plots fronting the Meir, occupied by houses and courtyard houses that were set back from the street.

Franchoys Gielis and the Sint-Arnoldus House on the Meir

The complex history of the block that incorporates the parcel under discussion can be partly reconstructed from descriptions in surviving sale contracts. However, it is not always easy to interpret the situation correctly, and much remains unclear, due to the fact that plots were on several occasions split up or joined together. Here we will discuss only a few aspects that are relevant to the present study.[10] Before turning our attention to Rubens's purchase at the end of 1610, we must consider the state of the plot in the sixteenth century, and we will also make a digression into a house on the Meir that played a role in Rubens's life, or more accurately that of his family.

At the beginning of the sixteenth century the largely unbuilt *raamveld* belonged to a cloth worker and it was then sold to the merchant Franchoys Gielis (? d. shortly before 1579). Simply put, this Gielis owned roughly one half of the block. His property did not include the east side, with the shooting range of the Guild of the Arquebusiers, or the two west corners, occupied by blocks of houses. In other words, Gielis's property fronted three streets: the Meir, the Wapper and the Hopland.

On 24 November 1545, Franchoys Gielis sold a section of his land, with a house on it, to the tapestry dealer Hendrik Pypelinckx and Clara de Thovion, who were Rubens's maternal grandparents. The property, with a gateway and courtyard, faced onto the Meir and had been made into a separate dwelling but was part of the larger Sint-Arnout House, also referred to as Sint-Arnoldus, the remainder of which stayed in the hands of Franchoys Gielis.[11] Most of the unbuilt plot adjoining the house – which in the seventeenth century was still frequently referred to as 'Franchoys Gielis' *raemhoff* – also remained in his possession.

Rubens's mother, Maria Pypelinckx (1538–1608), grew up in this house on the Meir, and she may have continued to live there after marrying the lawyer

---

10. Two recent studies that discuss this, with some different conclusions, are Devroe, *Rubens' huis*, 2008, I, pp. 49–51; Maclot, *Rubenssite*, 2016, esp. pp. 26–49.
11. Génard, *Rubens*, 1877, pp. 269–270. It should be noted that Maria Pypelinckx's parental home cannot simply be identified with the Sint-Arnoldus House (as assumed by Génard, and something that is repeated often in the Rubens literature), but only with an unnamed, but separate part of this extensive property on the Meir. We learn from the sale contract of 1545 that a party wall was to be installed to create a separate dwelling ('een wooninghe op heur selven') and it also clearly states that the house being sold is situated *next* to the Sint-Arnoldus House and courtyard, which were to remain the property of Franchoys Gielis (ibid., p. 269).

CHAPTER I - A HISTORICAL SKETCH OF THE PROPERTY ON THE WAPPER

Jan Rubens (1530–1587) in 1561.[12] An alderman of the Antwerp magistracy, Rubens's father felt threatened, with good reason, under Alva's reign of terror and it is well known that he fled the Netherlands with his family in 1568 to settle in Cologne. In the spring of 1589, after her husband had passed away, Maria Pypelinckx returned to Antwerp, a widow with three children, Blandina, Philip and Peter Paul.[13] Both her parents had died and, with her sister Susanna, she had inherited the house on the Meir. Did she at that point move back into the Sint-Arnoldus House, as is often assumed?[14] There is no evidence to confirm this. Indeed, it seems unlikely. The house may still have been let to tenants when Maria returned to Antwerp, as it was when her mother Clara de Thovion died in 1583, a fact that emerges from the inventory of Clara's estate, which includes an account of her rental income.[15] It should also be observed that, when she drew up her will in Antwerp in the same year, Maria Pypelinckx was not living on the Meir but at an address on the Kipdorp.[16]

Although it is safe to assume that Rubens lived with his mother for several years before going to Italy in early May 1600, it is far from certain whether he ever inhabited the Sint-Arnoldus House on the Meir, nor indeed do we know where Rubens had his studio before he departed for Italy. What we know is what appears in Maria Pypelinckx's will of 1606: that Rubens left with his mother in Antwerp a number of paintings 'he had made'.[17]

At any rate, at the time of her death (in 1608), Maria Pypelinckx was not living on the Meir but in a house on the Sint-Michielsstraat (now Kloosterstraat), for which she paid an annual rent of 125 guilders to the Norbertines of St Michael's Abbey.[18] It is perfectly possible that Philip and Peter Paul Rubens stayed here first on their return from Italy. The house in question was situated next to the abbey's monumental entrance portal, so on the west side of the street, and

12. It is often repeated in the literature that Jan Rubens moved in with his parents-in-law after his marriage and so lived in the house on the Meir (for example, Thys, *Historiek der straten*, 1893, p. 403; Maes – Laenens, *Juristen*, 1977, p. 96), but this is also contested (Douxchamps et al., *Rubens*, 1977, p. 65).
13. For the date of her return to Antwerp, see Baudouin, *Rubens' Kinderjaren*, 1991, pp. 133–159, and esp. pp. 139–140; reprinted in Baudouin, *Selected Studies*, 2005, pp. 45–65.
14. Génard, *Rubens*, 1877, p. 323, assumes that she moved into the house on the Meir and therefore that Rubens also lived there; this is followed by, for example, Rooses, *Rubens*, 1904, p. 28; Douxchamps et al., *Rubens*, 1977, p. 65; Baudouin, *Rubens' Kinderjaren*, 1991, p. 146; Heinen, *Garten*, 2002, p. 7; id., *Gesundheit*, 2004, p. 151.
15. According to the inventory of Clara de Thovion's estate, the house was divided into two separate dwellings, each rented out to tenants, who paid respectively 300 and 180 guilders a year; see De Bruyn, *Rubens*, 2006, appendix II, p. 133.
16. She was unwell at the time and had taken to her bed 'int Kipdorp', where she was staying (will of 18 November 1583; Antwerp–Beveren, Rijksarchief, Notariële archieven, notaris Lieven van Rokeghem, inv. no. 23772.
17. Génard, *Rubens*, 1877, p. 373.
18. Prims, *Kloosterstraat*, 1927, pp. 215–216, 218. The amount received from rent (not mentioned by Prims) can be derived from the accounts of Pypelinckx's estate: expenditure on rent for eight months amounts to 83 guilders and 6 stivers (Génard, *Rubens*, 1977, p. 434). For a full discussion of the abbey, and Rubens's later relations with it, see Herremans, *Rubens Unveiled*, 2013, pp. 60–88.

– significantly – opposite the house of Jan Brant and Clara de Moy, home to Rubens's bride, and where, as we have seen, he lived for several years after his marriage.

When, in late 1610, and after an absence of eight years in Italy (1600–1608), Rubens bought the plot in the same block as the house on the Meir where his mother grew up, he may have felt that he was coming home to familiar surroundings. It is possible that the rear façade of the Pypelinckx house was visible from Rubens's property, although this is difficult to ascertain as the exact location of the 'parental' quarters within the large Sint-Arnoldus House, in amongst the houses and courtyard houses on the Meir, is not known.[19]

However, by 1610 the Pypelinckx's house on the Meir, which passed to their two daughters, was no longer in the family. On 31 October 1601, while Rubens was in Italy, Maria and Susanna Pypelinckx had sold it to their next-door neighbour, a merchant by the name of Hendrik Hoons (Hoens). He owned the adjoining west section of the Sint-Arnoldus House, so that the two parts of the spacious residence could be reunited as a single dwelling, or at least had one and the same owner again.[20]

It is worth mentioning that in the nineteenth and early twentieth century, Rubens was firmly believed to have spent his youth in the Pypelinckx house. Indulging a certain romanticism, for which there was no historic basis, the memory of Rubens's supposed first home in Antwerp was kept alive. In 1854 the broad property occupying number 54 on the Meir, corresponding to the whole of the Sint-Arnoldus House – not to be confused with the Pypelinckx home, which occupied only part of the property – was given a new and elaborately decorated façade, crowned with a bust of Rubens. Underneath it, a Latin inscription commemorated the mansion's erstwhile occupants: Rubens's parents if not the great artist himself (Text ills 1 and 2).[21] It is understandable that prior to the restoration and reconstruction (in 1939–1947) of the house on the Wapper, visitors to Antwerp were sometimes misinformed, and so mistook this spacious and grand property on the Meir for the house of the illustrious painter.[22]

---

19. An idea of the correct location of the property, and the width of the façade, can be gained from the 1846 survey by Losson (Fig. 2). The building is located on the north side of the block (so on the Meir), second from the left. At the time it had a large courtyard (or garden) and a generous extension at the back spanning the entire width of the building. For this survey see Chapter II, pp. 79–80, n. 91.
20. Génard, *Rubens*, 1877, pp. 345–350.
21. '1567. Has ædes illustrissimi Rubeni Joannes & Maria Pypelincx inhabitaverunt parentes. re æd: 1854.' (Naeye, *De Proost*, 1976, repr. p. 220; Van Aerschot, ed., *Bouwen / Antwerpen*, 1979, pp. 329–330, repr.). The Pypelinckx house undoubtedly only occupied one section (on the east side) of the very long property at no. 54, the whole of which was known as the Sint-Arnoldus House (see p. 25, n. 11; see also Aerts et al., *Meir*, 1983, p. 40).
22. Conrad Busken Huet (1826–1886), who visited Antwerp in 1878, thought that the impressive (much restored) main façade of Rubens's house was on 'Place de Meir'; he describes the house on the Wapper as 'a second entrance, located in a side street round the corner' ('een tweede ingang, aangebragt in eene dwarsstraat om

CHAPTER I - A HISTORICAL SKETCH OF THE PROPERTY ON THE WAPPER

Text ill. 1. 'Maison de Rubens' (Antwerp, Meir 54), picture postcard (c. 1900).

Text ill. 2. Detail of the house represented in Text ill. 1: Bust of Peter Paul Rubens on top of the façade.

In 1903, the house was purchased by the art dealer Eugène Van Herck (1854–1941) and it then became the premises of the well-known antiques business that he ran with his sons. The Van Hercks circulated pictures of the façade and the interior of the house, which was filled with art and antiques, calling it the 'Maison Rubens'[23] – a somewhat misleading name in that it suggested the house had belonged to the artist himself, and perhaps also that some of the antiques had a 'Rubensian provenance'. We digressed to look at the Pypelinckx house and can now go back to the property (forming part of the same block) that was later acquired by Rubens.

The Round Walloon Church

It is important to state that in 1566 this unbuilt plot between the houses on the Wapper had been the scene of a historic event, memory of which lingered for a long time with many people. The event was connected with the beginnings of the Reformation and the conflicts surrounding it, developments that were also at the root of Rubens's parents' decision to emigrate.

de hoek') (Busken Huet, *Land van Rubens*, 1881, p. 136). At the start of the 20th century it was apparently still the case that city guides, led tourists to believe that the house on the Meir was Rubens's (Delen, *Rubens' huis*, 1933, p. 60).
23. Baudouin, *Charles Van Herck*, 2000, p. 16, repr. pp. 16–17.

After the eruption of the Iconoclastic Fury in Antwerp on 20 August 1566, the city council was forced to negotiate with the Calvinists and Lutherans. As a result, the Reformers were granted permission, on 2 September 1566, to give sermons on six vacant lots ('leege erven') within the city walls, and to erect churches there. In the event, only four such houses of prayer were built.[24]

One of these unbuilt plots, which is described as situated on the Wapper and behind the Kolveniershof, was 'a vacant lot belonging to Franchoys Gielis, which was only used for bleaching'. It was allocated to the 'Walloon Calvinists', a community of Reformed Christians with French as well as Walloon groups. One of the anonymous chronicles that described the event reports that they began without delay, meaning in September 1566, 'to dig and to lay the foundations for their new church',[25] and that they were able to celebrate Christmas there in that year.

Little is known about the actual appearance of this Walloon Church, which was located on the strip of land that was to become Rubens's garden. According to the chronicle mentioned above, 'this church or temple was completely round, just like the Temple of Solomon, and for this reason it was called the round church'. Other chroniclers describe it as octagonal in shape, or round like an egg.[26] Comparison with other early Protestant houses of prayer in France and the Netherlands suggests that the building had an elongated, octagonal ground plan and walls of stone to head height, the upper part made of timber and with a slate roof (Text ill. 3).[27]

This structure remained in place for only a short time. The Governor of the Netherlands, Margaret of Parma (1522–1586), gradually gained more control over the situation and ordered the 'temples' to be removed. In May–July 1567, the Protestant buildings were completely demolished so that the city could be freed from the memory of the 'false synagogues'. On 13 June the demolition of 'the round Walloon Church' on the Wapper began.[28] However, the 'temples'

---

24. For the context of these historical events, see Marnef, *Antwerp*, 1996, pp. 88–108; see also Thys, *Historiek der straten*, 1893, pp. 430–431. A full discussion of the lost Protestant edifices in Antwerp and elsewhere can be found in the publications of Joris Snaet (Snaet, *Tempels*, 1999, pp. 45–58; id., *Glory of God*, 2007, pp. 251–254; id., *Reformatie versus contrareformatie*, 2008, I, esp. pp. 74–82). For his reconstruction of the 'temple' in Ghent, see below, n. 27.
25. 'te graven ende fonderen haerlieden nieu kercke' (Antwerp, FelixArchief, inv. no. PK#105, *Chronycke van Antwerpen sedert het jaar 1500 tot 1575*, p. 97; cited by Snaet, *Tempels*, 1999, p. 54, appendix IV. See also Prims, *Waalse kerk*, 1948, pp. 143–146.
26. Snaet, *Tempels*, 1999, p. 53, appendix I; pp. 45, 53, appendix II; pp. 54–55, appendix IV.
27. Id., *Reformatie versus contrareformatie*, 2008, I, p. 77. Joris Snaet discusses at length the form of the lost 'temples' (all with a central ground plan) and reproduces a reconstruction drawing of a building in Ghent (Text ill. 3) that may have been similar, although possibly much larger, with a diameter of more than 40 m (Snaet, *Tempels*, 1999, fig. 4; id., *Glory of God*, 2007, fig. 259). One relevant example of a surviving church with layout based on similar 16th-century structures (a 17th-century wooden building on a central plan, but with its interior completely transformed) is the Amstelkerk in Amsterdam (Jacobs, *Amstelkerk*, 1990, pp. 48–53, 66–69). Many thanks to Joris Snaet for information about 'lost temples' and for permission to reproduce his drawing.
28. For mentions of the demolition in three different chronicles, see Snaet, *Tempels*, 1999, p. 55, appendices IV–VI.

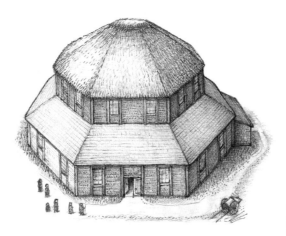

Text ill. 3. Joris Snaet, *Reconstruction of a Protestant Temple in Ghent*, drawing. Private Collection.

were not forgotten quickly. In October of the same year, large wooden crosses were erected on the four sites formerly occupied by the churches, and these remained in place for ten years, until their removal in 1577 (Text ills 5–7).[29] Twenty years after the destruction of the 'round temple', around the time that Rubens returned from Cologne with his mother (in 1589), plots of land on the Wapper were still occasionally described as 'by the Walloon Church' ('aende Waelekerck').[30]

No convincing traces of the foundations could be found when the garden of the Rubenshuis was dug up during the restoration, nor has anything been discovered since then. This is not surprising, given that the instruction had been for the four heretical buildings to be removed completely, including their foundations ('van welcke kercken het fondeersel uytgeroeyt was').[31] It has been suggested that certain difficult to identify remnants of a construction, which were unearthed in the garden, might have come from pillars belonging to the demolished building.[32] Whatever the truth, there is absolutely nothing to support the idea that parts of the sixteenth-century Protestant building were

---

29. For the locations of the four crosses, see Snaet, *Tempels*, 1999, p. 47, fig. 2 (bird's-eye view of Antwerp by Hoefnagel, indicating the four locations).
30. See, for example, the reference in the cadastral ledger of 1584–1585 (Degueldre, *Kadastrale ligger*, 2011, X, p. 15, no. 193) and in a tax register of 1588 (Vande Weghe, *Antwerpse straatnamen*, 1977, p. 402).
31. Snaet, *Tempels*, 1999, p. 54, appendix II.
32. Four masonry pillars were found in the garden during the restoration; it was believed – without justification in our opinion – that these might be part of a group of eight pillars belonging to a round building with a diameter of approx. 16 m. According to Émile Van Averbeke (1876–1946) and Frederik Clijmans (1893–1969), the pillars could have been remains of 'the temple', but they also considered other identifications, such as Rubens's 'Pantheon', which is certainly incorrect (E. Van Averbeke, cited in Clijmans, *Wederopbouw Rubenshuis*, 1941, p. 52; Clijmans, *Wederopbouw Rubenshuis*, 1946, pp. 64–66); see also Snaet, *Tempels*, 1999, p. 57, n. 11; Devroe, *Rubens' huis*, 2008, I, p. 77, fig. 39; Snaet, *Reformatie versus contrareformatie*, 2008, I, p. 77, n. 231.

still standing in 1610, when Rubens bought the property.[33] We can therefore be sure that Rubens did not rebuild this structure; nor did he convert it to suit his own needs, as has mistakenly been thought.[34]

B. The Thys Family and the Sale of the Parcel to Rubens

The Owners / Vendors

The successive owners of the parcel of land prior to 1610 can be identified more or less completely from the surviving archival records.[35]

Following the demolition of the 'Walloon' Church, title to the vacant lot was the subject of a dispute, but eventually, in 1579, it returned to the heirs of Franchoys Gielis. A number of the heirs were bought out between 1580 and 1584, after which the lion's share of the former *raamveld* fell into the hands of Franchoys's daughter Martha Gielis (d. 1586) and her husband, the Mechelen-born dealer in jewels, Christoffel Thys (c. 1522–1591). The couple were Protestants and they left Antwerp for good in 1584. At the time of his departure Christoffel Thys was one of the city's wealthiest merchants; he carried on a successful business and eventually settled in Frankfurt.[36]

The use to which the plot on the Wapper was put in the period between 1566 and 1610 can only be surmised. The wooden frames used in the preparation of cloth may already have been dismantled when the Walloon Church was erected in 1566 (see below); at any rate, the vacant lot was by then being used as a bleaching green, a function it probably still retained in 1610. Virtually no information is available about the occupants or tenants of the adjoining house (or houses) on the Wapper, which belonged to Christoffel Thys. We only know one name: in 1584–1585 a house with the relatively high rental value of 240 guilders was let by Christoffel Thys to Marie de Brimeu, widow of the merchant Koenraad Schets. But whether this is the house that was later bought

---

33. Considered possible by Tijs, but he was mistaken (Tijs, *Rubens en Jordaens*, 1984, p. 104).
34. For the unfounded hypothesis that Rubens converted it to a free-standing studio in his garden, see Chapter VII, pp. 214–215 and Chapter VIII, p. 237, n. 18.
35. A summary can be found in one of the sale contracts (Appendix I.2: [5]); more details are provided by the title deeds ('transporten voor schepenen gepasseert') preserved in the archives of the Rubenshuis, Fonds 'Expropriation'.
36. On the history of the Thys family (the name has many different spellings and is also Latinised to Thysius), who distinguished themselves in the field of business as well as learning, see Van Royen, *Familiecorrespondentie*, 1942, pp. 124–150, family tree p. 150; Heijnen, *Familie Thys(ius)*, 1984, pp. 111–116; Gelderblom, *Kooplieden*, 2000, passim, family tree, pp. 272–273. For Christoffel Thys's activities as merchant, see ibid., pp. 48–60, and passim. The name of the family lives on in the remarkable Bibliotheca Thysiana at Leiden (Mourits, *Thysius*, 2016, passim, with family tree, pp. 310–311).

CHAPTER I - A HISTORICAL SKETCH OF THE PROPERTY ON THE WAPPER

by Rubens is not clear.[37] That the owners of the property, the Thyses, once lived in a house on the Wapper, as is sometimes assumed, can safely be ruled out.[38]

When Christoffel Thys died in Frankfurt in 1591, his share of the block on the Wapper was inherited by his six children, all of whom had also moved away from Antwerp long previously and set up home in Amsterdam, Leiden and various German cities.[39] Two of these heirs are mentioned in the documents pertaining to the sale of the Antwerp plot to Rubens: Christoffel's eldest son, Hans (Johannes), and his youngest daughter, Magdalena, as well as her husband Andries Bacher. Hans Thys (1556–1611) grew up in Antwerp, but had left the city with his parents in 1584. He first moved to Amsterdam and a year later relocated to Prussia. In 1595 he returned to Amsterdam where he remained until his death. He, in turn, made a fortune by trading in various commodities, including jewels, leather and hides.[40] The inventory of his estate reveals that he was interested in painting.[41] His sister Magdalena Thys (1569–1622) followed a similar route: Antwerp – Germany – Amsterdam.[42] She married Andries Bacher (also Backer or Backaert; 1546–1616), a doctor from Poperinge. Until 1607, the couple lived in Halberstadt, where Bacher was personal physician to Duke Heinrich Julius von Braunschweig-Wolfenbüttel (1564–1613). Later they also lived in Utrecht for a while, and finally in Amsterdam.[43]

In the years between 1595 and 1602, a number of transactions concerning the properties that had been left behind in Antwerp took place between Andries Bacher and the heirs of Franchoys Gielis and Christoffel Thys, and these simplified somewhat the complex division of the estate.[44] As far as we can tell, the parcel on the Wapper had two owners when it was purchased by Rubens in 1610, namely Hans Thys and the Bacher – Thys couple. It is not clear which part of the property belonged to whom, nor is it out of the question

37. Degueldre, *Kadastrale ligger*, 2011, X, pp. XIV, XVII, 15, no. 192. The house has no name. The tenant should not be confused with the aristocratic spouse of Charles de Croÿ III (1560–1612) of the same name. According to Maclot, this building was situated to the north of the house later acquired by Rubens (Maclot, *Rubenssite*, 2016, p. 45).
38. That the house on the Wapper was the 'parental home' of Hans Thys is a persistent misunderstanding; see for example Heijnen, *Familie Thysius*, 1984, p. 113; Gelderblom, *Kooplieden*, 2000, p. 185. The affluent couple possessed several properties in Antwerp (and elsewhere) and before leaving the city they did not live on the Wapper but in the 'Drie Gulden Coppen' in the Korte Nieuwstraat, next door to the Sint-Annagodshuis; see for example ibid., pp. 56–57 (n. 114), 60; Degueldre, *Kadastrale ligger*, 2011, II, p. 48, no. 519.
39. For the Thys family, see above, p. 31, n. 36; on their trading activities, which extended into a large part of Europe (including Stockholm, Königsberg, London, Bayonne and Venice), see Gelderblom, *Kooplieden*, 2000, pp. 36–37, 48–60, 73–74, 97, 122–144, 482–485, and passim.
40. On the trading business of Hans Thys, who started out as a specialist in jewellery and became a general wholesaler, see Gelderblom, ibid., pp. 55, 57, 122–144, 164–171, and passim.
41. 'He was a genuine art collector' (Montias, *Art at Auction*, 2002, p. 156); on the paintings from his estate, auctioned in Amsterdam on 22 April 1614, see ibid., pp. 161–163.
42. This Magdalena Thys is one of the few 16th-century Dutch women by whom we have an ego-document, a *Memoriael* containing summary data about the family. The document makes no reference to the Antwerp properties. Leiden, Universiteitsbibliotheek Leiden, archives of the Bibliotheca Thysiana, inv. no. 655.
43. Van Royen, *Familiecorrespondentie*, 1942, pp. 127–129.
44. Full information about these transactions in 1595, 1599, 1601 and 1602 can be found in the archival documentation at the Rubenshuis, Fonds 'Expropriation'.

that the property transfers to Bacher were partly or even wholly fictitious.[45] As we shall see, the plot on the Wapper also had mortgages (hereditary rents or *erfelijke renten*) secured on it, the oldest of which went back fifty years, to the time of Franchoys Gielis.

It is striking that the two known sale deeds – one drawn up in Amsterdam, the other in Antwerp[46] – each give the names of the same two 'vendors' but that their status is described differently. Acting as vendor in Amsterdam on 1 November 1610 was Hans Thys; however, the concluding lines of the agreement state that the property will be passed from 'the esteemed Doctor Andries Backer, adviser and physician to the Duke of Bruynswyck, as well as the aforementioned vendor Hans Thys himself' (Appendix I.1). Yet a couple of months later, on 4 January 1611, the signatory vendors in Antwerp are Doctor Andreas Backaert [Bacher] and Magdalena Thys, his wife, while 'Jan Thijs, merchant residing in Amsterdam' is represented only by his proxy (Appendix I.2).

Thus, more than twenty-five years after their emigration from Antwerp, the Thys family resolved to sell off the properties they had left behind. Perhaps they only then realised that none of Christoffel Thys's children would ever move back to live in the city again. In several places the correspondence between the siblings refers to their hope for a return, especially a nostalgic yearning to live once more in 'onse vaders stede' ('our father's city').[47] Like other families, the Thyses waited a long time before finally selling their properties in Antwerp. They hoped to return one day, but the decision not to sell naturally also involved financial considerations. The exodus that took place after 1585 reduced Antwerp's population by approximately fifty per cent, leading to a substantial drop in house prices and making it unattractive to sell. All the same, former citizens of Antwerp remained very attached to the property they had left behind, and with the Thys family this manifested itself in the visits that they made to the city.[48]

Without question, the Twelve Years' Truce (9 April 1609) also contributed to the decision to sell. The truce with Spain made it easier for Antwerp citizens who had fled to the Northern Provinces to settle their 'abandoned' affairs.[49] Rubens's decision to move back to Antwerp more or less coincided with the

---

45. If so, this might have been prompted by a fear that Antwerp possessions could be sequestered; a proprietor living in the 'hostile' Northern Netherlands was potentially more at danger than Bacher, who at the time of these transactions was working in the service of a German duke. For fear of sequestration, see Van Eeghen, *Rubens en Rembrandt*, 1977, pp. 59–61; Montias, *Art at Auction*, 2002, pp. 155, 289, n. 510.
46. See below, pp. 34–35; Appendix I.1–2.
47. Van Royen, *Familiecorrespondentie*, 1942, pp. 126–128; for Hans Thys's hope in this regard, see Gelderblom, *Kooplieden*, 2000, pp. 130, 182–184.
48. By Hans Thys in 1595 and 1603 (Gelderblom, ibid., pp. 131, 142), and in 1606 by a son of Andries Bacher in the company of François, a brother of Hans (they walked around Antwerp for two days inspecting all the houses belonging to the family; Van Royen, *Familiecorrespondentie*, 1942, p. 130).
49. Montias also points to this: 'The truce in the war with Spain, signed on 9 April 1609, gave citizens of

CHAPTER I - A HISTORICAL SKETCH OF THE PROPERTY ON THE WAPPER

beginning of the Twelve Years' Truce, and he seems to have made clever use of the surge of vacant properties entering the market and turned this situation to his advantage. It meant that for a reasonable price he could scoop up a large piece of land that had been well known to him for years. Not only was the plot generous in size and in a central location, but, crucially, it was unusually 'open', with plenty of light that was protected by ancient rights of access to the bleaching green.[50] It was thus the ideal plot on which to build the studio he envisaged. What is more, it was also well suited to creating a beautiful and pleasant garden: it was perfectly oriented, with virtually unimpeded sunlight from the south and bordered along the entire length of the eastern side by a tree-lined yard. In Brussels such a plot would have been difficult if not impossible to find and would undoubtedly have been considerably dearer. The fact that access to Antwerp via the Scheldt was blocked was a drawback for merchants like Hans Thys, but it made hardly any difference to Rubens's 'business'.

The Two Sale Deeds (Amsterdam and Antwerp)

On 1 November 1610 an agreement was signed in Amsterdam between Rubens and Hans Thys (Appendix I.1). The Antwerp refugee, or at any rate his family, were not complete strangers to Rubens; as already mentioned, Hans Thys's grandfather, Franchoys Gielis, had in 1545 sold a house on the Meir to the parents of Maria Pypelinckx. Gielis remained the owner of the adjacent house until his death. It is quite possible that he continued to live there and that Maria Pypelinckx knew him as well as his children, including Martha Gielis, who was the mother of Hans Thys.

The agreement in Amsterdam between Rubens and Hans Thys came about through the help of an intermediary called Nicolaes Coop, who was a maker of musical instruments and also ran a tavern, which served as a meeting place for artists and musicians.[51] The signing of the agreement took place at his home. From 'Hans Thysz', Coop bought, 'for and on behalf of the aforementioned Pietro Pauli Rubbens', a property in Antwerp, which is described in the following terms:

[…] een huijs ende Bleeckhoff erven ende gronden met eenen vryen gangh aen't Bleeckvelt, streckende nae den Lammekens raem, in allen schijne 't voorsz. huys, genaemt de Wapper binnen de stadt van Antwerpen voorsz. op de Wapper gestaen ende gelegen is […] ([…]

    Amsterdam who had fled Antwerp for religious or other reasons a chance to settle their affairs in their native city' (Montias, *Art at Auction*, 2002, p. 154).
50. For more on this, see below, p. 48, n. 95.
51. In addition to these activities, Nicolaes Coop (or Cop or Coops) was probably also a painter; at any rate his son, Nicolaes Coops II (1592–1629), was a painter. On this son, see Bredius, *Rubens-document*, 1912, p. 216; Montias, *Promise*, 2001, p. 96; id., *Art at Auction*, 2002, p. 154.

a house and bleaching green or yard and ground with a right of access to the bleaching green, stretching to the Lammekensraem [the Hopland], the aforementioned house, in all probability called the Wapper, situated and standing on the Wapper in the aforementioned city of Antwerp [...]) (Appendix I.1: [2]).[52]

The keys were to be handed over 'around this coming Christmas' (that is Christmas 1610). Two months later, on 4 January 1611, a second deed concerning the same sale was registered with the aldermen of the Antwerp magistracy. As mentioned, the vendors named in this Antwerp contract are Doctor Andreas Backer [elsewhere also called Bacher or Backaert] and Magdalena Thys, his wife. They were represented in Antwerp by a 'merchant-jeweller' by the name of Christoffel Caers (Appendix I.2: [2, 8]).[53] The description of the property in the Antwerp sale deed of 1611 is more elaborate than that in the Amsterdam document and refers to 'eene huysinge, met eender grooter poorten, plaetse, gaelderije, coeckene [keuken], camers, gronde en allen den toebehoorten, gestaen ende gelegen op den Wapper' (a house with large gates, a courtyard, a gallery, a kitchen, rooms and ground including outbuildings, standing and situated on the Wapper). The property also included 'eenen bleijckhove daerneffens suytwaert gelegen' (a bleaching yard, adjacent on the south side).

Rubens's new house and courtyard was surrounded by the following properties: to the north by 'the yard of the house of Henrick Hoons' ('derve vanden huysinghe van Henrick Hoons');[54] to the south, that is on the side of the Hopland and the Lammekensraem, by 'certain small houses' ('seker huyskens') and finally to the east 'by the wall of the yard of the Guild of the Arquebusiers' ('aen den muer van de gulde van de coloveriers hove') (Appendix I.2: [3]).

The Purchase Price / Finances

In spite of the detailed information in the sale deeds, some ambiguity has arisen in the Rubens literature about the exact amount paid by Rubens for his property. The reason for this is that the deeds refer to what seems to be a relatively complicated payment scheme rather than specifying one simple amount. In addition to a sum of money, there is also a requirement to 'free' the

52. For the mistaken supposition concerning the name of the house, see above, p. 24, n. 7.
53. Undoubtedly a relation of Hendrick Kaers, who had represented Hans Thys's interests in Antwerp on previous occasions, for example in 1594 and in 1596 (Gelderblom, *Kooplieden*, 2000, p. 171, n. 280). It is interesting that in 1584–1585, the merchant Hendrick Kaers (Caers) is recorded as living on the Meir in a rented property belonging to Dionys Pypelinckx, which appears to have been part of the Sint-Arnoldus House (Degueldre, *Kadastrale ligger*, 2011, X, p. 14, no. 188).
54. This 'erf' (yard) therefore adjoined the houses that Hoons owned on the Meir, including the Sint-Arnoldus House and the house he had bought from Maria and Susanna Pypelinckx. This does not mean that Rubens's property directly adjoined his mother's former house, which was situated considerably further to the north (see the survey by Losson) (Fig. 2).

CHAPTER I - A HISTORICAL SKETCH OF THE PROPERTY ON THE WAPPER

purchased property from a number of hereditary rents secured on it, something that has often been overlooked.[55]

The following agreement can be extracted from the two deeds. The total amount owed by Rubens to the Amsterdam family was 8960 guilders.[56] Rubens was to pay this sum in three equal instalments (of 2986 guilders, 13 stivers and 1 groat), and on three specific dates: the first payment was to be made in cash by Christmas 1610, the agreed date for the handover; the second payment was due a year later, so Christmas 1611, and the third by Christmas 1612 (Appendix I.1: [3].

This simple schedule is complicated by additional stipulations. In mentioning the first and last instalments, the documents refer to a reduction of the outstanding amounts if Rubens agrees to take over a number of 'erfelijke renten' (hereditary rents), which the Thys family were still obliged to pay in Antwerp. In other words: if Rubens takes over these rents – which were calculated at the normal interest rate of 'the sixteenth penny' ('de penning zestien', 1/16 of the capital or 6.25 per cent) – he is allowed to deduct the 'hoofdsom' (capital sum) from the purchase price. Included in the first instalment are four of these rents, together amounting to eighty-five guilders a year, and it is made an 'expresse conditie' (explicit condition), imposed by the vendor and accepted by the buyer, that Rubens pays them. For the third instalment, the outstanding rents are in the order of sixty guilders; here Rubens can choose if he wants to take up the offer. His decision is not known.

In this way it was agreed that Rubens could deduct the *hoofdsom* of 1360 guilders (16 × 85 guilders) from the first instalment. There was a certain logic to this financial construction, which was advantageous to both parties. The Amsterdam vendors no longer needed to worry about hereditary rents stemming from the time the Thyses lived in Antwerp, and which they owed to local individuals, while Rubens did not need to raise as large a sum in cash at the time of the purchase.

This agreement means that when the Antwerp deed was drawn up in January 1611, Rubens no longer owed the Bachers 8960 guilders but 7600 guilders (8960 guilders minus 1360 guilders), which were to be paid in three instalments (Appendix I.2: [2, 9]).[57] It is this mention of 7600 guilders in the Antwerp deed – which before the publication of Bredius's article in 1912 was the only deed

---

55. But accurately explained in Prims, *Waalse Kerk*, 1948, p. 145; much simplified but also given correctly in Tijs, *Rubens en Jordaens*, 1984, p. 110.
56. More precisely the document refers to 560 guilders 'erffelyck tot 40 gr[ooten]. den gulden, bedragende in hooftsomma (tegens den penninck sestien te reeckenen) 8960 gulden' (Appendix I.1: [3]).
57. The three instalments are now specified thus: one payment of 1626 guilders, 13 stivers and 1 groat, and two payments of 2986 guilders, 13 stivers and 1 groat. First the full amount of 8960 guilders was divided by three (2986 g. 13 st. 1 gr.) and then 1360 guilders were deducted from the first instalment, as agreed. The fact that the total figure of 8960 could not be divided by three was solved by rounding off the instalments (which resulted in Rubens having to pay half a stiver more).

known – that led incorrectly in the Rubens literature to the conclusion that this was the price at which the house was bought by the artist.[58]

The four rents, amounting to eighty-five guilders, which Rubens was required to redeem, are specified in the Antwerp deed. Among the creditors were the chapter of Antwerp Cathedral and two widows (Appendix I.2: [6]).[59] We know that Rubens did not immediately pay off these outstanding rents, but chose to spread them over several years. We know from the surviving receipts that it was not until March and May of 1613 that he 'cleared' his property of the above four rents: along with the *hoofdpenningen* he paid all remaining arrears (Appendix I.4).[60] A few months earlier, at the end of 1612, he had paid the Thys family the final instalment of the 8960 guilders he owed them.

The total price paid for the house is evidently higher if one adds to the purchase sum of 8960 guilders the amounts paid by Rubens over several years to third parties to free the property from the hereditary rents. Bredius rightly points out that the cost of Rubens's property exceeded 9000 guilders, possibly totalling 'well over 10,000 guilders'.[61] This valid observation was then misconstrued and led to the misunderstanding in the Rubens literature that the purchase sum was simply 10,000 guilders.[62]

The complex payment scheme can be summed up as follows: the purchase price was neither 7600 nor 10,000 guilders, but 8960 guilders; however, in real terms the deal costs Rubens more, because for several years he also invested an indeterminable sum in paying hereditary rents that had been passed on to him by the previous owners.

---

58. For example, by these early authors (who were not aware of the Amsterdam deed): Van den Branden, *Schilderschool*, 1883, p. 505; Rooses – Ruelens, eds, *Correspondance*, 1887–1909, II, p. 153; Rooses, *Maison*, 1888, p. 217; repeated by later authors, including Baudouin, *Rubenshuis*, 1951, p. 99.
59. The hereditary rents were due to two widows (each 23 guilders), the chapter of the Cathedral of Our Lady (19 guilders, 13 stivers, 9 *oords*) and a Godefridus Verreycken (20 guilders); see Appendix I. 2: [6]). The total amount Rubens was allowed to deduct from the first instalment was apparently rounded down (so to the disadvantage of Rubens). As observed by Prims (Prims, *Waalse Kerk*, 1948, p. 145), the rents did not total 85 guilders, but 85 guilders, 13 stivers and 9 *oords*. The overall capital (a sum corresponding with the interest multiplied by sixteen) thus came to 1371 guilders; in other words 11 guilders more than the agreed amount of 1360 guilders.
60. The payments by Rubens were notarised on the following dates: 1) 2 March 1613: rent of 46 guilders, to the two widows; 2) 28 March 1613: rent of 19 guilders, 13 stivers, to Godevaert van Santvoort on behalf of the chapter of the Cathedral of Our Lady; 3) 13 May 1613: 20 guilders, to Godefridus Verreycken; the three documents registered with the Antwerp magistracy are preserved at the Rubenshuis, Fonds 'Expropriation'; for 1) and 3) see also the documents in the Antwerp FelixArchief, Schepenregisters, inv. nos SR#503 and SR#506, available online through Büttner – Heinen, eds, *Quellen und Dokumente*, 2011, nos 112 and 114; Buttner, *Rubens berühmt*, 2006, p. 178, n. 70.
61. Bredius, *Rubens-document*, 1912, p. 215. It is unclear if Rubens also owed interest to the vendors on the two instalments of the purchase sum he paid in 1611 and 1612.
62. Baudouin, *Rubens House*, 1977, p. 183; id., *Summary Guide*, 1977, p. 3.

Two Further Conditions from Hans Thys

Besides financial specifications, the Amsterdam agreement included two additional stipulations, both of which benefitted Hans Thys, who is the vendor mentioned in this deed. 'In recognition and in memory of the sale' Rubens was expected – as was customary in these situations – to make a 'hand-to-hand gift' to Hans Thys, namely an autograph painting 'as large or small as seemed appropriate to Rubens' ('soo groot en cleyn als hem Rubbens goetduncken sal') (Appendix I.1: [6]).

Especially interesting is the second demand, which stipulates that Rubens will teach one of Hans Thys's sons 'the art of painting' without keeping anything hidden from him. The young man will receive 'vrye leering' (free tuition) from the master and be granted free access to undergo his training. But in all other respects he will have to provide for himself (Appendix I.1: [7]). The 'value' of this special favour to the vendor should not be underestimated. We know from Rubens himself that he was inundated with requests to take on young pupils and that he was forced to turn down the majority of these approaches, including those from friends and family.[63]

It is not clear what Hans Thys's objectives may have been in adding this condition, nor do we know which of his four sons he had in mind, and this has fed quite a few speculations in the literature. For one thing, the youngest of Thys's sons, Anthony (1595–1634) – who later married his cousin, the daughter of Magdalena Thys and Andries Bacher – was already fifteen years old in 1610 and so actually too old to embark on an apprenticeship in Rubens's workshop. Was Thys perhaps more interested in obtaining a training in art connoisseurship, something that would be useful to a person setting up a business in this area? In that case he may have been thinking of his son Hans II (1592–1647), who indeed went on to become an art dealer.[64]

Whatever the case may be, in September 1611 Hans Thys died in a boating accident on the Zuiderzee forcing his sons, including Anthony, to break off their training and apprenticeships early in order to deal with the large estate and maintain their father's business.[65] In the end nothing may have come from this stipulation in the contract. None of Thys's sons became a painter, and as far as we know, no other member of the family made use of the clause. Yet

---

63. Anne-Marie Logan calls the stipulation in the contract 'astonishing' (Logan, *Rubens as a Teacher*, 2006, p. 248). For the frequently quoted letter of 11 May 1611, in which Rubens declines a request from Jacques de Bie, see Rooses – Ruelens, eds, *Correspondance*, 1887–1909, II, pp. 36–38, no. CXXVIII; Magurn, ed., *Letters*, 1955, p. 55, no. 22; Van de Velde, *Rubens' Brieven*, 2006, pp. 149–151, 165–166, no. 1).
64. On this question, see Van Eeghen, *Rubens en Rembrandt*, 1977, p. 62; Balis, *Studio Practices*, 1994, p. 100; id., *Rubens and his Studio*, 2007, p. 49, n. 71; Gelderblom, *Kooplieden*, 2000, pp. 202, 208. John Michael Montias believes that Hans II was the most likely candidate, at least intentionally, but that the intention was never followed up. See Montias, *Promise*, 2001, p. 99; id., *Art at Auction*, 2002, pp. 153, 156.
65. On the trading activities of Anthony Thys and his brothers, see Gelderblom, *Kooplieden*, 2000, pp. 197–210.

an unfounded notion has crept into the Rubens literature that one of the sons indeed went to stay in Antwerp and was apprenticed to Rubens.[66]

The Antwerp deed, in which as we have seen, Hans Thys is replaced by the Bachers as the selling party, omits these two additional conditions. However, this does not mean that the conditions had been dropped. We know, because there is evidence for this, that the gift of a painting was still included in the sale. For a long time it remained unclear if the promised painting was ever supplied to the Thys family, but eventually the missing piece of the puzzle was discovered by Montias in the carefully maintained accounts of Hans Thys's heirs.[67] These refer to expenses that were incurred 'to speak about the painting that Rubens had promised us' ('om te spreecken wegen de schildery ons van Rubens belooft'). On two occasions discussions took place – in 1616 at the house of Rubens's representative Nicolaes Coop, who is mentioned in the contract, and a second time in 1617 – but these seem to have come to nothing,[68] and it was not until 1618 that the matter was finally settled: a record in the accounts of Thys's heirs refers to expenses in connection with the purchase and gilding of 'a frame for the Rubens painting' ('een lyst tot de schilderije van Rubbens').[69] Finally, on 4 November 1619 the cost of transporting Rubens's painting from Antwerp was noted in the account book.[70] This shows that Thys's heirs only received the painting that had been promised to them nine years after the agreement had been made. Why Rubens waited so long before fulfilling his commitment cannot be explained.

The subject of Rubens's painting is not mentioned, nor is it clear with which family member it ended up or what happened to it in later years. Montias was unable to find a record of a painting from the hand of Rubens in property inventories of the Thys family. Conceivably it is the *Judith Beheading Holofernes* which in 1621 was in the collection of Theodoor Schrevelius in Leiden and that has been tentatively identified with the version in the Herzog Anton-Ulrich-Museum in Braunschweig.[71]

---

66. Schama is of the view that 'Anthonie or his brother Hans [...] spent a time in Rubens's studio' (Schama, *Rembrandt*, 1999, p. 458). Logan agrees with Montias (see n. 64) that Hans II was the most likely candidate and does not rule out the possibility that he was actually a pupil of Rubens. See Logan, *Rubens as a Teacher*, 2006, pp. 248, 258.
67. Montias, *Promise*, 2001; id., *Art at Auction*, 2002, pp. 153–163: chapter 'Art Collectors and Painters I: Rubens's Promise to Hans Thijsz.'.
68. Ibid., 2001, p. 101; ibid., 2002, pp. 157, 290, n. 532.
69. Ibid., 2001, p. 101; ibid., 2002, pp. 158, 290, n. 536.
70. 'for freight from Antwerp for the painting of Pieter Paulus Rubbens' ('oncosten ... aen vracht van Antwerpen voor de schilderye van Pieter Paulus Rubbens' (id., *Art and Promise*, 2001, p. 101; id., *Art at Auction*, 2002, pp. 158, 290, n. 536).
71. d'Hulst – Vandenven, *Old Testament (CRLB)*, 1989, p. 105, under no. 51. For the possible identification of this work with the painting that belonged to Thys, see Montias, *Promise*, 2001, p. 102; id., *Art at Auction*, 2002, pp. 158–159; Büttner – Heinen, *Leidenschaften*, 2004, p. 121, under no. 1; Büttner, *Rubens*, 2015, p. 233, fig. 37.

It seems likely that Hans Thys's go-between, Nicolaes Coop, who travelled to Antwerp on his behalf, was also given a painting in return for his mediation. At any rate, a large '*Petrus*' from the studio of Rubens appears in the inventory of the property of Nicolaes Coop's son Aert Cop (Coop) of 16 July 1621.[72]

Rembrandt

Finally a curious 'coincidence' should be mentioned, that has repeatedly been brought up in the Rembrandt literature: in 1639 Rembrandt (1606/07–1669) bought his house on the Breestraat, now the Rembrandthuis, from Christoffel Thys (1603–1680), who happened to be the son of Hans's brother François and so belonged to the same well-to-do 'Antwerp' family.[73] However, the similarities end there. While Rubens prospered and was able to develop his house into a prestigious residence, Rembrandt struggled to pay the large sum of 13,000 guilders owed to Christoffel Thys and he eventually lost the house.[74]

C. *The Houses on the Parcel on the Wapper and the Composition of the Purchased 'Huysinge'*

Let us return to Rubens's purchase of 1610–1611. How did the parcel acquired by Rubens look, and what can we find out about the house (or houses) on the Wapper? Clarification has frequently been sought from a number of bird's-eye views of the city, which, as was customary in those days, give not only a more or less reliable impression of the streets but also of individual buildings and dwellings. It should be noted that the creation of these maps does not coincide with the moment Rubens bought the plot; we have to make do with sixteenth-century plans which show the city as it was some fifty, or at least thirty years earlier.

We will first take another look at the map of Virgilius Bononiensis, which is dated 1565, but shows the layout of the 1550s. This unique document presents a detailed – although certainly not photographically correct – bird's-eye view of Antwerp from the east.[75] A detail of this map (Fig. 1) provides an interesting

---

72. Bredius, *Rubens-document*, 1912, p. 216.
73. Contract in Strauss – Van der Meulen, *Rembrandt*, 1979, p. 159, doc. no. 1639/1. For this, see also Van Eeghen, *Rubens en Rembrandt*, 1977, p. 62; id, *Art at Auction*, 2002, p. 160; Schwartz, *Rembrandt*, 2006, pp. 131–132. Rembrandt produced an etching which shows the country house of Christoffel Thys (*Panorama near Bloemendael Showing the Saxenburg Estate*, 1651); see ibid., p. 263, fig. 437. The idea, put forward by Schama, that in buying a house from the same family, Rembrandt was deliberately following Rubens's example seems far-fetched (Schama, *Rembrandt*, 1999, p. 459: 'was it part of the irresistible attraction?').
74. After Saskia van Uylenburgh's death (in 1642) the house became the property of their son Titus, and it played an important role in Rembrandt's bankruptcy (see Bosman, *Rembrandts plan*, 2019, passim).
75. Virgilius Bononiensis, *Bird's-eye View of Antwerp from the East*, 1565; hand-coloured woodcut, 120 × 265 cm, printed on 20 sheets; unique impression preserved in Antwerp, Museum Plantin-Moretus, inv.

impression of the block containing the parcel later purchased by Rubens. Behind a wall running along the street that connects the Meir to the Hopland (the Kolveniersstraat) can be seen an elongated stretch of land with trees. This is the shooting range of the arquebusiers (*kolveniers*), which bordered the entire east side of Franchoys Gielis's property. The crowns of the tall trees on the sixteenth-century map prevent us from seeing the actual partition between the arquebusiers' practising ground and the *raamveld*. We can assume, however, that the wall mentioned in the sale deed of 1611 ('den muer vande gulden vande coloveriers hove') (Appendix I.2: [3]), and which was repaired in 1615,[76] was already in position. It seems likely that the area reserved for target practice with firearms was safely screened off from the *raamveld*.

Perpendicular to the Wapper, about halfway along this street, on the site of the present Rubenshuis, is a house with a stepped gable at both front and back, and with south-facing windows. However, we cannot know with absolute certainty that this is the house that Rubens bought half a century later. After all, the map reflects a different point in time, and we must be vigilant not to interpret details too literally.

To the left and right of this house, parallel to the Wapper, runs a wall, and on the left-hand side there is a gateway that appears to be crowned by three merlons. Further along to the left, at the corner, are a number of houses, some of which are fronting the Wapper, while others face the Hopland and look out over the much larger *raamveld* of the Lammekensraam.

In all probability a small part of Gielis's *raamveld* – possibly a narrow strip running parallel to the yard of the arquebusiers – extended to the Hopland, as described later in the deed of 1610: 'stretching to the Lammekens raem' (Appendix I.1: [2]). No such passageway can be detected on the map; the only surviving copy is unfortunately damaged in this area.

In other bird's-eye views from the sixteenth century, the houses have a more stereotypical appearance and do not exhibit the same level of accuracy, making them of little use to our research. The elongated, tree-lined plot of land of the arquebusiers is a consistent feature, but there is considerable variation in the arrangement of the houses along the edge of the block and also in the walls that separate individual plots, and we have no means of knowing which of these images is closest to the truth.[77]

no. MPM.V.VI.01.002. It is not possible to give a more precise date than 'the 1550s', as the map does not reflect the layout at one particular moment, but rather combines existing elements with buildings that were still under construction, while also omitting certain buildings; see Voet et al., *Antwerpen*, 1978; Maclot, *Portrait Unmasked*, 2014; Lombaerde – Geerts, *Antwerpen verbeeld*, 2015, pp. 11, 15, no. 14.

76. On this common wall, see below, Chapter IV, pp. 123–124.
77. Concerning the maps to be discussed there is a considerable amount of literature (with some disagreements about dating); for a general overview, see Couvreur, *Iconografie*, 1975, pp. 565, 559–560 (figs); id., *Stadsplattegronden*, 1985, pp. 539–541; De Brabander, *Na-kaarten*, 1988, pp. 19, 56–57, 60–61; Bedeer – Janssens, *Steden in beeld*, 1993, pp. 24–25; Tijs, *Historisch portret*, 2001, pp. 76–77, 85; K. Geerts in Lombaerde – Geerts,

CHAPTER I - A HISTORICAL SKETCH OF THE PROPERTY ON THE WAPPER

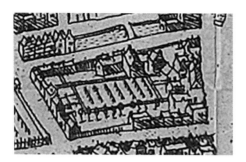

Text ill. 4. Hieronymus Cock, *Bird's-eye View of Antwerp* (1557), engraving, detail. Antwerp, Museum Plantin-Moretus.

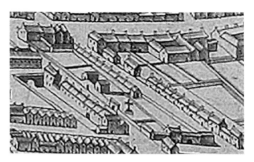

Text ill. 5. Petrus (Pieter) Van der Heyden after Lambert van Noort, *View on the City of Antwerp* (1569), engraving, detail. Antwerp, Museum Plantin-Moretus.

An entirely different layout can be seen, for example, in the view of the city from the east published by Hieronymus Cock (1557). Here the buildings on the side of the Wapper not only include a house with its gable perpendicular to the Wapper, but also a large building with its roof running parallel to the street (Text ill. 4).

Further examples in which the cartographers undoubtedly took liberties when depicting the buildings on the side of the Wapper are the maps by Petrus van der Heyden (1569) and by Frans Hogenberg (1572), both views from the south (Text ills 5–6), and that by Joris Hoefnagel, which shows the city from the east (Text ill. 7).

But these maps do include the interesting detail of the large cross erected in the vacant lot on the Wapper after the church of the so-called Walloon Calvinists had been demolished in 1567, on the orders of Margaret of Parma. It is further worth noting that the *ramen* ('frames') in the yard along the Wapper no longer appear in these maps, in contrast to the nearby Lammekensraam where they are still in evidence. This suggests that the frames had already been removed by then and that the yard was only being used as a bleaching green, something that fits in with the descriptions in the deeds: 'Bleeckhoff' and 'Bleeckvelt' (1610) and 'bleyckhove' (1611) (Appendix I.1: [2] and 2: [3]).

The maps mentioned here only give a rough indication of the location and boundaries of the property bought by Rubens, as is apparent from a comparison with the cadastral plan of Losson of 1846 (Fig. 2), which shows, seen from the west, the individual plots in their correct relative positions.[78] The above observations furthermore demonstrate that, in the absence of sufficient detailed and reliable visual documentation, we cannot form an impression of

Antwerpen verbeeld, 2015, nos 11, 19, 21, 27. The following authors have carefully studied 16th-century maps in relation to Rubens's property, and also reproduce details: Tijs, *Rubens en Jordaens*, 1984, pp. 88, 91; Devroe, *Rubens' huis*, 2008, I, pp. 11–17; II, pp. 2–10, nos 1–9; Maclot, *Rubenssite*, 2016, pp. 36–46.

78. For this cadastral plan, see Chapter II, pp. 79–80, n. 91.

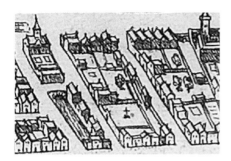

Text ill. 6. Frans Hogenberg, *Map of Antwerp with the Citadel and the Head* (1572), etching, detail. Antwerp, Museum Plantin-Moretus.

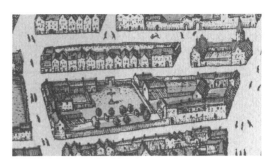

Text ill. 7. Joris Hoefnagel, *Panoramic View of Antwerp* (1574), detail of engraving in Braun – Hogenberg, *Civitates*, 1575.

the dwelling or buildings constructed on the Wapper side of the plot. It is thus impossible to determine the configuration of the elements of the *huysinge* listed in the sale deed of 1611 (a large gate, a courtyard, a gallery, a kitchen and rooms) (Appendix I.2: [3]).

Be this as it may, it would be reasonable to assume that the 'old' ('Flemish') wing of Rubens's house was formed out of an existing house, and that an open, then unbuilt part of the bleaching green became the site for the new ('Italian') wing. Yet, the situation seems not to have been quite so simple. The mention of a 'plaetse' (courtyard) as well as a 'gaelderije' (gallery) suggest that the 'huizing' (property) bought by Rubens already consisted of at least two houses, or wings, which were somehow interconnected. The size of these elements and their location in relation to each other and to the Wapper are matters that cannot be ascertained. The large gate referred to in the deed may correspond to the gate with three merlons on top, which stands some distance away from the houses in the wall that runs along the Wapper, and which can be seen in Bononiensis's map and, in a simplified form, that of Hoefnagel (Fig. 1 and Text ill. 7).

The *gaelderije* probably consisted of an open colonnade along one side of a courtyard or 'patio', an arrangement that was frequently used in sixteenth-century Antwerp to connect the main house with a section lying behind or next to it.[79] Given that we know nothing about the location of the wings and the courtyard, the question of the location of this walkway also remains unresolved. None of the suggestions in the literature are backed by conclusive arguments.

The suspicion that the 'Italian' wing was built on the site of a previous dwelling stems from the unusual layout of the cellars underneath this wing. In the sixteenth and seventeenth centuries, it was common practice to leave

---

79. Rutger Tijs refers to 'Huyzingen' with internal gardens and Tuscan peristyles (Tijs, *Historisch portret*, 2001, pp. 63–65; id., *Atlas*, 2007, pp. 166–168). Petra Maclot, who describes four main types of private houses in 16th-century Antwerp (Maclot, *Portrait Unmasked*, 2014, pp. 34–38), mentions 'the elegant arcades along the courtyard, a major typological feature of the Antwerp building tradition' (ibid., p. 36).

CHAPTER I - A HISTORICAL SKETCH OF THE PROPERTY ON THE WAPPER

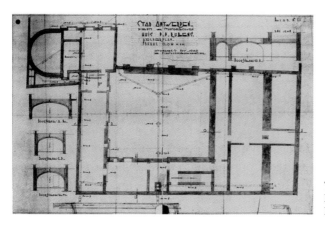

Text ill. 8. Plan of the cellars of the Rubenshuis, blueprint. Antwerp, Rubenshuis Archive.

unchanged the original cellars and foundations of buildings that were rebuilt and we have no reason to believe that a different path was followed in the case of the extension to Rubens's house. What is striking, however, is that underlying the studio are not one but two elongated vaulted cellars, both perpendicular to the Wapper: one spanning the normal width of a cellar, the other, next to it on the north side and aligned with the courtyard, constructed to a narrower format (Text ill. 8).[80] It is tempting to conclude that the largest cellar (on the south side) belonged to an older house and that a second, narrower chamber was added so that the cellar continued underneath the entire width of the studio.

The presence of the old cellar makes it likely that the property bought by Rubens included a dwelling on the south side of the courtyard. The question remains whether Rubens retained parts of the existing house, and substantially altered others.[81] A more likely scenario is that he razed the old structure to the ground (leaving the cellar intact), and built from scratch a new, much broader wing, to his own design – something that is also implied by the term 'aedificavit', used by Philip Rubens to describe the construction of the studio (Appendix I.26).[82]

80. Tijs, who was the first to draw attention to the layout of the cellars, has a different interpretation; according to him, the walkway (the above mentioned 'gaelderije') was situated above the narrow cellar, so perpendicular to the Wapper and aligned to the south side of the present courtyard (Tijs, *Rubens en Jordaens*, 1984, p. 96).
81. This is the view of several authors, including Rutger Tijs, who believes that Rubens never constructed an entirely new, rectangular studio wing, but that, on the contrary, he only converted an existing building into his studio (Tijs, *Rubens en Jordaens*, 1984, p. 96, see also p. 116).
82. Less clear is the wording used by De Piles, *La vie de Rubens*, pp. 12–14 who writes that Rubens purchased a large house which he 'rebastit […] et en embellit le dedans' (Appendix I.31).

D. Subsequent Extension of the Property: The Purchase of a Group of Houses Adjacent to Rubens's Plot

For the sake of completeness we should explain that, in the course of the 1620s, Rubens enlarged the property he had bought from the Thys family. He acquired a number of small houses with their gardens, which bordered his large garden – some situated (to the west) on the Wapper, others on the Hopland (to the south). On 23 December 1621 Rubens purchased a dwelling consisting of two houses on the Hopland (one of which was named 'Breda'), and which adjoined the passageway leading from his garden to the street (Appendix I.15). On 18 July 1627, from a man called Hans Smekens and his wife Tanneke Hendricx, he bought 'sesse huyskens oft wooninghen elck met een hoffken' (six small houses, each with a garden), three of which faced onto the Hopland and three onto the Wapper. The couple kept possession of the large house in the middle known as De Witte Roos, and which occupied the corner between the Wapper and the Hopland (Appendix I.18). A year later Rubens purchased another of the couple's small houses on the Hopland, adjoining those he already owned there (Appendix I.19), so that – as far as we know – he then possessed a total of nine adjacent houses.

More details can be found in the inventory of the 'Staet van goederen' (estate) of Isabella Brant (d. 1626), which was approved 28 August 1628 (Appendix I.20).[83] It lists the houses with a note of their location and the amount of rent collected for each. A total of eight adjacent houses are mentioned, five on the side of the Hopland and three by the Wapper. In 1628 the houses were rented out for various amounts ranging from sixteen to forty-four guilders a year.

The small houses are next mentioned when Rubens's substantial estate is settled. In October 1641 a request is made to obtain permission to sell Rubens's great house along with 'eenighe cleyn huyskens' (a few small houses) that are situated on the Hopland; it is argued that these are in a deplorable state and require major restoration (Appendix I.22).[84] The three houses on the Wapper were apparently in better condition and a decision had been made to include them with the sale of the 'great house'.

---

83. Six of these houses were bought by Rubens after his wife had passed away, but they were part of her estate because the sum paid for these dwellings – 4000 guilders – came from them jointly. The sum constituted a small part of the money (84,000 guilders) Rubens had received from the Duke of Buckingham through the sale of paintings and antique sculptures, a transaction completed in August 1627; since these sculptures were acquired during Isabella Brant's lifetime (in 1618), they had also been her property.
84. It is deemed appropriate to sell the houses because they are 'audt ende caducq syn ende groote reparatien souden behoeven' (old and damaged and would need a great deal of repair work) (Génard, *Nalatenschap*, 1865, p. 168). The request was granted but the houses failed to sell because no acceptable offers were forthcoming.

CHAPTER I - A HISTORICAL SKETCH OF THE PROPERTY ON THE WAPPER

The final settlement of Rubens's estate (the so-called *Staetmasse*, submitted in November 1645) lists the eight adjacent houses, numbering them anti-clockwise from 1 to 8, starting from the one next to the great house on the Wapper and ending with the buildings on the Hopland (Appendix I.23: [4–6]).[85] Additional information is given for no. 8, the house with the highest valuation. Apparently the last tenant had moved out in December 1639 (only six months before Rubens's death), since when Rubens had been using the house himself: he had installed his library there, while it also provided storage for 'slechte' ('insignificant') paintings and copies (Appendix I.23: [5]).[86] As it happens, this last tenant was a hapless painter, David Ryckaert II (1589–1642), by whom only a few works are known and who died in poverty.[87] The description in the *Staetmasse* clearly shows that house no. 8 was situated on the Hopland side and that part of it extended over the entrance or gateway from this street to Rubens's garden. We can therefore reject without hesitation two tentative suggestions for the location of the library mentioned in the literature. It was certainly not in a house near (or partly above?) the other gateway to the garden, leading from the Wapper, on the south side of the studio;[88] nor was it in the small house with stepped gable visible in the background of the 1692 Harrewijn print (Text ill. 37).[89]

No image is known of the houses on the Hopland side. They are not visible in the 1692 Harrewijn print: they must be concealed behind trees, and it is certainly wrong to suggest that Rubens had demolished them.[90]

The only images we have of the houses on the Wapper as they must have looked in the seventeenth century are in Harrewijn's print of 1692. Their fronts are illustrated in the detail at the foot of this print, where they form part of the street façade (Text ill. 9). However, the image shows an alteration in the layout that was realised between 1660 and 1680, during which time the three houses were converted into two dwellings.[91] Their backs are concealed by the trees

---

85. The document records the income generated by the eight houses (rent received from 1641 to September 1645; Appendix I.23: [6]), as well as 20 items of expenditure for maintenance (Appendix I. 23: [7–9]). Valuations for the dwellings on the Hopland range from 1200 guilders (nos 6 and 7 together) to 2650 guilders (no. 8); valuations for the houses on the Wapper were omitted because these were being sold together with the great house.
86. For the library, see Baudouin, *Pictor doctus*, 2001, pp. 72–74 (his theory about the possible location of the library needs to be rectified; see below, n. 88).
87. This David Ryckaert was the father of the well-known genre painter David Ryckaert III, and a brother of the painter Maarten Ryckaert, whose impressive portrait by Anthony van Dyck is preserved at the Museo Nacional del Prado in Madrid. Rubens's former tenant died a few years after leaving the house (buried 3 October 1642); his meagre estate was seized because of debts (Van den Branden, *Schilderschool*, 1883, p. 604).
88. Suggested by Baudouin, *Pictor doctus*, 2001, p. 74.
89. Uppenkamp, *Rubens's palazzetto*, 2018, pp. 219–220, 230, n. 3, as 'the servants' house' (but more likely the stables; see Chapter III, pp. 108–109).
90. Suggested by Heinen, *Garten*, 2002, p. 1; id., *Gesundheit*, 2004, p. 106.
91. For this conversion, see below, Chapter III, p. 102.

CHAPTER I - A HISTORICAL SKETCH OF THE PROPERTY ON THE WAPPER

Text ill. 9. Detail of the 1692 Harrewijn print (Fig. 18): the remodelled houses on the right of Rubens's house on the Wapper.

in their gardens that can be seen behind the high wall that lies between the entrance gate and the small house with stepped gable at the left (Text ill. 37).[92]

Did Rubens buy the plot with the intention of rebuilding some or all of the adjacent houses, or at least a wish to incorporate them in his property? Whatever plans he may have had, it seems that the houses remained independent dwellings until his death and, with the exception of the earlier mentioned house on the Hopland, were rented out to third parties.

We should mention at this point that there is no reason to believe that Rubens used the adjacent houses to put up pupils and assistants ('at times rent free'), as has sometimes been suggested.[93] Likewise it seems unlikely that they served as accommodation for domestic staff.[94]

In any case, the rental houses were undoubtedly an investment. By adding them to his property, Rubens moreover procured an advantage which may have outweighed the financial benefit: it allowed him to have more control over the view from his garden and, significantly, the sunlight entering it. While

92. Comparison with the Bononiensis map (Fig. 1) reveals that the four stepped gables that rise above the trees are the street fronts of the large houses on the far side of the Wapper, opposite the houses in question, and on the west side of the canal.
93. With thanks to Nils Büttner for explaining the misunderstanding that arose from a suggestion which he expressed only orally, but was taken for a documented fact by Jakumeit, *Review Rubens – Baroque Passion*, 2005, p. 334; followed by Logan, *Rubens as a Teacher*, 2006, p. 263, n. 64: 'Nils Büttner found documents showing that Rubens bought houses […] and allowed artists to live in them, at times rent free').
94. A possibility considered by Bert Watteeuw, who has investigated what is known about the servants in Rubens's household and points out that we have no idea where they slept in the house (Watteeuw, *Domestic Staff*, 2015, p. 60).

the east side was taken care of by the unbuilt and 'green' shooting range of the arquebusiers, the acquisition of the adjacent houses meant that Rubens also gained control over large parts of the west and south of the block. That this was one of the reasons, indeed the principal one, for buying the houses emerges from an unusual stipulation in the two contracts exchanged between Rubens and the Smekenses in 1627 and 1628. As mentioned, Rubens bought from them a total of seven small houses to the south and west of his garden. The contract mentions an easement, which, as we know from the sale deed, already existed when the plot was still being used as a bleaching green. The contract stipulates that the vendors are not allowed to raise the height of the houses remaining in their possession. In the backyards of these houses, they were also prevented from constructing any new buildings – in stone or timber – above the existing height. The condition was made to ensure that 'the sun would not be taken away from the yard' ('om nyet te benemen de sonne van de hoff') – i.e. the former bleaching green, which now belongs to Rubens.[95]

95. More or less the same wording is used in the deeds of 18 July 1627 and 15 June 1628 (Appendix I.18–19); in order to bleach linen it was essential to have enough sunlight. The deeds also include agreements about communal walls, wells and water drainage; see also Maclot, *Rubenssite*, 2016, p. 57.

Chapter II
Eye Witnesses to the House:
Written and Pictorial References

All the evidence indicates that after buying the property in 1610–1611, Rubens altered it substantially to suit his needs. It should be stressed that we only have a fragmentary impression of what the house looked like during his lifetime. Indeed, the available sources are simply too few to allow us to form much of a picture. The idea that we have sound knowledge of Rubens's house is a misconception, something that is partly reinforced by the current house, which has been turned into a museum but which is for the most part a reconstruction of the years 1939–1946.

Nonetheless the building itself, or what remained of it in 1938, can be regarded as an important source which provides essential information. This is true not only for the elements that survive in more or less original form – the portico, the garden pavilion, the roof trusses of the studio wing, and the cellars – but also for specific aspects such as dimensions and exact locations. In preparation for restoration and reconstruction, all possible original traces that could be retrieved from the walls, floors, the roof structure, the cellars and the garden were scrutinised. A number of aspects of this research, and the conclusions drawn, will be discussed elsewhere in this volume.[1]

Written and visual sources give an idea of the house as it was after it had been altered and extended by Rubens, and these were of course used as the basis for the restoration. They provide interesting information, but also leave many questions unanswered, and at times they contradict each other. Records that survive from Rubens's own lifetime are very scarce and they give us almost no concrete information about either the exterior or interior of the building.

A. The House in the Time of Rubens and his Family: History and Written Sources (1611–1648)

Information from Rubens Himself

We have little information from Rubens himself about the house. One of the few interesting documents in this respect is the deposition that Rubens signed

---

1. For the restoration and the extensive literature on this issue, see below pp. 82–85.

before a notary in 1621, and which came to light only recently. In it he states that in 1615 carpenters had failed to install the (wooden) boarding on his roof correctly (Appendix I.14).[2]

In Rubens's extensive correspondence there are only three passages in which mention is made, one way or another, of the house he owned for almost thirty years.[3] In 1618 he remarks in a letter to Sir Dudley Carleton (1573–1632) that the building work has been very costly (Appendix I.10). On only two occasions does he mention a specific location in the house. Writing to Nicolas Claude Fabri de Peiresc (1580–1630) on 3 August 1623 he refers, in connection with the installation of a perpetual motion machine, to a room that he calls 'mio studiolo secreto' (my private study) (Appendix I.16). A sentence in a letter to Lucas Faydherbe (1617–1697) written from Elewijt fifteen years later, on 17 August 1638, reveals a rare detail about the interior: Rubens urges his young assistant to make sure that no originals or sketches are left out upstairs in the studio (or the studio wing) ('datter geen originaelen en blyven staen *boven op het schilderhuys* oft eenige schetsen') (Appendix I.21). Later we will return more fully to these locations in the house mentioned by Rubens.

The correspondence tells us nothing about the conditions that affected the people who lived and worked in the house: Rubens,[4] his family, their live-in servants and the many workshop assistants.

Philip Rubens, Rubens's Nephew

Rubens's relatives and members of his immediate circle remain silent on the subject of the house, with one notable exception: a short passage in the Latin *Vita Petri Pauli Rubenii*, the biography of Rubens written by his nephew Philip (1611–1678) around 1675, and which is based on a lost memoir of Rubens by his son Albert. Philip, who spent part of his childhood living on the Meir, and so just around the corner from his uncle (and guardian), was undoubtedly well acquainted with the house, and his involvement with it continued even after Rubens's death. At the moment when Rubens's sons Nicolaas and Albert died (in 1655 and 1657 respectively), Philip was next-of-kin of their children. He was directly involved in the initial attempts to sell the property and in the final sale in 1660 (Appendix I.22, 25).

2. For more details on the contents of this deposition, see Chapter IV, pp. 124–125.
3. A few other references that tell us nothing about the building have been omitted here. For example, his wish to be able to return to his home ('in casa mia'), 'that really has need of my presence' (Letter to Pierre Dupuy, written in London on 8 August 1629; Magurn, ed., *Letters*, 1955, p. 321, no. 195; Rooses – Ruelens, eds, *Correspondance*, 1887–1909, V, pp. 148–149, under no. DCXV.
4. A somewhat unexpected situation, which apparently affected Rubens himself – if we are to take his comment literally – occurs in a letter to Pierre Dupuy, dated 27 January 1628. Rubens is writing from Antwerp, so presumably from his house, and observes that it is so cold there '… that the ink freezes in the pen' (Magurn, ibid., p. 235, no. 145; Rooses – Ruelens, eds, *Correspondance*, 1887–1909, IV, pp. 358–359, under no. DXXXIII).

In his *Vita* Philip devotes a few lines to describing his famous uncle's house (Appendix I.26). The short passage, in Latin, can be rendered as follows: while Rubens was still living with his parents-in-law, he bought himself a house ('aedes proprias emit'), next to which was a large yard ('magnamque aream'); there he built a large extension in Roman style ('ubi diaetam amplissimam romanâ formâ aedificavit'), which lent itself well as a painting studio ('picturae studio aptam'); the special garden also gets a mention. One puzzling word in this brief description is 'diaeta', which can have several meanings: not just 'a place of residence', 'a dwelling', but more specifically 'an extension' or an outbuilding, such as a garden pavilion or a summer house.[5] This word, and also the phrase 'romanâ formâ' (in Roman style) may have been copied from Albert Rubens's lost Latin text, and the terminology employed is possibly based on information from Rubens himself.

'Tourists' Visiting Rubens (1614–c. 1635)

Soon after Rubens's move back from Italy to Antwerp, and even before he built his studio wing on the Wapper, his well-organised and successful studio with many assistants had become widely known. In 1611 he had already been forced to turn down, by his own testimony, more than a hundred applicants who hoped for an apprenticeship in his studio.[6]

Together with the Officina Plantiniana and the *Tapissierspand* the famous painter's studio became one of the unmissable sights of a visit to Antwerp. It seems to have been a standard part of the Grand Tour of Europe that was undertaken by young men as the completion of their education. But other travellers also made sure to include in their programme a visit to Rubens's house, which from the 1620s meant not just the celebrated studio but the possibility of seeing his extraordinary art collection. Giovanni Pietro Bellori (1613–1696) reports that '… [there was] no foreigner passing through Antwerp who did not see his collection …'.[7] According to Roger de Piles (1635–1709), 'persons of all conditions, including the most exalted princes and nobles visited the collection'.[8] It was not only the collection that attracted interest, but also, apparently, the well-organised studio, which – as was widely known – allowed the clever artist to make a lot of money with relatively little effort.

---

5. We owe thanks to our late colleague Jeanine De Landtsheer (d. 2020) for help with translating and interpretation of this term. Lind, *Rubens*, 1946, p. 39 translates 'diaeta' as summer house (see Appendix I.26). For a further discussion of this, see also the section on the studio wing (Chapter V, p. 156, nn. 45, 46).
6. See Rubens's often cited letter of 11 May 1611 to Jacques de Bie (see Chapter I, p. 38, n. 63).
7. Appendix I.28; citation from Muller, *Collector*, 1989, p. 65.
8. Ibid., p. 65. For a full discussion of the visitors to Rubens's famous collection, see ibid., pp. 65–66; Muller, *Rubens's Collection*, 2004, pp. 65–66; Büttner, *Rubens berühmt*, 2006, pp. 91, 93, 96.

CHAPTER II - EYE WITNESSES TO THE HOUSE

During the artist's lifetime numerous 'tourists' paid a visit to Rubens and thus saw his house as well as the studio working at full capacity, but only four have left written testimony. It is important to add that it is not always apparent how reliable their information is; at times we wonder whether their descriptions match what they really saw, or if they have spiced up their account with details from other sources. Either way, these written sources tend to be no more than a few lines long and mostly express praise for the splendid house and the great master's unique collection.

It seems likely that Rubens received visitors in his famous studio before the moment it was established in the south wing of his house on the Wapper, or before this section of his house had reached its final state. This can be inferred from the account of a visit that took place in early 1614. The earliest surviving record of a visit to Rubens's studio comes from a group of German noblemen who stayed in Antwerp with their entourage from 31 January to 6 February 1614. Two members of this party published an account of their journey that took in several European countries. The report by Johann Wilhelm Neumayer von Ramssla (1572–1641), published in 1620, gives an almost day-by-day account of the visit to the city. We are informed that the company has been to visit the 'vortreffliche' ('outstanding') painters Peter Paul Rubens and Jan Brueghel I (1568–1625). They were surprised by the large amount of money Rubens was able to earn (100 guilders a week) (Appendix I.13). Thomas Sagittarius (1577–1621), who described the same journey in Latin verse (published in 1621), devotes twenty lines to the visit to the famous painters: he pays tribute to their talent by comparing them to Apelles.[9] The German tourists do not mention any particular paintings, but we know that in February 1614 they would have been able to see the side panels of *The Triptych of the Descent from the Cross*, since they visited the studio just a few weeks before the panels were taken to the cathedral (Appendix I.3). Neither of these authors gives any information about the location of the house and studio, and in any case, as discussed, we cannot be certain that Rubens had actually established his workshop in the property on the Wapper as early as February 1614.[10]

In his *Ulysses Belgico-Gallicus* of 1631, which is more a travel guide with detailed comments than a personal travel journal, Abraham Golnitzius writes

---

9. Sagittarius, *Ulysses Saxonicus*, 1621, p. 232; Goris, *Lof van Antwerpen*, 1940, pp. 64–65 (with Dutch translation, p. 65, n. 1); Arents, *Bibliotheek*, 2001, pp. 292–293, no. Q6; Büttner – Heinen, eds, *Quellen und Dokumente*, 2011, under 'Viten und Werkungszeugnisse'. Both Jan-Albert Goris and Prosper Arents wrongly date the Antwerp visit of these noblemen to 1613, misled by the departure date which is given in the title of Sagittarius's book.
10. For the assumption that the studio was in Jan Brant's house, see Chapter IV, pp. 131–132, n. 46. Jan Brueghel I (1568–1625) had his studio in a large house called De Meerminne (The Mermaid), which he had bought in 1604 in the Lange Nieuwstraat, the street in which Hendrick van Balen (1573–1632) also lived (Woollett, *Rubens and Brueghel*, 2006, pp. 10–11). The fact that the German 'tourists' mention Rubens and Brueghel in the same breath suggests the possibility that in early 1614 their studios were not far apart (or even in the same house?).

about his visit to Rubens ('vivum Europae miraculum') in the 1620s. But he merely describes works of art that he saw in the workshop – although his claim to have seen certain paintings is doubtful.[11]

Equally concise is the passage referring to the Italian painter Mattia Preti (1613–1699), who was received, probably in the 1630s, by Rubens in his 'magnifica Casa', which housed a remarkable collection of artworks.[12]

Otto Sperling

A more elaborate eyewitness report with regard to the interior of the house, and without question one of the most frequently quoted passages in the entire Rubens literature, is that of Otto Sperling (1602–1681), a German medical student at Leiden University who called on the famous painter in 1621 (Appendix I.27). His account seems at first sight to be wholly reliable, but we need to be cautious. Parts of it are difficult to interpret and seem at odds with the facts. It is important to note that Sperling wrote his report more than forty years after his visit to Antwerp, at a time when he was in prison in Copenhagen, from 1664 until his death in 1681. It is fair, therefore, to query the accuracy of his memories. In addition, it appears that Sperling tried to make his story more interesting by presenting certain details that he heard from others as though they were first-hand experiences. For example, he describes an improbable encounter that he and his travel companion had enjoyed at the house of the Jesuit Schottius: they happened to find Hugo Grotius there who had just escaped from Loevestein Castle and he allegedly told them in person the exciting story of his getaway. However, such a meeting is chronologically impossible. According to Sperling, he and his travel companion arrived in Antwerp two days before the Feast of Corpus Christi (29 May 1621), while Grotius had already left Antwerp for Paris on 3 April.[13]

According to Sperling's account, the two students received a friendly welcome at Rubens's house. They were introduced to the master himself and a servant had then shown them round his magnificent palazzo ('seinem

---

11. Golnitzius, *Ulysses*, 1631, pp. 71–72; Rooses, *Reizigers*, 1898, pp. 223–224. Golnitzius (also Golnitz or Göllnitz) came from Danzig. Little is known about him; in 1642 he is recorded as secretary to Christian IV of Denmark. It is hard to believe that he saw the 22 paintings of the *Medici* series in Rubens's workshop, as he claims. Based on these works, the date of the visit was assumed by Rooses to be 1624, but there is no further information to support this and the date remains uncertain. The visit has also been dated to around 1620 (Büttner, *Rubens berühmt*, 2006, p. 96) and 1625 (Simson, *Rubens*, 1996, p. 214). Interestingly, in a later French edition of the *Ulysses* the Medici paintings are omitted (Coulon, *L'Ulysse*, 1643, pp. 50, 51). On 2 March 1633 Rubens ordered a copy of the *Ulysses* from Balthasar Moretus for his son Albert (Arents, *Bibliotheek*, 2001, pp. 293–294, no. Q8; De Schepper, ed., *Rubens' Bibliotheek*, 2004, p. 62, no. 27).
12. Published a century later in De Dominici, *Vite*, 1742, pp. 319–320.
13. This incongruity as well as further rather improbable details in Sperling's account were observed by Carl Van de Velde (Van de Velde, *Rubens's Letters*, 2011, p. 3); for Grotius's sojourn in Antwerp, and his departure, see Nellen, *Hugo de Groot*, 2007, pp. 259–260.

CHAPTER II - EYE WITNESSES TO THE HOUSE

herrlichen Palatio') full of Greek and Roman sculptures. They also saw a large room that had no windows, but was lit only from above, and which had many young painters working in it. Sperling remarks on the organisation of the studio and the production process of the paintings; according to him, the paintings were retouched in just one or two places by Rubens but he was still happy to release them as 'Rübbens Werck'. Like Neumayer von Ramssla, Sperling feels the need to mention the great wealth that Rubens has managed to accumulate and the precious gifts he has received from kings and princes (Appendix I.27).

In all probability Sperling and his travel companion did visit Rubens's house, but as already mentioned, it is difficult to know how much his memories are distorted after forty years and how much he added to his account in order to make it more interesting. Max Rooses questioned Sperling's reliability. He was particularly concerned by the description of Sperling's encounter with Rubens who, like a 'braggart', could simultaneously paint, conduct a conversation, dictate a letter and listen to a book being read to him.[14] We will return to Sperling's 'large top-lit room' in Chapter VII.

Princely Visitors (1625–1635)

There are various brief mentions and reports of noble visitors coming to honour Rubens. After the fall of Breda, the Infanta Isabella went to Antwerp, where she paid a visit to Rubens on 10 July 1625. Although it is possible that she had called on her court painter on a previous occasion, this was probably her first visit to the house on the Wapper.[15] In mentioning the visit in his journal, Philippe Chifflet (1597–1657) only informs us that the Infanta was particularly taken with the Egyptian mummy which Rubens kept in his 'Panthéon' (Appendix I.17). Chifflet's focus is somewhat unusual – given the presence of so many art treasures in the house – and it may reflect his own interest in this rare object in Rubens's collection, rather than that of the Infanta.[16]

---

14. Rooses, *Huis van Rubens*, 1910, p. 203 [p. 15].
15. During a visit to Antwerp ten years earlier, in August 1615, the archdukes visited the mint building (De Munt) and the *kunstkamer* of Cornelis van der Geest (1575–1638). Whether they paid Rubens the honour of a visit on that occasion, as claimed by some, cannot be confirmed. But it seems unlikely that Rubens would have received them in his house, which was still unfinished at the time (we know that the construction of a staircase was subcontracted more than a year later; see Appendix I.9 and No. 19). In September 1631 the Infanta visited Antwerp in the company of Maria de' Medici who had fled from France. The Queen visited Rubens (Puget de la Serre, *Histoire curieuse*, 1632, p. 68; see also n. 17), but it is not known if the Infanta was also present on this occasion, as Puget de la Serre does not mention this explicitly.
16. His mention certainly seems to relate to a book by his brother, the physician Jean-Jacques Chifflet (1588–1660), about ancient burial rites as well as Jesus's grave (Chifflet, *De linteis*, 1624). Rubens bought two copies of this publication at the end of 1624 (Arents, *Bibliotheek*, 2001, p. 170, E94; De Schepper, ed., *Rubens' Bibliotheek*, 2004, pp. 77–78, no. 40). For the mummy and coffin in Rubens's collection, see Muller, *Collector*, 1989, p. 150, cat. III, no. 1, pl. 125; Van der Meulen, *Antique (CRLB)*, 1994, I, p. 29, n. 12; Belkin – Healy, *House of Art*, 2004, no. 78.

In September 1631 the exiled French Queen-Mother Maria de' Medici (1573–1642) stayed in Antwerp and went to Rubens's workshop to admire his paintings. Her chronicler Jean Puget de la Serre (1594–1665) devotes just two lines to the occasion and then goes on to sing the praises of Rubens and his art.[17]

Jan Gaspar Gevartius (1593–1666) writes at some length about the visit paid by the Cardinal-Infante Ferdinand in April 1635, but this is a purely rhetorical eulogy that adds nothing to our knowledge of the house itself.[18]

Colleagues and Patrons

Finally, it should be remembered that Rubens's house was of course familiar to numerous artists, but none of these seems to have produced any written testimony. The same holds true for the various patrons and envoys who visited Rubens on the Wapper. All we have is a brief passage in a letter from John Wolley to Dudley Carleton, dated 8 February 1620, from which very little can be deduced; Wolley reports that he has been round to Rubens's house to look at a painting by Bassano. The two had a conversation, after which Rubens had taken him to 'a chamber' to show him the painting in question.[19] From this short reference we can obviously not deduce whereabouts in the house the men had conducted their conversation, nor where the painting was kept.[20]

The Heirs, Including Helena Fourment (1640–1648)

After Rubens's death, the house together with a number of the adjacent small houses passed undivided to his eight heirs. Half of the property was assigned to his two 'voorzonen' ('sons from the first marriage'), Albert and Nicolaas, because it was also counted as part of the estate of their mother, Isabella Brant. The remaining half was split in two again, and one half (i.e. a quarter of the

---

17. 'La Reyne eut la curiosité de voir toutes les belles & riches peintures qui sont dans la maison de Monsieur Rubens' (Puget de la Serre, *Histoire curieuse*, 1632, p. 68). Although a precise date is sometimes given (at least once as 10 September), the queen's visit cannot be dated more accurately than between 4 September (the day she left Brussels for Antwerp; Henrard, *Marie de Médicis*, 1876, p. 92) and 2 October (the date of a letter from Balthasar Gerbier (1592–1663), in which he mentions her contact with Rubens; Rooses – Ruelens, eds, *Correspondance*, 1887–1909, V, p. 449). With sincere thanks to Nils Büttner for helping clarify this. We know that Rubens owned a copy of the *Histoire Curieuse*, bought from the Plantin publishing house, on 18 February 1632 (Arents, *Biboliotheek*, p. 181, no. E132).
18. Gevartius points out that the prince was following the example of Alexander the Great who visited the studio of Apelles; he refers to Rubens as 'aevi nostri Apelles', and also compares him to the Greek painter and philosopher Metrodorus of Athens (mid 2nd century bc), who depicted the Triumph of Lucius Aemilius Paulus (Gevartius, *Pompa Introitus*, 1642, p. 171); see also Büttner, *Rubens berühmt*, 2006, p. 93, n. 46; Knaap – Putnam, eds, *Pompa Introitus*, 2013, p. 28; for the Apelles anecdote recorded by Pliny (Pliny, *Natural History*, XXV.135), see McHam, *Pliny*, 2013, pp. 45–46, 318, 334, anecdote no. 82.
19. Rooses – Ruelens, *Correspondance*, 1887–1909, II, pp. 244, 246, under no. CXCIX.
20. During the reconstruction of the house it was concluded from this vague passage that the ground floor very likely included an antechamber or audience room (Van Averbeke, *Rubenhuis. Restauratie II*, 1938, p. 48), and a corresponding room was created on the street side, adjoining the studio.

total) then went to the artist's widow, while the other was divided into eight 'child's portions' (so 1/32 of the overall property) to be distributed equally among all eight heirs. In other words, Albert (1614–1657), Nicolaas (1618–1673) and Helena Fourment (1614–1673) each owned one quarter plus 1/32 of the property, while the five younger children each owned 1/32 part.[21]

The house was thus not simply inherited by Helena Fourment, as is often assumed in the literature, but after Rubens's death she did not leave the house immediately. Before moving permanently to Brussels, she continued to live there for a number of years as a tenant paying rent, first as widow with her five children, and then also for a shorter time after her marriage (probably in early 1644) to Jan-Baptist van Broechoven van Bergeyck (1619–1681). That she rented the house emerges from a passage in the so-called *Staetmasse*, the account of Rubens's estate, which was submitted in November 1645. Entries recording income for the estate or *sterfhuis* mention that since Rubens's death his widow has continued to live in the house; the initial lease was for two years, and this was then extended for three more years, until 'bamis' (1 October) 1645.[22] The annual rent was set at 400 guilders, half of which was due to the *sterfhuis* (Appendix I.23: [3]).

The *Staetmasse*

There is no information at all about the house for the period when it was occupied by Helena Fourment, her children and second husband. From the *Staetmasse*, the account of Rubens's estate, we know that in these years a large part of the contents of the house – 'all the art objects, paintings and antiquities' ('alle de consten, schilderijen en antiquiteiten') – had been sold, and it seems likely that the spacious studios and other areas used for his profession by Rubens soon acquired new functions.

It should be remembered that no inventories of the contents of the house survive. A comprehensive document of this kind, specifying the location of each object, was customarily drawn up for the benefit of children who were minors at the death of a parent. Such lists must therefore have been made both when Isabella Brant died and at Rubens's death, but, regrettably, no copy of these extremely important documents survive.[23] Nor do we have domestic inventories for any of the subsequent seventeenth-century residents of the house. This means that for the whole of the seventeenth century we lack

---

21. For this division, see the sale deed of 1660 and the accounts of the estate (see below, p. 72, n. 71).
22. Bamis or 'bamisse' is a contraction of 'Baafmis' or 'Bavomis', the feast of St Bavo.
23. The *Staetmasse* indicates that an inventory of the house of the deceased was drawn up on Rubens's death by the notary Toussaint Guyot (8 June 1640 and following days); see Génard, *Nalatenschap*, 1865, p. 71; Muller, *Collector*, 1989, p. 92.

CHAPTER II - EYE WITNESSES TO THE HOUSE

detailed inventories of the contents of the house, documents we might have expected to provide information about the layout of its interior.

A few scattered details, however, can be retrieved from the 1645 account of Rubens's estate or *Staetmasse*. It lists close to five hundred items of income and expenditure, including many debts outstanding at the time of Rubens's death. Only six of the entries in this voluminous document make reference to the property on the Wapper. Besides the rent paid by Helena Fourment (as mentioned, an annual sum of four hundred guilders), there are the usual repairs and maintenance costs: to the windowpanes, and to the 'slate roofs on the *groote huyssinge* [main building] on the Wapper'.

There are two entries connected with the studio or the studio wing ('het schilderhuys') which are interesting but difficult to interpret. We are informed that a house painter or *kladschilder* has been paid for applying a grey wash to the studio (Appendix I.23: [7]). It is not clear from this what exactly has been painted, or even whether it was the interior or exterior.[24] Another entry mentions three guilders paid for making 'blaffeturen' ('window shutters') in the *schilderhuys* (Appendix I.23: [9]). Some have believed that these were shutters fixed to the outside of the studio windows, but this possibility can be firmly ruled out and the hypothesis was ignored in the restoration.[25] In any case, the document clearly states 'in' the *schilderhuys*. It seems possible that these 'blaffeturen' were blinds which were somehow attached to the insides of the windows in order to soften the light in the studio, a matter which will be discussed in a later chapter.[26]

Only one record in the *Staetmasse* offers slightly more precise information about the structure, function and decoration of the interior: the estate or *sterfhuis* is credited with more than one hundred guilders from the sale of ivory from the 'thoren' ('tower') in which Rubens's antiquities were kept (Appendix I.23: [1]).[27]

Attempts had been made to sell the house as early as 1645, but they were not immediately successful. It was not until 1660 that the remarkable house finally found a buyer who was willing to pay the large sum demanded. Given that the undivided property belonged to eight and later ten heirs (following the deaths of Nicolaas and Albert, in 1655 and 1657 respectively, their share passed to their

24. Tijs infers from this entry that the inside of the house must have been whitewashed (Tijs, *Rubens en Jordaens*, 1984, p. 141; id., *Rubens*, 2004, p. 235); Maclot also sees other possibilities, such as the outer walls, or maintenance of plinths, etc. (Maclot, *Rubenssite*, 2016, p. 60).
25. It was thought that the studio windows originally had exterior shutters, because the window openings were all found to have iron hinges on which shutters could have moved (notes from Van Averbeke, with drawing; see Devroe, *Rubens' huis*, 2008, I, pp. 72–73; II, p. 76, no. 61); this idea was rightly dismissed by authors, including Tijs and Maclot, who believed that the *blaffeturen* were interior screens (made of parchment, paper or textile). See Tijs, *Rubens en Jordaens*, 1984, p. 141; id., *Rubens*, 2004, p. 235; Maclot, *Rubenssite*, 2016, pp. 60, 170.
26. On the light in the studio, see Chapter VII, p. 209, n. 22.
27. We will return to this 'ivory from the tower' in Chapter VIII, p. 244, n. 37; Chapter XI, p. 329.

children), it seems most unlikely that any important changes were made to the property between Rubens's death in 1640 and the sale of the house in 1660.

B. The House in the Time of Rubens and his Family: Contemporary Depictions (up to c. 1645)

Unfortunately Missing: Designs by Rubens

There can be no doubt that Rubens made designs (drawings or perhaps also oil sketches?) for architectural components and decorative elements of his house, yet almost nothing of this material survives, arguably not even in copied form.[28] At present we know of only two drawings for scenes that decorated the studio façades (No. 10a and No. 13a; Figs 65 and 96) and indistinct architectural studies in black chalk that can be found on the verso of two of Rubens's drawings (No. 7a and No. 13b; Figs 54 and 97).

At the end of the eighteenth century there were perhaps still four sheets surviving with architectural designs for the house, together with a design for the façade of the Antwerp Jesuit Church. These were in the collection of Pierre Wouters which was auctioned in Brussels in 1801.[29] However nothing more is known about these drawings, which were described as 'dessins d'architecture pour sa propre maison', and so – regardless of whether they were originals or copies[30] – it is not possible to establish exactly what they showed.

Therefore what little remains of Rubens's preparatory work is so minimal that it contributes more or less nothing to our knowledge of the house.

Panneels and the *Rubens Cantoor* (c. 1622–c. 1630)

Only two of Rubens's many collaborators (who would of course have known parts of the house very well) have left us drawings representing elements of the building. One is by Anthony van Dyck and shows a detail of the portico (No. 24, Copy; Fig. 139). A more interesting group, however, and forming a separate category in the contemporary visual sources, are the drawings firmly

---

28. For discussion of drawings that may have been copies after Rubens's designs rather than after a wall painting on the façade, see under Nos 11–12 and 18.
29. Wherebouts unknown, probably lost; technical details unknown. prov.: Pierre Wouters, his sale, Brussels, 16–18 November 1801 (catalogue of 1797), lot 528, as 'La façade de l'église des Jésuites à Anvers [...] et 4 diff. desseins d'architecture pour sa propre maison'; lit.: T'Sas, *Catalogue*, 1797, p. 246, no. 528; Delen, *Rubens' huis*, 1933, p. 26; Fabri – Lombaerde, *Jesuit Church (CRLB)*, 2018, pp. 74 (n. 57), 218 (n. 15).
30. It seems very doubtful that they were originals. Pierre Wouters was canon of the Church of St Gommarus in Lier, but he lived in Brussels. His estate contained a collection of 2000 drawings, in 1527 lots, including 120 sheets attributed to Rubens – a large group which raises questions. Michiel Plomp understandably queried the validity of the attributions in Wouters's catalogue, describing the extensive collection of so-called Rubens drawings as 'Rubens school rather than Rubens originals' (Plomp, *Collecting*, 2005, pp. 53, 54).

attributed to Willem Panneels (1600 or 1605–1634), which date from the 1620s. They include some of the earliest known images of the house, or at least of certain details. As Rubens's pupil (from 1622) and then as his assistant, Panneels had known the house very well in the 1620s. Moreover, while Rubens was away on diplomatic missions in Madrid and then London, from the end of 1628 until about March – April 1630, he entrusted the care of the closed-up workshop to Panneels.[31] As we know, during this time – and possibly already in the years before – he produced a series of drawings after works by his master, a collection that was supplemented with anonymous copies, in all totalling five hundred sheets, now preserved in Copenhagen and known as the *Rubens Cantoor*.[32]

A number of drawings in the *Cantoor* show decorative details of the house which would have been visible from the courtyard, and so were not necessarily made 'clandestinely' during Rubens's absence abroad. One of these features a striking sculptural element of the portico, namely one of the satyrs in the spandrels (Fig. 174), two others show scenes taken from the painted frieze on the façade of the studio (Figs 71, 84).[33] Other sheets in the *Cantoor* collection are possibly also related to the house, among them copies after an *Andromeda Liberated by Perseus*, but with these it is harder to be certain (see under No. 18 and No. 37).

On two of these copied sheets with decorative details of Rubens's house, the location of the original is written by Panneels in his secret code. The satyress in high-relief is described as 'in Rubens's courtyard' ('op de pledts tot rubbens'). Particularly interesting is the inscription under a scene with Alexander the Great (No. 12, Copy; Fig. 84), which explicitly states that this scene was *painted* on Rubens's house ('geschildert opt huys van sino[r] rubbens').

Interestingly, two locations in the interior of the house are also mentioned on the drawings. On several sheets it is noted that the originals copied by Panneels had been 'fetched' from Rubens's *cantoor*. Rather than a cabinet or cupboard, this may have been the name of a room – although it should be added that no such room can be located in the house, a matter to which we will return later.[34] Similarly, it is not possible to establish the location of 'het Saelken' (the room) where, according to inscriptions on two of the sheets, there was a painting of a Silenus.[35]

---

31. For the biographical data of this little-known master, his stay with Rubens and the problems of attribution, see Huvenne, *Rubens' Cantoor*, 1993, passim; Duverger, *Panneels*, 1993, passim; Balis, *Panneels*, 2020, pp. 3–6.
32. A selection from this group of drawings was published in Garff – de la Fuente Pedersen, *Panneels*, 1988; Huvenne – Kockelbergh, eds, *Cantoor*, 1993; see also Held, *Review Garff – de la Fuente Pedersen*, 1991; Svenningsen, *Rubens Cantoor*, 2013.
33. For more information about these sheets, see the respective entries, under Copies in Nos 11, 12 and 31.
34. For the location of the 'Cantoor', see Chapter VII, pp. 225–226.
35. Garff – de la Fuente Pedersen, *Panneels*, 1988, nos 56–57.

CHAPTER II - EYE WITNESSES TO THE HOUSE

The House as a Background in Paintings

Contemporary sources include images of sections or details of the house in Rubens's own paintings as well as those of a number of contemporaries who undoubtedly knew the house well. It should be stressed, however, that these works were not made with the intention of documenting the house. They by no means provide a 'realistic' impression, and so we must be careful not to take them too literally when it comes to details.

Sections of the house – or more accurately, architectural elements that bear a strong resemblance to the property on the Wapper as it must have looked in Rubens's day – served as a natural and stylish backdrop for portraits of members of the Rubens family. Rubens's *Portrait of Hélène Fourment au carrosse*, in the Musée du Louvre (1630s; Appendix III.7; Fig. 21), shows an idealised image of the 'Italian' house on the Wapper.[36] More interesting, but problematic in terms of its attribution, is the painting *The Walk in the Garden* in the Alte Pinakothek in Munich (Appendix III.6; Fig. 25); this offers a detailed view from around 1630 of the garden and pavilion, but with some imaginative changes: the architecture has a 'richer' appearance and the artist has added elements which allude to the theme of love.[37]

Anthony van Dyck (1599–1641) used the portico as the backdrop for his *Portrait of Isabella Brant* (Appendix III.5; Fig. 19), while Philip Fruytiers (1610–1660) depicted Rubens's children walking through a vine-decked arbour which incorporates elements of the garden pavilion (Appendix III.26).[38] A simplified version of the portico – with some important differences in the details – appears in the anonymous portrait of an unidentified man, painted in 1636 (Text ill. 119).[39]

We should also consider a work that has hitherto received little attention in relation to the study of Rubens's house: a life-size portrait, now in Berlin, of a man and woman dressed in costumes that suggest a date of about 1655 (Appendix III.10; Fig. 22). We do not know their identities or who painted them, but the allusion to Rubens's house is unmistakable. The couple are standing in front of an archway that is reminiscent of Rubens's portico, but of particular interest is the faithfully rendered garden pavilion with its statues in the background, partly cut off by the edge of the painting.

Elements of Rubens's house were also used to depict architecture of an entirely different order. The gallery with antique sculptures seen in the background of Willem van Haecht's *Studio of Apelles* (Appendix III.8; Text

36. See below, Chapter V, passim and esp. pp. 159–161.
37. See below, Chapter X, pp. 301–302.
38. See below, Chapter X, pp. 304–305, n. 22.
39. See Chapter IX, p. 272, n. 65.

ill. 100; Fig. 128) is based on Rubens's 'antiquarium'. In a scene from the story of Cupid and Psyche, which is dated around 1640–1650, Jacques (Jacob) Jordaens (1593–1678) combined not one but two images of the portico with the garden pavilion and also a fountain to represent the palace of Cupid (Appendix III.9; Fig. 20). It goes without saying that the allusions to Rubens's famous house in these historicising scenes, though explicit, are in no sense intended to be realistic. We will discuss these pictures further when we go on to analyse the particular elements of the house depicted. An overview of this iconography of Rubens's House, including more or less 'realistic' images as well as variations, can be found in Appendix II.

Finally, mention should be made of a painting in Stockholm which has been erroneously thought to represent a part of Rubens's house. It is a unique and, in itself, fascinating interior with two women and children, dated c. 1622 and attributed to Cornelis de Vos (1584/85–1651) and Frans Francken II (1581–1642). The idea that this interior shows a room in Rubens's house[40] has rightly been rejected, as has the title, 'Le Salon de Rubens'. In actual fact the scene is set in the house of Jan Wildens (1585/86–1653).[41]

Topographical Paintings from the Seventeenth Century; the Aylesbury 'View of the Courtyard'

It would be reasonable to expect the seventeenth century to have yielded topographical paintings of the famous house that had become a visitor's attraction, but very little evidence of such works survives.

A painting on marble – now lost – is mentioned in the inventory of the estate of a certain Benedictus van de Walle in 1652. Among his possessions were 'two perspectival views on marble: one showing the house of the late Sir Peeter Paulus Rubens and the other a church' ('Twee Prospectiven van marmer: d'een wesende naer de wooninge van wylen heer Peeter Paulus Rubens ende d'ander een Kerkxken').[42] A few years later, the inventory of the estate of the widow

---

40. It used to be cautiously suggested that the *Salon* (Stockholm, Nationalmuseum, inv. no. NM 407) showed a formal room in Rubens's house with the hostess, Isabella Brant; see, for example, Rooses, *Huis van Rubens*, 1910, p. 205 [17]; Muls, *De Vos*, 1932, pp. 32–33; Delen, *Rubens' huis*, 1933, pp. 35–36; Speth-Holterhoff, *Cabinets*, 1957, pp. 88–89); not expressing a view: Tijs, *Rubens en Jordaens*, 1984, p. 112; for more information on the attributions, and an extensive bibliography, see Cavalli-Björkman et al., *Cat. Stockholm (Flemish Paintings)*, 2010, pp. 157–158, no. 79.
41. The correct identification is given by Van der Stighelen, *Cornelis de Vos*, 1990, pp. 86–93, no. 37. It was clear before this that the lady of the house is not Isabella Brant; it is worth mentioning a further argument in support of her identification as Maria Stappaert, the wife of Jan Wildens: what is probably the same young woman, holding her son in her lap, can be recognised in a portrait by Van Dyck in London, The National Gallery, inv. no. NG3011 (see N. De Poorter in Barnes et al., *Van Dyck*, 2004, pp. 103–104, no. I.110, as probably representing Maria Stappaert and her son).
42. These anonymous works were at his house on the Kipdorp, in 'de groote Neercamer aen den Hoff' (inventory of 7 and 9 December 1652; Duverger, *Kunstinventarissen*, 1984–2009, VI, p. 390). Possibly the 'kerxken' showed the interior of the Antwerp Jesuit Church; if so, for a similar (or the same?) work, see the

CHAPTER II - EYE WITNESSES TO THE HOUSE

of Andries Snellinckx (1587–1653) lists a painting by this master after Rubens representing 'het Hoff of Mr Rubbens',[43] but this represented one of Rubens's country estates rather than the house (or the garden) on the Wapper.[44]

Another work that has been problematical to identify is a large painting attributed to Dirk van Delen (1605–1671), which Gustav Friedrich Waagen saw in the collection of the lawyer and author Edmund Phipps (1808–1857), before it was auctioned in London in 1859 as *The Courtyard of Rubens's House, at Antwerp, with Figures Seated at a Table; a Garden in the background*, a description that seems rather to suggest an imaginary genre scene.[45]

The only known surviving 'topographical' painting from the seventeenth century representing Rubens's house is a large anonymous work in the Discover Bucks Museum in Aylesbury (Appendix III.3; Fig. 16) The canvas went unnoticed until 2007, when it was given a major conservation treatment in order to improve its horribly damaged condition.[46]

The canvas gives a view of the courtyard, looking from the entrance on the Wapper, with in the distance the garden pavilion glimpsed through the central arch of the portico. This is more or less the same view as the Harrewijn print of 1684, but it deviates from the print (and apparently also from the actual house) in several details, highlighting the Italian character of the house. To the left, the 'old' or Flemish wing is replaced by the corner of a façade modelled on the Italian wing opposite, extending to about the same height and with an identical projecting eaves cornice supported by modillions. Two of the five bays, to the right, are largely hidden by a puzzling structure (an arcade?) with massive columns. The painting is brought to life with an image of Rubens, Helena Fourment and their daughter, a group corresponding to Rubens's *Family Portrait* in the Metropolitan Museum of Art in New York.[47]

---

painting in oil on Carrara marble by Wilhem Schubert van Ehrenberg (1630–1676), in the Rubenshuis (inv. no. RH.S.189; Baudouin, *Willem van Ehrenberg*, 1981, pp. 7–14; Baisier, ed., *Divine Interiors*, 2016, pp. 142–143, no. 37).

43. Inventory of 1–3 January 1656: 'Een schilderye wesende het Hoff van mynheer Rubbens sonder lyst geschildert door Andries Snellinck naer Rubbens' (Duverger, *Kunstinventarissen*, 1984–2009, VII, p. 300).
44. The painting probably was a copy after Rubens's *The Park of a Castle* (Vienna, Kunsthistorisches Museum, inv. no. 696; Adler, *Landscapes (CRLB)*, 1982, no. 42; K. Schütz in Kräftner *et al.*, *Rubens in Wien*, 2004, pp. 324–331, no. 84; a copy is in the Rubenshuis (inv. no. RH.S.081, as *The Castle Grounds at Ekeren*; Adler, *Landscapes (CRLB)*, 1982, under no. 42). See also Bresseleers – Kanora, *Rubens te Ekeren*, 1957, pp. 13, 47–52. The existence of a signed copy by Snellinckx seems to confirm that a copy after this composition was indeed made by him (sale, Paris (Tajan), 28 June 1996, lot 60). Katlijne Van der Stighelen's cautious suggestion that the work mentioned in the inventory of 1656 could be an image of Rubens's garden in Antwerp, interpreting 'het hoff' (mansion or court) as 'den hoff' (meaning garden), and that it was a copy after *The Walk in the Garden* (Van der Stighelen, *Andries Snellinck*, 1989, p. 336, n. 129) is untenable.
45. Waagen, *Treasures*, 1854, II, p. 228, as Dirk van Delen, 'a large picture of singular power for the painter, and very carefully executed'; sale, London (Christie's), 25 June 1859, lot 54, as Dirk van Dalen [sic]; Tijs, *Rubens en Jordaens*, 1984, pp. 13, 17.
46. Van Beneden, *Rubens's House Revealed*, 2009. In the house of a previous owner is had been used as a dartboard.
47. Vlieghe, *Portraits (CRLB)*, 1987, no. 141, fig. 195.

Although, as said, more or less the same viewpoint is used as in the Harrewijn print, the painted view is certainly not based on the well-known print. This emerges from several details, most notably from the *Calumny of Apelles* scene in the frieze above the entrance to the studio: in the canvas this scene (No. 13; Fig. 91) is more detailed and cannot possibly have been copied from the corresponding small image etched by Harrewijn (Fig. 90).

It is difficult to date the painting. Conceivably, it was made after Rubens's death and predates the print of 1684.[48] A dating in the 1660s seems plausible. The huge marble columns to the right, the decorated floor of the courtyard, the predilection for costly materials (black marble in the façade) are alien to Rubens's house, and are features of the kind that might lead us to the author. Indeed, similar elements that exaggerate the grandeur of a place can be found in works by or attributed to Anton Gheringh (1630–1668), who specialised in church interiors and was active in Antwerp in the 1660s.[49]

In short, the painting cannot be regarded as an accurate representation of the house in every detail; comparison with the Harrewijn print (to which we will return in the next chapter) leads to the conclusion that it must be a combination of keen observation (of the house itself) and fantasy, with the aim of giving a grander appearance to the house. Furthermore, the rather strange dark colour scheme of the portico and façade, probably partly due to darkening of materials, is not a reliable source of information.

Nevertheless, the canvas is a document of great importance. Not only is it the only known image of the decoration of the studio façade besides the Harrewijn print, it also appears to be the work of an artist who was better able to represent architectural details than Van Croes or Harrewijn. It is therefore a welcome addition to the print, as will emerge in the discussion of details in Chapters V and VI, and in the Catalogue.

Cartographical Sources: 1628–c. 1650

It is interesting to note that cartographers had the idea of marking the celebrated (and often visited) house on their maps of Antwerp. The earliest example found is a bird's-eye view of the city from the south, dated 1628, which is a reworking

48. The arrangement of the window glazing bars (probably in their original form in the painting and in altered form, thus later, in the print (cf. Figs 16–17) may indicate that the painting was made before the print; see under No. 7.
49. Rightly observed by Arnout Balis; see, for relevant examples: the *Interior of the Antwerp Jesuit Church* (which has fictitious elements, for example the double columns) in the Musée d'Ixelles; canvas, 139 × 163 cm (Van Calster et al., *Flemish Painting*, 1988, no. 1, as Wilhelm Schubert von Ehrenberg, but more likely by Anton Gheringh); Anton Gheringh, *Elegant Figures in a Baroque Church Interior*, canvas, 120 × 140 cm; signed and dated 1667(?), sale, London (Christie's South Kensington), 7 July 1994, lot 219; De Maere – Wabbes, *Dictionary*, 1994, II, p. 471, fig.: *Interior of an Italian Church* (as Anthon Günther Gheringh). Gheringh's name has also been put forward previously as the possible artist (Van Beneden, *Rubens's House Revealed*, 2009, p. 104, n. 4).

CHAPTER II - EYE WITNESSES TO THE HOUSE

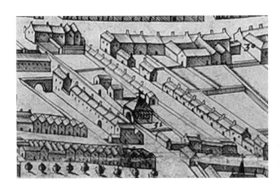

Text ill. 10. Pieter Verbiest, *The Siege of Antwerp by Prince Maurice of Orange in 1605* (1628), engraving, detail.

of the sixteenth-century map of Van der Heyden mentioned before. The cross that marked the location of the Walloon Church has been replaced by 'Rubbens huys', a large building with a pyramid-shaped roof (Text ill. 10).[50]

From the mid-seventeenth century onwards, the famous painter's house is regularly marked as a site of interest on maps of Antwerp. However, no useful information about the house can be derived from the various miniscule representations of the property shown in these documents. It seems that marking its location was the only consideration.

Rubens's house is also marked on the bird's-eye view from the east included in Jan Gaspar Gevartius's sumptuous book on the *Pompa Introitus Ferdinandi*, published in 1641 or 1642 (Text ill. 11). This map is an adaptation of the sixteenth-century plan by Joris Hoefnagel (Text ill. 7), mentioned above: as well as the decorations for the Joyous Entry in 1635 (arches and stages), a number of buildings have been added. Rubens's house is listed in the key as 'Domus Petr. Rubenij'. Little effort has been made to give an impression of the building itself: the maker has simply crowned one of the two adjacent buildings on Hoefnagel's map with a pyramid-shaped roof, topped by a weathervane.[51] In the same book, Gevartius also describes the Cardinal-Infante's visit to Rubens and praises the house and its splendid art collections in grandiloquent Latin prose.[52]

50. Published by Pieter Verbiest (d. 1642/43); Van der Heyden's map was re-engraved with additions turning it into *The Siege of Antwerp by Prince Maurice of Orange in 1605*, of which there are several editions: 1605 (naturally without an image of Rubens's house); 1628; 1648 (details reproduced in Bedeer – Janssens, *Steden in beeld*, 1993, pp. 36, 47, 53). Whether the engraved date of 1628 can be trusted – in which case a map with Rubens's house would indeed have been for sale in his lifetime – has not been further investigated.

51. Gevartius, *Pompa Introitus*, 1642, between pp. 172 and 173. See also Tijs, *Rubens en Jordaens*, 1984, p. 140; Muller, *Rubens's Collection*, 2004, p. 66; Devroe, *Rubens' huis*, 2008, I, p. 18, fig. 11; II, no. 10. On the plan, based on a 16th-century layout of Antwerp, the representation of the house is very approximate; the plot with gateway onto the Wapper is still unbuilt, while the house marked as Rubens's lies too close to the Meir; it looks as though the maker tried to indicate the portico. To avoid confusion: it is not the plan included in Gevartius's *Pompa Introitus* book, but a detail from a different map, by Verbiest (see below), that is reproduced in Martin, *Pompa (CRLB)*, 1972, fig. 1.

52. See above, p. 55, n. 18.

CHAPTER II - EYE WITNESSES TO THE HOUSE

Text ill. 11. Theodoor van Thulden, *Map of Antwerp with the Joyous Entry of Cardinal-Infante Ferdinand*, etching and engraving, detail.

Text ill. 12. Joan Blaeu, *Map of Antwerp* (1649), engraving, detail. Antwerp, Museum Plantin-Moretus.

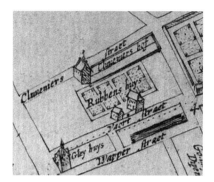

Text ill. 13. Pieter Verbiest, *Bird's-eye View of Antwerp from the West* (c. 1650), engraving, detail. Antwerp, Felixarchief.

A dozen or so maps which were published around 1648 and in the following decades, some based on earlier plans, feature the house but in an equally unreliable form. One example is the panoramic view from the east of 1649, by Joan Blaeu (Text ill. 12).[53] Lastly we should mention a different type of map: a view from the west, probably produced around 1650 and published by Pieter Verbiest, with images only of landmark buildings rather than 'every single house'. Rubens's house appears in a large rectangular plot showing the garden (Text ill. 13).[54]

Meanwhile, during Rubens's lifetime, a few changes had occurred in the vicinity of his house. On the map just mentioned we can now see the new premises of his neighbours, the arquebusiers – known as the Kolveniershof – with its expansive saddle roof, which was built between 1631 and 1636. And on the other side of the Hopland, in the plot known as the Lammekensraam, the

---

53. Tijs, *Atlas*, 2007, fig. pp. 90–91; Devroe, *Rubens' huis*, 2008, I, pp. 18–19, fig. 12; II, no. 11.
54. First edition of c. 1650; also used as a folding plan of the city in Le Roy, *Notitia Marchionatus*, 1678 (see Martin, *Pompa (CRLB)*, 1972, fig. 1; Devroe, *Rubens' huis*, 2008, I, pp. 19–20, fig. 14; II, no. 13). For a variant, published in 1662 (?), see Couvreur, *Ikonografie*, 1989, fig. 2.

65

frames that had been used in the working of woollen cloth have disappeared and been replaced by the Church of the Discalced Carmelites, which – although still awaiting completion – had been inaugurated in 1626.[55]

C. Later Residents: the Cavendishes, the Van Eyckes and Hillewerve

William and Margaret Cavendish (1648–1660)

The first people to occupy the house after Rubens's widow and her family were William Cavendish (1592–1676), at the time Marquess, later First Duke of Newcastle, and his wife Margaret Lucas (1623–1673). Taking refuge from the Civil War at home, they rented the house from Rubens's heirs from 1648 to 1660, paying an annual rent of six hundred guilders.[56]

There is a wealth of information about their stay in Antwerp but unfortunately it yields little of use to this research. However, it is clear that the noble refugees avoided expenditure on their temporary home, undertaking no building work. Having been stripped of their fortune, they were forced to live on credit while in Antwerp. They incurred large debts and they had in any case clear priorities for spending the money that they borrowed. Their prime concern was to return to England as soon as possible. We can safely assume, therefore, that the architecture of the house was left unchanged at the couple's departure in 1660.

While the aristocratic couple were living in Rubens's former home, they entertained numerous eminent guests. Without doubt the high point of their social life in Antwerp was a visit from the exiled Prince Charles (1630–1685), the future Charles II, in February 1658, when he was travelling from The Hague to Paris in a company that included his brothers James and Henry as well as his sister Mary, widow of William II of Orange.[57]

Both refugees had made something of a name for themselves as philosophers and their visitors also included famous members of the intellectual world, for example Descartes. The eccentric Margaret Cavendish furthermore

---

55. Rubens supplied two of the seven altarpieces for this church: *St Teresa of Avila Interceding for Bernardino de Mendoza* (Vlieghe, *Saints (CRLB)*, 1972–73, II, no. 155) and *The Education of the Virgin*, both in Antwerp, Koninklijk Museum voor Schone Kunsten Antwerpen, inv. nos 229 and 306. For a full discussion of this lost church and its interior, see Herremans, *Rubens Unveiled*, 2013, pp. 112–132.
56. For a full account of this noble couple, and their stay in Antwerp, see Van Beneden – De Poorter, eds, *Royalist Refugees*, 2006; see also Worsley, *Cavalier*, 2007, p. 169 ff. The sum paid in rent by 'den Marquis van Nieuw-Casteel' is recorded in the inventory of the estate of Albert Rubens, d. 1657 (Appendix I.24).
57. In honour of their visit the Cavendishes held a banquet and ball. The records of the event do not specify in which rooms the festivities took place (Härting, *Entertainment*, 2006, pp. 331–339). The Prince is also said to have called on the couple in 1649 and on other occasions (ibid., p. 338, n. 17).

CHAPTER II - EYE WITNESSES TO THE HOUSE

Text ill. 14. After Abraham van Diepenbeeck, *William and Margaret Cavendish Watching while William's Sons Charles and Henry are Demonstrating a Courbette and a Ballotade*, engraving.

Text ill. 15. The Riding House in Bolsover Castle (UK).

had a passionate interest in scientific experiments of many kinds. In 1657 she corresponded with Constantijn Huygens (1596–1687) about a scientific experiment involving 'Prince Rupert's drops',[58] and he may also have been one of her guests in Antwerp. Years earlier, in 1636–1640, Huygens had corresponded with Rubens about architecture, and he was no doubt interested in the house, which he had not seen during Rubens's lifetime.[59]

But above all, visitors came to the house to experience the art which Cavendish practised passionately: dressage. It is unclear which areas of the house and garden were used for the marquess's riding school. A great deal of visual documentation on Cavendish's horsemanship can be found in his luxurious manual *La méthode nouvelle*, published in Antwerp in 1658. The plates for the book were engraved after drawings by Abraham van Diepenbeeck (1596–1675) and they feature architectural elements in the background of dressage scenes, which in reality took place in Rubens's house. Yet none of these can be connected with the house directly. For example, a plate like *William and Margaret Cavendish Watching while William's Sons Charles and Henry are Demonstrating a Courbette and a Ballotade*, shows the family seated in a pavilion with five arches (Text ill. 14),[60] which was not, it seems, based on an actual building. No such pavilion, with a gallery of five arches resting on Ionic columns, and with a lantern above (or

---

58. For the correspondence about these glass drops (in Dutch 'Bataafse tranen'), see Akkerman – Corporaal, *Margaret Cavendish*, 2010, pp. 203–233.
59. Huygens and Margaret Cavendish probably met in Antwerp, either with the Duarte family (on the Meir) or at Rubens's house (Akkerman – Corporaal, *Margaret Cavendish*, 2010, pp. 225–227); see also J. Knowles and L. Hulse in Van Beneden – De Poorter, eds, *Royalist Refugees*, 2006, no. 45. The correspondence between Rubens and Huygens was cut short by Rubens's death (Ottenheym, *Rubens en Huygens*, 1997; Ottenheym, *La Vera Simmetria*, 2007, pp. 148–151).
60. Cavendish, *Méthode nouvelle*, 1658, pl. 42; Van Beneden – De Poorter, eds, *Royalist Refugees*, 2006, fig. p. 223, pl. 42.

behind) and smoking chimneys in the background, can be located on any side of Rubens's garden.

For his houses in England, Welbeck Abbey and Bolsover Castle, the marquess had gone to great lengths to provide the infrastructure required for riding demonstrations. Besides the usual stables, he built riding houses consisting of a spacious, high-ceilinged hall with a soft floor and windows positioned high up, on a rectangular ground plan. The riding house at Welbeck Abbey, built in the 1620s, was the largest (approx. 36 × 12 m), while the one at Bolsover Castle (Text ill. 15), built in the 1630s, was much smaller (approx. 27 × 9 m).[61]

Rubens's property came with stables where Cavendish could keep his expensive horses.[62] However, it seems pertinent to ask if the marquess turned part of the building into an indoor riding house, or whether the dressage training sessions and demonstrations were always held in the open air (with the spectators seated in a pergola or arcaded pavilion, as seen in the plate mentioned above; Text ill. 14). The existence of an indoor riding house in Antwerp seems to be confirmed by a sentence in the introduction to Cavendish's second manual of horsemanship, published after his return to England (1667). He proudly gives an account of the resounding success of his riding school in Antwerp, writing that he was visited by 'gentlemen of all nations', and his 'private riding house at Antwerp, though very large, was often so full that my esquier, Captain Mazin, had hardly room to ride'.[63] This tells us two things about the location: the demonstrations did not take place in the garden but in a 'very large' area inside the house, and the spectators, or at least a substantial number of them, were in the same space as the horsemen rather than watching from a raised gallery. It seems that this situation was ideal neither for the riders, nor the visitors, who had to stand close to the leaping horses.

Lucy Worsley, who has made a thorough study of Cavendish as patron of equestrian architecture in England, thinks it possible that Rubens's studio was used as a riding house. She points to the suitably high ceiling, the elevated placing of the windows (which would not distract the horses) and the 'first-floor balcony', which was similar to the 'raised viewing gallery at Welbeck'.[64] Although much smaller than the riding houses at Cavendish's English houses (see above), the floor area of the workshop – which was 8.5 m across and at least

---

61. For a full discussion of Cavendish's riding houses, see Worsley – Addyman, *Riding Houses*, 2002; see for the measurements: ibid., pp. 204, 208; for the soft floor: ibid., p. 208. See also Worsley, *Cavalier*, 2007, passim.
62. The *Staetmasse* lists 'stallingen' ('stables') in the description of the property on the Wapper (Appendix I.23: [2]). On the stables in Hillewerve's time, and on the stables indicated later in the drawing by François Mols, see Chapter III, pp. 108–109, n. 43.
63. Cavendish, *New Method*, 1667, ['To the readers', n. pag.]; see also Worsley – Addyman, *Riding Houses*, 2002, p. 217.
64. On the former studio as riding house, see Worsley – Addyman, ibid., pp. 212, 214–215; Worsley et al., *Horsemanship*, 2006, p. 37; Worsley, *Cavalier*, 2007, pp. 169–174. For Ursula Härting it is also highly likely that the studio was transformed into a manège (Härting, *Entertainment*, 2006, p. 333).

CHAPTER II - EYE WITNESSES TO THE HOUSE

Text ill. 16. View of the open gallery in the studio of the restored Rubenshuis.

14 m in length – would, according to Worsley, have been adequate. Nonetheless, problems remain with this hypothesis. It is particularly hard to imagine the horses doing their leaps and turns on the hard stone flooring overlying the cellars instead of on the usual soft ground.

There has been discussion of the possible existence of a 'viewing gallery' in Rubens's house but the evidence for this is vague. As far as we know there was a mezzanine at the street side of the studio wing,[65] but it is unclear if there was originally an open gallery, or platform, that provided a view into the studio, as today in the restored house (Text ill. 16). It is important to note that Worsley's hypothesis is not weakened by the fact that she assumes that a gallery existed in Cavendish's time. No doubt such a structure was practical both from the point of view of the horsemen and the audience, and it certainly makes her comparison with Cavendish's English riding houses more compelling. But it was not essential. As we know from Cavendish's own description, some of the audience were in any case positioned on the ground floor.

A remnant of Cavendish's horsemanship can be seen in the garden in Harrewijn's 1692 print: close to the stables – the building with the stepped gable and which is decorated with a pair of caryatids – is a dressage pole (Text ill. 17). We know from the elaborate descriptions and illustrations in Cavendish's manual *La méthode nouvelle* that such poles played an important part in his dressage method (Text ill. 18).

There is a persistent misunderstanding in connection with the dressage method, which is based on the mistaken assumption, first made by Floris Prims and followed by others, that Cavendish used a round arena, not unlike a circus ring.[66] This prompted Prims to develop a bizarre hypothesis. He supposed, incorrectly, that when Rubens bought the plot at the Wapper, vestiges of the

65. For the mezzanine, see Chapter VII, pp. 203–204.
66. Prims, *Manège van Cavendish*, 1939, pp. 205, 209.

69

CHAPTER II - EYE WITNESSES TO THE HOUSE

Text ill. 17. Detail of the 1692 Harrewijn print (Fig. 18): the dressage pole in the garden.

Text ill. 18. Lucas Vorsterman II after Abraham van Diepenbeeck, *Courbette de côté à gauche*, engraving.

'round' Calvinist church built in 1566–1567 were still present. Moreover, he thought it likely that Rubens had converted these remains in his garden into a round building, and that this construction was subsequently converted into a 'round' manège by Cavendish.[67] However, Cavendish certainly did not use a circular manège, and after the demolition of the 'round' church, no round constructions were ever erected in Rubens's garden. In spite of this, Prims's completely ungrounded hypothesis was absorbed into some literature on Rubens's house.[68]

As already mentioned, the plates in *La méthode nouvelle* feature no architectural elements that can be recognised as part of Rubens's house. An image that may come closer to what the house actually looked like is the illustration *William Cavendish and his Family Seated in Front of a Fireplace in Rubens's House*, which appears in one of the works published in Antwerp by Margaret Cavendish (Appendix III.28; see also Text ill. 19). It is possible that Van Diepenbeeck, who made several design drawings for the scene (showing variations), was partly inspired by the existing interior. It is hard to see, however, where such a room with tall windows on two sides would have fitted into the house. That said, the monumental fireplace with life-size herms could certainly be based on decorative elements that were part of Rubens's interior. The two caryatids, one male, the other female, with tall baskets of flowers on their heads, bear some resemblance to other *canephorae* found in his inventions.[69]

---

67. '[Rubens's House] had a large carousel ('een groote rotonde') which could serve as a manège' (Prims, *Cavendish*, 1939, pp. 199–201). According to Prims, the round building in the garden was used by Rubens as the 'Pantheon' and top-lit studio (regarded as one and the same area). For more on this, see Chapter VIII, p. 237, n. 18.
68. Tijs, *Rubens en Jordaens*, 1984, pp. 110–113, 143–144; also mentioned as a possibility by Devroe, *Rubens' huis*, 2008, I, pp. 111–112. See also Chapter VIII, pp. 237, n. 19.
69. For full-length statues of 'basket bearers' which Rubens used in one of his altar designs, see Herremans, *Architectural Sculpture (CRLB)*, 2019, pp. 169–170. For the use of caryatids and herms in Rubens's work, see Lombaerde, *Rubens / Vredeman de Vries*, 2018, pp. 117–127. See also No. 4.

Text ill. 19. Petrus Clouwet after Abraham van Diepenbeeck, *William Cavendish and his Family Seated in Front of a Fireplace [in Rubens's House]* (Appendix III.28b), engraving.

It should be observed at this point that the full-length double portrait in Berlin of c. 1655, mentioned above, and which shows a well-to-do couple standing in front of a portico with Rubens's garden pavilion in the background (Fig. 22), does not represent the Cavendishes, as argued by Ursula Härting in an extensive article (see Appendix III.10). Their physiognomy is entirely different and rules out the identification.

William and Margaret Cavendish, who saw themselves as pitiable exiles who were forced to live abroad in shabby accommodation, seem to have been pretty much indifferent to the fact that they had moved into Rubens's house. Apparently, the significance of the famous painter, who had worked for their own king, Charles I, in London, and who had occupied the house until eight years before their arrival, had no meaning in the fairy-tale world in which they lived. Compared with the couple's splendid residences in England, the house was indeed rather modest. Margaret's *Sociable Letters* (published in London in 1664), a collection of more than two hundred letters addressed to an imaginary correspondent, include a number of passages about her life in Antwerp. Her many anecdotes and reflections make no mention of the famous painter; she does not refer to the house or any of the rooms in it, so that we learn nothing about the interior or even the use to which the different rooms were put. There is only one anecdote that holds a clue, of sorts. It is a humorous tale set in the garden, about a jealous neighbour who suspects her husband of delivering presents to one of Margaret's 'waiting-maids'. It must be that the couple taking centre stage in this anecdote lived in one of the adjacent houses along the

CHAPTER II - EYE WITNESSES TO THE HOUSE

Wapper or the Hopland, and that this house – as the story reveals – had in the past been accessible from Rubens's garden by a door in the common wall.[70]

The Sale of the House (1660)

After the noble couple's return to England, a buyer was finally found for the great house and the adjacent houses along the Wapper. In a public sale at the Vrijdagmarkt, on 3 September 1660, the property was sold to Jacomo van Eycke the Younger for 20,000 guilders. More on this Jacomo van Eycke in a moment. The deed of sale was drawn up on 16 September 1660 (Appendix I.25).

Before going further, we should point out that there had been a change with regard to Rubens's heirs since his death in 1640, as three of his children had died in the meantime: Isabella Helena (d. 1652), Nicolaas (d. 1655) and Albert (d. 1657); in addition, Constantia Albertina had become a nun and relinquished her share of the estate. This means that in 1660 the heirs were: Albert's daughters, Nicolaas's children, Helena Fourment and her two sons and a daughter from her first marriage.[71]

Jacomo van Eycke and Cornelia Hillewerve: 1660–1680

For twenty years, from 1660 to 1680, the house was home to the prosperous merchant and alderman Jacomo (also Jacob) van Eycke the Younger (c. 1620–1679), his wife Cornelia Hillewerve (1631–1686) and their family.[72] We have no records concerning the house itself during this period, and it remains an open question to what extent the architecture or decorative elements were altered in any significant way. As will be seen in further chapters, the only indication

---

70. The woman complains in a letter to the marquess; from a window her husband can peer into the garden, where the handsome girl can often be seen strolling. Separating the houses is a common wall with a door which 'belongs to our garden, but opens into the man's garden'. The door is 'nailed close up', but there is 'a little hole' the man can 'fill full of flowers' for his sweetheart (Cavendish, *Sociable Letters*, 2004, pp. 178–181, Letter 124).
71. For the heirs, and their representatives when the deed of sale was drawn up – among them Rubens's nephew Philip Rubens, who was then a municipal secretary – see the full contract, Génard, *Rubens*, 1877, pp. 106–111; see also Maes – Laenens, *Juristen*, 1977, pp. 160–161, where it is wrongly assumed that Constantia Albertina had also died. She had joined a convent (Génard, *Rubens*, 1877, p. 108) and had passed her inheritance to her brothers and sister; she lived until around 1710. In the 1657 inventory of the estate of Albert, his share of the as yet unsold house is included *pro memorie* (Appendix I.24); following the sale, Albert's share of the poceeds (one quarter plus 1/32 of the 20,000 guilders, or 5625 guilders) were paid out to his three daughters (Rooses, *Afrekeninghen*, 1910, p. 63).
72. For the Van Eycke family, including genealogical data, see Prims, *Van Eycke*, 1939, pp. 223–228; Maufort, *Duarte*, 2002, pp. 944–945, [genealogical table: pp. 956–957]. In 1667 the rental value of Jacomo's dwelling (formerly Rubens's house) was estimated at 600 guilders, and he belonged to a group of six Antwerp citizens whose properties were in the top rental bracket (Timmermans, *Patronen van patronage*, 2008, p. 31). His younger half-brother was Giovanni Battista van Eycke (Jan Baptist van Eyck), who co-owned Rubens's patterns for the *Decius Mus* series (Duverger – Maufort, *Decius Mus*, 1996, passim; Baumstark – Delmarcel, *Decius Mus (CRLB)*, 2019, I, pp. 171 (n. 98), 223–224, 249 and passim.

CHAPTER II - EYE WITNESSES TO THE HOUSE

Text ill. 20. Gonzales Coques, *Portrait of Maria Agnes van Eycke as St Agnes*. London, The National Gallery.

that work was undertaken to alter the property concerns the south side of the former studio and the adjoining small houses on the Wapper.[73] But it remains possible, of course, that the Van Eycke couple altered or embellished the house in other ways.

Linked to this family's stay is one image in which a part of Rubens's house can be identified: a small portrait of a young woman painted on silver of c. 1675 by Gonzales Coques, in The National Gallery, London (Appendix III.11; Text ill. 20). The architecture in the background clearly shows the portico. The fact that the woman is depicted as St Agnes, with her attributes of the lamb and

---

73. On the problematic (and important) question of this south side of Rubens's studio – with or without windows –, see below in Chapter V (pp. 158–159) and Chapter VII (pp. 205–210).

73

the sword, firmly suggests that she is Maria Agnes van Eycke, a daughter of Jacomo van Eycke and Cornelia Hillewerve.[74]

Incidentally, it should be noted that the Van Eycke family were previously thought to be the subject of another painting by Coques, a family portrait showing eight figures playing music on a terrace, which survives in several versions, including one in Budapest.[75] In pursuit of this identification, Prims concluded that the architecture seen in this portrait – which includes a portico with round arches supported by Corinthian columns – was that of Rubens's house.[76] But this is certainly a misconception; the costumes of the young ladies indicate that the portrait was painted no later than the 1640s, and it has been shown convincingly that the sitters are the musical family of the successful jeweller and diamond merchant Gaspar Duarte (1584–1653), who lived on the Meir.[77]

Cornelia Hillewerve and Hendrik Hillewerve (1680–1694)

In January 1680, shortly after Jacomo van Eycke's death, his widow sold the house to her brother, Canon Hendrik Hillewerve (1621–1694). In the next chapter we will return to this important occupant of Rubens's house and also to the prints that he had made by Jacob Harrewijn, which count as an essential source of information about Rubens's house.

Written Sources: Rubens's Biographers and Nicodemus Tessin (1672–1681)

Once the famous master's studio and his magnificent art collection were both gone, the house lost some of its appeal to visitors. Nonetheless interest continued in a house that had occupied such a special place in Rubens's life and its memory lived on. It is praised by Rubens's biographers, not all of whom had seen the house with their own eyes. During the period of the Van Eycke's occupancy it was mentioned by Giovanni Pietro Bellori (1672) and Joachim von

---

74. The Van Eyckes married in 1651 and had four sons – two of them Jesuits and one a Carmelite – and three daughters; see Prims, *Van Eycke*, 1939, pp. 226–227; Maufort, *Duarte*, 2002, pp. 956–957). The life dates of Maria Agnes are unknown; according to Prims, she entered the convent prior to her mother's death in 1686; a possible earlier *terminus ante quem* for her entry is 1682, the date of Hillewerve's donation to his sister Cornelia and her children (Appendix I.33), on which occasion she is not mentioned (see below).
75. Budapest, Szépművészeti Múzeum, inv. no. 573; Lisken-Pruss, *Gonzales Coques*, 2013, pp. 137–141, 214, n. 722, no. 20, as 'Die Familie Van Eyck (?)'; for six other versions, of lesser quality, see ibid., nos 20a–20 f. See also n. 77.
76. Prims, *Van Eycke*, 1939, p. 227.
77. Maufort, *Duarte*, 2002, pp. 941–960; her arguments that the group portrait should be dated c. 1644 seem very plausible. One of the other versions, in the Museum der Bildenden Künste in Leipzig (inv. no. G 1609), bears a date that can be read as 1656 or 1653 (ibid., p. 942; Lisken-Pruss, *Gonzales Coques*, 2013, p. 237, no. 20a), but the young ladies' costumes contradict this later date.

Sandrart (1675–1679) (Appendix I.28–29); in 1681, when Hillewerve was living there, it is described by Roger de Piles (advised by Rubens's nephew Philip) and by Filippo Baldinucci (Appendix I.31–32). Of particular interest is the information passed on by the Swedish architect Nicodemus Tessin, who visited the house in 1687 (Appendix I.34). We will look more closely at these authors when we discuss the decorative and architectural elements about which they inform us: the painted façades (in Chapter VI) and Rubens's 'museum' or 'antiquarium' (in Chapter VIII).

D. Aftermath (1695–1947): Residents after Hendrik Hillewerve; Mols's Drawing; Destruction, Nostalgia and Reconstruction

Residents after Hendrik Hillewerve

Following Hendrik Hillewerve's death, on 22 February 1694, the house passed to his two nieces who had moved away from Antwerp to Brussels (see below). In 1695 they sold the property to Michiel van Steencruyse, and he in turn sold it one year later to Thomas de Letter. The sale deed of 8 December 1696 contains some interesting information: besides itemising a number of parts of the property, it includes some detail about the interior decoration of the time (Appendix I.37). Thus, it refers to stables in the garden, a large hall ('de groote salette'), stone and marble statues, vases, pedestals; for the interior it mentions the furnishings in the large hall, including mirrors and paintings, and also decorations in the chapel; the deed further specifies that, to the south of the main house, are a wagon house, a coach house or wash house ('wagenhuyse, coetshuyse oft waschuyse') with a large gate. Two of the adjoining houses on the Wapper to the south, which had until then been part of the property, were kept back from the sale, since the vendor wanted to retain them. These houses had been added to the property by Rubens in 1627 and were now being separated from the parcel. It is interesting that the deed mentions seven windows in the coach house, overlooking the garden of the adjacent house, and these were not to be bricked up.

A few years later, the house changed hands once again. The contract, drawn up on 7 April 1701, repeats the previous descriptions in almost identical terms, but this time it also mentions a 'cleyne salette' ('small hall') and some gilt-leather decoration (Appendix I.38).[78]

---

78. See also the advertisement in the *Gazette van Antwerpen* (26 December 1755), announcing the public sale on 9 January 1756, and stating that the sale of the property includes: the copper vases in the garden, a gilded 'reliquair' and other ornaments in the chapel, as well as tapestries hanging in the 'groote salette' – undoubtedly the former studio (Appendix I.40); Tijs, *Rubens en Jordaens*, 1984, p. 157; Maclot, *Rubenssite*, 2016, pp. 89–90.

Interestingly, thirteen years after Hillewerve's death, the house was rented out for several years to the wealthy merchant and banker Justus (Justo) Forchondt (1647–1710), who had returned to Antwerp in 1707, after a long period living in Spain. He was one of the six sons of Guilliam Forchondt (also spelt Forchoudt) (1608–1678) and the last male descendant of this famous family of merchants.[79]

The subsequent residents or owners of Rubens's house in the eighteenth century and the period thereafter can here be ignored. For information about this period, ending in the requisition of the property by the City of Antwerp in 1931–1937, reference can be made to the publications of Hervé Douxchamps and Rutger Tijs, and to the comprehensive studies of the building history by Annika Devroe and Petra Maclot.[80] However, we must mention one later owner who played a crucial role in the history of the house: in 1763 the house was purchased by the De Bosschaert family, who went on to make far-reaching alterations to the property, and they will come up several times in what follows.

François Mols's Plan and Comments

Not a single image of Rubens's house, or even a part of it, is known to survive from the eighteenth century. Indeed, there is a gap of almost one hundred and fifty years between Harrewijn's prints and the house's next appearance in a handful of paintings and prints in the second quarter of the nineteenth century, followed around 1860 by the first photographs.[81]

What we do have from the eighteenth century, however – and this is as essential a document for an understanding of the house as the prints by Harrewijn – is an annotated drawing by the dedicated Rubens researcher François Mols (1722–1790), whose extensive collection of notes is preserved in the Royal Library in Brussels (Text ill. 21). Mols visited the house on several occasions: in 1763, before it was auctioned, but also later, after it had been substantially altered. Of crucial importance is the summary plan which he drew from memory, clearly in an attempt to render the 'original' situation prior to 1763 (Fig. 3; Appendix I.43).

---

79. Having lived in Cadiz for many years, he died at Rubens's house on 5 April 1710 (and not, as is sometimes claimed, in 1709). On this important trading firm, and in particular Justus, see, for example, Denucé, *Kunstuitvoer*, 1931, pp. 9, 14, 20; Jordens, *Forchoudt*, 2010, passim [with genealogical table, p. 82]; Van Ginhove, *Forchondt*, 2011, pp. 135–138. A rental contract survives, to which is attached a list of 16 items: household goods and works of art (including sculpture) then present in the house and garden (Denucé, *Kunstuitvoer*, 1931, pp. 265–266).
80. Douxchamps et al., *Rubens*, 1977, pp. 133–136; Maes – Laenens, *Juristen*, 1977, pp. 160–164; Tijs, *Rubens en Jordaens*, 1984, pp. 157–170. Devroe, *Rubens' huis*, 2008, I, pp. 59–64; Maclot, *Rubenssite*, 2016, pp. 87–147; id., *Rubenssite*, 2019, pp. 27–29.
81. For these 19th-century sources, see below, pp. 80–82 and Appendix III. 50–53.

Although this summary ground plan was made one hundred and twenty years after Rubens's death, and was 'fait de mémoire', as Mols puts it, it is the only document that gives an impression of the interior layout of the house. Obviously, not everything in the drawing is correct – the relative dimensions and proportions of the spaces, for example – but we can confidently assume that it is a fair reflection of what Mols saw when he was there, and especially that his comments and notes about certain details correspond to the actual situation. It should be noted that Mols – contrary to his contemporary Van der Sanden (see below) – says absolutely nothing about the sculptural decoration of the house. This means that from him we can learn nothing about these elements (reliefs, statues or busts).

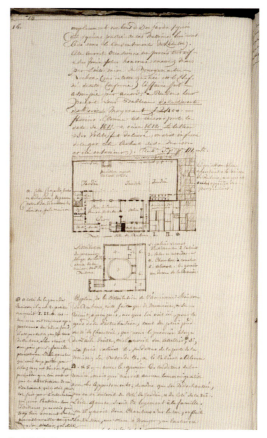

Text ill. 21. Page including the plan of Rubens's House in the Notes of François Mols. Brussels, KBR, MS 5726.

Mols is surprised by the strange and unconventional form of the house and the rather impractical way in which it was divided ('d'une forme si singuliere en apparence, si irreguliere et si peu commode'), which went against what he would have expected of Rubens 'qui etait un si habile homme' (Appendix I.43: [4]). He was also curious about how the house was used by the painter and speculated about the functions of the various rooms and areas. He guessed that the family's living quarters were in the small houses along the Wapper – in other words, not in the 'Flemish' wing – which is certainly wrong. He particularly questions the location of the studio, in a position where he felt that Rubens would not be able to work in peace because of the proximity of the staircase, which he saw as a source of noise (Appendix I.43: [11]).

In about 1770 Mols noted that little of the original building remained besides the portico, the garden pavilion, the so-called chapel with its 'antichambre', and parts of the left wing. What is more, the portico had suffered 'une altération assez considérable'. On the garden side, at first-floor level, a 'corridor' had been added to the portico, connecting the two wings. Only the central arch had been left open to provide access to the garden. At this point the mural paintings, which had still been visible when Mols visited the house before the sale, had probably also disappeared.

We know that major changes were indeed made to the house some three years after it was acquired in 1763 by the new owner Charles-Nicolas de Bosschaert (de Pret) (1715–1792), and subsequently by his son Charles-Jean (1759–1828).[82] It is understandable that in later years there was considerable disquiet about what was seen as the destruction of the remarkable house belonging to the famous citizen of Antwerp. A good example is the comment of an indignant Augustin Thys who accuses the family of wrecking large parts of both interior and exterior of the house with 'une main sacrilège et barbare'.[83]

Jacobus van der Sanden

From around the same time as Mols's notes, we also have a brief commentary by Jacobus van der Sanden (1726–1799), who was the secretary of the Antwerp Academy of Fine Arts, and author of a lengthy art-historical treatise entitled *Oud Konst-Tooneel van Antwerpen*, completed in c. 1770 but never published.[84] The bulk of the information he provides matches that of Mols. He reports that after 'Jonker de Bosschaert' had moved in, 'the building had undergone continuous change from the year 1766 onwards' ('is den Bouw zedert het jaer 1766 maer veranderd'). In other words, the building had been substantially altered. Van der Sanden had visited the house before the changes and had seen at first hand the extent to which the building with its portico and garden pavilion was richly embellished with sculptural decorations. He had also seen the painted façades (Appendix I.42: [2]).

The Nineteenth Century

The first nineteenth-century author to draw our attention to the house is the Antwerp historian and man of letters, Victor Charles Van Grimbergen (1810–1859), who published a monograph on Rubens in 1840, on the anniversary of his death. He briefly mentions the extensive alterations carried out in the

82. The house was bought by Charles-Nicolas in 1763; after his death it passed to his son, whose wife, Catherina de Vinck (1775–1857), was a descendant of Rubens (through Nicolaas Rubens's daughter); the house remained in the family until the 20th century. For this family de Bosschaert (de Pret), see Douxchamps et al., *Rubens*, 1977, p. 134 (with genealogical table, p. 135).
83. Thys, *Historique*, 1873, p. 350; id., *Historiek der straten*, 1893, p. 429.
84. This manuscript in three parts, preserved at the Antwerp FelixArchief; the publication was announced in 1771, but not published due to a shortage of subscriptions. For the author, see Vercoullie, *Van der Sanden*, 1913, cols 310–311; De Clercq – Van Deyck, *Letterkundigen*, 1952, p. 250. We know that Van der Sanden was working on volume III in 1767 (see Baudouin, *Altaren / Sint-Elisabethgasthuis*, 1993, pp. 47–48).

eighteenth century and goes on to give a short description of the house as it was in his time. Not long before ('a few years earlier') the property had been split in two. In the garden pavilion there were still a number of statues to be seen – in his opinion, not the original works – as well as a marble table which he considered to be authentic.[85] Meanwhile, the house was still attracting interest from local as well as foreign tourists. What they witnessed was no more than 'a splendid ruin' that provoked 'involuntary reverence, mingled with regret'.[86] People knew that the garden pavilion and the stone table were original, and they tried to imagine the house as the place where Rubens had worked.[87]

When art historians looked into the site of Rubens's house at the end of the nineteenth century, they found only two original elements: the portico, which had been partly incorporated into later structures, and the dilapidated garden pavilion at the back of the garden. The rest had been drastically altered or demolished during the eighteenth and nineteenth centuries. With a sense of nostalgia, the art historians reported what had been lost to their city.

The first person known to have visited the house out of art-historical interest (in the 1870s) was Auguste Schoy, who found that very little of the original construction remained.[88] Frans Jos Van den Branden (1837–1922) writes that only 'the picturesque triumphal arch' with 'behind it the stone pavilion with its statues were preserved, faintly reminding future generations of how magnificent Rubens's palace had once been'.[89] Max Rooses (1839–1914), who wrote about Rubens's house more than once, reminds us each time that major rebuilding had been undertaken after 1766, so that '[…] all that was original and beautiful in the buildings constructed by Rubens disappeared, except the portico and the pavilion'.[90]

Survey by François Antoine Losson (1846)

A correct impression of Rubens's house and garden within the block can be derived from Losson's survey of 1846, referred to above (Fig. 2).[91] The majority

---

85. Van Grimbergen, *Rubens*, 1840, p. 387, n. 10; at the end of his book, which is largely based on Jean Francois Marie Michel's monograph on Rubens, published almost 70 years earlier – both in French (Michel, *Rubens*, 1771) and in Dutch (id., *Rubens*, 1774) – Van Grimbergen included a long endnote commenting on the house. With regard to the statues, see also Chapter X, p. 310, n. 33. For the table in the garden pavilion, which according to him, was 'installed there by Rubens', see Chapter X, p. 299, nn. 14, 15.
86. Roscoe, *Belgium*, 1841, p. 177.
87. Van Vyve, *Guide*, 1854, pp. 114–115; De Clercq et al., *Rubens' tuinportiek en tuinpaviljoen*, 2014, p. 18.
88. Schoy, *Rubens*, 1878, pp. 33–34; id., *Influence Italienne*, 1879, pp. 339–340.
89. Van den Branden, *Schilderschool*, 1883, p. 509.
90. Quotation from Rooses, *Rubens*, 1904, p. 154; see also Rooses, *Maison*, 1888, p. 228; Rooses, *Rubens*, 1904, pp. 148–149, 154.
91. Cadastral plan (survey map) from the west, drawn up by F.A. Losson in 1846 and published in 1848. For an image of the whole plan, see Tijs, *Historisch portret*, 2001, p. 119; id., *Atlas*, 2007, pp. 102–103. Concerning Rubens's property, see Devroe, *Rubens's huis*, 2008, I, pp. 21–22, fig. 18; II, no. 17; Maclot, *Rubenssite*, 2016, p. 108. The earliest known survey, the 'primitief kadasterplan', hand-drawn in 1824 by the surveyor

CHAPTER II · EYE WITNESSES TO THE HOUSE

of the plots in the block between the Meir, the Hopland, the Kolveniersstraat and the Wapper preserve their boundaries as in the seventeenth century. The plan not only shows the various components of Rubens's house in their correct relative positions, but also other properties that have been mentioned above: the Kolveniershof, the Sint-Arnoldus House on the Meir, and the small houses on the Wapper that Rubens acquired. But the boundaries of Rubens's old property have undergone one notable change. The plan shows the splitting of the large parcel into two lots, as described by Van Grimbergen. The dividing line cuts right across the courtyard and through the portico. It is not known when this radical split – which involved the building of a long wall – came about. As mentioned, Van Grimbergen reports that this had happened 'a few years' before 1840, but it may well have been a few decades earlier – in any case before 1824, as is clear from a survey of that year.[92] In the course of the nineteenth century the boundary of the property underwent one further change: in 1888 a number of houses on the Hopland were extended to the north, resulting in the removal of a strip of Rubens's former garden along the southern extremity (establishing the present boundary).[93]

Depictions by Romantic Artists (1814–c. 1880) and in Photography (c. 1860)

Not surprisingly, Rubens's house – or what was left of it – drew the interest of Romantic painters and graphic artists who used it as a background for scenes depicting the life of the 'national hero' Rubens (App. III, 40).[94] For the courtyard these artists could draw on Harrewijn's first print (Fig. 17), though sometimes they preferred the altered situation that could be observed *in situ*, so with the raised portico (but omitting the partition wall, of course). It is essential that we approach these romantic images critically in our research into the house, as they combine seventeenth- and nineteenth-century elements with fictional motifs.[95]

The remains of the house stimulated some archaeological interest, something that is reflected in a pair of line engravings made to coincide with the Rubens celebrations of 1840. Erin Corr (1803–1862) produced two plates after line drawings by Nicaise de Keyser (1813–1887) and J. Stordiau, one in collaboration with Jozef Linnig (1815–1891), showing the garden pavilion (appendix III.46),

    A.J. Noël Reuflet, mostly shows the same layout (Devroe, ibid., I, p. 21, fig. 17; II, no. 16; Maclot, *Rubenssite*, 2016, fig. p. 105 and passim).
92. In Reuflet's plan of 1824 (see previous note) the partition line is already visible. A *terminus post quem* cannot be established; Maclot places the splitting of the parcel between 1801 and 1824 (Maclot, ibid., pp. 104–105) or 'shortly after 1815' (Maclot, *Rubenssite*, 2019, p. 28).
93. Id., *Rubenssite*, 2016, p. 116.
94. See, for example, Appendix III.40–42, 44.
95. For a misconception, based on 19th-century images, concerning the fountain with bagpiper, see Chapter III, p. 115, n. 53.

CHAPTER II - EYE WITNESSES TO THE HOUSE

Text ill. 22. Edmond Fierlants, *The Garden Pavilion of the Rubens House* (1860), photograph. Antwerp, FelixArchief.

Text ill. 23. Edmond Fierlants, *The Portico of the Rubens House* (1860), photograph. Antwerp, FelixArchief.

CHAPTER II - EYE WITNESSES TO THE HOUSE

and another the portico (Appendix III.45). They give a detailed impression of the situation at the time, albeit with a few concessions to contemporary taste – especially in the facial expressions of the statues.

The first truly 'realistic' images of elements of Rubens's house appear with the emergence of photography around 1860. The earliest known photograph, belonging to a series of stereoscopic views of Belgium, by Louis Schweig (1807–after 1886), features the garden pavilion in 1856 or 1857 (Appendix III.50).[96] A few years later, in 1860, the Brussels photographer Edmond Fierlants (1819–1869) was commissioned to make photographs of the garden pavilion and the altered portico as part of a major project by the City of Antwerp (Appendix III.51–52; Text ills 22–23).[97] An excellent photograph of the garden pavilion was produced in 1864 by the French photographer Adolphe Braun (1812–1877) (Appendix III.53).[98]

Restoration and Reconstruction (1939–1946)

Visitors to the Rubenshuis comparing the present-day layout to what can be seen of the complex in the prints by Harrewijn (Figs 17–18) will find that the two look fairly similar. This is not surprising, given that two of the most important elements – the portico and the garden pavilion – survive largely intact, while the reconstructed parts were closely modelled on Harrewijn's prints. These, along with the ground plan by Mols (Fig. 3), served as a guide for the reconstruction of the house in the years 1939–1946. Of course, these documents were not a simple blueprint; many questions were left unanswered by the prints so that a number of key issues became subjects of controversy during the reconstruction. The majority of these problems remain unresolved to this day, and in a few cases we have come to realise that the decision taken at the time was wrong. It should be remembered, however, that the reconstruction was based on a series of compromises, which at times led to pragmatic solutions that were at odds with the historical truth.

This study does not examine the history of the reconstruction of the Rubens House – which began with the City's requisition of the properties in 1931 and the following years[99] – or the numerous problems that unfolded in the process.

96. Deposited in 1857; The German-born photographer Louis Schweig was active in the Netherlands and Belgium in the mid-19th century (he lived in Antwerp from 1847 to 1857); Van Goethem, *Fotografie en Realisme*, 1999, pp. 30, 390–392.
97. The photographs taken by Fierlants (one of the portico and two of the garden pavilion) are part of a series of 300 photos of Antwerp, selected by a group of painters including Henri Leys (1815–1869). The series is no longer complete; it is preserved at the Antwerp FelixArchief; see Joseph – Schwilden, *Fierlants*, 1988, pp. 35–40, 107, 211, no. 594 (two photographs of the garden pavilion), p. 211, no. 593 (portico); Ceuleers, *Verloren Stad*, 2016, nos 94 and 96.
98. Ibid., no. 95.
99. On the requisition by the City of Antwerp, see, for example, Maes – Laenens, *Juristen*, 1977, pp. 161–164; Van Driessche, *Herschepping*, 2013, p. 17.

An extensive archive survives at the Rubenshuis, while a good deal of material about this complicated undertaking by the City of Antwerp is also held at the Antwerp FelixArchief. Reference should further be made to the comprehensive preparatory study that was drawn up by Ary Delen in 1933, and to publications written as the work was taking place, including a periodical entitled *Het huis van P.P. Rubens: periodisch bulletin*, of which only two volumes appeared, both in 1938.[100] Results of later studies are presented in the well-documented book by Rutger Tijs, and in three unpublished texts, a final analysis with an overview of the state of affairs by Annika Devroe, a research report by Thomas Van Driessche, and lastly the comprehensive study of the building history by Petra Maclot.[101]

The city architect Émile van Averbeke (1876–1946) was put in charge of the project.[102] Following a period of preliminary research, work on the restoration and reconstruction began in January 1939. It was completed just over eight years later, in 1947.[103] The bulk of the project thus coincided with the difficult war years. But, in spite of the shortage of building materials and other problems, work continued throughout the war,[104] so that on 21 July 1946 the house could be opened by the then mayor of Antwerp, Camille Huysmans.

The complexity of this undertaking, which besides requiring careful interpretation based on archaeological science, also involved aesthetic and of course museological considerations, should not be underestimated. Looking at photographs taken before and during the reconstruction, one gets an idea of the determined way in which many of the original elements had been remodelled, and the challenges that had to be overcome (Text ills 59–60, 67,

---

100. Delen, *Rubens' huis*, 1933; id., *Geschiedenis Rubenshuis*, 1938, pp. 7–21; Van Averbeke, *Eerste bevindingen*, 1938, pp. 27–45; Buschmann, *Huis-Rubens*, 1938, pp. 51–81.
101. Tijs, *Rubens en Jordaens*, 1984; Devroe gives a clear account of the state of affairs on the basis of extant research- and restoration reports (Devroe, *Rubens' huis*, 2008, esp. I, pp. 103–126); Van Driessche, *Herschepping*, 2009 (also published in abbreviated form as id., *Herschepping*, 2013; id., *Herschepping*, 2019); Maclot, *Rubenssite*, 2016. In addition to these studies, the following documents in the archive at the Rubenianum were also consulted: reports by Van Averbeke (Van Averbeke, *Rubenshuis, restauratie I*, 1938; Van Averbeke, *Rubenshuis, restauratie II*, 1938); a short report compiled in 1954 by Theo Ruyten (Ruyten, *Opzoekingswerken Rubenshuis*, 1954). Further information about the restoration is contained in the detailed restoration report for the portico and the garden pavilion (De Clercq et al., *Restauratienota*, 2014, passim) and in the reports on the technical research on these constructions (see under No. 24 and No. 34).
102. On Van Averbeke and his views on the restoration, see Van Driessche, *Herschepping*, 2009, pp. 3–5 and passim; Van Driessche, *Herschepping*, 2013, pp. 17–18 and passim. The architect was forced to abandon his work due to ill health; he died on 1 February 1946, six months before the opening ceremony of the restored house. His role as project leader was taken over by Theo Ruyten (1884–1975), who went on to become the first curator of the Rubenshuis (until 1950).
103. The construction site diaries, which were kept from 2 January 1939 to 26 May 1947, contain a detailed record of what was demolished, repaired and built each day (Antwerp, FelixArchief, inv. nos MA#9878–9880; see Devroe, *Rubens' huis*, 2008, I, pp. 67, 124).
104. The reconstruction of the house was fully backed by the German occupiers, who regarded the famous master as an important exponent of the 'deutsch-flämische Kultur- und Geistesgemeinschaft', making him suitable material for propaganda purposes (for an extensive discussion, see Büttner, *Rubenshaus*, 2020, pp. 137–156). On construction activities during the war, see also Tijs, *Rubens en Jordaens*, 1984, pp. 224, 228; Van Driessche, *Herschepping*, 2009, pp. 13–17; id., *Herschepping*, 2013, pp. 23–26.

104–107).[105] A concrete summary of all the problems is provided by the long and comprehensive list of questions that was presented in the summer of 1938 by Van Averbeke to the restoration committee.[106]

It should be repeated that a number of contentious issues that were discussed in the 1930s and 1940s – at times giving rise to heated debate – remain unresolved today. It is worth noting also that discussions did not merely focus on historical and archaeological aspects. With the decision to purchase the house, and to restore it to its former state, came questions of a more fundamental nature that also needed to be addressed. Some were in favour of converting the requisitioned houses into a functional museum and documentation centre dedicated to Rubens, without going to the length of recreating every detail of the original architecture. And then there were people who were driven by a romantic-nostalgic aspiration to restore the magnificent house to its former glory and to show it 'as it had been'. As might be expected, the second option won, despite protests and harsh but valid criticism – including from Paul Buschmann (1877–1924) – that the whole thing would be 'a misleading illusion', 'a shameful scam'.[107]

We must also mention a temporary reconstruction of the house which the City of Antwerp made for its pavilion at the 1910 World Exhibition in Brussels. It was designed by the architect Henri Blomme (1845–1923) with help from Max Rooses, and it was executed in *staff* (reinforced plaster), gypsum and filler.[108] Apart from true-to-scale replicas of the portico and the garden pavilion, visitors could also admire lavishly decorated reconstructions of the interior of Rubens's studio and the façade facing the courtyard. Besides attracting much praise, there was justified criticism, but the ambitious project proved a true crowd-puller at the exhibition. The temporary pavilion in Brussels was seen as an opportunity to test the ground and it undoubtedly paved the way for the

---

105. See also Chapter V, passim. For the numerous photographs (preserved in the Antwerp FelixArchief and the archive at the Rubenshuis), see Delen, *Rubens' huis*, 1933, figs on pp. 57, 59 (the remodelled portico); Delen, *Geschiedenis Rubenshuis*, 1938, figs on pp. 16 (façade facing the Wapper), 17–19 (courtyard); Van Averbeke, *Eerste bevindingen*, 1938, figs on pp. 24–25 (façade facing the garden), pp. 41–42 (studio façade); Buschmann, *Huis-Rubens*, 1938, fig. on p. 57 (excavation); Clijmans, *Wederopbouw Rubenshuis*, 1941, figs 16–19; comprehensive documentation with a series of photographs in Tijs, *Rubens en Jordaens*, 1984, figs on pp. 171–175, 177, 180–182, 188–195, 209, 218–217. These and other photographs can also be consulted online at DAMS (URL: dams.antwerpen.be); search for 'fotoboek ontstaansgeschiedenis van het Rubenshuis', and the FelixArchief website (Verzamelingen, Beeld en geluid, Foto's, Fotoverzameling losse foto's [URL: https://felixarchief.antwerpen.be/archievenoverzicht/539321]).
106. Devroe, *Rubens' huis*, 2008, I, pp. 115–119; for the committee's answers, see ibid., I, pp. 119–122.
107. Buschmann, *Huis-Rubens*, 1938 (esp. pp. 59, 62). For the debate about the form the reconstruction should take, and the various restoration approaches, see also Van Driessche, *Herschepping*, 2009, pp. 6–9; Van Driessche, *Herschepping*, 2013, pp. 15–19.
108. Rooses, *Huis van Rubens*, 1910, pp. 193–207 [pp. 5–19]; Blomme, *Huis van Rubens*, 1910; Tijs, *Rubens en Jordaens*, 1984, pp. 163, 167–169, figs on pp. 167–168; Jaumain – Balcers, *Bruxelles 1910*, 2010, p. 116, figs 13–15; Devroe, *Rubens' huis*, 2008, II, nos 85a–85e; Van Driessche, *Herschepping*, 2013, p. 16.

later decision to requisition the Antwerp house, so that it could be returned to its former glory.

Ludwig Burchard

Of course, we must also acknowledge in this volume Ludwig Burchard's involvement in the restoration. From London he corresponded with the Antwerp city architect Émile van Averbeke. The correspondence began in December 1938 but was brought to a halt in March 1939 when Van Averbeke fell ill and, soon after, by the outbreak of the war, which meant that Burchard could no longer be contacted. In answer to Van Averbeke's question whether Burchard was aware of other images of Rubens's house besides those that were already known, Burchard wrote a long letter to the architect on 6 February 1939, commenting on Jordaens's *Cupid and Psyche* (Appendix III.9; Fig. 20) as well as three drawings that could be linked to the frieze on the façade of the studio.[109] It was agreed that Burchard would write an article on these painted murals for the third volume of the *Periodisch Bulletin*. In the event, however, this volume did not see the light of day, and the article that Burchard sent to Antwerp in March 1939 – of which sadly no copy survives – was never published. Contact between Burchard and Antwerp was not re-established until after the war, in January 1948 – eighteen months after the restoration and reconstruction of the Rubenshuis had been completed.[110]

---

109. A carbon copy of this typed letter was preserved in the Rubenianum (now lost). For those drawings, see No. 11, Copy; No. 12, Copy and No. 13a.
110. Curator Theo Ruyten, who had obtained Burchard's London address from the art dealer Sam Hartveld, sent him a letter on 7 January 1948. In his reply Burchard promises: 'one of my first visits to the continent will surely be Antwerp, and I shall not fail to see you there […] and visit the Rubens House' (Correspondence of Ludwig Burchard at Antwerp, Rubenianum, box 'Rubenshuis').

Chapter III
The House in the Time of Hendrik Hillewerve: A Closer Look at Jacob Harrewijn's Prints

A. The Art-loving Canon

In January 1680, shortly after Jacomo van Eycke's death, his widow, Cornelia Hillewerve, sold the house to her brother, Canon Hendrik Hillewerve (1621–1694).

This man, who spent the last fourteen years of his life in Rubens's house, seems to have followed a rather unusual path. His father, Cornelis, was an art dealer and Hendrik initially took over the family business. After the death of his wife, Margareta Goos (1631–1657), he became a priest. In 1661 he was appointed canon of St James's Church.[1] As one of the church's principal benefactors he funded a number of important embellishments, including the building of the main altar in 1686.[2]

Text ill. 24. Detail of the 1692 Harrewijn print (Fig. 18): the portrait of Canon Hendrik Hillewerve in a tondo.

Like his brother Franciscus (d. 1700), who was canon of Our Lady's Cathedral in Antwerp, Hillewerve remained active as a dealer in paintings. We have almost no written information, however, about pictures or other art objects that Hillewerve may have kept in Rubens's house.[3] A codicil that was added to his will in 1692 mentions furniture, books and paintings which

---

1. For biographical details, see Prims, *Hillewerve*, 1932, pp. 145–152. It is remarkable that two of his brothers were also canons, Frederik in Bruges, and Franciscus (d. 1700) at the Cathedral of Our Lady in Antwerp.
2. For a full discussion of Hillewerve's contribution to the ornamentation of the church, see Muller, *St Jacob's Church*, 2016, pp. 129–132, 171–174 and passim. He also made a bequest to the church (see n. 4).
3. Archival documents include numerous references to a 'Hillewerve' (with or without the title of canon) in connection with paintings that were sold; it is not always clear which of the brothers is being mentioned (see, for example, Denucé, *Kunstuitvoer*, 1931, p. 115; id., *Musson*, 1949, passim; Duverger, *Musson*, 1968, passim); for a *Battle of the Amazons* that (Hendrik?) Hillewerve bought from Matthijs Musson, see B. Schepers in McGrath et al., *Mythological Subjects I (CRLB)*, 2016, I, pp. 158, 160, 168, n. 97. An *Ecce Homo* by Titian, from the estate of Buckingham, was purchased by (Hendrik?) Hillewerve in 1648 and sold by him to Archduke Leopold Wilhelm (now Vienna, Kunsthistorisches Museum; Wethey, *Titian*, 1969–75, I, pp. 79–80). Franciscus was involved in a trial about a series of the apostles that had been incorrectly attributed to Van Dyck (N. De Poorter in Barnes et al., *Van Dyck*, 2004, p. 67).

Hendrik bequeathed to his brother Franciscus; only one painting is identified by title in this document: 'The Church of Rome' ('de Kercke van Roomen'), which is for 'd'heer Balthazar Moretus'.[4]

The large sum that Hillewerve paid his sister for the house – 36,000 guilders[5] – suggests that he wanted to provide financial support to the widow and her three children. Two years after the purchase of the property he extended his generosity even further. Although he continued to live there until his death in 1694, Hillewerve ceased to own the house long before this. On 17 June 1682, he gave the property as a 'donatio inter vivos' to his sister and her three children, Joanna, Teresia and Joseph van Eycke (Appendix I.33). There were a number of conditions attached to the gift: Cornelia Hillewerve was not allowed to sell the house; instead, she was to come and live there (or remain there) with her children, while her brother retained the use of a number of rooms (see below). It is clear from this that Cornelia Hillewerve took over responsibility for her brother's household. On top of an annual rent, he paid her a sum for food and drink, and she also received rent from the two adjacent houses on the Wapper towards the annual maintenance costs of the larger property.[6]

Cornelia Hillewerve's son, Joseph van Eycke, became a priest in the Antwerp Carmelite Order (Brothers of the Blessed Virgin Mary of Mount Carmel), and in 1683 he in turn gave his portion of the property to his two sisters. Thus, when their mother died in 1686, Joanna [Maria Justa] and [Anna] Teresia van Eycke, who were both 'pious daughters', took over ownership of the house in which their uncle was living. To formalise this arrangement a new act was drawn up in 1692 (Appendix I.35). In his will of 1686 Hendrik Hillewerve had bequeathed the bulk of his moveable property to his nieces, but he revoked this provision in a codicil of 1692, stating that they were wealthy enough and, furthermore, that they had moved to Brussels.[7]

Finally, it should be remembered that although Hillewerve's residency in the house lasted for fourteen years, he actually owned it for just two years and a few months. In light of this it seems unlikely that he undertook substantial alterations to the house, unlike the Van Eyckes, who not only occupied the house, but also owned it for twenty years.

The sale and donation deeds drawn up in 1660 and in the 1680s provide little or no information about the property that helps in our research. The

4. For Hendrik Hillewerve's will, with codicil stating that the bulk of his possessions are to be left to his brother Franciscus and the St James's Church, see Duverger, *Kunstinventarissen*, 1984–2009, XI, pp. 388–389. Balthazar Moretus III (1646–1696) was the nephew of his deceased wife, Margareta Goos.
5. The sale deed of 1680 only mentions 'a certain sum of money' but the amount paid for the house can be calculated from a receipt for a duty payment of 450 guilders (= 1 1/4 percent), this amount being a fraction of the purchase price of 36,000 guilders (Antwerp, Rubenshuis, archive, no. RH.D.054.4.02.11).
6. For more on this donation, and the conditions attached to it, see Devroe, *Rubens' huis*, 2008, I, p. 58; Maclot, *Rubenssite*, 2016, pp. 79–80.
7. Duverger, *Kunstinventarissen*, 1984–2009, XI, pp. 388–389.

descriptions of it in these documents are concise and sound almost identical: the house with its many upper and lower rooms ('opper- en neercamers'), basements and attics; a large garden, and the two adjacent houses with their gardens. The last mention of the *schilderhuys* as a section of the house comes in 1660 (Appendix I.25). The 1682 'donatio' has an interesting passage in which Hillewerve lists the parts that he wishes to retain for his own use: his bedroom, 'quarters' for himself and his servant, and the 'chapel room'(Appendix I.33: [3]).

That Rubens's house played a significant role in the life of the art-loving cannon is plain. This is borne out by the two prints of the grand home that he commissioned from Jacob Harrewijn but there are other testimonies as well. When the canon comes in for praise, then the house inevitably also receives a mention. In his Latin eulogy, published around 1695, Franciscus Desiderius de Sevin (b. 1644) devoted forty-six verses (out of a hundred and eighty) to the house and garden that had belonged to the famous painter (*Amplissima Domus Rubeniana nunc Hilwerveriana*). He reports that Hillewerve's very splendid chapel (*splendidissimum sacellum*) was decorated with a large number of sacred relics (Appendix I.36).

B. The Two Prints by Jacob Harrewijn: General Remarks

Two documents that are of central importance for our knowledge of Rubens's house are the well-known prints (Appendix I.1–2; Figs 17–18), which were commissioned by Canon Hendrik Hillewerve, who moved into Rubens's house forty years after his death, living there from 1680 to 1694.

As the inscriptions at the bottom of the prints tell us, they were made by Jacob Harrewijn (1660–1727) after drawings by Jacob van Croes, an artist about whom virtually nothing is known.[8] The successful and talented etcher Harrewijn was born in Amsterdam in 1660, where he was a pupil of Romeyn de Hooghe (1645–1708).[9] He travelled south and established himself in Antwerp, where he became a Master in the Guild of St Luke in 1688, before moving to Brussels in about 1694. There he died in 1727 and was buried in the Collegiate Church of St Michael.[10]

---

8. We have very little information about Jacques (or Jacob) van Croes – also (incorrectly?) referred to as Jan van Croes. We only know that he produced topographical drawings in the second half of the 17th century (and possibly at the beginning of the 18th century); see also his drawing representing Frans Floris's House (Chapter VI, pp. 197–198; Text ill. 81).
9. Van Nierop, *Romeyn de Hooghe*, 2018, pp. 46, 114, 257, 303.
10. For these biographical data, see the publication by Émile Van Heurck (1871–1931), whose source was the transcription of the original family chronicle preserved in the Kempuseum in Brecht (Archief en Bibliotheek van de Geschied- en Oudheidkundige Kring van Brecht); Van Heurck, *Harrewijn*, 1920, pp. 8–9, 28, 31. Van Heurck published a list of 111 works by Harrewijn (ibid., pp. 10–19). It is sometimes mistakenly assumed

CHAPTER III - THE HOUSE IN THE TIME OF HENDRIK HILLEWERVE

These extremely important etched views of Rubens's house, are dated 1684 and 1692. However, we should note that the date of the drawings by Van Croes, on which they are based, can only be guessed. It is possible that they were made on the same occasion rather than eight years apart. If so, and it remains entirely a matter for speculation, both prints show the premises as they appeared between 1680 (the date of the purchase by Hillewerve) and 1684.

As the prints are essential for our knowledge of the many lost parts of the house we will draw on them extensively in the chapters to come as well as in the catalogue. An assessment of their reliability is therefore appropriate.

First, a general observation: the prints are certainly not 'photographic' in terms of how they show the overall structure. The Harrewijn views show the architecture incoherently and in slightly distorted perspective: there is something not quite right about the proportions.[11] It is clear that the artist who made the drawings, Van Croes, constructed his images from more than one vantage point. Everything suggests that his views are an amalgamation of a number of individual details which he appears to have drawn on separate sheets (possibly from different viewpoints) before combining them.[12] The final result is acceptable, although closer inspection reveals quite a few inconsistencies of detail. The most striking thing is that the artist failed to apply the use of vanishing points correctly. One by-product of this is that the different storeys of the north façade are shown with different proportions in the same print.[13] Comparison with a surviving part of the house illustrates these oddities. Although the principal details of the portico (in the first print) are faithfully rendered, the proportions are not quite right: the satyrs in the spandrels are too small, while the niches and the busts above them are far too big.

The draughtsman's fragmentary way of working may also explain another peculiarity: on closer inspection we find that some elements of the house are shown in reverse. This is most noticeable in the representation of the north façade of the studio in the 1692 print. The workshop wall could not actually have been seen from the apparent viewpoint since the portico would have been in the way. Van Croes, found an easy way around this difficulty by simply inverting the north façade depicted in the first print. This is apparent from

---

that Harrewijn returned to Holland and died in The Hague in or after 1732 (see, for example, 'RKD-Artists' database URL: https://rkd.nl/nl/explore/artists). In 1689 he married Anna-Catharina van Cleemput, in Deurne (near Antwerp). The couple had 15 children. Two of his sons, Jacob-Gerard and Frans, were also etchers and worked – rather confusingly – in a similar style (making the right attribution to one of these three Harrewijns not always easy).

11. Rutger Tijs, also, pointed to the impossible viewpoint, the distorted perspective and other details such as shadows suggesting light falling from the north (Tijs, *Rubens en Jordaens*, 1984, p. 151).
12. This was observed by Arnout Balis, who looked into the question of the reliability of the prints, and wrote an extensive (unpublished) note about it.
13. It is therefore not easy to determine from the prints the exact dimensions of certain details for the catalogue descriptions.

CHAPTER III - THE HOUSE IN THE TIME OF HENDRIK HILLEWERVE

Text ill. 25. Detail of the 1684 Harrewijn print (Fig. 17): two scenes of the frieze on the north façade of the studio wing.

Text ill. 26. Detail of the 1692 Harrewijn print (Fig. 18): the same scenes as in Text ill. 25, in reverse.

asymmetrical details: the dog lying in the doorway is reversed (Text Ills 51 and 52), as are the scenes in the frieze above (cf. Text ills 25, 26). The subjects are the same and presented in the same order, but closer inspection reveals that the compositions are mirror images of those in the 1684 print. The statue in the niche of the garden pavilion is also shown in reverse (No. 36; Fig. 187).

A more subtle deviation in the print of 1684 from the true situation is the light shown falling from the left (i.e. from the north) and which gives form to the portico's sculptures in the round, and its relief (Fig. 142); a similar impossible situation appears in the presentation of the garden (through the arches of the portico): there, shadows are consistently created by direct light falling from the north (Text ill. 27).

It was certainly Van Croes and Harrewijn's intention to present the details of the striking house as accurately as possible, and they achieved this on the whole. Their work thus remains of greater documentary than artistic value. Indeed it is fair to say that a degree of clumsiness is noticeable in the way certain architectural and decorative details have been rendered. But otherwise they provide a surprisingly detailed and faithful impression of the complex as it would have looked in Hillewerve's day, and the information provided is very valuable.

It has sometimes been doubted that the prints provide a truthful depiction of what could be seen in Hillewerve's time. Émile Van Averbeke, one of the architects responsible for the modern reconstruction of the house, believed that certain details had been added or modified to enhance the appearance of the actual house, and that this was done at the request of Hillewerve, who had – in his opinion – a penchant for 'ostentatious display'.[14]

---

14. Van Averbeke, *Rubenshuis, restauratie II*, 1938, p. 27. In his report, Van Averbeke makes clear his disapproval of certain elements of the house as depicted: he uses phrases such as 'ridiculous' (ibid., p. 27 and passim), 'another mystification by Hillewerve' (ibid., p. 41), and states that 'The documentary value of this print is nil' (ibid., p. 42).

CHAPTER III - THE HOUSE IN THE TIME OF HENDRIK HILLEWERVE

Text ill. 27. Detail of the 1684 Harrewijn print (Fig. 17): the light falling from the left (the north) in the garden.

However, we have found no indication that Van Croes or Harrewijn indeed added anything with this in mind. The question applies especially to the statues on top of the portico (Fig. 227), which were never present, according to some, neither in Rubens's time nor when Hillewerve lived in the house.[15]

Yet there is perhaps one exception. It seems possible that a few minor adjustments were made to the true situation for the sake of 'decency': the scantily clad mythological figures of Mercury, Andromeda and Venus (Nos 5, 18 and 37) may have been provided with a little more clothing in the print than was actually present.

It can also be observed that certain parts of the architecture are left out or have been changed to give the image greater clarity and especially to make room for extra details. In the second print it is obvious that the portico is left out (indicated only by its footprint) (Text ill. 28) to provide an uninterrupted view into the courtyard from the east.

Less obvious (and not indicated by a footprint this time) is the omission in the same print of the arcade perpendicular to the north studio façade, thus allowing an unimpeded view of this façade.[16] The view of Hillewerve's chapel is also 'impossible': from the much lower adjoining room, it could not have been seen as presented in the print (where it is shown full-height and with a curtain either side) (Fig. 127).[17]

In short, there is no evidence of Van Croes or Harrewijn deliberately 'falsifying' the image of the house and, taking into account the deviations

---

15. For further discussion of this, see Chapter IX, pp. 278–285 and under Nos R1 and R2.
16. The print can be compared to the Aylesbury painting (Appendix III.3; Fig. 16), where the arcade is represented, and hides a part of the façade.
17. See Chapter VIII, pp. 239–240, n. 26.

CHAPTER III - THE HOUSE IN THE TIME OF HENDRIK HILLEWERVE

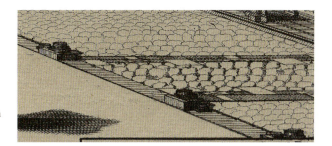

Text ill. 28. Detail of the 1692 Harrewijn print (Fig. 18): the footprint of the omitted portico.

mentioned, we can confidently use their detailed views to describe the lost parts of the house in the following chapters and the catalogue.

The essential question for our research remains: how closely do Harrewijn's images correspond to the situation at the time of Rubens's death? The garden has obviously partly been redesigned in the French style, while the interiors shown in the prints had, of course, also been rearranged by Hillewerve and other residents after 1640. But with regard to the architecture and the exterior of the house itself, the question is harder to answer. As outlined above, the house almost certainly underwent a number of substantial alterations between 1660 and 1680, when it belonged to the Van Eycke family. Some work may also have been undertaken by other occupants prior to 1660, although this seems less likely. Similarly, it is unlikely that Hillewerve, who lived in the house for fourteen years (1680–1694) but was its owner for only two years and a few months, would himself have altered the exterior of the building. That said, it is possible that Van Eycke or Hillewerve made changes to the 'free-standing' sculptural decorations, including the busts and statues.[18]

C. *The Subjects of the Two Prints: A Closer Look*

The Orientation of the Property

Before we go on to look at the prints it is worth remembering the orientation of what is shown, something we touched on in the discussion of the plot's history in Chapter I. For an understanding of the description of the house it is important to note that Mols's plan (Fig. 3) and the majority of later plans and drawings reproduced in the literature give no indication of orientation. The Wapper and the entrance are often depicted 'at the bottom' of the sheet, which is in fact west in orientation rather than south. In other words, entry to the house is from the west, and straight ahead towards the east, at the far end of the garden, is the

---

18. We will return to the problematical matter of the busts and the statues in Chapters IX and X.

CHAPTER III - THE HOUSE IN THE TIME OF HENDRIK HILLEWERVE

Text ill. 29. Detail of the 1684 Harrewijn print (Fig. 17): the coat of arms of Canon Hendrik Hillewerve.

pavilion; thus – and this may seem rather confusing at first, but is nevertheless correct – in the Harrewijn print and in Mols's drawing, the buildings facing the courtyard are: to the right, the north façade of the south wing and, to the left, the south façade of the north wing (see Fig. 6).

The First Print (1684): A View into the Courtyard from the West

Harrewijn's first print, dated 1684, shows the courtyard looking east (Fig. 17), and it presents the general view on entering the property from the main gate on the Wapper. To the left, on the north side of the courtyard, is the plain, undecorated façade belonging to the so-called family quarters, or 'Flemish' wing. In the centre is the portico, and stretching out beyond it, towards the east, the garden, in the middle of which the perspective leads to the pavilion; on either side of this are hedges forming a covered walkway with gaps for 'windows' and two entrances along the length of the Kolveniershof (Text ill. 31), hiding the wall between the two properties that was, as we know, restored in 1615.[19] To the right, on the south side, is a large building with a richly decorated façade: the *schilderhuys* or studio wing, which is often referred to in the literature as the 'Italian' wing.

In this print which he commissioned, Hendrik Hillewerve, the proud owner of the magnificent house, gives prominence to himself. His coat of arms, with a swimming dolphin, alluding to his motto 'tranquilis (or tranquillus) in undis' (calm amidst the waves) appears at the bottom (Text ill. 29).

In one state of the print (Fig. 17) and therefore not appearing on all impressions – a tondo can be seen at the top with his portrait as a bust in profile (Text ill. 24).

---

19. See Appendix I. 5 and Chapter IV, pp. 123–124.

CHAPTER III - THE HOUSE IN THE TIME OF HENDRIK HILLEWERVE

Text ill. 30. Detail of the 1692 Harrewijn print (Fig. 18): the trees on the Wapper.

The Second Print (1692): The House and Garden Seen from the North-East

The second print, dated 1692, presents a general view of the house and garden, this time looking south-west (Fig. 18). To the left can be seen the garden pavilion and to the right the east façade of the workshop. The portico has been omitted so that we are granted an unimpeded view of the courtyard, seeing once more the broad north façade of the workshop. Perpendicular to the studio façade, and continuing in the same style, is the inner façade of the building that fronts the street, and adjoining part of the living quarters with the entrance gate to the street. Protruding above the roof over the gateway are the crowns of tall trees that must be growing in the street behind, on the Wapper (Text ill. 30).

No houses can be seen in the distance along the southern edge of the plot (running along the Hopland), not even the houses which Rubens had bought in the 1620s. They seem to be hidden from view: to the right by a wall, and to the left by a latticed pergola and walkway (Text ill. 31).

Furthermore the rear façades of the houses along the Hopland are obscured by tall trees rising from the small gardens. What we can see in this direction is the roof of the Church of the Discalced Carmelites, which is situated on the far side of the Hopland (Text ill. 32).[20]

To the right, near the stables (the small house with the pointed stepped gable; see below) we can see an interesting detail: the dressage pole that was installed for William Cavendish's riding school (Text ill. 17).[21]

---

20. For this church, see Chapter II, p. 66, n. 55. We have not been able to identify the roof (of a chapel?) with small bell tower that appears between the trees to the left.
21. For Cavendish and his dressage method, see Chapter II, pp. 67–70.

CHAPTER III - THE HOUSE IN THE TIME OF HENDRIK HILLEWERVE

Text ill. 31. Detail of the 1692 Harrewijn print (Fig. 18): the latticed pergola and walkway at the south side of the garden.

Text ill. 32. Detail of the 1692 Harrewijn print (Fig. 18): the roof of the Church of the Discalced Carmelites.

Life in Hillewerves's Garden

Six figures are shown in Hillewerve's garden. Near the stables are two men standing by a fence (or more likely a hitching post for horses) (Text ill. 17). Two others are looking after a pair of horses which they have unharnessed from the carriage that stands in the passage leading to the Wapper (Text ill. 37).

In the foreground, slightly out of sight behind the columns of Rubens's garden pavilion, two men are shown sitting at a table in the shade as they enjoy a glass of wine (Fig. 183). One of these, wearing a wide cloak that reaches down to the ground, is raising his glass. In all likelihood this is Canon Hillewerve himself, entertaining a visitor, who is also a clergyman, judging from his costume.

It should be noted that the six men in the garden are the only living souls to be seen in the two prints; the figure standing behind a balustrade looking out over the courtyard is part of a *trompe-l'oeil* painting (Fig. 107).[22]

Three Supplementary Images as Insets

Inserted in a strip across the bottom of the 1692 print are three supplementary images of the house. In the middle, represented as a sheet of paper or canvas loosely draped over a rod and with its corners curling up, is an image showing the façade fronting the Wapper, without the adjoining houses belonging to the neighbours (Fig. 26). Two extremely interesting images are shown either side, namely a pair of rooms as arranged in Hillewerve's time: to the left a semi-circular domed chapel (Fig. 127) and to the right a spacious interior

---

22. For the loggia in *trompe-l'oeil*, see Chapter VI, pp. 183–184 and No. 17.

with a four-poster bed and low-domed ceiling (Text ill. 47). Evidently these are the chapel room ('capelcamer'), which impressed De Sevin, and the canon's bedroom – two of the rooms in the 'quarters' ('kwartier') allocated to the canon and his servant in the contract for the 1682 'donatio inter vivos'.

Hillewerve's coat of arms with a dolphin appears three times on the print: in the top right corner (Fig. 18), on the pergola at the far end of the garden (Text ill. 40) and at the foot of the inset view of the bedroom, where it can be seen side-by-side with the arms (three stars) of his late wife Margareta Goos (Text ill. 47). The motif of the dolphin is also woven into the image in another way: at either end of the strip at the bottom, perched on a pedestal, is a sculpture of a writhing dolphin with its head pointing down (Text ill. 33), possibly based on an actual object in Hillewerve's possession. Heraldic connotations may have played a role in the choice of this motif in the print.[23]

It should be noted that the title of the second print, on the banderole, no longer refers to the house as '*hostel Rubens*', as in the 1684 print, but it is now named only after the occupier: '*La maison HILWERUE*'.

Text ill. 33. Detail of the 1692 Harrewijn print (Fig. 18): a dolphin (a sculpture ?) at the bottom left of the print.

D. *The Components of the Property*

From the surviving sources, the prints by Harrewijn, the plan by Mols and of course the actual building as it survived into the twentieth century, we can deduce that at the time of Rubens's death his house consisted of four wings, three of them forming the sides of a quadrangle which was closed off by the portico connecting two of the wings; in addition there were outbuildings such as the pavilion that was built against the wall of the Kolveniershof, and the stables in the south-west corner of the garden. A number of adjoining small houses were also added to the property in 1627 and 1628.

In Rubens's day the four wings, listed clockwise, were as they stand today in the reconstructed house (Figs 6–7):

---

23. A twisting dolphin with its tail pointing upwards also crowns the coats of arms of the Hillewerve – Goos couple on their tombstone in St James's Church; see Génard et al., *Inscriptions funéraires*, 1856–1903, II, p. 5: the same coats of arms are also depicted in a 'Sepulcher Book', preserved in this church (Muller, *St Jacob's Church*, 2016, pp. 526, 528, col. ill. fig. 10.26).

CHAPTER III - THE HOUSE IN THE TIME OF HENDRIK HILLEWERVE

a) the south wing, that is the studio wing, the 'schilderhuys' or 'Italian' wing;
b) the west wing, i.e. the street front on the Wapper (partly an old structure and a new part);
c) the north wing, the family quarters, also known as the 'Flemish' wing;
d) the east, or garden wing, that is the structure adjoining the east side of (c), and extending behind the neighbouring plots to the north, parallel to the Wapper.

Unfortunately, certain parts of the house are not visible in Harrewijn's prints, which is all the more regrettable as – and it is important to stress this – there are no other visual records for these sections at all. The least troubling of the omissions are parts of the façades facing the courtyard, which were almost certainly without decoration and so of limited interest for our study. These include most of the 'old' west wing (the part to the right of the entrance) and a few bays on the left side of the north wing.

More disconcerting is that we have no visual record at all of the garden side, or 'rear' of the portico, which, like the front, was certainly designed by Rubens. Another significant gap in our knowledge is the entire exterior of the east wing, with the exception of a narrow strip of façade to the left of the portico. This means that there is no known image of this intriguing part of the house which is indicated in Mols's schematic plan, and included a special architectural element: a 'tower' or 'pantheon'.

Finally, it should be noted that the prints do offer some information about the south side of Rubens's former studio wing, but the situation seems to have undergone substantial alteration in Hillewerve's time, meaning that the images are unhelpful if we want to learn about the original appearance of the studio's south façade (see below).

The three elements of the house that are interesting from an art-historical perspective and which are depicted by Harrewijn – the studio wing, the portico and the garden pavilion – will be discussed further in separate chapters. In the remainder of this chapter we will focus on the other parts of the house, and we will also consider the information provided by the prints about two rooms in the house during the time it was occupied by Hillewerve. Finally, we will discuss the ornaments that appear in the courtyard: a water pump, a fountain and a carved dog.

The North Wing or 'Flemish' Wing

In both of the prints by Harrewijn we gain an impression of the north (or 'old') wing of Rubens's former house. In the print of 1684 we can see, to the left of the courtyard, a substantial part of this north wing's south façade (Text ill. 34); this

CHAPTER III - THE HOUSE IN THE TIME OF HENDRIK HILLEWERVE

Text ill. 34. Detail of the 1684 Harrewijn print (Fig. 17): a part of the south façade of the north wing.

Text ill. 35. Detail of the 1692 Harrewijn print (Fig. 18): the old part (at the left) of west façade.

façade is very simple, with just one upper storey, narrow cross-windows and a saddle roof with a single small dormer window. Two string courses provide the only decoration. Standing against the wall is a water pump crowned by a wrought-iron ornamental structure.[24] The west or street side of this wing is incorporated in the west wing and can be seen in the inset at the foot of the second print (Text ill. 35). Here the façade spans two windows and is crowned by a stepped gable, which is decorated with six finials as well as a weathervane.

It is safe to assume that the north wing with its simple construction and plain exterior belonged to the original 'huysinge' purchased by Rubens in 1610. Hoping to gain an impression of this construction, researchers have tried to locate it in early bird's-eye views of Antwerp, but in vain. As mentioned above, the houses depicted on Rubens's plot on the Wapper are shown in these maps in widely differing forms, meaning that no reliable information can be derived from these documents.[25] The literature often assumes that Rubens's north wing corresponds to the house that can be seen in the famous map of 1565 by Virgilius Bononiensis. About halfway along the Wapper, the plan shows a fairly large house with a stepped gable towards the street and windows on the south side (Fig. 1). But this identification is far from certain. Within the block, the house

24. For more on this water pump, see below, p. 113.
25. See Chapter I, pp. 42–43.

CHAPTER III - THE HOUSE IN THE TIME OF HENDRIK HILLEWERVE

depicted by Bononiensis half a century earlier seems to lie closer to the Meir. It also looks noticeably bigger and more prominent than Rubens's long, narrow north wing, which was no more than four metres wide (a single room), and which probably had just a blind wall backing onto the neighbouring parcel to the north (see Fig. 6). It is worth repeating that this plan of Antwerp is of course not a photographically accurate record of individual houses or their locations.[26]

Whatever the case, the plain façade of the north wing seen in the Harrewijn print of 1684 (Text Ill. 34) suggests that it indeed formed part of a pre-existing dwelling whose architecture was left largely untouched by Rubens. The same observation can be made for the west or street front that adjoins the north wing to form an L-shape, and which is built in the same 'old' style (Text Ill. 35).

The general assumption in the literature has been that the older parts of the house, the entire north wing as well as the adjoining part of the street wing, and also the newly built adjoining upper storey of the east wing, were used by Rubens and his family as their living quarters, and this premise was followed in the modern reconstruction. The reconstructed rooms have been assigned particular functions and were furnished more or less accordingly. They were given names such as the parlour ('where visitors waited to be admitted to the master'), the kitchen, the serving room, the dining room, the bedrooms (including 'Rubens's bedroom'), the linen room ('where the linen was kept') and the family room ('where the family assembled around the hearth in the evenings').[27]

Although it is more than likely that the north wing and part of the west or street wing were indeed used as the domestic quarters, it should be pointed out that none of this is corroborated by contemporary sources. The seventeenth-century interior layout of these wings is completely unknown, and the functions assigned to the reconstructed rooms are not based on any evidence. Moreover, the names they have been given are anachronistic in that they ignore the fact that in Rubens's time most domestic rooms had several functions.[28]

At the time of the restoration, the original façades of the north wing had been lost. In order to emphasise its traditional 'Flemish' character, this section

---

26. Petra Maclot carried out a comprehensive study on de Bononiensis map, concluding that in terms of type the houses are shown accurately (that is with meaningful differentiation), but that considerably less attention was paid to the number and the exact location of houses (Maclot, *Portrait Unmasked*, 2014, pp. 35–36).
27. See, for instance, the visitor guide of 1977 (Baudouin, *Summary Guide*, 1977, passim; for the rooms in the east wing, assumed to be downstairs, the art gallery and, upstairs, for Rubens's bedroom or 'the large bedroom', see Chapter VIII, pp. 230–231.
28. For instance, except for the kitchen and one two other rooms including a 'comptoir', none of the names introduced at the time of the reconstruction occur in the Antwerp probate inventories of the first decades of the seventeenth century; rooms are labelled simply according to their location in the house ('neercamer', 'voorcamer', 'middelcamer', 'hangende camer' etc.) (Duverger, *Kunstinventarissen*, 1984–2009, I–III, passim). For the meaning of 'comptoir' (cantoor), see Chapter VII, pp. 226–227.

was reconstructed in a style which deviates distinctly from what can be seen in the prints. The walls are now decorated with courses of sandstone and brick, known in Dutch as 'speklagen' (bacon motif), a typical façade decoration in the Netherlands in the sixteenth and seventeenth centuries.

The West Wing / Street Front

An inset at the bottom of the second print shows the west or street front of Rubens's house, omitting the neighbours' adjoining houses (Fig. 18). The broad façade – measuring some forty-three metres across and consisting of eighteen bays – forms an impressive, roughly symmetrical ensemble. A higher central section spanning five bays, the west façade of the studio wing, is flanked by lower structures with gateways: to the left the so-called old or 'Flemish' wing, and to the right the wing with the houses which Rubens purchased in 1627.

The left-hand section of the west façade (Text ill. 35) incorporates the stepped gable mentioned above (the west side of the north wing). It is an oblong two-storey façade, which is interrupted by the entrance gate leading to the courtyard. The style is traditional and plain apart from a string course between the two storeys. To the right of the stepped gable, the saddle roof has two small dormers, each also with a stepped gable.

The entrance gate from the Wapper in this 'old' wing is enclosed within a moulded frame, with two round niches with busts or lion's heads above (Text ill. 36).[29] These decorative elements cannot be dated and so it cannot be established whether they were installed on Rubens's initiative. As with the north wing, the undecorated façades were rebuilt in the twentieth-century restoration, probably incorrectly, with alternate courses of brick and sandstone ('speklagen'), a style that was regarded as 'traditional Flemish'.

The central section of the street front, forming the west façade of the studio wing, is taller than the two 'old' side wings and spans five bays that are distinctly larger in scale. This façade will be discussed in Chapter V.

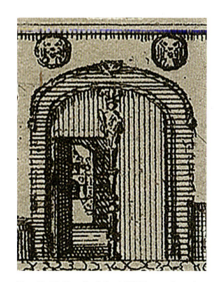

Text ill. 36. Detail of the 1692 Harrewijn print (Fig. 18): the entrance gate to the courtyard.

---

29. Reports drawn up during the restoration mistakenly refer to horse's heads, presumably placed there by Cavendish (Devroe, *Rubens' huis*, 2008, I, pp. 118–119; Maclot, *Rubenssite*, 2016, p. 182).

CHAPTER III - THE HOUSE IN THE TIME OF HENDRIK HILLEWERVE

The Houses on the Wapper

The right half or southern part of the street front offers an impression of the houses Rubens acquired in 1627, or rather the restructured houses as they looked in Hillewerve's day (Text ill. 9). The sale deed of 1627 speaks of three houses lying next to each other on the Wapper. This is repeated in the deed of 1660, when the property was transferred to Van Eycke. But when it was sold again twenty years later, in 1680, an important change seems to have occurred. Included in the sale this time are 'two more houses which used to form three separate houses or dwellings' ('twee andere huijsen eertijts drije huijskens off wooningen geweest sijnde […]') (Appendix I.30). From the description in the deeds we can deduce that the three houses had been converted into two dwellings between 1660 and 1680, in other words while the property belonged to the Van Eycke couple.[30]

This restructuring is confirmed by the print, which indeed shows only two separate dwellings, each with its own front door. As mentioned above, these two dwellings were let under Hillewerve, and the rent contributed to the maintenance of the main house (Appendix I.33: [4]).

The pattern of the roofs was apparently also altered. The three original houses probably each had a saddle roof with a stepped gable front and back. It seems that at a certain point Rubens's houses were provided with a single continuous roof, parallel to the Wapper and with modillions (rectangular corbels) underneath, harmonising more or less with the large roof of the studio alongside.

The South Wing. Its South Side: The Passageway from the Wapper to the Garden: In Hillewerve's Time a Coach House

The south wing, the most important part of Rubens's house, will be discussed extensively in later chapters. The present chapter will concentrate on what can be learned about the problematic south side of this wing in Hillewerve's time.

The inset with the street front in Harrewijn's print of 1692 shows a large gateway to the right of the tall studio façade – mirroring the entrance to the courtyard to the left of the studio – which is overarched by an upper storey with window (Fig. 26 and Text ill. 9). It emerges from the main scene of the print that the gate gave access to a passageway leading from the Wapper to the garden. On the garden side, level with the east façade of the studio, we can see this passageway, with a high blind wall above, crowned by a saddle roof with a small dormer (Text ill. 37).

30. Rutger Tijs also assumed that the conversion from three to two houses took place between 1660 and 1680 (Tijs, *Rubens en Jordaens*, 1984, p. 149).

CHAPTER III - THE HOUSE IN THE TIME OF HENDRIK HILLEWERVE

Text ill. 37. Detail of the 1692 Harrewijn print (Fig. 18): the stables (at the left) and (at the right) the gateway used as a coach house.

This structure, the covered passageway from the Wapper to the garden, is mentioned in a sale deed dating from 8 December 1696, which is the moment when the two small houses on the Wapper ceased to belong to the large house and were transferred to a new owner. Because of an easement on the property, the deed specifies that the south side of the main house consists of a coach house (also used as a wash house), which is lit by seven windows receiving light from the garden or courtyard of the adjoining house on the Wapper (Appendix I.37).[31]

The situation described also corresponds to Mols's drawing of about eighty years later (Fig. 3): next to the former studio is an elongated coach house ('remise'); above it, on the street side, is a small room with a single window, a 'cabinet' (indicated as '2'), which can be reached from the long 'galerie' that runs parallel to the street (indicated as '1'), as well as an attic ('6. grenier au-dessus de la remise') to which there is no access from inside the house.

There are indications that the layout of this part of the house, as shown in the print, in Mols's drawing, and as described in the sale deed of 1696, was different in Rubens's day, or at least up until 1627. From the sale deed of 1627

---

31. See also Maclot, *Rubenssite*, 2016, pp. 87–88.

CHAPTER III - THE HOUSE IN THE TIME OF HENDRIK HILLEWERVE

Text ill. 38. The recreated open passageway from the Wapper to the garden in the Rubenshuis.

(Appendix I.18) it can be deduced that there was then an open – that is uncovered – passageway between Rubens's property and the adjacent row of houses he bought. Rather than being adjacent to Rubens's house, the three houses on the Wapper are described as adjoining Rubens's bleaching green to the north.[32] From this description it follows that the original south façade of the studio wing was freestanding, with a gap of approximately four metres separating it from the adjacent house to the south. It is difficult to determine when this area was roofed over, with a 'new' south side joined to the neighbouring house and its garden. We cannot be absolutely certain that Rubens left this strip untouched after 1627, when he became the owner of the house adjoining the south side of his property. However, it seems more likely that this alteration was carried out by a later owner, quite possibly the Van Eyckes when they came to rebuild the small houses on the Wapper.[33]

In other words, at a certain point the original south façade of the studio became an internal wall. Of course, what matters in this context is what we can learn about the original façade of the studio wing at this side, and especially whether or not there once were windows that allowed sunlight to stream into the studio from the south. We will return to this intriguing question in the chapter dealing with the interior of the studio wing.[34]

During the modern reconstruction it was decided to recreate the open passageway from the Wapper to the garden (Text ills 38 and 86), moving away substantially from what can be seen in the Harrewijn print.[35]

---

32. 'drye daeraff neffen malcanderen opden Wapper alhier, tusschen den naerbescreven Bleyckhoff nu tertyt de voors. coopere toebehoorende aen deen zijde noortwaerts …'(three [houses] thereof next to each other on the Wapper here, between the said bleaching green, currently belonging to the aforementioned buyer on the north side…) (Appendix I.18).
33. For the restructuring of the houses (converting them from three houses into two dwellings) between 1660 and 1680, see above, p. 102.The sale deeds of 1660 and 1680 both refer to a passageway between the south wing Rubens's former house (in 1660 still denoted as the 'schilderhuys') and the houses lying to the south of this passageway (Appendix I.25, 30), without specifying whether it was covered.
34. See Chapter VII, pp. 205–210.
35. Later, in 1998, the passageway was covered over again (with a glass roof); see Maclot, *Rubenssite*, 2016, p. 245.

The Portico

In the Harrewijn print of 1684 we see the front of the portico, which connected the north and south wings, and functioned as a gateway into the garden (Fig. 17); since it is a surviving element of the house, and one moreover documented by earlier seventeenth-century sources, it will be described and discussed at length in a separate chapter (Chapter IX); information is also given under Nos 24–33.

The East or Garden Wing

The east wing was a two-storey structure, situated perpendicular to the so-called living quarters or north wing, and thus parallel to the Wapper. This wing jutted out significantly to the north, so that the neighbouring plot was enclosed by that of Rubens on two sides (south and east) (Fig. 6).

In the absence of visual records we can only guess at the appearance of the exterior of this wing, which – as can be deduced from Mols's drawing – contained Hillewerve's 'chapel room', the round or semi-circular domed space that had served as Rubens's 'antiquarium'. Apart from one narrow strip, the exterior of this wing is not visible in the views by Harrewijn. To the left of the portico in the 1684 print, is a slim section of façade facing the courtyard: a wall with two windows, one above the other, with leaded lights. It is striking that the lower window, and therefore, of course, the floor level of the room behind it, is noticeably higher than the rooms on the ground floor of the 'old' wing (Text Ills 34 and 94). Through an open door in the north wing we can just catch sight of a second door inside, which leads to this elevated room.

The same narrow section of wall with two windows, to the left of the portico, appears in the background of Gonzales Coques's small *Portrait of Maria Agnes van Eycke as St Agnes* (Appendix III.11; Text ill. 20). Moreover, through the left-hand arch a vague fragment can be seen of a façade with a single window, also with leaded lights (Text ill. 95).

Apart from this detail in the Coques portrait, the appearance of the south and east-facing façades of the east or garden wing thus remain completely unknown. Was this wing one of the existing structures on the site when it was bought by Rubens in 1610, and so executed in a plain, traditional style? When the property was restored, these façades, like those of the adjoining assumed 'family quarters', were reconstructed in 'Flemish' style with 'speklagen' (bacon motif) (Figs 14–15), although there was no original material on which to base the decision. If the wing was newly constructed by Rubens, it seems possible that the two façades visible from the garden would have followed something like the style of the Italianate east façade of the studio and (perhaps) of the unknown rear of the portico.

CHAPTER III - THE HOUSE IN THE TIME OF HENDRIK HILLEWERVE

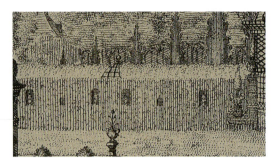 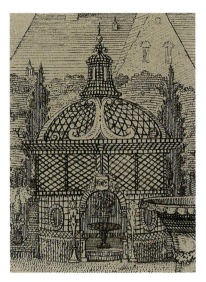

Text ill. 39. Detail of the 1692 Harrewijn print (Fig. 18): the walkway with 'windows' and busts at the south side of the garden.

Text ill. 40. Detail of the 1692 Harrewijn print (Fig. 18): the pergola at the south side of the garden.

The Garden

Both Harrewijn prints give an impression of part of the garden in the time of Hillewerve. Through the arches of the portico, against the wall of the Kolveniershof, the first print offers a glimpse of the garden pavilion symmetrically flanked by hedges forming a covered walkway with numerous window-like openings as well as two entrances. To the left and right of the central path that leads to the garden pavilion are parterres featuring exceptionally large vases on high pedestals (Text ills 27 and 41).

Looking south-west, the 1692 print, showing parterres and more vases, mostly on pedestals, provides further information about the garden.[36] Along the southern edge of the garden, parallel to the Hopland, is another walkway in which 'windows' or 'niches' with busts can be discerned (Text ill. 39). Midway along and rising over the walkway, we can see a curving mesh construction, made of metal or latticework, and crowned with a globe (possibly gilded?).

To the right of this walkway is a large latticework pergola in the shape of a rotunda, with a table inside. Inside at the back is a panel with figures, perhaps a painting. It is crowned with a dome-shaped roof topped by a lantern, and above the entrance we can make out Hillewerve's coat of arms (Text ill. 40).

---

36. The vases and pedestals in the garden are mentioned in the sale deeds of 1696 (Appendix I.37); see also Chapter II, p. 75) and 1701 (Appendix I.38; see also Chapter II, p. 75); a rental contract of 1707 refers to a copper vase in the flower bed (Appendix I.39).

CHAPTER III - THE HOUSE IN THE TIME OF HENDRIK HILLEWERVE

Text ill. 41. Detail of the 1692 Harrewijn print (Fig. 18): the parterres 'de broderie'.

It is difficult to determine to what extent Hillewerve's garden still contained elements from Rubens's time. It is striking that it bears no resemblance to *The Walk in the Garden* in Munich which was painted around 1630 (Appendix III.6; Fig. 25). Hillewerve's geometric parterres with decorative twirly patterns modelled on the French 'parterre de broderie' show that a large part of the garden had been redesigned according to contemporary French fashion (Text ill. 41).

Although hedges forming a covered walkway, concealing the garden's boundary walls to the east and south, are not visible in *The Walk in the Garden*, we can nonetheless assume that they formed part of the original design. A similar covering appears in many other images inspired by Rubens's garden and pavilion dating from before the sale of the house (1660), i.e. before the garden was redesigned by a later owner. Take for example the anonymous scenes from the 1640s of an *Elegant Company in a Garden* (Appendix III.36–37). A similar hedge with 'doorways' can also be seen in Teniers's *Elegant Company in a Garden*, dated 1651, to the right of a variant of the pavilion (Appendix III.34). Moreover, related motifs can be recognised in garden scenes by Rubens himself, for instance, *Susanna and the Elders*.[37]

Several seventeenth-century texts express admiration for the curious plants that were to be seen in Rubens's garden, which was exceptionally large for a

---

37. See, for instance, a variant (hedges with 'windows') in the background of *Susanna and the Elders*, in the Alte Pinakothek, Munich (d'Hulst – Vandenven, *Old Testament (CRLB)*, 1989, no. 65, fig. 170).

107

CHAPTER III - THE HOUSE IN THE TIME OF HENDRIK HILLEWERVE

plot in the centre of Antwerp, as well as ideally oriented. Authors who mention it include Philip Rubens (as *hortus latissimus*) and Roger de Piles.[38]

The plot that belongs with the restored house today still gives a good idea of the garden's impressive size for a city-centre location; the boundaries to the north, east and west remain unchanged; the removal of a strip of land in the nineteenth century, however, to be divided among houses along the Hopland, meant that the garden was slightly reduced along its southern edge.[39]

Rubens's garden has been studied from various different angles. Ursula Härting wrote several articles considering its place in garden history.[40] In connection with the house's reconstruction, attempts were made to return it as far as possible to its original state, which is something of a challenge given that so little information is available. Research was done into the possible appearance and planting of the original garden.[41] Taking a different approach, Ulrich Heinen rightly stressed that the garden formed an essential part of Rubens's house, following neostoical ideas about gardens shared by Rubens and his contemporaries.[42]

The Garden Pavilion

The Harrewijn print of 1692 gives a detailed view of the garden pavilion, seen from the north (Fig. 183), more or less from the same viewpoint as in the *Walk in The Garden* (Appendix III.6; Fig. 182). As it is a surviving part of the house, it will be discussed in a separate chapter (Chapter X) and in the catalogue (Nos 34–36).

The Stables

The small house with pointed, stepped gable in the south-west corner of the garden (Text ill. 37) served very probably as the stables, a function it may already have had in Rubens's and Cavendish's days. From the summarily listed components of the property on the Wapper in the *Staetmasse* of 1645 we know that it included stables ('stallingen'; Appendix I.23: [2]). When the house was sold in 1696, after Hillewerve's death, and only four years after the Harrewijn print, stables are mentioned in the garden ('inden hove'; Appendix I.37). The

---

38. Appendix I. 26, 31; see also Sandrart, Appendix I.29.
39. Maclot, *Rubenssite*, 2016, p. 116. In terms of its general atmosphere we should endeavour to forget that the plot is now surrounded by much taller buildings added in the 19th and 20th century (many of them showing their ugly rear side).
40. Härting, *Rubens' Garten*, 2000, pp. 59–66; id., *Prestige and Magnificenza*, 2004, pp. 120–125.
41. For a comprehensive overview of this research, with special attention to plants that might have been found in a 17th-century garden, see the report by Klara Alen (Alen, *Rubenstuin*, 2021).
42. Heinen, *Garten*, 2002, pp. 1–8; id., *Gesundheit*, 2002, pp. 71–182.

CHAPTER III - THE HOUSE IN THE TIME OF HENDRIK HILLEWERVE

Text ill. 42. Detail of the 1692 Harrewijn print (Fig. 18): the caryatids on the north façade of the stables.

Text ill. 43. The reconstructed so-called gardener's lodge (previously stables) in the garden of the Rubenshuis.

position of the small outbuilding in the Harrewijn print corresponds to that of a stable block ('Écuries') which François Mols encountered about a century later, and which is indicated on his manuscript plan of the property by a rectangular block divided into individual stalls (Fig. 3; Appendix I.43).[43]

An interesting element of this building in the garden is the narrow north-facing façade, which has decorations that may stem from Rubens's time. Above the tall, narrow window is a niche with a bust. Flanking the window and perched on tall pedestals, are two half-naked caryatids with raised arms, one probably male (to the left), the other female (right) (Text ill. 42). It is not clear what they are holding above their heads, and from the print we cannot tell if these decorative elements were sculpted or painted.

When the house came to be restored in the 1930s, the small building had disappeared and had been replaced by a more substantial construction extending to the north as well as the east. A new house with stepped gable – more or less like the one shown in the print – was built (Text ill. 43), but this was not laid out as stables (in the reconstructed house there is no building with this function).[44]

---

43. If his drawing (done from memory) is correct, the building then included an extension to the north (running as far as the passageway to the Wapper). The announcement of a public sale in 1797 describes the house as having stables for five horses (Tijs, *Rubens en Jordaens*, 1984, p. 160).
44. It was originally intended as a porter's lodge (Devroe, *Rubens' huis*, 2008, I, p. 118) but was eventually described as the 'gardener's lodge'.

CHAPTER III - THE HOUSE IN THE TIME OF HENDRIK HILLEWERVE

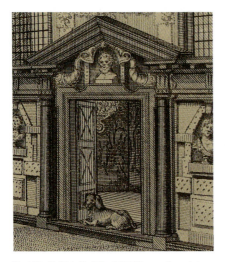

Text ill. 44. Detail of the 1684 Harrewijn print (Fig. 17): the open door (in the courtyard), giving a view into the former studio.

Text ill. 45. Detail of the 1684 Harrewijn print (Fig. 17): the view through the windows of the north façade of the studio wing.

E. Information on the Interior of the House in the Time of Hillewerve

Rubens's Former Studio Transformed into a 'Salon'

In both Harrewijn prints open doors allow a glimpse of the interior of the former studio as it was when Hillewerve occupied the house: transformed into a luxurious salon. In the 1684 print we can see through the courtyard doors the bottom half of a large crystal or glass chandelier, and the walls are completely covered with figures in a landscape, most likely part of a series of tapestries (Text ill. 44).[45] The two large windows on the left of the façade afford a further glimpse of the interior, revealing a partial view of a beamed ceiling and two arched windows on the garden side, one of which seems to be covered by a half-drawn curtain (Text ill. 45). The open door on the garden side, represented in the other print (Text ill. 46), reveals a fireplace, which is therefore on the eastern half of the south wall (where it is now reconstructed).

Hillewerve's Chapel

We know that Canon Hillewerve installed a private chapel in his house. The space is explicitly mentioned in the deed of gift of 1682, which states that

45. Tapestries are recorded in the 'grote salette' of the house more than half a century later (announcement of a public sale in 1756; see Chapter II, p. 75, n. 78).

the 'kapelkamer' (chapel room) shall remain at the priest's disposal. The chapel with its collection of relics is also praised and admired by De Sevin (b. 1644) (Appendix I.36). As we learn from Mols's drawing, this chapel was situated in the east wing (Fig. 3) and everything points towards it occupying the space of Rubens's former 'antiquarium', a part of the house to which we will return in Chapter VIII.

The inset at the bottom left of the 1692 print offers a view of this chapel (Fig. 127). Through open curtains we peer into a semi-circular space with a large window that extends up to the ceiling on the right. The chapel is furnished with an armchair and a prie-dieu; in the middle, at the top of a couple of carpeted steps, is the altar. Two prominent statues decorate the room: above the altar, in a niche crowned by a shell motif, is a seated Virgin Mary with the Christ Child standing beside her; to the left, opposite the window in a tall niche, is a taller than life-size St Joseph holding the hand of the Christ Child.

Text ill. 46. Detail of the 1692 Harrewijn print (Fig. 18): the open door on the garden side of the south or 'Italian' wing.

To either side of the altar, the curving wall is divided into a number of arch-topped niches – six on each side – in which dozens of reliquaries are displayed. Clearly these contain the holy relics mentioned in the eulogy by De Sevin. Above these is a second row of oval-shaped niches – again six on each side – with busts of similar sizes and shapes. Above these are six rectangular landscape compositions with figures, the subjects of which cannot be identified. The panels are separated by volute-shaped pilasters, each topped by a bust (ten in total). As with the north façade of the studio wing, it is not possible to establish by looking at the print whether elements (for example the pilasters and the various rows of busts) are sculpted in the round or painted in *trompe-l'oeil*.

The ceiling of the chapel room is a semi-circular construction with an *oculus*. The entire vault is covered with a *trompe-l'oeil* showing a balustrade and above it a view of Heaven (Fig. 127). Running over the semi-dome is a strip with clouds and angels playing music, motifs partly taken from Rubens's designs for the *Eucharist* series.[46] In the corners, left and right, angels are draping a cloth over

---

46. Motifs from this tapestry series indeed appear to have been used as models for the ceiling decoration. For the angel (to the left) playing the cello and another playing the lute (to the right), see the *Angels Playing Music* (De Poorter, *Eucharist (CRLB)*, 1978, nos 2 and 3); the angel playing the harp corresponds to *King David Playing the Harp* (ibid., no. 6), while the small angels with a cloth on either side of the balustrade were probably based on those who can be seen draping a fictional tapestry over the architecture in several of the *Eucharist* compositions (ibid., passim).

CHAPTER III - THE HOUSE IN THE TIME OF HENDRIK HILLEWERVE

Text ill. 47. Detail of the 1692 Harrewijn print (Fig. 18): Hillewerve's bedroom.

the balustrade. The vault itself is painted with clouds, putti and, in the middle, the Dove of the Holy Spirit with its rays fanning out towards the altar beneath.

We will return to Hillewerve's chapel when describing and discussing the room's original function as Rubens's 'antiquarium'.[47]

Hillewerve's Bedroom

The separate images inserted at the bottom of Harrewijn's 1692 print include a view of a room with a four-poster bed, evidently Hillewerve's bedroom (Text ill. 47). Otherwise the furniture in this room consists of two chests, a harpsichord and a series of armchairs. The walls are covered from top to bottom with strips of material with a vine motif, conceivably a precious gold-leather covering.[48]

47. See Chapter VIII, pp. 232 ff., and Nos 20–22.
48. A sale deed of 1701 mentions the presence of gilt-leather decorations in the house (Appendix I.38).

CHAPTER III - THE HOUSE IN THE TIME OF HENDRIK HILLEWERVE

On the walls hang paintings, a mirror and large heraldic panels. At the centre of the furthermost wall is a fireplace over which hangs a portrait of a seated clergyman, possibly Hillewerve himself. On either side, through open doors, we get a partial view into two adjoining rooms with windows.

The most curious feature of this room is the ceiling which has a shallow dome in the form of a small cap, and with a central opening and an *oculus* on either side. Like the walls, its curved sides are decorated with a prominent vine pattern. Mols's drawing informs us that this unusual room, which he labels the 'Salon en rotonde', is situated on the upper floor of the studio wing. A full discussion of this room follows in Chapter VII.

Text ill. 48. Detail of the 1684 Harrewijn print (Fig. 17): the water pump against the façade of the north wing.

F. *The Courtyard in the Time of Hillewerve*

The Water Pump

Mounted against the façade of the north wing in Harrewijn's print is a water pump crowned by a wrought-iron structure and decorated with three heads that are difficult to discern; two have a waterspout protruding from their mouths (Text ill. 48). When the house was restored, this pump with two cranks was still in position and largely intact (Text ill. 49). The decorative grille at the top had disappeared, but the cistern with two heads – actually, male heads stylised to look like lions – and the ornamental stone work underneath, with volutes and a (blank) tablet in the middle, were still there.[49] Whether this pump stems from Rubens's time

Text ill. 49. The water pump in the courtyard of the Rubenshuis.

---

49. The ornamental crown was reconstructed; the third head (on top of the cistern), which is unlikely to have been, but looks like a giant skull, was omitted. See also a photo of the façade with the pump before the reconstruction (Maclot, *Rubenssite*, 2016, p. 212), and the reconstruction drawing (Tijs, *Rubens en Jordaens*, 1984, p. 207). For a colour illustration, see Van Driessche, *Herschepping*, 2013, p. 38.

113

CHAPTER III - THE HOUSE IN THE TIME OF HENDRIK HILLEWERVE

Text ill. 50. Detail of the 1684 Harrewijn print (Fig. 17): the fountain with bagpiper in the corner between the portico and the former studio.

is a question that cannot be determined. However, the existence of an almost identical pump which bears the date 1684[50] suggests that a later date is more likely.

The Fountain with Bagpiper

Seen in the courtyard in Harrewijn's 1684 print is an element that was not included in the modern reconstruction of the house. Tucked into the corner between the portico and studio is a fountain decorated with a statue of a shepherd playing the bagpipes, with an animal, probably a goat, by his side. From one of the instrument's pipes a jet of water shoots high into the air. The pastoral scene is surrounded by an artificial grotto constructed from unworked natural stone (Text ill. 50).

50. In the Groot Begijnhof in Leuven; this pump has a comparable cistern with two heads with spouts over a similar stone with large volutes.

114

CHAPTER III - THE HOUSE IN THE TIME OF HENDRIK HILLEWERVE

Looking at the fountain in the print one cannot avoid noticing the strange and rather unlikely way in which it joins the façade: the artificial rock setting obscures the bottom part of a window and it hides the niche with a bust furthest to the left. In the print of 1692 the whole façade is visible, but without any evidence of the fountain. Its bizarre position raises the possibility that Harrewijn depicted it against the studio façade while it was actually situated somewhere else, for example near the garden side of the portico. The motif of the rocky grotto is in any case a feature that belongs to the decoration of a garden rather than a courtyard.[51]

More important than the question of its location is of course whether the grotto and the bagpiper date from Rubens's time. And even if the fountain was in position somewhere in the garden before 1640, was it indeed designed by Rubens? To our mind this is doubtful and we have therefore rejected it as Rubens's invention, and it is not included in the catalogue section.[52] Rutger Tijs was nonetheless convinced of its authenticity and made detailed comment on it in several publications. He rightly connects it to a statuette attributed to Giambologna (1529–1608), and to the publication of Solomon de Caus's book *Les raisons des forces mouvantes* (1615), of which Rubens owned a copy.[53] But the question remains whether these observations provide sufficient evidence for its existence in Rubens's house during his lifetime. Perhaps a more plausible suggestion is that it was added by one of the later residents.[54]

It should be noted that an entirely different type of fountain, featuring a dolphin and a putto or Amor, can be seen in *The Walk in the Garden* (Appendix III.6; Figs 25, 182, 218), and this is indeed included in the catalogue (No. 41; Fig. 218). While dolphin fountains do appear in Rubens's work and that of his contemporaries, the only image we have of the un-Rubensian bagpiper is the Harrewijn print. Yet who would have added this old-fashioned fountain, modelled on De Caus, to the courtyard or the garden between 1640 and 1684? It is also impossible to know where a cistern could have been installed in the house in Rubens's or Hillewerve's time that could produce such a high jet of water.

---

51. See, for example, Uppenkamp – Van Beneden, *Symbolism*, 2011, p. 121.
52. Ludwig Burchard also expressed his doubts. He wrote that it seemed to him far removed from Rubens ('für mein Empfinden Rubens fernsteht'), and he placed it after 1650 (letter to Émile Van Averbeke, dated 6 February 1939; see Chapter II, p. 85, n. 109).
53. Tijs, *Herdersgrot*, 2002, pp. 115–138; id., *Hirtengrotte*, 2002, pp. 9–18; id., *Rubens*, 2004, pp. 49, 134, 138, 140, 154–169. 19th-century images of the courtyard with the bagpiper fountain are not proof that it still existed then, as Tijs argues; they were intended as recreations of the 17th-century situation, which was simply based on the well-known print by Harrewijn.
54. Several authors mention the fountain but hesitate to express an opinion on its dating or invention; Ulrich Heinen does not come to a conclusion on the matter, saying no more than 'kann vielleicht Rubens' eigener Plannung entstammen' (Heinen, *Gesundheit*, 2004, pp. 84–85, 157–158, nn. 36–37); as possibly original in Uppenkamp – Van Beneden, *Symbolism*, 2011, p. 121; as possibly second half of the 17th century in Maclot, *Rubenssite*, 2016, pp. 67–68.

CHAPTER III - THE HOUSE IN THE TIME OF HENDRIK HILLEWERVE

The Lying Dog

Lying on the doorstep of the former workshop, in both prints (once in reverse), is a long-eared dog with its head turned towards the viewer (Text ills 51–52). The animal looks real enough, but in reality it is a sculpture – a *trompe-l'oeil* –, which was placed in the doorway as a *cave canem* (beware of the dog).[55] An old photograph taken in 1860 by Edmond Fierlants (Text ill. 53) shows a store in the courtyard, with a marble dog on top, which is now in a Belgian private collection (Text ill. 54).[56] Evidently this is the dog owned by Hillewerve, but it is difficult to establish whether it goes back to Rubens's time. A later date seems more likely.[57]

Text ill. 51. Detail of the 1684 Harrewijn print (Fig. 17): the dog on the doorstep of the former studio.

Text ill. 52. Detail of the 1692 Harrewijn print (Fig. 18): the dog (in reverse) on the doorstep of the former studio.

Text ill. 53. Detail of Text ill. 23: A marble dog on top of a store in the courtyard.

Text ill. 54. *A Marble Dog*, sculpture. Belgium, Private Collection.

55. It is worth remembering an ancient example of a *trompe-l'oeil* mentioned by Pliny: a miraculously lifelike bronze statue of a dog licking its wounds (Pliny, *Natural History*, XXIV.38; McHam, *Pliny*, 2013, pp. 37, 317, anecdote no. 46).
56. Lying dog (marble, h. 60 × w. 130 cm); Baudouin, *Herinneringen*, 1958, p. 22, no. 28. Not to be confused with a smaller, badly damaged dog in terracotta and of unknown provenance (Antwerp, Museum Vleeshuis, now on view in the Rubenshuis, inv. no. RH.B.049).
57. Muller (*Collector*, 1989), arguably rightly, omits the *Dog* from his catalogue of Rubens's collection of sculptures. Had it perhaps previously belonged to a funerary monument? An almost identical *Dog* forms part of the monument in the church of Broechem for Philip le Roy and Marie de Raet, who died in 1679 and 1662 respectively (Roosens, *Le Roy*, 1999, p. 155, fig. 8; Hedley, *Van Dyck*, 1999, pp. 71–72, figs 69–70).

Chapter IV
Construction and Remodelling: Evidence for a Chronology

A. Scope of Construction and Remodelling: The Timing

In a previous chapter we looked at the composition of the house in the time of Hillewerve when the overall situation was still the same as in Rubens's day. Around 1680 the property was made up of four adjoining wings, the portico connecting two of the wings, and there were a number of separate constructions, including the garden pavilion and stables in the garden.

Past authors have tried to identify the years in which Rubens's house was built and remodelled. In addition there have been attempts to establish the order in which the various parts of his property were realised. However, precise answers to these questions cannot be given. The following pages present an overview of the information that can be gleaned from contemporary documents. Although some important things can be learned from the records, they offer little in the way of concrete facts, especially as different parts of the property on the whole remain unspecified. As a result, attempts by authors to put the information into an order are, in our opinion, no more than hypothetical and do not merit discussing at length. For this reason we will mostly ignore the widely differing conclusions about the chronology of the construction of the various parts of the property.

Nor will we repeat the divergent opinions about the way in which the various wings came into being – ranging from remodelling existing structures to demolishing and replacing them, or building a new wing on the previously unbuilt bleaching green. As set out in Chapter I, there is little precise information about the 'huysinghe' Rubens purchased. The sale deeds of 1610 and 1611 inform us that the property comprised several structures centred on a courtyard, and with a 'gallery'. Certain parts are summarily listed in these documents, but no idea is provided of their relative positions, their state of repair or indeed how suitable they were for use by Rubens. We do not have the means to judge, therefore, the extent to which existing structures were altered and remodelled by Rubens, or which parts were built from scratch. All we can say with near certainty is that most of the north wing and the northern part of the west wing were already standing in 1610. For the remainder of the property the evidence is too thin to draw any useful conclusions.

CHAPTER IV - CONSTRUCTION AND REMODELLING

Construction Begins (?1613–1615)

As explained in Chapter I, Rubens had agreed to pay the purchase sum in three annual instalments that were due by Christmas 1610, 1611 and 1612, and there is no reason to doubt that these transactions took place as planned. In addition, Rubens had taken on a number of hereditary rents, which he paid off in March and May of 1613. It is more than likely that in the meantime – before completing the final payment – he had started to use his property in some way or other and he may even have been in the early stages of altering and extending the house. However, there are no records that allow us to verify this.

We can point to a few vague indications in Rubens's work that he was engaged in designing, if perhaps not yet building, the portico and the Italianate wing of his house by about 1614. A drawing with designs for a window surround (No. 7a; Fig. 54) can be found on the verso of a figure study for a lost *Discovery of Erichthonius by the Daughters of Cecrops*, a painting that has been dated c. 1613–1614. A most interesting combination of several architectural elements from the portico, as well as a few details of the studio façade, probably predating their construction, can be seen in Rubens's *Homage to Ceres*, in the State Hermitage Museum in St Petersburg, which is dated on stylistic grounds to c. 1612–1615 (Appendix III.13; Fig. 23).[1] Finally, Rubens's design for a book illustration for Justus Lipsius's 1615 *L. Annaei Senecae Philosophi Opera Quae Extant Omnia* features a niche in rustic style of a similar (though simplified) form as a niche in the decoration of the north façade of the studio (Text ill. 63).[2]

Rubens and Family Move to the House on the Wapper (c. 1615)

There is no certainty, but there is evidence to suggest that Rubens and his family did not move to the Wapper until four or five years after the date of the purchase. The couple's first child, Clara Serena (b. 21 March 1611), and their eldest son Albert (b. 5 June 1614) were both baptised at St Andrew's Church rather than St James's, which was the parish church for residents of the Wapper.[3] This very likely means that the family were still living in St Andrew's parish in the summer of 1614, that is to say with Isabella Brant's parents in the Sint-Michielsstraat (now Kloosterstraat).[4]

A little more than eighteen months later Rubens is first recorded as living on the Wapper: the funeral roll of Martina Plantin, who died on 17 February

---

1. Details such as the geniculated arch, the banded Doric columns, the bossed quoins and the oil lamps will be discussed in further chapters.
2. See Chapter V, p. 148, n. 31.
3. The couple's third child, Nicolaas, was baptised at St James's Church on 23 March 1618; for the baptismal records of the three children, see Génard, *Rubens*, 1877, pp. 17–18, 414 (n. 1), 460, 464.
4. For Rubens living with his parents-in-law, see Chapter I, p. 23.

1616 – and not in 1617, as is often stated incorrectly[5] – names 'Peeter Pauwels Rubbens' under the heading 'Arenbergstraet', which gives a list of people living in that neighbourhood (Appendix I.7).[6] In September of the same year, 1616, he appears in the list of members of the Guild of St Luke as living 'Opden Wapper' (Appendix I.8); ten other painters are registered in the same street, including Tobias van Haecht (1561–1631), Sebastiaan Vrancx (1573–1647) and Joos de Momper II (1564–1635).[7]

We can tell from these records that Rubens and his family probably moved to the Wapper after June 1614 and in any case before February 1616. This period can cautiously be defined more precisely. A publication of 1615 mentions an antique sculpture – the so-called Seneca bust (Text ill. 63) – which was displayed in Rubens's 'museum' ('in elegantissimo museo suo') (Appendix I.6). As explained in a further chapter, the term 'museum', was used in humanist circles to denote a study rather than an area for the storage and display of art objects.[8] Rubens no doubt had a study in the house of his parents-in-law, yet it cannot be ruled out that the 'museum' in question was situated in the house on the Wapper. This would mean that in the course of 1615 Rubens's house was already furnished and lived in.

It seems likely that even before 1615 Rubens was already using part of his property for his professional activities, be it to accommodate his workshop or as a store. Especially important, of course, is the question of when his productive workshop with its many assistants was established on the Wapper, a matter to which we will return below. It should be remembered that a group of German 'Grand Tourists' visited Antwerp in January 1614 and saw Rubens's workshop (Appendix I.13), but whether this was already located on the Wapper remains a question.

Thus, by the beginning of 1616, and probably already in the course of 1615, substantial modification of the 'old' house and some new building work had been done so that some or all of the property could be brought into use. However, this is not to say that Rubens's property had by this time more or less assumed the appearance of the finished house seen in the Harrewijn prints. We know that major alterations were still underway when the painter and his family were living at the house. Indeed, from the scant information that is

---

5. Erroneously dated 1617 by Max Rooses (Rooses, *Huis van Rubens*, 1910, p. 195 [p. 7]), and this incorrect date then copied by most authors (for example: Delen, *Rubens' huis*, 1933, p. 3; Delen, *Rubens' huis*, 1940, p. 23; Tijs, *Rubens en Jordaens*, 1984, p. 103; Devroe, *Rubens' huis*, 2008, I, p. 86; Maclot, *Rubenssite*, 2019, p. 25); corrected by Baudouin, *Fresco's*, 1998, p. 6, n. 10. With thanks to Dirk Imhof for providing information about this document. Martina Plantin (1550–1616) was the daughter of Christopher Plantin and the widow of Jan Moretus I; she ordered Rubens's '*Moretus Triptych*' (Freedberg, *Christ after the Passion (CRLB)*, 1984, nos 1–3) and was portrayed by Rubens (Jonckheere, *Prototypes (CRLB)*, 2016, no. 19).
6. The Arenbergstraat is located to the south of the Wapper (roughly 200 m from Rubens's house).
7. The entry for 'Opden Wapper' lists fifteen members; ten are described as 'scilder', while Rubens – remarkably – is a 'pintor' (Rooses, ed., *Boek gehouden*, 1878, p. 5).
8. See Chapter VII, pp. 227–228.

available, it is clear that the property was converted and extended in several campaigns over a number of years, possibly into 1618 and beyond.

It is possible that the large purchase sum, payment of which was spread over three years (1611–1613), stopped Rubens from immediately taking on the further financial commitment that came with altering the house, but it is difficult to gauge what risks he was willing to take. Certainly he was doing well financially. His contemporaries expressed their surprise about the apparent ease with which he earned large sums of money through his well-organised workshop.[9] Their impression is certainly confirmed by figures that are available from archival sources: between 1609 and 1614, from three important commissions alone, Rubens was paid a total of 6800 guilders (which was just over three quarters of the purchase price of his property).[10]

Architectural Treatises and Purchases in 1615–1617

Rubens's purchase of architectural treatises from the Plantin publishing house in the years 1615–1617 indicates that during these years he was taking an interest in such theoretical works, which would be essential tools for anyone engaged in the design or study of architecture.[11] However, although this is certainly interesting material to which we will return in the following chapters, we should not exaggerate the significance of the date of these purchases for the construction of Rubens's house. Indeed, it is important to remember that during these same years, Rubens's architectural activities were not limited to the alteration and extension of his own house but that he was also involved in the most remarkable architectural project that was then being realised in Antwerp, namely the Jesuit Church.[12]

Moreover, it should be noted that Rubens had already expressed interest in architectural theory at an earlier stage, prior to his return to Antwerp from Italy. He was familiar with Serlio's work, or in any case Book IV of his *Regole generali di architettura*, which first appeared in Venice in 1537; this emerges from thirty sheets copied from Rubens's lost 'Notebook' with drawings after illustrations from Serlio's chapter on the 'orders' and which Rubens annotated in Latin. The 'Notebook' was a compendium of theoretical knowledge useful

9. Wilhelm Neumayer von Ramssla, who visited the studio in 1614, speaks of 100 guilders a week (Appendix I.13); François Sweerts, writing in 1618, even mentions 100 guilders a day (Appendix I.11).
10. Payments known to have been made in this period include: 1800 guilders for *The Adoration of the Magi* (Madrid, Museo Nacional del Prado), 2600 guilders for *The Triptych of the Elevation of the Cross* and 2400 guilders for *The Triptych of the Descent from the Cross* (both in Antwerp, Cathedral of Our Lady); this last payment was only completed in 1621. Naturally these 6800 guilders were not 'net' profits.
11. On the architectural treatises in Rubens's possession, see also Tijs, *Rubens en Jordaens*, 1984, p. 96, with illustrations of entries in the *Journal* of the Officina Plantiniana, pp. 97 and 99; Rott, *Palazzi (CRLB)*, 2002, I, pp. 86–87, n. 6; Van Beneden, *Architecture*, 2011, pp. 26–29; Lombaerde, *Rubens the Architect*, 2011, pp. 126, 130–132.
12. Fabri – Lombaerde, *Jesuit Church (CRLB)*, 2018.

CHAPTER IV · CONSTRUCTION AND REMODELLING

to painters; it contained illustrations with comments by Rubens on a range of subjects from anatomy, optics, symmetry and proportions to the human passions. Architecture was then one of several theoretical studies pursued by intellectuals as part of their cultural education and not necessarily because they intended to put it into practice in the construction of actual buildings.[13]

Let us return to what is known about the architectural treatises in Rubens's possession, and the date of their acquisition. An important source is the *Journal* in which Balthasar Moretus I (1574–1641) carefully recorded customers' purchases, listing two hundred and thirteen titles on a range of subjects which were bought by or bound for Rubens between March 1613 and March 1640.[14] In addition to these there will have been other volumes in his rich library. Not all of the publications acquired from the Officina Plantiniana are necessarily entered in the *Journal*, and Rubens certainly also acquired numerous books by other means; some works he may well have brought back from Italy.

The entries with architectural treatises in the *Journal* are concentrated in the years 1615–1617. The entry for 2 February 1615 includes two different editions of Vitruvius's famous treatise *De architectura libri decem*.[15] On 2 May 1616 there is mention of a folio edition of Sebastiano Serlio's treatises ('van Architectura Serlii'), which Rubens has had bound.[16] In 1617 the *Journal* records the purchase of two architectural tomes: *L'idea della architettura universale* by Vincenzo Scamozzi and Jacques Francart's *Le premier livre d'architecture*, which was published in the same year.[17]

A large number of the books that were in Albert Rubens's possession are likely to have come from his father's library, although we have no indication of when or how Rubens had acquired them. Authors on architecture in Albert's collection include Vitruvius (c. 85–20 bc), Andrea Palladio (1508–1580), Giacomo Barozzi da Vignola (1507–1573) and Philibert de l'Orme (1514–1570).[18] Two works in Albert's library should be mentioned especially, since they include an image of the Porta Pia, which may have provided inspiration for Rubens's portico: the collection of Roman architectural prints published by Antonio

---

13. On this 'notebook' in general, see Balis, *Rubens und Inventio*, 2001; Balis et al., *The Theoretical Notebook (CRLB)*, forthcoming; on architecture and copies after Sebastiano Serlio (1475–1554) in particular, see Jaffé, *Antwerp Sketchbook*, 1966, [facsimile], II, fols 74v–89v, pp. 244–278; Fabri – Lombaerde, *Jesuit Church (CRLB)*, 2018, pp. 19–20, nn. 37–40.
14. Arents, *Bibliotheek*, 2001, pp. 133–206, nos E1–E213; Imhof, *Aankopen van Rubens*, 2004, pp. 22–26.
15. Identified as published in Venice (1567) and Lyon (1586); Arents, ibid., p. 144, nos E28 and E29; De Schepper, ed., *Rubens' Bibliotheek*, 2004, pp. 67–68, no. 32.
16. Arents, *Bibliotheek*, 2001, pp. 147–148, no. E35. From the title (beginning with 'van') it can be inferred that this is the Dutch translation by Pieter Coecke van Aelst (1502–1550), probably the Amsterdam edition of 1616. It is assumed that this is the volume that was later in Albert Rubens's library: *De Vijf Boecken van d'Architecture van Sebastiaen Serlio* (Arents, ibid., p. 346). On the many editions of Serlio's treatises (translated into six languages including Latin and Dutch), see Vène, *Bibliographia Serliana*, 2007.
17. Arents, ibid., p. 150, nos E41 and E42 (with the date of purchase given incorrectly as 26 May 1616 instead of 26 May 1617; with thanks to Dirk Imhof for checking this in the *Journal*).
18. Ibid., pp. 295–299, 346–347.

Lafreri (1512–1577) under the title *Speculum Romanae Magnificentiae*, and an edition of Vignola's *Regola delli Cinque ordini d'architettura*, bound with a series of portal designs by Michelangelo (Text ill. 127).[19]

In both Balthasar Moretus's *Journal* and the sale catalogue of Albert Rubens's library, the listed books are described very succinctly with just the author's name and an abbreviated title, but no indication of the place or year of publication. Consequently, with popular treatises that were reprinted often it is sometimes unclear which edition Rubens owned.

Archival Documents (1615–1616) and Two Letters (1618)

It is noteworthy that we know of only three archival documents that provide information about the dating of building works on Rubens's property on the Wapper. The year 1615 is mentioned twice: in the summer of 1615 the wall between Rubens's garden and the 'Kolveniershof', the shooting range of the arquebusiers, is repaired or reconstructed (Appendix I.5; see below); in a legal deposition of 1621, Rubens refers to work on his house in 1615 (Appendix I.14). Although interesting in themselves, neither document tells us much about the construction of the house, as will be explained below. The third mention of a date is in a contract for the construction of a staircase, drawn up in November 1616 (Appendix I.9). While the information provided by this document is more concrete and many details are forthcoming, there are problems again with its content and it is difficult to interpret.

These dates pertaining to certain parts of the house – a wall, a roof, stairs – provide little help in establishing a chronology for the remainder of the property, be it altering existing structures or constructing new ones. The lack of archival records also means that besides the names mentioned in these three documents – the sculptor Hans van Mildert (1588–1638), the joiner Jasper Bulliau and the slater Abraham van den Bossche – we have no information whatsoever about suppliers, stonemasons, sculptors or other tradesmen and artists involved in the construction of Rubens's house. With one exception: thanks to a number of quarry marks, including that of Jean Delfontaine (c. 1580–1667) from Arquennes in Hainaut, we know the provenance of the bluestone that was used for the portico and the garden pavilion.[20]

A further indication of a date is given by a letter which Rubens wrote on 12 May 1618 to Sir Dudley Carleton (1573–1632), the English ambassador in The Hague, with whom he was negotiating the exchange of antique statues for paintings. Rubens writes that he has already spent several thousand

19. Arents, *Bibliotheek*, 2001, pp. 298 (no. R.13349), 347, 349. For a fuller discussion of these books, see the commentary on the portico in Chapter IX, pp. 285–286, nn. 106–107.
20. For the quarry marks, see Chapter IX, p. 250; Chapter X, p. 296, n. 4.

guilders ('qualque migliaia di fiorini') on his property that year ('questo anno') (Appendix I.10). However, the term he uses – 'mia fabrica' – is too general to allow us to identify which part of the property was meant (if not rather the whole building in general).[21] We will return to this letter in a moment, as well as to another letter written two months later, not by Rubens but François Sweerts (1567–1629) (Appendix I.11).

The Wall between Rubens's House and the Kolveniershof (1615)

When Rubens bought his property, there was already a wall dividing it from the arquebusiers' shooting range. This can be deduced from the 1611 sale deed, which specifies that the eastern side of the plot he bought bordered the wall of the Guild of the Arquebusiers ('…aenden muer vande gulden vande coloveriers hove') (Appendix I.2: [3]).

The arquebusiers' accounts demonstrate that in the summer of 1615 plans were made to repair or reconstruct this wall 'at the side of the garden of Sr Rubbens' (Appendix I.5: [1]). To this end a contract was signed, on 25 July, with Franchoys de Crayer, a member of the guild and probably a contractor. In addition, surveyors ('erfscheiders') were paid to measure up 'the new wall', a fact that might suggest that its position was altered somewhat.[22] On 13 August, De Crayer was further tasked with making a 'little house with a privy' ('huysken ende secret'), which, again, could mean that the existing *secreet* was moved to a different location.

It goes without saying that Rubens was involved in these changes to the eastern edge of his property. It is possible that he initiated them, but this cannot be verified. The guild's accounts contain no explicit reference to a contract or agreement for the wall with Rubens. As mentioned above, the contract signed on 25 July 1615 formalised an arrangement between the guild and De Crayer, not Rubens, as is sometimes stated.[23] Nonetheless, certain entries in the guild's accounts reveal that – at an unspecified point in time – the arquebusiers had

21. The interpretation of 'fabrica' as 'industrial building' (so referring to the studio) – as proposed by Tijs *Rubens en Jordaens*, 1984, p. 126 – can be discarded. Translators of the letters give 'mia fabrica' a broader meaning: 'mes bâtiments' (Rooses – Ruelens, eds, *Correspondance*, 1887–1909, II, p. 151) and 'my estate' (Magurn, ed., *Letters*, 1955, p. 62). This is certainly correct. In his preface to the *Palazzi di Genova* Rubens twice uses the word 'fabrica' for buildings that are nothing to do with a workshop; one is the Palais du Luxembourg, Paris; see Rott, *Palazzi (CRLB)*, 2002, I, pp. 254–255 ('fabrica' translated as 'building').
22. The few lines in the accounts do not provide enough information to establish exactly what happened to the 'old' wall in 1615. While work to repair ('opmaecken') to the wall is mentioned, we also learn that surveyors were to be involved, which suggests that the position of (a part of?) the wall was altered. Most of the original boundary wall between the two plots remains in place today, incorporated in the later stonework. We have not been able to verify if Max Rooses was correct in calling De Crayer a master mason rather than a contractor (Rooses, *Rubens*, 1904, p. 163).
23. This error first appears in Génard, *Rubens*, 1877, p. 500 ('Aanteekening over het verdrag tusschen P.P. Rubens en de Colveniersgilde, rakende het opbouwen van eenen gemeenen muur'); copied by, for example, Delen, *Rubens' huis*, 1933, p. 25; Baudouin, *Kolveniershof*, 1975, p. 196; Tijs, *Rubens en Jordaens*, 1984, p. 103.

CHAPTER IV - CONSTRUCTION AND REMODELLING

discussions with their neighbour about the common wall. Rubens was not required to contribute anything to the cost of the wall itself (materials or labour). He did, however, pay half of the surveyor's fee for measuring up the wall, and he also had to contribute to the cost of the three hundred and twenty-three pots of beer drunk by the workmen (calculated as half of the beer consumed during work on the walll; Rubens did not pay for the pots consumed during the building of the arquebusiers's 'huysken') (Appendix I.5: [3]).

It is conceivable that the construction of a (partly?) new wall – which may have involved changing its position slightly to benefit Rubens – was in some way or other included in the price the arquebusiers paid Rubens for *The Triptych of the Descent from the Cross* for their altar in the Cathedral of Our Lady. An agreement about this important commission had been drawn up four years earlier, on 7 September 1611, but beyond the date we know nothing about the content of this document.[24] So whether or not the wall was mentioned is unknown. Whatever the truth, anecdotes have persisted which exaggerate a connection between *The Descent from the Cross* and Rubens's property, and have been repeatedly included in commentary on the famous triptych. One popular story even suggests that the arquebusiers paid Rubens for the altarpiece with the land on which he built his house.[25]

A misconception that has arisen more recently in the literature is that the 'huysken' built in 1615 can perhaps be identified with the garden pavilion.[26] This can be firmly ruled out; the fact that it is mentioned in the same breath as the privy ('secret') (Appendix I.5: [2]) makes it more than likely that this small building was part of the sanitary provisions of the arquebusiers, and in any case it was erected on *their* ground and at *their* expense, with Rubens (rightly) not even required to share in the cost of the beer drunk by the builders.

Carpenters and Slaters at Work on the Roof (1615)

On 5 January 1621, at the request of the slater Abraham van den Bossche, Rubens testified before a notary (Appendix I.14). The unnamed carpenters who built his house ('timmerlieden die gemaect hebben syne huysinge') in 1615 had also covered his roof with a wooden boarding ('berderinge') as a support for

24. The accounts tell us only how much was spent on consumption on the date that the commission was assigned to Rubens (Van den Nieuwenhuizen, *Descente de croix*, 1962, p. 40, doc. 2).
25. Two examples can be given: Rooses reports that in addition to a sum of money Rubens may have received 'une bande de terrain prise sur leur jardin pour etre jointe à sa propriété' (Rooses, *Oeuvre*, 1886–92, II, p. 118); according to an anecdote apparently told in Antwerp, and repeated by Joshua Reynolds (1723–1792), the altarpiece 'was given in exchange for a piece of ground, on which Rubens built his house' (Mount, ed., *Reynolds*, 1996, p. 33); see also De Poorter, *Kolveniers*, 1988, pp. 217–218, n. 67. See also the story about a lawsuit, recorded by François Mols in his notes (Appendix I.43: [5]).
26. A suggestion made by Heinen, *Gesundheit*, 2004, pp. 102, 168, n. 42; followed by Büttner, *Rubens berühmt*, 2006, p. 88, n. 17; id., *Rubens*, 2015, p. 93. Rightly rejected by Maclot, *Rubenssite*, 2016, p. 54.

the slates. However, they failed to do their work correctly: the covering had not been fixed (with nails) in the proper manner. Rubens testifies that the slater had put right the botched job, and no payment was requested for this task other than the cost of the nails.[27]

This document is interesting because we hear Rubens himself on the subject of construction work on his house, and also because at this point, six years later, he mentions the date 1615. He speaks of 'his house' and 'his roof'. Yet, there is no indication of what the construction work by the unnamed carpenters entailed, nor even which wing or wings are being referred to. A schematic drawing of the present roof structure of the Rubens House shows how complex 'his roof' was (Fig. 9).[28] It is interesting that in 1640 and 1641 – that is twenty years after Rubens's testimony – the roof is repaired by a Bastiaen van den Bossche, who was probably a relative of Abraham (Appendix I.23: [8]).

Contract for a Staircase (1616)

There is evidence that important construction work was still taking place after Rubens and his family had moved into the house in about 1615; as mentioned above, the date for their move cannot be given more precisely than between June 1614 and February 1616. The most concrete indication for ongoing work is a contract dated 2 November 1616, which, as it happens, is the only known contract connected to the building and furnishing of the house. On this date the sculptor Hans van Mildert, who is acting on Rubens's instruction, signs a contract with the joiner ('schrynwercker') Jasper Bulliau for a staircase that is to be made and installed in Rubens's house on the Wapper (Appendix I.9).[29]

This document is particularly interesting not only because it provides a date but also because it reveals that the work has to be executed following Rubens's instructions and to a design that he has made. An explanatory note in the margin states: following the existing drawing of it ('volghens de teeckeninghe daervan synde'). So there can be no doubt that Rubens made design drawings for architectural components and decorative elements of his house, yet almost nothing of this material survives, not even in copied form. At present we have a mere two drawings for scenes that decorated the studio façades (Nos 10a and 13a; Figs 65 and 96) and two sheets with indistinct architectural studies in black chalk (Nos 7a and 13b; Figs 54 and 97).

The fact that Hans van Mildert was acting on behalf of Rubens may indicate that, at any rate in late 1616, he was entrusted with organising and overseeing

---

27. Rubens had asked Van den Bossche, 'his' slater, to renail the entire slate roof ('wederom doen hernaegelen'). The document does not specify when this was done: it may have been in 1615, but perhaps it was six years later? Nor is it clear why the slater asked Rubens to testify about this.
28. Van Driessche, *Herschepping*, 2013, p. 28; Maclot, *Rubenssite*, 2016, p. 326, repr.
29. For more details on the contract, see also under No. 19.

CHAPTER IV - CONSTRUCTION AND REMODELLING

the construction work. Although this cannot be deduced from the contract, it seems probable that Van Mildert supplied the sculptural decorations for the staircase, and likely for other parts of the house as well.[30]

The contract is a rather confusing document, which unfortunately does not specify clearly the location of the staircase. Words have been deleted and corrections inserted, suggesting that even the person who drew up the document was struggling to understand everything. The inclusion of the drawing probably meant that there was less need to provide a detailed description in writing.

We can be confident that the staircase was intended for the wing with the workshop rather than somewhere in the domestic quarters. The staircase, it seems to us, is very likely the one represented in the Harrewijn print of 1692: on the west side of the courtyard, behind an arcade next to the entrance, a bottom flight can be partly glimpsed, open to the air and leading to the upper floors of the studio wing (Figs 30 and 124). If these are indeed the stairs in question, the richly decorated banister could well be Van Mildert's work following a design by Rubens (No. 19). We will return at more length to the problem of the location of the stairwell in a later chapter dealing with the interior of the studio wing.[31]

If Bulliau's staircase was indeed intended for the studio wing, as we believe, then the contract also demonstrates that work on this part of the building was nearing completion in early November 1616, or in any case was sufficiently advanced for the replacement of temporary flights of stairs. This does not, of course, rule out the possibility that the studio was already being used before this date.

Expenditure for the Alteration and Extension of the Property (1618)

As is clear from the above, a lack of information prevents us from establishing a chronology, or even proposing a plausible order for the building work. We likewise remain in the dark about the financial aspect of the enterprise, although from a handful of incidental remarks it is clear that Rubens spent a fortune on his house. In his letter of 12 May 1618 to Sir Dudley Carleton, mentioned earlier, Rubens writes: 'Besides, I have spent this year some thousands of florins on my estate ["nella mia fabrica"], and I should not like for a whim, to exceed the limits of good economy') (Appendix I.10).

That Rubens had indeed already spent a considerable sum on his house in 1618 is confirmed a few months later by another letter. On 18 July 1618 the Antwerp tapestry dealer and humanist François Sweerts (1567–1629) writes to Jan de Gruytere (1560–1627), informing him that he has received from Rome

30. Van Mildert's contribution to the decoration of Rubens's house is discussed in Chapter XI, pp. 327–329.
31. See Chapter VII, pp. 201–203.

a marble sculpture with an inscription. He goes on to say: 'In Antwerp, we eventually want to include Italian monuments. Petrus Paulus Rubenius, who is the Apelles of our age, has recently received from England more than 100 marble heads and statues'. Finally, he feels the need to comment on Rubens's finances: 'This Rubbens earns 100 guilders a day, [...] He has already squandered over 24 thousand guilders on his house' ('Desen Rubbens windt dagelyckx 100 guldens, [...] heeft alreede over 24 duysent guldens versnoept in syn huys') (Appendix I.11).

Sweerts belonged to the circle of Rubens's intellectual friends[32] and at the time he was involved in negotiations for the *Decius Mus* series.[33] Without question he is a reliable witness. A sum of more than 24,000 guilders does sound like an exaggeration and it is not clear whether this includes the purchase price of approximately 10,000 guilders, but the comment chimes with Rubens's own words about the great financial demands brought by building, decorating and furnishing his house.

Two *Termini ante quem*: Autumn 1621 for the Portico and 1622 for the Garden Pavilion

By 1618 the bulk of the construction was very likely done and work on the house was nearing completion.[34] The question is whether the portico – the most impressive element of Rubens's house, as well as the best preserved – was also already standing around 1618. As will emerge from Chapter IX, dealing with the portico, this cannot be ruled out. In any case we can be certain that the portico was finished in the autumn of 1621 at the latest, because Van Dyck must have seen it before his departure to Italy, as evidenced by several of his early works (Appendix III.15–16).

Given that the garden pavilion is the focal point of the garden perspective and was clearly conceived in combination with the portico, it was very likely constructed at the same time or just after, though a few years later cannot be

---

32. François Sweerts (Franciscus Sweertius) was a friend of Rubens's brother Philip and he undoubtedly knew Rubens in person; he wrote the earliest publication which includes an analysis of the qualities of Rubens's art (1628); see Martin, *Sweerts*, 1971, p. 96. In his *Monumenta Sepulcralia* (1613) he published the epitaphs of Philip Rubens and Maria Pypelinckx (see N. Büttner, in Van Beneden, ed., *Rubens in Private*, 2015, pp. 162–163, no. 15). Jan de Gruytere (Janus Gruterus) was also a practitioner of *bonae litterae*; he was a professor at the University of Heidelberg, and served as librarian of the famous library there.
33. See below, p. 134, n. 56.
34. This view had already been put forward by Rooses: 'Ce fut donc de 1615 à 1618 que Rubens bâtit la superbe demeure [...]' (Rooses, *Maison*, 1888, p. 218). But some authors think differently: Tijs is doubtful that before 1618 Rubens would have extended his property or carried out any major alterations to the house he bought in 1611 (Tijs, *Rubens en Jordaens*, 1984, p. 103). However, his opinion is based mainly on the false interpretation of a passage in Rubens's letter to Carleton (12 May 1618; Appendix I.10): Tijs understood the term 'capriccio' to refer to the semi-circular 'museum' (ibid., pp. 112–113), but what Rubens actually meant by this was simply the significant expenditure on his house in general.

CHAPTER IV - CONSTRUCTION AND REMODELLING

excluded. A *terminus ante quem* of 1622 is provided by a sketch for the *Medici* series dating from that year, and which features an architectural backdrop that is almost identical to the garden pavilion (Appendix III.18, Text ill. 135).[35]

The Purchase of Antique Sculptures (May–June 1618): A *Terminus post quem*?

As mentioned, it is more than likely that work on the house was still going on when Rubens and his family began using it as their home. An area that is important to mention in relation to this is the so-called 'antiquarium', a room that Rubens built in the east or garden wing of the house, specifically to accommodate a collection of ancient sculpture, and which he may not have completed until after his acquisition of a large collection of antique sculpture in 1618. The purchase date for these objects was 20 May and they arrived in Antwerp on 1 June.[36] If this assumption is right, then May – June 1618 can be taken as a *terminus post quem* for building the 'antiquarium'.

Another Letter: Arousing Admiration (1620)

Finally, there is a letter which indicates that in 1620 work on Rubens's house was far advanced, and perhaps even complete in most areas. On 1 October 1620 Jan van den Wouwer (Joannes Woverius, 1576–1636) writes a letter to his friend Balthasar Moretus I (1574–1641). Having praised the latter's work on the renovation of the Plantin House, which had started in March of that year (and which would come to a temporary halt in 1623), Woverius goes on to say: 'Our town of Antwerp is fortunate to possess two such great citizens as Rubens and Moretus. Foreigners will gaze at their dwellings, which will arouse the admiration of travellers'(Appendix I.12).[37]

B. Location of the Workshop: First Commissions in Antwerp (1609–c. 1617)

After his return from Italy, Rubens would doubtless have been impatient to find a studio that met his requirements. In the previous paragraphs we saw that Rubens and his family moved to the Wapper around 1615 (or more precisely, between June 1614 and February 1616). One question that arises from this is:

---

35. See Chapter X, esp. pp. 295–296.
36. Extensively on the 'antiquarium', see Chapter VIII; for details on the purchase in 1618, see Chapter VIII, pp. 237–238, n. 21.
37. On the renovation of the building of the *Officina Plantiniana*, see Voet, *Golden Compasses*, 1969, I, pp. 278–281.

where did he work before his new and spacious workshop was ready for use? We will look at Rubens's painted oeuvre up to c. 1617 to see what can be learned about the space in which these works were produced.

In Chapter I we considered whereabouts in Antwerp Rubens had previously lived (but not necessarily worked), and we will now summarise what we know. Before going to Italy he probably lived with his mother, but the exact location of her dwelling, and whether he also worked there remain open to question. We do know that when he travelled to Italy, he left some of his possessions, including paintings, in his mother's care. At the time of her death Maria Pypelinckx (d. 1606) was living in the Sint-Michielsstraat (now Kloosterstraat), in a house she rented from the Norbertines of St Michael's Abbey, and it is quite possible that Rubens and also his brother Philip stayed first at this address on their return from Italy. According to Philip's son, once Rubens was married (on 13 October 1609), he moved in with his parents-in-law, Jan Brant (1559–1639) and Clara de Moy (1570–1637), who also lived in the Sint-Michielsstraat (Appendix I.26).

There is of course a good chance – in fact every likelihood – that rather than having his studio under the same roof as his living quarters, Rubens worked in rented accommodation elsewhere in the city. However, we have no information about this. It is clear that soon after his return from Italy he must have had a reasonably large and successful workshop, which rapidly acquired an excellent reputation both at home and abroad. By May 1611, as we know from Rubens's often-cited letter to Jacques de Bie (1581–c. 1540), and so certainly before the spacious studio on the Wapper was established, he was attracting large numbers of aspiring artists who wanted apprenticeships.[38] In fact as early as six months before we have an indication that training places in Rubens's studio were in great demand: when Rubens bought the property on the Wapper, one of the vendors, Hans Thys, added a clause in the sale deed of November 1610, in which he stipulated that Rubens was to teach one of his sons 'the art of painting' (Appendix I.1: [7]).

Interest shown by 'tourists' is another indication that even before it was established on the Wapper, the studio was a hive of activity. The earliest mention of a visit by touring foreigners (German noblemen) to the well-organised and successful workshop of the 'Antwerp Apelles' comes in February 1614 (Appendix I.13).[39]

It was not just to accommodate a large team of assistants that Rubens needed ample space. From the beginning of his career he was working on canvases and panels to a very large format and if he did have a studio in one of the Sint-

---

38. Rubens had been forced to turn down more than a hundred applicants, many of whom were staying with other masters, waiting for a 'vacancy in my studio' (letter dated 11 May 1611; see Chapter I, p. 38, n. 63.
39. For these tourists, see Chapter II, p. 52.

CHAPTER IV - CONSTRUCTION AND REMODELLING

Michielsstraat dwellings – his mother's, or later that of his parents-in-law – it is likely to have been modest in size and so not ideal for this kind of practice.[40]

It is not known, for instance, where Rubens produced his first large-scale work following his return from Italy, *The Adoration of the Magi* for the Antwerp town hall, a canvas of nearly four metres across.[41] That he painted this huge scene in the town hall itself is unlikely. We can probably also rule out Jan Brant's house, not only because of the size of the canvas, but also because Rubens started on the commission – and possibly finished it – before he became Brant's son-in-law in October 1609.[42]

We are better informed about the place of production of the monumental *Triptych of the Elevation of the Cross*, a commission that came to Rubens in 1609 or 1610 from the church wardens of St Walburga.[43] There is evidence that he painted the panels – over four and a half metres high – in the church *in situ*. In early June 1610 a payment was made to the workers (perhaps sailors) of the Admiral of the Scheldt for hanging a sail in front of the high altar; this was to close off the choir so that Rubens could work there in peace.[44]

The *Triptych of the Descent from the Cross* (1611–1614): A Workshop in the Attic?

We also have information about the production of the Antwerp *Triptych of the Descent from the Cross*, a work that was commissioned from Rubens on 7 September 1611 by the arquebusiers, his neighbours on the east side of his property, for their altar at the Cathedral of Our Lady (Text ill. 55). This ensemble is slightly smaller than *The Triptych of the Elevation of the Cross*, but it is still of a sizeable format, with panels over four metres high.[45] It is clear from the accounts of the arquebusiers that Rubens did not on this occasion work in the church. The accounts include several references to panels which are at the house of the painter ('ten huize van de schilder') (Appendix I.3), and it is here that the deans

40. On Rubens's predilection for oversized supports – exceeding the size previously produced in Antwerp – from the moment he establishes himself in Antwerp, see Bulckens, *Rubens and Workshop*, 2019; for altarpieces in particular, see ibid., p. 1, n. 2.
41. Madrid, Museo Nacional del Prado, inv. no. P001638; originally approx. 256 × 381 cm; enlarged by Rubens in Spain to 355.5 × 493 cm. Devisscher – Vlieghe, *Youth of Christ (CRLB)*, 2014, I, no. 23; II, fig. 70 [with incorrect current width as 438 cm].
42. It is likely, though not certain, that the painting was already in place in the *Statenkamer* (State Room) at the time of the Twelve Years' Truce negotiations in March–April 1609; for a discussion of the dating, see Devisscher – Vlieghe, *Youth of Christ (CRLB)*, 2014, I, pp. 114–115.
43. Antwerp, Cathedral of Our Lady. The central panel measures 460 × 340 cm; the side panels 462 × 150 cm; see Judson, *Passion (CRLB)*, 2000, pp. 88–114, nos 20–22, figs 61, 64); d'Hulst et al., *Kruisoprichting*, 1992, passim; for the dating of the commission given here, see F. Baudouin, in ibid., p. 52.
44. Rooses, *Oeuvre*, 1886–92, II, pp. 79–80; Judson, *Passion (CRLB)*, 2000, p. 94. In the document the workers are called 'gasten'.
45. The central panel measures 421 × 311 cm; the side panels 421 × 153 cm; see Judson, *Passion (CRLB)*, 2000, pp. 162–182, nos 43–45, figs 135, 144, 151.

CHAPTER IV - CONSTRUCTION AND REMODELLING

Text ill. 55. View on Rubens's *Triptych of the Descent of the Cross*. Antwerp, Cathedral of Our Lady.

of the guild go three times, in October 1611, to check the progress on the project and inspect the panel's quality.

More details in connection with the same triptych pop up a year later, when the central panel is transported to the cathedral. In September 1612 the guild pays workers for 'bringing down the painting from the attic to the ground floor (?) at the house of the painter Rubens' ('affdoen van de schilderye vanden solder tot in den vloer, ten huyse van den schilder Rubbens') (Appendix I.3: [2]). This intriguing entry in the accounts is, however, difficult to interpret and raises a considerable number of questions.

If we take 'the house of the painter' to mean the house where Rubens was living in 1612, then the logical conclusion is that he painted the large panels at his parents-in-law's house in the Sint-Michielsstraat (now Kloosterstraat). This has frequently been taken for a fact,[46] while there is no direct evidence. With a façade extending over six bays, Jan Brant's mansion was certainly generous,[47] but even so it is doubtful that there would have been sufficient space for a

46. Baudouin, *Altars*, 1972, p. 62; Judson, *Passion (CRLB)*, 2000, p. 168; Christopher White calls Brant's dwelling 'a much grander house which could provide a studio with sufficient room for the artist to paint […] the *Descent from the Cross* (White, *Rubens*, 1987, p. 61); Vermeylen, *Antwerp Beckons*, 2004, pp. 19–20. For justified doubts about the existence of a studio in Brant's house, see Bulckens, *Rubens and Workshop*, 2019, p. 87, n. 26.
47. For the house, which was knocked down in 1977, see Chapter I, p. 23, n. 1. An impression of the division of the property into a large number of rooms is provided by the inventory drawn up on Jan Brant's death in 1639 (Duverger, *Kunstinventarissen*, 1984–2009, IV, pp. 267–271).

CHAPTER IV - CONSTRUCTION AND REMODELLING

workshop, quite apart from the question whether the bustling workshop was compatible with the domestic life of the municipal secretary and his family. It certainly seems possible that Rubens was working elsewhere, perhaps on his own property on the Wapper, for example in a makeshift workshop in the 'old' wing. We must also consider the possibility that he rented space somewhere else in the city,[48] although the designation 'at the house of the painter', if taken literally, seems to contradicts this.

Regardless of which house is being specified, the mention of the attic ('den solder') is surprising. From the entry in the accounts we can deduce that the panel had to be moved down, and that it was located in a space under the roof trusses. Or should the term 'solder' rather be interpreted as denoting a room on the first floor and not an attic?[49]

Attics were indeed sometimes used by painters, albeit probably as a storage space rather than a workshop.[50] An attic seems to be a rather problematical space for a studio, not least because of the difficulty of providing light but also maintaining a comfortable temperature. Was the panel placed here temporarily – in order to dry – before being moved to the cathedral? It strikes us as odd, indeed unlikely, that Rubens would have chosen to install his studio in such a space, and especially that he would have used this area to paint the large and extremely heavy oak panel with *The Descent from the Cross*, a work measuring more than thirteen square metres. Nonetheless, the entry in the accounts mentioned above has led to a widely held belief that Rubens had an attic workshop.[51]

Leaving aside the question of whether it was an attic that served as a studio or a store where the panel could be housed temporarily, it remains unclear how the monumental panel could have been moved into and out of this attic room via the narrow stairs of an Antwerp house. It is possible that 'den vloer' refers to a floor outside the house (in a courtyard?), rather than the ground floor inside. If so, the panel may have been lowered by a pulley on the outside of the building, perhaps through a large opening with shutters such as found in warehouses.

48. See the comment about Rubens's studio in February 1614 (it may then have been in close proximity to that of Jan Brueghel I; Chapter II, p. 52, n. 10).
49. This was suggested by Koen Bulckens (Bulckens, *Rubens and Workshop*, 2019, p. 87, n. 25). Max Rooses took 'de solder' literally, writing that 'le triptyque fut descendu du grenier de Rubens jusqu'au rez-de-chaussée' (Rooses, *Oeuvre*, 1886–92, II, p. 116).
50. For details, gathered from inventories, about the use of attics by Antwerp painters, see Van der Stighelen, *Zelfbeeld*, 2000, pp. 239–240.
51. Frans Jos Van den Branden believes that this attic was in the house where Rubens's mother died, on the west side of the Sint-Michielsstraat (Van den Branden, *Schilderschool*, 1883, pp. 503–504). Rooses places 'den solder' (the garret) in the Sint-Michielsstraat, implying that it was in Brant's house (Rooses, *Leven*, 1903, p. 150); in a second passage he takes a more cautious line and talks of 'the painter's house' (ibid., p. 162). See also Vermeylen, *Antwerp Beckons*, 2004, pp. 19–20: 'The Brant house […] was fitted with a studio in the attic where Rubens could paint'.

CHAPTER IV - CONSTRUCTION AND REMODELLING

About a year and a half after the main panel was brought down, on 18 February and 6 March 1614, the wings of the triptych were transported to the cathedral, apparently from the same location, and once more having to be 'brought down'. Workers were paid for moving down the wings of the altarpiece at the painter's house and carrying them to the church' ('van de deuren van den aultaer ten huyse vanden schilder aff te doene, ende in de kercke te draegen') (Appendix I.3: [3]).

1614–1616

Probably only a few months later (c. May 1614), Rubens painted another large panel extending to a height of more than four and a half metres and featuring an *Assumption of the Virgin*, now at the Kunsthistorisches Museum, Vienna.[52] This work was originally intended for the high altar of Antwerp Cathedral, but was eventually – in or shortly after 1622 – installed on one of the side altars of the Jesuit Church. Where Rubens painted it is unknown, nor is it clear where the panel was stored for eight years.

With a few exceptions, Rubens's paintings from around 1613–1615 are smaller in size than those just mentioned, and so their production and storage will have posed no problems. However, from 1616 onwards, he was again working on large-scale paintings, indicating that in the course of 1616 – that is prior to the contract for the staircase mentioned earlier – he could already avail himself of a suitably equipped studio at the house on the Wapper. This is corroborated by the funeral roll of Martina Plantin, mentioned earlier, which records that Rubens was living on the Wapper in February 1616 (Appendix I.7).

An exceptionally large painting is mentioned in two letters from Tobie Matthew to Sir Dudley Carleton. On 30 December 1616 the former writes about a *Wolf Hunt* which is more than five metres wide; the piece is 'so very bigge that none but great princes have houses fit to hange it up in'.[53] A subsequent letter, dated 6 February 1617, informs us that the painting has been purchased by the Duke of Aarschot after it was turned down by Archduke Albert, who would have bought it 'if any roome of his house in Brussels [the Coudenberg Palace] would have held it, excepting alwaies his great hall'.[54] This correspondence suggests that the huge hunting scene, which had been completed in late 1616, was not painted as a commission. In order to sell it, Rubens must have put it on

---

52. Inv. no. 518; 458 × 197 cm; Van de Velde, *Rubens' Hemelvaart*, 1975, pp. 245–277; Freedberg, *Christ after the Passion (CRLB)*, 1984, pp. 149–153, no. 37, fig. 87; Baudouin, *Intervention*, 2000, pp. 19–23; Fabri – Lombaerde, *Jesuit Church (CRLB)*, 2018, p. 198.
53. The sizes given by Matthew are 11 or 12 feet high and 18 feet wide (approx. 315 or 344 × 516 cm); see Rooses – Ruelens, eds, *Correspondance*, 1887–1909, II, p. 93, doc. CXLVI; according to Balis this *Wolf Hunt* can be identified with the canvas in the Metropolitan Museum of Art, New York, which was later reduced in size (Balis, *Hunting Scenes (CRLB)*, 1986, pp. 95–104, no. 2).
54. Rooses – Ruelens, eds, ibid., II, p. 97, doc. CXLVII; Balis, ibid., p. 102, n. 3.

display in a suitably large area for a while, so that it could be seen by potential buyers.

1617: Gigantic Production

The archival records reveal almost nothing about the whereabouts of Rubens's studio in the years 1616–1617. There is only one, vague, reference: early in 1617 the unpainted panels ordered for the *Triptych of the Adoration of the Magi* for the Church of St John the Baptist and St John the Evangelist in Mechelen were shipped from Mechelen to Antwerp; a payment is made to unload them and 'to carry them to the house of the aforementioned Rubens' ('te doen draghen ten huijse van de voors. Rubens').[55] While in 1612 the location of the 'painter's house' was unclear, at least we can now be confident that this refers to Rubens's studio on the Wapper.

Other projects can be mentioned which necessitated a spacious workshop. In the first place there are the eight large canvases which Rubens painted in preparation for the series of eight tapestries depicting *The History of Decius Mus*. On 9 November 1616, seven days after drawing up the contract for the staircase in the house, an agreement was signed about this tapestry series between, on the one hand, the Brussels tapestry weaver Jan Raes I (1574–1651) and the Antwerp tapestry dealer and humanist François Sweerts (Sweertius), and, on the other, the Genovese merchant Franco Cattaneo (1582–1617).[56] Altogether these canvases covered a substantial area, measuring circa seventy-two square metres, and they were completed in 1617, in less than twelve months (Text ill. 56).[57]

This large-scale series was nevertheless just a small part of the workshop's total production for that year. Reinhold Baumstark points out that 'during Rubens's long career there hardly was another year so filled with major projects'. He lists eighteen other large-format works on panel or canvas that can be dated to the same year, calculating that the total production must have amounted to approximately two hundred and sixty square metres.[58] Among the works that Rubens realised in this period was *The Great Last Judgement* for the high altar of the Jesuit Church in Neuburg, now in the Alte Pinakothek in

---

55. Devisscher – Vlieghe, *Youth of Christ (CRLB)*, 2014, I, pp. 137, 139, n. 5; II, fig. 88. The triptych was ordered on 27 December 1616, completed in September 1617, and installed in the church the same month (ibid., pp. 135–136).
56. Duverger, *Decius Mus*, 1976–78, pp. 17, 23, 37–38; Baumstark – Delmarcel, *Decius Mus (CRLB)*, 2019, II, pp. 219–220, appendix I.A.1; for Sweerts and his contacts with Rubens, see also above, p. 127, n. 32.
57. The canvases were all less than 3 m high; two were approximately 5 m wide, two nearly 4 m, and the rest were narrower (Baumstark – Delmarcel, ibid., passim). For the total surface, see ibid., pp. 12, 175.
58. Baumstark describes in detail the surge in Rubens's production during 1617 ('an overwhelming accumulation of commissions'); see ibid., 2019, I, pp. 150–154.

CHAPTER IV · CONSTRUCTION AND REMODELLING

Text ill. 56. *Decius Mus* series in Vienna, Gartenpalais Liechtenstein.

Munich and which is probably the largest altarpiece he produced, measuring 610 by 460 cm. We know that it was finished in October 1617.[59]

It is clear from this that in late 1616 and in the course of 1617 Rubens must have had access to premises large enough for the production of gigantic commissions such as these. In our opinion there can be no doubt that by then his new 'schilderhuys' was operational. It seems reasonable even to ask if the studio was indeed spacious enough to accommodate the impressively large canvases and panels.[60] Without question, a studio that had the capacity for work on a large scale was of key importance for Rubens's ambition to expand his 'business'. It is worth repeating here one of Rubens's most often-quoted remarks, in which he expresses his liking for large-format works: '[…] my talent is such that no undertaking, however vast in size […] has ever surpassed my courage'.[61] It seems only logical that he built as soon as possible a studio equipped for the production of such works.

59. This date can be deduced from a payment instruction issued on 31 October 1617; that the canvas was completed is furthermore confirmed by a letter dated 14 November, which reports that the painting has incurred some damage during transport; see Freedberg, *Christ after the Passion (CRLB)* 1984, pp. 201–206, no. 49, fig. 137; Renger, *Altäre für Bayern*, 1990, pp. 55–56, 87–88, docs 2–4.
60. Baumstark wonders if the workshop was spacious enough for the painting of the *Decius Mus* series, and suspects that Rubens also used other locations, including the studios of colleagues (Baumstark – Delmarcel, *Decius Mus (CRLB)*, 2019, I, p. 157).
61. Letter (in French), dated 13 September 1621, from Rubens to William Trumbull (1639–1716) (Rooses – Ruelens, eds, *Correspondance*, 1887–1909, II, pp. 286–287, doc. CCXXV; English translation from Magurn, ed., *Letters*, 1955, p. 77, no. 46. On Rubens's predilection for large formats, see, for example, Büttner, *Rubens*, 2015, p. 106; for a full discussion of this topic, see Bulckens, *Rubens and Workshop*, 2019.

Chapter V
The Exterior of the Studio Wing or 'Italian' Wing

In the courtyard, opposite the 'Flemish' or north wing, is the 'schilderhuis' or workshop containing the studios and other rooms in which Rubens and his numerous assistants and apprentices worked (see Fig. 7). This is a much taller and larger building than the 'Flemish' wing and is also entirely different in style. In the literature it has been dubbed the 'Italian' wing, an apt appellation, as closer study shows.

As they are for the rest of the house, surviving designs by Rubens for the workshop wing are extremely scarce. Only two autograph drawings with architectural motifs can be associated with it, and these are no more than vague sketches in chalk (No. 7a and No. 13b; Figs 54, 97). There are in addition two other Rubens drawings which can be linked to the narrative scenes incorporated into the decoration of the façade (No. 10a and No. 13a; Figs 65, 96). Nevertheless, it does not seem too far-fetched to suppose that Rubens had his workshop built to his own design, specifying the general layout as well as the architectural and decorative detailing of the façades.

Several points relating to the creation of this wing have already been discussed (in Chapter IV) and it is worth reviewing the conclusions that were arrived at. As can be inferred from the structure of the cellars which partly stemmed from an earlier building, the workshop wing very likely completely replaced one of the wings of the house that Rubens bought in 1610. As to the date, there are indications that the workshop wing may have been well advanced or even complete by 1615 or 1616. There is the document in which Rubens refers to carpentry work carried out on his house, including the construction and covering of a roof, in 1615 (Appendix I.14), and the contract dating from November 1616 regarding the installation of a staircase (Appendix I.9). Although neither document specifies which wing of the property these works relate to, it seems likely that Rubens was able to use the workshop from at least the end of 1616, when he accepted the commission for painting the very sizeable *Decius Mus* series. Then again, by that time it may already have been operational for several months or even a year. For it seems obvious that he would have begun working in his new studio – even if it was not yet completely finished – from the moment that he and his family moved to the Wapper, which was before February 1616.[1]

---

1. For a discussion of the location of Rubens's workshop in Antwerp before its installation on the Wapper

CHAPTER V · THE EXTERIOR OF THE STUDIO WING OR 'ITALIAN' WING

To determine what the exterior of the workshop wing originally looked like we can turn to the aforementioned seventeenth-century images: the two prints by Jacob Harrewijn dating from 1684 and 1692, and the anonymous Aylesbury *View of the Courtyard of Rubens's House*, probably made c. 1660 (Appendix III.1–3; Figs 16–18, 27). In addition, Rubens himself appears to have incorporated certain elements of his workshop wing in a building seen in the background of *Hélène Fourment au carrosse*, dating from the 1630s (Appendix III.7; Figs 21 and 31), though this should certainly not be regarded as a realistic rendering, as will be explained further in this chapter.

A. General Plan and Roofing of the 'Italian' or Studio Wing (see Fig. 7)

The workshop complex – the largest part of Rubens's house – was built on an L-shaped plan. The short leg of the 'L', which runs parallel to the Wapper, is a narrow building, approximately five metres deep, with one side facing onto the street and the other onto the courtyard. The long leg, perpendicular to the Wapper, is rectangular in plan with exterior measurements of around nine by nineteen metres.

The first Harrewijn print, of 1684, gives a detailed illustration of the north façade, while the later print, of 1692, provides additional information, as it shows not only the two Italianate façades fronting the courtyard but the east or garden façade as well. Moreover, a separate picture inset at the bottom of this sheet depicts the complete house frontage (Figs 18, 26), with its centre section formed by the workshop's west façade. In neither print is the workshop's south wall illustrated, an issue we shall return to later.

Roof and Eaves Cornice

The prints give us an idea of the way the roofs of the L-shaped wing are constructed (see the present roof plan, Fig. 9). The smaller part of the building facing onto the street – the short leg of the L – has a hipped roof that abuts the higher hipped roof of the workshop (Text ill. 57).

At the west ridge end of the higher roof was a weathervane consisting of a sphere on a tall foot with a compass rose above (in shape rather like a radiant sun); a large arrow projecting from the compass rose indicated the prevalent wind direction. No doubt the sphere and weathervane were gilded. We can make out, through the transparent fabric of Helena Fourment's *huyck* (her

(1609–c. 1617), see Chapter IV, pp. 128 ff.; on the earliest date of the presence of Rubens and his family in the house (after June 1614 and before February 1616), see also Chapter IV, pp. 118–119.

CHAPTER V - THE EXTERIOR OF THE STUDIO WING OR 'ITALIAN' WING

Text ill. 57. Detail of the 1692 Harrewijn print (Fig. 18): the roof of the L-shaped studio wing.

black cloak-like garment), a very similar 'golden' sphere topped with a sun on the roof of the house containing elements of the workshop façade that is depicted in the background of *Hélène Fourment au carrosse* (Fig. 21). According to the Harrewijn prints there was also a more or less related motif – a finial in the form of a flaming urn or smoking brazier – on the other two ridge ends of the roofs of the 'Italian' wing: on the street side and on the garden side, as well as a matching brazier on the garden end of the ridge of the north wing on the other side of the courtyard.

The eaves of the workshop complex project quite some way beyond the wall below. They are supported by consoles (or modillions) separated by rectangular compartments containing various decorative elements, not all of which are clearly legible on the print although a number of cornucopias and *bucrania* are recognisable (Text ill. 58 and Fig. 168). The larger roof, perpendicular to the Wapper, was pierced by a dormer on the courtyard side, and this was no doubt replicated on the other, south-facing side. We shall return to this means of illuminating the roof space when we come to discuss the interior of the studio wing.[2]

B. *The North Façade*

The 1684 Harrewijn print and the Aylesbury painting both show the courtyard of Rubens's house as seen from the entrance from the Wapper and both give, to the right, a detailed image of the workshop's striking north façade in foreshortened perspective (Figs 27–28). The same wall can also be seen in the 1692 print but there the foreshortening is more acute, reducing its legibility (Fig. 18). Apart from a few drawings that can be associated with the figurative scenes in the frieze, no other images of this remarkable façade decoration, in whole or in part, are known.

The prints are assumed to show a building whose exterior had not essentially changed since Rubens's day and thus to provide a reliable basis for

2. See Chapter VII, pp. 217–219.

CHAPTER V - THE EXTERIOR OF THE STUDIO WING OR 'ITALIAN' WING

Text ill. 58. Detail of the 1684 Harrewijn print (Fig. 17): the eaves cornice of the studio wing.

the description that follows. Even so, questions remain. For we must certainly bear in mind the possibility that some of the decorative elements and maybe, to a lesser extent, some of the half columns and mouldings as well, were not fully in the round or in relief, as the images suggest, but were painted in *trompe-l'oeil* on the plastered wall. This painted decoration will be looked at in more detail in the next chapter, in which we will investigate what can be learned about this matter from the seventeenth-century visual sources mentioned above.[3]

It should be said that when the decoration of the façade was reconstructed during the modern restoration of the house, nothing was recreated in *trompe-l'oeil*, but everything shown in the prints was sculpted in relief (Fig. 10).

In the 1930s, when it was still standing, examination of the north façade had yielded only scant information on this point: what had survived was a completely plain wall, without any trace of moulding or decoration (Text ills 59–60).

What was found, however, were the bases of the engaged columns on the ground floor,[4] indicating that the decoration of the lower part of the façade was built of durable material – if not entirely then at least in part. There were other finds, too; not in the wall but elsewhere on the site on the Wapper. In the garden, pieces of bluestone were found that may have come from the façade: remnants of mouldings, possibly from the windows,[5] and a pedestal that was reused in the modern reconstruction of the house.[6] Nonetheless, in the description that follows we can in some cases do no more than leave open the question of 'real' or painted.

3. See Chapter VI, pp. 170–171 and passim.
4. Ruyten, *Opzoekingswerken Rubenshuis*, 1954, p. 2.
5. See p. 143, n. 11.
6. The pedestal supporting the bust furthest to the right on the first level of the restored house bears the 17th-century quarry mark of Jean Delfontaine (Maclot, *Rubenssite*, 2016, p. 330) and could be an original component.

CHAPTER V - THE EXTERIOR OF THE STUDIO WING OR 'ITALIAN' WING

Text ill. 59. The north façade of the studio wing before the restoration.

Text ill. 60. The north façade of the studio wing during the restoration.

The Ground Floor Level

The north façade of the studio wing represented in the Harrewijn prints and the Aylesbury painting (Figs 27–28) comprises a cornice front with five vertical bays; it is divided into three horizontal levels, of which the bottom one is lowest in height. The five bays of this first, ground floor level, which correspond to those of the upper storeys, are separated by engaged Doric columns that support a heavily moulded entablature with a frieze of triglyphs (alternately plain, and with small volutes either side). In the centre bay the entablature is interrupted by a triangular pediment above a double door leading to the studio, surrounded by a substantial frame. The tympanum incorporates a niche housing a bust under a shell, and with a trailing cornucopia either side (Fig. 36) In the Aylesbury painting details of this motif (Fig. 37) differ from the print: the shell and the bottom of the niche are of a different – perhaps more Rubensian – design, and the bust is not a 'herm bust' but stands on a narrow base (see below).

CHAPTER V - THE EXTERIOR OF THE STUDIO WING OR 'ITALIAN' WING

In each of the two bays on either side of the door we see wall sections, separated by the Doric columns just mentioned. Each of these four sections is decorated in a rusticated manner with a complicated pattern of smooth bands, contrasting with heavy, bossed blocks and bossed bands of a lighter colour (Figs 33, 34).[7] The upper part is structured as a niche inside a geniculated arch accommodating a bust, a motif to which we shall return below.

It should be noted that the rusticated style on the ground-floor level of Rubens's studio very much follows the Italian practice of executing the façade of the bottom-most storey in this rugged style, to contrast with the higher storeys.

The Second Level: The *Oculus* and Round-Headed Windows

Seen from the outside the second or middle level of the north wall suggests that behind it lies a *piano nobile*. In reality, the first and second levels correspond to one vast space that Rubens used as his workshop. The central bay on the second level contains a large *oculus* beneath which floral garlands hang (Fig. 38). The two bays either side are taken up almost entirely by four very large arch-topped leaded lights composed of numerous rectangular quarrels – a window type of a size and shape that is rare in the domestic architecture of the seventeenth-century Low Countries.[8] In each of the spandrels, reposing on the curve of the top of the *oculus* and the windows, is a curly-tailed dolphin, which may be painted rather than made in relief (Fig. 151; see under No. 26). Between each of these is a broad, crest-like volute, tapering towards the bottom, with a row of *guttae* above and a vertical pearl motif down the middle (Text ill. 45).[9] Below, in the narrow sections of the wall between the windows, and as if standing on the entablature of the low first level, are pedestals supporting busts, four in total.

---

7. There is no reason to assume that marble was used in these wall sections. This was the belief at the time of the modern reconstruction – possibly a misreading of the boss pattern – resulting in the use of reddish marble. Rutger Tijs mentions the use of different kinds of marble in the modern façade, including white 'Botticino marble' and red 'rouge de Rance' (Tijs, *Rubens en Jordaens*, 1984, p. 216). See also the reconstruction drawing by Victor Blommaert with red coloured elements described as in marble (Maclot, *Rubenssite*, 2016, repr. p. 184 (bottom)).
8. The rarity of this shape in Rubens's house was noted by Jan Jehee in his study of window types in the Netherlands (Jehee, *Licht*, 2010, p. 127); he cites similar examples in religious architecture (see, inter alia, a window in the Groot Begijnhof in Leuven; ibid., p. 129, fig. 216), and he supposes that in Rubens's house the large expanses of quarrelled glass were reinforced by an armature of iron bars. Whether this was indeed the case cannot be deduced from the print.
9. The two outer-most crests in the Harrewijn prints are left undecorated. In the Aylesbury painting only one of these motifs is worked up in detail and has a palmette at the top.

The Third Level: The Rectangular Windows (No. 7)

On the third and uppermost level of the north wall the corners at either end have long and short quoining: the short quoins are rectangular; the long quoins are narrower and pointed at the inward end (Text ill. 66).[10]

In all three of the workshop façades that are represented in the prints – north, west and east – the third level contains rectangular lights composed of small quarrels and with window surrounds that may have been sculpted in bluestone rather than painted in *trompe-l'oeil*.[11] These window surrounds (No. 7; Figs 51–53) are comparable to Italian types that Rubens may have seen in situ or was familiar with from treatises on architecture. Similar windows were used by Palladio and Scamozzi and their followers and there are innumerable examples to be found, including in the Palladian architecture of the following centuries.

Characteristic of such windows is the use of 'ears' or 'crossettes', projections on either side of the window aperture where the lintel and sill meet the jambs.[12] A second characteristic, regarded by 'classical' architects as a virtually self-evident principle, can be seen above the windows: pediments that are alternately triangular and segmental. Countless examples of such alternating pediments, 'an innately understood device for instilling an interesting visual rhythm to a series of bays or openings,' as Calder Loth puts it, are to be found from Antiquity through to the twentieth century.[13]

The alternating window pediments in Rubens's three façades are broken or open-topped – the segmental type has inward-turning scrolls – and each contains a footed hemispherical ornament, a flower vase or a smoking brazier (Figs 51–53), or an oil lamp (Text ill. 61).[14]

---

10. For this unusual motif, see also the description of the east or garden façade (below, pp. 152).
11. Investigations carried out during the restoration brought to light stone sewer channels in the basement bearing the same stonemasons' marks as on the portico. According to Van Averbeke, these could have been the original mouldings surrounding the windows (Van Averbeke, *Rubenshuis. Restauratie II*, 1938, p. 8; Devroe, *Rubens' huis*, 2008, I, p. 73).
12. On the use of 'ears' or 'crossettes' in window frames, sometimes only at the lintel, see Ottenheym, *Scamozzi*, 2010, passim; see also Forssman, who uses the term 'Ohrenfenster' (Forssman, *Dorisch*, 1984, p. 79); on the motif of a Corinthian crossetted architrave in Francart, see De Vos, *Francart*, 1998, p. 67.
13. Loth, *Alternating Pediments*, 2013; he points out that this principle was taken so much for granted that hardly anything was written about it. Two examples will suffice: Michelangelo's façade of the Palazzo Farnese in Rome (Ackerman, *Architecture of Michelangelo*, 1961, fig. 39) and Inigo Jones's Banqueting House in London (Worsley, *Inigo Jones*, 2007, fig. 107).
14. The Harrewijn prints provide conflicting information: in the print of 1684 the ornaments of the north façade seem to be simply flower vases. In the print of 1692, however, smoking braziers (or oil lamps?) with a puff of smoke rising above the pediments can be discerned in the garden façade as well as in the north façade. In the Aylesbury painting the objects seem to be braziers (made of shining metal). Together with several other details corresponding to the architecture of the house, smoking oil lamps can also be seen in Rubens's *Homage to Ceres* in The State Hermitage Museum, St Petersburg (Appendix III.13; Fig. 23). For 'golden' flaming or smoking braziers on the rooftop of the house, see above, p. 139.

CHAPTER V - THE EXTERIOR OF THE STUDIO WING OR 'ITALIAN' WING

Text ill. 61. Detail of the 1692 Harrewijn print (Fig. 18): two windows at the upper level of the garden façade (with a smoking oil lamp at the right).

The shape of these ornaments also alternates: those in the tympanums of the segmental pediments are smaller and stand on a base, in front of which is a modest flower garland suspended from the scrolls. There seem to be few direct precedents for these hemispherical ornaments, although there is a related example in the garden façade of the Villa Medici in Rome (1576–1587), where we find, above the entrance and in the two towers, windows with crossettes, an open-topped pediment, and a sphere on a pedestal (Text ill. 72, Fig. 56).[15]

In connection with the upper windows in the three workshop façades represented in the prints, attention should be drawn to a chalk drawing by Rubens now in the Museum Plantin-Moretus in Antwerp: a study of a kneeling nude that corresponds to the figure of Aglaurus in a lost painting, the *Discovery of Erichthonius by the Daughters of Cecrops*. According to Fiona Healy, the lost original should be dated around 1613–1614, and in any case before April 1614.[16] On the verso of the sheet are some vague sketches in black chalk (No. 7a; Fig. 54), including a rectangular window similar to those of the Villa Medici. This drawing could thus be a study by Rubens for the framing of the windows on the top floor of his workshop, making it one of only two drawings by Rubens featuring architectural components that can be associated with his house.[17]

The Third Level: Panels and Herms (Nos 8–16 and No. 4)

Beneath each of the five windows in the third level of the north façade is a rectangular panel containing a figurative scene. Three similar panels on the garden façade and one on the short east façade facing the courtyard bring the total to nine. Painted in *grisaille*, and meant as a frieze of classical or classicised reliefs running in continuous series around at least three walls of the studio wing, they form an important part of the decoration, and will be discussed in detail in Chapter VI.

15. Toulier, *Villa Médicis*, I, 1989, passim; details of the windows in question: ibid., pp. 308, 309, figs 390 and 395; diagrams of the types of window in the façade of this villa: ibid., pp. 306–307, 432.
16. F. Healy, in McGrath et al., *Mythological Subjects I (CRLB)*, 2016, I, pp. 400–402; II, no. 40b, fig. 331.
17. For the other drawing, see No. 13b (Fig. 97).

The five panels on the north façade are separated and terminated by columnar pedestals. Four of these 'support' herms, while the two terminal pedestals bear large vases (Fig. 28). Both the herms and the vases were probably painted on the flat surface of the plastered wall rather than executed in high or low relief in stucco. In any case we can assume that they were monochrome and made to appear as if carved in stone. In the Aylesbury painting they are whitish, contrasting with the reddish wall around them (Fig. 42)

The four herms on the north façade and the two on the adjacent short east façade are almost identical (see also No. 4). Each is clad in a short cloak that conceals the torso, arms and hands. Emerging beneath the cloak is a shaft, proportioned to the height of a human figure and tapering downwards to a narrow foot. In the print they are perhaps shown broader than in reality and this would explain why their shoulders are touching the pediments.

The six herms have no attributes of any kind, which seems to suggest that they should be regarded as purely architectural motifs, bearing no allusion to identifiable mythological or historical characters. In the modern reconstruction of the workshop façades, however, the herms do not follow the simple design seen in the Harrewijn prints and the Aylesbury painting. They underwent a radical change of form and in the process acquired specific meanings. Arms, attributes, and differentiated garments were added, resulting in eight Olympian gods – two on the garden façade, four on the north façade, and another two on the short east façade overlooking the courtyard (Figs 10–12) – rendered in high relief and largely based on the deity herms adorning the *Portico of the Emperors* erected for the *Pompa Introitus Ferdinandi* (Text ill. 62).[18] It should be noted that the herms' unsubstantiated alteration led some authors astray in their interpretation of the original façade decoration.[19]

The Nine Busts on the North Façade (Nos 1–3)

According to the two Harrewijn prints the workshop's north wall was enhanced by nine busts (Figs 17–18): four set into niches on the first level; one above the central doorway, in a niche with a shell motif, and cornucopias on either side, and four mounted on pedestals in the second level. The Aylesbury painting (Fig 27) is less informative, showing only four of the nine busts and vaguely at that.

---

18. For the herms on the *Portico of the Emperors*, see Martin, *Pompa (CRLB)*, 1972, figs 37–43; only *Juno* on the north façade was adopted almost literally, while the other gods differ in details; for a diagram of these modern deity herms on the three reconstructed façades, see Stutz, *Residenz*, 1985, p. 144, fig. 7.
19. Stechow, *Classical Tradition*, 1968, p. 85; Warnke, *Rubens*, 1977, p. 39; a diagram in Stutz, *Residenz*, 1985, p. 144, fig. 7; Hans-Peter Schwarz sees in the deities 'Symbolfiguren der Kräfte der Natur' (Schwarz, *Künstlerhaus*, 1990, p. 83); Von Simson, *Rubens*, 1996, p. 212; Zimmermann, *Rubenshaus*, 2004, p. 171.

CHAPTER V - THE EXTERIOR OF THE STUDIO WING OR 'ITALIAN' WING

Text ill. 62. Theodoor van Thulden after Rubens, *The Portico of the Emperors*, etching, detail of *Frederick III and Albert II, with Mars Ultor and Ceres*.

We can assume that the busts were intended as portrayals of specific historical or mythological figures, but except for the faun in a niche to the right of the door, mentioned before (Fig. 34),[20] there is too little detail in the visual sources for secure identification of the other six busts visible in the earlier Harrewijn print, four – each representing a man with a curling beard and hair – are not greatly differentiated. There is also one beardless youth and one bald-headed man with a long beard. The remaining two busts are concealed behind the towering rocky surround of the fountain with a bagpiper on the left of the façade.[21]

It should be noted that none of the nine busts can be convincingly associated with the series of engravings depicting portraits of twelve famous Greek and Roman philosophers, poets, orators and statesmen (six Greek and six Roman) that were produced in 1638, around twenty years after the completion of the workshop. The engravings were based on drawings by Rubens and some of the busts in those drawings were actually in his own collection.[22] With one debateable exception there is nothing to suggest that the busts in the workshop façade – whether they were copies of sculptures, or plaster casts, or paintings in *trompe-l'oeil* – are related to the antique portrait busts Rubens owned. There

20. On this faun, see also below, pp. 147, 148 (n. 28), Chapter IX, p. 277; and No. 1, Copy.
21. On this fountain, see Chapter III, pp. 114–115.
22. See Van Mulders, *Twelve Busts*, 2008, pp. 106–114, nos 44–55.

CHAPTER V - THE EXTERIOR OF THE STUDIO WING OR 'ITALIAN' WING

is no discernible similarity, unless the head above the doorway (No. 2; Fig. 36) could be thought to bear some resemblance to the well-known pseudo-Seneca bust (Text ills 63–65), but this not a very convincing hypothesis (see below). It hardly needs saying that the valuable antique marble originals Rubens owned would certainly not have been used in the façade's ornamentation.[23]

Given that the busts are vaguely represented and virtually impossible to identify, we can only conjecture about a programme on which the wall decoration would be based. No doubt some of the busts – perhaps only the four between the windows and the one in the niche above the door – represent famous names from ancient times which Rubens 'chose and arranged [...] as part of a carefully conceived representation of ethical and artistic ideals expressed in the figures of classical Antiquity,' as Jeffrey Muller has put it.[24] The master may have adopted the principles set forth by Pliny and Vitruvius on the placing of busts in the atriums of Roman houses,[25] and he would certainly have seen examples of busts set in façades in Italy.[26]

As has already been mentioned, when restoration work started in 1937 the north façade was completely flat, without any trace of niches, pedestals or busts (Text ill. 59), while the Harrewijn prints represent all the busts as three-dimensional sculptures. It is therefore understandable that doubts have been expressed about the existence of real busts on the façade.[27] Whatever the case, for the busts in the niches on the ground floor there is an indication that they were carved fully in the round. It seems likely that the engaged columns (whose bases were found) as well as the four niches did actually exist and housed real busts. Strengthening that supposition is the fact that one of those busts, the aforementioned *Faun*, has survived in a free-standing plaster version, most likely a cast taken from an original that was already in very eroded condition (see No. 1; Cf. Figs 34 and 35). In the nineteenth century, and up until the start of the restoration works, this bust occupied the left-hand niche in the portico (Appendix III.52 and Text ill. 23).

---

23. See also below on the function of antique busts and the place in which they were kept in humanist circles, Chapter VII, pp. 227–228.
24. Muller, *Collector*, 1989, p. 26. In connection with the potential presence of busts of philosophers on the façade, Muller refers to what the Italian art theoretician Gian Paolo Lomazzo (1538–1592) wrote in his *Trattato*, published in 1584. Lomazzo proposed that 'schools and gymnasiums of the sciences were to be decorated with philosophers, beautifully posed, holding famous sayings and books [...]' (Muller, *Collector*, 1989, p. 27; Italian text: ibid., p. 27, n. 9). For a detailed discussion of the use and meaning of busts in humanist circles, see id., *Moribvs Antiqvis*, 2008.
25. Uppenkamp – Van Beneden, *Architectural Symbolism*, 2011, pp. 112, 113, n. 124.
26. See, for instance, the spectacular decoration of the first courtyard of the Palazzo Mattei di Giove in Rome (Text ill. 71); see below, p. 164, n. 65.
27. See, inter alia: Jeffrey Muller, who writes about the busts 'it is impossible to know for sure whether they were painted illusions or real sculpture' (Muller, *Rubens's Collection*, 2004, p. 39); see also Uppenkamp – Van Beneden, *Architectural Symbolism*, 2011, p. 112. Busts that are certainly *trompe-l'oeil* illusions can be seen in Harrewijn's image of Hillewerve's chapel (No. 22; Fig. 127).

CHAPTER V - THE EXTERIOR OF THE STUDIO WING OR 'ITALIAN' WING

During restoration the niches were reconstructed and all nine busts of the façade (not just those on the first level) were executed as sculptures in the round (Fig. 10). A copy of the plaster cast of the *Faun* was made, carved in stone; and, true to the print, was set in the niche to the right of the doorway. To fill the other three niches on the first level, busts were designed and carved of iconographically related figures, including a *Satyr* and a *Silenus*. These were not made after existing sculptures in stone or plaster but were more or less based on Rubens's mythological paintings.[28] It is hard to judge whether this choice was justified thematically. The bald, long-bearded head on the right of the print could indeed be that of Silenus but it could equally well be some other antique character. As with the herms, authors describing and interpreting this façade were sometimes misled by the modern reconstruction. Wolfgang Stechow, for instance, assumed that the lower level of the façade was adorned with busts of these 'lesser' nature deities.[29]

The shape of the four niches on the first level, described above, is remarkable, rendered in bossed *'alla rustica'* style, and with a so-called geniculated arch.[30] In this connection it is worth mentioning a close relationship with an engraving made after a design by Rubens showing a similar niche with a rusticated geniculated arch and containing a bust of Seneca – or more correctly a bust that Rubens and contemporaries saw as that Stoic philosopher – that was used as an illustration in Justus Lipsius's *L. Annaei Senecae Philosophi Opera Quae Extant Omnia*, published by Balthasar Moretus (Text ill. 63).[31] Interestingly, that book appeared in 1615 – just around the time that Rubens was probably working on the designs for his workshop wing. It also gives information about the sculpted head: in the preface Moretus writes that the engraving depicts a marble bust of Seneca that Rubens had brought back from Rome (Appendix I.6). The present whereabouts of Rubens's pseudo-Seneca are unknown. There are more than forty known copies of the expressive head, one of which was acquired by the Rubenshuis in 1952 (Text ill. 64).[32]

28. The titles given to these newly carved busts are somewhat confusing: a Satyr, a Faun, Pan and Silenus (and not the new 'Faun', but what is called 'Pan' is a copy after the surviving *Faun*); see Clijmans, *Wederopbouw Rubenshuis*, 1946, p. 80; Baudouin, *Summary Guide*, 1977, p. 8.
29. He describes them as follows: 'They are the symbols of pulsating life, of fertility, and of the *flatus divinus*; in many works of the master they had received, […] a place of great dignity while at the same time reveling in their animal powers' (Stechow, *Classical Tradition*, 1968, p. 85); Stechow's misreading is pointed out by Muller, *Collector*, 1989, p. 26, n. 6. Among others who based their interpretation on the divergent modern reconstruction are: Warnke, *Rubens*, 1977, p. 39; Stutz, *Residenz*, 1985, p. 144, fig. 7; Von Simson, *Rubens*, 1996, p. 212.
30. For a detailed discussion of the geniculated arch or flat arch, a major motif in the portico, see Chapter IX, pp. 265–267.
31. On the engraving by Cornelis Galle I (1576–1650) and the so-called Seneca bust, see inter alia Prinz, *Philosophers*, 1973, pp. 410–417; Judson – Van de Velde, *Title-pages (CRLB)*, 1978, I, pp. 165–166, no. 32; II, fig. 111; Muller, *Collector*, 1989, p. 151, cat. III, no. 7, pl. 130; Morford, *Stoics*, 1991, pp. 5–10; Muller, *Moribvs Antiqvis*, 2008, pp. 15–16.
32. Inv. no. B. 37; Baudouin, *Cat. Antwerp Rubenshuis*, 1974, no. 17; Herremans et al., *Heads on Shoulders*, 2008,

CHAPTER V - THE EXTERIOR OF THE STUDIO WING OR 'ITALIAN' WING

Text ill. 63. Cornelis Galle I, after Rubens, *The Bust of Seneca*, engraving.

Text ill. 64. Roman, the so-called *Bust of 'Seneca'*, sculpture. Antwerp, Rubenshuis.

Five of the busts – four between the windows and one in the niche above the door, and made of stone or plaster or painted in *trompe-l'oeil* – most likely represented illustrious Greek and/or Roman characters who, as mentioned earlier, cannot now be identified. It should be noted that in the 1684 Harrewijn print – and not in the Aylesbury painting – these five busts are 'archaic' in style, with the shoulders cut vertically and without a base, a type called a 'herm' or a 'herm bust'. If the print can be trusted, this type may suggest that Rubens intended the busts to represent Greeks rather than Romans.[33]

The modern reconstruction was based on the assumption that these five busts included philosophers, and new heads carved in the round and derived from well-known antique examples were set into the façade (Figs 10–11).[34] As is the case for the herms between the windows and the busts on the ground level, the modern reconstruction encouraged the false belief that the busts now

no. 35. For the pseudo-Seneca owned by Rubens, see also Van der Meulen, *Antique (CRLB)*, 1994, II, no. 117, fig. 218; Belkin – Healy, *House of Art*, 2004, no. 65, repr.
33. See under No. 3.
34. Placed between the windows of the north façade are Plato, Socrates, Sophocles and Marcus Aurelius and above the door, in the place of honour, the so-called Seneca. For the façade on the garden side – where there had originally been no busts – Demosthenes, Democritus, Homer and Julius Caesar were chosen (Fig. 12). On these 'modern' sculptures and their makers, see Clijmans, *Wederopbouw Rubenshuis*, 1946, pp. 78–81.

CHAPTER V - THE EXTERIOR OF THE STUDIO WING OR 'ITALIAN' WING

Text ill. 65. The so-called *Bust of Seneca*, sculpture in the reconstructed north façade.

on the north and east façades of the studio correspond to figures from Rubens's original programme.[35]

The bearded man in the centre, in the niche beneath the pediment and above the door (No. 2; Fig. 36), undoubtedly held a special significance for Rubens. The bust was often regarded as a version of the aforementioned so-called Seneca, and a copy of that work was chosen to fill the niche during the restoration (Text ill. 65).

That around 1615 the head was renowned among humanists does perhaps argue for that identification, but it remains no more than a hypothesis and the supposed resemblance is not wholly convincing. The herm bust in the 1684 Harrewijn print has curlier hair and a longer beard than the pseudo-Seneca that Rubens owned, though this may be more a matter of inaccurate rendering than actual difference.[36] The only other image of the north façade, the Aylesbury painting, is not very helpful either. It shows a quite different bust, on a narrow base (Fig. 37). Furthermore, if it really was a herm bust, as the Harrewijn print – but not the painting – clearly shows, then it was probably a Greek figure and not Seneca. It seems likely, therefore, that it was a different figure from Antiquity to whom Rubens gave pride of place in his workshop façade. After all, it is not hard to imagine him ornamenting his workshop wall with busts, invented by himself, of Apelles and the other ancient Greek painters, who played an important role in the iconography of the north façade.

35. See for instance, Stechow, *Classical Tradition*, 1968, p. 85; Von Simson, *Rubens*, 1996, p. 212. For a diagram of the busts on the reconstructed façades (considered to be the original program), see Stutz, *Residenz*, 1985, p. 144, fig. 7.
36. Among those who saw the pseudo-Seneca in the bust above the door: Evers, *Rubens*, 1942, p. 43; Stechow, *Classical Tradition*, 1968, p. 30; correctly described as 'impossible to identify' in Prinz, *Philosophers*, 1973, p. 412.

While there is not necessarily a connection with the decoration of the studio, it may be relevant to mention that Rubens may have owned more than one bust of what he believed to be the Stoic philosopher – not only the antique marble head but copies as well, carved or in plaster. Could it be that, somewhere in his house, he had set a copy above a door and beneath a shell motif similar to the one in the workshop's north façade? A 'Seneca' portrait bust appears in an almost identical arrangement (Text ill. 151) in Willem van Haecht's *Art Gallery with Van Dyck's 'Mystic Marriage of St Catherine'* of c. 1630, in a Scottish private collection (Appendix III.31).

C. The Italianate East Façade Next to the Entrance (Facing the Courtyard)

The Harrewijn print from 1692 shows the east-facing wall on the west side of the courtyard. The height is the same and the structure is partly similar to the north wall just described, but it is significantly narrower, comprising only three bays instead of five (Fig. 18). It connects with a wall of the older wing, with the arch over the passage leading from the Wapper to the courtyard, and with an *oculus* window above.

On the upper level of this façade are three windows framed in the same way, with alternating pediments, as the windows in the north wall and with the same type of herms between them. Interestingly, through these windows we can detect the outlines of three windows on the far side of the room, looking onto the Wapper (Fig. 51).[37]

The ordering of the first level, with engaged Doric columns supporting a heavily moulded cornice with a frieze of triglyphs, also corresponds to the north façade. Otherwise, however, the two walls are different. On the ground floor is an arcade consisting of three semicircular arches supported by smaller columns or pilasters clustered with the Doric columns. In the open space behind the arcade a staircase is visible and, on the left, a door to the workshop. On the first floor, according to the print, is an open gallery or loggia in which an exotic dark-skinned figure can be seen, as well as two parrots perched on the balustrade and a small dog in front. As will be explained in Chapter VI, the entire first floor was really one huge *trompe-l'oeil* painting on a flat blank wall. Notably, the print also shows what looks like an unframed painting, suspended beneath two windows and thus concealing part of the 'loggia', the suggestion

---

37. When Mols visited the house in 1763, and perhaps also originally, this was a long room with five windows which ran the entire length of the façade on the street side (referred to by Mols as 'Galerie servant d'Antichambre'; see Appendix I.43: [6]); see, for this room, Chapter VII, p. 202.

CHAPTER V - THE EXTERIOR OF THE STUDIO WING OR 'ITALIAN' WING

being that this is a painting by Rubens – an *Andromeda Liberated by Perseus* – hanging there to dry (No. 18; Figs 107 and 110).

D. *The East Façade on the Garden Side*

With only three bays the workshop's garden-facing east façade (Figs 18, 29) is much shorter than the north wall. On the upper level the corners of the building are quoined in the same long-and-short style as the north-facing courtyard façade, with alternating rectangular and inward-pointing quoins. In the print of 1692, these heavy blocks with their rusticated character are shown in more detail, indicating that the pointed quoins are bossed (Text ill. 66). While quoined façades were the rule for Italian Renaissance houses, we have not managed to find an architectural example of Rubens's unusual alternation with pointed elements. Interestingly, however, the same rare motif, with pointed and bossed quoins, does occur in Rubens's painted oeuvre: in the section above the pediment in the *Homage to Ceres* (Appendix III.13; Fig. 23). It is not easy to determine whether this Italianate architectural element of the façades was really in stone, as suggested in the print, or whether it was simply painted or in stucco.

The similarity of the quoins and the continuing figurative frieze apart, the articulation of the garden façade is very different from the north and east walls facing the courtyard. Instead of herms between the third-level windows there are two full-length figures, apparently standing on shallow bases. They were evidently derived from well-known antique statues, the *Hermes Belvedere* and the *Flora Farnese* (see Nos 5–6; Figs 45 and 48). Perhaps they were rendered as monochrome marble sculptures rather than lifelike figures in colour, a question that can, of course, not be resolved by the print, which is the only known image of this façade. Nor is it clear whether they were painted or made in relief. It seems more likely that they were paintings reminiscent of the kind of full-length figures that Rubens could have seen on Italian façades.[38] As with the herms of the two courtyard façades, it seems that the Harrewijn print does not represent the two

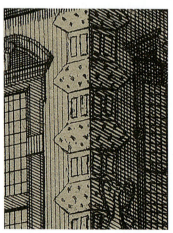

Text ill. 66. Detail of the 1692 Harrewijn print (Fig. 18): the quoins at a corner of the studio wing.

---

38. See e.g. the figures between the windows on the façade of the Palazzo Ricci-Sacchetti in Rome, with frescoes by Polidoro da Caravaggio (Baumstark – Delmarcel, *Decius Mus (CRLB)*, 2019, I, text ill. 29).

CHAPTER V - THE EXTERIOR OF THE STUDIO WING OR 'ITALIAN' WING

figures in their true proportions: they appear too broad, in fact, so that they overlap the window surrounds in several places.

The most obvious difference between the north and east façades, however, is the number of levels: on the east side there are only two. The height of the upper storey is the same as on the north wall, but below that the two levels have become one, filling the space between the ground and the bottom of the figurative frieze, with no suggestion of a *piano nobile* as there is on the north wall, making it much clearer that the room inside – Rubens's workshop – is also this high. The division of the façade into three bays is emphasised by very high banded Doric columns or pilasters that – although not really spanning more than one storey – could be described as an application of the giant or colossal order.

It should be noted that the architecture of this lower part of the garden façade, corresponding in height to the studio, is rusticated. The planar sections of wall between the columns are made up of large clearly defined blocks, and these blocks, as well as the three bands around each column, have a bossed surface (Fig. 29).

As with the north façade, it is also hard to tell which of the east wall's architectural elements were 'real' and which might have been painted in *trompe-l'oeil*. It might be supposed that the engaged columns or pilasters were entirely fictive but what we see in the print tells a different story: from the presupposed viewpoint (the right) the right sides of the bases and capitals are consistently visible, indicating that these elements have depth, a suggestion reinforced by the equally consistent shadows they cast.

In each bay much of the wall is occupied by a large, segmental-arched window; the centre bay also incorporates a double door with a fanlight, forming the rather unusual combination of a door with a very high window. Seen from the garden, the lower level of the east façade, from the ground up to the frieze and corresponding to the studio, looks almost like one great glass wall interrupted only by the two narrow masonry sections. An open conformation like this is more generally found in garden architecture – an orangery, for instance – and is certainly unusual for a workshop. Some have connected this distinctive form with the term *'diaeta'*, used by Philip Rubens for Rubens's studio, and possibly meaning a summer house or garden pavilion (see below).

The Disappearance of the Original Garden Façade and the Reconstruction

When the twentieth-century restoration and reconstruction of the Rubenshuis began, the original and somewhat impractical 'glass' east façade had long since vanished. This certainly happened after Hillewerve's death (in 1694), and most likely during the major renovation of the house that can be placed between 1763 and 1770.

What was encountered in 1938 matched more or less the information provided by François Mols, who visited the house in 1763 and then again later once important alterations had been carried out. This situation is not reflected in his drawing (Fig. 3), but it is described in his written comment: in order to connect the south and the north wings of the house a 'corridor' was built against the garden (or rear) side of the portico at first-floor level (Appendix I.43: [9]). We can assume that on the same occasion the workshop wing was extended by about two and a half metres on the garden side in order to connect with the 'corridor'. The large hipped roof was extended in proportion, and a completely new east façade was constructed.

We can obtain an idea of the substantial alterations to the garden side of the house, still in place in the 1930s, from architectural plans that were drawn up for the expropriation (Figs 4 and 5),[39] as well as several photographs. They show a long, three-storey garden façade, parallel to the Wapper (see e.g. Text ills 105–106). During the modern reconstruction the additional wing on the garden side of the house (including the extension of the former studio) was removed completely, leaving the south wing without an east façade (Text ill. 67). A new wall was built in the original position, in line with the rear side of the portico (Fig. 12).

It must be said that the architects responsible for the reconstruction deviated wrongly and quite considerably from the garden façade as illustrated in the Harrewijn print. Van Averbeke placed no faith whatsoever in the reliability of that depiction, maintaining that it exhibited 'structural inventions' that were entirely due to Hillewerve's predilection for 'ostentatious display' and lambasting the composition of the façade as 'simply ridiculous'.[40]

The façade with its very high windows is indeed rather unusual in design, but it should be noted that a similar arrangement of a window with a door underneath (as in the central bay) could be found elsewhere in Rubens's former house. It appears to the right in the interior of Hillewerve's chapel, in one of the insets at the bottom of the Harrewijn print of 1692 (Fig. 127).

The architects also dismissed Harrewijn's image because it lacked what they considered to be architectural orthodoxy. They found it inconceivable that Rubens would have devised a scheme for the garden façade that differed so greatly from the three-level arrangement of the two Italianate façades facing onto the courtyard. But there can be no doubt that the print reflects that wall's

---

39. For the ground floor, see the plan of July 1932 in Antwerp, FelixArchief, inv. no. MA-PLAN 11961 (Devroe, *Rubens' huis*, 2008, II, p. 63, no. 50, incorrectly as 'July 1937'). For the first floor, see the plan of 1936 in the Archive of the Rubenshuis (ibid., II, p. 64, no. 51).
40. Van Averbeke, *Rubenshuis. Restauratie II*, 1938, p. 27.

CHAPTER V - THE EXTERIOR OF THE STUDIO WING OR 'ITALIAN' WING

Text ill. 67. The studio wing with the demolished apocryph garden or east façade.

original appearance. Their point of view is quite easily refuted. In reality the portico (left out in the print for reasons outlined above) makes it impossible to see the dissimilar lower levels of the walls at the same time – unlike the upper levels, which are largely alike.

There was also another, quite different argument which critics of the Harrewijn version of the garden façade, with its great windows, felt strengthened their view. Rubens himself, they contended – albeit erroneously – had included in the background of *Hélène Fourment au carrosse* (Appendix III.7; Fig. 21) an image of this façade, with a portico and a balcony above it (see below).[41]

As said, the modern reconstruction of the lost east façade (Fig. 12) is not based on the Harrewijn print, nor – as might perhaps be expected – on the detail in the background of Rubens's portrait of his wife. Notwithstanding his criticism, Van Averbeke produced a design that followed the print to a degree, with tall windows and two banded columns at ground level, and with two full-length statues above,[42] but this was never realised. In the end it became a somewhat strange concept, partly based on the north façade, both in the three-

41. For more on this painting as a visual source for the house, see below, pp. 159–161.
42. See his detailed drawing for the restoration of the garden façade, 1939 (Tijs, *Rubens en Jordaens*, 1984, pp. 186–187; Devroe, *Rubens' huis*, 2008, p. 96, no. 77); the same design can be recognised in the wooden model of the house made in 1939–42 (Maclot, *Rubenssite*, 2016, p. 223).

CHAPTER V - THE EXTERIOR OF THE STUDIO WING OR 'ITALIAN' WING

level organisation and, to an extent, on the ornamental sculpture with busts and herms and vases. The heavy first level is striking, with two niches housing modern in-the-round statues of Neptune and Amphitrite that can hardly be called a successful integration.[43] Not only are they carved in a 'swollen' pseudo-baroque style, their subjects are entirely unrelated to the original decoration of Rubens's house. The three windows above them are flanked by busts in the round, while between the upper windows are deity herms, matching those in the reconstructed north façade, instead of the images of the two well-known full-length antique statues (No. 5 and No. 6).[44]

The Workshop as '*Diaeta*'

The east façade as shown in the 1692 Harrewijn print, with its uncommonly open aspect onto the garden, has been associated with the term used by Philip Rubens in his uncle's *Vita* to describe the latter's house. He called it a '*diaeta amplissima*' (Appendix I.26), a phrase that was translated by L.R. Lind as 'a large summer house',[45] but this is not the only possible translation. The Latin term '*diaeta*' can mean both a dwelling-place in general and more specifically an outbuilding or a garden pavilion. So exactly what Philip meant is difficult to determine and is open to interpretation. The importance of a relationship between the house and the garden does, however, seem to be indicated, something to which Ulrich Heinen drew attention. In an elaborate argument he emphasises that, in accord with the 'Lipsian' neo-Stoic school of thought, the connection with the garden is an essential element of the house that Rubens built.[46]

E. The West or Street Façade

The 1692 Harrewijn print includes a view of the west or street side of Rubens's house (Fig. 26). The higher workshop complex is in the centre, flanked more or less symmetrically by the 'old' part of the property in 'Flemish' style on the left, and on the right by a large doorway and the row of small houses that Rubens bought in 1627 (in their drastically remodelled later form).

The central workshop façade is an austere cornice front without an entrance. It has two rows of windows arranged in five regular bays (Fig. 32). This wide façade gives a somewhat misleading idea of the size of the wing behind. The

43. Both statues were made by the Antwerp sculptor Victor Van Esbroeck (1911–2010).
44. The herms represent Apollo and Diana; for the busts, see above, p. 149, n. 34; on the craftsmen who were responsible for the sculpture of this reconstruction, see inter alia Clijmans, *Wederopbouw Rubenshuis*, 1946, p. 80.
45. Lind, *Rubens*, 1946, p. 39; on this topic, see also above, Chapter II, p. 51, n. 5.
46. Heinen, *Gesundheit*, 2004, passim.

CHAPTER V - THE EXTERIOR OF THE STUDIO WING OR 'ITALIAN' WING

workshop itself extends to the width of slightly less than three bays of the street façade, while somewhat more than two bays (to the left) belong to the adjoining, very narrow, 'short leg' of the L-shaped complex – the part at right-angles to the workshop.[47]

The five upper windows are rectangular, almost square, with 'crossettes' and no further decoration; the bottom row consists of very tall windows with semicircular arches at the top with a decorative motif in the solid tympanum; in the lower section they are protected by wrought-iron grilles. Closed shutters, fixed to the insides of the windows and apparently made of wood, can be seen behind the grilles, leaving – interestingly – a strip of glass uncovered at the top (Text ill. 68). This rather unusual layout confirms the assumption that behind the five very tall windows there is not one high storey – as appears at first glance – but two: ground floor and mezzanine.[48] In the design of the façade these two lower storeys are not visually separated from each other, as the windows continue uninterrupted. But they are divided, about half way up, by a horizontal stone architrave.

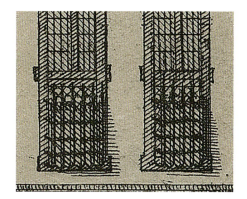

Text ill. 68. Detail of the 1692 Harrewijn print (Fig. 18): two windows of the lower section of the west façade.

Text ill. 69. The street façade in 1930.

At the time of the reconstruction of the house in the 1930s, the seventeenth-century street façade of the studio had completely vanished (Text ill. 69), and the new façade faithfully followed the Harrewijn print, but for a few details:

47. It should be noted that the bays of the street front and two east façades do not correspond in width. The three bays of the garden façade of the workshop (in total c. 8.5 m) are slightly narrower than those of the street front, while those of the courtyard façade are narrower still (in total c. 6.5 m).
48. We can assume that, when the shutters were closed, the uncovered strip of glass under the horizontal architrave provided light for a room at street level (underneath a mezzanine). For the mezzanine in the studio wing, see also the chapter dealing with the interior of this wing (Chapter VII, pp. 203–204).

the architraves of the high windows acquired more 'bands' (Fig. 13), in a form based on the façade of the sacristy of the former Antwerp Jesuit Church.[49]

To what extent the street façade depicted in the Harrewijn print corresponds to its appearance in Rubens's day is difficult to say. In any case the buildings shown to the right (the south) of the former workshop were largely remodelled. What was originally an open passageway to the garden was turned into a roofed-over coach house and the small houses were also rebuilt, with the three dwellings (bought by Rubens in 1627) becoming two.[50]

A more important question is the degree to which details in the workshop façade were altered after 1640. Did that frontage really display the robust character it had in Hillewerve's time? One can imagine that this side of the workshop was also enlivened with decorative details, painted or otherwise, though perhaps less exuberantly than the garden and courtyard façades. There are no indications that the five windows in the top storey were surrounded by painted decorative elements of the kind we know from the north and east façades; there is also no sign of a frieze of rectangular narrative panels below them, but it is not impossible that it had actually been there in Rubens's time.

Lastly it should be noted that in *Hélène Fourment au carrosse* (Appendix III.7; Fig. 21) Rubens depicted a completely different type of street front that bore little relationship to reality (see below).

F. The Problematic South Façade: The South Side of the Workshop

Neither of the Harrewijn prints shows the south wall of the workshop wing. Nor does it appear in any other image, unless the building in the background of *Hélène Fourment au carrosse* (Fig. 21) is considered as something more than an idealised and fictional image of the house. In the portrait we see a narrow vertical strip of a wall perpendicular to the Wapper, with windows and ornamental elements that in many respects match those of the north façade, but to what extent this is a depiction of the south façade as it really existed is hard to judge (see below).

As explained above, it is evident from archival sources that when the studio was built, this façade was an exterior wall alongside an open passageway, which was around four meters wide and led from the Wapper to the garden. In Hillewerve's time the lower part of this original façade had become an interior wall, while a storey had been built over the passageway, a situation that can

---

49. Illustrated in Lombaerde, *Significance*, 2002, figs 13, 14 (p. 62); Fabri – Lombaerde, *Jesuit Church (CRLB)*, 2018, fig. 133.
50. For this conversion, see Chapter III, p. 102.

CHAPTER V · THE EXTERIOR OF THE STUDIO WING OR 'ITALIAN' WING

be seen in the Harrewijn print of 1692: on the garden side (Fig. 29) as well the street side (Fig. 26).

One important aspect of the south façade that is omitted here, because it primarily concerns the interior, is whether or not there were windows on this side in Rubens's day. Did the studio perhaps not only have large windows on the north and east sides, but also – contrary to expectation – to the south? We shall attend to this question in more detail in the chapter dealing with the interior of the studio wing.[51]

G. *The Idealised Street and South Façades: The House in the Background of 'Hélène Fourment au Carrosse'*

Thus far the descriptions of the façades have been based on the Harrewijn prints and the Aylesbury painting, with additional information coming from the surviving house itself, including data revealed during the restoration. But there is another important visual source to consider, one which has already been mentioned several times, that being the Italianate house that Rubens depicted in the background of *Hélène Fourment au carrosse*, dating from the 1630s (Appendix III.7; Fig. 31). It should be emphasised that the house in the picture is not the house Rubens actually built on the Wapper – all the indications are to the contrary – but rather what he saw as his ideal home in the 1630s, and possibly also while it was being built twenty years earlier.

Rubens's handsomely dressed young wife is going out, wearing a *huyck* (a black cloak-like garment) made from the most expensive, finely pleated transparent silk.[52] She is leaving her palatial home, descending from a porch that is vaguely defined by steps, a column and pilasters.

Although this porch cannot be associated with any actual residence on the Wapper, the street is undoubtedly a more or less faithful rendition of the Wapper. On the left the canal known as the Vaart disappears under an arch. Running alongside it is a row of tall trees (whose tops appear on the right of the 1692 Harrewijn print, rising above the roofs of Rubens's house (Text ill. 30). In the distance, at the end of the Wapper, a house on the north side of the Meir can be seen. It is a traditional stepped-gable house in brick and sandstone, and with three bays, a type of town house that was very common in the Low Countries in the sixteenth century, and most of the houses on the Meir were of the same basic type but with slight variations. The impressive Italianate urban palace on

---

51. See Chapter VII, pp. 205–210.
52. Extensively on the *huyck* (*huyck* in 17th-century Dutch, 'huik' in Dutch, 'huke' etc. in English), see Watteeuw, *Material Girl*, 2019, pp. 183–223.

CHAPTER V - THE EXTERIOR OF THE STUDIO WING OR 'ITALIAN' WING

the Wapper is in marked contrast to this 'old' or 'Flemish' style. We see its street frontage as well as part of the wall perpendicular to it –i.e. the south façade.

Although depicted on a small scale and somewhat vaguely, it can nonetheless be established that the Italianate house has a number of general characteristics that correspond to the workshop wing as we know it from the Harrewijn prints: the same volume with three levels, a hipped roof, a strongly projecting eaves cornice supported by modillions, and heavy quoining. A number of details, both architectural and decorative, are also very similar. The gilded sphere and sun-shaped weathervane on the ridge end, which appears in the Harrewijn print, can also be seen here, shimmering through the transparent fabric of Helena Fourment's *huyck* (Fig. 31).

As was the case in Rubens's property, to the right of the main façade a lower wall with a gateway is depicted. Foliage above it suggests a garden, when in reality the gate gave access to an open passageway that was probably devoid of greenery, leading to the garden and stables. The street front of the idealised house on the Wapper consists of three bays with a prominent centre ressault: the front door is framed by a porch with Doric (?) columns supporting a balcony with a balustraded parapet. This arrangement is a simplified version of what is seen in the façades of several Roman palazzi.[53]

There are no indications that such a façade, with portico and balcony, was ever part of Rubens's workshop wing, not even on the garden side, as was once erroneously believed.[54] Then again, this type of articulation, with a powerful central ressault, does bring to mind what Rubens had to say about the town house Constantijn Huygens had built to his own design in The Hague. In Rubens's judgement the excessive simplicity ('la troppo simplicità') of both the entrance gate to the forecourt and the front door was to be regretted, as it was too modest for a town mansion; the design of the whole façade demanded more dignity and relief ('magior dignità e relievo à tutta la facciata').[55]

The acute perspective and rather vague rendering of the street side of the idealised house in Rubens's portrait make a reading of the features of the upper levels problematic. In the wall perpendicular to the Wapper, on the other hand, details can be distinguished, at least in the first and only bay that can be seen (Fig. 31). On the second level is a round-headed window with a few blocks that bears some resemblance to the windows in the actual street façade of Rubens's

---

53. For example, the façades of the Palazzo Borghese (Cresti – Rendini, *Palazzi*, 1998, fig. pp. 17, 256) and the Palazzo del Quirinale; for a version without free-standing columns, see the façades of the Palazzo Farnese, the Villa Giulia (ibid., fig. pp. 110, 168) and the rear façade of the Villa Medici (Toulier, *Villa Médicis*, I, 1989, pp. 292–293, figs 361–363). On this type of entrance porch, with other examples, see also Lombaerde, *Significance*, 2002, p. 59, n. 28.
54. Delen saw the detail in the portrait as probably representing the corner of the east and north façades (Delen, *Rubens' huis*, 1933, p. 42); repeated, among others by Devroe, *Rubens' huis*, 2008, I, p. 34; II, p. 41, cat. 34.
55. Citations from Ottenheym, *Rubens en Huygens*, 1997, pp. 6–7, Appendix IV, pp. 8–10; id., *La Vera Simmetria*, 2007, 149–150.

CHAPTER V - THE EXTERIOR OF THE STUDIO WING OR 'ITALIAN' WING

workshop. The rectangular pedimented window in the upper level (Fig. 55) more or less matches the windows in the actual north façade, although it is ornamented on either side with a small pendant festoon, of which there is no trace in the Harrewijn prints.[56]

Of particular interest as regards our knowledge of the real workshop wing is the clearly discernible *grisaille* panel directly beneath the window in the idealised south façade, which seems to be of the same type as the panels of the frieze on the real north and east walls. Rubens may also have represented (vaguely) matching panels in the street front of the imaginary house, but these are harder to see. Nevertheless, as mentioned above, it raises the question of whether, in the real house, the frieze of figurative panels, rendered in monochrome like *trompe-l'oeil* stone reliefs, adorned not only the north and east façades but continued on the other walls as well.

Finally, there is another interesting factor that emerges from the portrait: it gives us an image in colour of the idealised house on the Wapper. The heavy quoining, the architraves and the mouldings are all pale (as if in whitish stone), and the areas of wall in between are reddish, a colour combination found in Italian façades that Rubens would certainly have known and might have replicated in his house.[57] Indeed, it seems quite possible that this white and red colour scheme, represented by Rubens himself, was a characteristic of the real studio wing.[58]

H. The Italianate Character of the Studio Wing

It can be assumed that Rubens had the wing containing his workshop built to his own plan and that this would have involved both the general layout and the ornamental details. So what did he base his design on? The façades of that wing have a distinctly Italianate character, but apart from certain details discussed above, there is no immediately obvious model.

Genoa

It might be expected that Rubens would have drawn inspiration from the façades of Genoese palaces of the second half of the sixteenth century, of which

---

56. A similar motif can also be seen on either side of the round niches in the garden pavilion in *The Walk in the Garden* in the Alte Pinakothek in Munich (Fig. 182).
57. See, for example, the Porta Pia; the street façades of the Palazzo Borghese (Cresti – Rendina, *Palazzi*, 1998, fig. pp. 17, 256), the Palazzo Farnese (ibid., fig. p. 110) and the rear façade of the Villa Medici in Rome (Toulier, *Villa Médicis*, I, 1989, fig. 361).
58. In the only other coloured image of Rubens's studio wing – the Aylesbury painting of c. 1660 (Appendix III.3; Figs 16, 27) – the walls are again reddish, but besides the white decorative elements, the architraves, pediments, mouldings, etc. are mainly black.

CHAPTER V - THE EXTERIOR OF THE STUDIO WING OR 'ITALIAN' WING

he owned a series of detailed drawings that he reproduced as engravings in his *Palazzi di Genova*, published in 1621.[59] But, surprisingly, that is not in fact the case. In the older literature it was sometimes taken as read that the striking north façade was based on borrowings from Genoese palazzi, from which it may be concluded that the unmistakable Italian influence was simply and uncritically seen as 'Genoese'.[60] This misconception was convincingly corrected by Konrad Ottenheym and Piet Lombaerde, however, and likewise by Herbert Rott, who rightly said of the north wall that 'the façade decoration, with its luxuriant architectural and figurative embellishments is not based on a specific model'.[61] Indeed, the similarities that some claimed to see are hardly convincing. As mentioned earlier, the device of alternating pediments, which was employed in most Genoese palace façades, is too general and, as such, is hardly a valid argument. Equally inconsequential is the fact that in two examples of the *Palazzi* façades, herms – of a different type from those adorning the workshop wall – appear between the windows.[62]

Just as striking to note is that the north façade is not the only part of the house to lack Genoese elements in its decoration. The portico and the other façades of the studio wing (the street front, the 'glass' garden wall and the façade with the *trompe-l'oeil* loggia) have even fewer similarities to images in the *Palazzi* prints. The only possible conclusion is that the design of his new house bears no relationship to the drawings he brought from Italy and had in his possession at the time of its construction.

This observation is somewhat surprising, for in his foreword ('Al benigno lettore') to the *Palazzi di Genova* Rubens himself writes that in promoting the beauty of cities in the provinces north of the Alps the palaces depicted in its pages can be taken as examples. The palazzi of Genoa's urban elite, he points out, are not intended for ruling princes with a court to accommodate, but are ideal as town houses for gentry and wealthy patricians, whom he describes as 'private gentlemen' ('Gentilhuomini privati').[63] It may be wondered – assuming Rubens's recommendation was not purely rhetorical – which gentlemen in Antwerp and the Netherlands he would have had in mind. In any case, the

---

59. For this well-known publication, see Rott, *Palazzi (CRLB)*, 2002, I–II.
60. Indebtedness to the *Palazzi di Genova* was suggested by, for example Schoy, *Rubens*, 1878, p. 36; Rooses, *Rubens*, 1904, p. 146; Parent, *L'Architecture des Pays-Bas*, 1926, p. 49; Delen, *Rubens' huis*, 1933, p. 20. For a survey of this erroneous point of view, see also Lombaerde, *Distribution*, 2002, pp. 103–106. Italian influence in Rubens's house described simply as 'Genoese', also in Zimmermann, *Rubenshaus*, 2004, passim. One who disagreed with that prevalent opinion was Van de Castijne, *Question*, 1931, p. 111.
61. Ottenheym, *Rubens en Huygens*, 1997, p. 10, n. 20; id., *Palazzi di Genova*, 2002, pp. 86–87; Lombaerde, *Distribution*, 2002, pp. 103–106; Rott, *Palazzi (CRLB)*, 2002, I, pp. 87–89.
62. See No. 4.
63. For the text of the Foreword, a single page in length, see inter alia: Tijs, *Rubens en Jordaens*, 1984, fig. p. 20 (facsimile); Lombaerde, *Significance*, 2002. pp. 78–80 (English translation and facsimile); Rott, *Palazzi (CRLB)*, 2002, I, p. 254 and p. 255 (English translation from which the citation above was drawn); Antwerp, 2011, p. 9, fig. 1 (facsimile), cat. no. 23.

Genoese palazzi were built for a clientele whose financial resources far exceeded his own. The purpose the building was to serve was also an essential factor. Rubens had little need of representative spaces like the salons and reception rooms that were important to Genoese patricians. His Italianate south wing on the Wapper had a different and more specific function, and its dimensions were also different from those of the examples he published in *Palazzi di Genova*. It was a commercial space with a surface area of approximately nine by nineteen metres and outer walls of twelve metres in height. It was therefore considerably smaller in volume than the imposing Genoese urban palaces, which often took the form of a solid cube.

Mantua

Nothing in the workshop wing indicates that Rubens took the architecture he had encountered in Mantua as a model. It was once suggested that he had Giulio Romano's Mantuan house (Text ill. 70) in mind when he was designing the north façade of his atelier, whose basic articulation was seen as comparable to the street façade of the Italian artist's house. That building too had large arched windows over a rusticated ground floor and a central portal with pediment above it.[64] The decorative elements are entirely different, however, and the existence of a similar basic organisation, or rather the same number of bays, seems too meagre a reason to speak of influence.

Rome

Rubens's nephew, Philip Rubens, tells us that his uncle built his workshop in the Roman style ('romanâ formâ') (Appendix I.26), information that was repeated literally by Roger de Piles, who writes that Rubens bought a large house that he rebuilt 'à la Romaine' (Appendix I.31). On closer examination there seem to be some grounds for the reference to Rome.

As has already been mentioned, in the workshop façades there are reminiscences of the garden façade of the Villa Medici in Rome (1576–1587)(Text ill. 72), a building which Rubens would certainly have known. Similarities can be seen in several windows in that façade. In the same façade, moreover, antique reliefs have been set into frames in the wall, a motif that Rubens apparently sought to imitate in his *grisailles*. There are some striking similarities to the north façade of Rubens's workshop to be seen in another Roman building too, the Palazzo Mattei di Giove. In the opulently ornamented façades of the first

---

64. Rott, *Palazzi (CRLB)*, 2002, I, p. 88, text ill. 18; originally the façade had six bays, with five windows, enlarged by two bays in 1800. On this house, see Chapter VI, p. 200, n. 101. In connection with Rubens's house, see Stutz, *Residenz*, 1985, p. 142.

CHAPTER V - THE EXTERIOR OF THE STUDIO WING OR 'ITALIAN' WING

Text ill. 70. Façade of Giulio Romano's house, Mantua.

courtyard we find not only similar window framing and archaicised reliefs but also a series of busts set in niches (Text ill. 71).[65] Last, but not least, as we will see below, Rubens's impressive portico is also 'Roman' in character.

It hardly comes as a surprise to find that when Rubens built his house he looked for a model not so much in the architecture of Italy in general but rather, and more particularly, in the buildings of Rome. That Rubens should be enraptured by the Eternal City was virtually a matter of course, given that around 1615 he was part of a culture whose highest good was the revival of Antiquity.[66] In sixteenth-century Rome, patrons and architects had taken initiatives in pursuit of their ideal, which was no less than the reconstruction of classical Rome. This was reflected in the relaying of streets and squares

---

65. Cresti – Rendina, *Palazzi*, 1998, pp. 126–127; Uppenkamp – Van Beneden, *Architectural Symbolism*, 2011, p. 112, fig. 150. We have not been able to establish if the decoration of this Roman courtyard was completed before Rubens left Italy, and therefore if could have seen it as it appears today.
66. For this aspect of Rubens's art, see the chapter 'Reconstructing the Ancient Past' in Baumstark – Delmarcel, *Decius Mus (CRLB)*, 2019, I, pp. 65 ff.

CHAPTER V - THE EXTERIOR OF THE STUDIO WING OR 'ITALIAN' WING

Text ill. 71. Façade in the first courtyard of the Palazzo Mattei di Giove, Rome.

and the construction of new buildings. Scholars and artists made intensive studies of the architecture their antique forbears had left behind in the city, and they pored over the writings of Vitruvius, seen as the foundation of all good architecture.[67] This said, to return to the above remarks about Genoa, one cannot help wondering why 'Rome-oriented' Rubens published the large collection of 'Genovese' drawings he owned, but did not use them at all for the design of his own house, not even for the decoration of the façades.

---

67. For a detailed discussion of the connection between Rome and Rubens's house, see Uppenkamp – Van Beneden, *Vera simmetria*, 2011, pp. 34–42.

Chapter VI
The 'Italian' Wing:
The Wall Paintings

A. Painted or 'Real': A Problematic Matter

There is no doubt that some of the decorative elements on three of the workshop complex walls – the north and east courtyard façades and the east-facing garden façade – were painted in *trompe-l'oeil* on a flat surface rather than rendered in relief or in the round.[1] As we have already seen, it is not always possible to be absolutely sure what was painted and what was 'real' – that is modelled in stucco or carved in stone. What is certain, however, is that painting formed an essential and striking part of the decoration, a fact supported by sufficient evidence, as we shall see below.

The Witnesses: Written Sources

The earliest and also completely reliable reference stating that parts of the studio façade were painted occurs in an inscription in a drawing by Willem Panneels, who lived in Rubens's house for several years in the 1620s.[2] One of the many copies he made shows a scene from the façade, *Alexander with the Thunderbolt*, which he captioned, in the cryptographic code he devised, as follows: 'Dit is een ordinansi die geschildert is opt huys van sinor rubbens [...]' ('This is a design that is painted on the house of seigneur Rubens') (see No. 12, Copy; Fig. 84).

Also important are the eyewitness accounts by those who had seen the paintings before radical alterations were made to the house in the late eighteenth century. The Swedish architect Nicodemus Tessin (1654–1728), who passed through Antwerp on his way home from Italy in 1687, visited the house, then occupied by Hendrik Hillewerve, and recorded the fact in his travel diary: 'We also saw Rubens's house where he lived and painted his works, which was painted in *al fresco* in several places on the exterior' ('welches al fresco auf ettzliche stellen ausswendig war geschillert') (Appendix I.34).

---

1. As far as is known there is no reliable image of the south façade so it will not be considered here; the section of what is possibly an imaginary south façade, seen in the background of the *Portrait of Hélène Fourment au carrosse* (Appendix III.7; Fig. 31), provides too little certain information (see Chapter V, pp. 159–161). On the possibility of the existence of paintings on this south façade, and also on the street façade of the workshop, which was built in a sober style (according to the Harrewijn print), see below, Chapter V, pp. 158, 161; and below, p. 175.
2. See above, Chapter II, pp. 58–59.

CHAPTER VI - THE 'ITALIAN' WING - THE WALL PAINTINGS

François Mols, who viewed the house several times when it was up for sale in 1763, mentions the wall paintings in his notes. Amongst his observations – written in the past tense – is the following: 'It was mostly on the large walls facing onto the courtyard and the garden, between the first and second floors, that we saw these paintings, which survived for a long time and would have survived even longer had they not been neglected. They represented several mythological subjects in different compartments the same width as the windows ("plusieurs sujets de fable en différents compartiments de la largeur des fenêtres")', without any doubt referring to the frieze panels (Appendix I.43: I[2]). He went on to describe in fuller detail a fairly large picture of *Andromeda Liberated by Perseus* that could be seen in the courtyard, and to which we shall return.

Jacobus van der Sanden, author of the manuscript *Oud Konst-Tooneel van Antwerpen*, which was completed around 1770,[3] also uses the past tense when referring to the painted façades of Rubens's house. He writes that a good deal has changed since 'Jonker de Bosschaert' became owner of the house. Van der Sanden had seen the building before and adds that 'gelijk ik ook de mueren van buijten heb beschilderd gezien in fresco met colossale en klijndere Belden' (I have also seen the outside walls painted in fresco with colossal and smaller figures) (Appendix I.42: [2]).

Mols and Van der Sanden were both writing around 1760–1770 and, as said, both used the past tense. Almost 150 years after their creation, when the house was for sale in 1763, the wall paintings were still to be seen, albeit in poor condition, and it seems that they disappeared completely a few years later, around 1766, when major alterations to the property were carried out by the new owner, the De Bosschaert (de Pret) family.[4]

The wall paintings are also mentioned in a number of printed biographies of Rubens. The Florentine art historian and artists' biographer Filippo Baldinucci (1624–1697) gives the most details in his 'notizia' on Rubens, written in 1681 and published posthumously in 1702. Rubens, he tells us, '[…] built himself a large and most noble palace all in the modern Italian style, with pools ("bozzi") and other adornments, inside of which he painted with his hand a loggia with perspectives, architecture, and bas-reliefs of rich invention […]' (Appendix I.32). He also relates how the Infanta Isabella was taken in by a piece of *trompe-l'oeil* painting during a visit to Rubens's house (see below). One wonders what Baldinucci's source was for his description of the façade painting. Perhaps his informant was someone from the Netherlands who had joined the Florentine art world and who had known the house of the celebrated Rubens in his youth.[5]

3. On this manuscript and its author, see above, Chapter II, p. 78, n. 84.
4. See above, Chapter II, p. 78, n. 82.
5. One might think of Justus Sustermans (1597–1681), who was trained in Antwerp and stayed there until

It may have been on the basis of Baldinucci's text that the Parisian engraver Pierre-François Basan (1723–1797) also made a brief mention of the wall paintings in the biography of Rubens with which he prefaced his catalogue of Rubens prints, published in 1767: 'il orna la façade de Peintures à fresque' (he adorned the façade with frescoes) (Appendix I.41).

The Part Played by Paintings on the Façade: The Ratio between Real and Fictional

From the above witness accounts it is clear that there is sufficient documentation establishing the presence of paintings on the façades of the studio wing. But the sources cited tell us little about which parts were painted as opposed to 'real'. In other words: how significant were the paintings within the overall programme of the façade?

Baldinucci mentions bas-reliefs, a loggia and a painting in *trompe-l'oeil*, by which he clearly means the frieze and what can be seen on the east façade facing the courtyard in the Harrewijn print of 1692 (Fig. 30).

We can be certain that the figurative scenes of the frieze were painted, as emerges from the annotation on the drawing by Willem Panneels, and is confirmed by François Mols. Mols is the only eyewitness to provide detailed information on what exactly was painted on Rubens's walls. He mentions the painting representing *Andromeda Liberated*, and he unequivocally refers to the frieze panels labelling them as 'sujets de fable' on the façade, located under the windows, between the first and second floors. Mols knew the Harrewijn prints and he no doubt used them to complement what he remembered seeing when drawing up his description.

It is less obvious what Van der Sanden is referring to when mentioning 'colossal and smaller figures' (Appendix I.42: [2]). Possibly these too are figures appearing in the history scenes, the large *Andromeda* painting but also the smaller frieze panels. However, it may be that the 'colossal figures' refer to the herms between the third-level windows (No. 4, Fig. 41) and the two full-length figures on the garden façade (Nos 5–6, Figs 44 and 47), while the 'smaller figures' refer to the frieze (Nos 8–16, Figs 57, 60, 64, 69, 82, 90, 98, 101 and 106).

An important aspect, about which the sources mentioned teach us nothing, is whether or not some of the architectural elements – niches, window surrounds, pediments, half-columns – were painted in *trompe-l'oeil* rather than carved in stone or modelled in stucco. After all, as we shall see below, this type of painted

---

going abroad around 1616; for this date, see Martin, *Cat. London, NG (Flemish School)*, 1970, p. 250. In any case, when describing the façade in his 'notizia' written in 1681, Baldinucci could not have derived his information from the Harrewijn prints (dated 1684 and 1692).

decoration was an important component of the façades decorated with fresco paintings, which Rubens had encountered in several Italian cities.[6]

Archaeological Research

As stated in the previous chapter, when research was carried out in the 1930s in preparation for the modern reconstruction, nothing whatsoever remained visible on the façades – or more specifically the north façade, the only one still standing at the time – that might provide an answer to this question. The north façade was completely flat, and without elements carved in stone or modelled in stucco (Text ills 59 and 60). But did such elements once adorn the façade, and were they later removed? Remains uncovered in the course of archaeological research demonstrate that this is indeed what must have happened with parts of the decoration: discovery of the bases of the engaged columns on the ground floor suggests that these columns (and perhaps also the niches) had existed. A further indication that the façade used to contain actual niches is the existence of a bust fully in the round (No. 1, Copy; Fig. 35). Another significant discovery was made in the garden: bluestone fragments that may have come from the façade.[7]

A Closer Look at the Visual Sources: The Harrewijn Prints and the Aylesbury Painting

By the 1930s the two original east façades had disappeared, while the north façade was, as said, entirely flat and without decoration. The only images of the façades we are currently aware of predating the photographic records of the 1930s, are the anonymous Aylesbury *View of the Courtyard of Rubens's House* from about 1660 and the two Harrewijn prints. What can be deduced from these visual sources in connection with our present question: real or fictional? We have focused our investigation on the north façade, as shown in the painting and the print of 1684 (Figs 17 and 28), ignoring the second print.[8] Both images show the richly decorated north façade more or less from the same viewpoint – it appears to the right – in foreshortened perspective, and with the light falling from the left (the east). Parts that jut out are accentuated by deep shadows, which consistently fall on the right.

It is striking that in both images all of the decorations adorning the north façade are defined, to a greater or lesser extent, as carved in relief or in the

6. For detailed discussion of the Italian façades, see in the present chapter, pp. 190–196.
7. See Chapter V, pp. 140 (nn. 4, 6), 143 (n. 11).
8. The print of 1692 shows the two east façades, but it adds little information on the question discussed here; the north façade is simply depicted in reverse (on the use of mirror image in the prints, see Chapter III, pp. 90–91).

round – so much so that we would be deceived by their appearance if it were not for the written testimonies. In the Aylesbury painting the relief of the north façade is much more pronounced (Fig. 27). Compared with the smaller format of the etching, the medium of the work was more amenable in this respect. The detail is given on a much larger scale, in a medium that allows more subtlety, through the use of the colour, and moreover it was produced by an artist with more talent for the representation of complicated architecture. But even so we should not take too literally what we see. The frieze pictures are shown deceptively as if they were reliefs in a whitish stone. The same applies to a number of decorative elements such as the festoons underneath the *oculus*, the cornucopias, the little dolphins in the spandrels, and the herms between the windows. Like the frieze, these parts were probably also not really in relief. For other parts it is harder to be so sure. Pilasters and some mouldings are clearly shown as having depth with shadows on the right. The pediment above the double door, for instance, is plainly three-dimensional: the way it is depicted suggests a projection of quite some depth (Fig. 37). Also conspicuous is the furthest herm which stands out in high relief against the sky (a detail, however, which cannot accord with what was actually visible).[9]

The majority of these elements are also shown unmistakably as in relief in the Harrewijn print of 1684. For instance, the herm busts between the windows and their pedestals are depicted as projecting forward, in the round: we see their profile and they therefore seem to be 'real' (Figs 33, 36, 38). For most decorative elements, e.g. the volute-like ornaments in the window spandrels, we can see their right-hand side. The majority of architectural elements are also clearly shown as in the round, in perspective with shadow on the right-hand side. As in the painting, parts that project (cornices of the pedestals) intersect the adjoining window frames.

Theoretically speaking it would be possible to paint *trompe-l'oeil* decorations onto a wall in this manner – that is with elements that overlap one another – but this can be ruled out in the case of Rubens's façade. It is especially the overlapping of architectural details such as the large pediment in front of the windows (i.e. covering real panes of glass) that simply cannot be interpreted as *trompe-l'oeil* painting. Furthermore, one would expect that a different viewpoint would have been preferable in order to realise the *trompe-l'oeil* effect: from the centre rather than at such an acute angle to the right.

In short, a firm answer to the question 'real' or 'not real' can only be given to a limited degree, and originally there were undoubtedly a good many 'real' elements on the façade in stone or stucco, of which no trace remains.

---

9. As can be seen in the Harrewijn print, there was no herm at the far left of the façade. To left and right the façade was closed by a row of quoins, and a footed vase (Fig. 17).

CHAPTER VI - THE 'ITALIAN' WING - THE WALL PAINTINGS

Discussion and the Modern Reconstruction of the Façades

Given the written sources cited above it is quite surprising that the existence of wall paintings on the façades of Rubens's 'Italian wing' has long been disputed or even flatly denied. The series of figurative scenes that run like a frieze across the three façades, for instance, was seen as being carved in bas-relief and was also executed as such during the Rubenshuis reconstruction (Figs 10–12). Even more baffling is the fact that more than seventy years after that reconstruction, which has meanwhile come to be generally regarded as a misinterpretation, the theory that there had never been even a hint of painting on Rubens's walls was once again put forward, supported by lengthy arguments.[10]

Max Rooses was familiar with only two of the aforementioned testimonies – those of Tessin and Mols – yet quite correctly he had no doubt that paintings covered a part of the workshop walls.[11] That conviction was shared by Ary Delen, who reacted pretty sharply against the persistent misreading by those responsible for the restoration: as early as 1933, thus several years before the work started, and again in 1940, when it was underway.[12] He evidently found it impossible to accept the inclusion of carved reliefs in the reconstruction of the façades, although it has to be said that he failed to propose a plausible alternative.

Émile Van Averbeke, the architect in charge of the restoration, was well aware that the façades had been painted yet still opted for a sculptural solution, adducing two reasons for doing so. He was convinced that painting would not last long in 'our climate' and he also believed that Rubens himself had regarded the painting as merely a stop-gap at a time when adequate funds were lacking: '[…] he sought to create the illusion that the façades were finished, until such a time as circumstances allowed him to complete the ensemble'.[13] Obviously this notion can simply be dismissed.

---

10. Motivated amongst other things by the view that *trompe-l'oeil* is alien to Rubens's art ('n'entre pas dans son univers mental') (Coekelberghs, *Review Palazzo Rubens*, 2012, [pp. 9–13]; none of the cited testimonies seem to be valid to Coekelberghs; he doubts the authenticity of the inscription on Panneels's drawing in the Cantoor; he concedes that there were paintings in Mols's time but assumes that they were executed after 1681 to correspond to Baldinucci's account, which he believes should be regarded as entirely imaginary.
11. Rooses, *Rubens*, 1904, pp. 147–149; id., *Huis van Rubens*, 1910, p. 203 [p. 15]. When Rooses published his first studies of Rubens's house in 1888 (id., *Maison*, 1888, p. 220 and Rooses – Ruelens, eds, *Correspondance*, 1887–1909, II, pp. 153–159) Tessin's testimony was not yet known; Mols's account was sufficient for him to assume that a part of the walls were painted. But he was not sure whether that was also the case for the herms between the upper windows, which he thought could have been in relief; he refers to 'des cariatides peintes ou sculptées' (ibid., II, p. 153).
12. Delen, *Rubens' huis*, 1933, p. 34; Id., *Rubens' huis*, 1940, pp. 29–31. In this last work (p. 30) he writes that in contrast to earlier doubts, 'de termenfiguren tusschen de vensters van de verdieping en […] b.v. de dolfijnen en bloemfestoenen langsheen de vensters' (the herms between the first-floor windows and […] e.g. the dolphins and festoons of flowers along the windows) were painted.
13. 'Hij wou de illusie wekken dat de gevels áf waren, in afwachting dat de omstandigheden hem zouden toelaten het ensemble te voltooien'. Van Averbeke's opinion – that Rubens chose paintings as a temporary solution due to lack of money – can be found in his notes (Devroe, *Rubens' huis*, 2008, I, p. 104) and is

Ultimately, all that can be said is that today the reconstruction of the north façade, which more or less follows the decorative programme of the Harrewijn prints, but entirely in relief, gives us what is certainly an incorrect but still acceptable picture of the original façade.

However, in the case of the other façade looking onto the courtyard – the short east-facing wall (Fig. 11) – a misreading of the print resulted in a reconstruction which differs drastically from the seventeenth-century situation: the painted *trompe-l'oeil* loggia was created in stonework as if there had been a real one (see below).

B. Technique, Execution and Date

Which method was used to produce the wall paintings is not known. The literature often refers to them as 'frescoes' but whether or not they were actually executed in the Italian 'al fresco' technique remains to be seen. Hence the use here of the more neutral 'wall painting'.[14] Of course, this question also raises another: who was responsible for carrying out the many square metres of painting on the walls? Assistants from Rubens's workshop? That the master himself would have painted his own walls, as Baldinucci suggested ('dipinse de sua mano'; Appendix I.32), seems very unlikely. There is no reason to suppose that he would have been clambering about on scaffolding, brushes in hand, when he could have been spending his time far more profitably in every respect – not least financially – on the huge commissions that came his way from very early on.

As said, there is no information at all about who actually executed the wall paintings, and we are almost equally in the dark about when the work was done. The earliest evidence of their existence, and so providing a (not really useful) *terminus ante quem*, comes in the form of the copies drawn by Willem Panneels when he was resident in Rubens's house in the 1620s (c. 1622–c. 1630).[15]

We assume that Rubens designed the decorations of the façades – painted or otherwise – around 1615, or even somewhat earlier, making several drawings (possibly with variants) that have not survived. There is no trace of drawings except for two designs for the frieze panels (No. 10a, No. 13a; Figs 65, 96) and two vaguely sketched architectural studies in black chalk (No. 7a, No. 13b; Figs 54, 97).

---

   also mentioned in Clijmans' publications (Clijmans, *Wederopbouw Rubenshuis*, 1941, p. 49; id., *Wederopbouw Rubenshuis*, 1946, p. 60).
14. For suggestions about the possible technique ('some technique of oil painting on stone'), with a reference to Giorgio Vasari (among others), see McGrath, *Rubens's House*, 1978, p. 247, n. 7.
15. For Panneels and his drawings, see Chapter II, pp. 58–59..

CHAPTER VI - THE 'ITALIAN' WING - THE WALL PAINTINGS

As for any stylistic assessment, not much can be gleaned from the small and schematic depiction of the frieze in the Harrewijn prints, or even the more detailed depiction in the Aylesbury painting. More can be learned from compositional details, especially in the surviving drawings: it should be noted that scenes in the frieze contain hints of works that Rubens produced before 1616, specifically from the period between 1613 and 1615.[16]

Of course this possible date for the designs is not much help in dating the decoration of the façades; it remains an even greater challenge to establish a date of execution for the façade paintings themselves once the walls had been constructed. If we assume that Rubens did not leave his walls unpainted, whether completely or in part, for any great length of time, it follows that at least the architectural and ornamental elements – including the frieze depicted as a relief in stone – which all form an integral part of the architecture as it were, must have been painted as soon as the studio wing was finished. That is to say sometime in the years 1615 to 1617 and certainly no later than 1617, for in that year the workshop was already operational,[17] and very probably completely finished. We favour this assumption, and this is why all the selected decorative elements included in the catalogue, not only the frieze panels, but also the herms and busts – which cannot always be defined as painted or carved – are dated 'c. 1616 (?)'. But again, there are no data to either prove or disprove this cautious dating, while other views on this matter cannot be refuted.[18]

More problematic in many respects – and not only as regards its date – is the painting depicted on the short east façade, the *Andromeda Liberated by Perseus* (No. 18; Fig. 110). Comparison with other works by Rubens with the same subject, now in St Petersburg and Berlin (Figs 111, 113), prompts the question of whether a date as early as 'c. 1616' can realistically be considered. We shall return to this question in the catalogue.

Whatever the case, there is no reason to assume that every bit of the wall paintings, frieze included, would have been executed as late as 'around 1618' or 'between 1618 and 1621', as the literature usually states.[19] For as mentioned,

16. See for these hints under No. 9 (the frieze panel *The Triumph of Apollo* and *Victory Crowning a Hero* in the Gemäldegalerie Alte Meister in Kassel); under No. 15 (the frieze panel *The Drunken Hercules* and the same subject in the Gemäldegalerie Alte Meister in Dresden).
17. See above, Chapter IV, pp. 134–135..
18. In discussing this matter Arnout Balis expressed a quite different opinion. Assuming that the walls were painted by Rubens's assistants, he was of the opinion that they would not have prioritised painting the façade, but would have worked on it periodically, whenever possible, in what was a very busy period for the workshop. In that case the paintings would have been carried out over a much longer period, which cannot be precisely narrowed down.
19. See inter alia: Baudouin, *Fresco's*, 1998, p. 7 (as probably around 1618); McGrath, *Rubens's House*, 1978, p. 247 (as designed between 1618 and 1621); Healy, *Judgement of Paris*, 1997, p. 155 ('in 1618 Rubens embarked on the decoration of the façade'); Heinen, *Immolatio boum*, 2010, passim (as around 1618); Baumstark – Delmarcel, *Decius Mus (CRLB)*, 2019, I, pp. 102–103; II, p. 49, n. 109 (as 'painted from 1618 onwards' and 'around 1618').

that would mean that a significant area of the façades would have remained unpainted and therefore unfinished for quite a stretch (possibly as long as five years).

C. In Trompe-l'oeil: A Frieze of Bas-Reliefs, and a Painting on Canvas

In addition to all kinds of architectural and decorative elements a number of figurative scenes were to be seen on the façades of Rubens's studio. Directly below each window on the third level was a rectangular panel measuring about 1.5 × 2.5 m. Together they formed a series or frieze that continued along at least three façades (Nos 8–16; Figs 57, 60, 64, 69, 82, 90, 98, 101 and 106). On the short east courtyard wall there was also an *Andromeda Liberated by Perseus* almost three metres high, with life-size figures (No. 18; Figs 107 and 110).

We know that the frieze was in *grisaille* and the various scenes looked as if they were carved in relief. That it was not in colour can be inferred from the description by François Mols, who – to distinguish that work – specifically notes that the large *Andromeda* was painted 'in natural colours'. Corroboration comes from two paintings in which the frieze is shown as if consisting of pale monochrome stone reliefs. This is very clear in the three panels that can be seen in the north façade in the Aylesbury *View of the Courtyard of Rubens's House* (Figs 27, 70, 83, 91). Moreover, Rubens himself depicted a similar monochrome panel, vaguer but unmistakable, on the south façade of the building that gives an idealised impression of the workshop in the background of *Hélène Fourment au carrosse* (Figs 21 and 31).

In the Harrewijn prints, details of the scenes in the various compartments of the frieze are not easy to read. They are only a few centimetres high and, depending on their position, are seen in a more or less foreshortened form. Nevertheless, Elizabeth McGrath has managed to identify most of the subjects in what Julius Held rightly calls 'a thorough, and thoroughly fascinating article'.[20] She discovered that drawings by Rubens or one of his assistants – naturally more legible than the details in the prints – correspond to compositions on the façades. She identifies other scenes by relying on more or less similar compositions in Rubens's oeuvre, or on marble reliefs and other works of art from Antiquity.

Taking the frieze as it appears on the three façades in the two Harrewijn prints we see from left to right: three panels on the east or garden façade: *A Chariot Race*, *The Triumph of Apollo*, and *The Sacrifice of an Ox* (Nos 8–10; Figs 57, 60,

---

20. McGrath, *Rubens's House*, 1978; Held, *Review Garff – de la Fuente Pedersen*, 1991, p. 428.

64); five panels on the north façade: *The Sacrifice of Iphigenia, Alexander with the Thunderbolt, The Calumny of Apelles, Zeuxis and the Maidens of Croton* and *The Drunken Hercules* (Nos 11–15; Figs 69, 82, 90, 98, 101). On the short east wall of the workshop complex, facing the courtyard, only one panel of the frieze can be seen, representing an unidentified man with lance (No. 16; Fig. 106), while two more panels are seemingly (though not in reality) concealed by a much larger *Andromeda Liberated by Perseus* (see below).

The Famous Masters of Antiquity

The subjects depicted in the frieze are dealt with in greater detail in the catalogue section of this book (Nos 8–16). There is, however, a notable common characteristic that should be mentioned here. Four or more subjects depicted in the frieze, and also the *Andromeda Liberated by Perseus*, have a connection with ancient Greek painting. One scene illustrates an anecdote from the life of one of the famous Greek masters: *Zeuxis and the Maidens of Croton*. Other subjects correspond to paintings – which may or may not have been fictitious – known from ancient written sources. The most extensive information on Greek paintings is given in the *Natural History* of Pliny the Elder (23/24–79) and in the *Eikones* or *Imagines* of Philostratus (first half of the third century), while other ancient authors also occasionally described a painting.[21]

Of the nine frieze scenes, three can be unequivocally associated with a Greek masterpiece with the same subject: *The Calumny of Apelles* and *The Triumph of Alexander the Great* by Apelles, and *The Sacrifice of Iphigenia* by Timanthes. Two other suggested identifications seem less secure: *The Sacrifice of an Ox*, which is often thought to refer to a painting by Pausias, and *The Drunken Hercules*, which is – possibly erroneously – regarded as replicating a work by Parrhasius (these are discussed in greater detail in the catalogue, No. 10 and No. 15).

It should be emphasised that an inaccurate reading of McGrath's article led to a somewhat simplified idea about the scenes depicted in the frieze on Rubens's façades. It has been claimed that Rubens was aiming to recreate the famous masterpieces of Antiquity in his frieze and to equal them by *emulatio*.[22] First, this must be put into perspective as regards number, for as we have seen,

21. For the subjects of Rubens's frieze panels sources can also be found in the writings of Cicero (106–43 bc) for *The Sacrifice of Iphigenia* (No.11), of Lucian (c. 120 – c. 180) for *The Calumny of Apelles* (No. 13), and of Achilles Tatius (2nd century ad) for *Andromeda Liberated by Perseus* (No. 18). 17th-century authors who provide detailed information on classical painters include Karel van Mander (Van Mander, *Antijcke Schilders*, 1603) and especially Franciscus Junius, who wrote a lengthy study on the subject (Junius, *De pictura*, 1637). On the attitude of later artists to ancient Greek painting, see, inter alia, Joyce, *Ancient Painting*, 1992; Hecht, *Onbekende voorbeeld*, 1999; McHam, *Pliny*, 2013, passim. More specifically in relation to Rubens, see below, p. 180, n. 35.
22. See inter alia: Jacobs, *Vasari's Vision*, 1984, p. 415 ('Rubens' paintings are a statement about his ability to paint like Apelles, Pausias, Timanthes and others'); Baudouin, *Fresco's*, 1998, p. 17; Baumstark – Delmarcel, *Decius Mus (CRLB)*, 2019, I, p. 102.

only three of the nine scenes have a subject unambiguously analogous to that of a Greek master.

This idea is also incorrectly formulated as there is, after all, a significant difference between the frieze panels and a real *emulatio*: the classical subjects of the façade panels were in *grisaille*, not colour. It is true that according to Pliny the famous Greek masters produced 'white' monochrome paintings that were greatly admired, and which were emulated during the Italian Renaissance by the likes of Mantegna.[23] But – and this should be emphasised – Rubens had a different end in view. His scenes are intended to resemble stone bas-reliefs, not classical paintings that were celebrated for their deceptive realism.

That the scenes in the frieze are rendered as stone reliefs rather than paintings is entirely true to the type of logic that typifies Rubens's well-considered and intelligent creativity. There is no reason why Rubens would depict 'paintings' as permanent parts of his façade. Indeed, somewhere high up on a façade was certainly a rather odd place to display costly antique masterpieces, and not consistent with what we learn about the location of these works from Pliny and others. Stone reliefs, on the other hand, are perfectly in place – no less than busts carved in the round – incorporated between the decorative and architectural elements of a building.

McGrath also pointed out that the scenes are in *grisaille*, which puts Rubens's recreation of the ancient masterpieces in his façade into perspective. She also gives an explanation for the fact that Rubens made no attempt to use colours: he was 'restraining his own imagination within the bounds set by the visual remains available to him from Antiquity.' In other words, in the surviving antique stone reliefs he was 'seeing truer and more worthy reflections of the style and form of Greek painters'.[24]

One may wonder which programme could underlie the selection of the nine subjects in the frieze. Taking into account the foregoing – the fact that reliefs are depicted and not paintings – it may not be correct to assume that Rubens intended to provide a survey of the different genres or qualities of classical history painting, as has been thought.[25]

---

23. McHam, *Pliny*, 2013, p. 43. According to Pliny, Zeuxis also painted 'monochromes in white' (Pliny, *Natural History*, XXXV.64) and Apelles and others used a limited palette of four colours to execute their immortal works, namely white, ochre, red and black (ibid., XXXV.50). It is, however, very doubtful whether Pliny's information on the use of colour in paintings corresponded to reality. Antique sources that dealt with colour related not so much to the painter's practice but to complex theoretical systems that contradicted each other and above all led to much confusion (see Gage, *Color*, 1993, pp. 29–38). On Apelles's four-colour palette and the related 'sympathetic colours', see also Van Hout, *Dead colour*, 2010, pp. 59–61.
24. McGrath, *Rubens's House*, 1978, p. 276.
25. This possibility is cautiously suggested by McGrath, *Rubens's House*, 1978, p. 176; followed (as established) by, among others, Stutz, *Residenz*, 1985, p. 145). The following was assumed: Rubens's frieze might have drawn attention to allegory as a genre in *The Calumny of Apelles*; to the harmonious structure of the composition (or the genre of portraiture) in *The Triumph of Alexander the Great*; to pathos in Timanthes's *Iphigenia*; to strong sculptural design or to animal painting in Pausias's *The Sacrifice of an Ox*, and to humour in the *Drunken Hercules*,

In addition to a few of the historiated frieze panels on the façades, there was another scene that can be related to antique painting: the large (fictive) painting representing *Andromeda Liberated by Perseus* (No. 18; Fig. 110). A painting of this subject is described in Philostratus's *Imagines* and Pliny mentions an 'Andromeda' by Nicias.[26]

Although unarguably a painting with a classical subject 'in natural colours' and not in *grisaille* as the frieze, the *Andromeda Liberated* is certainly not simply a 'reproduction' of the work of a Greek master. It presents a modern work, the product of Rubens's own hand and *inventio*,[27] that is – only seemingly, of course – painted on canvas, as can be gathered from the edges nailed to a stretcher, and has been hung out to dry in his courtyard.

Finally, it ought to be mentioned that the two illusionistic forms that Rubens uses in the painting of his façade – stone sculpture (reliefs and busts in the round) and a canvas fixed to the wall – correspond to the recommendations on wall painting given by the architectural theorist Sebastiano Serlio (see below).

The Antwerp Apelles: Rubens and Classical Painting

In both the monochrome 'stone' frieze on his workshop walls and the colourful canvas ostensibly hanging out to dry, Rubens alludes to Greek masterpieces that in his day were deemed to have represented the absolute acme of artistic excellence. So it is easy to see why these vanished paintings, so highly praised by classical writers, appealed to the imagination. On a parenthetic note, we can form a better picture of those classical masterpieces today thanks to images derived from them that have been discovered in Pompeii and elsewhere.[28] Our knowledge of these allows us to state that such boundless admiration was perhaps not entirely justified, and that the qualities of the Greek masters must be seen in perspective. In particular, it is doubtful whether their work would stand comparison with what Western oil painting produced in later centuries.

Rubens was certainly acquainted with an example of Roman painting, the so-called *Aldobrandini Wedding*, a fresco measuring approximately 1 × 2.5 m that was found in Rome in 1601. He had studied this work, which was known

---

and to the creation of an ideal image from the observation of nature's diversity in *Zeuxis and the Maidens of Croton*.

26. Philostratus, *Imagines*, I, 29; Pliny, *Natural History*, XXXV.132.62. The copies found in Pompeii, which were still unknown in Rubens's time give an idea of the *Andromeda* by Nicias, an Athenian painter of the 4th century bc. (Ling, *Roman Painting*, 1991, p. 128, fig. 134, 135).
27. For related versions of Rubens's *Andromeda Liberated by Perseus* see F. Healy, in McGrath et al., *Mythological Subjects I (CRLB)*, 2016, pp. 213–214, nn. 12–13; see also No. 18.
28. A good idea of Roman wall painting, including images probably based on the famous Greek masterpieces, is given by the visual material in: Ling, *Roman Painting*, 1991, passim; see also n. 26.

and admired as a unique piece before the Pompeii finds, as appears from his praise of it in a letter to Peiresc, written years later.[29]

Of the long-lost Greek masterpieces, however, he could only form an approximate idea and they survived solely in his mind's eye. We hear Rubens's own words on the matter in a letter of 1 August 1637 – so about twenty years after the decoration of his façade – to Franciscus Junius (1589–1677) '[they] present themselves to us in imagination alone, like dreams; being sketched out only in words they are "thrice grasped at in vain" (as Euridice's shade by Orpheus) and often escape to disappoint us in our hope'.[30]

As explained, it is not these elusive images that Rubens represents in his frieze but simulated sculpture, undoubtedly in imitation of things he had seen in Italy, where countless bas-reliefs in imitation of ancient art could be seen on façades, either painted in *trompe-l'oeil* or carved. Even authentic classical reliefs would sometimes be used to ornament Renaissance walls. To name but two examples in Rome: the garden façade of the Villa Medici (Text ill. 72),[31] and the walls in the first courtyard of the Palazzo Mattei di Giove (Text ill. 71).[32]

When Rubens came to design the scenes for his frieze he turned to the writings of classical authors and to the vestiges of classical art he had seen and meticulously copied during his time in Italy: sarcophagi, from which he derived compositional arrangements and figures, and sculpture, on which he drew for facial expressions, postures and gestures. By using models like these, he tried to match his style as closely as possible to the art of Antiquity.

Moreover, Rubens's interest in sarcophagi found expression in his painting. For unlike the famous freestanding statues of single figures, the composition of the high reliefs involved several characters. In this connection Baumstark has drawn attention to the importance of Rubens's emulation of the principle in which the action is portrayed by 'a string of figures' in the foreground, without much depth, as can be seen in the *Decius Mus* series, for example.[33]

It seems from the letter to Junius, aforementioned, that Rubens was well aware of the perils involved in trying to recreate Greek masterpieces. Experience had taught him, Rubens wrote, 'how few among us, in attempting to reproduce in fitting terms some famous work of Apelles or Timanthes that is graphically described by Pliny or by other authors, will not produce something insipid or inconsistent with the grandeur of the ancients; but each one, following his

---

29. Letter dated 19 May 1628. In detail on this fresco and Rubens's letter: Baumstark – Delmarcel, *Decius Mus (CRLB)*, 2019, I, pp. 87–88, text ill. 11.
30. After McGrath, *Rubens's House*, 1978, pp. 245–246, n. 1 (with Latin text and comments); see also, with variations in the translation: Rooses – Ruelens, eds, *Correspondance*, 1887–1909, VI, pp. 179–181, doc. DCCCXXXI; Magurn, ed., *Letters*, 1955, p. 407, under no. 241; Van de Velde, *Rubens' brieven*, 2006, pp. 177–179, no. 9; on this letter in detail, see also Büttner, *Rubens und Junius*, 2011, pp. 342–361.
31. Toulier, *Villa Médicis*, I, 1989, passim, esp. pp. 322–348, figs 427–474. See, for these reliefs, also under No. 10.
32. Cresti – Rendina, *Palazzi*, 1998, fig. pp. 126–127; on this remarkable façade, see also Chapter V, p. 164, n. 65.
33. Baumstark – Delmarcel, *Decius Mus (CRLB)*, 2019, I, pp. 88–90.

CHAPTER VI - THE 'ITALIAN' WING - THE WALL PAINTINGS

Text ill. 72. Garden façade of the Villa Medici, Rome.

own bent, will [...] fail to do justice to those great spirits whom I honour with profoundest reverence, preferring indeed to admire the traces they have left, than to venture to proclaim myself capable of matching them even in thought alone'.[34]

Be that as it may, he more than met the challenge, if not in the *grisailles* of the frieze decorating his façades, then certainly in many other paintings in various genres. To mention just a few of the subjects: *Prometheus Bound* (after Euanthes), *Achilles among the Daughters of Lycomedes* (after Athenion), *The Birth of Venus* (after Apelles), *A Boy Blowing a Fire* (after Antiphilus) and *Andromeda* (after Nicias and Euanthes) – a subject to which we shall return in the Catalogue (No. 18).[35]

Rubens's admission that he considered himself incapable 'of matching them even in thought alone' thus seems something of a rhetorical exaggeration. The reality was probably quite the reverse, for there is every indication that the 'Antwerp Apelles' believed himself to be the equal of those exalted forbears.

---

34. For this letter, see above, p. 179, n. 30; the translation cited here is taken from McGrath, *Rubens's House*, 1978, p. 245.
35. On Rubens's emulation of lost classical works, see inter alia, in addition to the aforementioned article by McGrath: Dempsey, *Prometheus Bound*, 1967; Held, *Rubens*, 1982, pp. 109, 110; Baumstark – Delmarcel, *Decius Mus (CRLB)*, 2019, I, p. 102, nn. 113–114; Baumstark points to the fact that 'most of these reconstructed paintings date from the decade after Rubens's return from Italy' (ibid., p. 102) and he finds allusions to famous Greek masterpieces in the *Decius Mus* series painted in 1617 (ibid., pp. 102–103).

No doubt he saw himself as one of the 'few among us' who could work in a style which was, as he put it in his letter to Junius, not 'inconsistent with the grandeur of the ancients' ('a veterum maiestate non alienum').

Indeed, very early on Rubens's contemporaries were already comparing him to Apelles, who according to Pliny 'surpassed all the painters that preceded and all who were to come after him [...]' and who 'singly contributed almost more to painting than all the other artists put together [...]'.[36] While he was in Italy and shortly after his return to Antwerp he was already being hailed as the new Apelles, and in humanist circles he was labelled 'the Apelles of our century' and 'the Apelles of the Netherlands',[37] a title he would keep, with variations, throughout the following decades.[38]

A Subject in the Artist's House: A Tribute to Painting

Unlike Frans Floris (1519/20–1570) in Antwerp or Bartholomeus Spranger (1546–1611) in Prague (see below), when Rubens decorated the walls of his house it was not with an allegorical glorification of 'Pictura' or the Liberal Arts. Nevertheless, by means of the frieze rendered in *grisaille* with its allusions to works by the celebrated masters of Antiquity, he too paid subtle tribute to painting.

In this respect, Rubens did pretty much what Giorgio Vasari (1511–1574) had done rather more elaborately in his house in Arezzo, in the rooms on the *piano nobile*. Some of Vasari's scenes can be associated with the *grisailles* on Rubens's workshop walls, such as *The Sacrifice of Iphigenia* after Timanthes (Fig. 79), *Zeuxis and the Maidens of Croton*, and Apollo as patron and protector of the arts.[39] Vasari also had a house in Florence, and there too Apelles and

36. Pliny, *Natural History*, XXXV.79; on Apelles's exceptional qualities, see inter alia: McHam, *Pliny*, 2013, pp. 47–50.
37. The earliest known reference to Apelles comes in a passage in a Latin elegy *Ad Petrum Paullum Rubenium navigantem*, written by Rubens's brother Philip in the winter of 1603–1604, and published a few years later in Rubens, *Electorum Libri*, 1608, pp. 122–124 (see inter alia Baumstark – Delmarcel, *Decius Mus (CRLB)*, 2019, I, p. 65). In a letter of 30 November 1608 to Philip Rubens, Justus Ryckius (1587–1627) refers to our 'Apelles Belgicus' (Arents, *Bibliotheek*, 2001, p. 291). In 1609 allusion is made to Apelles in poems written on the occasion of the marriage of Rubens and his bride Isabella Brant by both Daniel Heinsius (1580–1655) and Philip Rubens (Rooses – Ruelens, eds, *Correspondance*, 1887–1909, II, pp. 12, 13, doc. CXX, pp. 22, 23, doc. CXXII). Dominicus Baudius (1561–1613) uses the title of 'Apelles nostri aevi' in a letter dated 4 October 1611 (ibid., II, pp. 44–45, doc. CXXX). In 1615 Balthasar Moretus uses the same title in his foreword to Lipsius's *L. Annaei Senecae Philosophi Opera Omnia Quae Extant* (Appendix I.6), as, later, does Jan Gaspar Gevartius in his commentary on the *Pompa Introitus* (see Chapter II, p. 55, n. 18).
38. Variants include Apelles 'seculi nostri' (1618; see Appendix I.11), 'Belgicae nostrae' (imprimatur of *Palazzi di Genova*, by Canon Laurens Beyerlick, 1622; Rott, *Palazzi (CRLB)*, 2002, I, p. 256), or 'nostri temporis' (see Fabri – Lombaerde, *Jesuit Church (CRLB)*, 2018, pp. 66 (n. 6), 221, 225), and 'ce nouveau Apelle' (Puget de la Serre, *Histoire Curieuse*, 1631, p. 56). On Rubens dubbed as Apelles, see also Büttner, *Rubens berühmt*, 2006, passim (see 'Apelles' in the Index of Names).
39. For Vasari's houses in Arezzo (1541–1548) and Florence (1570–1579), see Albrecht, *Häuser von Giorgio Vasari*, 1985, pp. 83–100; Schwarz, *Künstlerhaus*, 1990, pp. 177–182, no. 18; McHam, *Pliny*, 2013, p. 21, figs 34, 35. For his house in Florence, see also Jacobs, *Vasari's Vision*, 1984, pp. 399–416.

Zeuxis are lauded in frescoes. It is here, in an artist's house, that for the first time the subject of the frescoed decoration is art itself. It represents a critical turning point in the history of the artist's self-representation: he is conscious of standing at the very pinnacle of artistic achievement.[40]

It was this idea that Rubens was acknowledging by including in the frieze around his workshop scenes that had once been depicted by his great classical predecessors. No doubt he was inspired by Vasari, but equally by his own erudite knowledge of the art of Antiquity. Moreover, by introducing a 'modern' mythological work of his own invention (*Andromeda Liberated by Perseus*) into his façade decoration he emphasised the relationship between the painting of his own day and that of the famous classical masters. He fully recognised the value of that tradition and saw his art as a logical continuation of it, affirming in the process the excellence of contemporary painting and also, of course, his own work. A healthy awareness of his own worth as an artist would certainly not have been alien to Rubens, who from a very early stage, and before he started building his workshop, was known as 'the Apelles of his day' and 'the god of painters'.[41]

D. The Short East-Facing Wall in the Courtyard: A Combination of Trompe-l'oeil and Reality

From the 1692 Harrewijn print it appears that the composition of the short east façade facing the courtyard was quite complex (Fig. 30), and at first sight it is not altogether clear what was 'real' and what was painted in *trompe-l'oeil*. This ambiguity was the cause of a number of problems during the restoration of the house, which led in turn to a partially incorrect reconstruction. Even today there is no consensus about how Harrewijn's image ought to be interpreted, as we shall see below.

The upper level continues the arrangement of the north façade: rectangular windows with a vase or brazier in the tympanum of a pediment above, and loosely-cloaked herms in between (Fig. 51). Presumably the same combination of genuine and fictive – that is to say real windows and painted herms – was used here too.

---

40. Albrecht, *Häuser von Giorgio Vasari*, 1985, p. 100.
41. For Rubens dubbed as Apelles, see above, n. 37; he was described as the 'god van de schilders' (god of the painters) in a letter of 12 March 1611 from Jan Le Grand (Monballieu, *Nachtmael*, 1965, pp. 186, 195, doc. 2).

A *Trompe-l'oeil* Loggia (No. 17; Fig. 107)

What the print shows on the first-floor level, between the ground-floor gallery and the upper level with its windows and herms, is undoubtedly an illusionistic image – artificial architecture painted in perspective on a blank façade (No. 17; Fig. 107). By 'breaking through' a wall and introducing characters who can be seen behind a balustrade in a loggia or balcony on a higher level, Rubens associated himself with a rich tradition in wall painting.[42]

The print gives us an inkling of the 'loggia con prospettive' that according to Baldinucci was on one of Rubens's façades (Appendix I.32). The faux loggia is seemingly open on both sides, front and back, and recalls – in simplified form and on a modest scale – the kind of 'double loggia' that Rubens may have seen in Italian villas and palaces (Text ill. 73).[43]

The front of the 'loggia' is divided into three bays by triple Corinthian or composite colonettes supporting an architrave; a balustrade fills the bottom part of each bay. On the far side we see a cloudy sky between two semicircular arches, and through the balusters at the front we get a glimpse of the balustrade on the other side. There is not much more of the loggia's interior to be seen: on the left, a wall with a similar triple colonette, and a ceiling of which only part of one caisson and a rosette are visible, the rest being hidden by the painting ostensibly hanging in front. This chimerical architecture is livened up by a figure with a dog and a pair of birds.

Text ill. 73. Detail of a façade in the courtyard of the Palazzo Farnese, Rome.

In so far as it can be determined on the basis of the print, we can work out from the perspective where the viewer of the illusory loggia was meant to stand in order to best appreciate Rubens's visual legerdemain. The loggia is seen from the right and – logically, of course – from below or, more precisely, from the point of view of someone standing at ground level. Using the sight lines we can deduce that our putative viewer was on a line with the portico and more or less in the middle of it. The

---

42. See No. 17.
43. A double loggia, with two open sides with semicircular arches, connects two wings in the courtyard of the Palazzo Farnese in Rome; similar examples, also in Rome, can be found in the Palazzo di Venezia (Cresti – Rendini, *Palazzi*, 1998, fig. p. 61) and the Palazzo Borghese (ibid., fig. pp. 23, 257).

likelihood is, therefore, that the perspective was calculated to create the best *trompe-l'oeil* effect as one entered the courtyard from the garden through the portico's central arch. It should be noted that when Van Croes did the drawing on which the Harrewijn print was based the viewpoint he chose was not this ideal position but one higher and more to the right, so that the print gives a picture of the loggia that is somewhat awkward and distorted, with seemingly 'incorrect' sight lines.

It was known from the writings of Max Rooses that the supposed loggia was actually a *trompe-l'oeil* painting.[44] Even so, and for reasons that are unclear, it was decided during the modern reconstruction to create as 'real' architecture something that had never existed. Thus, on the first floor, a genuine loggia was built (Fig. 11), overlooking the courtyard but not the street – as the painted fictitious loggia in the print apparently does.

On the Ground Floor: A Real Gallery and a Real Staircase

The ground floor is a different matter. We are convinced that what the Harrewijn print shows is the 'real' situation, not a painting in *trompe-l'oeil*, as has sometimes been thought.[45] We believe, in other words, that what we see beyond an arcade is part of a real staircase, probably the one mentioned in a contract dated 2 November 1616 between Hans van Mildert, acting for Rubens, and a joiner (see No. 19; Fig. 124).

There are many arguments to support the contention that the ground floor depicted in the print is 'real'. First and foremost is the direction of the light, which consistently falls from the east, casting shadows accordingly – compare, for example, the shadows of the columns on the ground floor with that cast by the garden pavilion. It seems to us virtually impossible that in his drawing of the house Van Croes would opt for exactly the same incidence of light as that used in a *trompe-l'oeil* painting of part of a façade. The 'real' shadows falling across the ground floor of the gallery therefore define the image as a real open space. What is more, the print also shows one side of the passage to the Wapper: what we see – the two arches, the first six steps of a staircase, and a door – cannot possibly belong to an illusionistic painting. For one thing, two blank walls with fictive arches and doors would leave no access from the courtyard to the part of the studio wing fronting the street – so we can rule that out.

There is a second clue in the Aylesbury *View of the Courtyard of Rubens's House*. On the right edge of the painting, though out of proportion and hardly

---

44. Van Averbeke, *Rubenshuis. Restauratie II*, 1938, pp. 42–43; Rooses was already referring to 'un mur couvert d'une peinture décorative' in 1888 (Rooses, *Maison*, 1888, p. 220); on the loggia see also No. 17.
45. E.g. in Muller, *Rubens's Collection*, 2004, p. 12. Tijs in particular was convinced that the lower level was fictive and discusses it at length (see below, p. 197, n. 90).

legible in the darkness, is part of a column and an arch that connects it to the column clearly visible forming the corner of the colonnade. Between these two columns, another arch can be seen, connecting the corner column to yet another one that is hidden behind the first. Together these form an open gallery (Fig. 16). Lastly, and decisively, we think, is the plan drawn by François Mols. Careful examination reveals something that has gone unnoticed until now: by the covered entrance to the courtyard there was indeed a kind of porch, which he labels the '*peron*' (Fig. 125).

As shown by both the print and the plan, much of the ground-floor space in the narrow part of the 'Italian' wing – the short leg of the L, facing the Wapper – was taken up by a staircase. The print only shows the bottom of the first flight, and how exactly the stairs continued beyond that with a second flight is not entirely clear (see below).[46]

The Connection Between the 'Old' and the 'New' Wing and the Need for a Blank Wall

A closer look at the façade on the west side of the courtyard leads to an interesting observation. The presence of an illusionistic painting on the first floor of this façade – and its specific position – may indicate that it was provided as the solution to purely architectural problems: how to join the new wing to the old one and how to accommodate a monumental staircase.

Two wings, dissimilar in style and proportions, with floors and windows on different levels, meet on the left side (seen from the courtyard) of the entrance gate. In the 1692 Harrewijn print only part of the 'old' wing is visible: the entrance passage with an *oculus* above it, a section of roof with a dormer window, and part of an upper-storey cross-mullioned window (Fig. 18). It would seem that Rubens never embarked on the drastic measures that would have been involved in the renovation or alteration of the old façade, nor did he strive for symmetry. The result is a façade with a rather unsatisfactory combination of the 'old Flemish' and 'Italian' styles. It can reasonably be said that the absence of symmetry in this façade (as well as the disparity between the south and north façades of the courtyard) is quite unexpected in the house of someone who was thoroughly steeped in the principles of Italian architecture.

Rubens was also faced with another problem: how to accommodate a very sizeable staircase within the narrow section of the studio wing. In all probability there was a second flight of stairs rising diagonally against the inside of the courtyard wall. It would make sense, therefore, to have a solid wall here, with the necessary light coming in from the windows in the street wall. And indeed,

---

46. The staircase will also be discussed in the next chapter, which deals with the interior of the studio wing.

Mols's plan shows part of the stairs built against the inside of the courtyard wall, which is represented without a single window (Fig. 125).

Fictive painted architecture offered a way to display a façade without having to take into account what lay behind it, in this case a mezzanine level and the stairs. It is also possible that a painted coat of plaster was added to the wall on the first floor to camouflage alterations in the masonry of this wall.[47]

In other words, the wall does not seem to have been left blank in order to provide space for a painting with a *trompe-l'oeil* scene. Rather on the contrary, it was painted because for technical reasons that part of the façade needed to be solid (as a design with windows would have been impossible). This hypothesis is in no way invalidated by the fact that a fine specimen of *trompe-l'oeil* would also have a relevance on the wall of a painter's house – about which, more later. We assume that Rubens devised this inventive solution and in doing so successfully combined the circumvention of an architectural problem with the expression of meaningful subject matter.

In *Trompe-l'oeil*: A Painting Hung Outside to Dry

On the short east façade, to the left of the entrance gate in Harrewijn's 1692 print, is an element painted in *trompe-l'oeil* that at first sight appears rather odd. Fixed just below the top-floor windows is a large unframed painting on canvas on a temporary stretcher – the nails are clearly visible. It covers two of the panels in the frieze, as well as part of the *trompe-l'oeil* loggia (Fig. 30). It is hardly surprising that on the basis of this print – the only image known of this façade – it was sometimes thought that in Hillewerve's time a real autonomous painting on canvas was actually attached to the outside wall of Rubens's house.[48] Yet as early as 1888 Max Rooses had correctly concluded from François Mols's notes that everything depicted on the first floor to the left of the entrance gate – including the *Andromeda Liberated by Perseus* – was painted in *trompe-l'oeil*.[49]

An earlier source, Baldinucci's aforementioned *Notizia* on Rubens, also tells us that a fictive painting was depicted on one of Rubens's walls. Baldinucci writes that the artist had built a 'palazzo' in the Italian style and decorated the façades with a rich variety of motifs. Among them was a painting that seemed to be attached to the wall, as if hung in the sun to dry ('attaccato un Quadro

---

47. Something similar was noted in the plastered and painted façades in Genoa; an attempt to attain more unity in renovated and modernised façades was even seen as one of the origins of the many façade paintings in that city (Musso, *Painted Architecture*, 2014, pp. 165, 167, 181).
48. Hans Gerhard Evers, who assumed that it was a real painting, suggested that it was a remnant of a triumphal arch that had returned to the master's workshop and simply been left hanging there. 'Aber das ist reine Vermutung', he added circumspectly (Evers, *Neue Forschungen*, 1943, p. 268). Even Elizabeth McGrath was fooled by Rubens, supposing that the frieze must have continued behind the (real) *Andromeda Liberated by Perseus* (hiding two more panels): McGrath, *Rubens's House*, 1978, pp. 269–270, 276.
49. Rooses, *Maison*, 1888, p. 220; Rooses – Ruelens, eds, *Correspondance*, 1887–1909, II, p. 154.

per asciugarsi al Sole'). We are not told what the subject of this fictive work of art was, but the optical illusion was apparently so successful that it deceived the Infanta Isabella. Baldinucci describes her reaction to it when she was visiting Rubens: never doubting that what she beheld was a real painting, not a deceptive imitation painted on the wall, she asked for it to be brought down for closer inspection (Appendix I.32).[50] Whether this story has any basis in fact is hard to say. The Infanta did indeed visit Rubens's house on the Wapper on at least one occasion.[51] Perhaps – if there is any truth to the tale – she was not really fooled but asked for the picture to be fetched down as a witty bon mot, meant as a compliment to her host.

Incidentally, is not that hard to imagine being taken in by the image of an unframed painting hanging outside on the façade of a painter's house. Evidently it was not uncommon in Rubens's day to allow a finished painting to dry in the sun before it was transported, or if need be to expose a work to sunlight for a while to restore the discoloration of oil.[52]

That Rubens made full use of this practice is clear from his letters. He mentions it several times in his correspondence with Sir Dudley Carleton, with whom he was negotiating the exchange of antique statues for a group of his own pictures. In his letter of 20 May 1618 he says of the paintings that 'They are not yet thoroughly dry, and still need to remain on the stretchers for some days before they can be rolled up without risk,' adding in the margin that 'In this fine weather they will be put out in the sun'.[53] And on 26 May: 'with the aid of the sun, if it shines bright and without wind (which raises dust and is injurious to freshly painted pictures) they will be ready to be rolled after five or six days of fine weather'.[54] In a second letter of the same date, he reports that the weather that day has been so beautiful ('we have had such a nice sun') that, with a few exceptions, all the paintings can be packed.[55] It seems clear from the reference to the wind and the dust it stirs up that the paintings were indeed placed outside in the open air. Or was it somewhere inside with open windows? There is no information that tells us how Rubens went about exposing finished paintings to the sun. In a way it seems unlikely that the west side of the courtyard, which

---

50. Baldinucci says nothing about the Infanta's motives in ordering the 'painting' to be brought down; perhaps he implies that she wanted a closer look at the interesting picture. In our view it is not very likely that he implies that the Infanta wished to see the panels of the *grisaille* frieze underneath the canvas (suggested by F. Healy in McGrath et al., *Mythological Subjects I (CRLB)*, 2016, I, p. 211).
51. For the Infanta's presence in Rubens's house, see above Chapter II, p. 54, n. 15.
52. On this method of bleaching discoloured oil, see Van Eikema Hommes, *Painters' Methods*, 1998, pp. 93, 124, nn. 10, 11 (with reference to Rubens's practice and to a recommendation by the Spanish painter Acisclo Antonio Palomino y Velasco (1655–1725) in his *El museo pictórico y escala óptica*, 1715–24).
53. Translation after Magurn, ed., *Letters*, 1955, pp. 63–64, no. 30; for the passage in this Italian letter, see Rooses – Ruelens, eds, *Correspondance*, 1887–1909, II, pp. 162, 163, no. CLXX; see also Muller, *Perseus and Andromeda*, 1981–82, p. 134, n. 9.
54. Rooses – Ruelens, eds, *Correspondance*, 1887–1909, II, p. 191; translation after Magurn, ed., *Letters*, 1955, p. 65.
55. Ibid., II, p. 194; translation after Magurn, ed., *Letters*, 1955, p. 66.

receives relatively little sunlight and is not particularly wide, was actually used, as suggested by the *Andromeda Liberated by Perseus*. Although of course it remains a possibility, and some have assumed that it was.[56] Certainly the façades of the sunny sides of the studio wing – especially the high an wide south façade – seem more suitable locations, but how many days in the year would have been fit for bringing paintings outdoors is debatable, and the inside of the house was undoubtedly more often used to dry the finished paintings.[57]

The letters to Sir Dudley Carleton relate to drying paintings in Antwerp before they were transported. But Rubens had something to say about post-transport treatment as well, recommending exposure to sunlight for a while for paintings that had been packed up, in order to restore their colours. This advice, complete with a technical explanation, was sent in a letter to Peiresc dated 9 August 1629,[58] and on 12 March 1638 to Justus Sustermans (1597–1681), then court painter to Ferdinando II de' Medici, Grand Duke of Tuscany.[59]

The Viewer Deceived

Tales of painted *trompe-l'oeil* effects confounding their viewers – as in the case of the Infanta Isabella – were far from unusual. All manner of variations on the theme of painting's deceptive realism – considered a hallmark of superior mastery – go into the making of anecdotal episodes in artists' lives.[60] They had antecedents in Antiquity, as we learn from *ekphrases* of famous paintings and anecdotes about classical painters, the best known being the competition between Zeuxis and Parrhasius, as told by Pliny the Elder. Parrhasius was deservedly judged the winner for he had fooled the eye of an artist (Zeuxis) with a 'curtain' behind which his painting was supposedly hidden, while Zeuxis had merely fooled the birds with his realistic grapes.[61]

---

56. Baumstark believes that Rubens put out paintings to dry in the spot where the *Andromeda* hangs 'without blocking any windows' and adds 'Thus the illusion took the place of reality whenever no actual painting was hanging there to dry' (Baumstark – Delmarcel, *Decius Mus (CRLB)*, 2019, I, pp. 158–159).
57. Perhaps one could think, for instance, of the long, narrow, well-lit room on the top floor of the studio wing with its windows overlooking the Wapper (which Mols labelled 'galerie').
58. About a self-portrait that might have been left in its case for too long, and 'taken on a yellow tone'; Rooses – Ruelens, eds, *Correspondance*, 1887–1909, V, p. 156; Magurn, ed., *Letters*, 1955, p. 323; Vlieghe, *Portraits (CRLB)*, 1987, pp. 156, 157, n. 8, under no. 135; Van Eikema Hommes, *Painters' Methods*, 1998, pp. 93, 124, n. 10.
59. The painting in question was *The Horrors of War*, now in the Palazzo Pitti Florence (Büttner, *Allegories (CRLB)*, 2018, I, no. 32, II, fig. 153). It was sent to Florence and remained wrapped up for some time, possibly to the detriment of the colours; Rooses – Ruelens, eds, *Correspondance*, 1887–1909, VI, pp. 207–211, Doc. no. DCCCL; Magurn, ed., *Letters*, 1955, p. 409, no. 242.
60. For a general discussion of these anecdotes and their meaning, see inter alia Kris – Kurz, *Die Legende*, 1934; id., *Legend*, 1979; for a collection of stories from classical Antiquity to the 20th century, see Erftemeijer, *Kunstenaarsanekdotes*, 2000; in extenso on the Plinian anecdotes and their influence of Renaissance painting, see McHam, *Pliny*, 2013, passim (with a list of 161 anecdotes, pp. 316–321).
61. Pliny, *Natural History*, XXXV.65–66; on this well-known anecdote, see also Gombrich, *Art and Illusion*, 1977, p. 173; Muller, *Perseus and Andromeda*, 1981–82, p. 137; Erftemeijer, *Kunstenaarsanekdotes*, 2000, pp. 12, 14; McHam, *Pliny*, 2013, pp. 47, 319, 321, anecdote nos 97 and 155.

This *topos* of praise for the illusionistic power of painting has enjoyed much imitation since the early Renaissance. As Paul Barolsky noted, '[...] art, said Vasari over and over again, is a trick, an *inganno*, a deception'. In his *Lives*, Giorgio Vasari gives many examples of deception caused by hyper-realistic paintings, such as the dog that was taken in by the realism of a painted one and attacked it, or the altarpiece with the Madonna in a laurel arbour that attracted real swallows who were nesting in the roof of the church.[62]

In his *Schilder-Boeck* Van Mander also gives an example that can be seen as a variant of the story about the two Greek painters attempting to outdo each other in skill. The scene is set in Frans Floris's workshop, where a young painter boasts of being sufficiently skilful to fool his master: so realistic was the spider he had mischievously added to a work that Floris had tried to brush it off with his hat.[63]

Even today deceptive *trompe-l'oeil* phenomena still fascinate artists and their audiences. They appear both inside and outside, in interiors or as part of the townscape.[64]

E. Painted Façades in Italy and Elsewhere

Serlio's Theory

It is worth reading what the architectural theorist Sebastiano Serlio (1475–1554) has to say on the subject of painted façades in his *Regole* (Book IV of his *I sette libri dell'architettura*), in a chapter with which Rubens was undoubtedly familiar.[65] Serlio had firm opinions on the matter. He maintained that the architect, not the painter should be responsible for the design of a façade. As to the painting itself he favoured monochrome images that simulated sculpture, rather than figures or objects in natural colours. He advises: 'If you are to decorate a façade with painting and do it with sound judgement, you could simulate marble or some other stone, "carving" whatever you wanted into it. You could also simulate niches containing bronze figures in high relief ...'.[66]

---

62. Barolsky, *Trick of Art*, 1998, p. 23.
63. Van Mander, *Leven*, 1604, fol. 243r; Miedema, *Kunst*, 1981, pp. 247–248; see also ibid., p. 75 and pp. 241–242.
64. There is an abundance of literature on this topic; the phenomenon gave rise to exhibitions and well-documented monographs; see inter alia Ebert-Schifferer et al., *Trompe l'oeil*, 2002; Matsier, *Bedrogen oog*, 2009; for interiors with illusionistic architecture, see Milman, *Architectures peintes*, 1986.
65. Book IV, Chapter XI: 'De gli ornamenti della pittura, fuori, e dentro de gli edifici' (unillustrated). For the English translation used in this chapter, see Hart – Hicks, *Serlio*, 1996, pp. 378–380. On Serlio's concepts, see also Schütte, *Fassadenmalerei*. 1992, pp. 113–132, and esp. p. 125. Stefano F. Musso points out that other treatise writers, including Gian Paolo Lomazzo (1538–1592), had in many ways recommended the use of wall paintings (Musso, *Painted Architecture*, 2014, p. 170). For Serlio and Rubens's house in this connection, see Muller, *Perseus and Andromeda*, 1981–82, p. 136, n. 18 (with variations in the translation).
66. Hart – Hicks, *Serlio*, 1996, pp. 378.

Serlio was particularly opposed to wall paintings that appeared to perforate the building with views of the sky or realistic landscapes. Such things destroy a building's character and transform it from a corporeal and solid form into a transparent one 'without solidity' ('senza fermezza'), like a building that is unfinished or ruined'. Characters depicted on façades should preferably be rendered in monochrome. 'Realistic' figures in colour were deemed unsuitable unless they were seen at a simulated window, for instance, and even then should be portrayed in 'calm postures rather than in bold movements'. Likewise animals, which could also be depicted at a window or 'above a cornice'.

Serlio's advice about painting scenes in natural colours is especially interesting. If the patron or the painter wished to 'take pleasure in the charm of the colours' he could simulate pieces of material attached to the wall as if they were furnishings ('panni attacati al muro, come cosa mobile') and anything desired could be painted on them without violating the integrity of the architecture.[67]

Serlio goes on to say that, in contrast to the façades, there is no objection to using colour when painting interior walls, providing it is done 'with good judgement'. Inside, simulated openings are appropriate, following the logic that from the inside one can look out and thus see the sky and landscapes.

Rubens, it must be said, largely adhered to Serlio's guidelines. As far as we know, the paintings on the walls of his house were mainly in monochrome and gave the impression of being carved reliefs that were part of the architecture. Only on the first floor of the short façade facing the courtyard was there a depiction of an open loggia that broke through the wall, and in which one figure and a number of animals could be seen. The simulated *Andromeda Liberated by Perseus* painted on canvas 'in natural colours' fulfilled the role of the 'panni' permitted by Serlio.[68]

Painted Façades: Italy

Rubens spent eight years in Italy (1600–1608) and would have looked with keen interest at the painted façades in the cities he visited in that time. Most of them have long since vanished, and only a few can still be summoned up in the imagination thanks to surviving visual material such as design drawings, drawn copies and sometimes photographs taken in the nineteenth or early twentieth century.

---

67. Ibid..
68. Rubens used a similar process (but one even more sophisticated, with scenes on fictive tapestries depicted in a series of real tapestries) on a monumental scale in his designs for the *Eucharist* series; see De Poorter, *Eucharist (CRLB)*, 1978, I, esp. pp. 69–76.

CHAPTER VI - THE 'ITALIAN' WING - THE WALL PAINTINGS

Text ill. 74. Giovanni Antonio Pordenone, *Design for the Façade of Palazzo d'Anna, Venice*, drawing. London, Victoria and Albert Museum.

Mantua, where Rubens served as Vincenzo Gonzaga's (1562–1612) court painter, must have looked particularly beautiful, with its painted houses contributing to the 'gay appearance of the town'.[69] Rubens saw painted façades elsewhere in Italy too, which are completely lost today. In Venice he was undoubtedly struck by the scenes from Roman history and classical mythology painted on the façade of the Palazzo d'Anna by Giovanni Antonio Pordenone (c. 1484–1539) (Text ill. 74).[70] In Verona, where he spent some time in 1602,[71] there were also numerous painted exterior walls, the Casa Trevisani-Lonardi being a particular case in point (Text ill. 75). We can tell from what remains of them today that the scenes were painted in light whitish colours ('con colori chiari, biancastri'), and thus, like the frieze on Rubens's workshop façades, gave the impression of being classical reliefs.[72]

---

69. In 1774 an eyewitness (Saverio Bettinelli) wrote of Mantua that 'no city used so much the best brushes in that century [i.e. 16th] and in the beginning of the 1600 [*sic*], so that all the streets were a real theater for various occasions. Unfortunately they are all destroyed by time, by new buildings, and by that barbaric desire to cover all with white [...]' (cited in Hartt, *Giulio Romano*, 1958, I, p. 69).
70. Wood, *Copies, Titian (CRLB)*, 2010, I, pp. 123, 126, n. 27; we can form some idea of them thanks to a number of preparatory drawings; see Cohen, *Drawings*, 1980, pp. 84–85, no. 2306, figs 78–79, and p. 112, no. 5429, fig. 80; Cohen, *Pordenone*. 1996, pp. 709–714, no. 79.
71. Van de Velde, *L'itinéraire italien*, 1978–79, p. 247; among the people Rubens met there were his brother Philip and Jan van den Wouwer (Woverius).
72. It is generally assumed that they were painted around 1510–1520 by Giovanni Maria Falconetto (1463–1535); Schweikhart, *Fassadenmalerei in Verona*, 1973, pp. 215–216, cat. no. 64, figs 106–110. A design for a wall painting by Bernardino India (1528–1590), born and active in Verona, was probably also intended for a house in that city (Koldewijn, *Wanden*, 1985, p. 14, no. 7).

CHAPTER VI - THE 'ITALIAN' WING - THE WALL PAINTINGS

Text ill. 75. Giovanni Maria Falconetto, *Frescoes on the Façade of the Casa Trevisani-Lonardi, Verona* (before 1908), photograph.

Apart from Mantua, Rubens spent most time in Rome.[73] He was especially intrigued by the façade frescoes that Polidoro da Caravaggio (c. 1495/1500–1543) designed and executed in collaboration with Maturino da Firenze. Amongst other things this is evidenced by the fact that he acquired quite a few anonymous drawn copies, which he retouched, sometimes to the point that they took on a distinctly Rubensian appearance.[74]

One of the earliest Roman palaces to be mentioned in this connection is the Casino del Bufalo (demolished in 1885), whose façades were decorated by Polidoro and Maturino da Firenze with episodes from Ovid's *Metamorphoses*.[75] Polidoro wall paintings in *grisaille* on the front of the Palazzo Milesi must have made a great impression on Rubens. No fewer than nine drawings with scenes borrowed from this impressive façade and reworked by him are known.[76]

At the Palazzo Gaddi, too, Polidoro and his collaborator covered the walls several floors high with dozens of paintings, likewise in *grisaille*.[77] Two drawings retouched by Rubens depict fragments from the long frieze that ran above the first-floor windows.[78] Although, for his own workshop walls,

---

73. Rubens's first visit to Rome lasted almost ten months from June-July 1601 to April 1602. His second and longest stay, which lasted two years and four months, began around the end of 1605 and continued until October 1608 (when he made a hasty return to Antwerp); Van de Velde, *L'itinéraire italien*, 1978–79, pp. 243–245, 249–252, 258.
74. On these drawings, see below nn. 75–76, 78; on Rubens's interest in Polidoro, see also Jaffé, *Rubens and Italy*, 1977, pp. 47–49.
75. We are fairly well informed about the compositions depicted thanks to the many drawn copies from the 16th and 17th centuries. For a 19th-century engraving of the façade, see Wood, *Copies, Raphael (CRLB)*, 2010, I, p. 373; II, fig. 208. Some of the frescoes were transferred to canvas (Museo di Roma, Palazzo Braschi; ibid., II, fig. 209). A copy worked up with gouache by Rubens is held in the Musée du Louvre: *Perseus Showing the Head of Medusa to Phineus and his Companions* (ibid., I, pp. 372–375, cat. no. 81; II, fig. 207).
76. Wood, ibid., I, pp. 380–402, nos 84–92. For an image of the entire façade, see the 19th-century print (Ravelli, *Polidoro*, 1978, pp. 367, 369, fig. 667; Wood, ibid., I, p. 381; II, fig. 216).
77. An anonymous drawing now in the Albertina in Vienna gives a good overall picture of the spectacular appearance of this façade (Birke – Kertész, *Albertina*, 1997, pp. 2104–2105, inv. 15462; Wood, *Copies, Raphael (CRLB)*, 2010, I, p. 376; II, fig. 210).
78. Ibid., I, pp. 375–380, nos 82–83, pl. 13; II, figs 211, 214.

Rubens took over none of the compositions or details found in Caravaggio's Roman frescoes,[79] it seems likely that he sought to imitate this frieze to some extent. With their dynamic design and sense of drama his scenes in *grisaille* reminiscent of classical reliefs show a certain affinity.

Genoa: Palazzi di Genova

Genoa was another Italian city with which Rubens was very familiar,[80] and there too many house-fronts were embellished not only with ornaments in relief but also a wide variety of paintings – to the extent, indeed, that they were regarded as a 'fundamental characteristic of the urban, artistic and social identity of Genoa'.[81] In many cases monumental figures, 'bronze' statues and herms were depicted between windows; there were innumerable instances of friezes with scenes occupying large sections of wall, of continuous series of ornaments running along the eaves cornice, and architectural motifs such as columns and window architraves with pediments above. Little of that splendour remains today, and what does survive is often not in good condition. Even so, we can still form a fairly good picture of it thanks to the very detailed documentation that survives, including nineteenth-century photographs which allow a clearer reading of the façade decorations.[82]

Of all the wall paintings to be seen in Genoa and its immediate surroundings those on the façades of the Palazzo del Principe Andrea Doria in Fassolo must have ranked among the most impressive. The numerous frescoes have disappeared but the designs by Pordenone (1448–1539) and Perino del Vaga (1501–1547) (Text ill. 76) still survive.[83]

---

79. Only one similarity can be spotted: the figure of the executioner in *The Sacrifice of Iphigenia* (No. 11), striding forwards in the foreground, sword in hand, is similar to the warrior in Polidoro's *Perseus Showing the Head of Medusa* (see under n. 75).
80. In 1628, Rubens wrote (in a letter to Pierre Dupuy dated 19 May) that he had been to Genoa several times (Rooses – Ruelens, eds, *Correspondance*, 1887–1909, IV, p. 422, doc. DLI; Magurn, ed., *Letters*, 1955, p. 265, no. 168). However, it is not possible to discover exactly when and for how long he stayed there. He was probably already there in 1602, and in 1603, 1604, 1605, and perhaps even for a final time in 1607 (Van de Velde, *L'itinéraire italien*, 1978–79, pp. 246, 254–255). On Rubens and Genoa, see also Rott, *Palazzi (CRLB)*, 2002, I, pp. 32 ff.; Musso, *Painted Architecture*, 2014, p. 161, n. 22.
81. Musso, ibid., p. 161; in detail on façades in Genoa: see Boccardo et al., eds, *Genua Picta*, 1982. On the symbiosis of architecture, sculpture and painting in Genoese façades, see also Lombaerde, *Rubens*, 2014, pp. 211–212; Lombaerde, *Rubens the Architect*, 2014, pp. 146–147.
82. Around 1980, attempts were made to restore as many overpainted or eroded remains as possible. Great efforts were also made to compile extensive documentation in order to reconstruct an image of the façades' original appearance. The results were published in Boccardo et al., eds, *Genua Picta*, 1982.
83. Boccardo et al., eds, ibid., pp. 147–153; for Pordenone's drawings, see ibid., p. 149, nos II.2 and II.3, figs 150–151. Two very detailed design drawings by Perino del Vaga are now in the Musée Condé in Chantilly and the Print Room of the Rijksmuseum in Amsterdam respectively (ibid., p. 150, nos II.5 and II.6, figs 153–154; Pasena Armani, *Perino del Vaga*, 1987, pp. 73–83).

CHAPTER VI - THE 'ITALIAN' WING - THE WALL PAINTINGS

Text ill. 76. Perino del Vaga, *Design for the North Façade of the Palazzo Doria, Genoa*, drawing. Amsterdam, Rijksmuseum.

The reader expecting that Rubens would show something of those lavishly painted Genoese façades in his *Palazzi di Genova* would be disappointed. There is not a single illustration of a figurative wall painting to be seen. What we can see, however, are the painted ornamental and architectural elements. The Palazzo Cattaneo Adorno is a good example. Comparison of the façade as it appears in the *Palazzi* print with a nineteenth-century photograph, shows that with the exception of the ground floor, which was largely constructed in durable materials, almost the entire façade was flat and painted. In the print the window architraves and all the decorative elements look as if they are executed in relief (either moulded in stucco or carved in stone).[84]

The imposing façade of the Palazzo Interiano Pallavicino, the 'Palazzo G' in the *Palazzi*, is another such case (Text ill. 77). As can still be seen today, the façade was painted not only with architectural features but also with full-length personifications of Virtues standing in niches (Text ill. 78). Components such as pilasters, capitals, the moulding around windows and the pediments above them, were also painted and not, as the engraving suggests, made of durable materials. But there is no trace of the Virtues or their niches in the print: those sections of wall are left.[85]

84. Boccardo et al., eds, *Genua Picta*, 1982, p. 53, figs 47–48 and pp. 255–256, nos 24.7 and 24.8, figs 369–370; Rott, *Palazzi (CRLB)*, 2002, I, pp. 211–213, nos 102, 102a, 102b; II, figs 212–213; Lombaerde, *Rubens*, 2014, p. 212, fig. 9b.
85. Not all the painted elements are depicted, however: there is no trace of the figures and the wall surface is left blank; see Boccardo et al., eds, ibid., pp. 223–229, no. 20, pl. VIa-b (colour ills); the paintings are more clearly distinguishable in a photograph from the end of the 19th century on p. 226, fig. 314; Rott, *Palazzi (CRLB)*, 2002, I, pp. 149–154, nos 46–46a (the photograph on p. 151, cat. ill. 14). See also Musso, *Painted Architecture*, 2014, pp. 176–177, figs 10–11.

CHAPTER VI - THE 'ITALIAN' WING - THE WALL PAINTINGS

Text ill. 77. Nicolaes Ryckmans, *Façade of the Palazzo Interiano Pallavicino (Palazzo G)*, engraving in *Palazzi di Genova* (*Palazzi Antichi*), 1st series, 1622.

Text ill. 78. Palazzo Interiano Pallavicino, Genoa.

It would appear, therefore, that the purpose of *Palazzi di Genova* was purely to illustrate the architecture of these buildings and avoid any excursus on the phenomenon of frescoed façades. If elements are illustrated that in reality were painted, that fact is not made explicit in the engravings – unlike, interestingly, some of the drawings on which the engravings were based. For instance, a drawing of the façade of the Villa Grimaldi 'Fortezza' (Palazzo D) bears the inscription: 'L'ornamento di detta facciata è tutta di pittura' (All the ornamentation of this façade is painted). In this case we can get some idea of the importance of the frescoes, described in a contract of 1566 as 'pintura chiamata chiaro et scuro' (*chiaroscuro*), from the extant façade, which appears to be almost completely flat, with no sign of pilasters, window mouldings and so forth.[86]

In the section of *Palazzi di Genova* titled *Palazzi Moderni*, a different solution was found for the illustration of a number of façades: all painted ornamental details were omitted. Features that were fully in the round are shown, such as the main entrance, balustrades and horizontal mouldings, but not window architraves nor the many pilasters and other elements that gave structure to the finished (painted) façades (Text ill. 79).[87] A particularly striking aspect of

86. Boccardo et al., eds, *Genua Picta*, 1982, p. 254, nos 24.3 and 24.4, p. 252, figs 263–264; Rott, *Palazzi (CRLB)*, 2002, I, pp. 134 (nos 23 and 23a), 137 (cat. ill. 9); II, figs 50–51. A similar inscription accompanies the drawing of 'Palazzo C': *L'ornamenta della faciata di sopra è di pittura* (the decoration of the top part of the wall is painted); see Boccardo et al., eds, ibid., p. 253, nos 24.1 and 24.2, figs 363–366; Rott, ibid., I, pp. 129–130, nos 16–17; II, figs 30–31. On this phenomenon, see also Ottenheym, *Palazzi di Genova*, 2002, p. 83; he also pointed out that in some drawings (but not in the engravings) there are notes about materials used in the façade, such as stucco or marble.
87. See the illustrations in Rott, *Palazzi (CRLB)*, 2002, II, figs 159, 166, 172, 184, 190, 196.

CHAPTER VI - THE 'ITALIAN' WING - THE WALL PAINTINGS

Text ill. 79. Nicolaes Ryckmans, *Façade of the Palazzo Gambaro* (without the painted decorations), engraving in *Palazzi di Genova (Palazzi Moderni)*, 2nd series, after 1622.

Text ill. 80. Hans Holbein II, *Design for a façade (Tanzgässlein) of the House 'Zum Tanz', Basel*, drawing. Basel, Kunstmuseum Basel.

these engravings is the strange astylar effect produced by windows without any kind of architrave or entablature, thus 'creating a rhythm of sharply cut out openings'.[88]

Painted Façades: North of the Alps

Rubens's workshop was by no means the only building north of the Alps to be adorned with wall paintings. Among the earliest known examples were the spectacular decorations (now lost) on two walls of the house named 'Zum Tanz' in Basel that were designed around 1520 by Hans Holbein II (1497?–1543) for the jeweller Balthasar Angelrot.[89] The designs involve a complex architectural structure that provides the basis for rising tiers of galleries bizarrely animated by a miscellaneous collection of characters (Text ill. 80).

It must be stressed that there is nothing to indicate that Rubens was familiar with Holbein's wall decorations, either from drawings or from seeing them first hand in Basel, as was previously thought. Nor is there any foundation for the view that Holbein's design somehow provided a model for Rubens's own house. Any notion of similarity falls

---

88. Ottenheym, *Palazzi di Genova*, 2002, p. 97; he points to the literal imitation of this stark appearance of the *Palazzi* façades in Northern Netherlandish architecture, to which no painting is added (ibid., pp. 96–97, figs 14–15). Of course this rather absurd 'naked' style is based on a misunderstanding.
89. For the surviving drawings of this façade, one original by Holbein and a number of copies, see Muller, *Holbein*, 1988, pp. 102–113.

to the ground when we recall that the lower gallery of Rubens's house was real, not the sort of *trompe-l'oeil* illusion conceived by Holbein.[90]

It was not only in Switzerland that frescoes were painted on exterior walls. They could also be seen in southern Germany (in Augsburg and Nuremberg, for example) and in other Central European countries right up until the late eighteenth century. There was a rich tradition of colourful scenes with both religious subjects and architectural elements depicted in *trompe-l'oeil*.[91]

Artists' Houses

It is not surprising that outside Italy artists should have been prompted to paint the fronts of their houses in the same sort of striking fashion they had seen there. The Antwerp-born Bartholomeus Spranger (1546–1611) is a case in point. He spent more than a decade in Italy before becoming court painter to Emperor Rudolf II (1552–1612) and settling in Prague, where in 1585 he bought a house and painted the street front with scenes and figures. The painting has almost completely disappeared but Karel van Mander (who had known Spranger personally) recorded a fairly detailed description of it. The front of the house was 'uyt den ghelen als van coper geschildert' (in yellow-coloured *grisaille*, as if painted in copper). Dozens of figures were portrayed: little children as large as life, who paint, draw and sculpt; a flying Mercury; Hercules; personifications of Fame, Justice and Rome; a frieze filled with captives and trophies or spoils. And, Van Mander adds: 'All this is wonderful to behold, the figures are astonishingly three-dimensional and beautifully posed'.[92] Clearly Spranger had painted an allegorical glorification of the fine arts on the front of his house, with figures such as Mercury, portrayed as the god of inspiration, and Hercules who symbolises Labour, the effort required to accomplish something.

In Antwerp, only one artist's abode with a painted street front is known, namely the house built by Frans Floris around 1563–1565 in the Arenbergstraat (demolished in 1816). A drawing of it produced in 1700 or thereabouts by Jacques van Croes gives us a general idea of what it looked like (Text ill. 81). There is also a series of eight engravings, published in 1576 by the monogrammist TG, showing parts of the façade: the scene above the entrance door, representing

---

90. Rutger Tijs was convinced that Rubens drew directly on Holbein's designs for the Basel wall paintings. He was particularly strengthened in this view by a design by Holbein that included an imaginary staircase for the Hertensteinhaus in Lucerne (drawing in the Kupferstichkabinett of the Kunstmuseum, Basel). He argues at length that en route to Italy Rubens must have passed through Basel and Lucerne, a hypothesis for which there are no grounds whatsoever. He also wrongly assumes that the staircase seen in the Harrewijn print is not a real staircase but painted in *trompe-l'oeil*, as in Holbein's design; see Tijs, *Renaissance- en barokarchitectuur*, 1999, pp. 131–132; id., *Herdersgrot*, 2002, pp. 118–121; id., *Rubens*, 2004, pp. 65–68, 140–141.
91. Banz-Heinhold, *Fassadenmalerei*, Munich, 1952.
92. Van Mander, *Leven*, 1604, fols 272v–273r; id., *Lives*, ed. Miedema, 1994–99, I, pp. 348–351; V, pp. 105–106. On Spranger in Prague, see Dacosta-Kauffman, *L'école de Prague*, 1985, pp. 42–44.

CHAPTER VI - THE 'ITALIAN' WING - THE WALL PAINTINGS

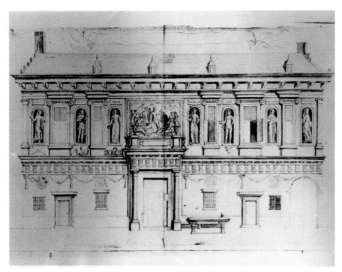

Text ill. 81. Jacques van Croes, *Façade of Frans Floris's House*, drawing. Brussels, KBR.

Pictura, Sculptura and Architectura (?), and the seven figures between the windows on the first floor, representing the attributes of the artist.[93] They were represented as statues in niches and according to Van Mander were painted in yellow, as if made of copper,[94] a peculiarity also found in Spranger's façade.

Presumably there were other artists in the Netherlands who also went in for pictorial house-fronts but nothing is known about them – other than from one reference by Van Mander to Cornelis Ketel (1548–1616) who, he tells us, painted the façade of his house in Amsterdam with all kinds of life-size figures. The most noteworthy aspect was the highly unorthodox method he employed, discarding the brush and painting with his hands and feet.[95]

When Rubens's wall paintings are compared with what could be seen in the Italian cities and the examples outside Italy mentioned above, it is striking that the façades as we know them from the Harrewijn prints are decorated with paintings on the garden and courtyard sides but not – or at least not to anything like the same extent, as far as we know – on the street side. If something did appear on the house-front, which cannot be determined, it was in a more

---

93. The figures depicted are personifications of Diligence, Skill (*Usus*), Poetry, Architecture, Labour, Experience and Industry (Van de Velde, *Floris*, 1975, pp. 64, 307–313, 421–423, figs 248–255; id., *Painted Decoration*, 1985, pp. 127–134; Wouk, *Façade of Floris*, 2014, pp. 189–125); id., *Frans Floris*, 2018, pp. 467–497); on Floris's house, see also Maclot, *Artists' Houses*, 2018, passim.
94. 'Hy hadde oock zijn huys uytwendich beschildert met *Pictura* en ander vry Consten, uyt den gelen, als oft van Coper waer gheweest' (Van Mander, *Leven*, 1604, fol. 241v).
95. Van Mander, *Leven*, 1604, fol. 278v; id., *Lives*, ed. Miedema, 1994–99, I, p. 373; V, pp. 152–154; see also Schwarz, *Künstlerhaus*, 1990, p. 216, no. 36; Chapman, *Cornelis Ketel*, 2009, pp. 267–268, 272, n. 70, 71. As regards the technique used for the façade paintings, it is interesting that Van Mander comments that Carel van Yper, a painter unknown nowadays, painted façades in fresco in Ypres, his native town ('op het nat kalck ghedaen'); see Van Mander, *Leven*, 1604, fol. 253r; id., *Lives*, ed. Miedema, 1994–99, I, pp. 270–271.

modest form, and did not include life-size figures. It may be assumed that, in Hillewerve's time, all the architectural components of Rubens's street façade seen in Harrewijn's print (Fig. 26), were 'real' and made in stone.[96]

F. Painted Interiors

Not surprisingly, painters also came up with the notion of displaying a sample of their painting skills – often with *trompe-l'oeil* effects – inside their own homes. An early example in Antwerp, which Rubens must have known, was the house named 'Sint-Quinten' built by Quinten Metsys (1466–1530) in the Schuttershofstraat. As we learn from a description in Alexander van Fornenbergh's biography of the artist, one of the rooms was richly decorated with paintings executed by Metsys himself: a frieze with a variety of decorative motifs as well as an opening in which a *trompe-l'oeil* gallery with a group of flute players appeared.[97]

There can be little doubt that in the seventeenth century the most remarkable illusionistically painted decorations in an Antwerp interior were to be found in the house of Jacques Jordaens. Much or perhaps even most of the interior wall space was covered with painted architectural components and *trompe-l'oeil* apertures filled with a whole range of characters. We can form an idea of what they looked like from surviving designs containing illusionistic features such as characters in a loggia, a motif for which Jordaens had undoubtedly found inspiration in Rubens's courtyard (Fig. 109).[98] Jordaens's imaginative compositions were not painted directly onto the wall itself but in oil on separate canvases, which were later removed from the house and dispersed. A version of *A Maidservant with a Basket of Fruit and Two Lovers*, for example, might have been part of this unique ensemble.[99] Jordaens also used his ceilings as supports for illusionistic decoration, depicting scenes glimpsed through an opening, as it were, in dramatically foreshortened perspective, a technique he took literally from the paintings Rubens produced for the ceiling of the Jesuit Church in Antwerp. Two series of ceiling pieces from the Jordaens house have

---

96. For the decoration of the street façade – perhaps with *trompe-l'oeil* frieze panels as in the other studio façades –, see Chapter V, p. 158.
97. In the upper part of the room was 'een uytspringhende gaelderijken, waer op vier figuerkens sitten, neven een, van coleur geschildert, spelende (te samen) op een accoordt van fluyten' (Van Fornenbergh, *Protheus*, 1658, pp. 29, 30; paraphrased in: Van den Branden, *Schilderschool*, 1883, pp. 122–123). see also Silver, *Massys*, 1984, p. 4. For the motif of *trompe-l'oeil* characters behind a balustrade, see also No. 17.
98. For Jordaens's drawings, which are assumed to have been intended for wall decorations in his house, see d'Hulst, *Jordaens*, 1974, p. 268, no. A180; Devisscher – De Poorter, eds, *Jordaens*, 1993, II, p. 79, no. B51; see also the illustrations in Tijs, *Rubens en Jordaens*, 1984, pp. 306–312; for a detailed description of Jordaens's house, see ibid., pp. 263 ff.
99. Versions in Glasgow, Kelvingrove Art Gallery and Museum, inv. no. 84; Antwerp, Koninklijk Museum voor Schone Kunsten Antwerpen, inv. no. 5049; see Devisscher – De Poorter, eds, *Jordaens*, I, pp. 138–140, no. A39.

CHAPTER VI - THE 'ITALIAN' WING - THE WALL PAINTINGS

survived: twelve *Signs of the Zodiac* and nine paintings telling *The Story of Cupid and Psyche*.[100]

In Italy too we know of artists' houses whose street fronts were left unpainted, while this was more than made up for by frescoes in halls, salons and corridors. Especially noteworthy were the frescoes in Giulio Romano's house in Mantua,[101] the palatial dwellings of Giorgio Vasari in Arezzo and Florence, and the houses of Federico Zuccari (1539–1609) in Florence and Rome.[102]

As far as we know, Rubens did not go in for this elaborate and more permanent type of wall decoration in his home or workshop. He probably lacked the wall space for it, particularly if we assume that he preferred to use his walls for displaying his large collection of paintings, both by himself and by other masters. Nothing is known of figurative scenes, either painted on to the plastered wall, or on canvases fixed to the wall (as in Jordaens's house), and indeed they may never have existed. Nor is there anything to suggest that there were painted ceiling pieces in Rubens's house.

Yet it is possible and perhaps even probable that certain ornamental and architectural features such as architraves, pilasters and festoons were painted in *trompe-l'oeil* inside Rubens's house. This conjecture is borne out by the only decorated part of the interior of which we have an illustration, namely Hillewerve's chapel, formerly Rubens's 'antiquarium' (Fig. 127). As will be explained below, in that room certain parts of the wall decoration, including niches containing busts, were very probably feigned.[103]

---

100. The *Signs of the Zodiac* ended up in Paris, where they were used as ceiling pieces in the Bibliothèque du Sénat in the Palais du Luxembourg (Tijs, *Rubens en Jordaens*, 1984, pp. 336 (fig.), 337–345, 348– 349; Devisscher – De Poorter, eds, *Jordaens*, 1993, I, p. 258). The *Cupid and Psyche* series (Tijs, *Rubens en Jordaens*, 1984, pp. 346, 347, 350, fig. pp. 286–290; Devisscher – De Poorter, eds, *Jordaens*, 1993, I, pp. 258–260, nos A84–A86) was recently acquired by The Phoebus Foundation, Antwerp; for a temporary reconstruction of the ceiling with these canvases, see the exhibition in the Frans Hals Museum in Haarlem *At Home with Jordaens* (2021–2022). See URL: https://www.franshalsmuseum.nl/nl/event/thuis-bij-jordaens/.
101. For this house (c. 1544), see Wirth, *Häuser*, 1985, pp. 62–68; Carpeggiani – Tellini Perina, *Giulio Romano*, 1987, pp. 128–140, figs 81–87; Schwarz, *Künstlerhaus*, 1990, pp. 172–174, no. 16; Müller, *Casa Pippi*, 2018. It is possible that there was originally a painted stucco decoration on the façade but this would have been unobtrusive since the large windows take up almost the entire wall.
102. For Vasari's houses in Arezzo (1541–1548) and Florence (1570–1579), see Albrecht, *Häuser von Giorgio Vasari*, 1985, pp. 83–100; Schwarz, *Künstlerhaus*, 1990, pp. 177–184, no. 18, pp. 194–196, no. 24, colour ill. pp. 136, 138; for the Casa Zuccari in Florence (1577–1579) and the Palazzo Zuccari in Rome (1593–1603), see Müller, *Casa Zuccari*, 1985, pp. 101–120; Schwarz, ibid., pp. 206–210, no. 30, colour ill. pp. 139–147.
103. See on this matter, Chapter VIII, pp. 242–243.

Chapter VII
The Interior of the 'Italian Wing' / the 'Schilderhuis'

Little is known about the inside of Rubens's house. Information about the decoration and the layout and function of the various rooms is in very short supply. Next to nothing of the original interiors has survived and there are no probate inventories or other documents that list the parts and contents of the house. Only two seventeenth-century illustrations provide a picture of the interior that corresponds to reality, albeit reality as it was fifty years after Rubens's death when the house had long since been adapted to the requirements of its later inhabitants, namely two views at the bottom of the 1692 Harrewijn print (Fig. 127 and Text ill. 47). Then, from almost a century after that, we have the simplified plan sketched from memory by François Mols, which gives an idea of the interior layout (Fig. 3). There are, however, several collector's cabinet or *kunstkamer* paintings in which we see not only decorative elements but also rooms that were apparently influenced by the interior of the home of the famous master.[1]

The most important section of Rubens's house, or at least an essential part of it, was of course the workshop complex. Italianate in style and built on an L-shaped plan, the short, narrow leg of the 'L' runs parallel to the Wapper and the longer leg forms one whole side of the courtyard. Thanks to the two Harrewijn prints we are very well informed about the appearance of the façades (with the exception of the south front) and the way the roofs were constructed (Figs 17, 18).

As to when the wing was built, we have already seen that work would have been well-advanced or possibly even finished in 1615 – apart from a staircase for which a contract was agreed towards the end of 1616 – and that the workshop was finished and in use no later than 1617.

A. The West Side of the Studio Wing

The Stairwell and Staircase, and a 'Galerie' Overlooking the Street

One of several puzzling parts of the workshop complex interior is the stairwell and staircase in the narrow part of the building parallel to the Wapper. Two

---

1. See Appendix III, 30–33.

CHAPTER VII - THE INTERIOR OF THE 'ITALIAN WING' / THE 'SCHILDERHUIS'

visual sources give information about stairs in this position: the Harrewijn print of 1692 and Mols's drawing of c. 1763. The print (Fig. 124) shows the start of a flight of steps apparently going up to the first or 'mezzanine' floor, but how the stairs exactly continued from there is far from clear. In Mols's drawing (Figs 125–126) two flights can be seen, the second one leading up to the top floor, to a room that he calls the 'galerie' (on which more below).

Most likely the wooden staircase consisted simply of two flights, with the second built against the blind wall (on the courtyard side) and leading up to a space on the top floor. But such a simple arrangement leaves a number of questions unanswered. In particular, it is not clear how the staircase connected with the rooms in the adjoining south and west wings. Moreover – and this is certainly important – we must ask how and where the upper floor or floors were closed off from the open air (while the bottom flight was open to one side).

Mols, who had seen the staircase (but made the drawing only 'de mémoire') evidently had difficulty fitting it correctly into the architecture on his plan, as can be gathered from the heavily hatched rectangle to the right of the stairs on the ground floor. So his drawing does not really offer a solution to our questions.

By the 1930s the staircase had completely disappeared (Figs 4 and 5) and the architects involved in the reconstruction of the house understandably found it hard to make anything of Mols's drawing of the second flight of stairs. It proved impossible, for example, to connect the 'open' ground floor to the upper levels. Several designs were proposed for the reconstruction, all with a more complicated staircase comprising three or four flights which did not combine into a continuous ascent. Eventually one of these, with a flight in the mezzanine (see Text ill. 16), was chosen, but its form undoubtedly deviates from the original design.[2]

As said, what can be determined from Mols's drawing is that when he visited the house, he found stairs that led to the top floor, which consisted of a long rectangular space occupying the entire length of the street front and lit by the top five windows of the street façade (Fig. 32). In his drawing Mols designates this room as no.1 and labels it the 'Galerie servant d'antichambre' (meaning an antechamber for the 'salon' on the upper floor).

As mentioned elsewhere, we can assume that the staircase with its richly carved banister represented in the Harrewijn print is that referred to in the contract between Hans van Mildert (1588–1638) and the joiner Gaspar Bulliau dated 2 November 1616 (Appendix I.9).[3] This document likewise offers little

---

2. See Van Averbeke, *Rubenshuis, restauratie II*, 1938, pp. 41–45, with three drawings of the house in section (nos 10–12), showing alternative arrangements; Devroe, *Rubens' huis*, 2008, I, pp. 105–106, 108; II, pp. 77–79, nos 62–64. In the reconstructed house, the flight of stairs that can be seen in the 1692 Harrewijn print has been followed, while the upper flights, rather than rising directly above, are sited in the adjoining south wing of the house, starting from the level of the mezzanine.
3. See Chapter IV, pp. 125–126; moreover, since we assume that the staircase was designed by Rubens, it is

CHAPTER VII - THE INTERIOR OF THE 'ITALIAN WING' / THE 'SCHILDERHUIS'

clarity about the construction and exact position of the stairs, stating only that they were to be placed in Rubens's house on the Wapper. It mentions, for example, 'the gallery' ('de gaelderye'), but its position between 'the two stairs' cannot be identified using the two visual sources.[4] Probably it was a landing somewhere between the two flights, on the same level as, and leading to the mezzanine.

In short, we cannot find a plausible solution for the problem of the 'open' staircase by combining the information given by the two visual sources. The construction cannot simply have been a stair with two flights, and a landing in between.[5]

In the 1692 Harrewijn print (Fig. 124) two doors can be seen under the colonnade either side of the staircase. To the left is a door leading to the studio, or rather to a room serving as an 'antichambre' (under the mezzanine). To the right, at the foot of the stairs, is a second door leading to what is probably a corridor on the other side of the stairs and parallel to the Wapper. This layout was retained in the modern reconstruction: there is now a narrow corridor with doors leading to the 'antichambre' and cellars.

A Mezzanine and an 'Antichambre'

There is reason to believe that on the Wapper side, the Italian wing was divided into three levels: a ground floor, a mezzanine and an upper storey. It is not possible to deduce this from Mols's plan of the interior layout of this wing, since he drew only two levels: the ground floor ('antichambre') and the top floor ('galerie servant d'antichambre') (Fig. 3).

As explained in the description of the west façade, the shape of the windows, according to the Harrewijn print, confirms that there was a low ground floor on the street side, with a mezzanine above.[6] The floor of the mezzanine must have been at the level of the horizontal stone architrave dividing the tall windows into two parts (Text ill. 68). In the part underneath the architrave, closed internal shutters can be seen that leave a strip of glass uncovered, thus allowing some light into the room on the ground floor; this suggests that the upper half of the high windows belonged to a different space.

During the preparatory research for the reconstruction it was believed, moreover, that traces of the existence of a mezzanine (assumed to be a gallery)

included in the catalogue (No. 19), where more details are given about its makers and decoration.
4. Described as: '[…] [de] voors. twee trappen de eenen beneden de voors. gaelderyen ende de anderen daer oppe […]' ([the] two flights of stairs mentioned, one below the aforementioned gallery and the other above) (Appendix I.9); of course, this was not the 'Galerie' indicated by Mols in his drawing; that room was to be found on the top floor and not between the two flights).
5. Many thanks are due to Brecht Vanoppen and Arnout Balis, both of whom looked into this matter carefully, without, however, reaching an acceptable conclusion.
6. See Chapter V, p. 157.

CHAPTER VII - THE INTERIOR OF THE 'ITALIAN WING' / THE 'SCHILDERHUIS'

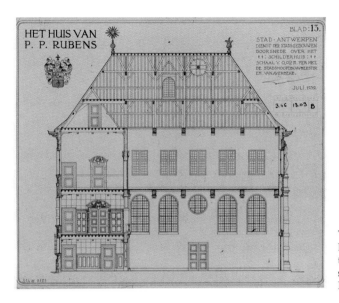

Text ill. 82. Émile Van Averbeke, Design for the reconstruction of the house: intersection of the studio wing, blueprint. Antwerp, FelixArchief.

had been found in the north and south walls.[7] This prompted the decision to create a low 'antichambre' with a mezzanine on top, in the form of an open gallery looking onto the studio (Text ills 16 and 82). We can be confident that a mezzanine did exist, but it is not certain that there was in Rubens's time an open structure like the one realised in the modern reconstruction.[8]

B. *The Large Workshop on the Ground Floor*

Rubens's large (or main) workshop took up a considerable part of the ground floor of the south wing.[9] As we have seen, an area containing, on the ground floor, an antechamber, with a mezzanine (or gallery?) above, was sectioned off at the street end of the space. The antechamber was entered through the door visible in the 1692 Harrewijn print, to the left of the staircase, within the arcaded gallery (Fig. 124). In his drawing Mols shows just such a ground-floor room, which he names 'antichambre', with windows looking onto the Wapper, and a wide doorway giving access to the former workshop, then a 'salon' (Fig. 3).

7. 'Ankers en openingen [in the north and south wall of the studio wing] waar vroeger een balk geplaatst werd, bewijzen dat wel degelijk een gaanderij in het atelier bestond' (Cramps and openings [in the north and south walls of the studio wing], indicating the former location of a beam, show that the studio indeed must have had a gallery) (Ruyten, *Opzoekingswerken Rubenshuis*, 1954, p. 4).
8. For the discussion regarding the existence of a gallery in William Cavendish's Antwerp 'riding house' (the former studio?), see Chapter II, p. 69.
9. The possibility, suggested during the restoration, that the large workshop was not at ground-floor level but three metres higher, like a *piano nobile*, while the space below was used for storage, can be dismissed; for a detailed discussion of the idea, with various hypothetical plans of the interior space, see Devroe, *Rubens' huis*, 2008, I, pp. 107–111; II, pp. 81–86, nos 66–68. See also below, p. 223, n. 67.

204

CHAPTER VII - THE INTERIOR OF THE 'ITALIAN WING' / THE 'SCHILDERHUIS'

Text ill. 83. View of the studio in the Rubenshuis.

Judging from the two Harrewijn prints and surviving parts of the building, the dimensions of the large room on the ground floor can be fairly accurately determined. The interior measured c. 8.5 m in width. It was 13 m long and 6.5 m in height, meaning that the ceiling was just above the tops of the windows and *oculus* in the north façade. The width and height correspond to the present, reconstructed studio (Text ill. 83).

In both Harrewijn prints open doors allow a glimpse of the interior as it was in Hillewerve's time when the room was furnished as a luxurious salon (Text ills 44 and 46).[10] In the prints there is virtually nothing to suggest the original appearance of the studio, except the probable location of a fireplace on the east half of the south wall (where it was reconstructed).

Windows and Lighting

When describing the exterior of the studio wing in Chapter V we discussed the unusual garden-facing east façade with a row of three tall windows filling most of the space between the ground and the bottom of the figurative frieze (Fig. 29). More noteworthy still was a discovery made during research that preceded restoration of the workshop's south wall, the appearance of which can only be conjectured as there is no known image of it – unless *Hélène Fourment au carrosse* (Appendix III.7; Fig. 31) is deemed to have documentary value (see above).[11]

The archaeological investigations carried out in 1938 that preceded the restoration revealed a surprise which presents a quandary. A particularly

10. See Chapter III, p. 110.
11. On the south façade in the background of this portrait, see Chapter V, pp. 159–161.

CHAPTER VII - THE INTERIOR OF THE 'ITALIAN WING' / THE 'SCHILDERHUIS'

striking and unexpected discovery was made in the masonry of the south façade, where traces believed to be of seven large round-headed windows were found, corresponding precisely in shape, size and also position to those of the north façade facing the courtyard. The discovery happened 'to general astonishment' during work taking place in February 1938, when large marble fireplaces were removed from the ground floor.[12] These traces seem to indicate that Rubens's studio not only had large windows to the north and east, but also on the south side, which is rather difficult to believe (see below). Unfortunately it is impossible to assess the accuracy of the observations made at the time. The only available information is a very brief note contained in the archaeological reports.[13] Furthermore, as far as we know, no drawings or diagrams were made; the only visual record is a photograph showing part of the excavated wall within which a (temporary) round arch has been reconstructed, and the outline of a window marked (Text ill. 84).[14]

Text ill. 84. The temporary reconstruction of a window with round arch in the south façade of the studio wing (c. 1940).

What later happened – or might have happened – to these windows is a matter of some confusion. As noted elsewhere, we know that the south side of this wing was originally an external wall, and beyond it was the passage leading to the garden from the Wapper. A floor was later added above the passageway, as can been seen in the Harrewijn prints, so that the external wall became internal. The once open passageway was converted into a coach house (also used as a wash house).

This situation is described in a sale contract drawn up a few years after the making of the second Harrewijn print

---

12. In his summary of the investigations (18, 19 and 21 February 1938) Théo Ruyten writes that first they found out that in the south façade: 'vijf ramen met halfronde waaiers bestaan hadden'. After removal of marble chimneypieces more was found: 'Er werden achter deze schouwen nog ramen gevonden. Derwijze dat er in de zuidergevel zeven ramen gevonden werden, welke juist dezelfde afmetingen hadden en op dezelfde hoogte geplaatst waren dan de halfronde ramen van de noordergevel' (Ruyten, *Opzoekingswerken Rubenshuis*, 1954, p. 3). See also Tijs, *Rubens en Jordaens*, 1984, p. 93; Devroe, *Rubens' huis*, 2008, I, pp. 70–71, fig. 37; Maclot, *Rubenssite*, 2016, pp. 169–170.
13. These very short passages are quoted in the note above, n. 12. Many thanks are due to colleagues for their help in this matter. Koen Bulckens, who is preparing a doctoral dissertation on Rubens's workshop, kindly shared his information; Arnout Balis tried (in vain) to find out more in the Rubenshuis archives. They came to different views about the possible existence of south windows. Bulckens believes that there may originally have been windows present (verbal communication; see also Bulckens, *Rubens and Workshop*, 2019, pp. 91–92), whereas Balis disagreed, finding there was insufficient evidence.
14. Devroe, *Rubens' huis*, 2008, I, p. 71, fig. 37; II, no. 88.

CHAPTER VII - THE INTERIOR OF THE 'ITALIAN WING' / THE 'SCHILDERHUIS'

(8 December 1696; Appendix I.37). At that moment, the adjacent small house on the Wapper, that had been part of the property since Rubens bought it in 1627, was split from the 'large house', and the status of the party wall became a legal matter in this contract. It emerges that the coach house of the large house was lit by windows (fitted with grilles) which gave directly onto the courtyard and garden of the small house next-door. It was a condition of the agreement that these windows should remain.[15]

In short, when the passageway was roofed over and turned into a coach house, the original south façade of the house became an internal wall. If there were any windows along the south side of the studio – which as we have seen, is not an established fact – they then ceased to provide light, and consequently may have been blocked up.

During the modern reconstruction of the house, an open passageway from the Wapper to the garden was restored, with a freestanding gateway onto the Wapper. The south side of the workshop thus became an exterior wall once more (Text ill. 38).[16] There were also plans to restore the seven windows in it, resulting in the making of several different designs (Text ill. 85),[17] but that idea was eventually dropped. On the ground floor two doors were introduced opening onto the passageway, one of them with a single large, round-headed window above.[18] As a compromise, however, bluestone architraves were set into the blank exterior wall in those places where the window apertures would have been, so that now a row of six blind, round-headed 'windows' can be seen (Text ill. 86). On the upper floor, where in all likelihood they had originally been, seven rectangular windows of a similar size to those of the north façade were installed (Text ill. 38).

It seems that Rubens had indeed conceived his workshop with windows on several sides. Nonetheless, that conclusion needs to be examined further. If he had windows put in the south as well as the north and east walls, he would have lit his workshop in a most unusual way, with light coming in from three sides. Then again, if all of those windows really existed, where could the fireplace in

---

15. The owner of the main house was required to install fixed panes in the window openings, while the owner of the small house was prohibited from building any construction in the garden which might exclude or reduce the light entering (see also Maclot, *Rubenssite*, 2016, p. 88). It is somewhat confusing that the contract refers to *seven* windows (the same number as were assumed to be in the lower level of the original south façade), while the wall overlooking the neighbour's garden must have been much shorter than the original façade, which ran the entire length of the open passageway (13 m).
16. Nowadays the passageway remains 'open', but it has been given a glass roof.
17. GN.29/5 - For designs for a proposed restoration of the façade with two rows of seven windows, see inter alia: Tijs, *Rubens en Jordaens*, fig. p. 204; Devroe, *Rubens' huis*, 2008, II, cat. nos 58, 66, 66a, 67d. The fourteen windows also appear in the wooden model of the house built in 1939–1942 (Maclot, *Rubenssite*, 2016, repr. p. 223).
18. The installation of a door leading from the studio to the passageway is based on Van Averbeke's assumption that there must have been a passage here to allow for the transport of large panels (Devroe, *Rubens' huis*, 2008, I, p. 105).

CHAPTER VII - THE INTERIOR OF THE 'ITALIAN WING' / THE 'SCHILDERHUIS'

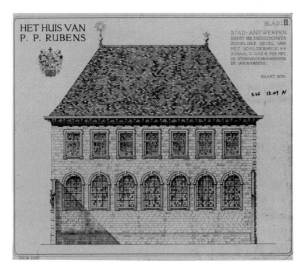

Text ill. 85. Émile Van Averbeke, Design for the south façade of the studio wing (1939), blueprint. Antwerp, FelixArchief.

Text ill. 86. Passageway from the Wapper to the garden (seen from the garden side).

the studio have been situated? Was it between two windows on the south side? And surely at least one area of solid wall would have been necessary to support large canvases or panels while they were being painted. There are two known images of a more or less Rubensian workshop (see below), but in neither of them is there anything to suggest the existence of windows on more than one side.

By any standard a workshop with direct light entering from more than one side is extraordinary. It could hardly be more at variance with the usual preference for a north light, as advocated in authoritative architectural tracts. Vitruvius recommended light from the north: 'Picture galleries [...] and painters' studios [should face north] in order that the fixed light may permit the colours used in their work to last with qualities unchanged'.[19] Vincenzo Scamozzi, in *L'idea della architettura universale*, published in 1615, offers a more detailed opinion on the direction from which light should ideally come, not so much in reference to a workshop but rather places used for the display of works of art. He too recommends a light from the north, which, he points out, is 'stable and firm for most of the year'.[20]

19. Vitruvius, *De architectura*, Book VI, 4, 2; id., *Ten Books*, trans. Morgan, 1960, p. 181; see Muller, *Rubens's Museum*, 1977, p. 576, n. 39. For light from the north, see also, for example, Sandrart, *Teutsche Academie*, 1675–80, Book III, part I, chapter II ('von dem Liecht und Mahlerzimmer'), p. 81; Stumpel, *Spiegelingen*, 2006, pp. 211–212.
20. For citations and references, see Muller, *Rubens's Museum*, 1977, pp. 576, 578; on Scamozzi's recommendations, see also Chapter VIII, p. 245, n. 42. Rubens bought a copy of *L'idea* in May 1617 (see Chapter IV, p. 121, n. 17).

CHAPTER VII - THE INTERIOR OF THE 'ITALIAN WING' / THE 'SCHILDERHUIS'

Yet Rubens planned to have light coming into the workshop not only from the usual direction, through the four tall second-level windows and the *oculus* in the north wall, but also from the east and possibly the south as well. Depending on the weather and the time of year, light could pour into the workshop with a greater or lesser degree of intensity from more than one side. Having several light sources is inconvenient when painting, and no doubt there would have been some way of shutting out or at least muting the light if required. The 1692 Harrewijn print shows a curtain over one of the east windows (Text ill. 45). This may not reflect the situation as it was in Rubens's day but, as mentioned above, there is reference to 'blaffeturen' ('window shutters') in the 'schilderhuis', for which a bill was settled by the estate (Appendix I.23: [9]).[21]

In this connection it is worth noting a piece of advice given by the Dutch art theorist Willem Goeree (1635–1711), who uses the same term 'blaffetuur' in his treatise on drawing. He too considers a north light ideal for a workshop. But if a room catches light from the south, 'one can, if the sunlight is too strong, put a thin sheet of oiled paper or fine linen in one's window'.[22] This he recommends as a means of diffusing the sunlight that often shines in for much of the day and distributing it evenly throughout the room. We can see just such a translucent light-diffuser over the window in the background of *A Young Painter Behind a Balustrade*, by Cornelis de Vos (Text ill. 87).[23]

Perhaps it was Rubens's intention to have as much light as possible in his workshop on overcast days, of which of course there were many in Antwerp.[24] A more sophisticated explanation, suggested by Hélène Dubois, is that the different light sources offered Rubens the opportunity 'to anticipate to some extent

Text ill. 87. Cornelis de Vos, *A Young Painter Behind a Balustrade*, detail with the window with light-diffuser in the background. Whereabouts unknown.

---

21. On the mistaken idea that these were external shutters, see Chapter II, p. 57, n. 25.
22. '[…] kan men bij voorval van te sterken zonne-schijn, een blaffetuur van dun ge-olijt post-papier, of dun lijn waat in sijn venster-sponning setten' (Goeree, *Teyken-Konst*, 1705, pp. 63–64); Sandrart makes a similar recommendation and refers to 'Plafeturi, vom oel getrenktem Papier gemacht' ('Plafeturi', made from paper soaked in oil; see Sandrart, *Teutsche Academie*, 1675–80, Book III, Part III, Chapter II ('von dem Liecht und Mahlerzimmer'), p. 81. On the 'blaffeturen', see also above, Chapter II, p. 57, n. 25. On the light in the workshop, see also Lemmens, *Atelier*, 1964, pp. 12–13; Stumpel, *Spiegelingen*, 2006, esp. pp. 209, 213.
23. Whereabouts unknown; Van der Stighelen, *Zelfbeeld*, 2000, pp. 246 (fig. 10), 260, n. 113 (as '*Portret van Jan Cossiers*'. Another type of light screening can be seen in the anonymous (Dutch or Flemish?) drawing *Interior of a Sculptor's Workshop*, now in the Kunsthalle Bremen, Bremen (Scholten, *Quellinus*, 2010, p. 38, fig. 46).
24. See on this (with Jordaens's comment on the 'short and foul days' of winter that prevented him from working at full speed): Bulckens, *Rubens and Workshop*, 2019, pp. 92, 100, n. 71.

the lighting conditions as they existed at the locations for which the paintings were intended'.[25]

Images of the Main Workshop (?)

There are two paintings that might give us an approximate idea of Rubens's workshop. The more 'realistic' of the two, at least as regards size and architecture, is the workshop that can be glimpsed in the background of *A Collector's Cabinet with the Figure of Pictura* attributed to Cornelis de Baellieur and now in the Graf Harrach'sche Familiensammlung, Schloss Rohrau (Appendix III.32; Text ill. 88).[26] Three painters are at work, all with their backs to the viewer. Two are at their easels – one busy with the portrait of a lady who sits for him – while the third perches high up on a scaffold, working on an enormous canvas nailed to a wooden frame and fixed against the wall.

As to the architecture of the room, we see part of a flat, beamed ceiling and, on the right, a windowless wall with a very tall doorway and an empty niche. Both features include motifs that were used elsewhere in Rubens's house: the 'ears' or 'crossettes' in the door frame and the carved scallop shell in the half-dome of the niche. The workshop's left wall is out of sight, but from the way the shadows fall we can tell that it contains the windows that allow the light to stream in. There can be no doubt that in this *Collector's Cabinet* an allusion to Rubens and his workshop is deliberately intended. Not only is the finely dressed gentleman led by Fame to Pictura probably Rubens himself, but in the atelier in the background the painter on the scaffold is working on a composition by the master, a version of *The Death of Decius Mus*.[27]

The second painting, a privately-owned *Allegory of Painting* by Jan Brueghel II (1601–1678), dated around 1625–1630 and possibly a copy of a lost work by his father, is interesting but certainly further removed from reality (Appendix III.33; Text ill. 89).[28] In the background is a large room in which painters are at work, sitting or standing in front of half a dozen easels, each placed next to a window. A lady in an armchair poses for her portrait. At the far end of the room a couple of servants bend to their toil at a table. It seems evident that this image is based on Rubens's famous workshop, which was considered to be one of the highlights of a visit to Antwerp. But the architecture should not be regarded as 'realistic' in any way. That Rubens's house would have contained such a grand room with a barrel vault and two rows of windows one above the other is

25. Dubois, *Grands tableaux de Rubens*, 2007, pp. 160–161.
26. See, in addition to the information in Appendix III.32, esp. on the detail showing the workshop: ibid., p. 162, fig. 4; Bulckens, *Rubens and Workshop*, 2019, p. 92.
27. Baumstark – Delmarcel, *Decius Mus (CRLB)*, 2019, I, pp. 156–157, text ill. 42, fig. 88; II, no. 5a.
28. See, in addition to the information in Appendix III.33, on the detail showing the workshop: Dubois, *Grands tableaux de Rubens*, 2007, p. 161, fig. 3.

CHAPTER VII - THE INTERIOR OF THE 'ITALIAN WING' / THE 'SCHILDERHUIS'

Text ill. 88. Cornelis de Baellieur, *A Collector's Cabinet with the Figure of Pictura* (Appendix III.32), detail of the studio in the background. Rohrau, Schloss Rohrau.

Text ill. 89. Jan Brueghel II, *Allegory of Painting* (Appendix III.33), detail of the studio in the background. The Netherlands, Private Collection.

inconceivable. The presence of children learning their trade in this room – one little lad, who uses the seat of a chair to work on, is not even breeched – also makes it questionable as a realistic image of Rubens's workshop.[29]

C. The Upstairs Studio (or So-called 'Pupils' Studio')

At the bottom right of the 1692 Harrewijn print is an inset with a picture of a spacious rectangular or square room furnished with a four-poster bed (Fig. 18 and Text ill. 47). Undoubtedly this is Hillewerve's bedchamber, described in the deed of gift of 1682 as being part of the quarters inhabited by Hillewerve himself and his servant, that were to be always at his disposal (Appendix I.33: [3]). On either side of the room is an open door through which part of a window in an adjacent room can be seen. What is particularly striking about the room is its circular cupola or 'calotte', which has a round opening at the top and an *oculus* on either side.

---

29. The material assembled by Anne-Marie Logan on Rubens as a teacher (Logan, *Rubens as a Teacher*, 2006) does not unequivocally answer the question of whether there were also young children in Rubens's workshop, something that seems rather unlikely. Training under Rubens was highly valued and consisted mainly if not exclusively of setting a pupil, youth or adult, to work on the paintings in the well-run studio. Children, on the other hand, spent a long time on drawing exercises before being allowed to hold a brush.

CHAPTER VII - THE INTERIOR OF THE 'ITALIAN WING' / THE 'SCHILDERHUIS'

The plan Mols sketched after visiting the house in 1763 indicates the location of this unusual room with cupola. On the top floor of the south wing – above what used to be the large workshop on the ground floor – he drew a circular form, marked with the number 3 (Fig. 3). In the key beside the plan he labels the room 'salon en rotonde' and in the adjoining notes he refers to it as 'la rotonde' – the rotunda (Appendix I.43: [6, 7]). So, strangely – contrary to what the Harrewijn print shows seventy years earlier – this would mean that in Mols's time not only the ceiling, but the room itself was circular.

Jacob van der Sanden, who, like Mols, had visited the house before it was radically altered, also made a brief note about the unusual (circular?) chamber, specifically stating that it was 'above the first floor'. Especially interesting is the fact that he knew what the room's function had been in Rubens's time, for he refers to it as: 'de groote Schilders camer in 't rond en verlicht, als een koupel…' (the large studio, round and lit like a cupola…) (Appendix I.42: [2]; see also Appendix I.42: [1, 3]).[30]

Taking all these sources together – the print and the information recorded by the eyewitnesses Mols and Van der Sanden – we can say with certainty that the room used by Hillewerve as his bedchamber was on the top floor, above what had been Rubens's large workshop.

An important matter that needs to be decided is the orientation of the room shown in the print, in other words: from which compass point are we looking at it? There seems to be only one possibility: the canon's bedroom is seen from the north, that is from the courtyard side, meaning that the north façade and its windows are not visible. If correct, then we can work out what it is that can be seen through the two doorways. The one on the left – the east or garden side – leads to what in Mols's day was a room with an 'alcove' (possibly Hillewerve's servant's room). On the right is the aforementioned long and comparatively narrow 'Galerie servant d'antichambre', with five windows overlooking the Wapper. The fireplace is placed against the south wall (corresponding to Mols's drawing). It should be noted that, in assuming this orientation, the distances to the façades and windows of the adjacent rooms are not represented realistically – these seem much nearer than they would actually have been; however, it is difficult to make the case for any other possibility.[31]

---

30. So like Mols, Van der Sanden gives the impression that the room itself was circular. However, his description of different parts of the house is somewhat vague, as he ostensibly combines what he had seen with his own eyes with information gathered from other authors (one of the sources he cites is Philip Rubens's *Vita*). Early on (as quoted above) he places the 'Cabinet en de groote Schilders camer in 't rond' on the upper floor (p. 205); but elsewhere he writes that the 'Cabinet van Rubens' (so not explicitly calling it his 'studio') was 'rondom verlicht als een koepel', and he refers loosely to seeing 'ruyme en heerlijke bovenplaetzen' (p. 528).
31. An eastern or western orientation seems more or less impossible. That would mean that one of the windows visible through the open door would be facing south; the fireplace would then be in the middle of the upper floor (and not where Mols places it); and finally there are the *oculi* in the cupola, which presumably correspond to the position of the dormer windows, i.e. on the north and south sides of the large hipped roof.

CHAPTER VII - THE INTERIOR OF THE 'ITALIAN WING' / THE 'SCHILDERHUIS'

According to the print the bedchamber was rectangular (or more or less square) in plan. Assuming that it spanned the full width of the south wing, the internal dimensions must have been in the region of eight and a half metres square with the flat part of the ceiling being around four and a half metres in height. The cupola would almost certainly have been built in timber rather than brick or stone.

As said, it is remarkable that some seventy years later both Mols and Van der Sanden describe this room not as a rectangular (or square) space with cupola, but circular. If we take their description as accurate, the only explanation is that the room was substantially altered (using timber?) to provide rounded corners (perhaps a rather far-fetched assumption).

Seen from the courtyard, the space occupied by the top floor – assuming that the location given above is correct – corresponded to the figurative frieze and the rectangular windows above. Hillewerve's bedchamber lay underneath the centre of the roof that covered the entire length of the south wing (street to garden), but its position was not central within the five bays of the north façade. The windows corresponding to the bedchamber are in fact the three to the right (Text ill. 90). This also explains why the dormer window allowing light into the cupola (about which, see below) was not centred above the north façade over the doorway, but closer to the street. At the time of the modern restoration there was in fact a large central dormer but it was evident from the roof construction that this was not where the original had been.[32] A dormer window was reconstructed in the original shape and position. The difference is clear when we compare a pre-restoration photograph (Text ill. 59) with the current location of the dormer (Fig. 10).

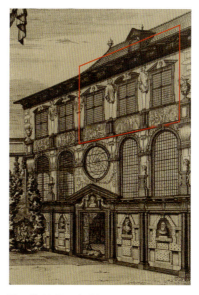

Text ill. 90. Detail of the 1692 Harrewijn print (Fig. 18): the location of Hillewerve's bedroom.

Otto Sperling's Description

In addition to the visual evidence of the Harrewijn prints and the testimonies of Mols and Van der Sanden, there is of course the well-known account by Otto Sperling, who visited Rubens in late May or early June of 1621. His

---

32. Ruyten, *Opzoekingswerken Rubenshuis*, 1954, p. 3; Devroe, *Rubens' Huis*, 2008, p. 74; Maclot, *Rubenssite*, 2016, p. 172.

autobiography includes a striking description of the place where he saw a lot of young assistants and apprentices at work: 'Wir sahen da auch einen grossen Sael, welcher keine fenstern hatte, sondern das Liecht fiel von oben drein Mitten im Sael durch ein grosses loch' (We also saw a vast room without windows but lit by a large opening in the middle of the ceiling) (Appendix I.27). It comes from one of the most frequently cited passages in the literature on Rubens and has occasioned all kinds of assumptions and comments concerning which room in the house Sperling could have seen and described.

In our view what Sperling saw could only have been the room on the top floor that Mols calls the 'rotonde'. As we have just seen, when we connect the evidence gleaned from the print with Mols's plan and Van der Sanden's manuscript, we can locate Sperling's 'vast room' with absolute certainty. Yet that connection has not always been made, and the whereabouts in Rubens's house of this room with an opening in the ceiling – and no windows, according to Sperling – has puzzled more than one Rubens scholar.

When Max Rooses published his article on Rubens's house in 1888, he took it as read that the spacious room with cupola on the top floor of the south wing (seen in Mols's drawing) was Hillewerve's bedchamber, but he did not believe that it was also the workshop described by Sperling. He suggested that the room where Rubens's 'pupils' worked ('la vaste pièce où travaillaient les élèves') was perhaps situated on the south side of the garden, in a separate building that could also be reached from the entrance on the Hopland. This building, a simple construction without decoration ('une construction sans apparat'), he submitted, vanished without trace after Rubens's death, which was why it did not appear in the Harrewijn prints, nor in Mols's drawing.[33]

This hypothesis can safely be rejected, but is not as strange as it might seem. There were painters in Antwerp who did indeed have a separate studio ('schilderhuis') in their garden or who put up a building to the rear ('achterhuis' or backhouse) for the purpose.[34] As an addition to his house 'Het Hoefijzer' on the Meir (bought in 1550), Frans Floris (1519/20–1570) had constructed an *achterhuis* that was undoubtedly used as a workshop. The grand town house he subsequently built in the Arenbergstraat on a plot purchased in 1562 consisted of two parallel (separate) buildings, one of which was an 'achterhuis' that was accessed by a gate from the street.[35] Archival records show that a century later, Antwerp painters still sometimes preferred to separate their work space from

---

33. Rooses, *Maison*, 1888, pp. 227–228; also in: Rooses – Ruelens, eds, *Correspondance*, 1887–1909, II, p. 158. In the Harrewijn print of 1692 the exit to the Hopland (as well as the small neighbouring houses facing the Hopland) are hidden by the covered walkway at the left of the pergola (Text. ill. 31).
34. Petra Maclot, among others, translates the Dutch word *'achterhuis'* as backhouse (see her article on artists's workshop in 16th-century Antwerp: Maclot, *Artists' Houses*, 2018, passim).
35. On the *'achterhuis'* used by Floris as studio, see Van de Velde, *Floris*, 1975, I, pp. 31, 451, doc. 37; id., *Painted Decoration*, 1985, pp. 127–128; on the *'achterhuizen'* of Frans Floris and his brother the sculptor Cornelis Floris, see Maclot, *Artists' Houses*, 2018, pp. 120, 122–123 (with a drawing by the author giving her impression of

CHAPTER VII - THE INTERIOR OF THE 'ITALIAN WING' / THE 'SCHILDERHUIS'

their domestic quarters. Cornelis Schut (1597–1655) and Jan Cossiers (1600–1671) both built a workshop in their gardens (in 1652 and 1653 respectively) and at his death in 1654 Jan Van Balen (1611–1654) owned a 'schilderhuys' 'achter den hoff' (beyond the garden).[36]

Rubens, who owned an unusual large plot, did not build his 'schilderhuis' as a separate 'backhouse', but the spacious and well-lit south wing he added to the older house to accommodate his business, was also (partly) located 'in the garden', so to speak. In any case, we can safely rule out the possibility that there was another studio somewhere else in his garden.

In his 1904 monograph on Rubens, Rooses was still sceptical about the top-floor atelier. As in his earlier article (of 1888), he found it inconceivable that Hillewerve's bedchamber had earlier been used as a workshop. Relying on Rubens's letter of 17 August 1638 to Lucas Faydherbe (Appendix I.21), he believed it was a place 'where items of little value were kept' while having no idea where Sperling's 'pupils' studio' might have been.[37] By 1910, however, Rooses had changed his mind. He was now convinced – quite rightly – that the room that was lit from the ceiling, and where Sperling has seen 'the pupils' working, was 'above the master's studio' (meaning the large studio on the ground floor), and that it was later furnished as Hillewerve's bedroom.[38]

Prior to the restoration, however, doubts were again raised, this time by Ary Delen, who pointed out that Sperling referred to 'a vast room without windows', whereas, as can be seen in the Harrewijn prints (Figs 17, 18), the rooms on the top floor above the studio had windows on the north and east sides.[39] 'Moreover,' he went on, 'there seems to be nothing in the building that resembles a round room with light from above. For now, the location of that room remains a mystery'.[40] It was doubted – rightly so, as we shall see below – whether the amount of light entering through an opening in the ceiling would be sufficient for a painter's workshop. In any case, during the restoration it was concluded that such a problematic room with cupola could not be original and must have been built by Hillewerve,[41] and in the end no attempt was made to reconstruct it. The top floor of the south wing is now a single large space with a

---

Cornelis's studio, which was a separate two-storey building – with an upstairs studio? – in the garden, fig. 6).

36. Kleinert, *Atelierdarstellungen*, 2006, p. 31; relevant archival documentation in Duverger, *Kunstinventarissen*, 1984–2009, VI, pp. 289 (Schut), 416–417 (Cossiers); VII, p. 29 (Van Balen); for Schut, see also Wilmers, *Schut*, 1996, pp. 23, 233 (doc. 118), 234 (doc. 132).
37. Rooses, *Leven*, 1903, pp. 150, 153; in the English version of a year later he corrects this: 'as for the studio upstairs, it was evidently not Rubens's, but one of less importance in which his pupils worked' (id., *Rubens*, 1904, p. 150).
38. Rooses, *Huis van Rubens*, 1910, pp. 203–204 [pp. 15, 16].
39. In the Harrewijn view the bedchamber is represented without windows, as the room is seen from the north (where the windows are).
40. Delen, *Rubens' huis*, 1933, p. 32.
41. Devroe, *Rubens' huis*, 2008, I, p. 121.

CHAPTER VII - THE INTERIOR OF THE 'ITALIAN WING' / THE 'SCHILDERHUIS'

Text ill. 91. The so-called 'Pupils' studio' in the Rubenshuis.

flat, beamed ceiling and rectangular windows of uniform size in the north, east and south walls (Text ill. 91).

Lighting was not the only issue that brought the location of the upstairs studio into question. There was another domed room in Rubens's house, the 'pantheon' or 'antiquarium' in the east wing – discussed in detail in Chapter VIII – and this also contributed to the confusion. A number of authors believed that Rubens's pantheon and the top-floor room with its cupola were in fact one and the same space. Floris Prims was one of them. He maintained that the 'museum' in the shape of the Pantheon and the so-called 'pupils' studio' were not separate rooms. Moreover, he thought that the circular structure with cupola might have been built in the garden and later converted by William Cavendish into his 'riding house' or 'manège'. The total lack of evidence for such a proposal – there has never been a circular arena in the garden – has already been covered.[42] Nevertheless, Rutger Tijs fell in with this bizarre 'manège' hypothesis. He too was convinced that what he called 'the apprentices' workshop' and Rubens's 'museum' of classical statuary were housed in the self-same circular structure in the garden, separate from the house.[43]

42. See Chapter II, pp. 69–70, nn. 66–67.
43. Tijs, *Rubens en Jordaens*, 1984, pp. 110–113, 143–144; he follows Prims's hypothesis and sees confirmation in

CHAPTER VII - THE INTERIOR OF THE 'ITALIAN WING' / THE 'SCHILDERHUIS'

Not every subsequent study rejected the opinions put forward by Prims and Tijs,[44] but even so it can be firmly dismissed. Rooses got it right in 1910. The cupola that was seen by Mols and Van der Sanden and depicted in the 1692 Harrewijn print did indeed exist in the south wing. There are two questions that make the doubts understandable. Firstly, it is not immediately obvious how a cupola could have been constructed under a hipped roof – and therefore without a lantern or something of the sort. And secondly, how was it possible to use as studio a room that, according to Sperling, had no windows and where the only light entered from above through an opening in the ceiling?

The Cupola in the Roof

Questions about the location of the room with cupola were prompted in part by doubts about the feasibility of constructing a virtually hemispherical vault, with light coming from above, underneath a hipped roof like the one covering the south wing. And indeed, on the outside of the roof there is no trace of a dome or a lantern to be seen. Nevertheless it had already been suggested that a dome could have been built into the roof truss, and a study of the beams, which are original, has confirmed this. The construction of the truss differs from the norm in a way that creates space in the centre and allows for a cupola without compromising the roof's stability.[45] The study has therefore removed all doubt about the possibility of a cupola being built in the roof.[46]

As can be seen in the detail showing Hillewerve's bedchamber at the bottom of the 1692 Harrewijn print (Text ill. 47), the cupola had a circular opening at the top and two additional *oculi*, on the north and south sides. All three openings received light from the roof space, which was lit in turn by dormer windows, one on the north or courtyard side of the roof and offset from the centre of the façade (Text ill. 90), as mentioned above; and presumably another on the south side.[47] However complicated and unusual in its construction, the cupola in Rubens's house was apparently not unique. We have found one example of a dome incorporated into a hipped roof and lit from the side, constructed in more

---

the fact that during restoration the remains of four bluestone columns were excavated in the garden. After measurements were taken, Van Averbeke concluded that they could have been the remains of a circular building, 16 m in diameter (E. Van Averbeke, cited in Clijmans, *Wederopbouw Rubenshuis*, 1946, pp. 64–66). However, this notion had grown from Prims's theory, and can be dismissed as an explanation for the presence of the bluestone remains.

44. See the comments in Devroe, *Rubens' huis*, 2008, pp. 88–91.
45. Discussed at length, with technical details and 3D reconstructions, in an unpublished study by Sigurd de Gruyter (De Gruyter, *Lichtinval*, 2012, pp. 6–12, figs 10–22; summarised in Lombaerde, *Rubens*, 2014, pp. 218–219, fig. 16).
46. There is thus no reason for scepticism about the possibility of this construction (for example, Van Beneden, *Rubens and Architecture*, 2011, p. 18).
47. In 1938, traces of a dormer window were found on the south side of the roof (Ruyten, *Opzoekingswerken Rubenshuis*, 1954, p. 3; Devroe, *Rubens' huis*, 2008, I, p. 74).

CHAPTER VII - THE INTERIOR OF THE 'ITALIAN WING' / THE 'SCHILDERHUIS'

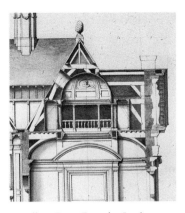

Text ill. 92. Pieter Post after Jacob van Campen, *North-South Cross-Section of the Mauritshuis, The Hague* (1652), drawing, detail. The Hague, Koninklijke Bibliotheek / Nationale Bibliotheek van Nederland.

or less the same manner. There was a cupola in the ceiling of the large upstairs hall of the Mauritshuis in The Hague, built between 1633 and 1644 to plans by the painter and architect Jacob van Campen (1595–1657). On the south side it had a large *oculus* that admitted light through an oblique shaft open at the roof plane (Text ill. 92).[48] It is worth mentioning that it was once thought – probably erroneously – that Van Campen may actually have seen Rubens's room with cupola.[49] Whatever the truth, his strong interest in the effects of zenithal light on paintings can also be seen in his design for the Oranjezaal in the Huis ten Bosch Palace, which he provided with a dome and lantern.[50]

Windows and Lighting

There is still the question of how to reconcile Sperling's account with the chamber depicted in the 1692 Harrewijn print and Mols's drawing. As noted, he states specifically that the room where he saw assistants and apprentices at work had no windows ('welcher keine fenstern hatte') but was lit from above by a large opening in the middle of the ceiling (Appendix I.27). Yet the chamber with cupola must have had windows – at least three on the north side, as can be gathered from the Harrewijn prints representing the north façade (Figs 17, 18) – and in Rubens's time there were probably windows on the south side as well.[51]

In theory it is possible, of course, that the room did not extend all the way to the north façade and that between the room and the front of the building there was a corridor or passage, but this seems rather far-fetched.

In short, however reluctant we may be to jettison the unique testimony Sperling provides about Rubens's workshop, we are left to conclude that part of his account is at odds with reality. Not only is it so that the architectural

---

48. The cupola was lost in the 1704 fire. See Terwen, *Johan Maurits*, 1979, p. 79, fig. 23; Lunsing Scheurleer, *Mauritshuis*, 1979, pp. 171–172, figs 99–102; Ottenheym, *Mauritshuis*, 2014, p. 47, figs 43, 52–84.
49. According to some biographers, Van Campen may have been apprenticed to Rubens (see Swillens, *Van Campen*, 1961, pp. 12–14), but there is no evidence for this (see Huisken et al., eds, *Van Campen*, 1995, pp. 15, 30, 53). J.J. Terwen does not rule this out, and even deems it possible that 'Van Campen probably spent part of his training as a painter under the domes of the recently completed building [Rubens's house]' (Terwen, *Johan Maurits*, 1979, p. 79). That, of course, is impossible if we take into account the fact that Van Campen was already registered as a master in the Haarlem Guild of Saint Luke in 1614 – thus before the completion of Rubens's workshop.
50. For extensive information about the light in this hall, see Van Eikema Hommes – Kolfin, *Oranjezaal*, 2013, pp. 179–253.
51. On the question of the windows in the south façade of the studio wing, see above, pp. 205–210.

evidence tells us there must have been windows. It should also be noted that there could never have been enough light for drawing or painting in a room that only received light from a cupola built beneath a roof. This was the conclusion reached by a study of the illumination in the upstairs workshop, based on computer simulations applied to a 3D reconstruction.[52]

That Sperling got things wrong is certainly not impossible; we have already commented on the inaccuracy of the account he wrote more than forty years after his visit to Antwerp in 1621.[53] Maybe his memory was at fault and he confused the domed room with the 'antiquarium', which he had also seen – as appears from his reference to the antique statues he saw in Rubens's collection ('seine antiquiteten und Griechische und Romanische Statuen') (Appendix I.27). Another explanation – and perhaps the most likely – is that while Sperling was there (in late May or early June) the windows were shuttered or covered in some way to diffuse the light, and he simply failed to notice them. We might recall in this connection that in Rubens's workshop there must have been some way of regulating light, as can be inferred from the aforementioned item in the accounts for making (or repairing) the 'blaffeturen' for 'the schilderhuys'.[54]

The Pantheon as Exemplar

The cupola into which light enters from above is obviously based on the Pantheon in Rome, lauded in numerous architectural treatises. The significance of this ancient building and the exceptionally even light that enters it will be examined further in Chapter VIII, when we discuss the second domed structure in Rubens's house, the 'antiquarium' in the east wing. Also discussed there are a number of aspects relating to both cupolas, including examples that Rubens may have known as well as probable imitations of those in his house.

D. The Two Workshops: Purpose and Names

Apart from the location and construction of the chamber with cupola, another factor we must take into account is the part the room played in the working process in Rubens's studio. Sperling states that in the room lit from above he saw many assistants whom he described as 'iunge Schilder' (young painters) or 'die jungen gesellen' (young journeymen) (Appendix I.27). His primary purpose was not to give information about the layout of the house but to show how tasks were allocated in Rubens's famous workshop, where several

---

52. De Gruyter, *Lichtinval*, 2012, pp. 13–17, figs 25–31.
53. See Chapter II, pp. 53–54.
54. See Chapter II, p. 57, n. 25 and above, p. 209, n. 21.

paintings were in simultaneous production, with assistants carrying out the largest part of the work.[55] He mentions that this ingenious production process brought Rubens both profit and renown. It surprised many of the visitors to his studio and indeed became something of a legend.[56]

Although consistent with the well-known cliché about the organisation of Rubens's workshop, we can assume that Sperling was not just repeating a Rubensian commonplace but describing what he had actually seen in the house in June 1621. To give an idea of the workshop's huge capacity: in the previous year, with the help of many assistants (including Anthony van Dyck), Rubens had completed thirty-nine ceiling pieces, each around 3 × 4 m in size, for Antwerp's Jesuit Church in a relatively short time.[57]

Following Sperling's account, the room lit from above where he saw the young painters at work has invariably been referred to in the literature as 'the pupils' workshop'. The term became entrenched in Rubens literature and is also used in the Rubenshuis museum as a name for the room above the main workshop.[58] Whether that name is meaningful and appropriate is another matter, however. The word 'pupil' itself is not in question, so long as it is not used in the narrow and literal meaning of a youth in training, but is understood to refer to a skilled assistant. Whereas Rubens and his contemporaries used the term 'discipel' ('disciple', synonymous with 'pupil') to refer to accomplished painters like Van Dyck,[59] it may be better to speak of 'assistants' or 'collaborators'. This is rightly noted by Arnout Balis, who points out that 'pupil' is not really a very useful term.[60]

That apart, we are still left with the following question: is it right to assume that the atelier with its cupola on the top floor was specifically intended to

55. Sperling's description of Rubens's workshop practice is one of the most frequently cited passages in the Rubens literature. It can be found in, for example, Rooses, *Rubens*, 1904, p. 153; Held, *Drawings*, 1959, pp. 19–20; Balis, *Studio Practices*, 1994, p. 98; Logan, *Rubens as a Teacher*, 2006, pp. 250–251; Büttner, *Rubens berühmt*, 2006, pp. 110–112; Balis, *Rubens and his Studio*, 2007, p. 37; Büttner, *Hands of Rubens*, 2017, p. 42; Baumstark – Delmarcel, *Decius Mus (CRLB)*, 2019, I, p. 160.
56. See Balis, *Rubens and his Studio*, 2007, p. 37; for a citation from Descamps, see ibid., p. 49, n. 98. For the easily earned money, see also Ramssla's account (100 guilders per week; see Appendix I.13) and the letter from Sweerts (100 guilders per day; see Appendix I.11).
57. The contract for the thirty-nine ceiling pieces was drawn up on 29 March 1620 and the paintings were delivered to the church within the year (Martin, *Ceiling Paintings (CRLB)*, 1968, pp. 31 ff.).
58. See, for example, Baudouin, *Summary Guide*, 1977, pp. 24–25, no. 14.
59. The contract for the Jesuit Church's ceiling pieces refers to Van Dyck (then 22 years of age) and 'sommige andere syne disipelen' (some other disciples of his) (Martin, *Ceiling Paintings (CRLB)*, 1968, p. 214); in the letter dated 28 April 1618 Rubens alludes to 'meglior mio discepolo' (translated as 'the best of my pupils'; Magurn, ed., *Letters*, 1955, p. 61, no. 28).
60. Balis, *Rubens and his Studio*, 2007, pp. 30–31, 41; on the various categories of workshop members and the terminology used to describe them, see also id., *Studio Practices*, 1994, passim, and esp. pp. 100–101; id., *Rubens and his Studio*, 2007, passim (wisely, neither article addresses the question of where exactly these workshop members worked, either before or after the house on the Wapper was built). On the extent to which Rubens actually had pupils – that is, gave youths lessons in drawing and painting – see Logan, *Rubens as a Teacher*, 2006. On the organisation and members of Rubens's workshop, see also Büttner, *Hands of Rubens*, 2017, passim; Baumstark – Delmarcel, *Decius Mus (CRLB)*, 2019, I, pp. 155–161.

CHAPTER VII - THE INTERIOR OF THE 'ITALIAN WING' / THE 'SCHILDERHUIS'

be used by Rubens's assistants, of whatever description, while the large space below served a different purpose? In our view this is a misunderstanding arising from Sperling's account, which suggests that Rubens himself worked somewhere other than among his collaborators. The lofty ground-floor room was perfect for painting the enormous panels or canvases to which his assistants often made a considerable contribution. That Rubens would have reserved it for his own use, as has sometimes been thought,[61] can therefore safely be ruled out.

Contemporary sources cannot help in this matter because they do not even mention the existence of more than one studio in the south wing, let alone inform us how these rooms may have been used in Rubens's highly efficient working process. The couple of references we do know only mention the 'schilderhuis' and this likely alludes to the south wing or studio wing as a whole rather than one particular room in it. That this was indeed the case is evident from, among other things, the 1660 deed of sale, in which a 'schilderhuys' and also a passageway next to the 'schilderhuys' are said to be part of the property (Appendix I.25). According to the terminology used in Antwerp in the seventeenth century, a distinction must be made between the term 'schildercamer' (a room) and 'schilderhuys' (perhaps not invariably, but more often than not an autonomous structure or separate wing).[62]

This subtle difference in meaning complicates the correct interpretation of the scarce seventeenth-century sources that mention Rubens's 'schilderhuys'. We know that Rubens used the term himself. Writing to Lucas Faydherbe on 17 August 1638, he urges him to make sure everything is well locked up and uses the phrase 'boven op het schilderhuys', where no sketches or originals are to be left lying about in his absence (Appendix I.21). In our view this relates to an otherwise unidentifiable room on the top floor of the studio wing. The difference may be subtle, but his words should probably be taken to mean literally 'upstairs in the studio wing', rather than 'in the workshop upstairs', and certainly not 'above the workshop'.[63] Nor can it be said with certainty

---

61. Seen thus by, among others: Rooses, *Rubens*, 1904, p. 150; see also Muller, *Rubens's collection*, 2004, p. 60: 'Rubens himself painted below, in the loftier and grander ground-floor workshop'; Logan refers to 'the workshop for Rubens' assistants', and states that 'Rubens' own studio was in a larger space on the ground floor' (Logan, *Rubens as a Teacher*, 2006, p. 251).
62. On the difference between 'schildercamer' (also 'werckcamer') and 'schilderhuys', see also Van der Stighelen, *Zelfbeeld*, 2000, pp. 238–240; Kleinert, *Atelierdarstellungen*, 2006, p. 31. For 'schilderhuizen' built by other masters in Antwerp, see above, pp. 214–215, nn. 34–36. It should also be noted that the word 'schilderhuis' (or 'schilderhuys' in seventeenth-century spelling), which was often used in Antwerp and elsewhere (also in the Northern Netherlands), is not included in the monumental dictionary of the Dutch language, the *Woordenboek der Nederlandsche Taal, 1864–1998*. For English translations, see n. 63.
63. The slightly different interpretations of Rubens's words (in Dutch) become somewhat clearer in translation; to give just a few examples: Rooses's 'dans l'atelier à l'étage', probably having in mind the cupolaed upstairs studio, is incorrect (Rooses – Ruelens, eds, *Correspondance*, 1887–1909, VI, p. 224, no. DCCCLXI); Held is mistaken in thinking that it means 'above the studio [...] meaning the upper storey or perhaps an attic' (Held, *Sketches*, 1980, I, p. 11); Magurn's 'upstairs in the studio' is correct but ambiguous (Magurn, ed., *Letters*,

CHAPTER VII - THE INTERIOR OF THE 'ITALIAN WING' / THE 'SCHILDERHUIS'

which space is meant in two entries in the *Staetmasse* (the account of Rubens's estate, submitted in November 1645) that refer to expenses: the grey-washing of the 'schilderhuis' and 'blaffeturen' for the 'schilderhuis' (Appendix I.23: [7, 9]).

In short, the existence of two workshops in the 'schilderhuis' is established, but it has not been determined what different functions they might have had. In any case the idea of a 'pupils' workshop' should be rejected and so must the term.

E. Communication Between the Two Workshops: A Windlass?

As mentioned earlier, the upstairs rooms in the studio wing could be reached by the stairs that appear in the 1692 Harrewijn print. Yet we should consider the possibility that this ornate staircase contributed to the functionality of the workshop. According to J.F.M. Michel, it was used to move paintings – a suggestion taken up by other authors.[64] It is not clear, however, on what his premise is based and he may simply have assumed as much by looking at the Harrewijn print.

The possibility that there was a second (less grand) staircase elsewhere in the south wing can, of course, not be ruled out. The stairs shown in the print seem rather impractical for intensive use by large numbers of assistants, who would have had to step out (into the arcaded gallery) every time they wanted to go from one studio to the other. On the other hand there is no indication of a second staircase in the south wing in Mols's drawing.

Apart from the stairs (whether one or more), another, more sophisticated device may have been used that would facilitate easy movement of paintings and materials between the two workshops. In the attic of the studio wing there is a wooden winch or windlass fixed into the roof truss. It has a striking large wooden wheel parallel to the ridge, which is equipped with iron two-pronged forks to keep in place the continuous loop of rope that ran around it (Text ill. 93).[65] Interestingly, in the ceiling directly below are two holes through which this loop could have passed so that the windlass could be operated from the top floor.[66] There is apparently no longer any evidence lower down in the house

1955, p. 411, no. 244). Muller's phrase 'upstairs in the "painter house"' is also correct as far as location goes (Muller, *Rubens's Collection*, 2004, p. 60). But it should be noted in passing that his translation of 'schilderhuis' given here (also in ibid., p. 74) as 'painter house' is debatable; in this Dutch compound noun 'schilder' refers not to the person ('painter') but to the action ('painting'), so 'schilderhuis' is literally a 'painting house', a place used for painting.

64. Michel, *Rubens*, 1771, p. 47; followed by Van den Branden, *Schilderschool*, 1883, p. 508; see also Devroe, *Rubens' huis*, 2008, p. 109.
65. For the windlass, which is still preserved in the roof space where it is now surrounded by equipment for the modern cooling system, see for example Clijmans, *Wederopbouw Rubenshuis*, 1941, fig. 6; Devroe, *Rubens' huis*, 2008, p. 109; Maclot, *Rubenssite*, 2016, pp. 58 (fig.), 172, 406.
66. For the holes in the ceiling of the upstairs studio, see Devroe, ibid., p. 73 (not illustrated); Maclot, *Rubenssite*,

CHAPTER VII - THE INTERIOR OF THE 'ITALIAN WING' / THE 'SCHILDERHUIS'

Text ill. 93. The wooden windlass with ropes in the attic of the studio wing (1938).

to suggest where or how the rope or ropes that were wound up and down by the mechanism were channelled.

Although no date can be put on this mechanism and it may therefore have been installed long after Rubens's time, it has been associated with the workshop operation. There is no consensus about the exact workings of the wheel, even among authors who firmly believe that it played a part in the workshop operation. It was thought, for example, that the winch played a role in the hypothesis – now rightly dismissed – that the ground floor served as a storage area below the actual workshop, whose floor was level with the sills of the large windows.[67]

Max Rooses (who was not aware of the existence of an upstairs studio) assumed that the windlass was probably used for lifting heavy panels ('à dresser et à hisser les lourds panneaux').[68] By this he meant manoeuvring the weighty wooden panels in one and the same space (the large workshop on the ground floor) by means of ropes that passed through the floors of the attic and first floor. This assumption makes sense, as some kind of mechanical assistance could save on manpower when panels or outsize canvases needed to be moved or repositioned, including being rolled up or unrolled.

2016, pp. 387–388, repr.

67. Incorporated in the reconstruction plans in 1938 was a suggestion that there was a staircase directly below the wheel, leading up from the low-ceilinged ground floor, which was thought to be used as storage space, to the workshop above (which would not in those circumstances have been level with the ground but located approx. 3 m above this store); in this scenario the winch would have served to hoist paintings and materials from the ground floor (through a stairwell) up to the workshop; however, the assumption that the workshop floor might have been higher was rightly abandoned; see Devroe, *Rubens' huis*, 2008, pp. 109–110, fig. nos 67a and 67b; Maclot, *Rubenssite*, 2016, p. 189, fig. 174.
68. Rooses, *Maison*, 1888, p. 18; id., *Huis van Rubens*, 1910, p. 206 [p. 18].

CHAPTER VII - THE INTERIOR OF THE 'ITALIAN WING' / THE 'SCHILDERHUIS'

That a windlass and ropes were used in the workshop cannot be ruled out, though neither written nor visual sources offer any confirmation that Rubens, or any other painter in Antwerp, employed such a device. In a wing of Jacques Jordaens's house, however, there is a similar wooden windlass in the attic above a room that could have been used as a studio.[69] But in Jordaens's house the windlass is combined with a hoist beam that projects beyond the top of a dormer window – in other words it is part of an apparatus for hauling loads up and down the wall outside, not inside the house. Moreover, there is no reason to consider the device as something exclusive to a painter's studio. Even today many houses in Antwerp and elsewhere have similar lifting gear in the attic (see below). It is important to state that it is very hard to date the surviving winches and it is not certain that the ones in the houses of Rubens and Jordaens do in fact date from the seventeenth century.

Not that this stopped authors from proposing an ingenious purpose for the windlass in the workshop-wing attic. It would, they suggested, have been used to move paintings vertically (i.e. through the floor) through the house. Intriguing and tempting as this hypothesis is, it is hard to judge whether there are firm grounds for it or not. The system has been seen as an important element in the way Rubens used the two workshops, the main one on the ground floor and the smaller one with its ceiling cupola. According to this theory, the windlass would have been used to bring paintings up and down through the upper workshop floor. This possibility was taken seriously by Sigurd de Gruyter who made a digital reconstruction (with a large square trap-door in the middle of the floor.[70]

There are indeed examples of somewhat similar systems for moving paintings. Koen Bulckens pointed to an 'invention' (perhaps never used) that can be seen in a drawing by Leonardo da Vinci (1452–1519): to be able to work on very large paintings without a scaffold, these could move up and down the wall through an opening in the floor while the artist simply stayed where he was.[71]

A more relevant example is a contraption that was designed to move paintings up and down and which was put into use at about the same time as Rubens was building his workshop. The high altar in the Antwerp Jesuit Church was fitted with a mechanism – probably the first of its kind – for

---

69. Rutger Tijs mentions, 'op de hoogste zolderruimte' (in the highest attic space), a wheel that was used 'om de doeken op te hijsen' (to hoist canvases) (Tijs, *Rubens*, 2004, p. 228). Further information kindly provided by Brecht Vanoppen: it is still to be seen in the attic of the south wing, an outbuilding bought by Jordaens in 1618 (wing no. 2 on the diagram in Tijs, *Rubens en Jordaens*, 1984, p. 267).
70. De Gruyter, *Lichtinval*, 2012, p. 13, fig. 23. Uppenkamp also thought this construction possible, *Rubens's palazzetto*, 2018, p. 221. The presence of a trap-door in the middle of the upper workshop floor seems highly unlikely. If there had been an opening connecting the two studios, this would surely have been a narrow shaft against one of the walls.
71. Bulckens, *Rubens and Workshop*, 2019, p. 95, n. 11.

substituting different canvases as altarpiece. Rather than one, four same-size paintings were made for the altar (two from the hand of Rubens), and these were shown in rotation, a system that remains in use today. To achieve this, a large vertical chest was constructed behind and below the altar, in which the (more than) five-metre high canvases are stored in sequence. The painting to be changed slides down and another is lifted up to replace it. The mechanism consists of pulleys, and not a windlass.[72]

To summarise, it is possible that the windlass played a role in the working of Rubens's workshops, but caution is called for in this matter and theories about its use may have been rightly doubted or rejected.[73] It could indeed simply be a winch used for lifting materials during building or repair work – an idea made all the more likely by the existence of very similar wooden winches in other houses in Antwerp,[74] and also in monumental buildings elsewhere.[75] In short, we do not think we can make any kind of definite statement on this subject.

F. Not Located: 'Elegantissimum Museum', 'Cantoor' and 'Studiolo Secreto' (Private Studio or Study?)

It seems obvious that in his large house Rubens would not always have worked side by side with his assistants. According to one hypothesis he would have kept the large studio on the ground floor for his own use, but as indicated above, that can be ruled out. A second theory involves the existence of a third workshop, a smaller 'private studio' where Rubens could work in peace and quiet. When Rubens's house was reconstructed, a room named as such was incorporated in the narrow part of the workshop complex fronting the Wapper, above the stairwell, though there was no basis for its location or even its existence.

We know from the inscriptions Willem Panneels added to his drawn copies that in the 1620s there was a 'cantoor' where Rubens kept drawings, among

---

72. On these alternating altarpieces, which became common in Jesuit churches, see Van Eck, *Jezuïeten*, 1998, pp. 81–94 (with an illustration of the shaft in the Antwerp church: ibid., p. 87, fig. 8); For the two canvases by Rubens, *The Miracles of St Francis Xavier* and *The Miracles of St Ignatius of Loyola*, now in the Kunsthistorisches Museum in Vienna, see Vlieghe, *Saints (CRLB)*, 1972–73, II, nos 104 and 115, figs 6 and 115.
73. Among the sceptics was Van Averbeke (see Devroe, *Rubens' huis*, I, p. 111, n. 264, with Devroe's contention that the windlass could not have been used for very large panels as it is not strong enough). Maclot assumes that it had a function in 'the raising and lowering of paintings or materials' (Maclot, *Rubenssite*, 2016, p. 172, figs pp. 58, 406).
74. For example in the Mercator Orteliushuis in the Hoogstraat (Derycke et al., *Mercator-Orteliushuis*, fig. on p. 161, as possibly dating from the 19th or early 20th century); in the house called 'De Gouden Schoen' on the Melkmarkt (Devroe, *Rubens's huis*, 2008, I, p. 111, n. 259), now Hotel 'De Gulde Schoen' with a suite under the attic beams where the windlass remains in place.
75. Similar winches still survive in the roof space in Leuven's town hall (Heirman-Staes, *Stadhuis van Leuven*, 1997, fig. p. 29) and in St Gommarus's Church in Lier (Van Tyghem, *Bouwwerf*, 1966, fig. p. 219). For the use of the windlass on building sites, see ibid., pp. 213 ff.

CHAPTER VII - THE INTERIOR OF THE 'ITALIAN WING' / THE 'SCHILDERHUIS'

other things.[76] But that is all we know. That most houses of any size in Antwerp had a 'cantoor', or 'comptoir' as the room was usually called, can be inferred from estate and probate inventories and other archival records. Some even had more than one. A constant factor seems to be that the 'cantoor' was largely the preserve of the master of the house, a place where important papers and valuables could be kept, and where works of art were often displayed. There was evidently a large variation in the size of such rooms and also in the objects stored in them. Some painters kept hundreds of works of art, including their own, in their 'cantoor', along with other useful work-related items such as sculptures, plaster casts, paintings, sketches, drawings, prints and books.[77] In 1622 the 'comptoor' of Deodaat del Monte (1582–1644) contained 'all that belongs to the art of painting'.[78] Joos de Momper II (1564–1635) had a 'comptoir' and a 'comptoir upstairs', though neither contained very much.[79] The probate inventory, dated 1653, of Jeremias Wildens (1621–1653), who died shortly after his father Jan Wildens (1585/86–1653), mentions a 'comptoir van den Ouden Wildens' containing 52 sketches and paintings and 'het Comptoir van des Overledene Vader' (the same room?) that held papers, money, jewellery, and some 60 books. There are also 96 entries listing quantities of 'verven' (pigments and dyes), while another 96 entries relate to hundreds of drawings and prints.[80] When Erasmus Quellinus II (b. 1607) died in 1678 the contents of his 'groot Cantoir' were found to be even more extensive, comprising more than 900 'items' including sculpture, paintings and drawings.[81]

Scholars, such as Jan Brant (1559–1639) and Nicolaas Rockox (1560–1640), undoubtedly used the room called 'cantoor' or 'comptoir' as a study, where they kept their books and perhaps appropriate works of art such as antique busts. When Brant, Rubens's father-in-law, died in 1639, his house contained two small 'comptoirkens' and a large 'comptoir'.[82] In the house of Nicolaas Rockox there was a small 'bovencomptoirken' (a small upstairs room), used by a certain Cornelis Janssens, and the 'comptoir' of Rockox himself, which at his death in 1640 contained among other things 16 paintings, 203 books and dozens of small sculptures.[83]

---

76. For Panneels and his copies, see Chapter II, pp. 58–59.
77. On the concept of the artist's 'cantoor', see also Huvenne, *Cantoor*, 1993, pp. 16–18; Muller, *Rubens's Collection*, 2004, p. 59.
78. 'alles tgene der consten raeckende is van't schilderen' (Duverger, *Kunstinventarissen*, 1984–2009, II, pp. 215–216).
79. In 1635; ibid., III, pp. 429–430.
80. Ibid., VI, pp. 491–492; VI, pp. 496–504.
81. Ibid., X, pp. 352–373.
82. Ibid., IV, pp. 268, 270. There is also reference to Brant's 'Comptoir standing in an attic on the street side', containing gold and silver medallions (ibid., IV, p. 271), but this is more likely to be a piece of furniture than a room.
83. Ibid., IV, pp. 385, 386 ff.; see also Muller, *Rubens's Collection*, 2004, p. 59.

CHAPTER VII - THE INTERIOR OF THE 'ITALIAN WING' / THE 'SCHILDERHUIS'

We know nothing about the character and purpose of Rubens's 'cantoor'. Did Rubens use it to paint in, and was it therefore a private studio? Or was it rather the study of a 'pictor doctus'? It was likely the room that is also known as the 'studiolo secreto', where Rubens put his 'perpetuum mobile', as he tells Nicolas Claude Fabri de Peiresc (1580–1630) when he writes to him on 3 August 1623 (Appendix I.16).[84] Instead of painting, a room like this could have been used for such things as private study and correspondence, and perhaps also for drawing on paper. Rubens probably kept his books there before they were moved, after Christmas 1639, to one of the small houses on the Hopland.[85]

In 1615 we find a mention of Rubens's 'elegantissimum museum', where he kept his precious marble *Bust of Seneca* (Appendix I.6). It should be noted that 'museum' must have been the Latin term for his study (or 'cantoor'), and it would be wrong to think that it refers specifically to a place in which works of art were displayed. It certainly does not refer to the 'antiquarium' or 'pantheon' that Rubens built to house his sculptures, as has been thought.[86] For one thing there is the early date: Rubens did not acquire his famous collection of antiquities until three years later.[87] Nor can we entirely rule out the possibility that 'the most elegant museum' mentioned in 1615 was a room in the house of his parents-in-law.[88]

We should note, too, that among scholars the term 'museum' ('mouseion'), a room dedicated to the muses, was commonly used for a study.[89] It did not necessarily contain works of art or antiquities. For instance, in his letters Justus Lipsius, who did not have a collection of art or even of antique coins, used the word 'musaeum' to refer to the room in which he worked.[90] Thus 'museum' was apparently the Latin name for what in Antwerp was called a 'cantoor' or 'comptoir'. This seems to be substantiated by Nicolaas Rockox's Latin inventory of his antiquities, in which they are referred to as being 'in museo', whereas according to the estate inventory in Dutch, the same objects are in his 'comptoir'.[91]

In passing it is worth pointing out that Rubens would very likely have kept a valuable antique bust – especially one like his Seneca – in his study. That such retreats were the perfect place for busts of classical celebrities is illustrated time

---

84. That the references are to the same room was also suggested by Huvenne, *Cantoor*, 1993, p. 17; Muller, *Rubens's Collection*, 2004, pp. 59–60.
85. See above, Chapter I, p. 46; Appendix I.23: [5].
86. Van Beneden, *Rubens and Architecture*, 2011, p. 13; id., *Portiek en tuinpaviljoen*, 2019, pp. 14–15.
87. See below, Chapter VIII, p. 237, n. 21.
88. This is also the opinion of Jeffrey Muller, who points out that in 1615 Rubens had not yet moved into the house on the Wapper (Muller, *Rubens's Collection*, 2004, p. 43).
89. See Van der Veen, *Studeerkamers*, 2000, p. 140.
90. My thanks to Jeanine De Landtsheer who drew this to my attention. See inter alia the letter in which Lipsius writes that his dog Saphyrus came to find him there ('in Musaeum') just before it died a tragic death (De Landtsheer, ed., *Iusti Lipsi Epistolae*, 1991–(ongoing), pars XIV: 1601, Letter 01 08 29).
91. Scheller, *Rockox*, 1978, pp. 17, 38; Muller, *Moribvs Antiquis*, 2008, p. 24.

CHAPTER VII - THE INTERIOR OF THE 'ITALIAN WING' / THE 'SCHILDERHUIS'

and again in portraits of scholars in their studies: Jan Gaspar Gevartius with Marcus Aurelius, Ludovicus Nonnius with Hippocrates, and Nicolaas Rockox with Demosthenes.[92]

Whether, generally speaking, 'elegantissimum museum', 'studiolo secreto', and 'cantoor' are names for the same space or not, in the context of Rubens's house they might well describe the same or a similar space, namely Rubens's study. Certainly, there must have been such a room in the house, but it cannot be established exactly where. Perhaps the domestic part of the house was the more likely location for a room dedicated to intellectual pursuits such as letter writing and reading – and especially activities Rubens undertook when his assistants were not present in the studio.[93] In this case a room somewhere on the upper floor of the east, north, or west wing might be considered.

Jeffrey Muller proposes another possibility: there might have been two 'cantoren' in Rubens's house, a small one (a private 'studiolo secreto' for maximum security, secrecy and privacy') and a larger one that was accessible to members of the workshop, where drawings, sketches, plaster casts and so forth were kept. This, of course, is not impossible. He suggests that these rooms would probably have been in the vicinity of the workshops – in the south wing, in other words. As mentioned, in our view this would not necessarily have been the case. Be that as it may, his attempt to locate these two 'cantoren' in the house on the upper floor of the south wing on the basis of Mols's plan (Fig. 3) – supposing that these are the rooms named as 'cabinet' – should certainly be rejected.[94]

One final point. In the State Hermitage Museum in St Petersburgh is a painting depicting an interior that may have been based on Rubens's study. The anonymous *Portrait of Rubens with his Son (Albert?)* (Appendix III.27) shows Rubens seated at a table and with several objects known to have been part of his collection of antiquities around him. Such a scene is undoubtedly meant to present a picture of the painter in his study but whether the wall in the background, with its large framed niche, represents an actual part of Rubens's house is an open question. Another (and incorrect) interpretation of the room in the Hermitage painting, suggesting the wall in the background is part of the north wall of the 'antiquarium', is discussed in the next chapter.

---

92. Respectively Vlieghe, *Portraits (CRLB)*, 1987, nos 106, 124, figs 122 and 152; Barnes et al., *Van Dyck*, 2004, pp. 99–100, no. I.105. In detail on the use and meaning of busts in humanist circles in Antwerp, see Muller, *Moribvs Antiquis*, 2008.
93. We know, for instance, that Rubens did not think about his designs for title-pages during 'normal working hours': he only found time on sundays and holidays (Judson – Van de Velde, *Title-pages (CRLB)*, 1978, I, p. 27).
94. Muller, *Rubens's Collection*, 2004, p. 60; the 18th-century French term 'cabinet' that Mols uses (no. 2. Cabinet [in the drawing], no. 5. Cabinet à alcove [in the comment]) need have no relation whatever to the interior in Rubens's time. In particular a 'cantoor' could not have been the 'Cabinet' (no. 2) above the entrance from the Wapper to the garden, for in Rubens's time this was an open passageway and the room on the floor above that Mols found there did not yet exist. On the restructuring of the houses and the passageway, see Chapter III, pp. 102–103.

Chapter VIII
The East or Garden Wing with the 'Antiquarium' (The Roman Pantheon): The Circular Structures

The east or garden wing was built at right angles to the north wing and therefore parallel to the Wapper. It extended quite a way northward, so that Rubens's house bounded his neighbour's plot on two sides (the south and east) (Fig. 6). Next to nothing is known about its exterior. All we have by way of visual evidence is the small strip of wall with its two narrow windows, one above the other, that abuts the portico in both the 1684 Harrewijn print (Text ill. 94) and the *Portrait of Maria Agnes van Eycke as St Agnes* by Gonzales Coques (Text ill. 95). In the portrait we can also see a small section of the east wing's south façade, including a window with leaded lights, visible through the portico's left arch. There are no known images of the east wing's east wall, overlooking the garden.[1]

Text ill. 94. Detail of the 1684 Harrewijn print (Fig. 17): a strip of wall (left of the portico) of the east or garden wing.

Text ill. 95. Detail of Text ill. 20: a section of the east wing seen through the portico.

1. For the reconstruction of the exterior of the east wing in 'Flemish' style (Text ill. 96, Fig. 14), see Chapter III, p. 105.

CHAPTER VIII - THE EAST OR GARDEN WING WITH THE 'ANTIQUARIUM'

A. An Art Gallery and a Bedroom (?)

In the Harrewijn print of 1684 an open door can be seen in the north-east corner of the courtyard, offering us a glimpse of the interior. We can detect the foot of a staircase,[2] and there is a second door, containing two panels with carved decoration, which opens on to a room on the ground floor. Apparently, judging from the position of its window, this room was much higher than the downstairs rooms in the north and west wings.[3]

When Rubens's house was reconstructed in the 1930s, the east or garden wing was rebuilt to what was thought to be more or less its original size. Based on the windows as they appear in the print, it was assumed that there were two storeys. Furthermore, although there was nothing to suggest this, the wing was provided with a steep saddle roof, which included a dormer window on the south side (Text ills 96 and 98). This contradicts the image of the print in which – strangely – no roof can be seen at all (Fig. 17).[4]

As to what this part of the property was used for, it was assumed that the top floor had belonged to the family's domestic quarters. It may originally have contained more than one room, but the entire top floor is now a single open area, with windows on the east and south, overlooking the garden, as well as a window looking west into the courtyard. In the reconstructed museum this room is described as 'the large bedroom', and is presented – although there is of course nothing to corroborate this – as Rubens's bedroom. Moreover it is assumed to be the room to which the master retreated during the last years of his life when illness prevented him from going out (allegedly he would sit by the upper window facing the courtyard, which conveniently allowed him to keep an

Text ill. 96. The reconstructed east wing (south and east façade).

---

2. Mols's drawing (Fig. 3) still has a staircase in this position. This had disappeared by the 1930s, but new stairs were installed in the same place during the modern reconstruction.
3. The fall of light in this part of the house, as represented in the print, is puzzling: on the upper part of the wall, light is shown coming from the north; it is also difficult to explain the source of light apparently emanating from the room on the ground floor.
4. See also below, n. 6.

CHAPTER VIII - THE EAST OR GARDEN WING WITH THE 'ANTIQUARIUM'

eye on what happened in the house), and it is also in this room, we are told, that he died.[5]

On the ground floor, there was almost certainly a spacious room about 4 or 4.5 m in height; this can be deduced from the position of the bottom window in relation to the adjoining portico.[6] At the time of the reconstruction this room was thought to have been an art gallery, a space purpose-built for the display of works of art, specifically to accommodate dozens of paintings hung next to and above each other, as seen in the works depicting such chambers by Willem van Haecht and others. It is hard to be sure whether there really was a room with that specific function in Rubens's day. It is not impossible, but there are no data to underpin the suggestion that Rubens used a separate room of this type as an exhibition space for his collection. At any rate, it is safe to assume that paintings were displayed throughout the entire house, using all of the wings.[7]

The idea that the high-ceilinged ground floor room of the east wing was used as an art gallery or a picture gallery seems to have grown from the fact that it adjoined a chamber that was indeed built especially to house a particular part of Rubens's collection, that being the 'antiquarium' intended for antique sculpture.

The reconstructed east wing that we now see in the Rubenshuis, gives an acceptable – if perhaps not quite correct – idea of the original arrangement of the interior in terms of its spatial volume (though not its decoration, which was quite different, and to which we shall return). In the modern reconstruction, the first room which, as said, now serves as an area for the display of paintings and precious objects and is known as 'the art gallery', is quite large and rectangular in plan (Text ill. 97). Adjoining it to the north is a semicircular room with a domed ceiling, and a lantern at the top of the dome (Text ill. 101).

---

5. 'They say that he would sit at this window to see the comings and goings of pupils, assistants and visitors' (Baudouin, *Summary Guide*, 1977, p. 19). We were unable to find the source of this romantic anecdote. If it was introduced in the 19th century, it must have been based on the 1684 Harrewijn print rather than the house itself, since the window in question was no longer in evidence at that time.
6. The portico is 8.1 m high and the ground-floor ceiling of the east wing can be theoretically placed somewhere halfway. Though not impossible, it seems rather unlikely that there was, behind the two windows, only one very high space (see below). As mentioned above, a strange and inexplicable detail in the Harrewijn print is that – unlike in the reconstructed house – no roof can be seen above the east wing. Was it perhaps much lower than the modern roof, and hidden behind the ('false') top of the façade?
7. For information on the display of paintings and other works of art in the house, see especially Muller, *Collector*, 1989, pp. 17–18.

CHAPTER VIII - THE EAST OR GARDEN WING WITH THE 'ANTIQUARIUM'

Text ill. 97. The 'Art Gallery' in the Rubenshuis.

B. The 'Antiquarium' or 'Pantheon' (also Called the 'Museum')

One of the parts of Rubens's house that had long since vanished when restoration began is the space referred to in the literature as the 'antiquarium' or 'pantheon' or 'museum'.[8] A survey of the extensive literature on this part of the east wing can be found in the catalogue, under No. 20.

During Hillewerve's occupancy of the house it was converted into a chapel and is depicted as such in the left inset at the bottom of the 1692 Harrewijn print (Fig. 127). In the lower tier of niches we can see the collection of reliquaries, that are praised as exceptional in an *encomium* (an eulogy) by Desiderius de Sevin (b. 1644) in which several verses are devoted to Hillewerve's splendid chapel ('splendidissimum sacellum') (Appendix I.36).[9]

It is not known when the remarkable semicircular structure disappeared and was replaced by 'normal', rectangular rooms. The high room with cupola served no purpose in a domestic interior and may have been remodelled during the substantial alterations that were carried out after 1763 by the

---

8. It should be noted that the term 'museum', which is often used in the literature for the room in question – as early as 1672, by Bellori (Appendix I.28) – can lead to confusion. As explained above (Chapter VII, p. 227), in humanist circles 'museum' described a study, not a space in which to display a collection.
9. For a detailed description of Hillewerve's much-admired chapel and its contents, see Chapter III, pp. 110–112.

CHAPTER VIII · THE EAST OR GARDEN WING WITH THE 'ANTIQUARIUM'

De Bosschaert de Pret family. Or was it much later, in the nineteenth century? Victor Van Grimbergen (1810–1859) puts the demolition of 'de koepel, of zaal in de smaak van Rome's Pantheon' (the cupola, or chamber in the taste of Rome's Pantheon) a few years before 1840, but this information is not necessarily to be relied on.[10]

The structure of Rubens's 'antiquarium' with a semicircular plan and lit by an opening in the top of the dome – evidently inspired by the Roman Pantheon – aroused considerable interest in the seventeenth century. A good deal of attention was paid to it by artists and writers, yielding interesting visual and written sources. As mentioned, there is the inset in the 1692 Harrewijn print. Moreover, there are paintings of picture galleries in which a separate space for sculpture can be seen in the background, and although there are usually variations in structure and details, they are plainly derived from Rubens's 'antiquarium'.[11] The seventeenth-century biographers of Rubens and their informants also deemed the unusual chamber worthy of report.

Written Sources

There is a reference in 1615 to Rubens's 'elegantissimum museum' in which he kept his antique *Bust of Seneca* (Appendix I.6) but, as explained above, that room may have been a study rather than a space expressly intended for the display of works of art.[12] Not until ten years later do we find the Pantheon-like room specifically and unmistakably referred to. On 10 July 1625 Philippe Chifflet noted in his 'diaire' that the Infanta Isabella had visited Rubens's 'Panthéon', where among the things to be seen was a well-preserved Egyptian mummy (Appendix I.17).[13]

Equally unambiguous is the allusion in an entry in the *Staetmasse* drawn up in 1645. The unusually high-ceilinged room is described as a 'thoren' (tower) in which the antiquities of the deceased [Rubens] were contained ('[den] thoren ten voors. huyse van den afflyvigen daer de antiquiteyten van den heer afflyvigen stonden' (Appendix I.23: [1]).

Biographers of Rubens knew about the room and mention it in their notes as something special. The earliest published reference comes in 1672 in Bellori's *Le Vite de' pittori*. He says of Rubens that 'in his house in Antwerp he built a round room with a single *oculus* at the top, similar to the Rotunda of Rome, for

---

10. Apparently, he is not aware of the fact that Hillewerve's chapel (which he knew from the Harrewijn print) and the 'pantheon' (which he knew from written sources) were one and the same room. For in the same paragraph he says that the former splendid chapel 'werd een kamer en dient thans tot salet' (was transformed into a room used now as a 'salet') (Van Grimbergen, *Rubens*, 1840, p. 387).
11. See catalogue, under No. 20.
12. See above, Chapter VII, p. 227.
13. For this mummy, see Chapter II, p. 54, n. 16.

CHAPTER VIII - THE EAST OR GARDEN WING WITH THE 'ANTIQUARIUM'

the perfection of even lighting,' and in it he placed his 'precious museum, with other rare and sundry curiosities' (Appendix I.28). A few years later Joachim von Sandrart, who had met Rubens in his youth, tells us much the same in the first part of his *Teutsche Academie*, which appeared in 1675: Rubens built himself a beautiful house which contained 'a "Kunstkammer" in the shape of a rotunda with light falling from above', adding that this room was 'next to the garden' (Appendix I.29).

Finally we have Roger de Piles, who would undoubtedly have been familiar with Bellori's text but also got his information directly from Rubens's nephew Philip. In his *Dissertation* of 1681 he describes the unusual chamber thus: 'Between the courtyard and the garden [Rubens] had built a rotunda, like the Pantheon in Rome, in which the light enters from a single opening from above in the centre of the dome' (Appendix I.31).

Invariably these seventeenth-century testimonies also refer to the function of this remarkable construction: it served to display works of art, valuables and curiosities. According to Sandrart, the rotunda was used not only to display statues and curiosities but – rather implausibly – also paintings by Rubens and other masters, illuminated to great advantage by the light falling from above (Appendix I.29).

Information from François Mols

When François Mols visited the house in 1763, the unusual room was still in existence, as can be seen from the plan he drew and the comments he added (Appendix I.43: [6, 8]; Fig. 3). In his drawing – made not in situ but from memory – he outlined a space that was neither circular nor semicircular but octagonal, calling it a chapel ('Chapelle'). Its proportions and dimensions are not accurate but by and large his drawing does appear to correspond to the room he found there. Did he realise that he had made the proportions of the 'Chapelle' too small? In what seems to be a correction in the margin he specifies: 'Cette Chapelle, bâtie en octogone, dépasse de tout son diamètre les limites de la maison' (In its diameter this octagonal Chapel exceeds the limits of the house).

It is of course no surprise that Mols describes Rubens's former 'antiquarium' as a chapel, for that was the use to which it was put by Canon Hillewerve, and it probably still had the appearance of a chapel when Mols visited the house. Moreover, he certainly knew the Harrewijn print of 1692,[14] which makes it all the more puzzling that, as mentioned above, he draws and describes 'the chapel' as octagonal in plan, and not semicircular.

14. Mols notes that the chapel 'once had a considerable number of relics in reliquaries placed from top to bottom in niches' (Appendix I. 43: [8]), information that is undoubtedly simply based on the Harrewijn print.

CHAPTER VIII - THE EAST OR GARDEN WING WITH THE 'ANTIQUARIUM'

Text ill. 98. Émile Van Averbeke, Design for the reconstruction of the east wing (intersection south-north), detail of a blueprint. Antwerp, FelixArchief.

In his general comments on the drawing, Mols noted how the curious edifice was connected to the rooms next to it, 'son antichambre' and the room above it (on the first floor). The room upstairs 'avait une tribune où on pouvait entendre messe' (had a gallery where one could attend mass) (Appendix I.43: [8]). According to this description, it had once been possible to look down from a gallery on the first floor to the ground floor where the altar stood, meaning that the octagonal chamber was at least two storeys high (the height of the ground floor and the gallery above).

Victor Van Grimbergen gives more or less the same information (derived from an unknown source and not from observation, as in his time the chapel had been transformed into a 'salet'). He maintains that on the first floor, next to the chapel that was two storeys high, had been a sickroom, and that by opening a window a bedridden patient could participate in the mass.[15]

A sectional drawing done in 1939 by Émile Van Averbeke for the reconstruction of Rubens's house (Text ill. 98) gives an approximate idea of how the chapel and the room upstairs could have adjoined each other. Whether it would also have been possible in Rubens's day to look into the 'antiquarium' from a window or gallery in a room on the first floor is, of course, a question to which there is no answer.

15. 'Nevens deze kapel [die twee verdiepen hoog was] was op het eerste verdiep eene ziekkamer uit welke by het openen eener venster de zieken op zyn bed den dienst die in deze kapel gedaen werd konde bywoonen' (Van Grimbergen, *Rubens*, 1840, p. 387).

235

CHAPTER VIII - THE EAST OR GARDEN WING WITH THE 'ANTIQUARIUM'

Text ill. 99. Foundation for the pilasters of the 'antiquarium' discovered in the 1930s.

The Location of the 'Antiquarium' in Rubens's House

The archaeological investigations that preceded the restoration work yielded more information about this special 'pantheon' room which is described by three seventeenth-century biographers, drawn and annotated by Mols, and was depicted as Hillewerve's chapel in the 1692 Harrewijn print. Where the building extended northwards, the foundations were discovered of a semicircular – thus not completely round – structure that had undoubtedly been Rubens's 'antiquarium' (Text ill. 99).[16] The discovery established clearly that Mols's information is only partly reliable: as stated, the shape of the 'antiquarium' was semicircular and not octagonal and, moreover, it extended further to the north than indicated in his drawing.

Vestiges of pilaster bases were found in the semicircular masonry, and from these the existence of seven niches could be deduced. The investigations also showed that this semicircular structure was put up later than the building with a rectangular ground-floor plan adjoining it, the so-called picture gallery ('kunstkamer').[17]

The rediscovered foundations were the starting point for the reconstruction of the 'antiquarium' and the 'picture gallery' as they can be seen today in the Rubenshuis (Text ills 97, 98 and 101). Based on those excavated foundations and the drawing by Mols, it can be assumed that these rooms are correctly

16. Van Averbeke, *Eerste bevindingen*, 1938, p. 27 (p. 30: drawing based on the excavations); Buschmann, *Huis-Rubens*, 1938, fig. p. 57; Muller, *Rubens's Museum*, 1977, p. 576, figs 3–5; Tijs, *Rubens en Jordaens*, 1984, p. 190, figs pp. 191 (top), 194 (bottom right); Devroe, *Rubens' huis*, 2008, I, p. 75, fig. 38.
17. During the investigations carried out on 14 February 1938 and the days following, indications that point to this were found; it appeared, for example, that the north side of the 'picture gallery' had been an outer wall, with putlog holes (Ruyten, *Opzoekingswerken Rubenshuis*, 1954, p. 3; Devroe, *Rubens' huis*, 2008, I, pp. 75–76, with reference to the notes by Van Averbeke held in the Rubenshuis archives).

sited. It should also be noted that the location corresponds fairly well to the accounts cited above: according to Sandrart this room was 'next to the garden', while de Piles described it as being 'between the courtyard and the garden' (Appendix I.29; Appendix I.31).

So it is hard to understand why there should still be any doubt about the correctness of the 'antiquarium''s location. One reason might be the existence of a second room with cupola in which light entered from above, namely the upstairs studio discussed in Chapter VII. In Rubens's house there were indeed not one but two top-lit round or semicircular rooms. Several hypotheses must be rejected; one of these is Rutger Tijs's notion that the two rooms with cupolas were in fact one and the same, a 'museum-cum-workshop' situated not in the house but in the garden.[18] It may also be recalled that, confusingly, references can still be found in the literature to 'round' structures incorrectly supposed to have stood in Rubens's garden.[19]

The Date: The Acquisition of Antique Sculpture in May-June 1618

As mentioned above, archaeological investigations revealed that the two main parts of the east or garden wing were not built at the same time. The semicircular extension was added at a later date to the north side of the existing rectangular structure.[20] It therefore seems very plausible to suppose that Rubens built his 'pantheon' not only after the 'domestic' north wing was already in use (at the beginning of 1616 at the latest), but also after the completion of a large part of the east or garden wing.

The building of the 'antiquarium' is logically and quite rightly associated with a collection of antique sculptures and objects that Rubens acquired from Sir Dudley Carleton on 20 May 1618. The collection, packed in twenty crates, arrived in Antwerp on 1 June 1618. Thus, in one fell swoop, when added to the antiquities he already possessed, Rubens became the owner of more than 140 pieces of classical sculpture, among which were 21 large statues, 8 figures of children, 4 torsos, 18 busts of emperors, 5 cinerary chests, and no fewer than 57 heads.[21]

---

18. He saw this as 'een licht geconstrueerd rond gebouw [...] hoogstwaarschijnlijk opgericht in hout en bepleisterd' (a lightly-constructed round building [...] probably built of wood and plastered); see Tijs, *Rubens en Jordaens*, 1984, pp. 143–144); he was following a hypothesis put forward by Max Rooses (though Rooses later revised his opinion (see Chapter VII, pp. 214–215, nn. 33, 38); Jeffrey Muller also rejected Tijs's assumption (Muller, *Collector*, 1989, p. 39, n. 77).
19. Certainly not to be seen in Rubens's garden were the remains of the 16th-century Calvinist 'Round Temple' (see Chapter I, pp. 28–31); nor was there a 'manège' or 'riding school', which some have misconstrued as a kind of indoor circular arena (based anachronistically on a false idea of what Cavendish 'manèges' looked like); for an accurate – and quite different – layout for such buildings, which in fact had a rectangular plan, see, Chapter II, pp. 68–70, nn. 66–67.
20. See above, p. 236, n. 17.
21. The acquisition also included 17 'piedestals', 4 reliefs and a number of fragments (Bastet, *Oudheden*, 1980,

Max Rooses was the first to suppose that it was this acquisition, in the summer of 1618, that prompted Rubens to build his pantheon as a place in which he could display his antique sculpture,[22] and this seems a very credible hypothesis. Jeffrey Muller, who wrote a detailed study about Rubens's so-called 'museum', thought likewise and he too dates 'the semicircular chamber' to 'around 1618'.[23]

A Closer Look at the Seventeenth-Century Images of Rubens's 'Antiquarium'

From a comparison with the image of Hillewerve's chapel it can be established beyond doubt that a room depicted by Willem van Haecht (1593–1637) in the background of his *Apelles Painting Campaspe*, painted around 1630 and now in the Mauritshuis in The Hague, was based on Rubens's 'antiquarium' (Appendix III.8; Text ill. 100). Glimpsed through an archway is a long, barrel-vaulted room that opens into a semicircular chamber illuminated by natural light admitted via a large round opening through which the blue sky can be seen. While certainly not a literal representation of an existing space, it is evident that in his depiction of Apelles's imaginary palatial studio, Van Haecht incorporated elements that he had seen in the notable home of the 'Antwerp Apelles'.

Both Van Haecht's painting and Harrewijn's 1692 print depict a semicircular chamber with very similar decoration (Figs 127 and 128). We assume that the richly ornamented curved wall with its tiers of niches and cupola above were designed by Rubens and have therefore included the remarkable interior of the 'antiquarium' in the Catalogue (Nos 20–22).

These two visual sources – the print and the painting – make it possible to compose a fairly detailed picture of what the original 'antiquarium' looked like. In Van Haecht's view the chamber with cupola is only partly visible, and somewhat simplified in comparison with the Harrewijn print, the wall consisting of only seven bays decorated with niches instead of nine. As said, the painted image is idealised, and has been relocated in Antiquity. This 'art gallery' with its 'antiquarium' dedicated to a collection of sculpture does not represent a part of Rubens's house, but the much grander abode where Apelles is at work in his studio, the 'officina', where according to Pliny, Alexander the Great frequently came to visit the famous painter.[24] Nonetheless, unlike the print, Van Haecht's image has the great advantage of being contemporary –

p. 72). On the entire transaction, see Rooses – Ruelens, eds, *Correspondance*, 1887–1909, II, pp. 145 ff., 189–190; Muller, *Rubens's Museum*, 1977, pp. 571–576; id., *Rubens's Collection*, 2004, pp. 62–63; Büttner, *Rubens berühmt*, 2006, pp. 94–95; Hill – Bracken, *Carleton*, 2014, pp. 171–178.
22. Rooses, *Rubens*, 1904, pp. 151, 256.
23. Muller, *Rubens's Museum*, 1977., p. 576.
24. Pliny, *Natural History*, XXXV.85 (without giving any particulars of this 'officina').

CHAPTER VIII - THE EAST OR GARDEN WING WITH THE 'ANTIQUARIUM'

Text ill. 100. Willem van Haecht, *Apelles Painting Campaspe*. The Hague, Mauritshuis (Appendix III.8).

Van Haecht died in 1637 – as well as, of course, showing a room that has not been transformed into a chapel. Moreover being in colour, it is one of the rare coloured impressions of an interior within Rubens's house.[25]

Looking at the seventeenth-century images, it cannot be deduced exactly how the two components of the east wing – the semicircular structure and the northern wall of the rectangular block on the plan – were joined together. Van Haecht's painting provides no indication useful for an understanding of the actual 'antiquarium' in Rubens's house. The Greek 'antiquarium' is shown from an oblique angle at the end of a high room with a coffered barrel-vault ceiling, which serves as a gallery in which statues are displayed along with paintings in three rows. Because the semicircular space beyond is wider and higher, we only get a partial view: the cupola, as well as the walls, especially to the left, are to a large extent hidden from view.

The print shows the former 'antiquarium' in a different manner. The structure adjoining the semicircular room has simply been omitted, reminding us somewhat of the way in which the portico is omitted from the view from the

---

25. Also referring to an interior in Rubens's house and also in colour, but probably further removed from reality, are the images of the studio (Appendix III.32–33; see Chapter VII, pp. 210–211, Text ills 88–89). The only other interior element appearing in a painting that can perhaps be related to Rubens's house can be seen in the background of the *Portrait of Rubens and his Son (Albert?)* in The State Hermitage Museum, St Petersburg (Appendix III.27; see below, p. 241 and Chapter VII, p. 228).

239

CHAPTER VIII - THE EAST OR GARDEN WING WITH THE 'ANTIQUARIUM'

east (above, in the main image of the same print from 1692). Unlike Van Haecht, Harrewijn offers a frontal view of Hillewerve's chapel, in which none of the elements are hidden allowing us to see the whole room. What the print shows us is not a realistic view but a cross-section of the structure, framed on either side by a tall curtain which masks the side walls.[26]

Finally we must attempt to assess the approximate height of the interior of the 'antiquarium' or 'den thoren'. Assuming that Hillewerve's furniture is represented at the correct scale in the print, the wall of the structure – that is up to where the cupola begins – would have been 5 to 5.5 m high. This wall was therefore probably somewhat higher than the adjacent ground-floor room, which we estimate to have come up to a height of 4 or 4.5 m.[27] The cupola itself would then have been some 2.5 m high and, of course, there was the lantern on top of that.

The Modern Reconstruction of the 'Antiquarium'

During the modern reconstruction of the Rubenshuis, the unusual 'antiquarium' was rebuilt in its correct position – namely where the foundations were found – and the replica is also acceptable in terms of its general form. However, no heed was paid to the decorative scheme shown in seventeenth-century sources. The detail in Van Haecht's painting had apparently escaped attention, while the decoration shown in the print was believed not to be original. This was certainly true for the chapel's cupola with its view of Heaven, but not for the northern wall. It was mistakenly thought that the elaborate pattern of niches shown in the print could not originate from the time of Rubens. Van Averbeke suspected that Hillewerve had filled in the original (prominently framed) niches and altered them to suit his taste when furnishing his chapel.[28] For this reason a completely new, more austere design was drawn up.[29] The division of the surface into prominently framed bays has indeed been retained but not the imaginative details seen in both the print and the painting. The dome and the semicircular north wall are largely executed in marble in contrasting colours (white, grey, yellow/orange and black). The cupola has a design of eight wide and rigidly defined 'ribs'. As said, the north wall has been greatly simplified in

---

26. It would not have been possible to see the whole room in this way from the adjacent (lower-ceilinged) room on the ground floor. In reality the walls at the top, left and right, would not have been visible at all (because they were built against the older northern wall of the east façade). Harrewijn solves this by showing two spandrels at the top filled in with neutral black cross-hatching, and by adding on either side a pulled back curtain – fixed to an imaginary point – elements which cannot possibly have been in this position in reality.
27. The calculation is based on the height of comparable existing furniture: 100 cm for the armchair and 85 cm for the prie-dieu; the statue of St Joseph in the tall niche on the left-hand side was probably larger than life-size.
28. Van Averbeke, *Rubenshuis, restauratie II*, 1938, p. 20.
29. For a drawing with a design by Victor Blommaert, see Tijs, *Rubens and Jordaens*, 1984, p. 225.

style, vaguely inspired by an Italian example: an apse in the loggia of the Villa Madama in Rome.[30] The wall is now divided into bays with monumental pilasters separating arch-topped niches, horizontal rectangular panels and tondi, all framed by dark bands of marble (Text ill. 101).

The round-headed niches of the reconstruction bear some similarity to the niche in the background of the anonymous *Portrait of Rubens and his Son (Albert?)* in The State Hermitage Museum in St Petersburg (Appendix III.27). Yet the idea that the austere background in the portrait was based on the interior of Rubens's 'antiquarium', as has been suggested,[31] seems to be a misconception founded on the inclusion of two antique objects that belonged to Rubens's collection: on the table a vase with a Medusa head, and in the niche the *Hecate Triformis*.[32] Whether this background is an accurate depiction of a room in Rubens's house or not, it can be assumed that the anonymous painter – who portrays Rubens seated by a table – was thinking of his sitter's study rather than sculpture gallery.[33]

Text ill. 101. The reconstructed 'antiquarium' in the Rubenshuis.

The Decoration of the Cupola

The two sources differ in their depiction of the decoration of the cupola. In Hillewerve's time, when the semicircular chamber was used as a chapel, the ceiling was befittingly adorned with a painted view of heaven, with music-making angels, and the dove of the Holy Spirit in the centre (Fig. 127). Van Haecht's painting, on the other hand, very likely presents a picture that approaches the original decoration of the cupola in Rubens's 'pantheon', intricately patterned with stemwork, and garlands in monochrome white on a yellowish background, painted in *trompe-l'oeil* or rendered in stucco relief (Fig. 128). It is noticeable that the cupola is not coffered like the dome of the Pantheon in Rome but is embellished more decoratively with motifs somewhat reminiscent of the fantastical grotesques encountered on authentic Roman domes and vaults. For this decoration, see also in the Catalogue, under No. 21.

30. Ibid, 1984, p. 224.
31. Bastet, *Oudheden*, 1980, p. 76.
32. For both objects, see F. Healy in Belkin – Healy, *House of Art*, 2004, p. 243, under no. 57; for the *Hecata Triformis* (now in the Rijksmuseum van Oudheden, Leiden), see ibid., no. 63.
33. See Chapter VII, p. 228.

CHAPTER VIII - THE EAST OR GARDEN WING WITH THE 'ANTIQUARIUM'

The Decoration of the Semicircular North Wall of the 'Antiquarium'

The north wall of the 'antiquarium', as depicted in the inset at the bottom of the Harrewijn print of 1692 (Fig. 127) is semicircular in structure and divided into nine bays. The two outermost bays left and right open up into a narrow barrel vault that follows the line of the semicircular cupola. To the right is a high window and to the left a large niche with an over-life-size statue of St Joseph (the Van Haecht painting shows a colossal antique statue to the right, in a corresponding position). The seven central bays are different in character; they are divided by pilasters that are the full height of the wall. Filling the bays there are numerous niches in different shapes and sizes, integrated into an elaborate light-coloured framework. In these, busts and other antique objects could be placed. For a detailed description, see No. 22.

In both the print and the painting there are also rectangular figurative panels above the top tier of niches. The Harrewijn print shows a frieze of six scenes, perhaps religious paintings that Canon Hillewerve installed in his chapel (Text ill. 102). In the far left picture a kneeling figure looks up at what could be celestial beams of light, perhaps suggesting a scene from the life of Christ or a saint. The scenes belonging to the original decoration had probably quite different subjects, inventions by Rubens that were in keeping with the subject matter displayed in the classicised 'pantheon'. Interestingly, the rectangular panels in Van Haecht's painting are monochrome scenes peopled by unidentifiable characters (Text ill. 103). Perhaps these are meant to represent painted *grisailles* that mimic (antique) reliefs, making them comparable to the monochrome frieze on the workshop façades (Nos 8–16).

The Busts in the 'Antiquarium'

As was the case for the studio's north façade, busts were an important part of the decoration of Rubens's 'antiquarium'. In Van Haecht's painting (Fig. 128) only the right-hand side of the chamber is visible; nonetheless there are no fewer than nine busts in the niches in the semicircular wall, as well as four larger ones standing on what seems to be a continuous stone ledge.

In Hillewerve's chapel, curiously, not all the busts have disappeared. A row of ten busts on bases, all placed at the same height, can be seen at the top: eight between the frieze with rectangular scenes and the cupola, and two more at the left and right-hand ends (at the edges of the image). More important are the twelve busts represented in the oval niches underneath the rectangular scenes (Text ill. 102). It is highly unlikely that these were actual in-the-round sculptures or plaster casts rather than *grisaille* paintings in *trompe-l'oeil* imitating stone. A clue can be found in the fact that we see the same narrow-footed busts in the

CHAPTER VIII - THE EAST OR GARDEN WING WITH THE 'ANTIQUARIUM'

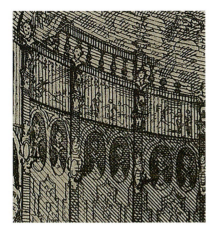 

Text ill. 102. Detail of the 1692 Harrewijn print (Fig. 18): decoration of Hillewerve's chapel (oval niches and rectangular scenes).

Text ill. 103. Detail of Text ill. 100: decoration of the 'antiquarium' (oval niches and rectangular scenes).

oval niches in both the Van Haecht painting (Text ill. 103) and the print. Indeed, it can be ruled out that 'real' three-dimensional busts which Rubens had placed in the niches of his 'antiquarium' would still have been in place in Hillewerve's chapel.

Koenraad Jonckheere made an interesting suggestion about these busts in the oval niches; He assumed that they might have been paintings of the first twelve Roman emperors by Rubens.[34] He points in particular to a partially surviving series of oval paintings on panel (all approx. 33 × 26.5 cm) that he dates to 1618–1620.[35] However, that specific identification is at variance with what can be seen in both the print and Van Haecht's painting: each bust clearly stands on a narrow foot and their shoulders are not 'cropped' by the oval frame, as they are in the *Emperors* series. Moreover, in Van Haecht's painting whitish busts are set against a dark background in the oval niches, and this colour scheme makes sense. As said, if the busts in the 'antiquarium' were painted they were probably meant to mimic sculptures and would therefore have been rendered in monochrome, not as portraits in lifelike colours. This, of course, is not to say that the twelve busts in the top tier of oval niches in Rubens's 'pantheon' could not have represented the twelve Roman emperors – they probably did, as it would have been an obvious choice of subject.[36]

---

34. Jonckheere, *Prototypes (CRLB)*, 2016, pp. 44–46, 106.
35. Ibid., pp. 40, 41, 104–115, nos 39–50, figs 158 and ff.
36. We learn from Arnold Houbraken that Govaert Flinck placed busts of the twelve emperors on top of the cornice in his large painting gallery (which according to Descamps was 'dans le gout de Rubens'); see below, p. 248, n. 55.

CHAPTER VIII - THE EAST OR GARDEN WING WITH THE 'ANTIQUARIUM'

Ivory 'from the Tower'

Was costly ivory used in some way in the decoration of the 'antiquarium'? An entry that is hard to interpret in the *Staetmasse*, the settlement of Rubens's estate, might suggest so. Gerard van Opstal (1605–1668), the son-in-law of Hans van Mildert who had died in the meantime, paid 100 guilders and 13 stuivers for 63 pounds of ivory that came 'Vuytten thoren' (From the tower) of the aforesaid house of the deceased in which stood the antiquities of the deceased (Appendix I.23: [1]). It remains unclear why it was necessary to specify in the entry that the ivory came 'from the tower'. It seems unlikely that part of the permanent decoration of the 'antiquarium' would have been stripped off to be sold, so perhaps the material in question was part of a consignment of raw ivory, which would certainly have interested ivory carver Van Opstal.[37]

C. Rubens's Two Domed Rooms: Inspiration and Imitation

We have seen from the above that when building his house, Rubens created two rooms that were lit from above. One was a studio in the workshop wing and had a domed ceiling; the other was a 'tower' in which his classical sculpture and antiquities were displayed, which was vaulted by a semi-dome. This was an unusual construction for a private house and was commented upon by Sperling and early biographers of Rubens. Indeed, these rooms were considered so special that they were the only parts of the interior depicted in the Harrewijn prints (Text ill. 47 and Fig. 127). Rubens's installation of domed ceilings was directly related to the quality of light that entered from an overhead position, or more specifically the effect such zenithal light had on paintings and other works of art.

The Roman Pantheon as a Model

Attention has rightly been drawn to the fact that in building domed rooms with natural 'overhead lighting', Rubens was putting into practice ideas that Italian architectural theorists had derived from Vitruvius.[38] The Pantheon in Rome was the pre-eminent example. For instance, Sebastiano Serlio (1475–1554), the most influential writer on architecture in the sixteenth century, bestowed lavish

---

37. We know that in the 1620s Rubens had statuettes carved in ivory by Georg Petel (1601–1635), and during his later years by Lucas Faydherbe (1617–1697), and these were part of the workshop production (Scholten, *Werkplaats-academie*, 2004, passim). So, on Rubens's death there may still have been a supply of raw ivory intended for this purpose in the house.
38. For a detailed account in relation to the 'antiquarium', see Muller, *Rubens's Museum*, 1977, pp. 576–581; see also below n. 43.

CHAPTER VIII - THE EAST OR GARDEN WING WITH THE 'ANTIQUARIUM'

praises on the Pantheon's interior in Book III (which deals with 'antiquita' in Rome and elsewhere) of his *Tutte l'opere d'architettura et prospetiva*. The building's beauty, he tells us, 'arises from the celestial light, which is not impeded by anything'. Such illumination was perfect for the temple's many statues, hence his recommendation: 'And therefore those who delight in keeping sundry statues and other things made in relief, ought to have a similar room which receives light from above'.[39]

Also interesting is Serlio's opinion that a room lit in this way would be 'very appropriate for paintings, on condition that they shall have been painted in a similar light'.[40] And the successful architect Vincenzo Scamozzi (1548–1616) gives similar guidelines in his *Idea della Architettura Universale*, published in 1615, a copy of which Rubens owned.[41] Scamozzi writes that, as Vitruvius had already prescribed, every room in which works of art are exhibited should face north in order to get 'a firm, stable and regulated light'. He then goes on to establish a hierarchy of six types of light. To bring out the best in works of art, 'bright and perpendicular light' is preferred, 'which we receive in courtyards or through the apertures in cupolas, such as that of the Rotonda [Pantheon] of Rome and similar places. Not being impeded by anything, this light is diffused equally as far as the ground'.[42]

Evidently the striking circular Roman temple, lit only by zenithal light, was the model for the 'antiquarium'. Chifflet was already calling it Rubens's 'panthéon' in 1625, and later on De Piles (in 1681), and De Sevin (c. 1695) also used that term for it.[43]

Clearly, therefore, when building his house, Rubens had followed the advice of the above-mentioned architectural theorists on how to achieve the optimum lighting in his 'antiquarium' and top-floor studio with cupola. He did not apply their theories to the letter, however, but adapted them to the space available in his house and to the weather in the Low Countries. In plan his 'panthéon' was not round but only semicircular. Of course, unlike Rome's Pantheon, in neither of Rubens's rooms was the *oculus* in the ceiling open to the heavens. Light would have entered the 'antiquarium' via a lantern on top of the dome,

---

39. Serlio, Book III (*Nel qual se figurano, e descrivono le antiquita di Roma [...]*), first edn. Venice 1540; citation taken from Muller, *Rubens's Museum*, 1977, p. 578 (Italian: ibid., p. 579, n. 46); for a slightly different translation, see Hart – Hicks, *Serlio*, 1996, p. 99; for Serlio's whole passage on the Pantheon, see ibid., pp. 99–111. On Serlio's publications in relation to Rubens, see Chapter IV, p. 121, nn. 13, 16; Chapter VI, pp. 189–190, nn. 65, 66.
40. Muller, *Rubens's Museum*, 1977, p. 579, n. 46 (with quotations in Italian and English); Hart – Hicks, *Serlio*, 1996, p. 99.
41. Scamozzi, *Idea*, 1615; Rubens bought this treatise from the Plantin printing house in May 1617 (see above, Chapter IV, p. 121, n. 17) and it appears in the sale of his books by Albert Rubens, sale cat. p. 9, col. 1 (Arents, *Bibliotheek*, 2001, p. 347).
42. Scamozzi, *Idea*, 1615, Book II, Chap. XIII, p. 137; citation taken from Muller, *Rubens's Museum*, 1977, p. 578.
43. See Appendix I: 17, 31 and 36; in the literature the Pantheon is often referred to as the model for the 'antiquarium', see inter alia Tijs, *Rubens en Jordaens*, 1984, pp. 44–60; id., *Rubens*, 2004, pp. 104–105; Van Beneden, *Rubens and Architecture*, 2011, p. 18, fig. 13.

CHAPTER VIII - THE EAST OR GARDEN WING WITH THE 'ANTIQUARIUM'

resulting in less light inside. A computer simulation on a 3D reconstruction shows that there would be insufficient illumination without additional light from somewhere, as was likewise the case in the studio with cupola on the top floor of the workshop wing.[44] Possibly the large window on the right (receiving light from the south) that can be seen in Hillewerve's chapel (Fig. 127) was intended as just such a compensatory light source.

Precursors: Top-Lit Circular Structures in Italy

We know of no other example in the Southern Netherlands of a room lit from above that was used as an artist's studio or a gallery in which to display sculpture. In building these top-lit chambers Rubens was undoubtedly partly inspired by authoritative architectural treatises, but he was also emulating the classical and Renaissance architecture that he had seen in Italy.[45] He had very probably visited the famous Pantheon in Rome and would certainly have been familiar with Mantegna's house in Mantua with its central circular courtyard, covered at that time by a dome with an large *oculus*, where Mantegna is thought to have installed his famous collection of antique sculpture.[46]

To what extent he may have known other spaces that became a source of inspiration for his own is harder to determine. Two examples will suffice. The first, in Rome, was the 'cortile interno' or inner courtyard of the Casa Sassi, where a collection of antique statues standing in niches and lit from above was displayed – though in this case the courtyard was not covered by a dome.[47] The second, in Milan, was in the Casa degli Omenoni, the house of renowned sculptor Leone Leoni (c. 1509–1590): on the *piano nobile* was a remarkable octagonal chamber measuring approximately 49 square metres, which was a repository for his most prized possessions. There were niches in all eight walls and the room was topped by a cupola with an *oculus*.[48]

---

44. For the study of the illumination of Rubens's *'antiquarium'*, see De Gruyter, *Lichtinval*, 2012, pp. 18–22, figs 37–40; Lombaerde, *Rubens*, 2014, p. 216, fig. 13.
45. For examples, see inter alia Helmstutler De Dio, *Leoni*, 2011, p. 137.
46. The house with its circular courtyard still exists, but the dome has disappeared; see Kraitrová, *Mantegna*, 1985, pp. 51–54, figs 3, 4; Schwarz, *Künstlerhaus*, 1990, pp. 152–154, no. 4.
47. See the drawing by Maarten van Heemskerck (1498–1574) in the Staatliche Museen zu Berlin, Berlin (Filippi, *Van Heemskerck*, 1990, p. 97, no. 4, pl. 4).
48. Schwarz, *Künstlerhaus*, 1990, p. 198; on the house, see ibid., pp. 197–199, no. 25; Helmstutler Di Dio, *Leoni*, 2011, pp. 136–137; on the house ('finer and more expensive than that of any previous painter or sculptor') in general, see ibid., pp. 46, 56–58. On Leoni's collection, and the question of Rubens having visited the Casa degli Omenoni or not, see Muller, *Collector*, 1989, p. 15, n. 35.

Imitations of Rubens's Domed Rooms: Sculpture 'Pantheon' or 'Antiquarium' and Workshop

Rubens's device of a 'pantheon' in which to display antique sculpture was much admired, and variations of it can be seen in paintings of picture galleries, including those by Van Haecht mentioned above.[49] Yet it remained an ideal. No one sought to imitate it in reality, as far as is known, and it is not hard to see why. Rubens's collection of antique sculpture was unique in the Netherlands, and therefore there was no need for such a specific space.[50]

Did the famous master's remarkable studio with its cupola become a prototype for other artists? Not as far as we know. There seem to have been no other examples at all in the Southern Netherlands. It would have been difficult to fit such a studio into an existing house, of course, and no details are known about the general structure or interior of newly built workshops. We have no idea whether the aforementioned studios ('schilderhuizen') built by Cornelis Schut, Jan Cossiers and Jan Van Balen in their gardens,[51] for example, had domed ceilings or let in light from above in some way. Nor is there anything resembling a ceiling allowing overhead light in the many pictures of painters at work in their ateliers. A room with a dome admitting zenithal light is nowhere to be found. What we can say is that the light usually does fall from above; often through a window high up, or through a window with the lower part covered.[52]

The situation is different when we look at the Northern Netherlands. Here we have a little more information about rooms that were domed or lit from above, be they picture galleries or painters' workshops. The large ingeniously illuminated picture gallery with cupola in the Mauritshuis in The Hague, and the *Oranjezaal* in the Huis ten Bosch in The Hague, both designed by Jacob van Campen, have been mentioned above.[53] Of particular interest in this context was a room in the house of Govaert Flinck (1615–1660) on the Leliegracht in Amsterdam, which seems to have been directly inspired by Rubens's house. Flinck began his career as a pupil and assistant of Rembrandt but from 1645 was increasingly influenced by the works of Rubens and Van Dyck. He possibly made a study trip to the Southern Netherlands that included a stay in Antwerp (after Rubens's death?).[54] If so, it can be assumed that he visited

---

49. For illustrations of a sculpture gallery in paintings, see under No. 20.
50. Muller also noted that 'no one in Antwerp or the rest of the Netherlands, North or South, followed Rubens's example' (Muller, *Rubens's Collection*, 2004, p. 48).
51. See Chapter VII, pp. 214–215, n. 36.
52. With regard to the latter, see also the comment by Van der Stighelen, *Zelfbeeld*, 2000, p. 258, n. 48; for 17th-century depictions of painters' workshops, see Lemmens, *Atelier*, 1964, pp. 12–13; Baticle – Georgel, *Technique*, 1976, passim; and esp. Kleinert, *Atelierdarstellungen*, 2006, passim.
53. See Chapter VII, pp. 217–218, nn. 48, 50.
54. According to his biographers Filippo Baldinucci and Arnold Houbraken, Flinck spent some time in Antwerp

Rubens's former house and thus had first-hand information about it. Flinck's now long-vanished room, was described by Arnold Houbraken, who in his *Groote Schouburgh* (1719) tells us that shortly after his marriage (in 1645) Flinck built 'a large chamber with lights high up' ('een groote schilderzaal met hooge lichten'). Busts of the Roman emperors stood along the cornice and there were also many plaster casts of the most famous antique statues, as well as a whole miscellany of painter's props.[55] Interestingly, from this description and other information it can be inferred that Flinck's chamber was a combination of an 'antiquarium' and a studio. Jean-Baptiste Descamps (1714–1791) knew about this remarkable room in Amsterdam, and saw the connection with Rubens's house. In his life of Flinck he writes that his 'beau Cabinet' was built 'dans le gout de celui de Rubens' and had its light ('sa grande lumière') entering through a dome pierced in the ceiling.[56]

A century and a half later we find another example of a studio with overhead light in Amsterdam in the premises known as 'Felix Meritis' (first stone laid in 1787), built on the Keizersgracht for the society of the same name. As can be seen in Adriaan de Lelie's *Drawing Gallery of the Felix Meritis Society* (1801) the room used by the drawing department was lit solely by a square skylight.[57]

Finally, it is worth mentioning the extraordinary and eccentric variant of Rubens's 'antiquarium' that was created in London around 1810 by the architect John Soane (1753–1837). He added to his house a top-lit tower called the 'dome' or 'museum', filled from top to bottom with sculpture and fragments of classical architecture. The uppermost floors of that remarkable structure have disappeared but a series of drawings provides a good idea, albeit with exaggerated perspective, of what it originally looked like.[58]

---

to study the work of the famous Flemish masters (without suggesting a date or a period in his life); see Jeroense, *Flinck*, 1997, pp. 83–84. J.W. von Moltke on the other hand considered such a trip to Antwerp by the very busy master rather unlikely (Von Moltke, *Flinck*, 1965, p. 12).

55. '[…] op welker bovenlyst de Borstbeelden der Keyzeren geplaatst stonden, vorder vele fraje afgietsels naar de geachtste marmere Antiquen […]'; among the props were '[…] all manner of exotic robes, garments, armour, firearms and bladed weapons, as well as old and costly velvet, and other hangings embroidered with gold thread […]' (Houbraken, *Konstschilders*, 1718–21, II, p. 22). On Flinck's studio with its 'lights high up', see also Von Moltke, *Flinck*, 1965, pp. 11, 33.

56. 'Ce beau Cabinet étoit bâti dans le goût de celui de Rubens. Sa grande lumière y venoit du haut percé en forme de dôme' (Descamps, *Vie*, 1753–64, II, p. 248). Later, the Uylenburgh art dealership was established in the same house (see Dudok van Heel, *Het Schilderhuis*, 1982, pp. 70–90).

57. Amsterdam, Rijksmuseum, inv. no. Sk-C-538, dated 1801; Middelkoop, ed., *Kopstukken*, 2002, pp. 250–251, no. 102.

58. Richardson – Stevens, eds, *Soane*, 1999, pp. 150–174, figs 137–138, nos 67–69; buildings with domes and overhead light were a constant in Soane's work. Jeffrey Muller points to a more general similarity between the houses of Rubens and Soane (the latter now the Sir John Soane's Museum, London); both belong to the same tradition, displaying a combination of knowledge and creativity in their collections (Muller, *Collector*, 1989, p. 64).

Chapter IX
The Portico

On entering the Rubenshuis from the Wapper, the visitor is struck by an impressive portico that separates the courtyard from the garden (Fig. 138). This triple-arched screen, which functions simultaneously as a bridge between the north wing on the left-hand side and the studio complex to the right, recalls a classical triumphal arch with three openings, an architectural form that was applied in new ways in villas as well as city gates during the Italian Renaissance. It is the most important part of the original house still standing and unsurprisingly the element that is most often reproduced and mentioned in the literature. A full list of bibliographic references can be found in the Catalogue (No. 24).

There can be no doubt that Rubens designed this impressive construction himself. However, this view is not shared unanimously and differing opinions have been put forward. For example, one name that is regularly mentioned in connection with the design of the portico is that of the sculptor Hans van Mildert, even though there are no obvious grounds for this.[1] We can also reject the idea that the design, rather than being an invention of Rubens, is based on a French example.[2]

As with all other elements of Rubens's house, the dating of the portico is a problematical business. We place it in about 1618, the argumentation behind which can be found in a previous chapter, where there is a general discussion of the dating of the components of the house.[3] Further on in the present chapter we will return to the question of the dating, examining the seventeenth-century pictorial material more closely.

Terminology

Rather than a 'portico', it would be more accurate to call the construction a 'gate', a 'portal', or possibly a 'screen'. Unlike what we see in Rubens's house,

---

1. For the attribution to Van Mildert as designer of the portico, see for instance, Van Aerschot, ed., *Bouwen / Antwerpen*, 1979, p. 548; Blommaert, *Barokarchitectuur*, 1982, p. 160; rightly, no mention of it is made by Leyssens, *Van Mildert*, 1941.
2. Oda Van de Castyne challenged the idea that Rubens was active as an architect, and she even went so far as to question his authorship of the portico and garden pavilion; she assumed that the portico was copied from a design by Salomon de Brosse, which Rubens had most probably seen in Paris, or in any case that he was strongly influenced by this French architect (Van de Castyne, *Rubens*, 1931, pp. 116–118; id., *Architecture*, 1934, p. 318); rejected by, for example, Baudouin, *Painter-Architect*, 2002, p. 15, n. 1.
3. See Chapter IV, p. 127.

CHAPTER IX - THE PORTICO

a portico is in fact a roofed structure underneath which people can shelter or walk, in other words it is not merely a gateway. Nonetheless, we will stick with this term, which is now well established in the Rubens literature. It was François Mols who defined the construction as 'le portique' (Appendix I.43: [9]), which made sense as in the eighteenth century it had been extended into a kind of portico with a depth of several metres.[4] Rooses adopted Mols's wording in his writings, and 'portico' thus became the habitual term, although other names have also been used.[5] It is not known what term was used for the construction in Rubens's time. The earliest mention found – and it is the only one that goes back to the seventeenth century – dates from considerably later: a document of 1689 mentions 'het portael' in Rubens's courtyard.[6]

A. The Portico in its Present State

Materials and State of Preservation

The portico is built from various types of stone. The visible parts, including the columns, the pilasters with thick bands and the pediment, are made of blue limestone from quarries in Hainaut as can be deduced from some dozens of quarry marks.[7] The decorative sculptural elements are carved from sandstone as well as limestone from various sources; the carved ornaments are dressed over a brickwork core.[8]

The description given below is based on the portico as it stands today. Although much is original in this best preserved part of the house, it should be stressed that the structure has suffered considerable wear and tear over a

---

4. He refers to the extension in his commentary, but it should be noted that in his drawn plan (Fig. 3) he represents the older, original situation (known to him from the Harrewijn print).
5. Mols's contemporary Van den Sanden talks about 'the balustrade or *afschutzel*' (Appendix I.42: [2]). Van den Branden refers to a *praalboog* (triumphal arch); Rott calls it an 'arcaded wall' (for the bibliographic references, see under No. 24). The inappropriate use of the term 'portico' for what should be defined as a 'portal' is explicitly pointed out by Coekelberghs, *Review Palazzo Rubens*, 2012, p. 7. It should be noted that the term 'portiek' used in the Dutch version of the *Palazzo Rubens* catalogue is consistently rendered as 'garden screen' in the English version (Uppenkamp – Van Beneden, *Palazzo Rubens*, 2011, passim); the same phrase is also used in Uppenkamp, *Rubens's palazzetto*, 2018, pp. 224–225. Authors writing (in Dutch) about the recent restoration of the structure all adhere to the established term 'portiek' (in *M & L, Monumenten, Landschappen en Archeologie*, XXXVIII, 4, 2019).
6. See below, n. 62.
7. Various quarry marks, including that of the master ('maître de carrière') Jean Delfontaine (c. 1580–1667) from Arquennes in Hainaut, can be found both on the portico and the garden pavilion. This is no help in dating the structure: Delfontaine supplied stone for buildings in Antwerp over a period of several decades, including the Kolveniershof, which was erected in 1631–33 (Adriaenssens, *Steenhouwersmerken*, 1976, pp. 82–83; Van Belle, *Signes lapidaires*, 1994, pp. 86, 92, and passim). On quarry marks, including those found on other parts of the house, see Chapter V, p. 140 (n. 6), p. 143 (n. 11); Chapter X, p. 296, n. 4; Maclot, *Rubenssite*, 2016, pp. 66, 68, 170. For marks on the portico, see also De Clercq, *Conservatie*, 2019, p. 74.
8. On the materials that were used, see under No. 24, p. 395, technical note.

CHAPTER IX - THE PORTICO

period of four centuries. Exposure to the elements has quite severely weathered the sculptural decorations, especially those in softer stone. Water erosion has occurred in places, and is particularly visible on the right dolphin, which has become virtually unrecognisable (No. 26; Fig. 150); in addition, areas of relief have broken off and disappeared altogether; for example, one of the satyrs has lost a hand (Fig. 171), while the eagles' feet are also damaged (Fig. 153).[9]

Photographs show that eighty years ago, at the time of the restoration, the damage was far less extensive (cf. Fig. 172). This is also revealed by a series of plaster casts of details of the portico that were made in 1942 out of concern for destruction being caused by the war.[10] Since some elements were less weather-beaten at the time, these moulds and casts provide a more accurate impression of the original forms, as is borne out, for example, by a comparison between the portico's keystone with the head of Medusa and its plaster counterpart (Figs 144 and 145). Surviving positive casts, complete or substantially intact, are listed as 'copies' in the catalogue.[11] Unfortunately, the moulds of other parts of the portico cannot be used to make new casts because it is not possible to identify the inserts required, hundreds of which are stored in crates, mixed together in disarray.[12]

It is especially important to note that the construction was substantially altered in the eighteenth century: the portico was made considerably higher, while at the back, level with the first storey, an extension was added to carry a corridor that connected the two wings of the house. Probably at this point, although it may have been later, the left arch of the portico was closed off. Some impression of the front of the raised structure can be gained from pictorial documentation that survives from the nineteenth century (see, for example, Appendix III.45, 49 and 52). Plans of the property drawn in the 1930s (Figs 4–5)

---

9. For more information about the portico's state of preservation, with references to detailed reports, see under No. 24.
10. Negative moulds of the portico's sculptural decorations were made in May 1942 by the sculptor Antoine Hoefnagels (1883–1964), and the positive casts were made in September 1942. The series is preserved almost in its entirety – although some are seriously damaged or broken into several pieces – in Antwerp, Centraal Depot Musea – Stad Antwerpen; see De Clercq, *Materieel-technisch onderzoek*, 1997, p. 15, figs 1–15; id., *Moulages*, 2012, p. 1, figs pp. 1–5, 18–19. De Clercq – Hayen, *Historische schets*, 2019, pp. 43, 51, nn. 19, 20.
11. See under Nos 25, 27, 30–33, and 35.
12. Adding to the confusion is the fact that the same store also contains a large number of casts made from sculptural elements created anew during the reconstruction of the house. For example the cast of a spandrel with dolphin (or rather a sea monster) was not made from the portico, as thought (De Clercq, *Materieel-technisch onderzoek*, 1997, pp. 5–6, fig. 7; id., *Moulages*, 2012, p. 1, repr. p. 4) but in fact corresponds to one of the 'dolphins' of the modern studio façade, added in the spandrels around the windows. On the other hand, there is also a cast of a caryatid from the garden pavilion that does not appear in the literature mentioned above.

CHAPTER IX - THE PORTICO

Text ill. 104. The portico with a raised structure (a corridor and a roof), 1937. Antwerp, FelixArchief.

and photographs made of the courtyard side around 1938 (Text ill. 104) show that these changes were still in place at the time of the restoration. A small number of photos also afford a view of the garden side of the three-storey structure with corridor that was added to the rear of, and on top of the portico. One of these, dating from 1906, shows the garden with the partition wall that divided the property into two parcels (Text ill. 105); another, made in 1938, shows the situation after the dividing wall had been taken down (Text ill. 106).

In the 1930s the garden side of the extension had a plain façade, harmonising with the adjoining eighteenth-century eastern façade of the studio wing, with windows on two floors above the two arches of the portico that remained open.[13]

During the restoration these extensions to the top and back were all removed and the portico was restored more or less to the state seen in Harrewijn's first print (Figs 17 and 142). That is to say, the front of the portico – the side facing the courtyard – was returned to its former state. As mentioned, there is no surviving image showing the original appearance of the rear or garden side, and so there was no pictorial material available that could guide an authentic reconstruction.

13. On the alterations to the east façade and the portico, see also Chapter V, p. 154.

CHAPTER IX - THE PORTICO

Text ill. 105. The garden with the partition wall (at the left), 1906.

Text ill. 106. The garden after the partition wall has been taken down, 1938.

Text ill. 107. The rear of the dismantled portico and (at the right) the reconstructed east wing, during the restoration (c. 1938).

The Unknown Rear of the Portico

When the later extension was removed, a plain, bare brick wall with remnants of plaster was revealed.[14] There are no photographs of the rear of the dismantled portico in its entirety, but a few do exist of details, which give an impression of its severely damaged condition (Text ill. 107).

From the findings at the time of the restoration, the architect Émile Van Averbeke concluded that the garden side of the portico had originally been 'just a plain wall'.[15] He then contradicts himself by reporting that a few pieces of moulding were discovered around the arches and near the 'de hoogste borstwering' (balustrade at the top). He furthermore suspects – and this seems

14. De Clercq et al., *Rubens' tuinportiek en tuinpaviljoen*, 2014, pp. 43, 44; see also Van Driessche, *Herschepping*, 2019, p. 36.
15. Van Averbeke, *Rubenshuis, restauratie II*, 1938, p. 16.

CHAPTER IX - THE PORTICO

Text ill. 108. The reconstructed rear of the portico.

plausible – that a good number of elements of the rear of the portico were cut away when the extensions were built. But, as said, he does not believe that the garden side was originally decorated. More important, in his view was that the portico needed reinforcing to ensure its stability, something that could only be achieved by adding a new façade to the garden side: nothing sumptuous, but a feature of some distinction and appropriate to the garden.[16] His advice was implemented. In 1939 the original wall at the rear of the portico, the surface of which was then bare, was provided with a cladding of sand-lime stone and bluestone after a design by Van Averbeke.[17] A neutral form was chosen, with the same thick banding in the lower section as at the front, and with no ornamentation besides a few moulded sections and shallow pilasters (Text ill. 108).

Visible on the jambs of the three arches is the vertical 'seam' between the original blocks of blue limestone and the new cladding, which continues the same forms (Text ill. 109).

It is worth comparing the current situation with the slightly broader jambs of the openings as they appear in the print by Harrewijn (Fig. 17) and in Jordaens's *Cupid and Psyche* (Fig. 20). A clearer understanding of the

16. Ibid., p. 17.
17. Van Driessche, *Herschepping*, 2013, pp. 27, 41, n. 113.

CHAPTER IX - THE PORTICO

 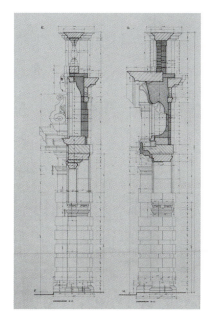

Text ill. 109. The portico seen from the rear, showing the vertical 'seams' on the jambs of the three arches.

Text ill. 110. M. Bonte, *Cross-sections of the Portico*, blueprint, detail. Antwerp, FelixArchief.

intervention made during the restoration can be gained from the drawn cross-sections of the restored portico in an architectural plan of c. 1980 by M. Bonte (Text ill. 110). This reveals the surprising depth of the niches in relation to the overall thickness of the portico.[18]

Van Averbeke's austere and modern design can hardly be said to achieve a convincing form. It lacks any affinity with Rubens's style or, for that matter, with seventeenth-century architecture in general. It is important to remember, of course, that he had no information whatsoever on which to base his design. Nevertheless, it seems more than likely that the rear of the portico, which was visible from the garden and adjoined the decorated east wing of the studio, was originally considerably less stark in appearance. In all probability it was decorated at the very least with painted or stuccoed ornaments. With regard to the decoration of the rear of the portico, it is worth mentioning an anonymous drawing from the second half of the seventeenth century which features an architectural design that may have been inspired by Rubens's house. The sheet shows a *palazzetto* viewed from the garden. A courtyard is closed off by a triple-arched construction crowned by statues on pedestals between sections of balustrade, and with rectangular historicising scenes underneath (Text ill. 111).[19]

18. The central niche is so deep (38 cm) that it goes through almost the entire thickness of the original structure leaving no more than about 6 cm between the niche and the newly added rear façade.
19. King Baudouin Foundation, on loan to the Antwerp Stedelijk Prentenkabinet (Museum Plantin-Moretus),

255

CHAPTER IX - THE PORTICO

Text ill. 111. Anonymous 17th-Century Artist, *Palazzetto Viewed from the Garden*, drawing. Antwerp, Museum Plantin-Moretus, Stedelijk Prentenkabinet.

In two contemporary depictions of the portico there are glimpses of architectural elements visible obliquely through the central arch. These are difficult to interpret, and should probably not be seen as literal depictions of the actual structure. Were there more columns of a similar type behind the columns with rusticated bands, and possibly part of the portico structure? Such a column can indeed be seen in Jordaens's *Cupid and Psyche* (Appendix III.9; Fig. 20). Further architectural elements can be made out behind the portico (which is rendered in reverse) in Van Dyck's *Portrait of Isabella Brant*: through the central arch can be seen a column, with a capital and an entablature with *guttae*, and through the left opening, an arch with a keystone (Appendix III.5; Fig. 19). However, as said, these should probably be regarded as fictional motifs, as is certainly the case with the balustrade behind the sitter in this portrait.

In any event, it is clear from Harrewijn's print of 1692, on which the footprint of the omitted portico is marked (Text ill. 28), that in Hillewerve's time there very probably was no additional construction behind the portico.

Colour

At the time of the restoration the entire portico was coated in paint.[20] This coating was removed, and the stonework was then left unpainted. Yet research has revealed that the portico originally almost certainly was covered in paint, meaning that the current appearance deviates from the seventeenth-century situation.

      inv. no. CVH.0444; pen and brown ink, ink wash, watercolour, 197 × 275 mm; see F. Baudouin, in Baudouin – Allard, eds, *Cat. Van Herck (Drawings)*, 2000, p. 112, no. 29.
20. For this, and on the paint and plaster removed in April–May 1939, see Lodewyck et al., *Conservation of the Portico*, 2003, pp. 30, 33, 35, 44, 67–68.

Researchers found remnants of some ten layers of paint. The oldest of these roughly matched the colours of the different types of stone, but there is no certainty that even this layer dates from the seventeenth century.[21] Indeed, we need to ask why the stonework was painted. Undoubtedly oil paint provided a layer of protection for softer types of stone. As for the colours, it is difficult to establish if the same hue, approximating to the colour of blue limestone, was used throughout to give a uniform appearance to the different types of stone. While this is a possibility, the oldest paint layers suggest that the portico may have been painted in differing hues, and this varied tonality may have been an essential element of its design.

Leaving aside the issue of paint, it is likewise difficult to determine to what extent the natural tonalities of the different stones played a part in the design. In other words, we do not know whether certain types of stone were chosen for their colour or simply because of the different ways in which they could be worked.[22]

Whatever the truth, it is noticeable that the portico is rarely portrayed as a monochrome structure in the pictorial records of the seventeenth century. In Jordaens's *Cupid and Psyche* (Fig. 20) a number of sculptural elements, including the satyrs, the ram's heads, the dolphins and Medusa head, stand out in a lighter colour. The same use of two tones – although less pronounced – can be seen in Van Dyck's *Portrait of Isabella Brant* (Fig. 19). The contrast is stronger in the 1684 print by Harrewijn (Figs 17 and 142), where there is a marked difference between the light parts and the dark pediment, columns, pilasters and niche surrounds. The contrast between light and dark tones is stronger still in the anonymous Aylesbury *View of the Courtyard of Rubens's House* (Figs 16 and 141), in which the portico is so dark that it seems almost black – something that may be due to darkening of paint or varnish – with a few elements such as the satyrs, the dolphins, the keystone and the Minerva bust accentuated in grey and white.

The Architectural Order of the Columns: Tuscan or Doric?

The openings of the portico are separated by heavy half-columns. Although the shafts of these columns are partly hidden by a series of six thick bands, it is nonetheless possible to tell that they belong to the Doric order. The same is true for the graceful free-standing columns of the side arches. Some authors have incorrectly defined the columns of the portico as Tuscan,[23] but, although

---

21. On the blue limestone the oldest layer was grey, approximating more or less to the colour of the underlying stone. Other types of stone were painted in beige, pale grey, dark grey and even pinkish hues (ibid., pp. 66–67; De Clercq – Hayen, *Historische schets*, 2019, pp. 42, 44).
22. Lodewyck et al., *Conservation of the Portico*, 2003, p. 68.
23. See, for example, Van Aerschot, ed., *Bouwen / Antwerpen*, 1979, p. 548; Baudouin, *Barok*, 1982, p. 112; Stutz,

CHAPTER IX - THE PORTICO

Text ill. 112. *Guttae* (detail of the portico).

it can be difficult to tell the two 'sturdy' orders apart, in this case, there can be no doubt.

To begin with, there are in the portico certain decorative elements which belong to the Doric order and not to the simple undecorated Tuscan order: the rosettes, the *guttae* and the *bucrania*. Rosettes can be found on the bands directly below the capitals of the four heavy and four light columns. *Guttae* are present in several places, 'hanging' from the cornice, for example, and over the eight columns just mentioned (Text ill. 112). At either end of the frieze is a *bucranium* (Figs 165 and 166). This decoration forms a standard part of the metopes of a Doric attic, and so it firmly establishes the architectural order of the construction as Doric. For this reason, it seems somewhat beside the point to search for a specific symbolic meaning for the *bucrania* in Rubens's portico. We discuss this motif in more detail in the Catalogue, under No. 29.

A second difference between Tuscan and Doric orders is that the column shafts are typically more massive in the Tuscan order (Text ill. 133). Careful measuring of both the engaged columns and the graceful free-standing columns supporting the arches shows that their proportions are Doric.[24] Nonetheless – and this should be stressed – the portico as a whole can justifiably be regarded as a successful example of the rustic or 'Tuscan' style, even if its architectural order is not actually Tuscan. This is a rather confusing matter to which we will return in the discussion of 'rustication' and the 'rustic order'.[25]

Residenz, 1985, p. 146; Baudouin, *Architecturale Motieven*, 2006, p. 199; Muller, *Rubens's Collection*, 2004, pp. 35–36. It is worth mentioning that some authors have also erroneously described the other columns of the house – in the studio façades and garden pavilion – as Tuscan.

24. I am grateful to Piet Lombaerde for letting me know that the shafts were carefully measured, which shows that there can be no doubt about their Doric character. The use of the Doric order is rightly pointed out by Uppenkamp – Van Beneden, *Vera simmetria*, 2011, pp. 62–65. On this, see below, p. 291, n. 123.
25. See below, pp. 290–291.

The Central Archway with Medusa Head and Dolphins

The central archway, which rises slightly above the height of the two other openings, has a so-called geniculated arch, that is a polygonal arch with bevelled corners. We will discuss this motif further in the present chapter.[26] At the centre of this arch is a protruding keystone featuring a striking decoration: a mascaron that can be identified as a Medusa head – the apotropaic (evil-averting) motif *par excellence* – combined with Jupiter's thunderbolt (Fig. 144). A full discussion of this remarkable detail of the portico can be found in the Catalogue (No. 25).

The two spandrels of the central archway each feature a dolphin with coiled tail in high relief (No. 26); to the right, the original has been virtually obliterated by erosion; the motif in the left spandrel is a modern copy (cf. Figs 150 and 149). Coiled dolphins, but with their noses angled downwards, were also used to decorate the ten spandrels in the top corners of the five windows of the studio's north façade (Fig. 151). We do not know whether this motif was chosen because of some special significance or for its decorative quality. It is therefore difficult to assign a specific meaning to the dolphin motif.[27]

The Side Arches: *Serlianas*

Stylistically, the two side arches differ markedly from the more robust central archway. Here the openings are crowned by profiled round arches, which rest on free-standing Doric columns. The manner in which the two types of arch with columns of different dimensions have been combined into a whole (Fig. 140) is remarkable. The smaller columns support not only the arches but also an architrave (decorated with *guttae*), which runs, as it were, behind the four heavy engaged columns. In addition, the architrave is accentuated by a second moulding underneath, and it continues, in sections, across the breadth of the entire portico. This second moulding is level with the small Doric capitals and continues the shape of these across the structure. Where this double architrave runs behind the large engaged columns, the stepped bands bracketing these columns are omitted so that there is a larger gap between the fifth and sixth bands than between those beneath. Projections from this double architrave can be seen on either side of the middle archway and they continue – at the same height – the profile of the capitals and architrave of the side arches. In the jambs of the large archway this double architrave creates the effect of two superimposed imposts, one with a simple moulding, and another above with Doric *guttae* (Text ills 109, 112).

---

26. See below, pp. 265–267.
27. For possible interpretations, see the catalogue entries in which the iconography of the dolphin is discussed: No. 26, and esp. No. 41.

CHAPTER IX - THE PORTICO

In order to understand the concept underlying this unusual and complex construction, we need to look at the portico in its entirety (Fig. 138). This reveals an interesting motif that is incorporated in the portico which has, rather surprisingly, not previously been noticed: the well-known motif of the *serliana*, part of which is recessed, as it were, behind the large columns. This Serlian motif – consisting of a central round arch, flanked on either side by a horizontal lintel or architrave supported by a column will be discussed in detail in the chapter dealing with the garden pavilion.[28] We have not been able to find other examples of *serlianas* used in this way, in combination with a structure in rusticated manner with heavy banding.[29] The relationship with the garden pavilion's 'pure' *serliana* – which is the focal point of the garden perspective seen from the courtyard through the central arch of the portico, and which allows us to see three *serlianas* in a line – is self-evident.

The Attic with Broken Pediment

The most impressive part of the portico is the storey above the three arches, the attic. Its main feature is a strongly articulated pediment, spanning all three arches and connecting them visually. Only the central section above the middle archway is complete; to either side, the pediment is broken by a panel with a hollow niche, and the two acute angles of the triangle stand in isolation above the outermost half-columns. Above each end of the pediment is a volute which coils forwards, surmounted by the *bucrania* already mentioned (Fig. 138).

The two niches rest on projecting pedestals, further accentuating the rectangular tablets below, which are inscribed with quotations from Juvenal's *Satires*, and are held up by satyrs in the spandrels (see below). Together with the niches, these rectangular elements form a structural unit on a vertical axis, which complements the upward movement rising from the base of the columns to the balustrade at the top. At the same time these vertical elements are perfectly integrated into the portico's overall horizontal design, an aspect stressed by the broad pediment.

The broken pediment was by no means a rare motif in the Netherlands. On a more modest scale it features in numerous sixteenth- and early seventeenth-century altars, as well as in funerary monuments. However, in those examples the sides remain intact and usually it is only the apex of the central section that is excised and replaced by a statue, a vase or family arms.[30]

28. See Chapter X, pp. 316–319.
29. However, (discrete) *serlianas* of three different types can be detected in the rusticated masonry of the *cortile* of the Palazzo Pitti in Florence; detail in Uppenkamp – Van Beneden, *Palazzo Rubens*, 2011, fig. 66); on this palace, which Rubens must have known, see p. 288, n. 112.
30. On the broken pediment, see Ottenheym, *Architectural Ornament*, 2007, pp. 128, 130, 132; Uppenkamp – Van Beneden, *Vera simmetria*, 2011, pp. 45–46. Anthony Blunt saw in the separation of the two ends in Rubens's

The Balustrade with Statues and Vases

Across the top of the attic runs a balustrade, which is punctuated by four pedestals that continue the upward movement of the columns. The middle section of this balustrade consists of a closed panel, centred between an open section composed of elegant balusters. The horizontal character of this storey is emphasised by lintels that run along top and bottom and span the entire width of the portico.

The bronze vases and the bronze statues of Mercury and Minerva which now crown the pedestals were made at the time of the restoration to replace the lost vases and statues shown in Harrewijn's 1684 print (cf. Figs 138 and 17). Whether or not the portico was crowned by statues in Rubens's time is an important question to which we shall return later in this chapter.[31]

Pairs of Eagles, Garlands and Ram's Heads

The main motif in the central part of the attic above the gateway, in the central section of the tympanum, consists of a rounded niche crowned by a shell-like motif set within a profiled frame (Fig. 153). On either side, eagles in high-relief elegantly frame the niche with their outstretched wings. In their beaks these birds of prey clutch a ribbon from which a fruit garland curves down towards the moulding of the architrave below. Several examples of this motif can be found in Italian sculpture (see under No. 27).

Placed on either side of the eagles are sturdy pedestals, cut off diagonally at the top, parallel with the sloping pediment moulding which projects forward above them. On the sides of each pedestal, carved in relief, is a ram's head in profile, terminating in a large volute (Figs 158 and 161). The long *vittae* (fillets) shown hanging from their horns make clear that these rams are presented as sacrificial animals. Similar ram's heads, inspired by ancient altars, occur more than once in Rubens's oeuvre, and the specific significance of this motif in the context of this portico is not obvious. For further commentary, see No. 28.

The Satyrs and the Verses from Juvenal

One of the most intriguing elements of the portico becomes visible to visitors once they have entered the courtyard: the pairs of satyrs, carved in high relief, in the spandrels of the side bays (Figs 171, 173, 175 and 176). Undoubtedly

---

portico a quotation from contemporary architecture in Rome, and he refers to the impressive broken pediment of the façade of the Villa Aldobrandini in Frascati – although in our opinion this comparison is rather far-fetched (Blunt, *Rubens and Architecture*, 1977, p. 613, n. 20).

31. See pp. 278–285; see also Nos R1 and R2.

CHAPTER IX - THE PORTICO

they were designed by Rubens, as can be deduced from similar figures in his painted oeuvre. They signify the realm of nature, which visitors will enter as they pass through the arches of the portico for a walk in the garden. The Catalogue provides further discussion of these sylvan creatures (Nos 30–33).

Both pairs of satyrs hold up a rectangular tablet, each of which is carved with verses from the Roman poet Juvenal's tenth *Satire*.[32] It is perhaps significant that satire is a literary genre which is commonly, but wrongly, said to derive from the Greek word 'satyr'.[33] The text on the left reads: 'Permittes ipsis expe[n]dere numinibus quid / Conveniat nobis rebusq[ue] sit utile nostris. / Carior est illis homo quam sibi' / Iuvenal. Satira X' ('You'll let the gods themselves estimate what will suit us and benefit our circumstances. They care more about people than people do themselves').[34]

The inscription on the other tablet reads: 'Orandum est ut sit mens sana in corpore sano. / Forte[m] posce aninum et mortis terrore care[n]tem. / Nesciat irasci, cupiat nihil. / Iuvenal. Satira X' ('You should pray for a sound mind in a sound body. Ask for a heart that is courageous, with no fear of death that can put up with any anguish, that is unfamiliar with anger, that longs for nothing').[35]

These inscriptions over the entrance to the garden hark back to the text that was fixed in such places in Italy in Antiquity and the Renaissance, a *lex horti* (garden law), giving the correct code of behaviour for visitors to the garden, sometimes joined with general words of wisdom.[36] An example that Rubens may have seen is the garden gateway in the Villa Medici in Rome (Text ill. 113). Over the rounded niches on either side of the central archway, stands a rectangular marble tablet, which bears a Latin inscription announcing the owner's name and welcoming visitors.[37]

Text ill. 113. Bartolomeo Ammanati, Garden portal with inscribed tablets. Rome, Villa Medici.

---

32. In full: Decimus Iunius Iuvenalis (life dates unknown; active late first–early second century ad; 16 Satires (*Satyrae*) by him are known.
33. Actually the name of this genre of Roman poetry derives from satura, a dish filled with a variety of fruits (a reference to a poetic medley).
34. Juvenal, *Satires*, X, 347–348, 350; Juvenal – Persius, *Juvenal – Persius*, trans. Morton Braund, 2004, p. 395.
35. Juvenal, ibid., 356–357, 360; Juvenal – Persius, ibid., p. 397.
36. Morford, *Stoic Garden*, 1987, p. 159; Heinen, *Garten*, 2002, p. 4; id., *Gesundheit*, 2004, pp. 124–125; Uppenkamp – Van Beneden, *Architectural Symbolism*, 2011, p. 92.
37. Toulier, *Villa Médicis*, I, 1989, p. 258, figs 297–298; Coffin, *Villa*, 1988, p. 231, fig. 142 (with translation of

A Gateway to the Stoic Garden

The inscription on Rubens's portico, consisting of six verses selected from Juvenal's tenth Satire, is intended not so much to remind visitors how they ought to conduct themselves when entering the garden, but more generally it recommends a life of virtue, accepting divine providence, keeping free from passions, and remaining steadfast in adversity and in the face of death.[38] Rubens was thus using the verses to express the right approach to life strongly influenced by neo-Stoic thinking, and which had been put into words by Justus Lipsius (1547–1606), especially in his *De Constantia*.[39]

It is worth noting, finally, that Rubens quoted from Juvenal's *Satyrae* on several other occasions, and he can certainly be regarded as one of Rubens's favourite authors.[40]

Although the inscription on the tablets is not exactly what one would normally expect to find on a *lex horti*, the verses are nonetheless apt for a gate that gives access to the garden. They are directly relevant in this sphere. Spending time in a garden was, according to Stoic philosophy, an essential means of maintaining bodily and spiritual health. This idea appears, for example, in a long passage in Lipsius's *De Constantia*, which describes in detail the beautiful garden of his friend Carolus Langius (1521–1573) on the banks of the river Meuse.[41] A walk in this garden one summer prompts a dialogue between Lipsius and Langius, in which they reflect on the healing properties of the garden. There is discussion of examples of figures from Antiquity who found respite in such places. Particularly interesting is the reference to painters coming to rest their tired eyes in a garden, a passage which Rubens undoubtedly knew. The text also includes a good many admonishments. Lipsius emphasises the right approach to adopt when in a garden: '*modesta voluptas*' (honourable desire) is permitted, but no '*torpor*' (indolence). Another temptation to be avoided is getting lost in a passion for collecting rare and exotic plants – an idle activity.

---

inscription); Heinen, *Gesundheit*, 2004, pp. 124–125, fig. 74; a detail given by Uppenkamp – Van Beneden, ibid., p. 92, fig. 115.
38. See for example Morford, *Stoics*, 1991, p. 190, remarking that Juvenal was not a Stoic author.
39. Lipsius, *De Constantia*, 1584 (published by the Plantin Press, both in Leiden and Antwerp; in the same year a Dutch edition was published entitled *Twee boecken vande stantvasticheyt*, in a translation by Jan Moretus I). For this and later editions and translations, see Hoven, *De Constantia*, 1997, pp. 75–81.
40. McGrath, *History (CRLB)*, 1997, I, p. 80; Arents, *Bibliotheek*, 2001, p. 216, under no. H5. Quotations from Juvenal can be found in a drawing after Hans Holbein II's *Dance of Death* (Belkin, *Copies (CRLB)*, 2009, I, pp. 117, 127, no. 19, fig. 62), and in a number of Rubens's letters (see Magurn, ed., *Letters*, 1955, nos 26, 120, 165). The *Satyrae* also tie in with the theme of *Seneca and Nero* (Jonckheere, *Prototypes (CRLB)*, 2016, pp. 33, 118–120, no. 52, fig. 177) and the *Decius Mus* series (McGrath, *History (CRLB)*, 1997, I, p. 80; Baumstark – Delmarcel, *Decius Mus (CRLB)*, 2019, I, p. 44; II, p. 11). Rubens had probably been introduced to Juvenal's verses at an early age when he attended Latin School.
41. Lipsius, *De Constantia*, 1584, Liber II, Caput I–III.

CHAPTER IX - THE PORTICO

The concept of the healing garden is discussed at length by Ulrich Heinen. He argues that Rubens's predilection for a well-designed, spacious garden should be understood in a philosophical context, and he characterises the artist's garden in Antwerp as 'Stoic' or 'Lipsian'.[42] It is important to take his remark into consideration when interpreting the meaning of the portico. Contrary to what might be expected, in terms of its symbolism, the portico belongs with the garden which lies on the far side, and not with the courtyard or façades of the buildings that surround it. Although the monumental Rubensian structure was the first thing that visitors saw on entering the artist's house, we must remember that it was a gateway to the garden. So, unlike the decorative scheme of the studio façades, one would not expect the portico to contain iconographical allusions to the occupation of the house's owner.

Niches with Concave Corners

Text ill. 114. One of the courtyard façades of Jacques Jordaens's house (detail), Antwerp.

We end this description with a note on two, rather unusual types of arches which are distinctive features of the portico. Upright rectangular niches are set into the attic panels flanking the central section, both of them enclosed by a moulded framework with concave corners at the top. It is difficult to say where Rubens found inspiration for this rather striking arch type. There are no illustrations of such an arch in architectural treatises, while the few known examples in Italy date from after Rubens's return to Antwerp.[43]

As with the geniculated arch, to be discussed below, the arch with concave corners became a recurrent motif in the Southern Netherlands. Unsurprisingly, Rubens included it in his decorations

---

42. Heinen, *Gesundheit*, 2004, pp. 71–182.
43. The motif appears over the portal of the Chiesa Sant' Orsola in Mantua, designed by Antonio Maria Viani (c. 1555/60–1629), who was architect to the Duke of Mantua; however, this church was not completed until 1608 and it is not certain whether Rubens saw it before it was finished. A few examples in Rome, two designs by Francesco Borromini (1599–1557), date from later: the windows of the Oratorio di S. Filippo Neri (Blunt, *Borromini*, 1979, fig. 67) and blind niches in the lower storey of the Collegio di Propaganda Fide (ibid., pp. 191–194, figs pp. 190, 193). It should be noted that arches with concave corners, as well as geniculated arches also occur in French architecture; see the portal of the former Collège des Jésuites in La Flèche (see Text ill. 117); a portal in Chaumont (Hautecoeur, *Architecture classique*, 1967, fig. 378).

for the *Pompa Introitus Ferdinandi*, in the *Front Face of the Arch of Ferdinand*.[44] Jordaens used it, no doubt after seeing it in Rubens's house, for the moulding surrounding the central window in one of his own façades (Text ill. 114).[45] Arches with concave corners, as well as the related so-called draped arches appear frequently until well into the eighteenth century, in church façades, altars, funerary monuments and other places.[46]

The Flat or Geniculated Arch

One of the most eye-catching elements of the portico is the flat or geniculated arch with angled corners in the central bay. As far as we know, the only earlier structure featuring a polygonal arch of this type is the *Porta Pia* (1561–1565) in Rome, a city gate designed for Pope Pius IV by Michelangelo, and which was certainly known to Rubens (Text ills 126 and 127).[47]

The geniculated arch is found not only in the portico. In Rubens's oeuvre are several paintings that show architecture with similar arches, including the *Homage to Ceres* (Appendix III.13; Fig. 23), which is among examples to be discussed later. An early instance of this 'Roman' motif, as a niche, can also be found in the title page which Rubens designed for Jan Hemelaers's *Imperatorum Romanorum Numismata Aurea*, published in 1615.[48] As mentioned in an earlier chapter, the niches on the ground floor of the studio's north façade are also similar in shape (Fig. 33).[49]

Rubens would go on to use the geniculated arch in later designs, notably in the architecture of the decorations constructed in the streets of Antwerp on the occasion of the *Pompa Introitus Ferdinandi*. The geniculated

Text ill. 115. Wenzel Cobergher, the façade of the Church of St Augustine, Antwerp, detail.

---

44. Martin, *Pompa (CRLB)*, 1972, no. 36, figs 67–68.
45. In the east façade of the west wing (Tijs, *Rubens en Jordaens*, 1984, ill. pp. 298–299, 334).
46. Examples include: the façade of the Church of St John the Baptist at the Béguinage in Brussels (Philippot et al., *Architecture*, 2003, ill. p. 104); the crown of the main altar in the St Martin's church at Duffel (Becker, *Altarbau*, 1990, fig. 37); a niche above the portal of the Thurn und Taxis Chapel of the Sablon Church in Brussels (Philippot et al., *Architecture*, 2003, p. 94); the tombs of Anna Maria van Berchem, in the church of St Willibrord in Berchem (Antwerp), and of Ambrosius Capello in Antwerp's Church of St Paul (ibid., pp. 396–397, figs 1–3); design for a portal of a chapel (F. Baudouin in Baudouin – Allard, eds, *Cat. Van Herck (Drawings)*, 2000, p. 330, no. CVH 221).
47. See below, pp. 285–287.
48. Judson – Van de Velde, *Title-pages (CRLB)*, 1978, I, no. 33; II, fig. 114. Or see URL: https://www.rijksmuseum.nl/nl/zoeken/objecten?q = RP-P-OB-26.640&p = 1&ps = 12&st = Objects&ii = 0#/RP-P-OB-26.640,0.
49. See Chapter V, p. 148.

CHAPTER IX - THE PORTICO

form was chosen for the central arches of *The Stage of Mercury*, *The Arch of the Mint* and *The Arch at St Michael's* as well as for the smaller arches and niches of *The Arch of Philip* and *The Stage of Isabella* (Text ill. 136).[50]

This distinctive shape of arch, invented by Michelangelo, was soon used by others. At about the time when Rubens was constructing his portico, Wenzel Cobergher adopted the motif for a window above the portal of the St Augustine's Church in Antwerp (Text ill. 115).[51]

In the following decades it became a distinctive element of Baroque architecture and sculpture in the Southern Netherlands. Many different examples can be found in a variety of architectural constructions: secular and religious buildings, funerary sculpture, civic displays, as well as in architectural motifs in the backgrounds of paintings. Two examples from church architecture will suffice: the bell tower and window mouldings of the Antwerp Jesuit Church, and the rood loft that stood in the (demolished) church of St Michael's Abbey, also in Antwerp.[52] One interesting example of a funerary monument is the drawing for a *Design for the Sepulchral Monument of a Young Nobleman* in the Fondation Custodia in Paris. The niche that contains the kneeling figure representing the deceased has a geniculated arch, and this motif was one of the formal Rubensian elements that led to the (misguided) attribution of this drawing to Rubens.[53]

Text ill. 116. Jacques Jordaens, *Design for a Wall Decoration*, drawing. Washington, National Gallery of Art.

Various painters followed Rubens in using this motif, especially Jordaens. In about 1640 he designed one of the façades of his house to include four windows with a geniculated arch, and this motif also occurs in a number of his drawings. He was undoubtedly directly inspired by Rubens's portico in his design for a *trompe-l'oeil* wall decoration, showing a portico with a loggia above. The design includes a geniculated arch, which is coupled by bands

---

50. For the central arches, see Martin, *Pompa (CRLB)*, 1972, nos 46, 50–52 and 54; for side arches, see ibid., no. 34; and for niches, see ibid., no. 13.
51. For this church, which is also discussed in connection with Rubens's garden pavilion (see Chapter IX, p. 297, n. 7), see Meganck, *Cobergher*, 1998, pp. 95–113, fig. 46.
52. For its usage in the Antwerp Jesuit Church, see Fabri – Lombaerde, *Jesuit Church (CRLB)*, 2018, pp. 207, 210, n. 27, text ill. 15. For interior views of the lost abbey church, see for example, Herremans, *Rubens Unveiled*, 2013, pp. 68, 70.
53. Herremans, *Architectural Sculpture (CRLB)*, 2019, p. 44, text ill. 13, as 'Anonymous seventeenth-century artist'.

to a Doric column, coiled dolphins in the spandrels, and two ram's heads in profile (Text ill. 116).[54]

However, it would be a mistake to see the geniculated arch as a phenomenon uniquely found in Antwerp or the Southern Netherlands. According to Konrad Ottenheym, this motif, which he calls 'one of the most remarkable new forms', appears at about the same time (c. 1615) in both the Northern and Southern Netherlands, probably independently, and thus in both regions inspired directly by Michelangelo's Porta Pia.[55]

Moreover, this form of arch is also encountered in France, although we should not necessarily assume that there was an influence in one direction or the other. One example to consider is the portal of the former Jesuit college in La Flèche (Fr.) (Text ill. 117).[56] It is worth pointing out that the connections between Rubens's portico and French architecture with its strong Italian influences, have understandably been little investigated. When he built his house, it is not obvious to what extent Rubens was already aware of French architecture, whether from books, drawings, or from observations he made while there. It is possible, but cannot be stated with certainty, that he had already visited France.[57]

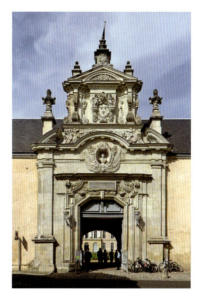

Text ill. 117. Portal of the former Jesuit college, La Flèche (Fr.).

54. *Design for a Wall Decoration*, Washington, National Gallery of Art, inv. no. 1975.131.a; d'Hulst, *Supplement I*, 1980, p. 365, no. A 175a, pl. 22; Tijs, *Rubens en Jordaens*, 1984, ill. p. 306. For a detailed discussion of Jordaens's house, see ibid., pp. 263 ff.
55. See the architectural treatise *Architectura Moderna*, published in 1631, with portal designs of c. 1615 by Hendrick de Keyser (Ottenheym, *Architectural Ornament*, 2007, pp. 125–127; see also Neurdenburg, *Hendrick de Keyser*, 1930, pp. 45 ff., figs 3–4, 7).
56. See also the portal of the former Carmelite Convent in Carpentras (Hautecoeur, *Architecture classique*, 1967, ills 325–326). These remarks about French examples were prompted by reading an unpublished typescript article by Robert F. Echols (*Rubens and Architecture*, 1986), in the files of the Rubenianum. Echols writes: 'The flat arch of demi-hexagonal shape was popular in France around the turn of the century', and refers to Hautecoeur, *Architecture classique*, 1967, figs 314, 325–326, 378, pp. 735–739, noting that: 'he [Hautecoeur] cites other examples in Paris, Rouen, Caen, Bourges, Vienne and several other locations'. The arch with concave corners also occurs in France; see n. 43).
57. Possibly Rubens travelled to Italy via France (visiting Paris and Fontainebleau?) and also came back again through France (as assumed by Jaffé, *Rubens and Italy*, 1977, p. 19; Merle du Bourg, *Rubens*, 2004, pp. 15, 16). Albert Rubens's library contained a copy of *L'Architecture* by Philibert de L'Orme (1514–1570), which he probably obtained from his father's books; it has been identified as the 1626 edition (Arents, *Bibliotheek*, 2001, p. 297, no. R8), but it may equally have been an older, 16th-century text. On connections with French architecture, see also the (mistaken) opinion of Oda Van de Castyne that it was not Rubens but a French architect who was responsible for designing the portico (see p. 249, n. 2). For similar rustication on the façades of the Palais du Luxembourg in Paris, see below, pp. 288–289.

CHAPTER IX - THE PORTICO

B. Depictions of the Portico and Related Architecture (1611–1621): Pointers Towards Dating

1611–1621

There is an architectural element related to the portico which can be found in Rubens's work a few years before its construction. A pediment supported by a banded column appears to the left in an anonymous drawing in Budapest depicting *The Assumption of the Virgin* (Text ill. 118), which is a copy after a – presumably lost – oil sketch by Rubens that can be dated to 1611.[58] The motif seems to foreshadow the central bay of the portico, but this certainly does not mean that Rubens was already engaged in the construction (or even design) of his house at this early date, a few months after taking possession.

Text ill. 118. Attributed to Willem Paneels after Rubens, *The Assumption of the Virgin*, drawing. Budapest, Szépművészeti Múzeum, Print Room.

There is a painting in which elements appear which have an undeniable similarity to the architecture of the house, and which has been dated on stylistic grounds to around 1612–1615: Rubens's *Homage to Ceres* in The State Hermitage Museum in St Petersburg, representing the goddess as an antique stone statue standing in a niche (Appendix III.13; Fig. 23). The architecture of the niche corresponds very closely to the central bay of the portico. The pediment has similar mouldings and is supported by engaged Doric columns with two bossed bands. As in the portico, the niche in this structure has a geniculated arch and is decorated on either side with two superimposed imposts between the bands. It seems likely that this work was made at the same time as Rubens's first designs for the portico. Interestingly, the similarity with elements of the portico is not the only link

58. Budapest, Szépművészeti Múzeum, Print Room, inv. no. 1558, as attributed to Willem Panneels after Rubens; pen, brown ink, brown wash, heightened with white, on paper, 407 × 224 mm (Baudouin, *Intervention*, 2000, pp. 19–20, fig. 25, as 'circle of Rubens'; id., *Drawings in Budapest*, 2004, pp. 9–11, fig. 1). For the complicated genesis of the altarpiece *The Assumption of the Virgin* for the Antwerp Cathedral, see Freedberg, *Christ after the Passion (CRLB)*, 1984, pp. 172–178, and esp. p. 174, no. 43, pp. 190–194, and esp. p. 192, no. 46; the drawn copy in Budapest, not known to Freedberg, can be attributed to Willem Panneels. The original after which the drawing was copied was probably one of the two *modelli* that Rubens submitted on 22 April 1611 to the canons, the chapter and church wardens, or a painting related to those *modelli*.

with Rubens's house. In the section above the pediment, details appear which also feature on the façades of the studio: the oil lamps and the alternating square and bossed pointed quoins. Two of the architectural motifs in the *Homage to Ceres* – the pattern of the alternating quoins, and the superimposed impost (which in the portico are an integral part of the incorporated *serlianas*) – can, as far as we know, only be found in Rubens's house.[59] This close parallel indicates that the *Homage to Ceres* should perhaps be dated to 1615–1616 rather than 1612–1615.

Elements of the portico can furthermore be identified in paintings by Rubens and Van Dyck that are usually dated a few years later, by which time the portico was very probably already standing. The Kunsthistorisches Museum in Vienna has a large canvas of *St Ambrose and Theodosius*, which Rubens painted with Van Dyck in about 1617–1618 (Appendix III.14). The portal of Milan Cathedral, visible behind the saint, is a construction with banded columns that bears a close resemblance to the central bay of the portico, although the scale has been reduced; we can see a Doric column with rosettes as well as a geniculated arch, in the spandrel of which is a curling motif reminiscent of the dolphin. It was probably shortly after this that Van Dyck painted the smaller variant of the same composition which is now in the National Gallery in London (Appendix III.15). Here the architecture is larger in scale, and a rounded arch has been added, more or less resembling the left opening of Rubens's structure, but lacking the smaller column. It is striking to note, on the left-hand side of the central archway, the unusual motif of the two superimposed imposts, which in the actual portico appear between the sixth and the fifth 'bands', forming the ends of the two architraves (Text ills 109 and 112).

It should be noted that in the work of Rubens and Van Dyck elements of the portico can be identified in numerous scenes where the action takes place by a gateway. Examples include Van Dyck's *St Martin*, in the Church of St Martin, Zaventem;[60] a large *Fish Market* in the Kunsthistorisches Museum, Vienna (recently identified by Elisabeth McGrath as representing *The Emperor's Mullet*), executed by assistants to a design by Rubens (Appendix III.17) and Rubens's versions of the *The Flight of Lot and his Family from Sodom*, in particular the one in the Musée du Louvre, dated 1625 (Appendix III.21). Scenes from Rubens's *Medici* series which should be mentioned because of their connection with the architecture of the portico are discussed below.[61]

From c. 1617 Van Dyck worked closely with Rubens for several years in the studio on the Wapper and he probably drew details of the finished portico *in situ*. Evidence for this can possibly be found in a chalk drawing attributed to

---

59. On these motifs on the façades, see Chapter V (for the quoins: pp. 143, 152, Text ill. 66; for the oil lamps: p. 143, n. 14, Text Ill. 61).
60. For other examples, see under No. 24 (pp. 396–397).
61. See p. 289.

him in the collection of the Fondation Custodia, Paris (No. 24, Copy; Fig. 139). The sheet shows the junction of the heavy Doric column with bands with the lighter, free-standing column of the right-hand bay, with the unusual and complex construction of the double architrave, described above. It seems reasonable to ask if this work is, in fact, not a copy of a lost architectural drawing by Rubens, but the recto of the sheet in any case suggests that it was produced by the younger master. On the reverse of the architectural drawing is a study of a pair of male legs, which Van Dyck used for the figure of John the Baptist in his *St John the Evangelist and St John the Baptist*, previously in Berlin and dating from about 1620 (Appendix III.16). The painting shows the two saints standing in front of an archway that is identical in every way – most noticeably on the right-hand side – to the central arch of Rubens's portico. It is quite possible that Van Dyck made other studies of the portico in addition to the sheet in Paris. Interestingly, a painting by Van Dyck which depicts the portico is mentioned in 1689 in the collection of the engraver and print publisher Alexander Voet I (1608–1689): 'Het Portael aen de plets van het huijs van Rubbens van Van Dijck geschildert' (The portal in the courtyard of Rubens's house, painted by Van Dyck).[62]

All of the paintings by Van Dyck mentioned above can be dated to the period between 1617 and the moment when the young artist set off to Italy in the autumn of 1621. The accuracy with which essential parts of the distinctive construction are rendered makes it highly likely that it was already standing. In the absence of archival material, it is impossible to specify the date of the portico's construction within this period more precisely. At any rate a dating of after 1621, as suggested by some authors,[63] can be rejected.

As stated, we know for a fact that Van Dyck saw Rubens's portico before he went to Italy, which implies that it was complete in the autumn of 1621 at the latest, and conceivably a few years earlier, in about 1618. The substantial sums of money ('some thousands of florins') Rubens had spent on his house during 1618, as he claims in his letter of 12 May 1618 to Carleton (Appendix I.10), may well have been used in large part for the portico. The material and labour

62. Inventory of the paintings Voet had bought after the death of his wife, drawn up on 18 February 1689 (Duverger, *Kunstinventarissen*, 1984–2009, XI, p. 531); the work appears a second time, as 'Het Portael van t' Huijs van Rubbens van Van Dijck geschildert', in the 'clijn sallet' (small reception room) on the garden side, in the inventory of his estate drawn up in November of the same year (ibid., XI, p. 573).
63. Oda Van de Castyne, who was convinced of a direct influence of Salomon de Brosse, dated the portico and the garden pavilion after Rubens's stay in Paris in February 1622 (Van de Castyne, *Rubens*, 1931, p. 117). Victor Blommaert wrote an article in which he inconsistently (and offering no evidence) described the portico as 'completed after 1623' as well as 'dating from 1623' (Blommaert, *Barokarchitectuur*, 1982, pp. 156–157); earlier, he dated it '1618–1622' (id., *Woonhuis*, 1980, p. 16). The question is discussed at length by Rutger Tijs, who does not rule out a later date (1620s or even 1630s), partly because of the lines from Juvenal, which he finds more in keeping with the mentality of an older Rubens (Tijs, *Rubens en Jordaens*, 1984, pp. 120, 122, 125). However, he argues that we should for now adhere to the assumption that the portico 'was probably built not long after the first alterations to the [16th-century] house were carried out' (ibid., p. 132).

costs for the monumental building must have been considerable, and the same certainly also applies to the creation of the sculptural decorations.

After 1621

Finally, there are a number of painted images of the portico that, although they provide no further information about its dating, are nonetheless extremely interesting because they were produced by artists from Rubens's immediate circle – colleagues who undoubtedly visited the house and therefore knew the portico from first-hand experience.

A painting that offers a contemporary and detailed impression of the portico – but, curiously, seen in mirror image – is Van Dyck's *Portrait of Isabella Brant*, in the National Gallery of Art in Washington, DC (Appendix III.5; Fig. 19). Although many authors describe it as painted *in* 1621 or *no later than* 1621, it needs to be said that there is no basis for this dating and that the portrait was very likely made posthumously, and therefore after 1626.[64] This means that despite assumptions often made in the literature, the Isabella Brant portrait cannot be used as a *terminus ante quem* for the portico (but of course we do not need it as there are sufficient other paintings that can be dated to 1621 or earlier).

Jacques Jordaens is another painter who made striking use of the portico: in his mythological painting *Cupid and Psyche* in the Prado in Madrid, which can be dated 1640–45 (Appendix III.9; Figs 20 and 159). Cupid's palace is suggested by a *capriccio* composed of several architectural structures that were part of Rubens's property. A variant of the garden pavilion can be seen, either side of which appears a version of the portico, one of them occupying an important place in the image and the other almost unrecognisable, and in extremely foreshortened perspective along the right-hand edge of the painting.

Painted in a similar vein and from about the same time, is a work attributed to Jan van Balen (1611–1654), *Bathing Women*, which shows the portico in the background (Appendix III.35). The visible part of the portico, mainly the central section, is faithfully represented with the exception of the satyrs, which have been transformed into semi-naked young women. The balustrade on the top is simplified and less high, and the apex of the pediment is crowned with a gilded sphere as in the painting by Jordaens.

A more drastic remodelling of Rubens's portico appears in another bathing scene: it has been absorbed into the façade of King David's palace in the background of an anonymous *Bathsheba Bathing*, in a Spanish private collection (Appendix III.38).

---

64. For arguments in favour of a later dating (after Van Dyck's return to Antwerp from Italy), see N. De Poorter in Barnes et al. *Van Dyck*, 2004, pp. 93–94, no. I.100.

CHAPTER IX - THE PORTICO

Text ill. 119. Anonymous, *Portrait of a Young Man*, 1636. London, The National Gallery.

An intriguing variant of an element of the portico appears in a portrait that was made in Rubens's lifetime. The background of a *Portrait of a Young Man*, dated 1636,[65] has an architectural feature that resembles one of the smaller archways (Text ill. 119). The banding is more or less accurately represented, but here too the figure in the spandrel of the arch has been altered; it has the same pose, but rather than a bearded satyr, it seems to show a (female?) winged monster with scaly or feathered hooves, possibly intended as a harpy.

There is a somewhat anaemic and strongly simplified variant of the portico in the anonymous life-size, full-length portrait of a couple in the Gemäldegalerie in Berlin (Appendix III.10; Fig. 22). The fashionable costumes suggest a dating of about 1655, but as yet no attempt to identify the sitters has been successful, and equally the identity of the artist who made this painting of evidently high quality has not been established. It would seem far-fetched to make a direct connection with Rubens's house, were it not for the accurate view of the garden pavilion visible through the central arch. Some elements of the gateway to the garden in the Berlin portrait are reminiscent of Rubens's portico: the heavy banding, the geniculated arch, the gilded sphere above the central pediment, and the balustrade. Moreover, as in the 1684 Harrewijn print, a statue can be seen on top of the balustrade. Partly obscured by the foliage of a tree, there is a free-standing whitish stone statue of a nude young man, who can be identified by his winged feet as Mercury (Fig. 230).

It should be noted that the strongly simplified image of the 'Berlin' portico is related to the pen drawings of about twenty variants (some also with a segmental pediment) on three sheets of the problematical 'Rubens' architectural sketchbook in The State Hermitage Museum, St Petersburg (Text ills 120 and 121). The drawings are from the hand of a later follower, whose identity has so far remained obscure, and they are certainly not copies after lost studies by Rubens, as some have believed.[66]

65. Anonymous, *Portrait of a Young Man*, dated 1636, London, The National Gallery, inv. no. NG 5631; canvas, 136 × 102 cm; Martin, *Cat. London, NG (Flemish School)*, 1970, p. 77, no. 5631.
66. St Petersburg, The State Hermitage Museum, Library, inv. no. 14741. This album contains a large number of

CHAPTER IX - THE PORTICO

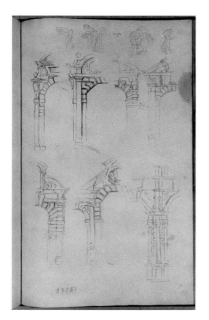 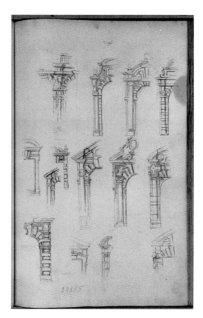

Text ill. 120. Anonymous after ? Rubens, Sheet from the *'Architectural Sketchbook'*, drawing. St Petersburg, The State Hermitage Museum.

Text ill. 121. Anonymous after ? Rubens, Sheet from the *'Architectural Sketchbook'*, drawing. St Petersburg, The State Hermitage Museum.

Two more seventeenth-century depictions of the portico appear in paintings that have already been mentioned: one is the anonymous and difficult to date Aylesbury *View of the Courtyard of Rubens's House* (Appendix III.3; Fig. 16) and the other Coques's small *Portrait of Maria Agnes van Eycke as St Agnes* of about 1675 (Appendix III.11; Text ill. 20). Finally, there is of course Harrewijn's print of 1684 (Appendix III.1), which gives a detailed view of the portico in Hillewerve's time.

After this print, we have to wait for nearly a century and half before we encounter another view of the portico, which had in the meantime been changed radically with an upward extension and a structure added to its rear.[67] The earliest nineteenth-century pictorial records of the portico are the line engraving of 1840, made by Erin Corr (1803–1862) (Appendix III.45) and a sheet from about the same date with a group of drawn studies of details

 pen sketches of window and door frames, altar mouldings, cartouches, pulpits, church fronts and church towers (including spires and domes). Apart from the portico variants (fols 78r, 81r and 81v), no further links with the architecture of Rubens's house can be found; among the many drawings of church towers, however, there are a number of variants of the bell tower of the Antwerp Jesuit Church. The attribution of the drawings to Rubens was rejected by Piet Lombaerde (Lombaerde, *Rubens the Architect*, 2011, pp. 128, 130, n. 28; id., *Painter-Architect*, 2014, p. xviii, fig. 9 (of fol. 81r); esp. on the tower, see Fabri – Lombaerde, *Jesuit Church (CRLB)*, 2018, p. 94, nn. 209–210, and pp. 118, 123, n. 8).

67. On this extension, see above, pp. 251–252.

CHAPTER IX - THE PORTICO

Text ill. 122. Detail of the 1684 Harrewijn print (Fig. 17): a sphere and a two-headed eagle in front of the balustrade.

of the portico by Nicaise de Keyser (1813–1887) (Appendix III.43).[68] The first photographic record, by Edmond Fierlants (1819–1869), was made in 1860 (Appendix III.52).[69]

C. Lost Elements of the Portico not Reconstructed: The Two-Headed Eagle, the Sphere and the Busts

A glance at seventeenth-century representations of the portico reveals a number of elements that are absent from the present structure, and which were evidently removed during the restoration, or if already lost, were not reconstructed.

The Two-Headed Eagle

In the Harrewijn print of 1684 a two-headed eagle with outstretched wings is shown in front of the central walled section of the balustrade, above the apex of the pediment; over the eagle is a sphere which projects above the balustrade (Text ill. 122). The heraldic eagle, which incidentally does not feature in any other image of the portico, is probably a later addition, for which there is no obvious explanation.[70]

---

68. There is an earlier 19th-century painting (Philippe Van Brée, *The Farewell of Van Dyck in the Courtyard of Rubens's House*, 1814; Appendix III.40), but as far as the portico is concerned, this has no documentary value: the image (with the two statues on top and the fountain with the bagpiper to the right) is entirely based on the Harrewijn print of 1684.
69. For the Brussels photographer Edmond Fierlants, see above, Chapter II, p. 82, n. 97.
70. Jeffrey Muller gives a tentative (but not very convincing) explanation: he assumes that the 'Hapsburg double-headed eagle', if it really did stem from Rubens's time, may have been present to indicate Rubens's loyalty to the house of Habsburg (Muller, *Collector*, 1989, p. 63).

The Gilded Sphere

The sphere which projects above the balustrade in the 1684 Harrewijn print was undoubtedly present in Rubens's time, but lower down, on top of the pediment. A prominently placed, central 'golden' sphere appears in all representations of the portico (and variations on it) in which the top of the balustrade can be seen: the Aylesbury *View of the Courtyard of Rubens's House*, Jordaens's *Cupid and Psyche*, the anonymous *Bathing Women*, and the anonymous double portrait in the Gemäldegalerie in Berlin (Figs 16, 20, 22 and Appendix III.35).[71]

In every one of these images it can be observed that the sphere does not rest on a cube but is set on a conical pedestal. It is therefore unlikely, as some authors have maintained, that the emblem of the sphere-on-a-cube is the idea underlying the choice of motif for Rubens's portico.[72] Furthermore, a gilded sphere on a finial recurs a number of times in seventeenth-century images of the house, as a feature crowning other parts of Rubens's buildings: on the roof of the garden pavilion (in *The Walk in the Garden*; Fig. 182); above the dormer windows (in the Harrewijn prints), and on the ridge of the roof, crowned with a weathervane in the form of a sun (in the Harrewijn print of 1692), and shimmering through the transparent fabric of the sitter's *huyck* in the *Portrait of Hélène Fourment au carrosse* (Appendix III.7; Fig. 31).[73] When discussing the possible emblematic meaning, we should not lose sight of the fact that in Italian Renaissance architecture a crowning sphere (as also a spherical brazier) is without doubt often used as a purely decorative element above doorways, balustrades and the like.[74]

---

71. A comparable arrangement with a 'golden' sphere on top of a pediment (crowning a niche) can also be found in Van Haecht's *Apelles Painting Campaspe* (Appendix III.8; Text ill. 100).
72. Teresa Esposito believes that a number of elements of the portico contain a hidden esoteric meaning. According to her, the sphere-on-a-cube refers to the 'fickleness of fortune' versus 'constancy, wisdom and virtue […]' as well as to the contrast between feminine and masculine (summarising an interview in *De Standaard*, see Van Maris, *Rubens*, 2018, p. D11). For an interpretation of the emblem of the sphere-on-a-cube as antithesis between fortune and virtue, see Uppenkamp – Van Beneden, *Architectural Symbolism*, 2011, pp. 103–104.
73. For the motifs of spheres and braziers on the roofs, see Chapter V, pp. 138–139. For braziers decorating the studio façades, see ibid., pp. 143 (n. 14), 182.
74. For a number of examples with spheres, see Coffin, *Villa*, 1988, figs 22 (design for a gateway), 102 (courtyard of the Villa Giulia), 200 (balcony over the loggia of the Villa d'Este); spheres as acroteria can also be found in the engraved portal designs of Serlio (Serlio, *Extraordinario libro*, 1551, pl. XVI), and of Francart (De Vos, *Francart*, 1998, figs 38 and 43); of the fifty portal designs by Bernardino Radi, twelve are crowned with spheres, always resting on a pointed pedestal (Radi, *Disegni de Architettura*, 1619, passim). Spheres placed on city gates (see for instance Michelangelo's Porta Pia; Text ill. 126) probably allude to cannonballs and thus the defensive function of these structures (Uppenkamp – Van Beneden, *Architectural Symbolism*, 2011, p. 102).

CHAPTER IX - THE PORTICO

Text ill. 123. Detail of Text ill. 20: the bust of a bearded man in the central niche of the portico.

The Busts in the Niches of the Portico

One difficult problem to solve is whether there were originally busts occupying the three niches of the portico, the round one in the middle, and the larger rectangular ones on either side – and if so, how to identify which figures might have been represented.

In the three earliest painted representations – Van Dyck's *Portrait of Isabella Brant*, Jordaens's *Cupid and Psyche* and the anonymous *Bathing Women* (Appendix III.5, 9 and 35; Figs 19–20) – the three niches are empty. Coques's small *Portrait of Maria Agnes van Eycke as St Agnes* (Text ill. 123) features in the central niche a bust of a bearded man, who somewhat resembles Marcus Aurelius. For comparison see the emperor's bust with a cloak draped over his shoulders in Rubens's *Portrait of Caspar Gevartius*.[75]

It is difficult to know, however, how much faith can be placed in these images as far as the busts are concerned. In these paintings, the portico has a specific function which does not imply a faithful documentary representation. In the *Cupid and Psyche* and the *Bathing Women*, the portico is part of a fictive palace. In the *Portrait of Maria Agnes van Eycke as St Agnes*, the striking detail of the vegetation growing in two or three places on the left-hand side of the portico is possibly also a fiction. It seems possible that Coques used this detail (as well as the bust?) to characterise the portico as an ancient building, hinting at Rome, in order to provide a fitting backdrop for the Roman martyr saint Agnes.

In the Aylesbury *View of the Courtyard of Rubens's House*, busts are vaguely indicated in the rectangular niches (Figs 16 and 141). More information can

75. Vlieghe, *Portraits (CRLB)*, 1987, no. 106, fig. 122. A head and a bust of a comparable type are both preserved in the Rubenshuis collection (inv. no. RH.B.006, as Hadrian or Aelius Caesar; inv. no. RH.B.027, as Marcus Aurelius), but these were not originally part of the house. In the Harrewijn prints, vague outlines of busts of bearded men with curly hair can be seen both on the studio façade and in the side niches of the portico.

CHAPTER IX - THE PORTICO

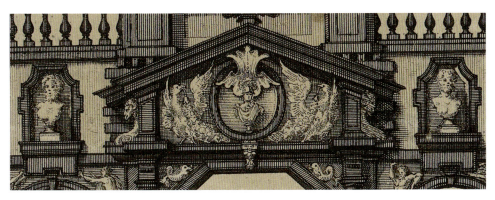

Text ill. 124. Detail of the 1684 Harrewijn print (Fig. 17): the busts in the rectangular niches of the portico.

be gathered from the 1684 Harrewijn print: ensconced in these niches, and almost as high as the niches themselves, we can see two huge, almost identical busts of unidentified men with curly hair and beards (Text ill. 124).

At an unknown moment (before 1840) these bearded men were replaced by two quite different busts, a faun and a bacchante, evidence for which can be found in pictorial documentation from

Text ill. 125. Detail of Text ill. 23: the bust of Minerva.

around 1840 (Appendix III.43, 45),[76] as well as in all photographs of the portico made before the restoration (Text ill. 104 and Fig. 143). In 1938 these busts were still in place. The faun in the left-hand niche, a plaster now in the Rubenshuis collection (No. 1, Copy; Fig. 35) was probably cast, as explained above, from a (lost) sculpted stone original that stood (in Hillewerve's time) in a niche on the north façade of the studio wing. On the portico, the faun was balanced (in the niche to the right) by a woman whose head was garlanded with vines, suggesting a bacchante. This work, which seems utterly un-Rubensian, judging from the photographs, was removed and can no longer be located.

76. The two busts are already visible at an earlier date – in the round niches of the garden pavilion, in Philippe Van Brée's *Rubens Painting in his Garden* of 1833 (Appendix III.42) But their placing here is undoubtedly a free invention of the painter, who 'transferred' to the pavilion what he saw in the portico.

CHAPTER IX - THE PORTICO

In the 1684 Harrewijn print and in the Aylesbury *View of the Courtyard of Rubens's House* the central round niche is occupied by a bust of Minerva, rather than the bearded man seen in the small portrait by Coques (cf. Text ills 124 and 123). This bust of the goddess was certainly there in Hillewerve's time, which is odd since there was also a second Minerva present as a full-length statue on top of the portico. The bust appears in all nineteenth-century pictorial documentation (Text ill. 125), and indeed it was still in place at the time of the restoration in 1938.

It was then removed and its current whereabouts are unknown. Judging from the photographs, it is difficult to tell if the sculpture might stem from Rubens's time. Jeffrey Muller includes the bust in his catalogue of sculpture in Rubens's collection and considers it possible that it was part of the original portico decoration, 'planned by Rubens'.[77] However, it remains unclear if the lost Minerva with the unusual fan-like feathered crest, should be considered an invention of Rubens.[78] There is no evidence to support this assumption, and we have therefore not included it in the Catalogue.

In other words, it is possible that Rubens placed busts in the niches of the portico, but as the pictorial documentation provides only conflicting information no firm conclusions can be drawn. The most categorical position taken on this matter is that of Ulrich Heinen, who was convinced that there were neither busts in the niches originally, nor statues on the top of the portico.[79] The issue was unresolved at the time of the restoration, and it was decided to leave the niches empty.

D. The Two Statues on Top of the Portico: Lost and Reconstructed

Finally, we should return to the two over-life-size statues which, according to the Harrewijn print, stood above the balustrade in Hillewerve's time (Fig. 227). No further information about them is available. They are not mentioned in any of the written sources, nor do we know of any other images in which they appear. Indeed, as we shall see below, it is thought that they may never actually have existed, although in our opinion that is being unnecessarily doubtful. Whatever the case, it is not known in what material they were executed,[80] and

---

77. Muller, *Collector*, 1989, pp. 29, 154, cat. III, no. 19. Followed, and so also regarded as original, by Uppenkamp – Van Beneden, *Architectural Symbolism*, 2011, p. 100.
78. We have found this type of helmet in just one other Minerva: the monumental marble fountain with a full-length statue of the goddess commissioned by the City of Amsterdam in 1660 from Artus Quellinus I (1609–1668) as a gift to Johan Maurits of Nassau-Siegen (now in Cleves, Museum Kurhaus Kleve; see Van Rooijen-Buchwaldt – de Jong, *Pallas*, 1994).
79. Heinen, *Garten*, 2002, p. 2; id., *Gesundheit*, 2004, pp. 112–115.
80. For a suggestion, see below, p. 283, n. 95.

we can only assume that they probably disappeared when the portico was raised and substantially altered in the eighteenth century.

The statues are problematic in many ways. To begin with, there is the question of attribution. Although in the print the etched statues appear no larger than 21 mm tall, the image is sufficiently detailed to rule out Rubens as designer, on stylistic grounds. There are enough Minervas of Rubens's invention known that we can state confidently that the goddess to the right above the portico has no connection with Rubens's art. We have therefore included the statues in the catalogue section dealing with rejected attributions (Nos R1 and R2). The authorship of the lost statues, and the date of their production, cannot for now be determined.

This conclusion gives rise to the question, even if these statues were not designed by Rubens, did they actually stand on the portico in his time, and if not, were other statues originally in position that were later replaced, certainly by 1684? In other words, there is good reason to doubt that in Rubens's time the portico was crowned by full-length statues, whether these or others.

Nevertheless the majority of authors take it for granted that the 1684 Harrewijn print shows Rubens's original concept for the two statues. It is often implicitly assumed, but sometimes also explicitly stated, not only that they are original but that they were designed by Rubens.[81]

Yet there has also been doubt that the original concept included statues on top of the balustrade. The most extreme position was that adopted by Émile Van Averbeke, architect for the modern restoration. In general he had little faith in the reliability of the Harrewijn prints and maintained that the top of the portico was too narrow to support the statues and vases shown in the print, and that consequently they could never have stood there, even in Hillewerve's time.[82] It is true that, as Van Averbeke observed, the shallow depth of the portico argues against the structure's fitness to provide a steady base for the weight of the statues, yet to our mind there seems insufficient ground to assume that the statues never existed and were merely an addition in the Harrewijn print.

In several publications, Ulrich Heinen has consistently rejected the presence of the two statues in Rubens's time. His rejection was based on his view of the portico's iconography, which he argues should be seen as the entrance to the 'Lipsian' garden,[83] a concept to which the two gods are alien. He found further confirmation of his view in the absence of statues in the seventeenth-century

---

81. See, for example, Jeffrey Muller, who not only includes the statues in his catalogue of sculpture in Rubens's collection (Muller, *Collector*, 1989, p. 154, cat. III, nos 17–18), but also regards them as 'carved after Rubens's design' (ibid., p. 26). For further literature and opinions, see Literature under Nos R1 and R2.
82. Van Averbeke, *Rubenshuis, restauratie II*, 1938, p. 16 (to this he added, somewhat ambivalently, that the statues and vases seemed 'almost essential' as a decorative element); on the portico's supposed lack of strength, see also Van Driessche, *Herschepping*, 2019, p. 36.
83. See above, p. 264, n. 42.

CHAPTER IX · THE PORTICO

paintings mentioned above.[84] Indeed, there is not even a hint of a statue above the balustrade in any of the painted versions of the portico, but this cannot in our opinion be regarded as decisive. After all, it is doubtful that these works – unlike the 1684 Harrewijn print – were intended to provide a realistic representation of the portico.

The Aylesbury painting (Appendix III.3; Fig. 141) shows a strange layout which may never have existed: each of the four pedestals supports an ornamental vase of giant proportions. In Jordaens's *Cupid and Psyche* (Fig. 20) no busts or statues are visible at all, neither those of the portico nor of the garden pavilion, but we should be careful not to draw any conclusions from this about the situation in Rubens's time. Jordaens places the elements of Rubens's house in a specific mythological setting, the palace of Cupid, an environment in which statues of gods might have seemed out of place. The same applies to the *Bathing Women* attributed to Jan van Balen (Appendix III.35).

There are also no statues to be seen above the portico in Van Dyck's *Portrait of Isabella Brant* (Appendix III.5; Fig. 19), although it should be observed that the top of the balustrade is for the most part cut off by the edge of the composition, so that in any case we would not be able to see more than the feet and lower legs of just one of the figures. As it happens, an indication that statues may have adorned the top of the portico in Rubens's time can be seen in the background of this portrait: in the distance, on the left-hand side, is a structure very similar to the portico balustrade and which is interrupted by a pedestal, on top of which rests a statue (Figs 19 and 232). The small, sketchy figure, draped in a classical robe and with a long spear in his or her right hand, cannot easily be identified. It is often thought to be a statue of Minerva, which the artist transposed from the portico to the side of his composition, aligning it with the head of the sitter, thus using the figure of the goddess of wisdom to allude to one of Isabella Brant's virtues.[85] That said, the statue above the imagined balustrade bears little resemblance to the helmeted Minerva with cuirass shown in the 1684 Harrewijn print. Closer inspection reveals that the identification with Minerva is in fact incorrect. Besides the spear, none of the usual attributes associated with the goddess are present, while the loose-fitting robe, which leaves part of the figure's torso exposed, is also inconsistent with Minervan iconography. It seems more likely that the statue represents a young man (with a laurel wreath?), possibly Honos.[86] Whatever the truth, from such a vaguely

84. Heinen, *Gesundheit*, 2004, pp. 113–115, p. 172, n. 179; id., *Text- und Bild-Formen*, 2008, p. 211; id., *Auctores*, 2009, p. 59. I am grateful to Ulrich Heinen for drawing my attention to the two last references and for sending an unpublished passage about this matter.
85. S. Barnes, in Wheelock et al., *Van Dyck*, 1990, p. 141, under no. 23; C. Brown, in Brown et al., *Van Dyck*, 1999, p. 154, no. 27; K. Belkin, in Belkin – Healy, *House of Art*, 2004, p. 238, under no. 56; B. Watteeuw, in Van Beneden, ed., *Rubens in Private*, 2015, p. 74, under no. 18.
86. For Honos (with spear, laurel wreath and cornucopia), see under No. 36.

CHAPTER IX - THE PORTICO

indicated figure, which may be fictive, we can draw no final conclusions about the possible presence of statues on top of the portico prior to 1640.

Another work that is intriguing in this connection is the double portrait in Berlin of c. 1655 in which a simplified variant of Rubens's portico appears in the background. Standing above this structure, to the right of the central gateway, is a statue placed on a pedestal connected to the balustrade (Fig. 230): a nude youth, half hidden by the foliage of a tree. His head cannot be seen, nor his hands, or any attributes they might hold, but from his winged feet it is clear that he is Mercury.

Although they were not designed by Rubens, and probably were never in his possession, we must nonetheless take a closer look at the two statues present in Hillewerve's time since many authors have seen in them a special symbolic meaning. As stated, a Minerva stands to the right (No. R2; Figs 227 and 231) with her usual attributes: wearing a helmet and cuirass, she clutches a very long spear in one hand and the shield with Medusa's head in the other. A matter that has not so far been touched on here is the much less straightforward identity of the figure to the left in the Harrewijn print (No. R1; Fig. 228). Most authors assume that it is a Mercury, but on closer inspection this is not so obvious. The figure does not have any of the god's attributes. We should not be misled by the two feathered wings that stick out above his head. In the print these are not part of Mercury's *petasus*, the winged sunhat, as might at first sight appear. There is no sign of a hat, but what we have is a figure with a winged head, garlanded, probably with flowers. We can find no trace of winged feet or sandals. The figure is not holding a caduceus but, strangely, a mahlstick, palette and several brushes, which – equally intriguingly – he holds in the wrong hand: right in place of left as one might expect.

Is Minerva's counterpart here a Mercury figure, presented holding a painter's equipment? There is indeed a well-known example of Mercury holding palette and brushes, by Hendrik Goltzius,[87] yet it seems that we can rule out the possibility that Hillewerve's statue was Mercury. The clothing especially, a long robe that sweeps down to the ground, is very out of place for the nimble 'flying' god. In images from Antiquity, the Renaissance as well as Netherlandish sixteenth and seventeenth-century art, including Rubens, he is depicted nude with the exception of a hat, a short loose mantle (a *chlamys*), and (usually, but not always) sandals.[88]

---

87. *Mercury as Painter*, painting dated 1611, pendant to a *Minerva*, Haarlem, Frans Hals Museum; the naked god holds palette and brushes in the correct (left) hand and caduceus/mahlstick in the right (Mai – Wettengl, eds, *Wettstreit*, 2002, pp. 198–199, no. 8; Leeflang – Luijten, eds, *Goltzius*, 2003, pp. 290–293, nos 106.1–106.3; Nichols, *Goltzius*, 2013, pp. 149–153, nos A-39, A-40).
88. Occasionally, it is true, Mercury appears more 'dressed up'; he is also traditionally shown as a Roman soldier with cuirass; one image shows him wearing a curious, loose costume, reaching to just above his knees (in the print of *Hermathene* by Aegidius Sadeler after Hans von Aachen; McGrath, *Musathena*, 1987, p. 242, fig. 69-b). He is certainly never shown tightly 'wrapped up', as in the statue on top of the portico.

CHAPTER IX - THE PORTICO

Judging from the attributes and drapery, the only conclusion that can be drawn from the Harrewijn print is that it is not a representation of Mercury, but rather a personification which, given the painter's equipment, could represent Pictura or an idea closely connected with painting or artistic activity. Frans Jos van den Branden had long ago inferred from the attributes that Hillewerve's statue could simply be Pictura, a view that was also shared by Ary Delen.[89] In his publications on Rubens's house, on the other hand, Rooses described the statue as a figure of Mercury.[90]

When the portico came to be restored in the 1930s, it was decided to reinstate the statues above the balustrade. As is clear from reports drawn up at the time, this prompted heated discussions among the members of the research committee about the possible identity of the left-hand figure.[91] They eventually followed the interpretation proposed by Rooses, and two statues, of Minerva and Mercury were cast in bronze. In July 1939, the two statues were commissioned from Edward Deckers (1873–1956), and in March 1942 these new over-life-size statues, based on Deckers's own invention, and differing substantially from those represented in the print, were installed on top of the portico (Fig. 138).[92]

The opinion reached by Rooses and authors that followed him is understandable. While the left-hand figure in Harrewijn's print cannot be Mercury because his attributes are missing and his attire is 'incompatible', there are other aspects of the statue that conflict with an identification as Pictura. For one thing, there is no certainty that the figure is actually female. The head with (short?) curly hair could just as well belong to a youth. Certainly, the 'macho', nonchalant hand-on-hip pose has a manly feel.[93] This pose does in general speak in favour of the youthful god Mercury, who was very often depicted thus by artists, including Rubens (Text ills 153 and 154).[94] Taking these

89. Van den Branden, *Schilderschool*, 1883, p. 507; Delen, *Rubens' huis*, 1933, p. 29; id., *Rubens' huis*, 1940, pp. 32–34.
90. Rooses, *Oeuvre*, 1886–92, p. 186; id., *Huis van Rubens*, 1910, p. 197 [p. 9].
91. Devroe, *Rubens' huis*, 2008, I, p. 123. See also Ary Delen's letter mentioned in the following note.
92. This issue of the statues and several other disputes arising during the restoration troubled Ary Delen so much that he reported his objections to the irresponsible actions in a long letter to Mayor Camille Huysmans (undated copy in the Rubenshuis archive, pp. 3–4). He considered it 'an outright scandal' that Deckers was commissioned to work up variants of statues he had produced thirty years earlier for the Rubenshuis reconstructions at the 1910 World Exhibition in Brussels, a task for which he received a very large sum of money (on the house in the exhibition, see Chapter II, pp. 84–85, n. 108). On the modern statues, see also Van Driessche, *Herschepping*, 2009, p. 22.
93. On the masculine nature of this pose, known as the 'Renaissance elbow', in portraiture between c. 1500 and c. 1650, see Spicer, *Elbow*, 1991, pp. 84–128.
94. Where Rubens is concerned, see for example: *Mercury* in the series for the Torre de la Parada (Alpers, *Torre (CRLB)*, 1971, no. 39, fig. 143); the ivory statuette, similar in composition (Text ill. 154) (Muller, *Collector*, 1989, pl. 117; see below, Chapter XI, p. 334, n. 48); Mercury in the *Stormy Landscape with Philemon and Baucis* painting in Vienna, Kunsthistorisches Museum (Adler, *Landscapes (CRLB)*, 1982, no. 29). Quellinus's high relief of *Mercury* in the Amsterdam Palace on the Dam – head in profile, left hand on hip, caduceus at an angle, legs crossed (Text ill. 153) – is distinctly similar in pose to the Harrewijn figure (Goossens, *Amsterdamse stadhuis*, 1996, fig. 49; Scholten, *Quellinus*, 2010, fig. 25).

282

different elements into consideration, it is tempting to think that Hillewerve's statue started off as Mercury and was subsequently transformed into a personification through the addition of certain items of clothing and attributes. This would also explain the mahlstick (instead of caduceus) in the figure's right hand. However, it is very difficult to see how such a metamorphosis, especially of the drapery, could have been realised in a three-dimensional sculpture. Or should we consider the possibility that Hillewerve's statues were in fact not three-dimensional?[95]

For the sake of completeness, one further argument in favour of an identification as Mercury needs mentioning here, which was unknown to the Mercury proponents at the time of the restoration and was not part of the discussions about the statues' identity. As described above, the god appears in his traditional nude state and with winged feet on top of the simplified version of the portico in the Berlin double portrait (Fig. 230).

But the principal argument brought by proponents of Mercury in support of their view is iconographic: the god most likely to be paired with Minerva is indeed Mercury. There was a long-standing tradition of depicting the two gods together, something that emerges from a range of sources. We know from a letter by Cicero, for example, that in his gymnasium (the area he used as a study) he placed a statue which combined the two gods as a Hermathena: Mercury (Hermes) as the patron of eloquence and Minerva (Athena) as goddess of wisdom. There are examples of Renaissance artists who took inspiration from this and depicted the two gods as conjoined figures.[96] We know from his *Theoretical Notebook* that Rubens was familiar with this passage from Cicero's letter, and he drew a design for a statue of Hermathena, with their two heads combined back to back.[97]

It is not surprising that artists chose these two gods for the decoration of their houses. They were regarded as joint guardians of the arts, with Minerva especially representative of 'wisdom' (the theory underlying art), and Mercury

---

95. This seems possible. Could they have been wooden cut-outs painted in oil, an arrangement that appeared on top of temporary street decorations, or over altarpieces? The fact that the clothing of both figures comes down to their feet – enhancing their stability – also points in this direction. This hypothesis would indeed weaken Van Averbeke's argument that the portico was too flimsy to support the weight of statues. On the subject of such cut-outs (known in archival records as *schroyeersels* [with variants]) made after Rubens's designs, see: an *Angel* in Flint, MI, Flint Institute of Arts (originally above the frame of the Antwerp *Elevation of the Cross*; Judson, *Passion (CRLB)*, 2000, pp. 120–121, no. 26; *Jupiter and Juno* in Antwerp, Private Collection (a part of the front face of *The Arch of Philip*; Martin, *Pompa (CRLB)*, 1972, p. 69, under no. 5, fig. 19).
96. For a full discussion of Hermathena and the two gods together, see McGrath, *Musathena*, 1987, pp. 239–245, figs pp. 68–69.
97. Ibid., p. 245; Muller, *Collector*, 1989, p. 38; Uppenkamp – Van Beneden, *Architectural Symbolism*, 2011, pp. 78–79.

CHAPTER IX - THE PORTICO

its practice.[98] Examples are the houses of Giulio Romano in Mantua, and Cornelis van Dalem in Antwerp.[99]

The doubtful interpretation of Hillewerve's statue as Mercury came about, as stated, because of the wings that stick out from the figure's head, suggestive of the god but not normally associated with the personification of Pictura. We have not been able to trace a single example of a 'winged' Pictura in Flemish painting.[100] Personifications of related concepts, however, in which inspiration plays a role, including *Furor Poetico* and *Imaginatione*, are described with a winged head and some are illustrated in Cesare Ripa's *Iconologia*; for a more detailed discussion, see No. R1.

These observations about winged personifications show that figures of this type were indeed known, but they do not help much in understanding the rather unusual statue above the portico. They tell us nothing concrete about the creation of the figures: who made them and when? If Rubens had nothing to do with the Minerva and her partner on top of the portico, it remains difficult to fathom which of the later inhabitants of the house (after 1640 and before 1684) might have come up with the idea of crowning the portico with these two over-life-size statues, including a Pictura or related idea. It is not likely that Rubens's heirs would have chosen to invest in further decoration of the property, and we can rule out the Cavendishes, who were only tenants of the property and were short of money. This leaves us with the Van Eycke couple or Canon Hillewerve himself, neither of whom is a more plausible candidate.

These considerations mean that there are insufficient grounds to assume that in Rubens's time Mercury and Minerva stood in prominent positions in the courtyard in order to accentuate the function of the house. As we have seen, there are reasons to believe that the portico should be considered in relation to the garden,[101] and it is not a foregone conclusion that it would also contain elements alluding to the profession of the illustrious owner. In other words it is far from certain that the statues would have formed an important part of 'a programme that refers to the artist as *pictor doctus* and *virtuoso*'.[102] Therefore, the commentaries of various authors, some of whom have gone into great detail about the significance of the pair of gods for Rubens's house, can probably

---

98. De Jongh, *Realisme en schijnrealisme*, 1971, pp. 161–165, n. 76 (with additional literature). For Minerva as guardian of the arts, especially of painting, see, for example, Mai – Wettengl, eds, *Wettstreit*, 2002, pp. 192–205. See also the two gods, connected directly with painting, in the pendants, *Mercury* and *Minerva*, by Goltzius (p. 281, n. 87).
99. The gods can be seen: either side of a doorway in Giulio Romano's house in Mantua (1539–1544) (Hartt, *Giulio Romano*, 1958, I, p. 240; II, figs 492–493); in Antwerp, seated in profile, on the façade of the lost house of Cornelis van Dalem (King, *Artists' Houses*, 2002, pp. 175, 178–179, fig. 2).
100. For representations of Pictura, see, for example, Mai – Wettengl, eds, *Wettstreit*, 2002, passim. With many thanks to Elizabeth McGrath, who looked (without success) for an example in the Warburg files.
101. See above, pp. 263–264.
102. As argued by Uppenkamp – Van Beneden, *Architectural Symbolism*, 2011, p. 76.

CHAPTER IX - THE PORTICO

be rejected as mere speculation.[103] Furthermore, several remarks made about the connection between the two gods and other elements of the house are questionable. There is indeed no ground for assuming a direct iconographic connection with the head of Medusa (see No. 25), or the ram's heads of the portico (No. 28),[104] the fictive painting of *Andromeda Liberated by Perseus* on the wall opposite (see No. 18), or with the statue of Hercules of the garden pavilion (see No. 39).

E. The Portico in the Context of Italian Examples and Architectural Theory

Michelangelo's *Porta Pia*

An important question pertaining to the portico is the extent to which Italian examples inspired its architectural form. As mentioned above, one particularly important element of the portico, the flat or geniculated arch, derives almost certainly from the Porta Pia (1561–1565) in Rome, a city gate designed by Michelangelo and commissioned by Pope Pius IV (Text ill. 126).[105]

Rubens certainly knew this gate. We can assume that he had

Text ill. 126. Michelangelo, *Porta Pia*, Rome.

seen it when in Rome, but images of the gate can, besides, be found in two publications which he probably owned, as can be inferred from their presence in the library of his son Albert. The entire front of the Porta Pia is reproduced in one of the engravings that Antonio Lafreri gathered in his *Speculum Romanae Magnificentiae* (c. 1568).[106] A detail of the central gateway is moreover included in

---

103. Discussion to be found, for example, in: Gordon, *Whitehall*, 1975, pp. 45–49; Muller, *Perseus and Andromeda*, 1981–82, pp. 141–143, figs 12–13; id., *Collector*, 1989, pp. 26–29, fig. 7, p. 154, cat. III, nos 17–18; Rosenthal, *Occasio*, 2000, pp. 202–203; Muller, *Rubens's Collection*, 2004, pp. 38–39, fig. 39; Rosenthal, *Rubens*, 2005, pp. 113–115; Uppenkamp – Van Beneden, *Symbolism*, 2011, pp. 76–81, fig. 94.
104. The *Palazzo* authors state that 'the meaning of the ram's heads is linked to the statues of Mercury and Minerva', and they point to the statue of Mercury with a ram, set onto the façade of Giulio Romano's house (Uppenkamp – Van Beneden, ibid., pp. 109–110).
105. Ackerman, *Architecture of Michelangelo*, 1961, pp. 114–122, fig. 74; for a full discussion of this gateway in connection with Rubens's portico, see Uppenkamp – Van Beneden, *Vera simmetria*, 2011, pp. 57–61, figs 67–68.
106. Albert Rubens owned an example of this collection of plates, which varies from set to set (mentioned in Arents, ibid., p. 349, but not catalogued as a book); for the *Speculum* in general, and its variable composition,

CHAPTER IX - THE PORTICO

Text ill. 127. Michelangelo, *Porta Pia*, detail, engraving in Vignola, *Regola delli Cinque ordini d'architettura*, 1602.

Text ill. 128. Michelangelo, Study for the *Porta Pia*, drawing. Florence, Casa Buonarotti.

a print from the series entitled *Nuova et ultima aggiunta delle porte d'archit[tetur]a di Michel Angelo Buonaroti* [...], which appears from 1602 onwards as addendum to editions of Vignola's *Regola delli Cinque ordini d'architettura* (Text ill. 127).[107]

Quotations from this remarkable gate can be found in Rubens's portico: in the form of the gateway in the central bay, in the heavy triangular pediment with its corners projecting on either side, the sharply profiled mouldings as well as the garland decoration contained within.

A number of Michelangelo's drawings for this city gate are preserved in the Casa Buonarotti in Florence and at Windsor Castle. These studies show variant designs for the central portal, almost all incorporating the geniculated arch (Text ill. 128).[108] Intriguingly, these sheets contain elements that can also be

see, for example, Zorach et al., *Virtual Tourist*, 2008. See also Uppenkamp – Van Beneden, *Vera simmetria*, 2011, pp. 35–36.

107. Albert Rubens had a copy of Vignola's *Regola delli cinque ordini d'architettura*, but it is not known which of the many editions it was. According to Prosper Arents, it was the Amsterdam edition of 1604 by Blaeu, in four languages (Arents, *Bibliotheek*, 2001, p. 298, no. R.13; De Schepper, *Rubens' Bibliotheek*, 2004, p. 69, no. 33), but this is doubtful. If the book did inspire Rubens for his portico, then it is in any case more likely that he consulted an earlier edition. This book should not be confused with Vignola's *Le due regole della prospettiva pratica* (Rome, 1611), which Rubens certainly did possess: he bought a copy from the Officina Plantiniana in 1613 (Arents, ibid., p. 137, no. E13).

108. The consistent occurrence of the geniculated arch in the series of drawings was also noted by Ackerman, *Architecture of Michelangelo*, 1961, p. 120, figs 77a–79b; see also Uppenkamp – Van Beneden, *Vera simmetria*, 2011, pp. 58, 60, fig. 71 (drawing in Windsor Castle).

found in Rubens's portico but naturally, while possible, it would be wrong to assume that he actually saw them.

Anthony Blunt emphasised correctly that in studying Michelangelo's architecture, particularly the late works, Rubens 'was showing an interest which was not shared by his Roman contemporaries'.[109] This does not mean, however, that Rubens simply borrowed motifs, leaving them unchanged; he mostly adapted them freely to fit in with his own designs. For example, he departed from Michelangelo's Porta Pia by replacing the 'rustic' blocks around the flat arch with an elegantly refined moulding, and with the insertion of a dolphin carved in high relief in the spandrels.

Rustication: Palaces in Mantua, Florence and Paris

When describing the façades of the Italian wing, we pointed out that the lower storey is characterised by areas decorated in a rusticated manner, with large bossed blocks of stone, while the corners of the upper storey have heavy quoins, partly bossed.[110] This scheme was entirely in line with the principle of Italian Renaissance architecture, according to which the lower storey as well as the corners of the building should be rusticated, thus projecting an image of strength.

One of the most striking features of the portico is another form of rustication, not bossed, but using bands of heavy blocks to attach the half-columns to the main structure. They give a strong structural unity to the whole and in addition they contribute to the pictorial effect that was certainly intended by Rubens. The bold sculptural structure of the whole screen comes to life especially in the afternoon light, when deep shadows are cast by the rustication of the half-columns.

Examples of such half-columns with smooth or bossed bands can be found in numerous sixteenth-century Italian buildings which may have been Rubens's inspiration. As is well known, immediately after his arrival in Italy in 1600, Rubens became court painter to Vincenzo Gonzaga, Duke of Mantua. Apart from a few periods of absence, he was principally active in Mantua until the end of 1605, and there he certainly became acquainted with two architectural masterpieces by Giulio Romano (c. 1499–1546): major sections of the Palazzo Ducale in the centre of the city, but especially the Palazzo Te, the Duke's *villa suburbana*. Here he would in particular have been struck by the *alla rustica* working of the stone in various parts of the complex, its roughness forming a distinct contrast to the refinement of the Doric columns (Text ill. 129).

---

109. Blunt, *Rubens and Architecture*, 1977, pp. 613–614.
110. See Chapter V, p. 152.

CHAPTER IX - THE PORTICO

Text ill. 129. A courtyard of the Palazzo Te, Mantua.   Text ill. 130. Giulio Romano, *Study for the Palazzo Te*, drawing. Vienna, Albertina.

In the Palazzo Te the Doric order and the rusticated manner were not combined in the way that Rubens used them in his portico. The combination of these two elements does appear in other work by Giulio Romano, including some of his designs for the Porta della Cittadella, which was erected in the vicinity of the Palazzo Te. It seems possible that as court painter Rubens may have seen and studied Giulio's drawings for these buildings in Mantua. There is a design sketch in the Nationalmuseum in Stockholm, and the Albertina in Vienna has two more detailed drawings (Text ill. 130).[111]

The application of different gradations of rustication culminated in the Palazzo Pitti (1558–1570) in Florence, especially the *cortile* which looks onto the garden (Text ill. 131).[112] The qualities that Rubens sought for his portico are already to be found here and he was certainly acquainted with this remarkable courtyard. It is likely that he got to know it fairly soon after arriving in Italy in early October 1600, when he went to Florence in the retinue of Vincenzo Gonzaga for the wedding by proxy of Maria de' Medici to Henri IV.[113]

Many years later Rubens would certainly also have seen the newly finished Palais du Luxembourg in Paris, when working there for a period of six weeks

---

111. Stockholm, Nationalmuseum, inv. no. NMH 360/1863 and Vienna, Albertina, inv. nos AZItalienunb. 1285–1286; Antwerp, 2011, p. 50, fig. 58, no. 4; Hartt, *Giulio Romano*, 1958, I, pp. 183, 194f, 226, and p. 306, nos 311–313; II, figs 415–417. The actual gateway was finally completed without recourse to Giulio Romano's drawings, after his death in 1546. Frederick Hartt correctly observed of these drawings that 'the general idea of a grandiose city gate with arches and a rusticated order was surely suggested by the Porta Maggiore [in Rome]' (ibid., I, p. 196). It is clear that this impressive monument from AD 52, which was undoubtedly known to Rubens, also influenced other 16th-century Italian architects.
112. Wolfgang Lotz called this three-storied courtyard, designed by Bartolomeo Ammanati (1511–1592), 'one of the most important cinquecento examples of the use of rustication'. Each storey has a different type of banded rustication. At the bottom, the Doric half-columns are made up of swollen drums, separated by grooves much narrower than in the heavier banding of the two upper storeys. These bands contribute greatly to the sculptural effect which is enhanced by the contrast of light and shade.
113. Rooses, *Rubens*, 1904, p. 54; Jaffé, *Rubens in Italy*, 1958, pp. 10, 104, n. 3; Smith, *Princesse de Toscane*, 1991, p. 79.

CHAPTER IX - THE PORTICO

Text ill. 131. Bartolomeo Ammanati, Courtyard of the Palazzo Pitti, Florence.

Text ill. 132. Central part of the front façade of the Palais du Luxembourg, Paris.

in January – February 1622 on an important commission for Maria de' Medici (1573–1642): a series of scenes from the Queen's life that were to decorate one of the galleries of the Luxembourg Palace. He must have been struck by how similar in style some of the façades of this building (Text ill. 132), designed by the French architect Salomon de Brosse (1572?–1626), were to those of the *cortile* of the Palazzo Pitti.[114]

It is thus no coincidence that in the background of three of the paintings of his *Medici* series Rubens included rusticated architectural elements that are reminiscent both of the Florentine palace courtyard and his own portico. Heavy banded columns can be found in *The Birth of Maria de' Medici* and *The Flight from Blois* (Appendix III.20). Particularly remarkable is the architectural background in *Henri IV Consigns the Regency to Maria de' Medici* (Appendix III.18; Fig. 24). The figures stand in front of a gateway which, although not completely identical, corresponds quite closely to the central arch of the portico, even including details such as the dolphins in the spandrels.[115] Moreover, standing behind it appears a structure which more or less corresponds to Rubens's garden pavilion.

---

114. The relationship reflected the explicit wishes of Maria de' Medici. In a letter dated 6 October 1611 the Queen asked her aunt, Maria Maddalena of Austria (1589–1631), Grand Duchess of Tuscany, to send plans and drawings of the Palazzo Pitti to Paris so that they could be used as a model for the palace she was planning to build in the French capital: '[…] en voulant en quelque chose me regler sur la forme et le modelle du Palais du Pitti […]' (Coope, *Salomon de Brosse*, 1972, p. 110). For the distinctive rustication of the entire building, see ibid., pp. 113–114.
115. There are notable differences: the head of Medusa is lacking, as are the double architraves (in the portico lying between the fifth and sixth bands), and a band has been added running at an angle over the broken shoulder. The portico elements in the *Medici* series have been mentioned frequently (Baudouin, *Architecturale Motieven*, 2006, pp. 199–203, 211, n. 3, with further references; Van Beneden, *Rubens and Architecture*, 2011, p. 20, fig. 14).

CHAPTER IX - THE PORTICO

Serlio on the Subject of Rustication and the 'Rustic Order'

In Sebastiano Serlio's series of architectural treatises, *Regole generali di Architettura* the subject of 'rustication' is discussed at length in Book IV. According to Serlio, the use of half-columns in combination with rustication was appropriate for buildings that were supposed to exhibit great strength (*fortezza*) and authority (*autorità*). The strength revealed by the rustication is further intensified 'when it is applied to the blocks which bind the columns and the keystones'. In his commentary on such combinations Serlio stresses that it 'is appropriate for fortifications, that is for city gates, citadels, castles, treasuries and places for storing munitions and artillery, prisons, ports and other such structures built for war'.[116]

It is thus no surprise that rustication is frequently applied in buildings with functions of the kind described, including city gates.[117] It should be pointed out that the introduction of such gates and fortresses in Italy coincides with the construction in Antwerp of embossed gates for the city walls, designed by the Bolognese architect Donato de' Boni di Pellizuoli (c. 1500–1556); this building project was begun in 1542 but not completed until 1562.[118] Rubens, therefore, would have come across architectural combinations of this type before his departure for Italy.

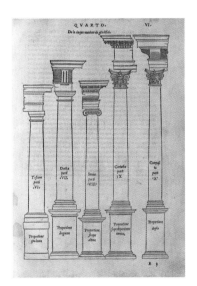

Text ill. 133. *The Five Orders*, engraving in Serlio, *Regole generali di Architettura*, Book IV, 1537.

Half-columns with deeply banded rustication can also be found in the portals of villas, for example the entrance of the Villa Giulia (1551–1555) in Rome, designed by Giacomo Barozzi, called il Vignola (1507–1573).[119]

It should be noted that the chapter in Book IV in which Serlio treats the topic of rustication is the one in which he deals with the Tuscan order. Its heading refers

---

116. Quoted from Onians, *Meaning*, 1988, p. 272; see also (with variant translations): Ackerman, *Tuscan/Rustic Order*, 1994, p. 495; Hart – Hicks, *Serlio*, 1996, p. 254; for Serlio's comments concerning *rustica*, see ibid., p. 254, and the whole of chapter V (ibid., pp. 256–280).
117. Examples include: the imposing city gates in Verona designed by Michele Sanmichele (1484–1559), the *Porta Nuova* (1533–1540) and the *Porta Palio* (1555–1560); see Onians, *Meaning*, 1988, figs 200–201; the Fortezza di Sant'Andrea, on the waterfront of the Venetian Lido, commissioned from the same architect, but not begun until 1543; see also public buildings that need to convey an aura of authority and impregnability, such as the *Zecca*, the Treasury of the Republic of Venice, designed by Jacopo Sansovino (1486–1570) and built in 1536–1545 (Howard, *Jacopo Sansovino*, 1975, pp. 43 and ff., figs 32, 36).
118. Lombaerde, *Antwerp in its Golden Age*, 2001, pp. 99–127, and esp. pp. 102–103.
119. Coffin, *The Villa*, 1988, p. 160, fig. 104; Cresti – Rendina, *Palazzi*, 1998, ill. p. 168.

to two terms which Serlio appears to regard as synonymous ('De Tuscano, et Rustico Ordine'), and he defines and illustrates the column, which has squat proportions and no decoration (Text ill. 133).

Another feature characteristic of the order is the plinth, which is round rather than square.[120] However, unlike Tuscan columns, which he counts as a separate order (additional to the four ancient canonical orders), he does not consider rustication to be part of a specific order, although he does not say so explicitly. Rather he viewed it as a genre which can be called 'Tuscan' or 'Rustic' and can be applied in many different ways.

In his study of the Tuscan/rustic order, James S. Ackerman remarks on the vagueness of Serlio's treatise.[121] Elsewhere, commenting on the Porta Pia, he clarifies this: 'Rustic can be characterized as a genre rather than an Order because there is more in it than a certain vocabulary of ornament. Associated with the countryside rather than with the city it may be thought of as an architectural equivalent to the pastoral genre in literature, connoting what we would call today a romantic or primitive rather than a classical spirit'.[122]

The somewhat ambiguous passage in Serlio's treatise explains to some extent the confusion that has grown up around the description of Rubens's portico; there is indeed reason to call it either 'Tuscan' or 'Rustic' even without the involvement of a Tuscan column.[123] As explained above, both the large half-columns and the smaller free-standing columns as well as part of the decoration are Doric.[124] This paradox also has its origins in Serlio. The application of rustication, according to Serlio, varies considerably in the building types he lists: 'the more coarsely bossed the construction is, the more it will match the quality of a fortress. A simpler rusticated design is then recommended for a city or castle gate, and a less heavily rusticated one for supporting terraces in gardens'.[125] Serlio states that in ancient Roman times examples could be found of a mixture of rustication with a classical order, and this is exactly what Rubens does in his portico. He combines rustication with the Doric order. A mixture of this kind 'represents […] partly *opera di natura* and partly *opera di artificio*'. John

---

120. Hart – Hicks, *Serlio*, 1996, ill. pp. 255, 257. For the proportions of the Tuscan order according to treatises by different authors, see Ackerman, *Tuscan/Rustic Order*, 1994, p. 497, table 16.1. Rubens copied Serlio's image of the Tuscan column with round plinth in his *Theoretical Notebook*, as is known from an extant copy (Jaffé, *Antwerp Sketchbook*, 1966, II, pp. 245–246, fig. 74v).
121. 'Replacing the *ordine toscano* with *opera toscana* he stealthily switches from the columnar order to rustication' (Ackerman, *Tuscan/Rustic Order*, 1994, p. 496).
122. Id., *Architecture of Michelangelo*, 1961, p. 122.
123. The portico is often rightly described as Tuscan; see Forssman, *Säulenordnungen*, 1984, p. 73 ('Ein besonders schönes Beispiel toskanischer Gartenarchitektur alla rustica'); Muller, *Rubens's Collection*, 2004, pp. 35–36. However, as mentioned above (pp. 257–258), the columns are sometimes erroneously referred to as Tuscan (Baudouin, *Barok*, 1982, p. 112; Stutz, *Residenz*, 1985, p. 146; Baudouin, *Architecturale Motieven*, 2006, p. 199), while they are unmistakably Doric.
124. See above, p. 258, n. 24.
125. Paraphrase of Serlio from Onians, *Meaning*, 1988, p. 275.

CHAPTER IX - THE PORTICO

Text ill. 134. Rubens, *The Garden of Love*, detail with the architecture in the background. Madrid, Museo Nacional del Prado.

Onians says in addition that 'the roughness of rusticated masonry presumably brings it close to natural raw stone, while the more the work is finished the more firmly it belongs to the world of art'.[126]

Serlio has more to say about this mixing of rustication with various orders in another publication, his *Libro extraordinario*, published in 1551. This contains a collection of fifty portal designs, including thirty plates illustrating gateways in rustic style mixed with the classical orders ('trenta porte di opera rustica mista con diversi ordini'). It is not possible to state with certainty that Rubens had this book and took inspiration from it directly, but there is an unmistakable relationship between the portico and several of the plates.[127]

Coarse rustication with bossed surface (*opera di natura*) was generally considered suitable for garden architecture. That Rubens was well aware of this emerges from the massive construction he depicted about 1630–1632 in *The Garden of Love* in the Prado in Madrid (Text ill. 134; Appendix III.24). In many respects, it recalls the appearance of the central bay of the portico. There is, however, one striking difference: the roughness of the bands of dripstone around the columns, in contrast to the smooth ones in Antwerp. Another difference is the addition of a herm on either side of the doorway. They represent giants (*Giganti*) and refer to Nature at its most primitive and powerful.[128]

---

126. Onians, *Meaning*, 1988, pp. 272–273.
127. A French and an Italian edition were published in Lyon in 1551 (Serlio, *Livre extraordinaire*, 1551; Serlio, *Extraordinario libro*, 1551) and numerous editions followed later, including one in Venice (Vène, *Bibliographia Serliana*, 2007, p. 180); not described as in Rubens's possession in Arents, *Bibliotheek*, 2001. For a more detailed discussion of the theory of rustication and Italian examples connected with Rubens's portico, see also Uppenkamp – Van Beneden, *Vera simmetria*, 2011, pp. 47–54.
128. Similar figures can also be found in a drawing for a fountain, dated 1637, by an unknown French architect, in Worcester College, Oxford (Fredlund, *Arkitektur*, 1974, fig. 22).

Architectural theory

Clearly, in conceiving the portico, Rubens had in mind certain buildings of the sixteenth and early seventeenth centuries that he had encountered during his stay in Italy. Probably he also took into account, with regard to the function required of the portico, what was maintained in general architectural theory about the meaning of the various orders and building types, while avoiding too literal an interpretation.

Rubens successfully incorporated these recollections into a concept which displays both unity and great originality. The harmonious combination of heavily banded half-columns, a central passageway with a geniculated arch and, to the left and right, bays with graceful semi-circular arches standing on slim Doric columns, each forming a *serliana*, is in itself an extraordinary achievement. In addition the attic brings into play a rich combination of niches, framed with elegant mouldings, within a vigorously articulated pediment. All of these elements have been combined into a whole that is powerful yet harmonious, and creates striking sculptural as well as pictorial effects.

When bringing the portico into the context of architectural theory as realised in comparable sixteenth-century buildings in Italy, we can see that Rubens followed a similar path to that exemplified by Michelangelo, interpreting ideas about the orders with considerable freedom, without completely throwing overboard the *regole* that applied in the individual case.[129] As with the late work of Michelangelo, but more consistently so, Rubens's architecture displays in the portico an unusual degree of fantasy and variety, and we can even detect a painterly approach.

The relationship between Rubens's architecture and that of his great predecessor Michelangelo and the subsequent generation of architects who were influential during the High Baroque in Italy, was commented on by Anthony Blunt. He noted in connection with Rubens's designs for title pages and triumphal arches for the *Pompa Introitus Ferdinandi* that 'none of these designs is an exact imitation of any particular work, but in all of them Rubens seems to be taking off, so to speak, from his ideas and developing in a highly inventive way, adding to them a liveliness which brings them very near to the full Baroque architecture of Borromini and Pietro da Cortona'.[130] This remark also applies to the portico, where Rubens in a similar way took forms and motifs he had observed in Italy and then developed them in an original manner which still allowed him to maintain an internal architectural logic.[131]

129. Ackerman, *Architecture of Michelangelo*, 1961, pp. 115, 122.
130. Blunt, *Rubens and Architecture*, 1977, pp. 609–611, and esp. p. 614.
131. Valerie Herremans came to a similar conclusion in connection with Rubens's designs for architectural ornaments. These respect inherent architectural ground rules, and this makes them less 'free' than other designs inspired by post-Michelangelesque mannerism (Herremans, *Architectural Sculpture (CRLB)*, 2019, p. 83).

Chapter X
The Garden Pavilion

Looking inwards from the entrance gate on the Wapper, the visitor can see a pavilion in the distance at the end of the garden. This small and elegant building is, besides the portico, the only original part of Rubens's house that survives. We assume that it was designed by Rubens, and have included it in the Catalogue (No. 34) with technical information and an extensive bibliography.

It is noticeable that the garden pavilion was situated at the focal point of the perspective, behind the central arch of the portico, which provides a pictorial framework for it (Fig. 138). The portico and the pavilion are both sited along a single central axis and they relate to one another rather like scenery elements, designed to create a dramatic illusion of depth. Piet Lombaerde saw this as an application of *oeillade* and *enfilade*. The distance from the entrance to the portico, and from portico to pavilion is in the ratio of one to three, while the height of the pavilion equals three times the height of the portico's central arch. This means that, standing by the entrance, the whole of the little building can be seen through the archway.[1]

In addition to this, another unifying element can be detected that connects the two constructions. As outlined in an earlier chapter, integrated in the architecture of the portico are two *serlianas*,[2] and this Serlian motif, which will be discussed more fully later, forms the principal, defining element of the garden pavilion.

Dating

As with other architectural elements of Rubens's house, we have no indications, archival or of any other kind, that inform us about the creation or dating of the pavilion. Given the close connection with the portico, it is safe to assume that the little building was conceived together with the portico, and was probably also built at the same time. If this is so, it means that the pavilion was constructed in about 1618, and before the autumn of 1621 when Anthony van Dyck, who had copied the portico (No. 24, Copy; Fig. 139), left for Italy.[3] A fixed *terminus ante*

---

1. Lombaerde, *Distribution*, 2002, pp. 111–112, fig. 13 ('reconstruction of the *oeillade* or central axis through the portico of the Rubens House'); id., *Rubens the Architect*, 2011, pp. 150–152; id., *Rubens*, 2014, pp. 208–211, figs 6–7; for more on this, with a digital, geometrical analysis of the relative positioning of the portico and garden pavilion in relation to the main entrance, see Boeykens, *Reflections*, 2014, pp. 231–235.
2. See Chapter IX, pp. 259–260
3. For a dating of the portico, see Chapter IX, pp. 269–271; for the misapprehension that the garden pavilion

CHAPTER X - THE GARDEN PAVILION

Text ill. 135. Rubens, *Henri IV Consigns the Regency to Maria de' Medici*, oil sketch (Appendix III.19). Munich, Bayerische Staatsgemäldesammlungen, Alte Pinakothek.

quem – for the invention of the pavilion if not its construction – is in any case 1622, the date of a preparatory sketch for one of the scenes of the *Medici* series, *Henri IV Consigns the Regency to Maria de' Medici*, in which it appears in the background (Appendix III.19; Text ill. 135).

Although there is no conclusive evidence for the pavilion and portico having been built at the same time, as we assume, it is worth noting that there are similarities in the materials used for the two constructions. The mortar has the same composition, and quarry marks indicate that the blue limestone used in the garden pavilion and portico comes from the same source.[4]

Another question that arises is whether or not a number of free-standing statues were part of the original concept and were placed there at the same time, or rather were added to the little building at one or more later dates, something to which we will return later.

A. Description of the Pavilion in its Present State

The pavilion (Figs 177–178) is built on a rectangular plan, adjoining the wall which separated Rubens's garden from the shooting range of the arquebusiers (Kolveniershof) to the east. The architectural motif that characterises both front and sides is a central round arch, flanked either side by a horizontal lintel or architrave, supported by columns. This motif, the *serliana*, will be the subject of further detailed discussion. As in the portico, to which the garden pavilion is related, the columns are of the Doric order, with a band of rosettes underneath

---

could be the 'huiske' (little house) that was built by the arquebusiers in 1615, see Chapter IV, p. 124, n. 26.

4. In addition, the brickwork core behind the shell on the portico's central bay contains a number of so-called black bricks (more accurately, dark grey), which are identical to those of the pavilion (De Clercq – Hayen, *Historische schets*, 2019, ill. p. 49). For the mortar, see ibid., p. 50; for the quarry marks on the pavilion, see De Clercq, *Tuinpaviljoen*, 2012, p. [1]; for the relative value of these marks for a dating, see Chapter IX, p. 250, n. 7.

CHAPTER X - THE GARDEN PAVILION

the capitals. To the front and sides, the arches are reinforced with wrought iron tie-rods.

In both spandrels of the arch at the front there is a circular niche, forming a blind *oculus*. These are both crowned by curved, eyebrow-like, hood mouldings, a combination that Rubens used again much later, in 1635, in one of his designs for the *Pompa Introitus* (Text ill. 136).[5]

Text ill. 136. Theodoor van Thulden, *The Stage of Isabella (Front Face)*, etching, detail of the lower storey.

Similar hood mouldings appear also in works from the years 1615–1617 by the architects Jacques Francart (1582/83–1651) and Wenzel Cobergher (1560–1634). Francart introduced one above an oval window in one of the portal designs of his *Premier Livre d'Architecture* of 1617,[6] while Cobergher used the motif above a tondo in the façade of the Church of St Augustine in Antwerp (Text ill. 115). In fact this church incorporates another Rubensian motif, the geniculated arch in the window above the entrance, and interestingly it was built at about the same time that Rubens was constructing his house and was probably working on designs for the portico and garden pavilion.[7]

Covering the full width of the front of the pavilion is a classical entablature, with a cornice which projects forwards, supported by modillions. On the Doric frieze, between the cornice and architrave, are triglyphs with *guttae* underneath: one at each end, and one in the middle. From seventeenth-century representations, including *The Walk in the Garden* (which gives an impression of the situation in c. 1630; Fig. 182) and the Harrewijn print of 1692 (Fig. 183), we can deduce that the central triglyph is not authentic. Originally there was a ram's skull (*aegicranium*) above the keystone, but in the eighteenth or early nineteenth century this disappeared and was replaced by the triglyph.

Above the cornice is a balustrade, closed on either side by pedestals, which are supported sideways by pressed-down volutes. Behind, and reserved as a dormer in the slated hipped roof, is a large niche, crowned by an open pediment. The pediment rests on two posts with sphinx-like female heads, with Ionic capitals above (No. 35; Figs 184 and 185). The plaited hair of these caryatids is tied into a bow over a quadrangular 'breast panel', with two volutes projecting

---

5. Two very similar round niches with an 'eyebrow' can be found in *The Stage of Isabella* (Martin, *Pompa (CRLB)*, 1972, no. 34a, fig. 64); there is also a related eyebrow-like moulding above the architectural framework in Rubens's drawn *Design for the Printer's Device of the Plantin Press*, dating from c. 1630 (Judson – Van de Velde, *Title-pages (CRLB)*, 1978, I, no. 74a; II, fig. 255).
6. De Vos, *Francart*, 1998, pl. 49; see also the window in the façade of the Church of St Augustine in Brussels, which was built after a design by Francart in 1620 (ibid., pp. 36–39, pls 16, 61).
7. The first stone of this church was laid on 7 March 1615 and it was consecrated on 2 September 1618 (Meganck, *Cobergher*, 1998, pp. 95–113, fig. 46).

CHAPTER X - THE GARDEN PAVILION

at the bottom. Slightly behind the niche, the sides are attached to a narrow, curved wing, which is again topped by an Ionic capital.

There is also, as mentioned, a *serliana* on both side elevations of the garden pavilion, though of a simplified kind (Figs 177–178). Here the semi-circular arch is supported by square columns made of 'black' (dark grey) brickwork, rather than rounded Doric columns in natural stone. Similar square columns also support the ribbed crossvault of the pavilion's interior. The sides differ from the front in not having round niches hollowed into the spandrels, nor do they have a cornice.

The combination of two types of column, round and square, is distinctly unusual, so much so that it has occasionally been suggested that the square ones might not be original.[8] However, there can be no doubt that the combination is indeed a seventeenth-century form, as is clear from the images of the pavilion in *The Walk in the Garden* (Fig. 182) and the 1692 Harrewijn print (Fig. 183). Moreover, both types of column are also represented in variants of the pavilion's lower level that appear in the background of small group portraits by Philip Fruytiers (Appendix III.26).[9]

Some commentary is needed on the use of striking dark bricks in several parts of the pavilion: the square columns at the back, the pilasters against the rear wall, the rounded arch and lintels. When the pavilion was restored in 1960, a decision was made to leave these elements bare of stucco, to create a strong contrast of light and dark. It was then felt that the colourful use of different materials – white statues and stucco work, blue limestone, dark brickwork and a gilded garland – was an essential characteristic of the garden building.[10]

In the most recent restoration, which was completed in 2019, this approach to the brickwork was maintained in the belief that the pavilion was originally a two-colour structure, with the black bricks left in their natural state.[11] This practice of leaving the brickwork exposed, with clearly visible pointing in a paler colour (Text ill. 137) was supposedly chosen by Rubens to create a picturesque effect. It was assumed that this plain appearance was in keeping with the alleged 'rustic character' of the pavilion's architecture,[12] but this does not seem tenable as a hypothesis. Although differences in colour can be detected in the seventeenth-century imagery (see below), it seems very unlikely that the current plain, unworked appearance of the brickwork elements listed

8. It was thought possible that the original round columns had been replaced by square ones (in the 19th century); Hayen – De Clercq, *Tuinpaviljoen*, 2010, p. 2.
9. See below, pp. 304–305, n. 22.
10. Van Aerschot, ed., *Bouwen / Antwerpen*, 1979, p. 548, fig. 345.
11. Mertens – Stoppie, *Conservatievisie*, 2019, p. 55.
12. An effect Rubens planned 'in the context of garden architecture in which other elements such as "grotti", with their building materials left unworked, played an important role' (De Clercq, *Rubens schilderend*, 2019, p. 54).

above corresponds with what Rubens envisaged for his elegant 'Italian' garden pavilion.

Today there are three stone, free-standing, statues of ancient gods in place in the pavilion. In front of a shallow niche, in the centre of the rear wall, stands an impressive over-life-size statue of Hercules (No. 40; Fig. 211). Around the niche, hanging above and draped either side, is a garland of fruits. To the right, standing between the columns, is a youthful Bacchus, his head crowned with vine leaves; he leans on a tree trunk, holding a bunch of grapes in both hands (No. 38; Fig. 202). He is balanced on the other side by a Venus that was installed in 1947 to

Text ill. 137. Detail of Fig. 177: the black bricks.

replace a Ceres (No. R4; Fig. 235) which was rightly thought not to be original.[13] A fourth statue, a young man with a cornucopia, can be seen in the niche on the roof, above the balustrade (No. 36; Fig. 187). We will return to look in more detail at these four free-standing statues further on in this chapter as well as in Chapter XI and in the Catalogue.

Inside the garden pavilion is a stone table with a baluster-shaped foot. This was already present in the nineteenth century and it appears in all the imagery of that period (e.g. Appendix III. 50–51 and 53). We do not know if it goes back as far as Rubens's time, as was believed by Victor Van Grimbergen and Auguste Schoy[14] (and probably many others in the nineteenth century), but this seems possible. There are three seventeenth-century illustrations of the pavilion in which a similar table can be seen, and evidently it functioned as part of the enjoyment of the garden in summer months.[15]

B. Depictions of Rubens's Garden Pavilion and Variants

A good deal of interesting iconographical material can be linked to Rubens's garden pavilion. It can be identified in a number of seventeenth-century paintings, by Rubens as well as other masters, but of course, care must be taken

13. For the modern Venus, see pp. 311–312, n. 38.
14. Van Grimbergen, *Rubens*, 1840, p. 387, n. 10 ('[…] [het] paviljoen, in 't welk men nog de zwarte marmere tafel ziet aldaer door Rubens gesteld'); Schoy, *Rubens*, 1878. p. 34; Schoy, *Influence italienne*, 1879, p. 340 (with the same text in both publications: '[…] le pittoresque pavillon […] – où on voit encore la table qui lui [Rubens] servait').
15. The table that is presently in place – original or copy? – (no inventory number; H. 88 cm) has an octagonal top made of pink marble (123 cm wide). In *The Walk in the Garden* the table is laid, and has been covered with a tablecloth ready for Rubens and Helena Fourment, who are walking towards it (Fig. 182); there is a table with a baluster foot in the Berlin double portrait as well as in the Harrewijn print, and in both it is being used: in the first by an unknown gentleman and lady (Fig. 181), and in the second (probably) by Hillewerve and his guest (Fig. 183).

because these pictures were not intended to provide an accurate representation of the actual architecture; depending on the context, certain details have been added and others omitted or changed.

In Works by Rubens

The earliest iconographical source of the pavilion is a composition from Rubens's *Medici* series, designed in 1622: *Henri IV Consigns the Regency to Maria de' Medici*. It can be recognised in the preparatory oil sketch in Munich (Appendix III.19, Text ill. 135) and – in more detail – in the large painting in Paris (Appendix III.18; Fig. 24). In both it can be glimpsed in the background through an arch that resembles Rubens's portico. Much of its lower part is obscured by foreground figures, while the top is truncated by the arch. The visible elements, however, are undeniably almost identical to those in Rubens's garden pavilion: the ram's skull (*aegicranium*) that was originally in the centre of the architrave, the balustrade with six balusters, the round niches and the niche in the roof above. In the large painting more details can be recognised, for instance the small volutes that are attached below the two sphinx-like caryatids. Further decorative elements can be made out that were perhaps also originally part of Ruben's pavilion. In the frieze either side of the skull there are garlands, triglyphs and metopes (consisting of helmets and libation vessels). Both of the round niches in the spandrels have small volutes on either side of the hood moulding, from which *vittae* (fillets) hang.[16] A distinctive feature of the pavilion that appears in the Medici painting is the use of a very dark colour for the mouldings, frieze and balustrade.

It goes without saying that Rubens did not intend to represent his garden pavilion in this allegorical history painting for the French queen. He merely used a similar structure, adapted to the context: it is on a more monumental scale and grander in appearance, suggesting a palatial backdrop. Replacing the blind back wall is a view through to a garden. The round niches as well as the roof niche are blank. But this should not be taken as evidence that in about 1622 statues had not yet been placed in the pavilion in Rubens's garden.

Rubens also used the architecture of the garden pavilion as a background in another completely different context, namely in *The Supper at Emmaus* of c. 1638, in the Prado in Madrid (Appendix III.25). The scene takes place before an open loggia with a view through to a landscape. In the interior of the loggia we see to the sides, both towards the front and further back, a number of columns that support the round arch as well as the cross-vaulted ceiling; the iron tie-rods are also present.

---

16. For *vittae*, which can also be seen on the portico, either side of the *bucrania* and tied to the horns of the ram's heads, see p. 261 and under No. 28.

CHAPTER X - THE GARDEN PAVILION

Text ill. 138. Rubens, *The Discovery of Erichtonius*, oil sketch. Stockholm, Nationalmuseum (Appendix III.23).

Echoes of the garden pavilion can be found in the architecture in the background of a sketch for the *Discovery of Erichthonius by the Daughters of Cecrops* of 1631–1632, now in the Nationalmuseum, Stockholm (Text ill. 138).[17] We can see the left-hand *oculus* of the roughed out *serliana*, here enriched with a pair of herms carrying flower baskets on their heads; the *oculus* is set in a frame and there are indications of the hood moulding above.

The Walk in the Garden

One important and extremely interesting iconographical source for the pavilion is the panel in the Alte Pinakothek in Munich, known as *The Walk in the Garden* (Appendix III.6; Figs 25 and 182). Unlike the two works mentioned above, this painting shows the pavilion in a setting that corresponds to its actual location, in Rubens's garden. The scene portrays Rubens, shortly after his second marriage (in December 1630) – so perhaps in the summer of 1631 – walking with his young bride Helena Fourment and his son Nicolaas towards their 'summer house', where a table has been laid, with a wine cooler and bottles on the floor next to it.

The painting is somewhat problematic: its attribution to Rubens has been doubted and there is no consensus about its dating.[18] Nonetheless, we can assume that it provides an impression of Rubens's garden in the early 1630s, but since it is an idealised rendition not every detail should be interpreted literally.[19]

17. F. Healy in McGrath et al., *Mythological Subjects I (CRLB)*, 2016, I, pp. 431–434, no. 42a; II, fig. 370; in the Stockholm sketch the right-hand side of the *serliana* is obscured by a fountain and it has simply been omitted from the many works deriving from this composition.
18. See the references under Appendix III.6.
19. Jeffrey Muller, for instance, calls the painting 'of questionable documentary value' (Muller, *Collector*, 1989,

CHAPTER X · THE GARDEN PAVILION

Certainly the setting is unrealistic, the garden appears to be surrounded by a wooded landscape rather than the city. Rising behind the garden pavilion, where in reality the arquebusiers' shooting range should be, is a tall building which can never have been there, and to which an (open?) door at the back of the pavilion appears to give access.

The pavilion shown in *The Walk in the Garden* features a ram's skull (*aegicranium*) on the front, above the keystone of the round arch, in the middle of the entablature. As mentioned above, this now lost element was part of the original decoration. Perhaps the same applies to the (now missing) stone basket containing flowers and fruits standing on top of the roof niche, and the gilded sphere that crowns the roof itself.

The appearance of the pavilion in the painting differs significantly from the current form in that its side is identical to the front, incorporating an *aegicranium* and rounded niche with 'eyebrow' hood moulding. Probably this elaborate decoration of the sides never existed – there is no niche in the side of the pavilion in the 1692 Harrewijn print either – but was shown this way in the painting in order to make the building more ornate. The mouldings around the circular niches are also more richly decorated than those in the Harrewijn print. Small volutes have been added to their tops on either side. Garlands can be made out hanging from these volutes on the niche on the side of the building; those to the front appear more like *vittae*, corresponding to a detail more clearly visible in the above-mentioned scene in the *Medici* series (Appendix III.18; Fig. 24).

The free-standing statues in the pavilion shown in *The Walk in the Garden* can be more or less clearly made out. Not much of the statue appears in the roof niche, although sufficient to conclude that it matches the youth still standing there (while ignoring for the time being the question of its being an original or a faithful copy). We can see his left hand resting on the curving base of the cornucopia. Between the columns on the ground floor level of the pavilion, are two nude statues on pedestals (Fig. 182). The female figure to the left is a Venus. The youth to the right, crossing his legs, largely corresponds with the Bacchus statue which is still in place, and it can be assumed that the statue in the Munich painting is also a Bacchus. It is worth noting that it differs in a few details: for example the animal skin around his loins is missing.

In the pavilion in *The Walk in the Garden* there is no trace of the full-length statue of Hercules with garlands. Instead, the painting shows a door frame, topped by the bust of a bearded man, probably Hercules (see in the Catalogue, no. 39; Fig. 210). The door itself was certainly fictive, since the rear wall of the garden pavilion backed on to the boundary wall between Rubens's garden

pp. 31–32, n. 33, referring to similar doubts raised by Hans Gerhard Evers, Matthias Winner and Hans Mielke).

and his rear neighbours, the arquebusiers. An actual doorway, like the one suggested in the painting, can never have been placed there.

It cannot be excluded that the arrangement with the door and bust is entirely fictional, and that it is a poetic alteration to the design in *The Walk in the Garden*, with the pavilion functioning as a portico leading to a larger building (a temple?) that, of course, never actually existed. Equally it is possible, however, that the Munich panel shows an earlier design for the rear wall, which was later replaced by the niche with the heroic-scale Hercules and garlands currently in place. Despite its uncertain status, we have included the bust in the Catalogue where further information is provided (No. 39).

In Works by Other Seventeenth-Century Painters

The garden pavilion in the distance was immediately visible to visitors when they entered the house, and it certainly also caught the attention of painters, both of Rubens's own generation, and in later years. In the paintings of these artists the Rubensian building recurs in several different variations, but always connected with the theme of love, or more particularly the garden of love.

The most striking rendition is that by Jacques Jordaens in the painting mentioned above in the chapter on the portico.[20] Jordaens included Rubens's garden pavilion in an architectural capriccio, sandwiched in between two images of the portico, and representing the imaginary palace of Cupid, in his *Cupid and Psyche*, which is in the Prado in Madrid, and can be dated 1640–1645 (Appendix III.9; Fig. 179). There are no full-length figures shown in the little building, but statues of Venus, Bacchus or Hercules would certainly have been inappropriate in the context of this tale. A large shell is shown placed in the empty roof niche. Jordaens also made other alterations to the building: the interior depicted repeats the structure, appearing to be double the depth, and has a ceiling with gilded ornamentation; the central ram's skull (*aegicranium*) was replaced by a cherub motif; sphynx-like heads appear above the large volutes.

In the *Elegant Company in a Garden*, dated 1651, by David Teniers II (1610–1690), we can see the garden pavilion in a much altered but still recognisable form (Appendix III.28). The building differs from the original in the absence of columns as well as having strongly contrasting colours. It is apparently constructed in red brick, with black mouldings and balustrade, and has a superstructure that is almost entirely white. There is a parrot perching on the iron tie-rod. The statue of a youth is present in the roof niche and, as in the Harrewijn prints, we can also see two small statues of putti above the volutes.

---

20. See Chapter IX, passim.

CHAPTER X - THE GARDEN PAVILION

Two full-length statues of semi-nude antique figures are placed in niches, a youth to the left and a female to the right, but these cannot be identified as they are partly hidden by the people gathering in front of it. What is certain is that they do not correspond to the statues that appear in *The Walk in the Garden*. Placed centrally in front of the pavilion, is a fountain with a putto riding side-saddle on a swan or goose, from whose beak a jet of water shoots upwards.

Rubens's pavilion can also be identified, in a form modified even further, in a number of scenes which are variants of his *Garden of Love*,[21] and have been wrongly attributed to Hiëronymus Janssens (1624–1693) (Appendix III.36). In these works a niche is visible in the rear wall which contains a single life-size statue of a goddess, Venus.

Of particular interest for the study of the pavilion is the image that appears in the background of the Berlin double portrait which can be dated to approximately 1655 on the basis of the costumes (Appendix III.10; Fig. 181). In front of a portico which is vaguely reminiscent of that of Rubens, stands an unidentified couple. In the background, glimpsed through the central arch of the portico – and so just as it would have appeared from Rubens's courtyard – is an image of the pavilion, which can be regarded as accurate. Unfortunately, in the painting the top of the pavilion is cut off, half-way up the roof niche, hidden behind the portico, while the left-hand portion lies beyond the edge of the canvas. In the pavilion the same couple can be seen, recognisable from their costumes, this time sitting at a table, the woman playing a lute while the man (with his distinctive blue stockings) poses nonchalantly, resting his head on his hand. In relation to the figures, the garden building and its statues are shown noticeably larger in scale than in reality. The round niche in the spandrel of the arch, glimpsed through the foliage of a tree, appears empty, as in *The Walk in the Garden*. In the centre of the architrave, the head or skull of a ram can be clearly made out, as in the later Harrewijn print. The statues, including the monumental Hercules, will be discussed in more detail shortly.

Finally, we should look at a contemporary image with architecture inspired by the garden pavilion, and which has previously escaped attention: *The Four Eldest Children of Rubens and Helena Fourment, with a Maid and Helena Fourment (?)* by Philip Fruytiers (1610–1666) in the British Royal Collection Trust, datable to c. 1639 (Appendix III.26). Because of its context, this work undoubtedly alludes to a setting in Rubens's garden. The troupe of children are moving about in an interior which corresponds more or less with the central space of the pavilion. The round arches and lintels are visible, supported by a combination of round and square columns, all in the same pale greyish colour (i.e. monochrome). It seems that Fruytiers is following the actual shape of the pavilion, although

---

21. Madrid, Museo Nacional del Prado, inv. no. P001690; Büttner, *Genre Scenes* (CRLB), 2019, no. 1, fig. 1.

he has modified its proportions and transformed the structure into an arbour covered with creeper.[22]

In the Prints by Harrewijn

We now come to the last of the seventeenth-century iconographical sources, the all-important prints by Jacob Harrewijn which have been mentioned several times in the previous chapters. In the print of 1684, the garden building is represented 'in the distance', seen from the front (Fig. 180); the four statues, although miniscule, are represented in such a way that they can be recognised. There are two putti standing on the volutes of the attic and, for the first time, busts appear in the round niches.

The second print, from 1692, shows the garden pavilion from closer to and the details can easily be appreciated (Fig. 183). It is viewed from the side, more or less as in *The Walk in the Garden*. Two clergymen, one of whom is probably Hillewerve himself, are sitting at a table enjoying a glass of wine.

The building is crowned with a number of decorative elements: placed on the apex of the pediment is a basket filled with fruit or flowers – something also to be seen in *The Walk in the Garden* – and on each of the outer corners is a small brazier. The two pressed-down volutes either side of the balustrade support small statues of putti (Text ill. 139).

Some decades earlier, Teniers had also shown putti standing in the same places in his variation on Rubens's garden pavilion, although their shapes are somewhat different (Appendix III.34). It is thus possible that the putti seen in the Harrewijn print were already crowning the pavilion in Rubens's time. This was assumed by Jeffrey Muller: he took the figures to be original, including them in his catalogue of sculpture in Rubens's collection.[23] In his view, they may symbolise virtue or liberty, an interpretation based on his opinion that 'the putto on the viewer's left [...] holds a money bag outstretched'.[24] But this is not an attribute visible being clutched by one of the statuettes of the print, nor is there any such evidence in the Teniers painting. Rather, the left-hand putto seems to be holding a cornucopia by his left side. Muller's suggestion that the right-hand putto might be holding a goose by its neck,[25] must also, on closer inspection, be rejected. The supposed goose is in fact simply a piece of drapery.

22. Fruytiers also employed variations of the same Rubensian background architecture in two other miniature group portraits: his *Portrait of a Lady with Maid and Three Children*, dated 1642 (Antwerp, Koninklijk Museum voor Schone Kunsten Antwerpen, inv. no. 824: Baudouin, *Fruytiers*, 1967, p. 174, fig. 11) and the *Portrait of an Unknown Family in a Garden* (sale, New York (Sotheby's), 26 January 2007, lot 121).
23. Muller, *Collector*, 1989, pp. 33, 154, cat. III, nos 21–22 (as 'Anonymous seventeenth-century Flemish master?').
24. Ibid., p. 33, n. 40; this interpretation, based on a false reading of the image, was followed by Uppenkamp – Van Beneden, *Architectural Symbolism*, 2011, p. 121.
25. Muller, *Collector*, 1989, p. 33, n. 40 (concerning the ancient motif of a child with goose).

CHAPTER X - THE GARDEN PAVILION

Text ill. 139. Detail of the 1692 Harrewijn print (Fig. 18): the putti on the volutes of the garden pavilion.

One of the spandrels on the side of the pavilion contains a decorative motif consisting of a bundle of attributes, either painted or worked out in relief (Figs 183 and 233). It is difficult to determine if these stem from Rubens's time or not. We can in any case reject the idea that this is an emblem of the art of painting designed by Rubens; for further commentary see the Catalogue under 'rejected attributions' (No. R3).

In Hillewerves's time busts had been added in the round niches of the spandrels. These are not easily discernible and so it is difficult to say if they are the same sculptures that were in place at the time of the restoration. Between the columns at ground level two statues are visible. As in the Munich painting, a nude female can be seen to the left, but this time of a different type, with drapery over her right arm; evidently she is Venus, since she is accompanied by a child, one of whose legs can be made out, as well as part of an arm that reaches up with an arrow. For further discussion of Hillewerve's Venus, which is curiously similar in composition to a statuette by Georg Petel (1601/2–1634), the reader is referred to the Catalogue (No. 37). Like the Venus, only more so, the statue of a nude youth to the right is concealed by a column. We can just see that he clutches a plate or cup in his outstretched right hand. This statue – in our opinion a figure of Bacchus – is discussed further in the present chapter and in the Catalogue (No. 38).

The Nineteenth Century and Early Photographs

A few paintings as well as early photographs give an impression of the garden pavilion's appearance in the nineteenth and at the beginning of the twentieth century, that is before restoration and reconstruction of the house started. The earliest images known from this period appear in two romantic scenes: one dating from 1827 by Mathieu van Bree (1773–1839), and another from 1833 by his brother Philippe van Brée (1786–1871). The former, in the Kunstsammlungen in Weimar, shows Rubens surrounded by ten of his colleagues and sitting at

CHAPTER X - THE GARDEN PAVILION

a table in the garden pavilion with the statue of Hercules in the background (Appendix III.41).

In the second, in the Brussels Royal Museums, Rubens is shown working at his easel in the garden accompanied by his wife and child, and a servant feeding peacocks and ducks. A large part of the pavilion, viewed from the front and showing the three statues, can be seen very clearly (Appendix III.42). Van Brée has introduced alterations to the structure above the *serliana*: the façade is not covered with white stucco – there is red brickwork showing – and in the round niches we can see the busts of a faun and a bacchante, which were then standing in the niches of the portico (and still were in 1938).

To coincide with the Rubens celebrations in Antwerp in 1840, large prints were published, showing the two original parts of the house still standing, accurately drawn in situ. The pavilion, with the statues included, was recorded in great detail in a line engraving by Erin Corr and Jozef Linnig, based on drawings by Nicaise de Keyser and J. Stordiau (Appendix III.46). At the foot of the print, the construction of the pavilion was shown in plan form with an additional inset image of the vaulting.

A good impression of the pavilion is provided by the earliest photographs, from about 1860: one by Louis Schweig (a stereophotograph), one by Edmond Fierlants and another by Adolphe Braun (Appendix III.50–51 and 53).[26] The pavilion was then in a rather dilapidated state; it was stuccoed, and therefore the same colour all over. There is another photograph in the Antwerp FelixArchief (city archives), probably taken in about 1914, which reveals – between two of the balusters, on the pedestal of the statue – the presence of a puzzling inscription with the date '1612'.[27] In a photograph published by Ary Delen in 1933,[28] the pavilion can be seen in an even more neglected state, but its general appearance remains unchanged.

Influence on Architecture

A final point to add is that interest in Rubens's remarkable garden pavilion was not limited to seventeenth- and nineteenth-century painting and early photography. Its direct influence can be seen in buildings that survive in the gardens of several Antwerp townhouses.[29]

---

26. For these early photographs, see Chapter II, p. 82, nn. 96–97.
27. Apparently this date was painted on later, and afterwards removed along with the stucco. In the light of what we know about the pavilion's building history, it is a mystery what this date – one year after the purchase of the property – can refer to. For the photo, see Tijs, *Rubens en Jordaens*, 1984, ill. p. 174; Muller, *Collector*, 1989, fig. 20.
28. Delen, *Rubens' huis*, 1933, p. 75.
29. A similar arrangement with two statues at ground level and a third in a niche at the top can be seen at a house called 'Salvator' in the Ambtmanstraat, on the façade fronting the courtyard garden (De Lattin, *Antwerpsche stadsbeeld*, 1940–55, III, ill. on p. 96; for this house, which had fallen into complete disrepair and

CHAPTER X - THE GARDEN PAVILION

Text ill. 140. The busts in the niches of the garden pavilion before the restoration, detail of Appendix III.53.

C. Sculpture in the Garden Pavilion

The Busts in the Niches

In all of the images of the pavilion which came before the prints by Harrewijn, including the Berlin double portrait, the round niches in the spandrels are empty (See e.g Figs 179 and 182). But the Harrewijn prints as well as the nineteenth-century images do show busts in these niches. It is hard to determine if these are the same sculptures each time. In the print dated 1692 we can see two full-face heads of youthful figures with curly hair (Fig. 183) and as far as we can judge they do not correspond to the busts visible in the nineteenth-century photographs, and which were still present in the 1930s at the time of the restoration. The left-hand bust was then a man in antique attire with a fibula on his right shoulder, and to the right was a woman looking upwards. Neither had a pedestal, and each was rounded at the bottom in order to fit into the curved niche (Text ill. 140).

These works, which are not carved but plaster casts, are now part of the Rubenshuis collection. The man is taken to be a *Bust of Cicero* (Text ill. 141) and the woman, reduced to a head by the removal of her (added) shoulders, is thought to be the fragment of a Niobe (Text ill. 142).[30] It is not clear when these two plaster casts were made, but it is certainly doubtful that these unrelated figures formed part of Rubens's design for the garden pavilion.[31] Besides, there are no indications that they should be regarded as inventions of Rubens and they have therefore not been included in the Catalogue.

is now being restored, see ibid., pp. 97–100). A simplified version, dated 1677, can be seen in the second court of the Osterrieth House on the Meir (Van Aerschot, ed., *Bouwen / Antwerpen*, 1979, p. 119 [not illustrated]; photo ACL B139446: or see URL: https://ney.partners/project/glazed-roofs-osterrieth-house/).

30. Anonymous artist, *Bust of Cicero*, inv. no. RH.B.025, plaster, H. 71.4 cm; Anonymous artist, *Head of a Woman* (fragment of a Niobe?), inv. no. RH.B.026, plaster on a stone socle, H. 64 cm.

31. Jeffrey Muller assumed that they belonged to Rubens's collection and he included them in his catalogue (Muller, *Collector*, 1989, p. 152, under cat. III, no. 8, p. 155, cat. III, nos 23–24, pl 139–140, as 'Anonymous early modern master in imitation of ancient sculpture'). According to him, the presence of Cicero may be explained by the fact that 'Rubens followed his advice in the decoration of his garden' (ibid., p. 33). On ancient originals which may have served as examples for these busts, see ibid., p. 33, nn. 41–42.

CHAPTER X - THE GARDEN PAVILION

Text ill. 141. Anonymous artist, *Bust of Cicero*, plaster. Antwerp, Rubenshuis.

Text ill. 142. Anonymous artist, *Head of a Woman (Niobe?)*, plaster. Antwerp, Rubenshuis.

The Statues in the Seventeenth Century

There is no consensus in the literature on the full-length statues placed by Rubens in his garden pavilion. The visual sources at our disposal – *The Walk in the Garden*, showing how the building might have appeared in c. 1630, the Berlin double portrait of c. 1655 and the prints by Harrewijn of 1684 and 1692 – are limited and allow us to reconstruct only partly what statues could be seen in the garden pavilion in the seventeenth century (Figs 181–182, 188 and 190, 195–196, 205–206, 212). Moreover, and this needs emphasis, it does not follow that the available information provides much clarity about the situation before 1640.

In the seventeenth-century pictorial records the following can be seen: in the niche at the top was a youth with cornucopia; below in the centre there was a Hercules (not present in *The Walk in the Garden*), and between the columns to the right, a Bacchus, with Venus to the left (not in view in the double portrait). Different versions of each statue can be seen among these images, and one figure, the Bacchus, does not fully correspond with the statue that was displayed in the pavilion in the nineteenth century, and which still stands there today.

The Statues after 1692

The eighteenth century is completely blank for information about the statues in the garden pavilion. Not even a single image survives for the period between the Harrewijn prints and the pictorial documents from the nineteenth century.

309

CHAPTER X - THE GARDEN PAVILION

Eighteenth-century written sources are also extremely scarce and from their very summary nature we can learn nothing. Documents connected with the sale or lease of the property tell us that there were statues in the house and garden, but the information is only general and gives no indication of their subject.[32] Nor can we gain anything concrete from the notes of Jacob Van der Sanden and François Mols, both of whom visited Rubens's house in about 1760. In his *Het Oud Konst-toneel*, Van der Sanden states that the summer house was a splendid structure built against the yard of the arquebusiers, from hewn stone and with appropriate statues ('het Zomerhuys tegen den Colveniers Hof groots was gebouwd met uytgehouwen Steen en toepassende Beldwerken') (Appendix I.42: [2]). Mols mentions the pavilion (as 'pavillon ouvert'), but not the statues, which were certainly standing there (Appendix I.43: [9]). It should be observed that besides the 'cariatides' that were part of the pavilion, Mols says absolutely nothing about sculpture in Rubens's house or garden, whether statues, busts or decorative elements such as the remarkable satyrs on the portico.

In the nineteenth century four statues were standing in the pavilion: the youth in the roof niche, the monumental Hercules, a Bacchus, and on the left-hand side not a Venus but a Ceres. For the authenticity of the statues, opinions recorded in the literature vary a great deal. In his Rubens monograph of 1840, Victor Van Grimbergen writes about the substantial alterations that the house underwent after 1763. Talking about the garden pavilion, he remarks that it had also lost a great many of its decorations both inside and out ('ook vele van zijne in- en uit-wendige cieraden'). He mentions three statues made by Lucas Faydherbe (1617–1697), two of which stood between the columns, and which have now been replaced by others ('thans door andere vervangen zijn'), while a third, a Hercules, had survived.[33] He does not talk about the figure in the roof niche. So, according to Van Grimbergen, Faydherbe was responsible for the three original statues, something to which we will return in the next chapter, and in the Catalogue (Nos 37–38, 40). The source of his information is not known.

Van Grimbergen's assertions are repeated almost word-for-word by Augustin Thys in 1893.[34] Frans Jos Van den Branden and Max Rooses knew the four statues that could be seen in the garden pavilion, but these authors tell us nothing that

---

32. A lease contract of 1707 mentions 'in de hof 3 losse beelden' (3 separate statues in the garden) (Appendix I.39); the announcement of the auction in 1755 describes only 'de figueren, pedestaelen […] in den hof" (the figures, pedestals […] in the garden) (Appendix I.40) In both cases we should be aware of the possibility that the statues listed were not those in the pavilion, but perhaps others standing somewhere in the garden itself.
33. Van Grimbergen, *Rubens*, 1840, p. 387, n. 10.
34. Thys, *Historiek der straten*, 1893, p. 429. Nothing is said about the statues in the passage about the Rubens House in the earlier (French) edition (id., *Historique*, 1873, pp. 344–358).

we cannot deduce from the earliest photographs.[35] To neither did it occur that the original sculptures might have been replaced by more recent works.

In the first more substantial study of Rubens's house in 1933, Ary Delen repeats the information provided by Van Grimbergen and Thys, which he incorporates without questioning it. According to him, the original statues – he does not name them or say how many there were – 'which were attributed to Faydherbe' had been replaced by others.[36]

The Statue of Ceres (No. R4; Fig. 235)

The appearance – certainly no later than the beginning of the nineteenth century – in the garden pavilion of a figure of Ceres in the position previously occupied by Venus (on the evidence of *The Walk in the Garden* and the second Harrewijn print), introduced ambiguity and a fair amount of confusion about the statues of the gods (Figs 182–183). The Ceres statue was removed during the restoration of the house in the 1930s and can no longer be traced. On several photographs, however, it can be seen in some detail, so we know fairly well what it looked like.

We can only guess why and when the seventeenth-century statue of Venus was replaced by a Ceres. The earliest known representation of the Ceres in the pavilion is in the painting by Philippe van Brée, *Rubens Painting in his Garden*, dated 1833 (Appendix III.42). The date of this swap can therefore not be narrowed down more closely than to a period of nearly a century and a half, between 1692 (the print by Harrewijn) and 1833.

On the basis of its style, we can rule out the possibility that the lost statue of Ceres came from Rubens's time. The idea that it could go back to an invention by Rubens must certainly be dismissed, and therefore it is placed among rejected works in the Catalogue. It is totally un-Rubensian and it differs from other representations of Ceres found in Rubens's work.

During the restoration of the house this discussion degenerated into a full-scale row about the question 'Venus or Ceres?' (see below), in which, finally, and in our opinion justifiably, Venus's supporters were victorious. But questions should certainly be asked about what happened afterwards. The Ceres which had stood in position for at least a century, was removed from the pavilion

---

35. In the pavilion, Van den Branden saw 'de forsche Hercules [...] tusschen Ceres en Bacchus, en daarboven zag men, in de gevelnis, eene halfnaakte maagd met den overvloedshoorn in den arm' (the mighty Hercules [...] between Ceres and Bacchus, and above, in the roof niche, you could see a semi-nude virgin holding the cornucopia in her arm) (Van den Branden, *Schilderschool*, 1883, p. 508). Rooses describes: 'une statue d'Hercule, à droite et à gauche, entre les colonnettes, les statues de Bacchus et Cérès; dans une lucarne élevée, formant niche, une statue de l'Abondance' (Rooses, *Oeuvre*, 1886–92, V, p. 186).
36. Delen, *Rubens' huis*, 1933, p. 54. In 1940 he again wrote, without naming Faydherbe, that the original statues (which he does not specify) had long since disappeared (id., *Rubens' huis*, 1940, p. 36).

CHAPTER X - THE GARDEN PAVILION

and 'disappeared' into private hands.³⁷ Moreover, its replacement was no more Rubensian: it was a newly carved figure, based not on one of the Venus types seen in *The Walk in the Garden* or the Harrewijn print, but on an original design by the Antwerp sculptor Willy Kreitz (1903–1982) (cf. Figs 182–183 and Fig. 177).³⁸

We should note that the decision to choose Venus rather than Ceres is still not generally accepted as correct. Some authors still maintain that the figure placed in his pavilion by Rubens was Ceres and not Venus (see below and under No. R4).

Short Chronological Summary of the Statues Appearing in the Pictorial Sources, and as Found in Situ at the Time of the Restoration

For the sake of clarity, a summary of what can be found in connection with the statues in the available pictorial documentation is given here. In simple terms the following years serve to provide a dating: c. 1630 (*The Walk in the Garden*; Figs 182, 196, 205, 210), c. 1655 (the Berlin double portrait; Figs 181, 208), 1684 (Harrewijn print; Fig. 180), 1692 (Harrewijn print; Figs 183, 195, 206), 1860 (the earliest photographs; Appendix III.50–52), 1938 (beginning of restoration work). It needs to be emphasised that the earliest image, *The Walk in the Garden*, shows a situation which may deviate from reality in some respects.

The following can be registered according to location:

a) in the niche at the top: consistently, to the present, a youth with cornucopia (sometimes only partly visible);
b) against the rear wall: c. 1630: a door frame with a bust of a bearded man above (probably Hercules); c. 1655 and 1684: a full-length Hercules; 1692: not visible; 1860 and to the present day: full-length Hercules (of the same type as in c. 1655);
c) front left: c. 1630 a nude Venus; c. 1655: not visible; 1684 and 1692: a Venus with Amor; 1860 until 1938: a Ceres with sheaf of corn; after 1943 to present: a modern Venus by Willy Kreitz;
d) front right: c. 1630: a nude youth with legs crossed, probably Bacchus; c. 1655: Bacchus with patera (shown in reverse); 1684 and 1692: Bacchus with patera; 1860 to present: Bacchus with bunches of grapes.

---

37. No trace of the Ceres can be found in the Antwerp municipal collections.
38. White stone, c. 200 cm; executed in 1943, and installed in the pavilion in 1947 (see Fig. 177); Van Ruyssevelt – Somers, *Kreitz*, 1998, p. 155, no. 132/3e, repr.); in 1940–1943, Kreitz produced a great deal of other work for the Rubens House, including bas-reliefs for the 'frieze' of the studio façades, and decorations for the monumental staircase (ibid., pp. 152–157, no. 132). Previously, in 1940, he had made a new Ceres statue of his own design (which did not end up in the Rubens House); ibid., pp. 152–154, fig. p. 153; De Clercq, *Moulages*, 2012, pp. 9–11).

CHAPTER X - THE GARDEN PAVILION

We should add that the presence of the same or a related statue type in these images does not imply that we are talking about the same object throughout the centuries. For the *Youth with Cornucopia* and the *Bacchus*, it is possible that at some point copies, either identical or with variations, have been installed to replace older works.

	Top niche	Rear wall	Front left	Front right
c. 1630	Youth with cornucopia (partly concealed, but cornucopia visible)	Door frame and bust of bearded man (Hercules?) – possibly fictive	Nude Venus (possibly fictive)	Nude youth with legs crossed (possibly fictive)
c. 1655	Youth with cornucopia (bottom part visible)	Hercules, full length, with garland	[not visible]	Bacchus with patera (in reverse)
1684	Youth with cornucopia (tiny)	Hercules, full length (tiny)	Venus and Amor (tiny)	Bacchus (tiny)
1692	Youth with cornucopia	Garland [statue hidden]	Venus and Amor	Bacchus with patera
1860 – 1938	Youth with cornucopia (current figure)	Hercules, full length (current figure)	Ceres with sheaf of corn	Bacchus with bunches of grapes (current figure)
1943 – **present**	Youth with cornucopia (current figure)	Hercules, full length (current figure)	Modern Venus	Bacchus with bunches of grapes (current figure)

Floris Prims's Interpretation: A 'Small Rustic Temple'

As we have seen, not everyone agreed with the view of the Venus supporters, nor, of course, with the switch-over of the goddesses during the restoration. The most strongly worded plea in favour of Ceres came from Floris Prims, who called the Venus replacement a 'capital error' which did not do justice to Rubens. He wrote a lengthy justification for the choice of Ceres, which was based on the conviction that Venus does not fit into the iconographic concept of the pavilion, which, according to him, represented 'a small rustic temple'. In what he believed to be Rubens's original choice of gods, Prims saw a coherent iconographic programme connected with fertility and nature, to which, in his view, Venus did not belong.[39]

This is an argument which evidently loses all credibility if we remember what we know from the 1692 print by Harrewijn, namely that in the seventeenth century a Venus certainly did occupy this position, thus before a Ceres was placed there. For Prims, who is determined to see a Ceres in the garden pavilion, this fact is no obstacle, because he does not interpret Hillewerve's statue as a nude Venus, but as a 'well draped' Ceres,[40] an untenable identification. In fact the piece of drapery behind the statue forms no part of it; it is the lower part of the cloak of the clergyman (probably Hillewerve) seated at the table. Prims makes no mention of the small Amor with arrow who stands beside his mother.

In his interpretation of the four statues Prims also makes the mistake of assuming that the figure in the roof niche is a female rather than a youthful male. He believed that she represents Ops, the Roman 'deity of the earth's fertility'. Finally, the presence of Hercules can only be accounted for by a far-fetched explanation of how he fits the proposed programme: according to Prims, Hercules is an agricultural god, protector of cornfields.

Interpretations since Prims

The notion that the figure in the roof niche is a female identifiable as Abundantia (assumed by Rooses) or Ops, a deity of the fertility of the earth (proposed by Prims), has been dismissed, and with good reason. It is undoubtedly a male figure, who has been seen, for example, as Honos or *Genius Loci* (see under No. 36). Despite the rejection of the impossible identification as Ops, certain authors have illogically held to the interpretation of the garden pavilion as a small rustic temple, in which Ops would logically play an essential role. This argument builds on Prims's mistaken identification of the gods on the ground

---

39. Prims, *Prieel van Rubens*, 1948, pp. 141–142; see also id., *Rubenshuis*, 1946.
40. Id., *Prieel van Rubens*, 1948, p. 141.

level, maintaining the belief that Ceres was the original statue and so rejecting Venus.[41]

Barbara Uppenkamp and Ben van Beneden also promote the idea of Ceres. They see the figure in the Harrewijn print as Ceres rather than Venus, and wrongly observe that Ceres is accompanied by a putto 'as in the St Petersburg painting', referring to Rubens's *Homage to Ceres* (Appendix III.13; Fig. 23).[42] However, the stone statue of Ceres in that painting is not 'accompanied by a putto' – six putti are decorating the niche with garlands of fruit – and the fact that in Hillewerve's print the child is clearly holding up an arrow is ignored. Assuming that the original figure was a Ceres, the authors expand on the possibility that the other statue does not represent Bacchus, but Ceres's son, Liber; they also make a connection with the Latin motto 'Sine Cerere et Baccho friget Venus'. Leaving aside the identity of the goddess, the authors offer a conclusion that nonetheless has some validity: 'A Hercules flanked by Bacchus and Ceres indicates that the garden was devoted to both the virtuous Stoic concept of leisure and the appropriate pleasures and joys, thereby expressing a balanced philosophy of life.'[43]

Similar explanations based on connecting such concepts as the garden, nature and fertility, recur often in the literature, but there are also explanations of a different kind. For example it has been suggested that in the four statues, Rubens sought to express the idea that labour (Hercules) leads to fertility (Bacchus and Ceres) and honour (the youthful male), something 'highly appropriate to Rubens's industrious and successful career'.[44] Rebus-like constructions such as this naturally remain no more than speculation.

Lastly it should be added that no simple and conclusive alternative can be offered as a 'reading' of the four free-standing statues. In the Catalogue the identification of the youthful male with cornucopia (No. 36) is discussed in more detail, as well as the possible meaning of the imposing Hercules figure in the context of the garden pavilion (No. 40). It is, however, reasonable to ask if an interpretation that links the four statues is really necessary. Indeed, it is far from certain that all elements of this sculptural scheme were placed in the pavilion at the same time, which brings us to the question of the makers of the statues and to their dating, a matter that will be considered in the following chapter.

---

41. This interpretation, the garden pavilion as a rural temple (with a Ceres), was followed by Baudouin, *Cat. Antwerp, Rubenshuis*, 1974, under no. 23; id., *Summary Guide*, 1977, p. 29; id., *Rubens House*, 1977, p. 183; id., *Rubens House*, 2005, p. 177; Tijs regards Ceres as 'possibly the original statue' (Tijs, *Rubens en Jordaens*, 1984, ill. p. 234); on the Venus – Ceres question, see also De Clercq, *Moulages*, 2012, pp. 7–10.
42. Uppenkamp – Van Beneden, *Architectural Symbolism*, 2011, p. 121.
43. Ibid., p. 121.
44. Baudouin, *Cat. Antwerp, Rubenshuis*, 1974, under no. 23; id., *Summary Guide*, 1977, p. 29; id., *Rubens House*, 1977, p. 183; id., *Rubens House*, 2005, p. 177; others that follow this include Zita Stutz: 'ein arbeitsames und tugendhaft geführtes Leben führt zu Wohlstand und Ehre' (Stutz, *Residenz*, 1985, p. 142).

CHAPTER X - THE GARDEN PAVILION

D. *The Serliana*

At the time of its construction, in about 1618, or a few years earlier, Rubens's garden pavilion was one of the rare examples in the Low Countries of a building incorporating a *serliana*: a central round arch, flanked either side by a horizontal lintel or architrave supported by columns. This architectural motif is named after Sebastiano Serlio, who was the first to promote it. In his *Regole generali di architettura*, the fourth in a series of treatises published in Venice in 1537, he included illustrations of six façades incorporating one or more *serlianas* (Text ill. 143).[45]

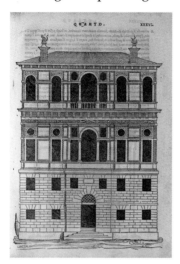

Text ill. 143. Sebastiano Serlio, *A Façade* ('with Serliana's') in the 4th volume of his *Regole generali di architettura*, 1537.

The motif first occurred in classical Antiquity and became popular again during the Italian Renaissance, in painting as well as in architecture.[46] One of the best known examples is the Basilica in Vicenza, with Palladio's two-storeyed loggia, constructed from a series of *serlianas*, which was begun about 1550 (Text ill. 144).[47]

In the Low Countries the motif had certainly become known through Serlio's treatises, which were available in Italian editions as well as in Pieter Coecke's Dutch translation.[48] Examples are known but these are rare, whether in painting,[49] or architecture.[50]

---

45. Hart – Hicks, *Serlio*, 1996, ill. pp. 307, 311, 313, 315, 335, 337. A second early and striking example of the motif – possibly inspired by Serlio's Book V (on temple architecture), and which can also be connected with Rubens – can be found in the lantern of the bell tower of Antwerp's Church of St Carolus Borromeus (Fabri – Lombaerde, *Jesuit Church (CRLB)*, 2018, p. 206, figs 133–135, 139–142).
46. For a full discussion of the motif in Antiquity and in the Renaissance, see De Jonge, *Travée alternée*, 1986; see also the chapter on the *serliana* in Worsley, *Inigo Jones*, 2007, pp. 37–182; specifically in connection with Rubens: Uppenkamp – Van Beneden, *Vera simmetria*, 2011, pp. 66–73.
47. Heydenreich – Lotz, *Architecture*, 1974, pp. 310–311, fig. 334; see also URL: https://nl.wikipedia.org/wiki/Basilica_Palladiana#/media/Bestand:Basilica_Palladiana_(Vicenza)_-_facade_on_Piazza_dei_signori.jpg.
48. For editions of Serlio's treatises, see Chapter IV, pp. 120–121, n. 16 and Chapter IX, p. 292, n. 127.
49. Fairly soon after the publication of Coecke's translation of Serlio's *Libri*, *serlianas* appear in the background of paintings by Pieter Aertsen (1503–1575) and Joachim Beuckelaer (c. 1530–1573); see Lunsingh Scheurleer, *Aertsen*, 1947, pp. 123–134; Buys, *Maria en Martha*, 1989, pp. 93–128.
50. The only early example of a *serliana* we can point to in architecture in the Netherlands is the impressive choir screen in the cathedral of Tournai, designed in 1570 by Cornelis Floris de Vriendt (1513–1575), and completed in 1574 (Steppe, *Koordoksaal*, 1952, pp. 260–274, fig. 92). Two other examples are sometimes presented as early *serlianas*, but they are less convincing and in any case they differ from Serlio's illustrations: the balcony of the palace in Breda, 1536 (Worsley, *Inigo Jones*, 2007, p. 143, fig. 170; Uppenkamp – Van Beneden, *Vera Simmetria*, 2011, pp. 66–67, n. 98) and the central bay of the Antwerp Town Hall, 1560–1564 (e.g. Steppe, *ibid.*, p. 268).

CHAPTER X - THE GARDEN PAVILION

Text ill. 144. Palladio, Basilica, Vicenza, detail.

We can assume that Rubens, like others, knew the *serliana* motif before he departed for Italy in 1600. But rather than Serlio's writings, it seems *likely* that his inspiration for using the motif for his garden pavilion came from seeing numerous sixteenth-century *serlianas* in Italy. Without question, an important source of inspiration for Rubens was the work of Giulio Romano (1499–1546), who introduced *serlianas* both in his paintings and his designs for architecture. We should especially mention the architecture he directed in Mantua, the city where Rubens spent most time while in Italy. The *serliana* features prominently in the Palazzo Te (c. 1527–1530) as well as in parts of the Palazzo Ducale (1536–1540).[51]

Rubens's familiarity with Giulio Romano's designs for architecture emerges from Giulio's drawing in the Albertina in Vienna, which shows a design for a monumental gateway, with loggia above, which was possibly never realised (Text ill. 145).[52] This loggia was crowned by a variant of the *serliana*, using a so-called Syrian arch, a segmental arch which itself supports a triangular pediment. Rubens must have known this invention in some form or other, since a very closely related motif can be seen in the rustic building in the background of his Italianate *Dancing Peasants and Mythological Figures* in the Prado, Madrid (Text ill. 146).[53]

---

51. See the garden façade, Palazzo del Te (Hartt, *Giulio Romano*, 1958, I, pp. 99–101; II, figs 158–160; Carpeggiani – Tellini Perina, *Giulio Romano*, 1987, pp. 47 ff., esp. figs 22–24); the loggetta in the Palazzo Ducale (Hartt, *Giulio Romano*, 1958, I, p. 169; II, fig. 355).
52. *Design for a Loggia with Rustic Portal*, Vienna, Albertina, Grafische Sammlung, inv. no. 1284: Hartt, *Giulio Romano*, 1958, I, pp. 253, 308, no. 364; II, fig. 525.
53. Madrid, Museo Nacional del Prado, inv. no. P001691; Díaz Padrón, *Cat. Madrid, Prado (Pintura flamenca)*, 1995, II, pp. 988–991, no. 1691; Büttner, *Genre Scenes (CRLB)*, 2019, pp. 215–230, fig. 150. On this borrowing from Giulio Romano, see Baudouin, *Architecturale Motieven*, 2006, pp. 203–206, figs 3–5; Uppenkamp – Van Beneden, *Vera simmetria*, 2011, p. 68, figs 84–85, no. 5; Büttner, ibid., p. 223.

CHAPTER X - THE GARDEN PAVILION

Text ill. 145. Giulio Romano, *Design for a Loggia with Rustic Portal*, drawing. Vienna, Albertina, Grafische Sammlung.

Text ill. 146. Rubens, *Dancing Peasants and Mythological Figures*, detail. Madrid, Museo Nacional del Prado.

Similarly, Rubens must have seen important examples of the *serliana* in the palaces and villas he visited in Rome. The motif features in the imposing garden façade of the Villa Medici (1576–1587) (Text ill. 72) (as well as in two structures that stand in its gardens: the Loggia di Cleopatra, a garden pavilion (Text ill. 147), and the Loggia del Bosco (or del Grotto), constructed underneath a terrace with balustrade.[54]

Another example in Rome can be found in the Villa Giulia, an elaborate building commissioned by Pope Julius III (1487–1555), construction of which began in 1551. As Anthony Blunt observed, Rubens's garden pavilion 'is closely reminiscent of that of the nymphaeum in the same villa' (cf. Fig. 177 and Text ill. 148).[55] The graceful central archway, flanked by architraves that rest on elegant, slender columns, as well as the round niches in the spandrels, are indeed very like elements found in the Antwerp pavilion.

One distinctive aspect of the *serlianas* in the Roman examples mentioned is that, just as in Rubens's house, the motif forms part of an architectural scheme which is closely connected with a garden. Giles Worsley, however, suggests a quite different meaning. He describes in detail how the *serliana* belongs to 'the architecture of sovereignty', or is an attribute of 'Majestas', but it seems that

---

54. For the first, see Toulier, *Villa Médicis*, I, 1989, pp. 466 ff., fig. 710; for the second, see ibid., pp. 439 ff., fig. 654. The two small buildings attracted the attention of Diego Velázquez, who reproduced them in two of his small landscapes (Madrid, Museo Nacional del Prado; ibid., ill. [p. 17], figs 226–227: López Rey, *Velázquez*, 1979, pp. 297–300, nos 46–47, illustrated).

55. Blunt, *Rubens and Architecture*, 1977, p. 613; Coffin, *Villa*, 1988, pp. 157–158, fig. 103; see also Uppenkamp – Van Beneden, *Vera simmetria*, 2011, p. 46, fig. 48.

CHAPTER X - THE GARDEN PAVILION

Text ill. 147. Rome, Villa Medici, Loggia di Cleopatra.

Text ill. 148. Rome, Villa Giulia, detail: upper part of the Nymphaeum.

the Italian 'garden' examples cited above do not quite carry this symbolism.[56] And so it cannot be taken for granted that the *serliana* of Rubens's pavilion was designed to emphasise the elevated status of Hercules, whose figure stands against the rear wall.[57] That view relies on too narrow an interpretation of the motif. Furthermore, as was explained above, it is possible that Rubens did not initially plan to have a statue of Hercules in the pavilion, but had the impressive statue made only later, in the 1630s.

---

56. Worsley, *Inigo Jones*, 2007, pp. 123–155.
57. As stated in Uppenkamp – Van Beneden, *Architectural Symbolism*, 2011, pp. 83–84; Van Beneden, *Portiek en tuinpaviljoen*, 2019, pp. 18–19. For Rubens's use of the Serlian motif in painting, see also De Staelen, *Rubens*, 2014, pp. 244–246.

Chapter XI
Sculpture and Sculptors

A. *Sculptural Decoration*

Sculptural decorations – figures carved in high relief, busts and full-length statues in the round – have already been mentioned in the sections dedicated to different parts of the house, the studio façades, the portico and the garden pavilion. Not all of these ornaments were necessarily carved in stone. Some of the reliefs decorating the façades and interior of the house may have been executed in stucco, while some of the free-standing sculptures may have been cast in plaster.

From early on, and through to the end of his life, Rubens would undoubtedly have enlisted the help of sculptors to embellish his house in a range of other ways. For example, to provide chimney pieces, doors, door frames, interior niches and other decorative elements, about which we know very little indeed, for almost everything was lost when the original interior was dismantled, including sculptural decoration.[1]

It is possible that remnants of the original interior decoration were still in place above a doorway in 1938: a head of Hercules below a shell, with garlands either side (Fig. 131). However, we must be careful how we approach these elements, since they cannot easily be dated, and some may in fact be later than the seventeenth century (see under No. 23).

A number of chimney pieces were probably ornamented with carving. A fireplace of a type that may well have been present in Rubens's house, featuring caryatids in the form of herms, can be seen in Van Diepenbeeck's drawing of *William Cavendish and his Family Seated in Front of a Fireplace in Rubens's House* (Appendix III.28–29; see also Text ill. 19).[2]

An intriguing 'Rubensian' chimney piece of another type needs to be mentioned in this context: a richly decorated piece of monumental proportions, sculpted in black and white marble and with ram's heads on its cheeks, in the Grand Hall of Mentmore, a mansion built between 1852 and 1854 in the neo-Jacobean style (Text ill. 149). This imposing chimney piece is said to have been

---

1. A list, drawn up by Annika Devroe, of elements that were probably part of the original interior and which can be seen in the present Rubenshuis, includes two doors with sculpted panels (Devroe, *Rubens' huis*, 2008, I, pp. 77, 79, figs 40, 43) as well a number of undecorated chimney pieces (ibid., I, pp. 78–80, figs 41–42, 44–45).
2. For the frequent use of herms in Rubens's work, see Lombaerde, *Rubens / Vredeman de Vries*, 2018, pp. 117–127; see also under No. 4.

CHAPTER XI - SCULPTURE AND SCULPTORS

Text ill. 149. The so-called Rubens Chimney piece. Mentmore (Buckinghamshire), Mentmore Towers.

designed by Rubens for his house, although there are no grounds for this claim. Its date is difficult to determine (second half of the seventeenth century or later?), and all we know about its provenance is that it was bought 'on the continent' around 1840–1850.[3]

As mentioned in previous chapters, architectural elements of Rubens's house appear in his painted oeuvre in a range of settings, for example in certain scenes from the *Life of Maria de' Medici* (Appendix III.18, 19 and 20; Text ill. 135 and Fig. 24) as well as *The Discovery of Erichthonius by the Daughters of Cecrops* (Appendix III.23; Text ill. 138) and *The Supper at Emmaus* (Appendix III.30).[4] It seems likely that his work contains further reminiscences of decorative sculpture from the house, but which we fail to recognise because the originals are unknown. A case in point is the intricate shell motif with small garland that appears above the back of Lars Porsenna's throne in *The Fortitude of Scaevola* (Budapest, Szépművészeti Múzeum), an interesting detail copied probably by Willem Panneels (Text ill. 150).[5] Such a motif could have been an actual mural decoration in Rubens's house. There is no immediate evidence to confirm this, but a similar arrangement can be seen in a *kunstkamer* (art gallery) painting by Van Haecht: as part of an overdoor in which the shell motif (of a simpler kind) frames a niche containing the familiar bust of 'pseudo-Seneca' that belonged to Rubens (Text ill. 151).[6]

3. Mentmore Towers, Mentmore (Buckinghamshire), was built by Mayer de Rothschild (1818–1874) to house his art collection; see, for the so-called 'Rubens chimney piece': *L'estampille*, April 1977, no. 85, p. 32, ill. p. 31.
4. See also the list given in the Appendix III.
5. For the painting, which is lost but known from, for example, a studio version in Budapest, see McGrath, *History (CRLB)*, 1997, I, fig. 163; II, no. 46. For the drawing, see anonymous seventeenth-century artist (Willem Panneels?), Copenhagen, Statens Museum for Kunst, Kongelige Kobberstiksamling, Rubens Cantoor, no. VI, 100; black chalk, 217 × 312 mm (ibid., II, p. 233, under no. 46, copy 10).
6. The niche, with a garland either side, crowns the round arch of a doorway in Willem van Haecht's *Picture Gallery* at the Isle of Bute (Scotland), Mount Stuart, Collection of the Marquess of Bute (Appendix III.31). It is possible, however, that Van Haecht borrowed the motif from Rubens's *Mucius Scaevola* composition (a version of which appears in the same *kunstkamer*).

CHAPTER XI - SCULPTURE AND SCULPTORS

Text ill. 150. ? Willem Panneels after Rubens, *Niche with Scallop and Bust*, drawing. Copenhagen, Statens Museum for Kunst, Kongelige Kobberstiksamling.

Text ill. 151. Detail of Appendix III.31: a niche with the bust of the pseudo-Seneca.

Naturally, in this chapter we will only look at sculptures that formed part of the decoration of Rubens's house and garden in some way or other, and not the 'separate' sculptures of various types and sizes that belonged to his art collection. Besides antique sculptures and statuettes carved in ivory and other materials, Jeffrey Muller's list of Rubens's sculpture collection includes twelve free-standing pieces: four busts and eight full-length statues.[7]

When it comes to separate works, it is of course not always clear if they were intended to be a permanent part of the decoration or were portable objects, which perhaps even in Rubens's time were occasionally moved around within the property. This problem arises in particular with the busts, which – with the exception of precious antique works – could in theory be placed anywhere inside the house, but also in the niches of the façades, portico or garden pavilion.

Besides the above-mentioned head of Hercules over a doorway, the only free-standing sculptures found at the house in the nineteenth century – not necessarily stemming from Rubens's time – were the five busts in the niches of the portico and garden pavilion, as well as four full-length statues in the pavilion, and a reclining dog.

The seventeenth-century visual sources for the sculptural elements are by no means easy to interpret, as emerges from the table provided for the statues of the garden pavilion.[8] It is doubtful, for example, that everything shown in *The Walk in the Garden* (Fig. 25) really existed. On the other hand, the Harrewijn prints (Figs 17–18), which in our opinion are a reliable source, include elements

---

7. Muller, *Collector*, 1989, pp. 145–146 (works offered for sale listed in the *Specification*), 150–155 (Cat. III).
8. See Chapter X, p. 313.

CHAPTER XI - SCULPTURE AND SCULPTORS

that were not part of the house in 1640. This is true, of course, for the religious sculptures that Hillewerve placed in his chapel, a Madonna and a St Joseph, but also for the reclining dog and the fountain with a bagpiper in the courtyard.[9] In particular the two statues on top of the portico (Nos R1–R2; Figs 227–228, 231) present considerable problems in terms of dating, a matter discussed in detail in Chapter IX and in the Catalogue.

Whatever the truth, examination of these images (*The Walk in the Garden* and the prints by Harrewijn) reveals elements that had disappeared from the house and garden by the nineteenth century, and these have been discussed in previous chapters: the two statues above the portico (which had in the meantime been provided with an extra storey); a carved staircase; all but one of the 'real' busts decorating the façades and the 'antiquarium'; a Venus in the garden pavilion as well as two putti on the top. There was also no trace of a fountain, whether with putto and dolphin or with a bagpiper.

We can assume that Rubens designed, if not all, then at least some of the sculptural decorations for the house and garden himself. But in the absence of preparatory drawings or sketches, or any other indications, this remains a problematical subject. It is therefore difficult to determine which sculptures – surviving or lost (but known from pictorial sources) – merit inclusion in the Catalogue.

The dating of this disparate and fragmentary material, for which no archival sources are available, must remain a matter of speculation. Assuming that the sculptural decorations that form an integral part of the architecture were created at the same time as the house, it is logical to follow the hypothetical dating of the building to which each element belongs. For the portico this date is c. 1618, and for the studio façades c. 1616 (?); this date can also be used as an approximation for the free-standing busts of the north façade.

Naturally, it is possible that in later years, in the 1620s and 1630s, the house or parts of its decoration were altered or extended. This certainly seems to be the case with the statues of the pavilion, or at least some of them: by referring to the known pictorial documentation, as well as using stylistic analysis, we can deduce that the statues do not all date from the same time, and that some must have been installed later. An obvious case is the monumental Hercules (No. 40; Fig. 211), which clearly dates from much later than 1618, the approximate date given to the pavilion. A more plausible dating for this statue is in the 1630s (see below).

---

9. For the dog and the bagpiper fountain, see Chapter III, pp. 114–116.

B. The Sculptors

We have already established that, apart from the contract for building the staircase, dated 2 November 1616, and Rubens's witness statement about the construction of the roof in 1615 (see Appendix I.9 and 14), there are no known archival documents that throw any light on the artists, workmen and suppliers employed by Rubens in building his house. We learn the name of a joiner and a slater. Of the artists who were involved in one way or another in the decoration of the house, only one is named: the sculptor Hans van Mildert (1588–1638).

It thus remains an important question which other sculptors might have contributed work to Rubens's house, whether in the form of free-standing statues, or sculptural elements integrated into the architecture. Making an attribution on stylistic grounds is very complicated, and not just for the lost sculpture. Those pieces that survive often present problems because of varying degrees of weathering or other damage.

Two sculptors have already been mentioned in previous chapters, Hans van Mildert and Lucas Faydherbe (1617–1697). Both are important figures who worked closely with Rubens, and they will be discussed in this chapter at greater length. It is reasonable to ask, however, if these were the only artists involved in work on Rubens's house. There were certainly other sculptors active in Antwerp who are known to have been in contact with Rubens.

For example, the very productive [Colyns] de Nole family of sculptors had various members who collaborated on several occasions with Rubens: Jan (or Hans) (before 1570–1624), his brother Robrecht (before 1570–1636), assisted by his nephew Andries (1598–1638), one of Jan's sons.[10] However, given that this collaboration did not always go well, it is perhaps rather unlikely that Rubens would have called on them to work on his house.[11]

In order to attribute the statues in the garden pavilion, some of which can be dated to the 1630s, it seems useful to look at which sculptors, besides Van Mildert and the De Noles, would have been capable of carving life-size statues in stone to Rubens's designs at the time. Some indication is given by the accounts for

---

10. We are well informed about their work thanks to the comprehensive study by Marguerite Casteels (Casteels, *De Nole*, 1961). An idea of the level of skill of the De Nole workshop can be gained from the statues of the apostles placed against the pillars of the nave in the Cathedral of St Rumbold in Mechelen in the 1630s, one of the most important sculpture series in the Southern Netherlands (Leyssens, *Apostelbeelden*, 1942, pp. 49–64; Casteels, *ibid.*, pp. 174–178, figs 75–88). On Rubens and the De Nole workshop, see Fabri – Lombaerde, *Jesuit Church (CRLB)*, 2018, pp. 105–108, and passim.
11. That relations between Rubens and the De Noles were strained emerges from a letter of 1614 to the Archduke Albert concerning the high altar for the Ghent Cathedral of St Bavo. In this letter, without naming the sculptors, Rubens makes negative remarks about their design. We know that he is referring to the De Noles because of the contracts drawn up between them and the cathedral (Herremans, *Architectural Sculpture (CRLB)*, 2019, nos 1–1a and App. II).

CHAPTER XI - SCULPTURE AND SCULPTORS

expenditure on the triumphal arches and stages made for the *Pompa Introitus Ferdinandi* in 1635. From the records of payments we know the names of the sculptors of the twelve over-life-size stone statues of emperors that were made to be installed in the colonnades of *The Portico of the Emperors* (Text ill. 62).[12] If we leave aside Van Mildert, who played an important role in the commission for the *Pompa Introitus* (see below), the accounts name a further five sculptors in connection with the lost emperor statues. Works have survived by two of these, Huibrecht van den Eynde (1594–1661) and Sebastiaan de Neve (1612–1676), meaning that we can form an idea of their artistry.[13] Three others are known only from archival documents: Jenin Veldenaar or Veldener (1607–1655), Forcy Cardon (master in 1606 – last mentioned in 1640–1644), and a certain Pauwel van de Mortel.[14] Erasmus Quellinus I (1584–1640) also supplied work for the *Pompa Introitus*, including a herm figure more than ten feet high.[15]

It is possible that one or more of these masters may have been involved in making sculpture for Rubens's house, and in particular in the carving of life-size stone statues. From what we know, however, it is clear that caution is required in attributing the sculptures.

One important 'Rubensian' sculptor, who for a time worked closely with Rubens, and should be mentioned in this context, is Georg Petel (1601/2–1634). He is not included in this chapter, but he is mentioned in the Catalogue in connection with one work, a statue of Venus and Cupid (see under No. 37). Finally it is worth considering whether Rubens may have given one or more commissions to the celebrated Artus Quellinus I (1609–1668), who was the most talented of all sculptors in Antwerp. We will return to him shortly, having looked more closely at the evidence concerning Van Mildert and Faydherbe.

---

12. *Génard, Intrede*, 1869–76, VII, p. 24; Martin, *Pompa (CRLB)*, 1972, pp. 110–112; the statues, 9 feet high (c. 2.50 m), were destroyed in the fire at the Brussels Coudenberg Palace in 1731 (Baudouin, *Keizersbeelden*, 2005, pp. 335–346).
13. Van den Eynde's known work consists of statues which originate from about 1630–1640, including the *Faustina Group* in the Maagdenhuis Museum, Antwerp; for a full account of this master: Jansen – Van Herck, *Van den Eynde*, 1945, pp. 5–90. For the *Faustina*, see ibid., pp. 47–48, no. 16, pl. 3; Verhelst, *Maagdenhuis*, 1996, p. 76, ill. pp. 75, 96). In about 1639 and 1643, De Neve made, for example, statues for the Chapel of Our Lady in the Antwerp Jesuit Church (Jansen, *O.L.Vrouwkapel*, 1938, pp. 50–58, pl. X; id., *Beeldhouwers*, 1940, pp. 112–139; Casteels, *De Nole*, 1961, pp. 183–191.
14. For the first, see Jansen, *Bijdrage*, 1946, pp. 46–48; for the second: Casteels, *Cardon*, 1964, cols 298–299.
15. *Génard, Intrede*, 1869–76, VII, p. 43 (no. CLXXX); XIII, p. 230; Martin, *Pompa (CRLB)*, 1972, p. 31. What we currently know about him is that he mainly worked in wood, and in a rather archaic style; the only object by him that survives is a wooden pulpit in the chapel of St Elizabeth's Hospital in Antwerp, now known as 'The Botanic Sanctuary' hotel (Gabriëls, *Erasmus Quellien I*, 1925, pp. 326–331).

Hans van Mildert (1588–1638):[16] Close to Rubens for More than Twenty Years

It is known that the sculptor Hans van Mildert signed a legal document on behalf of Rubens in November 1616, in connection with the making of a staircase for the painter's house (Appendix I.9; No. 19). The fact that he was representing Rubens suggests that he was responsible, certainly by late 1616, for directing and supervising building work in the house.[17] Although not explicitly mentioned in the contract, it can be assumed that Van Mildert provided carved decorations for the staircase in question. Furthermore, it seems likely that other sculpture, both for the interior and exterior of the house, can be attributed to Van Mildert.

In the first instance, the obvious sculptures to consider are those carved into the portico. The high reliefs representing pairs of satyrs (Nos 30–33; Figs 171, 173, 175–176) as well as the other sculpted elements, including dolphins, eagles, ram's heads, and *bucrania* (Nos 26–29; Figs 150, 153, 158, 165–166) have traditionally been assigned to Van Mildert. The attribution rests solely on the contract for the staircase mentioned, and on its own this is perhaps not sufficient evidence. Yet the attribution should not be discarded outright.[18]

Several pieces of information show that in the years 1615–1621 the two artists maintained friendly as well as professional contact. On 6 August 1615 Rubens was godfather to Van Mildert's third child, Peter [Paul].[19] In 1616–1617 Rubens designed the high altar in the Kapellekerk in Brussels, which was executed in 1617–1618 by Van Mildert.[20] They were also in touch in 1616, and possibly 1617, in connection with commissions given to Van Mildert but in which Rubens was not directly involved, for example the high altar of the cathedral in 's-Hertogenbosch.[21] Furthermore, in the years 1615 until 1621 the artists were

---

16. For this sculptor, see especially Leyssens, *Van Mildert*, 1941; for further bibliographical information, see Fabri – Lombaerde, *Jesuit Church (CRLB)*, 2018, p. 100, n. 12; see also Herremans, *Architectural Sculpture (CRLB)*, 2019, passim, and esp. pp. 65, 71–78.
17. This was also assumed by Leyssens (Leyssens, *ibid.*, pp. 101–102). For the untenable proposition that Van Mildert's contribution went much further, and that he should also be regarded as the designer of the portico, see above, Chapter IX, p. 249, n. 1.
18. There is no agreement about this in the literature. Leyssens believed that Van Mildert was responsible for more than just the staircase, but he mentions no other sculptures that Van Mildert might have provided (ibid., pp. 101–102). Kitlitschka takes a more critical view: he points to the lack of archival evidence and finds the stylistic affinities insufficient (Kitlitschka, *Van Mildert*, 1972, p. 224). Muller also wondered if the two statues seen above the portico in the Harrewijn print could be attributed to Van Mildert (Muller, *Collector*, 1989, p. 154, cat. III, nos 17 and 18).
19. Leyssens, *Van Mildert*, 1941, pp. 74, 118; Duverger, *Waeyens*, 1989, p. 391.
20. Now in the church of Sint-Joost-ten-Node; Leyssens, *ibid.*, pp. 117–118; Herremans, *Architectural Sculpture (CRLB)*, 2019, pp. 128–133, no. 2.
21. In 1616 Rubens was asked to advise on the design of the high altar (Herremans, *ibid.*, p. 71; Fabri – Lombaerde, *Jesuit Church (CRLB)*, 2018, p. 101). It is possible that they also communicated with each other about a metal altar rail for the altar of the Antwerp mercers in the cathedral; Rubens was consulted by their guild about this work in 1617 (Baudouin, *Altaartuinen*, 1985, pp. 163–169).

CHAPTER XI - SCULPTURE AND SCULPTORS

Text ill. 152. ? Hans van Mildert, *Honos*, sculpture. Antwerp, Museum Plantin-Moretus.

both involved in the construction of the Jesuit Church in Antwerp, Rubens as contributing architect and painter of altar and ceiling paintings, and Van Mildert as maker of sculptures, including the high altar.[22]

It thus seems almost inevitable that Rubens would have asked the talented Van Mildert to carry out the carving that needed to be done for his house, especially in the period 1615–1621. Did he also contribute parts of the garden pavilion, which was probably built around the same time as the portico? It seems possible that he carved the sphinx-like caryatids either side of the niche (No. 35; Figs 184–185). In addition, it is possible that Van Mildert made at least one of the free-standing statues for the garden pavilion, specifically the youth with cornucopia in the roof niche (No. 36; Fig. 187). The basic features of this statue correspond to those of a limewood *Honos* that stands on a chimney piece in the Museum Plantin-Moretus (Text ill. 152), and which is sometimes regarded as a work made by Van Mildert in about 1620, using a preparatory drawing by Rubens (Fig. 191). However, since both attribution and dating of the wooden statue have been doubted, this work does not provide a relevant comparison (see under No. 36).

In later years, after the period 1618–1620, Van Mildert went on to collaborate with Rubens on other projects. It is generally assumed that he made the three statues formerly crowning the main altar of the church of St Michael's Abbey in Antwerp. These can be dated to around 1624, and certainly before 1629.[23]

It is known that the two artists still had professional ties in the 1630s. As mentioned, the sculptor contributed to the *Pompa Introitus Ferdinandi* in 1635. He received the considerable sum of 3900 guilders 'for making various stone figures, capitals, terms and other pieces [...] as well as for various drawings and for his labour in bringing all the models to large scale'.[24] According to

22. Fabri – Lombaerde, *Jesuit Church (CRLB)*, 2018., passim, and esp. pp. 100–105.
23. Herremans, *Architectural Sculpture (CRLB)*, 2019, pp. 139–152, nos 4–6.
24. Génard, *Intrede*, 1869–76, VII, p. 73 (no. CCLIII); XIII, pp. 228–229; Citation taken from Martin, *Pompa (CRLB)*,

CHAPTER XI - SCULPTURE AND SCULPTORS

John Rupert Martin, he may have been responsible for making the large Spes statue, which was placed on the *Stage of Welcome* (Fig. 50).[25] A few years later, in 1637–1638, Van Mildert made sculptures to designs by Rubens for the high altar of the Church of the Calced Carmelites in Antwerp.[26]

Did the sculptor also carry out commissions for Rubens himself in the 1630s, and so perhaps for his house or collection? We know that at the time of Van Mildert's death on 21 September 1638,[27] Rubens still owed him a large sum of money. When eighteen months later Rubens died, this debt had not yet been cleared, as emerges from the settlement of Rubens's estate, submitted in 1645, known as the *Staetmasse*. This document states that Hans van Mildert's widow was paid 512 guilders for 'diversche wercken' (various works), which her husband had carried out for Rubens, without giving further details (Appendix I.23: [10]). Was this relatively large sum owed for work done in connection with the house on the Wapper? While this remains a possibility, nothing more precise can be said without resorting to speculation.

In the 1630s, the Van Mildert and Rubens families remained on friendly terms. By then, the Van Milderts were also living on the Wapper and so, like Rubens, they were parishioners of St James's Church. In 1615, Rubens had been godfather at the baptism of Van Mildert's third child (see above), and on 18 November 1634 it was Helena Fourment who presented the sculptor's eleventh child (Johannes) at the font.[28] The settlement of Rubens's estate informs us that a 'Jan van Milder' received 24 guilders for making a copy [of a painting].[29] This suggests that one of Van Mildert's sons – clearly not Johannes, who was born in 1634 – may have been active as a painter in Rubens's workshop (if the copy was made before Rubens's death), but it is equally possible that the heirs commissioned the copy between 1640 and 1645.[30] The last thing to note, and again this emerges from the same document, is that one of Van Mildert's sons-in-law, the sculptor Gerard van Opstal, bought a quantity of ivory from Rubens's estate.[31]

From the above we can conclude that both the contract of 1616 and the close ties between Van Mildert and Rubens over a sustained period of time make it a reasonable assumption that the sculptor played an important part in the decoration of Rubens's house.

     1972, p. 30; see also ibid., p. 38.
25. Ibid., p. 38, figs 2–3.
26. Herremans, *Rubens Unveiled*, 2013, p. 101; id., *Architectural Sculpture (CRLB)*, 2019, pp. 167–173, no. 13.
27. For the date of his death, see Leyssens, *Van Mildert*, 1941, p. 75.
28. Ibid., p. 74; Duverger, *Waeyens*, 1989, p. 391.
29. Duverger, *Kunstinventarissen*, 1984–2009, V, p. 279.
30. For this Jan van Mildert, see Hairs, *Sillage*, 1977, p. 226; Balis, *Studio Practices*, 1994, pp. 118, 127, n. 219; Id., *Rubens and his Studio*, 2007, p. 34, n. 42.
31. See above, p. 244; Appendix I. 23: [1].

CHAPTER XI - SCULPTURE AND SCULPTORS

Lucas Faydherbe (1617–1697):[32] a Talented Young Man in Rubens's House

The name of the sculptor and architect Lucas Faydherbe occurs at an early point in the nineteenth century in the literature in connection with the statues of the garden pavilion.

As early as 1840, Victor Van Grimbergen suggested that the sculptor was the maker of the three original statues, of which, according to him, only the Hercules survived,[33] and this attribution to Faydherbe of the monumental Hercules (No. 40; Fig. 211) was frequently taken over by later authors.[34] It is indeed true that twenty years after the contract with Van Mildert, another talented sculptor, Lucas Faydherbe, joined Rubens's circle, and so it is not surprising that sculpture in Rubens's garden has been attributed to him. As is well known, before returning to settle in his native town Mechelen, this artist lived and worked in Rubens's house for more than three years in his youth, between 1636 and 1640. While there, he mainly made small sculptures (statuettes and reliefs in ivory) to Rubens's designs. We learn all this from Rubens himself, in the favourable reference he wrote for Faydherbe on 5 April 1640, when the young artist left Antwerp to return to Mechelen.[35]

A second document, a letter from Rubens to the young sculptor written one month later, gives more information about Faydherbe's work for him in ivory: 'there is no hurry about the little ivory child'.[36] Frits Scholten points out that Faydherbe's activities undoubtedly formed part of the production of Rubens's workshop, alongside the paintings.[37] One work of astonishing virtuosity and skill that was probably made by Faydherbe while working for Rubens is the ivory statuette of *Cupid and Psyche Asleep on a Bed* in The State Hermitage Museum, St Petersburg.[38]

Besides work in ivory, Rubens's testimonial also mentions a large stone statue that was made in his house ('tot mijnen huijse'), a *Maria Mater Dolorosa*, which could then be seen in the Beguinage Church in Mechelen and is still

---

32. See especially, with a reference to further literature, De Nijn et al., eds, *Faydherbe*, 1997.
33. Van Grimbergen, *Rubens*, 1840, p. 387, n. 10. He does not mention the subjects of the two other statuettes, and says nothing about the fourth statue in the niche.
34. See Chapter X, pp. 310–311; and No. 40.
35. Rubens states that Faydherbe '[...] over de dry jaeren by my ghewoont heeft, ende mynen Discipel gheweest is [...] ende voor my ghemaeckt heeft diversche wercken van ivoor' (no subjects are mentioned); for the (lost) document, see Duverger, *Getuigschrift*, 1977, pp. 259–279; Vlieghe, *Faydherbe*, 1997, pp. 24–25, 27, n. 1.
36. Letter from Rubens to Faydherbe, dated 9 May 1640 (Rooses – Ruelens, eds, *Correspondance*, 1887–1909, VI, p. 281); quotation from Magurn, *Letters*, no. 250, p. 415.
37. Scholten, *Werkplaats-academie*, 2004, pp. 43–44 and passim.
38. Muller, *Collector*, 1989, p. 146, pl. 121 (as 'Faydherbe (?)'); Boele et al., eds, *Liefde*, 2002, p. 128, no. 71 (as 'anonymous'), repr.; Scholten, *Werkplaats-academie*, 2004, p. 41, fig. 9 (as 'Faydherbe').

preserved there.[39] It should be noted that we have no further information about the presence of the young sculptor in Rubens's house or his activities there. Undoubtedly there must have been a separate workshop somewhere, for carving works in stone and ivory.

In his remarks Rubens does not mention that Faydherbe's work included making stone statues for him as private commissions. However, this does not mean that none were produced. After all, his testimonial was intended for the authorities in Mechelen and it is understandable that Rubens singles out a statue by his 'disciple' that they would be able to see in their own city, so that they could judge his qualities for themselves.

Born in 1617, Faydherbe was of course too young to have made any of the sculpture that forms an integral part of the architecture, such as the satyrs on the portico and the caryatids of the garden pavilion. However, it is worth considering if in the short period he was living with Rubens, from 1636 until the spring of 1640, he made a number of free-standing stone statues or busts for the house. Can we indeed attribute one or more of the pavilion statues to Faydherbe, as was believed in the nineteenth century, an idea which remained attractive to several later authors? Given his age, it is impossible that he had anything to do with the statues that appear in *The Walk in the Garden* (Fig. 182), a painting which shows the situation of shortly after 1630. Thus the bust of Hercules against the rear wall of the pavilion, the youth with cornucopia in the roof niche, as well as the Venus and the Bacchus (Nos 36–39) can be ruled out as works attributable to Faydherbe.

The situation with regard to the full-length Hercules (No. 40; Fig. 211) is different. This statue might have been made in the course of the 1630s. Could it have been carved by Faydherbe? Stylistic comparison with other works from his hand cannot help much with this question, since so few examples are known from the earliest period of his production (c. 1636–1640). A number of Hercules busts by Faydherbe survive, but they are later and so do not provide a useful benchmark.[40]

39. Libertus, *Faydherbe*, 1938, pp. 55–56, fig. 2; De Nijn et al., eds, *Faydherbe*, 1997, p. 133, no. 11, repr. . For an illustration, see also URL: https://www.wga.hu/html_m/f/faydherb/lucas/1/dolorosa.html.
40. Several almost identical versions of a bust of Hercules with lion's skin hood over his head and shoulders survive, including terracottas in the Victoria and Albert Museum, London (c. 1640–1650?), and in the collection of the King Baudouin Foundation, Brussels (inv. no. 50), on loan to the Rubenshuis (c. 1675–1680; Rubenshuis, inv. no. RH.B.62); see De Nijn et al., eds, *Faydherbe*, 1997, nos 21, 59–60; Baudouin – Allard, eds, *Cat. Van Herck (Terracottas)*, 2000, no. 7; Docquier et al., *Mythologie*, 2016, pp. 17, 43, ill. p. 41. When comparing these busts with the statue in the garden pavilion, one is struck by the presence of a certain gracefulness and very different physiognomical types. Although dependent on Rubens's art, the manner of execution is decidedly 'post-Rubensian' in character.

CHAPTER XI - SCULPTURE AND SCULPTORS

More interesting in this respect is that there is documentary evidence that Faydherbe produced a statue of Hercules.[41] Very probably this was the life-size figure of the hero in Mechelen, standing in a niche at the back of the garden of the house of his son Jan Lucas (1654–1704), who, like his father, was a sculptor and architect. This is now lost but was certainly in place by 1657. The photos we have of this piece show it in a very battered state and without a head (Fig. 213) – it was severely damaged in a fire – making stylistic comparison impossible. It is nevertheless clear that this figure was modelled on the *Hercules Farnese*, and it can be linked to Rubens's sketch of *Hercules Overcoming Discord*, now in Museum Boijmans Van Beuningen, Rotterdam, and which can be dated c. 1615–1618 (for more information about the statue in Mechelen and Rubens's sketch, see under No. 40).

Faydherbe's name has also been suggested for the surviving *Bust of a Faun* (No. 1, Copy; Fig. 35), but this attribution is untenable. It is a plaster cast from an original that was so severely weather-beaten that nothing can usefully be said about it. Besides, the original bust was part of the decoration of the north façade of the studio, and so we can assume that it was already standing in a niche here in 1617, the year of Faydherbe's birth.

To conclude, despite assumptions often repeated in the literature, and despite the fact that Faydherbe worked for some four years in close contact with Rubens, none of the known works that formed part of the sculptural decoration of Rubens's house can with certainty be attributed to him.

Artus Quellinus I (1609–1668): the Most Talented Sculptor in Antwerp

Finally, it seems fair to ask if Rubens would have commissioned one or more works for his house from the celebrated Artus Quellinus I.

Quellinus is best known for the series of impressive marble statues and reliefs that he made with his assistants for Amsterdam Town Hall between 1650 and c. 1663, undoubtedly the most important commission carried out by sculptors from Antwerp in the seventeenth century (Text ill. 153).[42] The attention that has deservedly been paid to his contribution to this 'eighth wonder of the world' means that his works created before this period, in Antwerp and elsewhere, have been studied rather less well.

Very early on, before his journey to Italy, Quellinus's qualities must have been noticed. By then he had already made important statues for Frederik Hendrik, Prince of Orange. In 1634, when he was no more than twenty-five, he was paid for two hardstone statues, a Mars and a Venus, both larger than life-

---

41. Leyssens, *Hercules*, 1948, pp. 211–215.
42. For example: Fremantle, *Town Hall of Amsterdam*, 1959, passim; Goossens, *Schat*, 1996. passim; Scholten, *Quellinus*, 2010 (with bibliography).

CHAPTER XI - SCULPTURE AND SCULPTORS

Text ill. 153. Artus Quellinus I, *Mercury*, sculpture. Amsterdam, Paleis op de Dam (formerly Town Hall).

Text ill. 154. ? Artus Quellinus I after Rubens, *Mercury*, statuette. St Petersburg, The State Hermitage Museum.

size ('twee hartstene beelden eenen Mars ende eenen Venus, beijde grooter als t leven…'), destined for the steps of Honselaarsdijk Palace.[43] Also working for the stadholder, in the same period he made a monumental Minerva and other statues for the gardens of Nieuburch Palace at Rijswijk.[44] Since these statues have unfortunately not survived, we do not know what his work looked like before his period in Italy. That he had already achieved a great deal by then also emerges from the reference by Joachim von Sandrart, who met him in Rome.[45]

It is far from clear in which years Quellinus may have worked for Rubens. Given his age, it could only have been from about 1630, or shortly before, which leaves a period of about ten years in which Rubens was still alive. For a considerable part of this time, however, Quellinus was away in Italy and since there is no detailed knowledge of his stay there, it is difficult to provide an answer. There are reasons to believe that he left Antwerp in 1634 and was still

---

43. Slothouwer, *Paleizen*, 1945, p. 265.
44. For these statues, see Neurdenburg, *Beeldhouwkunst*, 1948, pp. 20, 174; Bezemer Sellers, *Tuinen*, 1997, pp. 131, 140. For a full discussion of Frederik Hendrik's palaces, see Slothouwer, *Paleizen*, 1945; see also Ottenheym, *Frederik Hendrik en de bouwkunst*, 1997, pp. 111–116 (Honselaarsdijk), 117–118 (Ter Nieuburg).
45. He wrote that Quellinus had already shown 'vielfältige Proben' (many proofs) of his artistry in his native city (Sandrart, *Teutsche Academie*, 1675–80, II, Book 3, p. 351; quoted by, for example, Fremantle, *Town Hall*, 1959, p. 148, n. 2).

CHAPTER XI - SCULPTURE AND SCULPTORS

in Rome in 1636.[46] There is no agreement in the literature about the date of his return to Antwerp. His return is often placed in 1639, although an earlier date (1638) as well as a later one (January or February 1640, i.e. a few months before Rubens's death) have both been put forward.[47]

With regard to possible collaboration with Rubens in the late 1630s, we should consider a pair of ivory statuettes, a Mercury (Text ill. 154) and a Venus, in the State Hermitage Museum in St Petersburg. They were certainly designed by Rubens, and perhaps also commissioned by him. It has been suggested that these works could be by the hand of Quellinus and that he produced them in 1639, shortly after his return from Italy.[48] However, it should be emphasised that this attribution is based solely on stylistic comparison.

In any case it seems possible that when needing to commission sculptural decorations or life-size statues Rubens would have turned to the highly talented sculptor, and if so this needs to have been before or after Quellinus's sojourn in the south. There were certainly close contacts between Rubens and members of the artistic Quellinus family. In 1631 Rubens became godfather to Erasmus I's seventh daughter, Catharina.[49] What is more, the painter Erasmus Quellinus II (1607–1678), Artus's brother, was an important assistant in Rubens's workshop, who produced large-scale paintings to designs by the master for the *Pompa Introitus Ferdinandi* and the Torre de la Parada.[50] It should also be noted that from the beginning of 1637, Erasmus Quellinus and Rubens collaborated on designs for book illustrations.[51]

Undoubtedly Artus Quellinus I was the sculptor best able to turn Rubens's ideas into stone. This is clear, for example, from the cartouche with the printer's mark above the entrance to the Plantin Press (Text ill. 155), a work which is in all likelihood based on an invention of Quellinus, but closely follows a drawing by Rubens.[52] It is possible that Quellinus made sculpture for Rubens's house. The work that should be considered in the first place is the monumental Hercules in

---

46. An earlier date for Quellinus's departure from Antwerp was wrongly suggested by Mariette Fransolet, who assumed that he arrived in Rome as early as 1625–1630 (Fransolet, *Du Quesnoy*, 1942, p. 136).
47. On 12 August 1639 'Quellinus stone carver' in Antwerp is paid for the cartouche for Plantin (see below, n. 52), but this has been interpreted in various ways: the Quellinus mentioned could be either Artus or his father Erasmus (died 22 January 1640); the payment would have included both the cartouche already ordered (and still to be made) and the finished cartouche; see Kitlitschka, *Rubens*, 1963, p. 282; Herremans, *Architectural Sculpture [CRLB]*, 2019, pp. 209, 212, n. 18.
48. Feuchtmayr – Schädler, *Petel*, 1973, pp. 179–180, under no. 140, figs 145–149; Muller, *Collector*, 1989, p. 145, pls 117–118 (as 'Quellinus').
49. Baptised on 5 May 1631 (De Bruyn, *Quellinus*, 1988, p. 21).
50. Martin, *Pompa (CRLB)*, 1972, pp. 30, 181, 187, no. 48; Alpers, *Torre (CRLB)*, 1971, nos 8, 12–13[?], 16, 21–22, 26–27, 47[?] and 51.
51. Judson – Van de Velde, *Title-pages (CRLB)*, 1978, I, p. 31, passim, e.g. under nos 75–76, 78–80.
52. Gabriëls, *Quellien*, 1930, pp. 82, 84, pl. III (p. 15); Fremantle, *Town Hall*, 1959, p. 149, fig. 164; for the drawing: Judson – Van de Velde, ibid., I, no. 74a; II, fig. 255.

CHAPTER XI - SCULPTURE AND SCULPTORS

Text ill. 155. Artus Quellinus I, *Labore et Constantia*, relief above the entrance to the Plantin Press. Antwerp, Museum Plantin-Moretus.

the garden pavilion (No. 40, Fig. 211), a piece that stands up to the comparison with the masterly sculptures for the Amsterdam Town Hall (Text ill. 153). So far, however, no concrete evidence has been found to corroborate Quellinus's contribution to the decoration of Rubens's house, which would have occurred before 1634 or in the short window from 1638 to 1640, and thus it remains no more than a hypothesis.[53]

53. For this, see also in the Catalogue, under the two statues sometimes attributed to Quellinus: the *Hercules* (No. 40) and the *Bacchus* (No. 38).

CATALOGUE

CATALOGUE RAISONNÉ

A. The Façades of the South Wing (Studio): Nos 1–19a

No. 1. *Four Busts in Niches, Including a Faun*: Sculptures (cf. Fig. 33)

Possibly carved in the round, or executed in plaster or stucco; approx. 88 cm.

Formerly on the north façade of the studio, lost

c. 1616 (?)

VISUAL SOURCES:
(1) Harrewijn print, 1684 (Appendix III.1; Fig. 17; detail: Fig. 33);
(2) Harrewijn print, 1692, scarcely recognisable (Appendix III.2; Fig. 18);
(3) Aylesbury *View of the Courtyard of Rubens's House*, 1660s, vague indication of two busts to the left of the entrance door (Appendix III.3; Fig. 16; detail: Fig. 27).

COPY: *Bust of a Faun*, hollow and on a socle (Fig. 35), Antwerp, Rubenshuis, inv. no. RH.B.021 (as 'attributed to Lucas Faydherbe'); plaster, 87.7 × 63.5 cm. PROV.: in 1860 in the left-hand niche of the portico (as seen in the photograph by Edmond Fierlants; see Appendix III.52) and still present at the start of the renovations in 1938. LIT.: Clijmans, *Wederopbouw Rubenshuis*, 1941, n.p., fig. 8; Baudouin, *Rubenshuis*, 1955, pp. 19–20; Baudouin, *Rubens's House*, 1955, p. 20 (as 'a faun' and 'very probably by Lucas Faydherbe'); Baudouin, *Summary Guide*, 1977, p. 18 (as 'Pan'); Baudouin, *Rubens's House*, 1977a, p. 17 (as 'a bust of Pan, very probably by Lucas Faydherbe'); Muller, *Collector*, 1989, p. 29 (as 'satyr' and 'a later addition').

LITERATURE: Clijmans, *Wederopbouw Rubenshuis*, 1946, p. 80; Stechow, *Classical Tradition*, 1968, p. 85; Prinz, *Philosophers*, 1973, p. 412; Stutz, *Residenz*, 1985, p. 144, fig. 7; Muller, *Collector*, 1989, pp. 26–27; Von Simson, *Rubens*, 1996, p. 212; Muller, *Rubens's Collection*, 2004, p. 39; Ben van Beneden in Herremans et al., *Heads on Shoulders*, 2008, p. 124, no. 63; Muller, *Moribvs Antiqvis*, 2008, p. 23; Uppenkamp – Van Beneden, *Architectural Symbolism*, 2011, p. 112.

We can tell from the Harrewijn prints (Figs 17–18) that the north façade of the studio wing was decorated with nine 'classical' busts. On the ground floor there were busts in four niches of a distinctive shape, namely an arch with angled corners – a so-called flat or geniculated arch – and executed *alla rustica*. They are somewhat reminiscent of the niche containing a bust of Seneca – or rather which Rubens and his contemporaries incorrectly identified as that of the Stoic philosopher – which appears in an engraving after a design by Rubens, and made as an illustration to Justus Lipsius's *L. Annaei Senecae Philosophi Opera Quae Extant Omnia* published in 1615 (Text ill. 63).[1]

The visual sources do not provide enough information to identify the four busts situated on the ground-floor level – with one exception. The most detailed source is the 1684 Harrewijn print (Figs 17 and 33); if we trace the niches from left to right, the following can be established: the first is half hidden by the fountain with rock structure adjoining the façade, also concealing the bust;[2] in the second niche, to the left of the doorway, a (young?) bearded man can be seen; to the right of the doorway is the *Bust of a Faun* (Fig. 34), which is the only one that can be recognised, because a plaster cast is known (see Copy; Fig. 35); finally, to the far right is a bust of a bald-headed man with a beard who is possibly intended as a Silenus, but could equally be a classical philosopher.

The cast of the *Faun*, that possibly goes back as far as the eighteenth century and was made from an original that was already in a rather weather-

CATALOGUE No. 2

beaten state,[3] shows a young man turning his head to one side and looking down, apparently smiling. Whether intended as a faun, or more specifically the god Pan, it is hard to tell. In any case it is a 'woodland creature' with pointed goats' ears. Because of its damaged state it is difficult to make out if he also has little horns. He has a raw animal hide on his right shoulder tied together by its paws, and his shock of curly hair is ringed with ivy or vine tendrils.

As can be seen in old photographs of the portico – including that by Edmond Fierlants of 1860, which is the earliest one known (Text ill. 23) – the plaster *Faun* stood in the left niche of the portico, and when the restoration began, he was still in position there. It was then one of three busts that decorated the niches of the portico, each of them standing on the same type of pedestal with a volute on either side (the left-hand volute of the *Faun* has been broken off). The two busts (material unknown), which stood in the remaining niches of the portico until 1939 (Text ill. 104) were removed at the time of the restoration, and they have disappeared. In the right niche was a Bacchante and in the central (round) niche there was a Minerva, which is visible in the Harrewijn print of 1684 (Text ills 124–125).[4]

There is no basis for the attribution of the *Faun* to Lucas Faydherbe (1617–1697), a possibility often mentioned in the literature, and which is also repeated in information given in the Rubens House and the KIK–IRPA database. That attribution can be ruled out for the surviving plaster copy, which was cast from an eroded bust and could not possibly have been made during Rubens's lifetime. But there is still no reason to think of the young sculptor as maker of the lost original bust. That would mean that the *Faun* was carved in the late 1630s at the earliest, some twenty years after completion of the studio wing. It is of course possible that one or more of the busts that stood in the niches were replaced by other works during Rubens's lifetime, but there is no evidence to support this assumption. Faydherbe's possible involvement in the sculptural decoration of Rubens's house is discussed in Chapter XI.[5]

As the subject of only one bust is identified (as a faun or Pan), we can only speculate about a possible iconographical programme linking the nine busts in the façade; for more on this, see Chapter V.[6]

1. See Chapter V, p. 148, n. 31.
2. For the rocky structure with bagpiper fountain, see Chapter III, pp. 114–115, Text ill. 50.
3. Recent technical research (by Studiebureau Lode De Clercq / 30 May 2019) concluded that this bust was cast (perhaps in the 18th century) from a badly eroded stone sculpture which had remains of polychromy.
4. See Chapter IX, pp. 277, 307.
5. See pp. 330–332.
6. See pp. 145 ff.

No. 2. *Bust in a Niche with a Scallop, Flanked by Cornucopias*: Sculpture or Mural Painting (cf. Fig. 36)

Possibly sculpted in the round, or executed in plaster or stucco, or painted in *trompe-l'oeil*; approx. 75 cm.

Formerly on the north façade of the studio, lost

c. 1616 (?)

VISUAL SOURCES:
(1) Harrewijn print, 1684 (Appendix III.1; Fig. 17; detail: Fig. 36);
(2) Harrewijn print, 1692 (Appendix III.2; Fig. 18);
(3) Aylesbury *View of the Courtyard of Rubens's House*, 1660s, a variant is vaguely discernible (Appendix III.3; Fig. 16; details: Figs 27, 37).

LITERATURE: Evers, *Rubens*, 1942, p. 43 (as 'pseudo-Seneca'); Clijmans, *Wederopbouw Rubenshuis*, 1946, p. 80; Stechow, *Classical Tradition*, 1968, pp. 30 (as 'pseudo-Seneca'), 85; Prinz, *Philosophers*, 1973, p. 412 (as 'impossible to identify'); Stutz, *Residenz*, 1985, p. 144, fig. 7; Muller, *Collector*, 1989, pp. 26–27; Von Simson, *Rubens*, 1996, p. 212; Muller, *Rubens's Collection*, 2004, p. 39; Ben van Beneden in Herremans et al., *Heads on Shoulders*, 2008, p. 124, no. 63; Muller, *Moribvs Antiqvis*, 2008,

p. 23; Uppenkamp – Van Beneden, *Architectural Symbolism*, 2011, p. 112.

The visual sources depicting the north front of the studio show a bust of a bearded man, placed centrally over the doorway. In the painting we see a bust on a socle, while the prints show a herm bust. Contained within a pediment, it stands in a niche topped by a large scallop shell, and with a cornucopia on either side. The most detailed image is provided by the 1684 Harrewijn print (Fig. 36), but even this is too vague to allow identification of the man with curly hair and beard, whose prominent position implies special significance. The head of the bust is usually regarded as a copy of the antique marble 'pseudo-Seneca' which Rubens owned,[1] and when the façade was reconstructed it was decided to place a modern copy (in the form of a herm bust) in the niche over the doorway (Text ill. 65). This may have been the right decision, but doubt remains.

For the ground floor, there are indications that it included actual niches containing busts in the round (No. 1; Fig. 33). For the niche with the bust over the doorway, however, there is no evidence, and so it cannot be determined if this part of the façade decoration was painted in *trompe-l'oeil* or executed in stone or stucco.[2] Interestingly, a similar arrangement, consisting of a head of Hercules under a large scallop, both executed in plaster, was still present in the interior of the house in 1938 (No. 23; Fig. 131).

1. See Chapter IV, p. 119; Chapter V, pp. 146–150; Chapter VII, p. 227.
2. For this, see Chapter V, p. 140; Chapter VI, pp. 169–171.

No. 3. *Four Unidentified Herm Busts*: Sculpture or Mural Painting (cf. Fig. 38)

Possibly sculpted in the round, or executed in plaster or stucco, or painted in *trompe-l'oeil*; approx. 70 cm.

Formerly on the north façade of the studio, lost

c. 1616 (?)

VISUAL SOURCES:
(1) Harrewijn print, 1684 (Appendix III.1; Fig. 17; detail: Fig. 38);
(2) Harrewijn print, 1692, very vaguely indicated (Appendix III.2; Fig. 18);
(3) Aylesbury *View of the Courtyard of Rubens's House*, 1660s, variants with a socle (one bust only vaguely indicated, another incomplete) (Appendix III.3; Figs 27, 37).

LITERATURE: see under No. 1.

According to the Harrewijn prints mentioned above, a row of busts decorated the second storey of the studio's north façade (Fig. 39). The three bearded men and a beardless youth are only vaguely indicated and they lack distinguishing features that would allow them to be identified individually. But it is also not clear if they were intended as a specific group of (historical) figures. There is reason to believe that they represent Greeks. The 'archaic' type of the busts, with shoulders vertically truncated and lacking a socle, a type called 'herm bust',[1] may indicate that Rubens intended them as Greeks rather than Romans. At least, this is a possible inference from an engraved series of busts of ancient celebrities based on drawings by Rubens, in which this difference of form is used to distinguish Greeks from Romans (Fig. 40).[2] Because of the vagueness of the visual sources it is impossible to establish whether one or more of these famous figures was also represented on the façade. Equally, no relationship can be detected with a group of about twenty anonymous drawings, retouched by Rubens, which include a number of busts of famous Greek authors and philosophers, almost all represented as bearded men.[3]

As is the case with other parts of the façade decoration, it cannot be determined if the four busts were painted in *trompe-l'oeil* or executed in stone or stucco. On this question, see Chapter VI.[4]

1. This 'archaic' type of bust is also called a 'herm', or 'herm portrait'. We do not use the word herm as Marjon van der Meulen does (Van der Meulen, *Antique (CRLB)*, 1994, II, nos 204–205, 208–210, 212–213, 215, 219) to avoid confusion with the herms with a shaft (No. 4).

2. See illustrations in Van Mulders, *Twelve Busts*, 2008, pp. 106–114, nos 44–55. We have looked in vain in the literature for confirmation of our belief that Rubens (and his contemporaries?) attached a specific meaning to this difference.
3. 230–245, nos 201–220; III, figs 405 and ff.
4. See pp. 169–171; see also Chapter V, p. 140.

No. 4. *Six Herms*: Mural Painting or Relief (cf. Figs 41–43)

Mural painting or relief; approx. 300 cm.

Formerly on the north and east (courtyard) façades of the studio wing, lost

c. 1616 (?)

VISUAL SOURCES:
(1) Harrewijn print, 1684 (Appendix III.1; Fig. 17; detail: Fig. 43);
(2) Harrewijn print, 1692 (Appendix III.2; Fig. 18; detail: Fig. 41);
(3) Aylesbury *View of the Courtyard of Rubens's House*, 1660s (Appendix III.3; Figs 16, 27; detail: Fig. 42).

LITERATURE: Rooses, *Maison*, 1888, p. 220 (as 'des cariatides peintes ou sculptées'); Rooses, *Oeuvre*, 1886–92, V, p. 185; Rooses – Ruelens, eds, *Correspondance*, 1887–1909, II, p. 153; Stutz, *Residenz*, 1985, p. 144; Lombaerde, *Rubens / Vredeman de Vries*, 2018, p. 124, n. 39.

The Harrewijn prints of 1684 and 1692 (Figs 17–18) show more or less identical herms on a narrow pedestal between the windows of the uppermost floor of the two façades of the Italian wing facing the courtyard: four on the north façade and two on the adjoining east façade; there seem to be five youths with curly hair and one man with a beard. Draped over their shoulders is a short, loose cloak which is arranged in several different ways, but neither arms nor hands are visible. Their uniformity and the complete absence of attributes suggest that these herms are to be interpreted as an architectural motif, making no reference to particular mythological or historical figures.[1]

The herms were probably painted in *trompe-l'oeil* and thus completely flat.[2] We should note that the image provided by the Aylesbury *View of the Courtyard of Rubens's House* (Figs 16, 27, 42) is different from the prints. The painting shows herms not only between the windows. To the left of the far window, on the corner of the north and east (garden) façade, we can see an additional herm (Fig. 42), which suggests that rather than four, there were five or more present on the north façade. In the painting these figures are monochrome, white, and apparently in relief, as shown by the corner herm which is silhouetted against the sky. However, this image seems less truthful than the prints, in which the façades are bordered by quoins (Fig. 43), a pattern which matches the building in the background in Rubens's *Hélène Fourment au Carrosse* (Appendix III.7; Fig. 31).

Various possible sources of inspiration can be identified for the armless herms. Similar, but female, red-yellow coloured herms with vases on their heads, and probably intended as made of metal, can be seen flanking 'Greek' paintings among the murals in the interior of the Casa Vasari in Arezzo (Fig. 79).[3] Piet Lombaerde observed that very similar herms with loose cloaks appear in the title-page of *Vestigi della antichita di Roma* […], published in Prague in 1606.[4] A herm of a similar type, without arms and with a cloak draped over the shoulders, but represented as a caryatid with a basket of flowers on the head, appears in the background of Rubens's *Portrait of Anne of Austria*.[5]

Several façades with herms are illustrated in Rubens's *Palazzi di Genova*, but there is no reason to regard these as a direct source of inspiration for his own house. These Genoese herms are not of the same type: on one façade they appear nude with arms raised, and on another they again have arms and also coiled fishtails as 'legs'.[6]

Rubens worked several other anthropomorphic elements into the house architecture and decoration. Still extant, and included in the catalogue (No. 35; Figs 184–185), are the two caryatids ('sphinxes') with Ionic capitals on the front of the garden pavilion. Other examples are known only from seventeenth-century illustrations of the house, and because insufficient information about them is available they are omitted from the catalogue. We know from a drawing by Abraham van Diepenbeeck (1596–1675) representing the Cavendish family in Rubens's house (Appendix III.28a.) that there were probably one or more chimneypieces with three-dimensional herms as caryatids. In Hillewerve's time two life-size caryatids (probably male and female) with upstretched arms, painted or in stone or stucco, could be seen on the north façade of Rubens's former stables (Text ill. 42).[7]

1. Unlike the comparable 'armless' herms that flank scenes of the *Achilles* series, which are intended as gods and personifications, as is clear from their attributes (for example a headdress or an animal underneath the shaft of the herm); see Haverkamp Begemann, *Achilles (CRLB)*, 1975, passim. For the frequent use of herms in Rubens's work, see Lombaerde, *Rubens / Vredeman de Vries*, 2018, pp. 117–127.
2. For a discussion of 'real' versus *trompe-l'oeil*, in relation to the façade decoration, see Chapter V, p. 140; Chapter VI, pp. 169–170. During the restoration of the house it was decided to create reliefs representing Olympian gods, with arms and attributes (see Chapter V, p. 145, nn. 1, 19).
3. Albrecht, *Häuser von Giorgio Vasari*, 1985, p. 91, figs 6–7; McHam, *Pliny*, 2013, figs 34–35, 195–196, 198.
4. Lombaerde, *Rubens / Vredeman de Vries*, 2018, p. 124, n. 39; for the book *Vestigi [etc.]*, see Judson – Van de Velde, *Title-pages (CRLB)*, 1978, I, p. 250; II, fig. 201. It is not known if Rubens had this book in his possession, but the engraving does contain a second link with Rubens's work: the use of a large animal hide as background in one of his designs for a title-page (ibid., I, no. 58; II, figs 199–200).
5. The original portrait in Madrid (Museo Nacional del Prado, inv. no. P001689) shows only one of these herms in full: a woman or a beardless youth (Huemer, *Portraits (CRLB)*, 1977, no. 2, fig. 43; Díaz Padrón, *Cat. Madrid, Prado (Pintura flamenca)*, 1995, p. 980, no. 1689; the copy formerly in the Metropolitan Museum of Art in New York shows more of the second herm, a bearded man (Huemer, ibid, no. 2, copy, fig. 44). For these caryatids, see Lombaerde, *Rubens / Vredeman de Vries*, 2018, p. 119.
6. Rott, *Palazzi (CRLB)*, 2002, II, figs 24 and 27; see also Tijs, *Rubens en Jordaens*, 1984, repr. pp. 54–55.
7. For Rubens's stables, see Chapter III, pp. 108–109.

No. 5. *Hermes Belvedere*: Mural Painting or Relief (cf. Fig. 44)

Mural painting or relief; approx. 300 cm.

Formerly on the east or garden façade of the studio, lost

c. 1616 (?)

VISUAL SOURCE: Harrewijn print, 1692 (Appendix III.2; Fig. 18; detail: Fig. 44).

LITERATURE: Muller, *Collector*, 1989, p. 35, n. 56 (as 'Bacchus'); Heinen, *Gesundheit*, 2004, p. 138 (as 'Bacchus'); Uppenkamp – Van Beneden, *Architectural Symbolism*, 2011, p. 117 (as 'Bacchus').

The Harrewijn print of 1692 (Fig. 18) shows a full-length nude youth between the windows of the top storey of the east or garden façade of the studio. The figure stands on a shallow base and was painted or possibly in relief (Fig. 44).[1]

The authors listed above believed that the youth represents Bacchus, because of the attribute in his outstretched hand (a *patera*?) and the drapery clinging to his shoulder, which they saw as the edges of a panther hide. However, this interpretation must be rejected. As with his counterpart on the other side of the window, this figure goes back to a famous ancient marble statue: the *Hermes Belvedere* (Fig. 45), a Roman copy after a work of Praxiteles (or, more likely, a follower), which was admired for its ideal proportions, and regarded as 'one of the most perfect statues that has come down to us from antiquity'.[2] Drawings of the Hermes were made by many artists when visiting Rome, including Rubens.[3] His drawings are lost, but they are known from two copies by Willem Panneels in the so-called Rubens Cantoor. One of these sheets shows a frontal view of the statue that corresponds to the figure on the façade (Fig. 46).[4]

What has been seen as an animal skin (with its paws hanging down) is in fact Mercury's *chlamys*, which has been gathered together in an unusual manner for optimal freedom of movement, forming a narrow strip which hangs over the shoulder and wraps around his left forearm. As

CATALOGUE No. 6

stated, the irregular and somewhat untidy folds that drape the ancient statue's left shoulder have thus been misunderstood in identifying Rubens's youth figure. Apart from the rolled-up *chlamys*, the ancient *Hermes Belvedere* is naked, while the figure on Rubens's façade has his hips covered with drapery, possibly added on the initiative of a later prudish resident. Or was it added by the printmaker?[5]

On the ancient statue (and also in Panneels's drawings) the hands are missing, but for the image on Rubens's façade these have been added. In the print, it is rather difficult to make out what the youth is holding in his right hand. Some have identified it as a drinking bowl or *patera*, but this attribute is not sufficient to identify the figure as the god of wine since a *patera* belongs in the hand of several gods or personifications.[6] The youth's left hand seems to be empty, and he has in any case none of the usual attributes of Bacchus such as vines, grapes or a *thyrsus*.

In short, both the full-length figure of the youth and his female companion (No. 6) between the windows of the east or garden façade derive from well-known and admired ancient statues seen by Rubens in Rome. It seems very likely that Rubens wanted to evoke images of the statues themselves – probably monochrome as if in marble – rather than intending them as personifications, or gods that could be connected iconographically with his garden.[7]

1. For this, see Chapter V, pp. 152–153.
2. Also called the Antinous Belvedere, referred to as 'le Lantin' or 'l'Admirable'; Rome, Musei Vaticani (Belvedere Courtyard), inv. no. MV_907_0_0; see Haskell – Penny, *Antique*, 1982, pp. 141–143, no. 4, fig. 73; Pasquier – Martinez, eds, *Praxitèle*, 2007, p. 306, fig. 215 (as after a follower of Praxiteles); Bober – Rubinstein, *Antique Sculpture*, 2010, pp. 62–63, no. 10. Other versions survive, for example in The British Museum, London (inv. no. 1864, 1021.1 (as 'The Farnese Hermes').
3. For Rubens's use of the statue in paintings, see F. Healy, in McGrath et al., *Mythological Subjects I (CRLB)*, 2016, I, p. 335, under no. 28.
4. Copenhagen, Statens Museum for Kunst, Kongelige Kobberstiksamling, inv. no. KKSgb16304 (Rubens Cantoor, III.26); Van der Meulen, *Antique (CRLB)*, 1994, II, no. 25; III, fig. 53; Garff – de la Fuente Pedersen, *Panneels*, 1988, no. 197, pl. 199); another sheet in the same collection (inv. no. KKSgb16376;

Rubens Cantoor III.25) shows the statue in three-quarter view, facing left (Van der Meulen, *ibid.*, II, no. 26; III, fig. 55; Garff – de la Fuente Pedersen, *ibid.*, no. 255, pl. 258).

5. If the *Hermes* was made in relief, it seems unlikely that an added drapery was actually present in the façade itself. For another example of drapery (in the Harrewijn print) that was probably not original, see the *trompe-l'oeil* painting *Andromeda Liberated by Perseus* (No. 18).
6. For the *patera* as attribute, see under No. 27.
7. See also under No. 6.

No. 6. *Flora Farnese*: Mural Painting or Relief (cf. Fig. 47)

Mural painting or relief; approx. 300 cm.

Formerly on the east or garden façade of the studio, lost

c. 1616 (?)

VISUAL SOURCE: Harrewijn print, 1692 (Appendix III.2; Fig. 18; detail: Fig. 47).

LITERATURE: Kieser, *Antikes*, 1933, p. 111, n. 4 (as a painted 'Flora'); Burchard, *Wildenstein*, 1950, p. 12, under no. 10 (as 'painted'); Martin, *Pompa (CRLB)*, 1972, p. 42, n. 9 (as 'Flora'); Muller, *Collector*, 1989, pp. 34–35 (as 'Flora'); Heinen, *Gesundheit*, 2004, p. 138 (as 'Flora'); Uppenkamp – Van Beneden, *Architectural Symbolism*, 2011, p. 117, as Flora.

In the Harrewijn print of 1692 (Figs 18, 47) a full-length woman can be seen between the windows of the top storey of the garden façade of the studio wing: she stands on a shallow plinth, holding a posy in one hand and lifting the corner of her dress with the other. It was probably a mural painting, although it is possible that it was a stucco relief.[1]

This figure goes back almost literally, in reverse, to the celebrated *Flora Farnese*, a Roman marble statue carved from a Greek prototype dating from the fourth century BC (Fig. 48).[2] Rubens probably made a drawing of this ancient masterpiece during his second stay in Rome (1605–1608), when it stood in the Palazzo Farnese. No drawing from his hand has survived, but one was used as model for an illustration in Philip

Rubens's *Electorum Libri II*, which was published in Antwerp in 1608 (Fig. 49).³

In the literature about Rubens's house it is consistently stated that Rubens chose this figure holding a posy as ornament for the façade in order to link it with the garden. A depiction of the goddess Flora, protector of gardens, is certainly appropriate on the façade facing the garden.⁴ Nonetheless it should be pointed out that the apocryphal identification of the ancient statue as Flora may not have played a decisive role in the selection of this figure on the façade. For it is not certain that Rubens intended to represent the goddess. In the *Electorum Libri II*, the statue is illustrated simply as a *statua tunicata* (Fig. 49) and the commentary by Philip Rubens makes no mention of Flora, but rather describes a statue representing some goddess or other ('[statua] Deae cuiusdam') in the Farnese Palace.⁵

Moreover, Rubens must have known the archaeologically correct interpretation of the famous 'statua tunicata', as it could be deduced from images in Roman coins. A female holding a growing crop in her hand, instead of a flower, and lifting the tip of her drapery (in order to move more freely, and thus appear or disappear swiftly), is a representation of Hope (Spes). This interpretation can be found, for example, in personifications in allegorical compositions by Otto van Veen (1556–1629)⁶ and it is also the meaning that Rubens later gave the statue in the decorations for the *Pompa Introitus*. A carved stone statue of Hope, modelled on the *Flora Farnese*, occupies a prominent position in the *Stage of Welcome* (Fig. 50).⁷

To our mind, the iconographical significance of the female figure – regardless of whether seen as Flora or Spes – did not play a role in her selection for the façade decoration, but rather this was a decision based on artistic or aesthetic considerations. Its significance seems to lie in representing one of the most famous and admired statues of the ancient world, celebrated especially for its fluid, 'clinging' drapery. One argument that favours this interpretation is the presence, as a pendant on the other side of the window, of a youth who is not connected in any way with the garden, but who does indeed correspond to another famous ancient statue: the *Hermes Belvedere* (see No. 5).

If this assumption is correct, it follows that both figures on the east façade of the studio wing, whether painted or in relief, were probably monochrome so as to resemble ancient marble sculptures.

1. For this discussion and other remarks about the figure on the façade, see also Chapter V, pp. 152–153; Chapter VI, 169–171.
2. Naples, Museo Archeologico Nazionale di Napoli, inv. no. 6409; Haskell – Penny, *Antique*, 1982, pp. 217–219, no. 41, fig. 113.
3. Judson – Van de Velde, *Title-pages (CRLB)*, 1978, I, no. 3; II, fig. 43 (as a 'statua tunicata'); Van der Meulen, *Antique (CRLB)*, 1994, I, pp. 55, 101–102, text ill. 54; Logan – Belkin, *Drawings, I*, 2021, no. 162; II, fig. 215.
4. For an interpretation as Flora in connection with the garden, see, for example, Muller, who refers to a lost Flora by Praxiteles, which according to Pliny 'had graced a garden' (Muller, *Collector*, 1989, pp. 34–35); Heinen, *Gesundheit*, 2004, p. 138.
5. Rubens, *Electorum Libri*, 1608, p. 67; Judson – Van de Velde, *Title-pages (CRLB)*, 1978, I, p. 82); the Latin description was noticed by Burchard (Burchard, *Wildenstein*, 1950, p. 12, under no. 10).
6. See for example *Man between Hope and Fear*, an illustration designed by Van Veen for his *Emblemata of Quintus Horatius Flaccus* (Vaenius, *Emblemata Horatiana*, 1607, p. 165).
7. The interpretation of this figure, which is inscribed below BONAE SPEI SACRUM, is based on ancient coins (see the commentary on this in Gevartius, *Pompa Introitus*, 1642, pp. 12–13); for the arch, see McGrath, *Pompa*, 1971, p. 42; Martin, *Pompa (CRLB)*, 1972, pp. 38–39, figs 2–3. A comparable Spes figure appeared on the rear of the *Arch of the Portuguese* ('Arcus Lusitanici'), designed by Ludovicus Nonnius; see Gevartius, ibid., pl. opp. p. 22; commentary, ibid. p. 23 ('spes dextrâ manu Surculum [twig], vel Florem tenet'); there is a description, but no illustration, in Martin, ibid., pp. 64–66.

No. 7. *Window Surround*: Architecture (cf. Fig. 52)

Probably bluestone (or painted in *trompe-l'oeil*?); approx. 300 m.

Formerly on the third level of the façades of the studio wing, lost

c. 1616 (?)

CATALOGUE No. 7a

VISUAL SOURCES:
(1) Harrewijn print, 1684 (Appendix III.1; Fig. 17; detail Fig. 53);
(2) Harrewijn print, 1692 (Appendix III.2; Fig. 18; Fig. 51);
(3) Aylesbury *View of the Courtyard of Rubens's House*, 1660s), variant (Appendix III.3; Figs 16, 27; detail: Fig. 52);
(4) Rubens, *Hélène Fourment au Carrosse*, Paris, 1630s, variant in the background (Appendix III.7; Fig. 21; detail: Fig. 31).

LITERATURE: Müller Hofstede, *Review Burchard – d'Hulst*, 1966, p. 446; Müller Hofstede, *Entwurfszeichnung*, 1967, p. 116; Devroe, *Rubens' huis*, 2008, I, p. 73.

We gain an impression of the rectangular windows of the third storey of the studio wing from the Harrewijn prints (Figs 17–18, 51, 53) and the Aylesbury painting (Fig. 16; detail: Fig. 52). A similar window type also appears in the background of *Hélène Fourment au Carrosse*, which gives an idealised image of Rubens's studio wing, although in that painting the window surround is decorated on either side with small garlands (Figs 21, 31 and 55).

The windows have distinctive projections at both upper and lower corners, features known as *crossettes* or 'ears', and each has a broken pediment. They closely resemble Italian window types used by Palladio, Scamozzi and their followers, of which there are many examples, not least in Palladian architecture of subsequent centuries. In the line of windows of the studio façade, variety was achieved through pediments that are alternately triangular and segmental, each broken and with a brazier (rather than a vase) or a smoking oil lamp in the middle. The broken tops of the segmental pediments terminate in volutes, and these are connected by a small garland. For more on these windows, see Chapter V.[1]

It is worth noting that in the three available images of the north façade, the two Harrewijn prints and the Aylesbury painting, the actual mouldings around the windows are more or less identical, while the arrangement of panes is different. In the painting (Fig. 52), the horizontal window bar runs, as might be expected, at the same level as the blocks that project from the moulding on either side of the window. This is not the case in the prints (Figs 51, 53), in which the bar is noticeably lower, suggesting that the original arrangement of the panes is the one shown in the painting and this might have been altered before Harrewijn made the first print (1684).

1. See, pp. 143–144.

No. 7a. *Architectural Study of a Window Surround and Other Elements*: Drawing (Fig. 54)

Black chalk on paper, foxed; 432 × 354 mm.

Recto: *Study for Aglauros Opening the Basket* for *The Discovery of Erichthonius by the Daughters of Cecrops* (see below, n. 1).

Antwerp, Museum Plantin-Moretus, Prentenkabinet. Inv. no. PK.OT.00113

c. 1614 (?)

TECHNICAL NOTES: with vertical crease, left, and diagonal cut, lower right. With embossed marks of the Museum Plantin-Moretus in the centre of the sheet at bottom. Unknown collector's mark in the lower left corner, and in brown ink, in an unknown hand, the attribution *P.P.Rúbens F.*, with current inventory number in graphite underneath; lower right, old inventory number: A.XV.1.

PROVENANCE: M. Mariën, from whom purchased in 1916.

EXHIBITED: Antwerp, 1991, no. 21.

LITERATURE: Müller Hofstede, *Review Burchard – d'Hulst*, 1966, p. 446, fig. 8; Müller Hofstede, *Entwurfszeichnung*, 1967, p. 116, pl. III/18, 4; C. Depauw in De Nave, ed., *Around Rubens*, 1991, p. 145, no. 21 (as 'door vreemde hand?'); F. Healy, in McGrath et al., *Mythological Subjects I (CRLB)*, 2016, I, pp. 400, 402, n. 1, under no. 40b (as 'by a different hand?').

Opinions have been divided about the attribution of the recto of this sheet with a kneeling figure in black and white chalk, which is so badly rubbed that it is difficult to judge. It is now generally accepted as a study by Rubens for a lost *Discovery of Erichthonius by the Daughters of Cecrops*, which can be dated c. 1613–1614, and in any case before April 1614.[1] The sheet had in the past been attributed to Rubens by Justus Müller Hofstede. Moreover, he correctly noted that the verso is connected with 'the framing of windows of the upper floor of the studio wing in Rubens's house', and he was the first to reproduce this interesting verso.[2]

It does indeed seem very likely that the drawing is a design – not carried out literally – for the windows in the studio wing and thus, with No. 13b, it is one of only two autograph architectural studies for Rubens's house that survive. It shows a rectangular moulded window frame with *crossettes* (or 'ears') top and bottom, and crowned with a sphere on a small plinth. Interestingly, this window type matches those of the garden façade of the Villa Medici in Rome (Fig. 56).[3]

The window in the drawing differs in several details from those that appear in the visual sources mentioned under No. 7 (the Harrewijn prints and the Aylesbury painting (Figs 53, 51, 52). For example, in those images the *crossettes* both top and bottom are slightly different in appearance, and the crowning is formed not by a sphere on a plinth, but by a broken pediment with a brazier (rather than a flower vase) or an oil lamp in the centre.

Faint indications also appear on the sheet alongside the window frame, and they might correspond to a first idea for other elements of the façade decoration: left, the plinth for a herm figure, and underneath a rectangular panel for one of the frieze paintings.

The windows and the drawing are also discussed in Chapter V.[4]

1. F. Healy, in McGrath et al., *Mythological Subjects I (CRLB)*, 2016, I, no. 40b; II, fig. 331.
2. Müller Hofstede, *Review Burchard – d'Hulst*, 1966, p. 446, fig. 8.
3. Toulier, *Villa Médicis*, I, 1989, I, passim; details of the windows in question: ibid., pp. 308, 309, figs 390 and 395; for diagrams of the window types on the façade of this Villa: ibid., pp. 306–307, 432.
4. See pp. 143–144.

No. 8. *A Chariot Race (The Lowering of the Cloth)*: Mural Painting (cf. Fig. 57)

Wall painting; approx. 120 × 175 cm.

Formerly on the east or garden façade of the studio, lost

c. 1616 (?)

VISUAL SOURCE: Harrewijn print, 1692 (Appendix III.2; Fig. 18; detail: Fig. 57).

LITERATURE: Rooses, *Maison*, 1888, p. 221 (as 'Pluton enlevant Proserpine'); Rooses, *Oeuvre*, 1886–92, V, pp. 185–186 (as 'Pluton enlevant Proserpine'); Delen, *Rubens'huis*, 1933, p. 29 (as 'Ontvoering van Proserpina'); Prims, *Rubenshuis*, 1946, p. 12, p. 33 (as 'de ontvoering van Proserpina'); Baudouin, *Summary Guide*, 1977, p. 29 (as 'the rape of Proserpina'); McGrath, *Rubens's House*, 1976–78, pp. 139–140, fig. 7; McGrath, *Rubens's House*, 1978, pp. 261–263, pl. 28b; Stutz, *Residenz*, 1985, p. 145; Van der Meulen, *Antique (CRLB)*, 1994, I, p. 100; Von Simson, *Rubens*, 1996, pp. 209–210; Logan – Belkin, *Drawings, I*, 2021, p. 217.

The wall painting in the form of a fictive stone relief, at the left on the east façade of the studio, shows a race with a *quadriga* (a chariot drawn by four horses). It has not been possible to establish if the subject is taken from one of many ancient stories about chariot races,[1] nor is it clear if Rubens had in mind a specific ancient painting of such a subject. It has been suggested that the frieze panel could be a reference to the chariot races which, as we know from Pliny, Aristides was famous for depicting.[2] However, Pliny's information is so brief – within a list of subjects treated by Aristides, he says no more than 'he also painted quadrigas racing', without description or commentary[3] – that it remains doubtful that this was Rubens's source for the frieze panel.

CATALOGUE No. 9

If Rubens simply wanted to represent a typical ancient relief scene, without drawing attention to a specific Greek painting – which certainly seems possible – then he had a good example at his disposal. To a large extent the composition is taken from a chariot race (*The Lowering of the Cloth*) shown on a fragment of a Roman relief which he had copied in Italy (Fig. 58)[4] and which was published as an illustration to Philip Rubens's *Electorum Libri II* (Fig. 59).[5]

The illusionistic relief on the studio façade represented a similar composition, incorporating almost all of the elements of the Roman relief. A *quadriga* awaits the starting signal, with the horses rearing; the figures in both ancient relief and wall panel are in the same poses: one gestures with his arm out in front, the second is ready to steer, stretching his arms in parallel, while a third holds a rod. A man wearing a toga stands at the far left; in the ancient relief, he is the *praetor* who gives the starting signal by letting a cloth (the *mappa*) fall, a practice specifically mentioned in Philip Rubens's book. Undoubtedly the man with his right hand raised at the far left in the wall painting corresponds to the man in the relief, and so rather than holding a staff as the Harrewijn engraving seems to suggest, he must also be 'dropping the cloth'. Both images likewise include the dramatic motif of a fallen man: in the marble relief fragment as well as in the book illustration only his feet are visible, bottom right. In Rubens's composition his whole body can be seen, curled into a ball with his head on the ground, underneath the rearing horses.

1. For detailed commentary on the theme of the victorious charioteer, see McGrath, *Rubens's House*, 1978, pp. 262–263.
2. Ibid., p. 262, as a tentative suggestion; as an established fact in Simson, *Rubens*, 1996, p. 209.
3. '[Aristides] pinxit et currentes quadrigas' (Pliny, *Natural History*, XXXV.99); not mentioned by McHam, *Pliny*, 2013.
4. In Rome Rubens made a drawing (now lost) from a fragment of a marble relief that was part of a circus constructed during the reign of Julius Caesar. It was in the Barberini collection and is now in the collection of the Vatican Museums (Van der Meulen, *Antique (CRLB)*, 1994, I, pp. 99–100, n. 14, text ill. 50; Logan – Belkin, *Drawings, I*, 2021, p. 217, no. 161; II, figs 214, 214a).
5. Engraving by Cornelis Galle I (Rubens, *Electorum Libri*, 1608, between p. 32 and p. 33), the plate is inscribed with title at top: ICONISMVS CIRCENSIVM ET MISSIONIS MAPPAE (Illustration of the circus game and the lowering of the cloth). See Judson – Van de Velde, *Title-pages (CRLB)*, 1978, I, pp. 80–81, no. 2; II, fig. 42; Van der Meulen, *Antique (CRLB)*, 1994, I, pp. 99–100, text ill. 51.

No. 9. *The Triumph of Apollo*: Mural Painting (cf. Fig. 60)

Wall painting; approx. 120 × 175 cm.

Formerly on the east or garden façade of the studio, lost

c. 1616 (?)

VISUAL SOURCE: Harrewijn print, 1692 (Appendix III.2; Fig. 18; detail: Fig. 60).

LITERATURE: Rooses, *Maison*, 1888, p. 221 (as 'Héros couronné par la Victoire'); Rooses, *Oeuvre*, 1886–92, V, pp. 185–186 (as 'Héros couronné par la Victoire'); Delen, *Rubens' huis*, 1933, p. 29 (as 'Een held door Victorie gekroond'); Prims, *Rubenshuis*, 1946, p. 12 (as 'de kroning van Apollo'); McGrath, *Rubens's House*, 1976–78, pp. 144–145, fig. 11; McGrath, *Rubens's House*, 1978, pp. 272–276, pl. 28b; Stutz, *Residenz*, 1985, p. 145; Heinen, *Immolatio boum*, 2010, p. 224; Uppenkamp – Van Beneden, *Architectural Symbolism*, 2011, p. 111, n. 120; Büttner, *Allegories (CRLB)*, 2018, I, p. 143.

The central frieze panel on the garden façade shows Apollo as victor in a musical competition, in which his gentle, harmonious lyre has defeated a shrill flute. Sitting with his lyre on his lap and his legs crossed, Apollo is crowned by Victory, a winged semi-naked woman who holds the wreath over his head with her right hand.

Some background information is required for the other figures in the scene. Ovid provides two stories about a musical contest won by Apollo, and gives a detailed account of the Metamorphoses that then followed. In the first story it was the woodland god Pan with his pipes who lost the competition. Also present were the mountain god Tmolus as judge, and the unfortunate king Midas who called out the wrong judgement – an insult which provoked Apollo to give him donkey's ears.[1] In the second Ovidian tale, Apollo's competitor was the satyr Marsyas. Neither Tmolus nor Midas are mentioned and the story ends in a horrific scene which is described in detail: the loser was flayed alive, and eventually the many tears shed in mourning by his 'fellow satyrs, fauns and nymphs' metamorphosed into the Marsyas, the purest river in Phrygia.[2] Thus the plot of the two Ovidian stories is quite different, and so are the characters who feature in them, with the exception, of course, of the god Apollo who won the contest.

Another short version of the story of Midas's ears appears in the *Fabulae* of Hyginus, in which he refers to Apollo's opponent as Marsyas or Pan ('cum Marsya vel Pane'), making no distinction between the two stories given by Ovid.[3]

There can be no doubt that in the frieze panel on Rubens's façade the figure to Apollo's right is King Midas who raises his arms in shock and grasps his altered ears. It is probably Tmolus who sits between Apollo and the figure of Victory. Finally, we need to identify which of the plucky flautists – Pan or Marsyas – is shown as the captive loser, with hands tied, in the foreground. The horned hybrid creature with goat's legs, and possibly with pan pipes tied around his middle – a detail not clearly visible in the print – has all the characteristics of both a satyr and the god Pan. So at first sight the Ovidian story with Midas, Tmolus and Pan seems to be the subject of the frieze panel. But is it? Is the captive figure not more likely Marsyas, who was cruelly punished for his *hubris*? Indeed, in Ovid's story Pan was not tied up, and certainly the immortal woodland god was never flayed or killed.

It should also be noted that if Rubens intended to represent Marsyas, then he might have been thinking of a painting by Zeuxis that Pliny mentions, but only by its title: he informs us that there was a *Marsyas Bound* ('Marsyas religatus') by the Greek master on display in Rome in the 'Shrine of Concord'.[4] Rubens perhaps assumed that Pliny's short title referred to a *Triumph of Apollo*. In that case it is possible that he had this lost work by Zeuxis in mind when making the design for his frieze panel.

Yet, there is more than one difficulty with assuming that the wall painting depicts Apollo defeating Marsyas. As noted above, Midas plays no role in the story of Apollo's contest with Marsyas, and furthermore it is not obvious that the captive creature with goat's legs is indeed meant to represent Marsyas. For Rubens was certainly aware that in Antiquity Marsyas was seen as a faun, that is a figure with horns and a tail, but – unlike the satyr Pan – having human legs.[5]

It should be clear that the two Ovidian tales are probably not the right starting point for an identification of the scene, as pointed out by Elizabeth McGrath in her comprehensive analysis of the subject.[6] Her primary conclusion was that, in accordance with the 'Renaissance pictorial convention', Rubens did not limit himself to classical sources in his images of Apollo's musical contest.[7] There is an obvious explanation for this inconsistent mixing of Ovid's two stories: the subject is not intended to illustrate a story but should be understood as an allegory. The figures of Midas and Pan (or Marsyas) are not so much 'characters', but rather personifications. Midas thus represents *Ignorantia*, with the long ass's ears which were the familiar trademark used to personify this vice.[8]

As in the allegorical scene *The Calumny of Apelles*, shown in another frieze panel (No. 13; Fig. 90), here too the long ass's ears adorn the head of a character that fails to make the right judgement. In the context of the musical competition, this Midas as *Ignorantia* can be seen more specifically as 'unenlightened aesthetic judgement'. The meaning of the allegory with the crowned Apollo is thus straightforward: it represents 'the symbolic final triumph, with good art victorious over bad'.[9]

Certain motifs in the composition of the *Triumph of Apollo* also appear in other works by Rubens and deserve attention. The figure of Victory can be connected with Rubens's painting *Victory Crowning a Hero* in the Gemäldegalerie Alte Meister in Kassel, which is dated around 1614.[10] One strikingly similar motif – a seated, half-naked Victory with a victor's wreath in her outstretched right hand, one knee drawn up and her body turning to the right – appears in a

CATALOGUE No. 10

pen drawing with *Sketches for a Figure of Victory* in the Hessisches Landesmuseum in Darmstadt, regarded as a preparatory study for this painting (Fig. 62).[11] Furthermore, on the verso of this sheet, two very sketchily drawn variants of a winged figure can be seen crowning someone (Fig. 63). The lower Victory composition is particularly interesting: rather than a hero in armour, as in the Kassel painting, it is Apollo – identified by his lyre – being crowned. To the right of the god, there are a few lines that possibly indicate the head and part of the torso of a bound captive. It is naturally difficult to determine if Rubens drew this composition on paper to record his first thoughts for the frieze panel. Burchard and d'Hulst believed that it was a design for a *'Crowning of Apollo after his Victory over Marsyas'*, without, however, making the connection with the façade painting.[12] In the Kassel painting as well as in the drawings, Victory holds a palm branch in her left hand. This cannot be made out in the small detail of the Harrewijn print. There, between Apollo and Victory, are two vertical and intersecting lines that are difficult to interpret. One of them possibly represents a long lance held by Victory.

We should note that in this fictive stone relief, as in a number of the other frieze panels, Rubens also borrowed a motif from ancient sculpture. For the torso and head of the captive satyr he used one of the chalk drawings he had made in Rome of the *Centaur Tormented by Cupid*, which was then in the collection of Scipione Borghese and is now in the Musée du Louvre.[13] The sheet that Rubens used as a model for the satyr with hands tied behind its back (like the centaur) and head turned to the left, is in the collection of the Wallraf-Richartz-Museum & Fondation Corboud, Cologne (Fig. 61).[14]

1. Ovid, *Metamorphoses*, XI.146–179; Ovid, *Metamorphoses*, transl. Miller, 1977–84, II, pp. 130–133.
2. Ovid, *Metamorphoses*, VI.382–400; Ovid, *Metamorphoses*, transl. Miller, 1977–84, I, pp. 314–317.
3. Hyginus, *Fabulae*, CXCI.
4. Pliny, *Natural History – IX*, trans. Rackham, 1952, XXXV.66.
5. See, for example, Bober – Rubinstein, *Antique Sculpture*, 2010, nos 29–32, 34; the best-known representations of the wretched Marsyas are the sculptures that show him strung up against a tree, suspended by his wrists (that is as 'Marsyas Legatus' as in the painting by Zeuxis; ibid., nos 32, 32a).
6. McGrath, *Rubens's House*, 1978, pp. 273–275.
7. Rubens saw no difficulty in representing Midas and Marsyas in one and the same scene. As McGrath notes, in Apollo's musical contest which forms part of the Torre de la Parada series, the flute player with human legs who performs in front of Midas, is certainly Marsyas and not Pan, as a number of authors have incorrectly assumed (see McGrath, *Rubens's House*, 1978, p. 273, n. 134). The flautist in the painting (executed by Jordaens) and in Rubens's preparatory sketch was correctly seen as the faun Marsyas until A.P. de Mirimonde wrongly assumed that it must be Pan because of the presence of Midas and the musical instrument (pan pipes); see De Mirimonde, *Duel musical*, 1971, pp. 56–57; followed by a number of authors, who give the (incorrect) title as *The Judgment of Midas* (for example: Alpers, *Torre (CRLB)*, 1971, nos 41–41a, figs 147–148; Devisscher – De Poorter, eds, *Jordaens*, 1993, no. A53).
8. McGrath, *Rubens's House*, 1978, pp. 274–276, n. 139.
9. Ibid., p. 275, with references to allegorical scenes, for example Spranger's *Allegory of Art* (ibid., pl. 36b).
10. Büttner, *Allegories (CRLB)*, 2018, I, no. 13; II, fig. 69.
11. Ibid., I, no. 13a; II, figs 78–79. The connection between frieze panel and drawing was noted by McGrath, *Rubens's House*, 1978, p. 272, pl. 35c.
12. Burchard – d'Hulst, *Drawings*, 1963, I, p. 107, under no. 63 verso; these authors date the Kassel *Victory Crowning a Hero* to 1615, i.e. a year later than Büttner (see n. 10) and thus closer to our probable dating of the frieze panel.
13. For the statue, see for example Haskell – Penny, *Antique*, 1982, p. 179, no. 21, fig. 93. For Rubens's drawings which show the statue from various viewpoints, three originals and copies (preserved in the so-called Rubens Cantoor), see Van der Meulen, *Antique (CRLB)*, 1994, I, nos 65–69; III, figs 124–125, 127, 129–132; Westfehling, *Zeichnungen Rubens*, 2001, pp. 202–211, figs 26–30; Logan – Belkin, *Drawings, I*, 2021, nos 183–187; II, figs 237–239.
14. Westfehling, *Zeichnungen Rubens*, 2001, passim, fig. 26; Logan – Belkin, *Drawings, I*, 2021, no. 184; II, fig. 238. The torso of the centaur, taken from the same drawing, can also be found in Rubens's *Ecce Homo* in the State Hermitage Museum, St Petersburg (D. Jaffé in Jaffé et al., *Rubens*, 2005, pp. 182–183, nos 83–84).

No. 10. *The Sacrifice of an Ox*: Mural Painting (cf. Figs 18 and 64)

Wall painting; approx. 120 × 175 cm.

Formerly on the east or garden façade of the studio, lost

c. 1616 (?)

CATALOGUE No. 10

VISUAL SOURCE: Harrewijn print, 1692 (Appendix III.2; Fig. 18; detail: Fig. 64).

LITERATURE: Rooses, *Maison*, 1888, p. 221 (as 'un sacrifice païen, rappelant la Chute du Paganisme'); Rooses, *Oeuvre*, 1886–92, V, p. 185 (as 'un sacrifice paien'); Delen, *Rubens' huis*, 1933, p. 29 (as 'een heidense offerdienst'); Prims, *Rubenshuis*, 1946, p. 12 (as 'offer van een witten stier'); McGrath, *Rubens's House*, 1976–78, pp. 138–139, fig. 6; McGrath, *Rubens's House*, 1978, pp. 259–261, 276, pl. 28b; Stutz, *Residenz*, 1985, p. 145 (as 'das Stieropfer des […] Malers Pausias'); Von Simson, *Rubens*, 1996, pp. 209–210 (as 'das Stieropfer von […] Pausias'); Heinen, *Immolatio boum*, 2010, pp. 221–223, and passim, fig. 26 (as 'Immolatio Boum'); Baumstark – Delmarcel, *Decius Mus (CRLB)*, 2019, I, p. 103, n. 117; II, p. 41.

The third frieze panel on the studio's garden façade shows a Roman sacrificial scene apparently in the form of a stone relief. To the left a priest invokes the gods, standing beside a tripod on which the sacrificial flames can be seen burning, while the victim is forced down. It is impossible to tell if the animal is a bull or an ox – both were sacrificed to the gods – but since the distinction is not important here, we will refer to it as an ox.[1] One assistant stands behind to control the animal, while the second pulls its head down to one side, and the third stands with axe raised ready to strike the blow.

For this subject, as with a number of the frieze panels presented as stone reliefs, Rubens took inspiration from motifs which he knew from Roman reliefs. For this sacrificial scene no exact prototype is known such as that used for the *Chariot Race* (No. 8). But we can identify a large number of Roman images which influenced the composition as a whole as well as many of the details.

In order to depict the ancient ritual in an archaeologically accurate way, Rubens very likely had at his disposal one or more drawings that he made in Italy. But even if he did not, he was probably familiar with Roman reliefs showing sacrificial scenes, since reliable and fairly detailed images were reproduced in antiquarian publications (Fig. 68).[2]

Roman sacrificial scenes that relate to compositions by Rubens with a similar theme, in the frieze panel as well as in paintings, have often been discussed in the Rubens literature.[3] In connection with the frieze panel, Elizabeth McGrath mentions a relief which featured on the *Arch of the Argentarii* in Rome and which is now in the Palazzo dei Conservatori.[4] A striking resemblance to it can be found in the central section of a sarcophagus type depicting the 'biography of a Roman general', which was used with variations for a number of deceased, meaning that several examples have survived, including one in the Palazzo Ducale in Mantua (Fig. 66),[5] and another in Le Gallerie degli Uffizi in Florence.[6] Besides these sarcophagi, there is also an interesting fragment with a sacrificial scene, again in the Uffizi.[7]

Finally, it is worth noting that a similar sacrificial scene also occurs on a fragment among the group of ancient reliefs fixed to the garden façade of the Villa Medici in Rome (Fig. 67). Rubens probably saw this façade, and it seems possible that this was one of the Roman examples which inspired him to create a similar frieze of ancient reliefs for his studio wall.[8]

One constant motif in the Roman reliefs listed is that of the sacrificial animal whose head is being held and pushed down by a half-naked sacrificial attendant, who is shown kneeling and in profile. This movement of pulling the head down and to one side is a realistic detail: it reflects the actual course of the ritual, achieving the required position of the neck for the fatal blow. Furthermore, the victim's eyes needed to be turned away from the weapon so that it would not notice what was about to happen: it was important to prevent the animal from panicking in order to maintain the illusion that it consented to the sacrifice.[9]

The officers responsible for keeping the animal in check and slaughtering it were the *victimarii*, recognisable by their bare torsos and the *limus*, a long apron tied around the waist. One of them, the *popa*, was responsible for rendering the victim unconscious with a hammer or axe. He is usually shown half hidden behind the animal's back, but occasionally, as in Rubens's wall painting, we see him as a full-length figure. The kneeling

351

CATALOGUE No. 10

victimarius, who holds the animal down by its horns and nose might be the *cultrarius*, and his job was to cut the victim's carotid artery with a knife as soon as it had been struck by the *popa*.[10] This figure in the wall painting is comparable to one in a woodcut in Du Choul (Fig. 68).[11] Moreover, as has been frequently noted, there is also a related scene in Raphael's cartoon for *The Sacrifice at Lystra* from the famous *Acts of the Apostles* tapestry series.[12]

Rubens inserted the same sacrificial attendants – the priest with head covered, the kneeling *victimarius* and the *popa* with axe – as well as the victim with its head pushed downwards, in his other compositions with images of Roman sacrifices. At about the same time as the wall painting, or rather shortly after completion of the studio, he was working on *The Interpretation of the Victim*, a design for one of the scenes of his tapestry series illustrating the history of Decius Mus (Fig. 78).[13]

The choice of this subject of the Roman sacrifice for the studio façade is certainly connected with Rubens's special interest in sacrificial rituals which were at the centre of public life in ancient Rome.[14] However, we should perhaps also consider the possibility that another quite different factor led to Rubens's selection of this scene for his façade decoration. Otto Brendel, who made a study of ancient sarcophagi and reliefs, believed that the sacrificial scene, as depicted in the sculpted examples given above, is connected with one of the celebrated ancient Greek paintings which Pliny mentions as being on display in Rome.[15] In Pompey's portico, together with *The Sacrifice of Iphigenia* (see under No. 11), there was, according to Pliny, a painting by the Greek painter Pausias, the subject of which was an '*immolatio boum*', a sacrifice of oxen. This painting was admired for the ingenious manner in which one of the victims was represented. Pliny writes: 'The chief point was that although he wanted to show the long body of an ox he painted the animal facing the spectator and not standing sideways, and its great size is fully conveyed'. And he adds: 'Next, whereas all painters ordinarily execute in light colour the parts they wish to appear prominent and in dark those they wish to keep less obvious, this artist had made the whole ox of a black colour and has given substance to the shadow from the shadow itself, with quite remarkable skill that shows the shapes standing out on a level surface and a uniform solidity on a broken ground'.[16]

Authors who have written about Rubens's images of sacrifice are convinced that, by copying Roman sculptural examples, he wanted also to evoke Pausias's masterpiece.[17] In the literature on the façade frieze panel it is often simplistically stated that Rubens intended to recreate the Greek painting, and authors replace the title *Sacrifice of a Bull* or *Sacrifice of an Ox* with the one given by Pliny to Pausias's work, '*Immolatio Boum*' (a sacrifice of oxen).

Yet, how certain is this proposed borrowing? There is no obvious reason to believe that the Roman sculptors who carved a scene that was such an important feature of contemporary life would have taken a Greek painting as their model, even a very famous one. Furthermore, there are details in the Roman images that differ substantially from Pausias's work. In the reliefs mentioned as well as in Rubens's related wall painting, only a single animal is shown rather than several cattle. Significantly, these authors fail to acknowledge the absence – both in the ancient reliefs and in Rubens's fictive relief which follows them – of the two most admired aspects of Pausias's *Immalotio Boum*. The victim is not shown foreshortened but mostly in profile. This is even clearer in the sketch-like drawing, which was probably made as a preparatory study for Rubens's frieze panel (No. 10a; Fig. 65). Naturally there can be no sign of the famous effect of colour which inverted light and shade, either in the stone reliefs or in the fictive monochrome relief. In short, Rubens was decorating his studio façade, his '*diaeta romana*',[18] with the intention of evoking a Roman relief, and not a Greek painting.

Nonetheless, Rubens must have known Pliny's commentary, and he made use of it elsewhere in his work. It is indeed possible to detect Pausias's unusual effect of light and shadow in the victim in *The Interpretation of the Victim*, mentioned above,[19] and probably Rubens emulated the remarkable foreshortening in the frightened ox (or bull) represented frontally and storming towards us in the dramatic scene of the disturbed sacrifice in *The Eucharist Overcoming Pagan Sacrifices*.[20]

1. In descriptions in the literature of similar sacrificial scenes in ancient sculpture the animal is variously seen as an ox or bull (Brendel, *Immolatio Boum*, 1930, passim, as 'Stieropfer'), and sometimes both without distinction. See, for example, Bober – Rubinstein, *Antique Sculpture*, 2010, p. 240 ('a bull'), p. 242 ('white oxen'); see also the relief mentioned in n. 8. Jack J. Lennon, who describes in detail the procedure of the Roman sacrifice, names the victim explicitly as a 'bull' (Lennon, *Victimarii*, 2015, pp. 69–70, 80–81, 83). In the important Roman sacrifice involving three animals, known as the 'suovetaurilia', the third animal besides the pig and the ram was of course a bull.
2. For example, the book by Guillaume Du Choul, which has woodcut illustrations of sacrificial scenes (Du Choul, *Discours*, 1581, pp. 315, 324). For this and other publications, see also Baumstark – Delmarcel, *Decius Mus (CRLB)*, 2019, II, p. 38.
3. See for example Heinen, *Immolatio boum*, 2010, passim; a comprehensive list is given in Baumstark – Delmarcel, *Decius Mus (CRLB)*, 2019, II, pp. 37, 47 (nn. 59–74). For literature specifically on Roman reliefs of the relevant type, see for example Brendel, *Immolatio Boum*, 1930, pp. 196–225; Huet, *La mise à mort*, 2005, pp. 91–119 (with further literature).
4. McGrath, *Rubens's House*, 1978, p. 259, pl. 33c; for this relief, see for example Huet, *La mise à mort*, 2005, p. 101, fig. 7.
5. Levi, *Cat. Mantua (sculpture)*, 1931, pp. 86–87, no. 186 (repr.); Heinen, *Immolatio boum*, 2010, p. 200, fig. 4; Baumstark – Delmarcel, *Decius Mus (CRLB)*, 2019, I, fig. 30; II, p. 37 (no. 5), p. 47, n. 70.
6. Inv. no. 82. Mansuelli, *Cat. Florence*, I, no. 253; Bober – Rubinstein, *Antique Sculpture*, 2010, no. 197; Baumstark – Delmarcel, *Decius Mus (CRLB)*, 2019, II, p. 47, n. 69; this sarcophagus was on display (until 1784) in the garden of the Villa Medici in Rome, meaning that Rubens may have seen it. A third sarcophagus of the same type is in the Los Angeles County Museum of Art (Bober – Rubinstein, *ibid.*, p. 249, under no. 197).
7. In no. 342. Mansuelli, *Cat. Florence*, 1958, I, no. 149; Heinen, *Immolatio boum*, 2010, pp. 200–201, fig. 5 (incorrectly as from the façade of the Villa Medici in Rome; see n. 8). The relief in the Uffizi was used as model for a woodcut in Du Choul, *Discours*, 1581, p. 324 (Fig. 68).
8. Toulier, *Villa Médicis*, I, 1989, p. 345, no. 473, repr. pp. 20–21 and figs 473A–473C (as *'Taureau conduit au sacrifice'*). This is a fragment of the *Ara Pacis Augustae* of Claudius, and on the façade it was enlarged into a rectangle and given a decorative moulding; a reconstruction of this altar, with a plaster cast of the fragment, is displayed in the Museo dell'Ara Pacis, Rome (see Laubscher, *Arcus Novus und Arcus Claudii*, 1976; La Rocca, *Arcus et area Claudii*, 1994).
9. Baumstark – Delmarcel, *Decius Mus (CRLB)*, 2019, I, p. 33.
10. For a clear description of the *victimarii*, their function, practices, dress and iconography, see Lennon, *Victimarii*, 2015, pp. 65–89.
11. Du Choul, *Discours*, 1581, ill. p. 315.
12. For Raphael's cartoon with the sacrificial, see Shearman, *Raphael's Cartoons*, 1972, pp. 122–124, 128, pl 34–38; Fermor, *Raphael Cartoons*, 1996, figs 12, 16; De Strobel, ed., *Sistine Chapel / Tapestries*, 2020, no. 9. In connection with Rubens's sacrificial scenes, see for example Heinen, *Immolatio boum*, 2010, pp. 201–202, fig. 6; Baumstark – Delmarcel, *Decius Mus (CRLB)*, 2019, I, p. 18, fig. 28; II, pp. 34 ff.
13. Ibid., no. 2a, fig. 25 (as '1617'). The same sacrificial attendants appear also in a later work by Rubens: the dramatic scene showing *The Eucharist Overcoming Pagan Sacrifices* (De Poorter, *Eucharist (CRLB)*, 1978, I, no. 16b; II, fig. 200).
14. Bober – Rubinstein, *Antique Sculpture*, 2010, pp. 240–245; see also Heinen, *Immolatio boum*, 2010, passim; Baumstark – Delmarcel, *Decius Mus (CRLB)*, 2019, II, pp. 32–33.
15. Brendel, *Immolatio boum*, 1930, pp. 117 ff. Lippold, *Antike Gemäldekopien*, 1951, p. 61, however, was less convinced of the link between the Greek painting and the Roman reliefs.
16. Pliny, *Natural History*, XXXV.126–127; see also, with different translation, McGrath, *Rubens's House*, 1978, pp. 260–261 (quotation in Latin: p. 261, n. 66). On the painting by Pausias, see also McHam, *Pliny*, 2013, pp. 45, 107, 319, no. 110, 338, no. 110.
17. Elizabeth McGrath was the first to connect Pausias's masterpiece with Rubens's frieze panel (McGrath, *Rubens's House*, 1978, pp. 260–261); followed, also in respect of Rubens's other sacrificial scenes, in the extensive commentaries by Ulrich Heinen (Heinen, *Immolatio boum*, 2010, passim) and Reinhold Baumstark (here in connection with *The Interpretation of the Victim*, a scene from the *Decius Mus* series; Baumstark – Delmarcel, *Decius Mus (CRLB)*, 2019, I, p. 103; II, p. 37); likewise as 'after Pausias' in the brief mentions by Zita Stutz and Otto von Simson (Stutz, *Residenz*, 1985, p. 145; Simson, *Rubens*, 1996, pp. 209–210).
18. For this description, taken from Philip Rubens's 'Life of Rubens', see Chapter V, p. 156; and Appendix I.42: [2].
19. Baumstark – Delmarcel, *Decius Mus (CRLB)*, 2019, I, p. 103; II, p. 37. Baumstark points out rightly that the Pausias motif also occurs more than once in works by Jordaens (ibid., I, p. 49, nn. 109–110).
20. De Poorter, *Eucharist (CRLB)*, 1978, I, no. 16b; II, fig. 200.

No. 10a. *The Sacrifice of an Ox*: Drawing (Fig. 65)

Pen and brown ink on beige paper; 24.9 × 38.4 cm.

Private collection, on loan to Cologne, Wallraf-Richartz-Museum & Fondation Corboud, Graphische Sammlung. Inv. no. 2011/001

c. 1616 (?)

TECHNICAL NOTES: the drawing is in generally good condition, with four dark spots on the right. The beige sheet is pasted onto another blue sheet (29.8 × 43.5 cm) for extra support. Pasted on the mount is a small strip of paper printed with text: *P.P. Rubens. Vorbereitung zu einem Stieropfer. Geistreich in Umrissen mit der Feder ausgeführt qu. fol.* For a more elaborate technical description, see Heinen, *Immolatio boum*, 2010, p. 226, n. 1.

PROVENANCE: Private collection; on loan to the Wallraf-Richartz-Museum & Fondation Corboud, Cologne, since 2010.

EXHIBITED: Cologne, 2011; Cologne, 2018.

LITERATURE: Heinen, *Immolatio boum*, 2010, passim (as 'Immolatio boum' and 'um 1618'); Baumstark – Delmarcel, *Decius Mus (CRLB)*, 2019, II, p. 41.

This freely executed sketch of a sacrificial scene was unrecorded until it was linked to the frieze panel (No. 10) in a substantial article by Ulrich Heinen in 2010. Indeed, although Rubens used a similar antique motif in other scenes, there seems to be enough evidence to consider this sheet as a preparatory drawing for the façade decoration.

The drawing closely resembles the composition of the frieze panel, and hence also the sculpted Roman reliefs mentioned in No. 10. To the right in the drawing is a very similar group of the victim (with its tail in the air) with the two *victimarii* who restrain it, one kneeling and the other behind the animal with his arm over its back. The *popa*, with his weapon raised above his head, is also vaguely indicated. The remainder of the composition differs from the wall painting. The priest with his arms in the air can be seen, but here he faces to the right. The most significant difference in the drawing's composition is the addition of a sacrificial assistant crowned with a laurel wreath, who crouches in front of the sacrificial animal. He is undoubtedly the *cultrarius*, recognisable by the knife sheath hanging around his waist as well as the bowl that he holds in order to catch the victim's blood. Although not present in the wall painting, this motif is also borrowed from Roman reliefs depicting the same subject. A very similar figure can be seen, for example, in the relief in Le Gallerie degli Uffizi in Florence, which is illustrated in the text by Guillaume Du Choul (Fig. 68).[1]

The rapid and summary way in which the elements are sketched also characterises other drawings of this period. One drawing which is relevant for comparison and can be linked to one of the other frieze panels, is a sheet which includes a rapid study for a seated Apollo being crowned: the *Sketches for a Figure of Victory* in the Hessisches Landesmuseum in Darmstadt (Fig. 63).[2]

Ulrich Heinen assumes that the wall paintings were executed around 1618 and he applies the same dating to the drawing. However, if the drawing is indeed a preparatory study for the decoration of the studio façade, then it must have been produced one or two years earlier, shortly before or during the completion of the studio, that is around 1616. For discussion of the dating, see Chapter VI.[3]

See No. 10 for the doubtful hypothesis that Rubens's theme was inspired by a celebrated masterpiece by the Greek painter Pausias and that the subject can therefore be identified as the 'Immolatio boum' (sacrifice of oxen) described by Pliny.

1. For the relief in the Uffizi, see No. 10, n. 7; in the drawing, borrowings from two of the woodcuts in Du Choul can be detected: one shows the ox in profile with its tail in the air (Du Choul, *Discours*, 1581, p. 315); the other is a faithful copy of the relief in the Uffizi (ibid., p. 324), and shows the crouching youth with his head wreathed.
2. See No. 9 and esp. n. 6.
3. See pp. 173–175.

No. 11. *The Sacrifice of Iphigenia*: Mural Painting (cf. Figs 17 and 69)

Wall painting, approx. 120 × 175 cm.

Formerly on the north façade of the studio, lost

c. 1616 (?)

VISUAL SOURCES:
(1) Harrewijn print, 1684 (Appendix III.1; Fig. 17; detail: Fig. 69);
(2) Harrewijn print, 1692, in reverse and scarcely legible (Appendix III.2; Fig. 18);
(3) Aylesbury *View of the Courtyard of Rubens's House*, 1660s, (Appendix III.3; Figs 16, 27; detail: Fig. 70).

COPIES: (1) Drawing (Figs 71, 75 and 77), by Willem Panneels, Copenhagen, Statens Museum for Kunst, Kongelige Kobberstiksamling, inv. no. KKSgb6362 (Rubens Cantoor, IV,28); black chalk, pen, brown ink, heightened with white chalk, 185 × 286 mm. Inscribed below: AGAMEMNON. EXH.: Antwerp, 1993a, no. 65; Braunschweig, 2004, no. 80. LIT.: McGrath, *Rubens's House*, 1976–78, p. 137; McGrath, *Rubens's House*, 1978, pp. 248, 256 ff., pl. 32a; Garff – de la Fuente Pedersen, *Panneels*, 1988, I, p. 182 ff., no. 246; II, fig. 249; Held, *Review Garff – de la Fuente Pedersen*, 1991, p. 428, no. 246; Huvenne, *Cantoor*, 1993, n. 28, pp. 157–159, 162 (no. 65); Baudouin, *Fresco's*, 1998, pp. 14–16, fig. 11; Baudouin, *Drawings in Budapest*, 2004, pp. 12–13, fig. 11; U. Heinen in Büttner – Heinen, *Leidenschaften*, 2004, pp. 300–302; Heinen, *Immolatio boum*, 2010, pp. 222–223, 232, n. 9, fig. 28; Baumstark – Delmarcel, *Decius Mus (CRLB)*, 2019, II, pp. 49–50, n. 110.

(2) Drawing (Fig. 72), by an anonymous artist,[1] Budapest, Szépművészeti Múzeum, Collection of Prints and Drawings, inv. no. K.58.821; black chalk, 170 × 265 mm. Inscribed below in brown ink: APELLIS IPHIGENIA. PROV.: collection of István Delheres. LIT.: Baudouin, *Fresco's*, 1998, pp. 14–17, fig. 13 (as 'circle of Rubens'); Huvenne, *Tekeningen*, 1993, p. 158; Baudouin, *Drawings in Budapest*, 2004, pp. 12–13, fig. 10 (as 'circle of Rubens'); Baumstark – Delmarcel, *Decius Mus (CRLB)*, 2019, II, p. 50, n. 110 (as 'apparently done by Rubens's workshop').

(3) Drawing (Fig. 73), by an anonymous artist, whereabouts unknown; red chalk, 670 × 880 mm. On *recto*, inscribed: *91* in ink (?) in bottom right-hand corner. Attached to the same mount, a drawing of St Catherine, by another hand. PROV: sale, Amsterdam (Christie's), 9 November 1998, lot 49 (as 'Circle of Sir Peter Paul Rubens').

LITERATURE: Rooses, *Maison*, 1888, p. 221 (as 'un sacrifice antique'): Rooses, *Oeuvre*, 1886–92, V, p. 185 (as 'un sacrifice antique'); Delen, *Rubens' huis*, 1933, p. 29 (as 'een heidense offerdienst'); Prims, *Rubenshuis*, 1946, p. 12 (as 'Het offer van Iphigiena [sic]'); Stutz, *Residenz*, 1985, p. 145; McGrath, *Rubens's House*, 1976–78, pp. 137–138, fig. 5; McGrath, *Rubens's House*, 1978, pp. 256–259, 276, pl. 28a; Van der Meulen, *Antique (CRLB)*, 1994, I, p. 109; Von Simson, *Rubens*, 1996, pp. 209–210; Baudouin, *Fresco's*, 1998, pp. 14–15, fig. 12; Baudouin, *Drawings in Budapest*, 2004, pp. 12–13; U. Heinen in Büttner – Heinen, *Leidenschaften*, 2004, pp. 300–302; Heinen, *Immolatio boum*, 2010, pp. 222–223; Uppenkamp – Van Beneden, *Vera simmetria*, 2011, p. 38; Baumstark – Delmarcel, *Decius Mus (CRLB)*, 2019, II, pp. 41, 49.

The frieze panel at the far left underneath the top windows of the studio's north façade depicted one of the best-known tragic Greek myths: the Sacrifice of Iphigenia. It is an episode from the Trojan war, mentioned by several authors but best known from the version of the disturbing story in Euripides's tragedy *Iphigenia in Aulis*.[2] When the Greeks gathered their ships in the port of Aulis to set off for war, the goddess Diana, who was angry with Agamemnon, king of Mycenae and leader of the Greek army, held back the winds to prevent the fleet's departure. The Greeks learned that they would not be able to depart unless Agamemnon's daughter Iphigenia was sacrificed. On the pretext that she was to marry Achilles, Iphigenia was lured to Aulis where the tragic sacrificial scene took place.

The subject is not shown clearly in the surviving representations of Rubens's façade, the Harrewijn prints (Figs 17, 69 and 18) and the

CATALOGUE No. 11

Aylesbury painting (Figs 16, 27, 70), and were it not for a group of drawn copies, including a sheet by Willem Panneels from the 1620s (Figs 71, 75 and 77), we would probably not have understood the exact meaning of this ancient sacrificial scene. The description that follows is therefore based on these drawings.

The *trompe-l'oeil* relief shows the luckless Iphigenia, kneeling in front of the altar with her hands bound, while the executioner forces her head down as he prepares to strike with his sword. Her hair hangs down loose, hiding her face. Elizabeth McGrath pointed out that the resignation with which she undergoes her terrible fate is not unlike Rubens's representation of another virgin who was sacrificed by being put to the sword: the saint in *The Martyrdom of St Catherine of Alexandria*, an altarpiece for a church in Lille which was made around the same time as the frieze panel.[3] Iphigenia's posture is also strikingly similar to that of the bare-shouldered kneeling figure of Mary Magdalen who leans forward in the same way in Rubens's *Lamentation with St Francis* in the Museés royaux des Beaux-Arts de Belgique in Brussels, which is dated between 1617 and 1620 (Fig. 74).[4]

One figure in the frieze panel recalls a detail from one of the many drawings after Italian frescoes that Rubens collected and retouched. The executioner, represented as an energetic man in profile, striding forwards in the foreground, sword in hand, is similar to the warrior in *Perseus Showing the Head of Medusa to Phineus and his Companions* after Polidoro da Caravaggio.[5]

In the *trompe-l'oeil* relief Rubens applied his meticulous knowledge of scenes of ancient Roman sacrifice. Standing around the altar are the high priest Calchas and his usual attendants, a second priest and two assistants, a fluteplayer (*tibicen*) and a *camillus*: a boy wearing a laurel wreath who holds the *acerra* (an incense box), a figure to whom we will return. Behind them can be seen the head of a bull or ox. The precious vessels used for sacrifice are in the right foreground: the pitcher (*guttus*) and the large dish in which the sacrificial victim's blood is collected, or in which entrails were placed to be interpreted.

As observed by McGrath, a number of elements of Rubens's composition – the postures of the officiating priest, the *tibicen* and the *camillus*, as well as the bovine head in the background – are remarkably similar to the central motif of the Roman relief showing *Marcus Aurelius Sacrificing before the Capitoline Temple*, in the Palazzo dei Conservatori in Rome (Fig. 76).[6] In addition, the altar in Rubens's composition is also inspired by an actual ancient model, a candelabrum base, formerly in the Palazzo Farnese in Rome (Fig. 80). The ram's heads at the top, as well as two crouching sphinxes at the bottom with their long tails decoratively intertwined, are taken from it almost literally.[7]

The most striking figure in Rubens's *Sacrifice of Iphigenia* is Agamemnon, who has brought his child to Aulis under false pretences and is about to have her sacrificed. He cannot be distinguished among the vague details of the images that record the façade, but the drawings show him quite clearly. He appears seated to the left, completely hidden underneath his cloak, a fold of which is draped over his head, covering his face except for the ends of his beard. With this *tristitia velata* motif Rubens is referring to a well-known feature of one of the lost works by Greek painters, *The Sacrifice of Iphigenia*, by Timanthes. This masterpiece, that could be seen in ancient Rome as part of the collection that was on public display in the Portico of Pompey, was described and praised by Pliny, Quintilian, Valerius Maximus and Cicero.[8] Its most admired feature was that, having exhausted every expressive device in showing the pity felt by onlookers for the girl about to be sacrificed, the painter could find no art to match her father's supreme suffering and so showed him simply with his head cloaked in mourning, leaving his feelings to the imagination.[9]

Timanthes depicted the high priest and Agamemnon's attendants with their faces imprinted with various gradations of sorrow and pity. They are described by the Roman authors mentioned as: the 'high priest Calchas looking sad, Ulysses sadder still, Ajax crying out and Menelaus sorrowfully lamenting'.[10] Among the seven Greek warriors shown attending the sacrifice in Rubens's frieze painting, McGrath attempted to identify individuals mentioned in descriptions of Timanthes's painting. Menelaus is probably the figure at the far left, standing beside his brother; the two men behind the executioner may be Ajax and Ulysses. She also remarked that Rubens has added a figure not mentioned in the *ekphrases*, but who does play a role in Euripides's tragedy, namely Achilles. He is undoubtedly the beardless youth with wavy hair who appears in the background, his hands raised in horror, 'who seems to advance in a state of more distressed astonishment than any of the others'. His extreme emotions, including rage, are understandable and appropriate. For Iphigenia was tricked into coming to Aulis with the false promise that she was to marry Achilles, making him the unwitting instrument of her tragic fate.[11]

Rubens was not the first painter who included in the decoration of his own house an allusion to the celebrated painting in which the ancient Timanthes succeeded ingeniously in expressing an emotion by not displaying it. Giorgio Vasari (1511–1574) had anticipated him in the mid-sixteenth century, although his composition was quite different. On one wall of his house in Arezzo Vasari created a scene in which Timanthes stands at work with the much admired painting on the easel (Fig. 79).[12] Unlike Rubens, Vasari thus created, as it were, a narrative within a narrative.

It goes without saying that we cannot judge how Rubens's composition compared to the lost masterpiece. It is worth mentioning, however, that in a house in Pompeii there was a wall painting (now in the Museo Archeologico Nazionale di Napoli) that has been taken as a copy of Timanthes's *Iphigenia*, although discrepancies with the literary descriptions rather argue against it.[13]

Whatever the case, the sober composition of Rubens's sacrificial scene is closer to a relief showing the *Sacrifice of Iphigenia*, with five standing figures, one of them Agamemnon wrapped in his cloak, which encircles the base of a Roman altar, the *Ara of Cleomenes* in the Museo Archeologico Nazionale di Firenze (Fig. 81).[14]

In *The Interpretation of the Victim*, the sacrifice scene from the *Decius Mus* series, Rubens paid particular attention to the *camillus*, the effeminate young boy crowned with a laurel wreath and with long blonde hair (Fig. 78).[15] Here it is worth noting, as McGrath observes, that Rubens may have been referring in his own wall painting not only to Timanthes's *Sacrifice of Iphigenia* but also to a second Greek work mentioned by Pliny. For in both scenes we should perhaps see the detail of the *Camillus* standing by the altar as a reflection of Parrhasius's painting of a priest with a boy beside him, who wears a wreath and holding an incense box.[16]

As mentioned, few of the details of the composition given here can be made out in the illustrations of the façade. In the Aylesbury painting (Fig. 70) the scene is so vague and dark that we cannot conclude very much. In the prints (Figs 17–18 and 69) it is noticeable that Harrewijn, or rather Van Croes (the artist of the drawing) seems to have had difficulty with making an accurate reading of the monochrome scene high up on the façade, which was – forty years after Rubens's death – probably no longer in optimal condition. There is no trace of the seated figure of Agamemnon, although he is essential to the scene; the kneeling victim holds her head upright, the altar is shown in simplified form, and the *camillus* (the youth with incense box) is also apparently missing. It is especially obvious with the rendering of the executioner figure that something has gone wrong in the print: his body has been joined to the head of one of the men behind, making him much too tall; no sword can be seen. It is also not clear how we should construe his legs: probably because the drawing copied the original inaccurately, there now seems to be a second kneeling figure to his left.

This absence of reliable information for the detail of the composition painted on the façade makes it difficult to judge if the surviving drawn copies were done from the wall painting itself or from a lost preparatory drawing by Rubens. Willem Panneels had access to the drawings which Rubens kept in his so-called Cantoor, and his frieze copies were perhaps based on designs by Rubens that he came across there. Equally he may have used the façade itself as model, rendering it in his slightly untidy drawing style. The chalk drawing in Budapest, which is quite different in technique and style, puts more emphasis on its relief-like quality, and it does perhaps render a faithful image of the actual monochrome fictive relief rather than a drawing. It might have been produced during Rubens's lifetime, but no plausible attribution for it can be proposed.[17]

As noted, it is unclear exactly what the model was for the three drawn copies of The Sacrifice of Iphigenia, a matter complicated by the fact that the two images of the studio façade, the Aylesbury painting and the Harrewijn print, differ in detail. The drawings do not closely follow either one of these visual sources, and furthermore there are different details in each. In other words, no two of the five images that reproduce the Sacrifice of Iphigenia frieze panel have matching details. The Budapest drawing corresponds closely with Copy 3, but several elements differ from Panneels's drawing (Copy 1), which means that these sheets are not based on the same model. To name just a few differences: in the Budapest drawing (as well as Copy 3), Iphigenia is seated on a step which runs from underneath the altar as far as the executioner's foot; the executioner has a beard in the Budapest drawing (as also in Copy 3); in the Budapest drawing we cannot see the executioner's left hand with which he forces down Iphigenia's head; as in the classical candelabrum base (Fig. 80), the sphinxes in the Budapest drawing have female heads, while Panneels's drawing shows griffin's heads. It is also worth noting that while the correct title AGAMEMNON appears on Panneels's drawing, the title on the Budapest sheet, APELLIS IPHIGENIA refers to the wrong Greek painter.[18]

In short, it is safe to assume that Rubens made a preparatory drawing for The Sacrifice of Iphigenia, as for all the other frieze panels, but there is insufficient evidence to determine if one or more of the surviving copies were made after a preparatory drawing rather than from the actual façade paintings that were visible to all entering the courtyard. In the absence of clarity on this matter, the three drawings are thus included in the catalogue simply as copies of the wall painting under discussion, and there is no catalogue entry for a (probably lost) preparatory drawing by Rubens.

1. For tentative attributions, see below under n. 17.
2. Euripides, Iphigenia in Aulis, esp. lines 1547–1560. This episode from the Trojan war – which is not described in Homer's Iliad, as might be thought – was treated in different ways by various classical writers; for the sacrificial scene, see authors mentioned under n. 8.
3. Vlieghe, Saints (CRLB), 1972–73, I, no. 78, fig. 133; Burchard dated the work '1615, or somewhat later' (ibid., I, p. 122). McGrath observed that, unlike her Christian counterpart, Iphigenia is not rewarded with a heavenly vision and consequently lets her head hang down, rather than looking up towards heaven (McGrath, Rubens's House, 1978, p. 257).
4. Brussels, Musées royaux des Beaux-Arts de Belgique, inv. no. 164. Judson, Passion (CRLB), 2000, no. 70, fig. 204. The figures of Iphigenia and Mary Magdalen are almost identical, although Mary bends over more deeply and in both hands (which are not bound) she clutches the nails of the passion.
5. Wood, Copies, Raphael (CRLB), 2010, I, no. 81; II, fig. 207.
6. McGrath, Rubens's House, 1978, p. 259, fig. 32b. For the relief, see Bober – Rubinstein, Antique Sculpture, 2010, no. 191; see also Van der Meulen, Antique (CRLB), 1994, I, p. 109, text ill. 56; Heinen, Immolatio boum, 2010, p. 213, fig. 19. For detailed discussion of Rubens's interest in Roman sacrificial scenes, with which he was familiar from Roman reliefs, and which he frequently included in his paintings, see ibid., passim; Baumstark – Delmarcel, Decius Mus (CRLB), 2019, II, pp. 9–42. See also under No. 10.
7. Now in the Musée Condé, Chantilly (Bober – Rubinstein, Antique Sculpture, 2010, no. 57); the shape of the ram's heads is changed somewhat and a festoon has been added. A similar altar with sphinxes with intertwined tails can also be found in The Interpretation of the Victim (Fig. 78) from the Decius Mus series (Baumstark – Delmarcel, Decius Mus (CRLB), 2019, II, no. 2a, see esp. detail figs 37–38).
8. Pliny, Natural History, XXXV.73; Quintilian, Institutio Oratoria, II.13.13; Valerius Maximus, Memorabilia, VIII, 11, 6; Cicero, De Oratore, 22:47. The relevant passages are quoted by Moffitt, Sluter's Pleurants, 2005, pp. 79–80.
9. For this ancient painting, see McGrath, Rubens's House, 1978, pp. 256–257; McHam, Pliny, 2013, pp. 249–250, 321, no. 147, 342, no. 147 (with references to the passages in Alberti, Vasari, Lomazzo and four further 16th-century Italian authors). Timanthes's tristitia velata motif, which is an image of deep mourning, has been treated at length by John Moffit in a quite different context: the mourners in flowing Carthusian habits with their heads completely hooded, in Claus Sluter's Pleurants around the base of the effigy of Philip the Bold, formerly in Champmol, now in the Musée des Beaux-Arts, Dijon (Moffitt, Sluter's Pleurants, 2005, pp. 78–81).

10. Taken from McGrath, *Rubens's House*, 1978, p. 257 (with references to the descriptions by various Latin authors).

11. Ibid., p. 257; Achilles's furious response features in Euripides's *Iphigenia in Aulis*; and Achilles also plays a role in later sentimental versions of the story (see ibid., p. 257, n. 45).

12. Vasari's composition, which shows a blindfolded Iphigenia sitting on the altar, her hands tied behind her back, also differs markedly from Rubens's frieze panel (McHam, *Pliny*, 2013, pp. 249–250, fig. 196). On the house in Arezzo, see also Albrecht, *Häuser von Giorgio Vasari*, 1985, pp. 83–94.

13. Apart from the admired motif of Agamemnon who can be seen standing hidden by his cloak, there is in the Roman painting no relationship with Rubens's composition. Iphigenia is not shown kneeling in front of the altar, accepting her fate, but rather she gesticulates as she is carried to the altar by two men, while the deer sent by Diana to replace her has already appeared in the sky. Scholars of ancient painting are divided on the question as to whether this Roman copy, which is characterised by 'Hellenistic pathos', is indeed modelled on Timanthes's masterpiece. Georg Lippold rejects the identification on stylistic grounds, arguing that the style suggests a Greek original of a much later date (Lippold, *Antike Gemäldekopien*, 1951, p. 53, fig. 39). Roger Ling questions the usefulness of Pompeian paintings to gain an impression of the composition of ancient Greek masterpieces (Ling, *Roman Painting*, 1991, p. 154, fig. 139). Stelios Lydakis on the other hand regards it as a mediocre copy after Timanthes (Lydakis, *Greek Painting*, 2004, p. 125, figs 98–99). On this, see also McGrath, *Rubens's House*, 1978, p. 258, n. 51.

14. McGrath, ibid., p. 258, fig. 26b; Lydakis, ibid., p. 125, fig. 97; Bober – Rubinstein, *Antique Sculpture*, 2010, no.105.

15. For a full discussion of this figure characterised by androgynous beauty, see Baumstark – Delmarcel, *Decius Mus (CRLB)*, 2019, II, p. 38, nn. 83–86, under no. 2a, fig. 32.

16. McGrath, ibid., p. 257. See Pliny, *Natural History*, XXXV.70 ('[pinxit] item sacerdotem adstante puero cum acerra et corona').

17. While coming to no definitive conclusion, Baudouin (Baudouin, *Drawings in Budapest*, 2004, p. 13) observes that the Budapest sheet recalls drawings attributed to two artists from Rubens's circle – Theodoor van Thulden (1606–1669) and Abraham van Diepenbeeck (1596–1675) – in the so-called Fontainebleau sketchbook and elsewhere (see, for example, Wood, *Drawings*, 1990, pp. 3–53).

18. The title on Panneels's drawing is clearly authentic, as shown by comparison with the letter type of inscriptions in his prints. The reference to the wrong Greek painter on the Budapest copy could be a later addition: the inscription is in brown ink, while the rest of the sheet is executed in black chalk.

No. 12. *Alexander with the Thunderbolt*: Mural Painting (cf. Figs 17 and 82)

Wall Painting; approx. 120 × 175 cm.

Formerly on the north façade of the studio, lost

c. 1616 (?)

VISUAL SOURCES:
(1) Harrewijn print, 1684 (Appendix III.1; Fig. 17; detail: Fig. 82);
(2) Harrewijn print, 1692 (Appendix III.2; Fig. 18), in reverse and scarcely legible;
(3) Aylesbury *View of the Courtyard of Rubens's House*, 1660s (Appendix III.3; Figs 16, 27; detail: Fig. 83).

COPY: Drawing (Fig. 84), by Willem Panneels, Copenhagen, Statens Museum for Kunst, Kongelige Kobberstiksammling, inv. no. KKSgb12474 (Rubens Cantoor, IV,35); black chalk, pen and brush, brown ink, 172 × 227 mm. Inscribed in pen and brown ink, on recto, at bottom 92 and (in Panneels's code): *dit is een ordinansi die geschieldert is opt huijs van sinor rubbens ende is een triomf van allexander mangnus [sic]*, and on verso, in pencil, in the centre: *6*. Watermark: post horn hanging from a star (cf. Briquet, 1923, no. 8074-countermark). EXH.: Antwerp, 1993a, no. 67. LIT.: Falck, *Rubenselevs Tegninger*, 1918, p. 70, repr. on p. 72; Oldenbourg, *Rubens*, 1922, p. 192; Prims, *Rubenshuis*, 1946, p. 22; McGrath, *Rubens's House*, 1978, p. 248, pp. 252–255, pl. 29b; Garff – de la Fuente Pedersen, *Panneels*, 1988, no. 248; Held, *Review Garff – de la Fuente Pedersen*, 1991, p. 428, no. 248; Huvenne, *Tekeningen*, 1993, pp. 156, 157, 163, no. 67; McGrath, *History (CRLB)*, 1997, I, pp. 91–93, under no. 16; II, fig. 65; Baudouin, *Fresco's*, 1998, pp. 12–14, fig. 10.

LITERATURE: Rooses, *Maison*, 1888, p. 221 (as 'tableau où on voit couronner une femme'); Rooses, *Oeuvre*, 1886–92, V, p. 185; Delen, *Rubens' huis*, 1933, p. 29 (as 'waar een vrouw gekroond wordt'); Prims, *Rubenshuis*, 1946, p. 12 (as 'Kroning van Alexander'); McGrath, *Rubens's House*, 1976–

CATALOGUE No. 12

78, pp. 134–136, fig. 4; McGrath, *Rubens's House*, 1978, pp. 251–256, 276, pl. 28a; Stutz, *Residenz*, 1985, p. 145; Von Simson, *Rubens*, 1996, p. 209; Huvenne, *Tekeningen*, 1993, p. 158; McGrath, *History (CRLB)*, 1997, I, pp. 91–93, under no. 16; Baudouin, *Fresco's*, 1998, pp. 12–14, fig. 8.

The second frieze panel on the north façade, to the right of *The Sacrifice of Iphigenia* (No. 11), was correctly identified by Floris Prims as an allegorical scene showing *The Triumph of Alexander the Great*. Neither the Harrewijn prints nor the Aylesbury painting provide a very detailed image (Figs 82–83). The latter is interesting in that it represents the façade in colour and shows the scene as it must actually have appeared: monochrome and with pronounced shadows (suggesting light from the left) in imitation of a stone relief. Much more detail can be obtained from a drawn copy by Willem Panneels, who was employed by Rubens and lived in the house in the 1620s (Copy; Fig. 84).[1]

That the Panneels drawing does indeed represent the panel on Rubens's façade rather than being a variant of the same subject, can be deduced from the coded inscription, which also confirms the identification of the subject: 'this is a composition painted on Mr Rubens's house, and it is a triumph of Alexander the Great'. Furthermore, the inscription states unequivocally that the frieze panel was indeed painted on the façade rather than carved in relief, as believed by several authors, and which is the form that was chosen in the restoration (for discussion, see above).[2]

Although we can be certain that the copy shows an image of the picture on the façade, it is not absolutely clear that Panneels made his drawing directly from the façade rather than from another drawing, possibly a detailed design by Rubens. We should mention in this connection that several differences (on which more later) can be detected between his drawn copy and the details given in the 1684 Harrewijn print, but these do not inform us definitively what Panneels used as model.

The description of the composition that follows is largely based on Panneels's drawing which, as mentioned, is more detailed than the Harrewijn print or the Aylesbury painting. Alexander is shown standing upright in the centre, nude apart from some drapery, the extremities of which appear over his left shoulder and right arm. Winged Victory holds a triumphal wreath over his head. One essential element that cannot be made out on the print is Jupiter's thunderbolt, which he clutches in his right hand. With his left hand on the bridle, Alexander holds Bucephalus, the horse that played a central role in his life. He was the only person who could tame him and Bucephalus became Alexander's loyal companion on military campaigns across Asia. There are captives standing to the left and lying at his feet. To the right, beneath a fold of drapery which suggests a baldachin, sits the king of the gods, Jupiter, with his sceptre and accompanied by his eagle. His raised hand seems to express surprise at what he sees: his lethal weapon in the hand of a mortal. Likewise, the eagle screeches in reaction to the scene, its beak wide open.

The details shown in the two images of *The Triumph of Alexander* (Figs 82–83) are not exactly the same, something for which there is no plausible explanation. It is certainly possible that by the time the Aylesbury painting and Harrewijn prints were made, some damage had been done spoiling the appearance of the paintings on the façade, meaning that details could no longer be correctly interpreted. Thus no eagle appears at Jupiter's feet either in the print or the painting. In the print, the arched top of Victory's wing has been misinterpreted as the head of an additional figure. One striking difference is the figure of the crouching captive with his hands bound, depicted frontally at Alexander's feet, and who only appears in the print. He is not visible in the painting, while in the drawing we see instead a partial view of two lying figures, one in profile. In this case, a misreading of the original seems less likely.

In this illusionistic stone relief, Rubens made use of a number of motifs taken from ancient sculpture, both reliefs and free-standing, as he did with most of the other frieze panels. For the *Triumph of Alexander* we have again benefited greatly from the knowledge and perceptiveness of Elizabeth McGrath, who identified the motifs summarised below.

Both the appearance and seated pose of the enthroned Jupiter are reminiscent of the type of bearded and seated divinity who often appears in profile on Roman sarcophagi and represents either Jupiter or Pluto with the dog Cerberus. One such Roman relief, showing Pluto, which Rubens may have seen in Italy, is the Proserpina sarcophagus, in the Palazzo Ducale in Mantua (Fig. 86).[3] The image of Bucephalus likewise goes back to classical sculpture. The motif of the hero holding a horse by the reins corresponds, of course, to the celebrated free-standing sculptures of the *Dioscuri* in Rome. Furthermore, the horse raising its front right hoof, largely hidden by the man who holds him by the reins in his left hand, as in Rubens's composition, can also be found in reliefs, for example in a detail from the *Sacrifice to Apollo* on the Arch of Constantine (Fig. 85).[4]

The most striking borrowing is of the two male figures to the left: they are 'barbarians' captured by Alexander, as is clear from their barbarian clothing with leggings down to their ankles. These are taken almost literally from the two large ancient statues of captured 'barbarian' chieftains, now in the Palazzo dei Conservatori in Rome (see e.g. Fig. 88). When staying in Rome, Rubens almost certainly saw them and possibly also drew them – in the garden of the Palazzo Cesi in the Borgo Vecchio.[5] In the absence of a drawing, he may have taken them from illustrations in publications such as the *Speculum Romanae Magnificentiae*, a collection of engravings of Roman monuments published by Lafreri, an example of which was in Albert Rubens's possession (Fig. 89).[6] The façade decoration is not the only composition in which Rubens put a version of the two captives. They also appear, in colour and with more detail, in *The Triumph of Rome* in the Mauritshuis in The Hague.[7]

In the selection and execution of this frieze scene Rubens undoubtedly had in mind one of the famous paintings by Apelles: *Alexander Holding a Thunderbolt*, in the Temple of Diana at Ephesus, which is described by Pliny and known also from three passages in the writings of Plutarch. Pliny provides the longest commentary: 'He [Apelles] also painted Alexander the Great holding a Thunderbolt, in the temple of Artemis at Ephesus, for a fee of twenty talents in gold. The fingers have the appearance of projecting from the surface and the thunderbolt seems to stand out from the picture – readers must remember that all these affects were produced by four colours; the artist received the price of this picture in gold coin measured by weight, not counted.'[8]

Thus the most remarkable aspect of the painting, according to Pliny, was the extraordinary effect of foreshortening demonstrated in the hand with the thunderbolt. Beyond the lines cited, Pliny gives no further detail, so that the composition of the masterpiece remains unknown. The few further mentions of it in classical literature also fail to give a more accurate description, but they are evidence of the significance and fame of Apelles's painting. An interesting passage can be found in Plutarch, who informs us that the sculptor Lysippus, maker of a statue of Alexander, voiced criticism of Apelles's painting: he thought it wrong to show Alexander with Jupiter's thunderbolt and believed that in his own statue he had celebrated Alexander with greater decorum, representing him with a commander's spear.[9]

What can Rubens have used as the basis for his Alexander figure, who is shown – quite exceptionally – as a nude hero? In other works by Rubens and not just in historical paintings in which he plays the leading role, Alexander appears as a general in armour.[10] In that traditional guise he appears in a very sketchy pen drawing, in Berlin, with studies for a composition showing *The Triumph of Alexander* and including several other figures, but conceived along very different lines to the wall painting.[11] Possibly Rubens took inspiration for his unconventional Alexander from an ancient Jupiter type, which would be logical because his image is somewhat similar to the king of the gods as he appears on Roman coins, which Rubens must certainly have known: represented frontally, nude and with thunderbolt in his hand (Fig. 87).[12]

As far as we can tell, the theme of Alexander with the thunderbolt remained a rare subject in Antiquity and in subsequent Western painting, despite the fame of Apelles's picture.[13]

1. On Panneels and the Rubens Cantoor drawings, see above, Chapter II, pp. 58–59.

CATALOGUE No. 13

2. Chapter VI, pp. 172–173.
3. Bober – Rubinstein, *Antique Sculpture*, 2010, p. 61, no. 9a; McGrath, *Rubens's House*, 1978, p. 252, n. 31, pl. 30b. A second example with an almost identical motif was undoubtedly seen by Rubens on the sarcophagus with *The Abduction of Proserpina*, now in Rome, Palazzo Pallavicini Rospigliosi, Casino dell' Aurora (Bober – Rubinstein, *ibid.*, no. 9, fig. 9iii); see the drawn copy attributed to Rubens (Van der Meulen, *Antique (CRLB)*, 1994, II, no. 139; III, figs 270–271). For a detailed discussion of the motif of the god enthroned in profile, in other ancient sculpture as well as reworked by Rubens in his paintings, see McGrath, *ibid.*, pp. 252–253, n. 31.
4. For this, as well as several further examples, see McGrath, *Rubens's House*, 1978, p. 254, n. 34, pl. 30 f.
5. Observed by McGrath, *ibid.*, pp. 252 (n. 31), 254 (n. 35), pls 30b, c and d. On these statues, see Haskell – Penny, *Antique*, 1982, p. 171 (3), under no. 17; Van der Meulen, *Antique (CRLB)*, 1994, I, p. 50 (as 'Captive Barbarian Chieftains'). The statue of *Roma Triumphans* standing between them is illustrated in profile in Philip Rubens's *Electorum Libri II*, after a drawing by Rubens (Judson – Van de Velde, *Title-pages (CRLB)*, 1978, I, no. 3; II, fig. 43).
6. For this compilation of plates, no two of which are put together in exactly the same way, see Chapter IX, pp. 285–286, n. 106.
7. Inv. no. 837. Büttner, *Allegories (CRLB)*, 2018, I, no. 41; II, fig. 188.
8. Pliny, *Natural History*, XXXV.92; see McHam, *Pliny*, 2013, pp. 107, 289, 303, 317, 325, [Anecdote] no. 21. See also, with a different translation, McGrath, *Rubens's House*, 1978, p. 252, n. 29; for other sources, see *ibid.*, p. 252, n. 30.
9. *Ibid.*, p. 253, n. 33 (with passage from Plutarch in Greek and English translation). The same note has detailed discussion of Apelles's image, which can also be traced in emblem books as an example of 'importuna adulatio' (inappropriate flattery); see Henkel – Schöne, *Emblemata*, 1967–76, I, col. 1153. McGrath also draws attention to a rather different representation by Rubens of Alexander and the thunderbolt, no longer nude, but wearing armour, and in a quite separate context: in the title-page for H. Goltzius's *Romanae et Graecae Antiquitatis Monumenta* (published 1645) he appears falling to the ground among other figures who represent lost kingdoms (ibid., pp. 254–255, nn. 37, 39, pl. 31b; the commentary on the title-page of this book, probably written by Jan Gaspar Gevartius (1593–1666), refers explicitly to Apelles's painting mentioned by Pliny; see also Judson – Van de Velde, *Title-pages (CRLB)*, 1978, I, no. 82; II, fig. 275 (text of the 'explicatio': ibid. I, p. 339, n. 2). Intriguingly, an unidentified (Roman?) general in armour and with a thunderbolt appears in Rubens's representations of *The Triumph of Rome* (Büttner, *Allegories (CRLB)*, 2018, nos 40 and 41).
10. The subjects are *Alexander and Roxana* (McGrath, *History (CRLB)*, 1997, no. 14) and *Alexander's Lion Hunt* (Balis, *Hunting Scenes (CRLB)*, 1986, no. 16, fig. 93 [copy]). McGrath believes that in the wall painting Rubens probably chose a representation of heroic nudity to lend Alexander 'a specifically Greek authenticity' (McGrath, *Rubens's House*, 1978, pp. 254–255, n. 38).
11. Berlin, Staatliche Museen zu Berlin, Kupferstichkabinett, inv. no. KdZ. 4249; McGrath, *ibid.*, pp. 255–256, n. 41; McGrath, *History (CRLB)*, 1997, II, no. 16; I, fig. 63.
12. For example, the variants illustrated in Hemelaers – de Bie, *Numismata aurea*, 1615, pls 21, 36, 39–40, 49. In the coins mentioned, note also the similar position of the upraised left hand. It is worth remembering that Rubens designed a title-page for this book; Judson – Van de Velde, *Title-pages (CRLB)*, 1978, I, no. 33; II, fig. 114.
13. For an engraved carnelian gem (*intaglio*) described as a nude Alexander with the thunderbolt, which is believed to derive possibly from Apelles's painting, see Trofimova, ed., *Alexander*, 2010, p. 156, no. 123, repr.

No. 13. *The Calumny of Apelles*: Mural Painting (cf. Figs 17 and 90)

Wall painting; approx. 120 × 175 cm.

Formerly on the north façade of the studio, lost

c. 1616 (?)

VISUAL SOURCES:

(1) Harrewijn print, 1684 (Appendix III.1; Fig. 17; detail: Fig. 90);

(2) Harrewijn print, 1692, in reverse and scarcely legible (Appendix III.2; Fig. 18);

(3) Aylesbury *View of the Courtyard* of *Rubens's House*, 1660s (Appendix III.3; Figs 16, 27; detail: Fig. 91).

LITERATURE: Rooses, *Maison*, 1888, p. 221 (as 'sujet inconnu'); Rooses, *Oeuvre*, 1886–92, V, p. 186 (as 'sujet inconnu'); Delen, *Rubens' huis*, 1933, p. 29 (as 'onduidelijk onderwerp'); Prims, *Rubenshuis*, 1946, p. 12 (as 'onontcijferd'); Müller Hofstede, *Rubens in Italiën*, 1977, p. 65; McGrath, *Rubens's House*, 1976–1978, p. 134, fig. 3; McGrath, *Rubens's House*, 1978, pp. 250–251, 275, pl. 28a; Cast, *Calumny*, 1981, p. 184, n. 40; Stutz, *Residenz*, 1985, p. 145; Braham, *Rubens*, 1988, p. 22, under no. 26; Scott, *Perseus and Andromeda*, 1988, p. 258; Massing, *Calomnie*, 1990, pp. 86–87, p. 384, nos 26.G.B. and 26.G.B.a, pl. 26.G.B.a; Von Simson, *Rubens*, 1996, p. 209; Baudouin, *Fresco's*, 1998, pp. 10–11, fig. 7; Muller, *Rubens's Collection*, 2004, p. 39; Van Beneden, *Rubens's House Revealed*, 2009, pp. 106, 107, fig. 10; Heinen, *Immolatio boum*, 2010, p. 223; Uppenkamp – Van Beneden, *Architectural Symbolism*, 2011, pp. 111–112, fig. 148; Neerman, *Calumny of Apelles*, 2016, p. 4; Neerman et al., *Calumny of Apelles*, 2018, p. 110.

The subject of the frieze panel above the entrance to the studio, in the centre of the north façade, is an allegory which is largely inspired by a lost ancient painting by one of the most famous Greek artists. It is a version of Apelles's *Calumny*, of which there is a fairly detailed description, an *ekphrasis*, in the (Greek) writings of the Syrian satirist and rhetorician Lucian (c. 125–180 AD). For more on this subject, and Rubens's interpretation of it, see under No. 5a.

The largest and most readable record of the frieze panels on Rubens's studio façades can be found in the anonymous painting in Aylesbury, that shows three panels decorating the north façade (Fig. 91). It has details that give a good impression of their appearance: they were monochrome and resembled reliefs in stone.

It is important to note that as with the scenes of *The Sacrifice of Iphigenia* (No. 11; Fig. 69) and *Alexander with the Thunderbolt* (No. 12; Fig. 82), several of the details of *The Calumny* in the Aylesbury painting do not match the Harrewijn print. Undoubtedly the anonymous artist gives the more accurate image of the original façade decoration as far as the frieze goes. It is not immediately clear how to explain this discrepancy between the visual sources. Possibly by Hillewerve's time, the murals were no longer in good condition, making them difficult to read, and leading to the misinterpretation of details by Harrewijn (or rather Van Croes, who made the drawing used as a model). Or should we assume that by 1684 a number of details had been altered by restoration? In the case of *The Calumny*, the Aylesbury painting shows, in the lower foreground, a hybrid monster in place of the female figure with human arms that appears in the print. The monster's left limb ends in an animal claw, as in Rubens's preparatory drawing (for more on this, see under No. 13a). Careful examination reveals that the image of the wall painting in the Aylesbury *View of the Courtyard of Rubens's House* corresponds closely to the drawing.

No 13a. *The Calumny of Apelles*: Drawing (Fig. 96)

Black chalk, pen and brown ink and brown wash; 30.6 × 38.5 mm. For the verso see No. 13b (Fig. 97).

London, The Courtauld Gallery, Princes Gate Collection. Inv. no. PG52

c. 1616 (?)

TECHNICAL NOTES: drawn on grey-brown laid paper; 309 × 391 mm. A vertical crease 1/3 from the right, seen from the recto. On the verso the crease creates a clear boundary between the architectural study and the figure studies, indicating that the latter were most likely drawn after the sheet was folded. Generally in good condition, though with some yellow stains. Inscribed on the verso, lower left: *46* (or *40*); and lower right: *de Rubens af-af*.

PROVENANCE: Acquired from Colnaghi, 31 December 1953, by Count Antoine Seilern (1901–1978), London; by bequest to the Courtauld Institute of Art, London, 1978.

COPIES: (1) Plaque (with alterations), attributed to an anonymous Flemish silversmith, the high relief is incorporated into a basin made in 1683 by an unidentified London silversmith (signed *IM*). Dundee (Scotland), The McManus: Dundee, Dundee's Art Gallery & Museum, inv. no. 1979–867; gilt silver, 56.1 (diameter) × 5.8 (depth) cm, lettered on the rim in Latin: *Georgio Armitstead Armigero D.D. Gul.E Gladstone Armitiae Benevolentiae Beneficiorum delatorum Valde Memor Mense Augusti A.D. 1894*. PROV.: William Ewart Gladstone (1809–1898), prime minister of the UK; by whom in 1894 presented to George Armitstead (1824–1915), 1st Baron Armitstead, Dundee; by whom bequeathed to the museum in 1916. LIT.: Massing, *Calomnie*, 1990, p. 382, no. 26.G.a.

CATALOGUE No 13a

(2) Copper plaque (with alterations), by an anonymous German artist, whereabouts unknown; repoussé, 14.5 × 20 cm. PROV.: sale, London (Sotheby's), 7 July 1988, lot 92. LIT.: Massing, *Calomnie*, 1990, p. 382, under no. 26.G.a.

EXHIBITED: London, 1988–89, no. 26.

LITERATURE: Seilern, *Cat. London, Princes Gate*, 1955, pp. 83–84, no. 52, pl. CIII; Norris – Popham, *Review Seilern*, 1955, p. 398; Müller Hofstede, *Ölskizzen*, 1969, p. 237, n. 91; Seilern, *Corrigenda and Addenda*, 1971, p. 35, no. 52; Müller Hofstede, *Rubens in Italien*, 1977, pp. 63–65, 67, nn. 71–67, fig. E36; McGrath, *Rubens's House*, 1976–78, p. 134; McGrath, *Rubens's House*, 1978, pp. 248, 250–251, 276, fig. 29a; Cast, *Calumny*, 1981, p. 184, n. 40, fig. 54; Stutz, *Residenz*, 1985, p. 145, n. 16; Braham, *Rubens*, 1988, p. 22, no. 26; Massing, *Calomnie*, 1990, pp. 86–87, 381, no. 26 G.A.; Logan, *Review Rubens*, 1991, p. 315 (as not by Rubens (?)); Baudouin, *Fresco's*, 1998, pp. 10–11, n. 23, fig. 9; Heinen, *Immolatio boum*, 2010, pp. 223–224, 232, n. 91.

It is very likely that Rubens made preparatory studies for all the figurative scenes painted on the façade and indeed for the remainder of the painted and sculpted decorations that adorned these walls. However, almost none of this material has survived. A mere two drawings can be regarded as autograph studies for the frieze scenes: a summary pen drawing (No. 10a; Fig. 65) and the sheet under discussion, which shows the composition worked out in more detail, and which by and large matches the frieze panel above the studio entrance (No. 13; Figs 90–91).

The subject of this scene, apparently rendered as a stone relief, was inspired by the well-known Greek text about slander by the Syrian satirist and rhetorician Lucian (c. 125–180 AD). His discussion of this subject is illustrated with a tale about the slander which was directed against the Greek painter Apelles, a dramatic event against which the artist protested by painting an allegorical scene known as the 'Calumny of Apelles'.[1] In the *ekphrasis* describing this celebrated picture, Lucian lists ten personifications who play a role in the allegory, adding that he is relying on the interpretation given to him by a guide who explained the picture. The (anonymous) guide is not absolutely sure of the identity of certain figures, and this is understandable because Calumny (Slander, 'Diabole' in Greek) is shown alongside characters who stand for closely related concepts which can be difficult to tell apart. In English translations of Lucian's text these malign and dangerous figures are sometimes named as Envy (or Jealousy), Ignorance (or Stupidity), Suspicion, Treachery (or Intrigue or Conspiracy), Deceit (or Deception) and Hatred (or Rage).[2]

Rubens no doubt knew the ancient allegory from depictions of the *Calumny* by earlier artists (as will shortly become clear) as well as from the actual text of Lucian,[3] and probably also from other authors citing the ancient text.[4] Broadly speaking, he followed the *ekphrasis*, but in a much simplified form. His is not a literal illustration of Lucian's writing, such as we see in the famous painting by Sandro Botticelli (1445–1510), or the *Calumny* by Maarten de Vos (1532–1603), who was one of the few artists in the Southern Netherlands to depict this subject.[5]

In his version of the image, Rubens takes over only six of the ten personifications listed by Lucian – five in human form and one in the guise of a monster – and he adds a further three not mentioned in the classical sources. He also deviates from Apelles's painting by altering the significance of a number of the characters (or ideas), as will be explained below. This means, as said, that Rubens's composition cannot be interpreted and described simply by following the details of Lucian's *ekphrasis*.

It is worth noting that Rubens was not the first to come up with a modified interpretation of the well-known Calumny subject. Antoine Seilern and later authors observed that Rubens complemented Lucian's description with figures introduced by Federico Zuccaro (1540/41–1609) in his representation of the *Calumny*, which was engraved in 1572 by Cornelis Cort (1533–1578) (Fig. 92).[6] In Rubens's allegory no less than four of the nine figures are taken from Zuccaro's composition.

Rubens's depiction of the central protagonist is striking. He does not show Calumny as the beautiful, seductive young woman portrayed by Apelles and those who followed him to the letter. On the contrary, Rubens depicts her true nature and presents her as an ugly old woman with wild loose hair and snakes writhing over her shoulders, a type related to the traditional image of *Invidia*. The concepts of *Calumnia* and *Invidia*, who appear as two separate figures in the *ekphrasis*, seem to have been combined by Rubens into a single menacing character. In Apelles's painting, Envy or *Invidia*, often the source of slander – as in Apelles's case – was represented quite differently: as 'a pale ugly man' who goes in advance, with Calumny trailing behind.

Rubens's Calumny cast as *Invidia* performs the same action as in Apelles's painting. She clutches *Innocence*, a young man who raises one arm desperately to beg for mercy. She uses all her might to drag him by the arm and hair towards a group of ominous figures who will condemn him. A significant difference is that Rubens depicts the figures moving towards the left, while Lucian says explicitly that the 'man with very large ears' sits to the right, a scheme that is followed in most representations, but not in Zuccaro's.

At Calumny's feet crouches a monstrous creature, a harpy with female torso and bird's or lion's paws, who spreads her bat's wings and hisses aggressively at her victim. Zuccaro introduced a similar terrifying monster into his composition, but seen from behind (Fig. 96). It is difficult to be sure if this personifies a specific idea. Antoine Seilern and Helen Braham thought of Deceit, but the monster with hateful grimace could equally be Hatred or another destructive passion.

Interestingly, Rubens introduced very similar hideous figures to another scene representing a victim of slander: in one of his oil sketches for the *Medici* series, *The Departure of Maria de' Medici from Paris* (Munich, Bayerische Staatsgemäldesammlungen, Alte Pinakothek). The long-necked flying monster with claws and bat wings, identified as personifying 'deceit' ('le mensonge'), now with a companion, is threatening the queen, hovering above her, spitting fire (Fig. 93). Calumnia, an ugly old woman holding a torch, attacks her as she approaches from the left, and stretches out a fist to punch her victim.[7]

In the *ekphrasis* and in the majority of illustrations, Innocence is dragged towards an authority figure who has long donkey's ears ('almost like those of Midas', as Lucian specifies) and sits in judgement on a throne. Lies are whispered in his ears by two figures whom Lucian's guide presumed to be Ignorance and Suspicion. The structure of Rubens's composition is quite different and tighter; there is no suggestion of space, the throne is absent. Apelles's three figures are reduced by Rubens to two, represented, as mentioned, not on the right of the composition, as Lucian describes, but to the left. The most important – a seated figure with donkey's ears denoting his stupidity – is possibly also intended as a ruler in judgement, as implied by the diadem (or crown) on his head and the chain or other ornament around his neck. The head of a scowling, malicious-seeming woman appears over his right shoulder; possibly she is Suspicion, giver of bad advice, and she bends down towards him to whisper something in his ear.

Lucian mentions *Furor*, not a person, but symbolised simply by the device of a flaming torch in the hands of Apelles's Calumny. In Zuccaro's composition, which is followed in this detail by Rubens, this is quite different. In the left foreground of Rubens' composition sits a chained and blindfolded man on top of certain objects which cannot be made out very clearly in either the drawing or in the visual sources that record the façade. The motif can be understood from Zuccaro's *Calumny*: it is the chained and blindfolded *Furor*, blind rage, who sits on top of a pile of plundered armour which includes a cuirass (with collar pointing towards the viewer), with a shield underneath and a helmet alongside. This motif is taken literally from a passage in Virgil's *Aeneid*: in peacetime, *Furor* is imprisoned in the temple of war, meaning the Temple of Janus: 'within, impious Rage, sitting on savage arms, his hands fast bound behind him with a hundred brazen knots, shall roar [...]'.[8] This is also how *Furor* or *Ira* is described in Cartari's *Imagini* (Fig. 94), and in some editions the figure is also illustrated thus: in the 1615 edition, for example, which reproduces the motif taken literally from Zuccaro's composition (Fig. 92).[9]

Zuccaro's version also helps explain the gesture with outstretched arms made by the ignorant man with ass's ears. He is on the point of opening the lock that binds *Furor's* chains, thus releasing blind rage which will destroy Calumny's innocent victim. This terrifying figure appears, unfettered but blindfolded and with a torch in hand, in other pictures by Rubens. In the title-page of Haraeus's *Annales Ducum seu principum Brabantiae* (1623), *Furor* can be seen pulling open the doors of the Temple of Janus, and in one of the Stages of the *Pompa Introitus Ferdinandi* he storms out of the Temple of Janus, blindfolded and with blazing torch and sword in hand.[10]

But hope is not entirely lost for the unfortunate victim. Two Olympian gods, shown in Zuccaro's image but not in Apelles's painting, arrive just in time to assist the falsely accused, and they will save him from destruction. Minerva, recognisable in Rubens's drawing by her helmet, long spear, as well as a vaguely indicated round shield fastened to her left arm, grabs the man with ass's ears by his arm to prevent him from releasing *Furor*.

An important role is also given to Mercury (on the right), wearing a winged hat and raising his caduceus. He introduces Truth, who is a completely naked woman, steering her into the scene with his hand resting on her shoulder, while she makes a rhetorical gesture which undoubtedly accompanies a plea that exonerates the victim. By intervening, the gods succeed in rescuing Innocence, just as Apelles was eventually relieved of the death penalty by testimony that brought to light the true facts.

The meaning of the two gods added by Zuccaro and Rubens to the personifications present in Apelles's allegory seems obvious. Minerva who counters the foolish gesture of the figure with ass's ears – a move that will unleash *Furor* – can be seen as wisdom triumphing over ignorance. Mercury who brings truth to the fore probably personifies reason or argument, succeeding in exposing the lies and rectifying the error.[11]

Thus, at the simplest level of interpretation, both Apelles's and Rubens's *Calumny* can be seen as a moral and didactic allegory which warns against the pernicious effects of envy, slander and hasty judgement.[12] Incidentally, both Zuccaro and Rubens omit one of Apelles's figures: *Poenitentia* (Repentance), who appears once *Veritas* has demonstrated that the accusations are false.

It is possible that Rubens's image was influenced by another interpretation, or rather a kindred idea: elements of his *Calumny* overlap with political allegories dealing with peace and war. Minerva and Mercury are bringers of peace and oppose the blind rage of war which sweeps away the innocent. Their opponents are *Furor*, chained up in the Temple of Janus, and the terrible *Invidia*, seen as the instigator and nurturer of war.[13] Minerva appears as protector of peace not only in Rubens's *Calumny* but also in other allegorical scenes. The clear link between Rubens's representation of *The Calumny of Apelles* and his later *Horrors of War* has been noted.[14]

There is no apparent reason to make a direct connection between this allegory and Rubens's profession and assume that beleaguered Innocence should somehow be viewed as the artist and his work.[15] It is also doubtful that the gods are acting here in their role as protectors of the arts. Some have assumed that there was a direct connection between the pair of gods in the *Calumny* frieze panel and the two statues above the portico (Nos R1 and R2).[16] As explained elsewhere, however, these statues are problematic in many respects: they were probably not present on the portico in Rubens's time, and therefore they are not a valid reference point in forming an interpretation.

Rubens's allegory – painted as if carved in stone – differs from representations by his predecessors, and not only because he puts his own interpretation on the characters. Even more striking are the differences he brings to the composition. As conceived by Renaissance artists, Apelles's scene is usually set in a palace room, or in the open air with an urban landscape behind: thus in a clearly identifiable setting. In contrast, Rubens constructs his composition as if it were a Roman relief, following the same scheme as the other frieze panels; in other words in a shallow space, and with the figures packed tightly together in the foreground. Thus, Rubens's

Calumny is presented as a single knot of energy, quite different from the deliberately didactic and carefully laid out composition with figures in groups that Lucian describes.

In seven of the nine frieze pictures, direct borrowings from classical sculpture have been detected, deriving from free-standing statues as well as reliefs, but none has been found in the composition of the *Calumnia* panel. Nonetheless there is reason to believe that Rubens used a (lost) drawing after an ancient statue of Venus, seen in profile. We can, indeed, point to a related motif that appears in a different context in Rubens's work: the nude figure of Venus, in a similar setting, in profile at the edge of the composition, who appears at the far right of Rubens's *Sacrifice to Venus in a Temple*, c. 1630, in the Courtauld Gallery, London (Fig. 95).[17]

Rubens did not return to Apelles's well-known theme in any other painting but it can certainly be said that he must have had it in mind twenty years later when he was working on the *Horrors of War* (Palazzo Pitti in Florence). As noted elsewhere, this dynamic, allegorical composition contains elements that echo the *Calumny* both in structure and to some extent in meaning.[18]

As far as the details in the two visual sources can actually be made out, the composition was taken over from the drawing unaltered, apart from one element: more space was left between Innocence and Truth. One further difference, the figure of the woman with human arms (in the Harewijn print) in place of a harpy with animal claws, probably resulted from an incorrect reading of the wall painting.

It is worth remarking that the drawing has not always been recognised as a design for the frieze painting on the façade, made by Rubens in about 1616, as here proposed. Antoine Seilern, who was the first to publish the drawing – without being aware of the relationship with the wall painting – saw it as a work by Rubens that was made 'c. 1605–1606' during his time in Italy, a view that was followed by Helen Braham and Justus Muller Hofstede (who suggested '1606–1607') and others.[19] The attribution to Rubens was not questioned by these authors, and Ludwig Burchard also regarded the drawing as original (as can be inferred from his notes in the Rubenianum).

This early dating in the Italian period, however, is not tenable; there can be no doubt that the drawing was made as a design for the frieze panel executed some ten years later. For one thing the composition corresponds in virtually every detail. Furthermore, we can rule out the possibility that it is an earlier drawing to which Rubens returned for the façade decoration. Several aspects suggest that it was made specifically for the frieze panel: it has the same proportions and the drawing imitates the effect of a monochrome relief. Any lingering doubt is eliminated by the horizontal lines in black chalk framing the composition top and bottom, which is an unusual procedure for Rubens. Surely this indicates part of the fictive relief, specifically the frame which was to be painted in *trompe-l'oeil*, like the scene itself. An additional argument for a dating after the Italian period is of course provided by the architectural studies on the verso of the sheet which can also be connected with the house.

Anne-Marie Logan was the first (in 1991) to question the early dating of this *Calumny* drawing. She rightly pointed out that a dating in Rubens's Italian period was untenable because of the undisputed connection with the frieze panel. Moreover, she also questioned the attribution to Rubens, which she described as a 'troubling drawing with regard to Rubens' authorship'. She drew attention to the unusual technique, which argues against an attribution to Rubens, and she was inclined to believe that it is a copy, or the work of a pupil or follower, probably based on the wall painting on the façade.[20]

This rejection seems too harsh, a view that is shared by Christopher White.[21] There are a number of *pentimenti* which are inconsistent with a copy, both in the reworking with pen and a fine brush in ink, and in the first draft in black chalk. The dynamic style and expressive vigour that distinguish the composition argue against the suggestion that the drawing is a copy. Certain weaker passages in the washed areas could be the result of a later intervention.

It is also worth noting that the unusual appearance of this *Calumny*, which is indeed difficult to fit into Rubens's drawn oeuvre, can be partly explained by the unique nature of the project for which it was made, which was not a painting, but a *trompe-l'oeil* version of a monochrome Roman relief. This explains the heavy shadows in grey wash.

Frans Baudouin, who believed in the drawing's authenticity and was aware of the direct connection with the frieze panel, was also of the view that a dating in Rubens's Italian period was untenable. He proposed that the drawing was more likely made after Rubens's return to Antwerp, possibly around 1611–1613, and had been reworked later.[22] There is, however, no apparent reason to think that Rubens would have been working on the design of the frieze panels so early. A dating of the designs and execution of the wall paintings to around 1616, as here proposed, seems more plausible (on this see above).[23]

Little attention has been paid to the verso of this sheet (No. 13b; Fig. 97), which has faint chalk sketches and figure studies in pen, very summarily indicated. It is nonetheless interesting because, as with the recto, parts can be linked with Rubens's house.

Finally, it can be observed that the *Calumny of Apelles* is the only one of the frieze panels to have been imitated, albeit in the form of derivative works of mediocre quality and with substantial alterations which include a clothed version of Truth. Curiously, this is in metalwork: Rubens's composition is known from two relief plaques, one in silver and the other in copper (see Copies 1–2). From the existence of these reliefs it can perhaps be deduced that Rubens's composition was (in his lifetime?) executed on a smaller scale as a relief plaque.

1. For a full discussion of the theme, including a catalogue of the many representations of it, see Massing, *Calomnie*, 1990. This particular painting by Apelles is not mentioned by Pliny (see McHam, *Pliny*, 2013, p. 48); Lucian's description was used by Leon Battista Alberti (1404–1472) in his discussion of literature as the painter's inspiration, in his *De Pictura* (Alberti, *De Pictura*, ed. Venatorius, 1540, III, pp. 102–103). The whereabouts of Apelles's celebrated *Calumny* during Lucian's lifetime are not known and it has even been suggested that it did not actually exist, something firmly contradicted by Massing (Massing, *Calomnie*, 1990, p. 17 ff.). See also Lydakis, *Greek Painting*, 2004, pp. 161–166.

2. On the many editions, published in various languages, see Massing, *ibid.*, pp. 29–45, 469–480. The majority of translations in Italian, French, English and other modern languages are not based on the original Greek text but a Latin translation. It is important to note that the Greek abstract nouns (the names of the personifications) do not have exact equivalents in other languages in every case. According to Massing, the main protagonist, called 'Diabole' in the original Greek and 'Calumnia' in Latin, can be better translated as 'Delatio', that is 'Delation' (to inform, betray; see ibid., p. 6). For a Greek–English translation, see Lucian, *Phalaris etc.*, transl. Harmon, 1913, pp. 365–367. For the editions of Lucian that Rubens may have owned, see following note.

3. It is difficult to establish which of the many editions Rubens may have consulted for the *ekphrasis*. A clue can perhaps be found in the library of Albert Rubens, who inherited books from his father. The sale catalogue of Albert's books records two editions of Lucian: one in four octavo volumes (Arents, *Bibliotheek*, 2001, p. 355) and one Latin translation described as *Opera*, published 'Parisis apud Vascosanume' (ibid., p. 356). Neither is identified by Arents, who makes no mention at all of works by Lucian in Rubens's possession. Elizabeth McGrath (personal communication) suggests that the first reference could be to the bilingual Greek–Latin edition published in Basel, 1602, by Gilbertus Cognatus and Ioannes Sambucus (Lucian, *Opera*, eds Cognatus – Sambucus, 1602; for the *ekphrasis*, see ibid., pp. 838–842). The second is probably the Latin edition of 1546 by Michel de Vascosan, Paris (Lucian, *Opera*, trans Erasmus et al., 1546; for the *ekphrasis*, see ibid., pp. 287–288).

4. See, for instance, Lucian's description cited by Vincenzo Cartari in his *Imagini*, of which Rubens probably had a French edition (Arents, *Bibliotheek*, 2001, p. 296, no.R5); for Lucian's text, see Cartari, *Images*, 1610, pp. 587–588; id., *Images, transl. Mulryan*, 2021, p. 365.

5. For Botticelli, see Massing, *Calomnie*, 1990, no. 4.A; for the *Calumny* by Maarten De Vos, see Neerman, *Calumny of Apelles*, 2016; Neerman et al., *Calumny of Apelles*, 2018. The theme appears in printmaking in the Southern Netherlands, but besides the work by De Vos and Rubens's lost wall painting, no other painted version is known.

6. For a full commentary on the composition by Zuccaro, with a catalogue of the many versions in painting and printmaking, see Massing, *Calomnie*, 1990, pp. 197–217, 356–380, nos 26–26.F.B.

7. The identifications as 'deceit' ('le mensonge') and 'calumnia' are based on the so-called Baluze memorandum. See Held, *Sketches*, 1980, p. 119, no. 76, fig. 78; Millen – Wolf, *Maria de' Medici*, 1989, p. 177; Renger – Denk, *Cat. Munich (Flämische Malerei)*, 2002, p. 428, no. 105.

8. Virgil, *Aeneid*, I. 294–296. For the motif, see Massing, *Calomnie*, 1990, p. 201, fig. 79.
9. Cartari, *Imagini*, 1615, p. 354 (as 'Imagine del Furore e dell Ira'), ill. p. 353; an illustration with a different *Furor* appears in an earlier edition (id., *Imagini*, 1608, p. 366, ill. p. 367). For a translation of the passage, see id., *Images*, transl. Mulryan, 2012, p. 312 (not illustrated): 'I have supplied this brief image of the angered person because I don't find that the ancients made any image of Anger [also called Fury]'.
10. Judson – Van de Velde, *Title-pages (CRLB)*, 1978, I, pp. 232–233, no. 52; II, figs 179–180; Martin, *Pompa (CRLB)*, 1972, p. 174, figs 82–83, 86–87; for the explanation, see Gevartius, *Pompa Introitus*, 1642, pp. 118–119.
11. Müller Hofstede described Minerva in this context as 'Weisheit' and Mercury as 'Meister der Rede und der Beweiskunst' (Müller Hofstede, *Rubens in Italiën*, 1977, p. 64).
12. Massing distinguishes three important interpretations of Apelles's *Calumny*: one moral-didactic (Massing, *Calomnie*, 1990, pp. 105–119), one juridical – that is as a warning against judging too quickly and coming to the wrong conclusion (ibid., pp. 127–138) – and one religious (ibid., pp. 145–149). The last two obviously do not apply to Rubens's wall decoration.
13. It is worth recalling the link between *Invidia* and war, as represented in a series of triumphal processions, *The Cycle of the Vicissitudes of Human Affairs* (*Circulus vicissitudinis rerum humanarum*) by Maarten van Heemskerck (1498–1574). One of the triumphal carriages in the series represents 'Envy Bringing Forth War' (Veldman, *Leerrijke reeksen*, 1986, no. 6–4, fig. 24). *Invidia*'s carriage is pulled by horses labelled *Calumnia* and *Detractio* ('Detraction', damaging someone's reputation).
14. For Minerva (understood as 'Wisdom') confronting war, see allegories in Büttner, *Allegories (CRLB)*, 2018, nos 27–31. For *The Horrors of War*, see below, n. 18.
15. This was suggested by Müller Hofstede; he sees it not just as a reference to the snide attack on Apelles, but also on 'die Würde des Künstlers und seines Werkes' (Müller Hofstede, *Rubens in Italiën*, 1977, p. 65). See also following note.
16. A connection with the statues was presumed by the *Palazzo* authors, who saw the *Calumny* frieze panel as 'directly linked to the trials and tribulations of the artist's profession', and as 'thematically closely related to' another frieze panel, *The Triumph of Apollo* (No. 9) (Uppenkamp – Van Beneden, *Architectural Symbolism*, 2011, pp. 111–112).
17. Belkin, *Copies (CRLB)*, 2009, I, no. 12, pl. 4; II, fig. 43 (as 'c. 1630'). Part of the scene – not the statue of Venus – was taken from Adam Elsheimer (*Il Contento*: Edinburgh, National Galleries of Scotland). Ludwig Burchard was the first to observe that the figure of Innocence in the drawing was later used for the statue of Venus (see Seilern, *Cat. London, Princes Gate*, 1955, p. 84).
18. Büttner, *Allegories (CRLB)*, 2018, I, no. 32; II, fig. 153; for parallels between the *Calumny* of Lucian's *ekphrasis* and Rubens's description and representation of *The Horrors of War*, see McGrath, *Rubens's House*, 1978, p. 250, n. 22.
19. Seilern, *Cat. London, Princes Gate*, 1955, p. 84; Müller Hofstede, *Rubens in Italiën*, 1977, p. 63; Braham, *Rubens*, 1988, p. 22.
20. Logan, *Rubens*, 1991, p. 315; following this hypothesis, she assumes that the drawing was made after completion of the house, which according to her was 'not built until 1618' (see above for this very late dating of the façade's completion, frequently adopted, Chapter VI, pp. 173–175).
21. I am very grateful to Christopher White, who is preparing a catalogue of the Courtauld Gallery drawings, for sharing his opinion (private correspondence, July 2020) and for kindly sending me his unpublished catalogue entry.
22. Baudouin, *Fresco's*, 1998, p. 12; his attribution as well as dating were followed by Heinen, *Immolatio boum*, 2010, pp. 223, 232, n. 92.
23. Chapter VI, pp. 173–175.

No. 13b. *Architectural Studies and Figure Studies for an Entombment*: Drawing (Fig. 97)

Pen and grey-brown ink, black chalk; 30.6 × 38.5 mm. Verso of No. 13a (Fig. 96)

London, The Courtauld Gallery, Princes Gate Collection. Inv. no. PG52

c. 1616 (?)

For more technical notes, provenance and exhibition history, see No. 13a.

LITERATURE: Braham, *Rubens*, 1988, p. 22, under no. 26; Baudouin, *Fresco's*, 1998, p. 12, fig. 18 (repr. upside down); Heinen, *Immolatio boum*, 2010, p. 224.

The main subject of the verso of the *Calumny of Apelles* (No. 13a; Fig. 96) is formed by a few architectural details sketched in black chalk, which are difficult to interpret, but include the image of a column or pilaster with moulded pedestal or capital. No details of the portico or studio façades can be recognised among them, but it is reasonable to assume that these studies have some connection with Rubens's house. Apart

CATALOGUE No. 14

from No. 7a (Fig. 54), on which there is a study for a window surround, also in chalk, this sheet is the only remaining evidence of the architectural drawings which Rubens undoubtedly made in preparation for the construction of his house.

The verso of the *Calumny* drawing was also (later?) used for pen studies for a completely different subject. On the left-hand side of the sheet, or at the upper edge if rotated by a quarter turn to the left, there are sketchy pen drawings which are certainly from Rubens's hand. Various figures are sketched in such a summary way as to be hardly distinguishable. Among these pen sketches, at the left (if rotated), a group of figures can be made out: two men carrying a lifeless body, and in the background behind them, further figures. This is probably a study for an *Entombment*.[1]

1. Compare, for instance, a more finished drawing of *The Entombment* in the Rijksprentenkabinet, Amsterdam: to the right, in a similar manner, a man appears who bends forward and supports the lifeless body by its feet (Judson, *Passion (CRLB)*, 2000, no. 76, fig. 222, as probably c. 1615). Seilern also thought of an *Entombment*; less convincing is *The Discovery of Callisto*, suggested by Braham as an 'alternative identification'.

No. 14. *Zeuxis and the Maidens of Croton*: Mural Painting (cf. Fig. 98)

Wall painting; 120 × 175 cm.

Formerly on the north façade of the studio, lost

c. 1616 (?)

VISUAL SOURCES:
(1) Harrewijn print, 1684 (Appendix III.1; Fig. 17; detail: Fig. 98);
(2) Harrewijn print, 1692, in reverse and scarcely legible (Appendix III.2; Fig. 18)

LITERATURE: Rooses, *Maison*, 1888, p. 221 (as 'le Jugement de Paris'): Rooses, *Oeuvre*, 1886–92, V, p. 185 (as 'le Jugement de Paris'); Delen, *Rubens' huis*, 1933, p. 29 (as 'Oordeel van Paris'); Prims, *Rubenshuis*, 1946, p. 12 (as 'Oordeel van Paris'); Müller Hofstede, *Rubens in Italien*, 1977, I, p. 59, fig. E31; Müller Hofstede, *Ut Pictura Poesis*, 1976–1978, p. 182; McGrath, *Rubens's House*, 1976–78, p. 142, fig. 9; McGrath, *Rubens's House*, 1978, pp. 268–269, 276, pl. 28a; Muller, *Theory and Practice*, 1982, p. 235; Jacobs, *Vasari's Vision*, 1984, p. 415; Stutz, *Residenz*, 1985, p. 145; Scott, *Perseus and Andromeda*, 1988, p. 258; Von Simson, *Rubens*, 1996, p. 210; Healy, *Judgement of Paris*, 1997, pp. 96, 155–156, fig. 164; Mansfield, *Zeuxis*, 2007, pp. 46–47.

The panel between the *Calumny of Apelles* (No. 13) and the *Drunken Hercules* (No. 15), in the frieze containing *trompe-l'oeil* paintings of stone reliefs, features a representation of one of the most celebrated anecdotes told about ancient painters: Zeuxis and the five maidens of Croton. In order to paint Helen of Troy, a woman of ideal beauty, Zeuxis asked his patrons, the citizens of Croton, to show him the most beautiful girls from the city so that he could choose a model from among them. However, instead of picking one, as expected, he selected no less than five beauties, skilfully combining the best parts of each to paint a woman of perfect beauty.

Several classical authors give accounts, which vary slightly, of how the famous Greek painter went about his work. The oldest, most complete and best known version, summarised above, comes from Cicero's *De Inventione*, where he compares the famous painter's method with his own approach to teaching rhetoric. As stated, according to him it was Helen of Troy who was represented by Zeuxis and the painting was intended for the Temple of Hera in the city of Croton.[1]

Naturally the story is included among the many anecdotes about painters which Pliny lists in his *Naturalis Historia*, but his reference to it is only summary and his story diverges from the usual one in several ways. He places the tale in Agrigento, and since he fails to mention the painting's title, he does not name the beauty who was to be portrayed. The kernel of the anecdote is nonetheless the same. He tells us that Zeuxis 'held an inspection of maidens of the place paraded naked and chose five, for the purpose of reproducing in the picture the most admirable points in the form of each'.[2]

The story became, moreover, one of the most often cited of Pliny's anecdotes, with mentions beginning in the Renaissance, and repeated later in numerous art-theoretical treatises.[3]

The frieze panel on the studio façade shows an interior (defined as such by the curtain to the left), in which a bearded Zeuxis sits with his legs crossed while he inspects the young women brought in for him. He has not yet begun to paint but appears to have a stylus in his hand and to be busy with preparatory work, probably drawing.

Three of the maidens have already taken their clothes off, with others in long dresses and veils awaiting their turn. It is far from clear what working method Zeuxis is using to create his ideal image. Is he perhaps making preparatory studies of separate 'parts'? Neither can we tell from the frieze panel which moment in Cicero's tale is depicted: the selection of five beauties from among the assembled daughters of Croton – which naturally requires more than five women – or the careful inspection of the chosen maidens? Probably it is the former. The figure in long robes trailing to the ground who appears between Zeuxis and the maidens is difficult to make out in the print. Conceivably it is an (old?) woman, her head veiled, who is there to chaperone the girls,[4] and possibly – as her raised left arm seems to suggest – to help them take off their clothes.

To the right, three maidens are shown still fully dressed and veiled, as was expected of virtuous patrician women. For their clothing Rubens took inspiration from classical statues representing the so-called Pudicitia type. There is a striking figure, second from right, dressed in a *himation*, a long length of which hangs covering the left arm, which she holds across her breast. Almost certainly Rubens's model was an ancient statue which served as prototype for female figures in many of his paintings: the so-called *Pudicitia Mattei*, a statue formerly in the Mattei Collection in Rome and now in the Vatican Museums (Fig. 100).[5]

In terms of both contents and composition, the image of the wall painting in many respects resembles another theme, the judgement of Paris. The frieze-like presentation of a seated man looking searchingly at an array of naked or semi-naked women standing together, is indeed very similar. The three naked women are also represented – as in Rubens's Paris scenes – each from a different angle: frontally, in profile and from behind. It is no surprise that until Elizabeth McGrath correctly identified the subject, the very small detail in the Harrewijn print led to the misapprehension that the painted scene on Rubens's façade showed a judgement of Paris.[6] There are differences, however, that leave no room for doubt: the events are set in an interior (see the curtain), there are too many women visible for this to be a scene with the three Olympian goddesses, and the man looking on is not clutching an apple as reward for the winner.

As far as we know, Rubens only treated the anecdote about the painter Zeuxis and the maidens of Croton in the monochrome *trompe-l'oeil* relief on the façade, and there is no painting of the subject from his hand, on panel or canvas, unlike the judgement of Paris, a story he represented often. This is in some ways surprising, given the scope the theme offers to combine an important story with an attractive image of five women in a range of poses and in various states of 'undress'.[7]

This anecdote about a famous ancient artist lent itself admirably to demonstrating the possibilities of the art of painting: the creation of an image of ideal beauty based on the diversity offered by nature itself. The theme touches on the discussion of the relationship between nature and art, and the question of which is superior. It can be interpreted as an illustration of the idea that the artist can create something that surpasses the model of nature, which might even lead to the attribution of divine status to the artist.[8] It is therefore not surprising that it was especially this story that artists chose to incorporate in the decoration of their houses. Long before Rubens, Giorgio Vasari had selected the theme for the decoration of the interior walls of his homes in Arezzo and Florence.[9]

As with the remainder of the frieze, Rubens designed his composition so as to give it the appearance of a fictive stone relief, with figures set in a flat, shallow plane. In this frieze-like arrangement with all the figures presented side-by-side, he departed from earlier representations of the theme such as Vasari's, mentioned above, but equally that of his teacher Otto van Veen (1556–1629), who depicted the undressed girls in a range of poses and in different spatial zones of Zeuxis's studio (Fig. 99).[10]

Finally, it is worth remembering that this story is connected with the *epithalamium* which Jan Gaspar Gevartius (1593–1666) wrote on the occasion of Rubens's marriage to Helena Fourment in 1630. Very appropriately, and with mildly tongue-in-cheek exaggeration fitting to the genre, he states that Rubens, who was the Apelles of his age (*Saeculi sui Apelles*), has outdone Zeuxis, since he did not require five beautiful maidens in order to discover perfect beauty. This he could find in a single maiden: his bride, Helen of Antwerp (*Helena Aduatica*), who far surpassed her Greek counterpart.[11]

1. Cicero, *De Inventione etc.*, transl. Hubbel, 1949, pp. 166–169; Mansfield, *Zeuxis*, 2007, pp. 19–20.
2. Pliny, *Natural History*, XXXV.64: according to him 'the picture' was made for the temple of Hera (Juno) Lacinia in that city. In a further passage Pliny refers to a *Helen* by Zeuxis – apparently not the same painting – which could be seen in Rome in the Portico of Philip (ibid., XXXV.66). For Pliny's version of the story, see Mansfield, *Zeuxis*, 2007, p. 20; McHam, *Pliny*, 2013, p. 321, [Anecdote] no. 162. There is also a version of the anecdote in Dionysius of Halicarnassus, *De priscis scriptoribus censura*, I (see Dionysius, *Opera*, ed. Reiske, 1774–77, V, p. 417).
3. For a list of Renaissance authors who refer to the Plinian anecdote, including Petrarch, Alberti, Castiglione and Vasari, see McHam, *Pliny*, 2013, p. 345, no. 161; a later author is, for instance, Karel Van Mander (Van Mander, *Antijcke Schilders*, 1603, fol. 67r). For the anecdote, see also Kris – Kurz, *Die Legende*, 1934, p. 69; id., *Legend*, 1979, pp. 44, 61; Erftemeijer, *Kunstenaarsanecdotes*, 2000, p. 12. For an extensive study of the theme, including a Freudian interpretation, see Mansfield, *Zeuxis*, 2007.
4. The figure is similar to the old woman (a nurse or chaperone?) who appears in other images with young women, for example *Achilles Discovered among the Daughters of Lycomedes* and *The Discovery of Erichtonius by the Daughters of Cecrops*. Given the veil and the long robes, it seems unlikely that the figure is a man, as proposed by Healy, *Judgement of Paris*, 1997, p. 156.
5. Haskell – Penny, *Antique*, 1982, p. 300, no. 74, fig. 157. Rubens's use of this statue in paintings was noted by, for example, Stechow, *Classical Tradition*, 1968, pp. 55, 58; Jaffé, *Rubens and Italy*, 1977, p. 81; Held, *Oil Sketches*, 1980, I, p. 505; Freedberg, *Christ after the Passion (CRLB)*, 1984, p. 41; Baumstark et al., *Liechtenstein*, 1985, p. 317. Rubens undoubtedly made one or more drawings of this statue, but nothing more is known of them (Van der Meulen, *Antique (CRLB)*, 1994, I, p. 61). Concerning the women's drapery, it is worth noting that these also resemble clothing in a Roman mural that Rubens knew: the *Aldobrandini Wedding* (see Chapter VI, pp. 178–179).
6. See, for example, Rooses and Delen (references under Literature, above); likewise this was the subject erroneously selected for the sculpted relief panel currently on the façade; see for example the Rubens House guides by Clijmans, *Wederopbouw Rubenshuis*, 1946, p. 79; Baudouin, *Rubens's House*, 1955, p. 12. id., *Summary Guide*, 1977, p. 9.
7. Perhaps even Rubens was reluctant to represent an abundance of nude women and experienced something of what Elizabeth Mansfield has suggested as explanation of the almost complete absence of the ancient theme in painting from c. 1750 to c. 1850: its problematic similarity to a brothel scene ('the incongruous evocation of a brothel'; Mansfield, *Zeuxis*, 2007, pp. xx, 117 ff.).
8. According to Ernst Kris and Otto Kurz, 'The conception on which this anecdote is based views the task of the artist, in accordance with Plato's theory of art, as surpassing the model of nature and, by improving on nature, to realize an ideal beauty in his works. [...This conception] gave rise to the idea that the artist creates like God, that he is an *alter deus*' (Kris – Kurz, *Die Legende*, 1934, p. 69; Kurz, *Legend*, 1979, p. 61).
9. For the Zeuxis scene in the Casa di Vasari in Arezzo (1541–1548), see McGrath, *Rubens's House*, 1978, pp. 249, 268, pl. 26a; Albrecht, *Häuser von Giorgio Vasari*, 1985, p. 88, fig. 4; Mansfield, *Zeuxis*, 2007, p. 45, fig. 8; McHam, *Pliny*, 2013, p. 228, fig. 171. The scene on the walls of Vasari's house in Florence (1570–1579) is an unusual variant, divided into two sections: in place of Zeuxis we see Apelles at work on a painting of Diana, surrounded by several nude models; and in the adjacent section yet more young women are approaching his studio (Albrecht, ibid., pp. 97–98, figs 10–12; Schwarz, *Künstlerhaus*, 1990, pp. 194, 196, figs 84, 87; Mansfield, ibid., p. 46, fig. 47; McHam, ibid., p. 228, fig. 170).
10. For a sketch in *grisaille* by Van Veen, in a private collection and on the art market, see Müller Hofstede, *Rubens in Italien*, 1977, I, p. 59, fig. E30; id., *Ut Pictura Poesis*, 1976–1978, pp. 181–182, fig. 5; Healy, *Judgement of Paris*, 1997, pp. 155–156, p. 207, n. 92, fig. 165.
11. Rooses – Ruelens, *Correspondance*, 1887–1909, V, pp. 344–347, no. DCXCII. For commentary on this see, for example, Healy, *Judgement of Paris*, 1997, p. 96.

No. 15. *The Drunken Hercules*: Mural Painting (cf. Fig. 101)

Wall painting; approx. 120 × 175 cm.

Formerly on the north façade of the studio, lost

c. 1616 (?)

VISUAL SOURCES:
(1) Harrewijn print, 1684 (Appendix III.1; Fig. 17; detail: Fig. 101);
(2) Harrewijn print, 1692, in reverse and scarcely legible (Appendix III.2; Fig. 18)

LITERATURE: Rooses, *Maison*, 1888, p. 221 (as 'la Marche du Silène'); Rooses, *Oeuvre*, 1886–92, V, p. 185 (as 'la Marche du Silène'); Delen, *Rubens' huis*, 1933, p. 29 (as 'een Gang van Silenus'); Prims, *Rubenshuis*, 1946, p. 12 (as 'Hercules dronken'); McGrath, *Rubens's House*, 1976–78, pp. 141–142, fig. 8; McGrath, *Rubens's House*, 1978, pp. 263–268, 276, pl. 28a; Stutz, *Residenz*, 1985, p. 145; White, *Rubens*, 1987, p. 62, fig. 80; Von Simson, *Rubens*, 1996, p. 209; Büttner, *Allegories (CRLB)*, 2018, I, p. 143; Grimmett, *Drunken Hercules*, 2020, p. 54.

The fifth and final frieze panel of the north façade represents the drunken Hercules in company with figures who are part of a bacchic procession. The staggering hero is shown frontally, accompanied by two woodland creatures who hold him under his arms to prevent him from falling over. To the right is a satyr, recognisable by his goat's legs and short horns; to the left is a faun, also horned, but with human legs. A merry time is being had by all: the group in the middle are joined by a satyr who hops around while playing a double-flute, and by a dancing bacchante or *maenad*, holding one arm above her head and lifting the end of her dress with her left hand. The athletic appearance of the staggering main figure leaves no room for doubt that it is Hercules, rather than Bacchus or Silenus, who is caught in this embarrassing situation.

The composition of the relief-like monochrome scene is constructed from motifs which Rubens had faithfully copied from ancient works of art. The central motif comes from a classical Roman relief that was in the collection of Cyriacus Mattei (1545–1614), and which Rubens had seen – and almost certainly drawn – while in Rome; it is now known only from an engraved illustration in an eighteenth-century publication (Fig. 104).[1] Besides the general position of the three central figures, the frieze panel also takes over details such as the empty jug between the feet of Hercules's companion to the left, and the up-raised club. In the Harrewijn print we cannot see who is holding the club, but as in the relief, it has perhaps been put into the hand of the satyr rather than the dancing bacchante. It is also not clear if Hercules is holding a drinking cup (rather than a tambourine) in his left hand, which hangs down limply. A few differences can be observed: Hercules's head is shown frontally and his loins are wrapped, unusually, in what appears to be his lion's skin.

Ancient sources can also be found for the two figures either side of the central group, the dancing bacchante seen from behind and the piping satyr: they come from the bacchic procession on the famous and much admired monumental neo-Attic *Borghese Vase*, now in the Musée du Louvre (Figs 102–103).[2] We know that Rubens copied details from this vase when it was in the collection of Scipione Borghese (1577–1633). This emerges from four figures extracted from it, which do not appear in the wall painting: a maenad and a drunken Silenus held by a faun, on an autograph sheet in Dresden,[3] and a dancing faun in a copy in the so-called Rubens Cantoor.[4] There are minor differences between the two figures in the frieze panel and those on the vase. In the vase the bacchante (Fig. 103) holds a tambourine above her head, but this cannot be made out in the Harrewijn print; the piping faun, a figure with human legs, but with the tail and ears of a goat (Fig. 102), was changed by Rubens into a hopping satyr, a more animal-like creature with goat's legs.

Of the nine frieze panels, this is the only subject which also appears as a painting in Rubens's oeuvre. Around 1613–1615 – and so probably a few years before the decoration of the studio façade – Rubens painted the drunken Hercules in a large, almost square panel, now in the Gemäldegalerie Alte Meister in Dresden (Fig. 105).[5] As in the wall painting, this shows the extraordinarily strong and courageous hero, normally the personification of virtue, in circumstances that reveal another side of his character. It shows the consequences of his great weakness, his excess in all actions and his penchant for the sensual, including an excessive fondness for alcohol which at certain moments lands him in ridiculous and embarrassing situations. Hercules's companions in the Dresden painting, as in the frieze panel, belong to Bacchus's train and this may indicate that Rubens had one particular episode of the hero's drunkenness in mind, that is the moment after the drinking contest into which Hercules – proud of his capacity for drink – entered with the god of wine himself, Bacchus.[6]

The Dresden painting was made with a pendant, *The Coronation of a Hero*, in the Alte Pinakothek in Munich, in which a hero in armour is crowned by Victory, while using his foot to restrain the defeated envy, lust and drunkenness (in the form of a satyr).[7] These two important moral allegories remained in Rubens's house until his death, and it seems possible that they formed a more or less constant feature of the decoration of his interior.

The theme of the drunken hero, as depicted in the classical relief and in Rubens's compositions in the Dresden panel and in the frieze painting, is closely related to an epigram from the *Greek Anthology*, published (in Latin) in Natale Conti's *Mythologia*: 'The man who could subjugate anything, the hero of the twelve labours, famous throughout the world for his manly strength and valour, is now, after the feast, rolling along with tottering steps, weighed down with wine, quite conquered by Bacchus, that subtle unlooser of limbs'.[8]

As noted, Rubens took inspiration for this theme of the drunken hero from ancient reliefs as well as written sources. We need to ask whether with his choice of theme for the fictive stone relief he may also have had one of the lost famous paintings by ancient Greek masters in mind, as is the case with some of the other frieze panels. This is not obviously so. No classical source mentions a painting of the drunken Hercules. Some have believed that there was a connection between this wall painting and the image of Hercules which Parrhasius boasted that he painted from a vision of the hero, who often appeared to him in dreams.[9] Pliny only mentions this painting as 'a picture of Hercules in Lindos' without further elucidating the subject, and there are insufficient grounds for assuming that it represented the drunken hero. Or rather, it seems unlikely that it would have occurred to Rubens that Hercules appeared in a drunken state to Parrhasius, and that this would have led him to paint Hercules in a situation unbecoming to his status as hero.[10] The fact that Parrhasius was notorious for his sarcastic and irreverent character, and especially for a disreputable, licentious way of life, was somewhat improbably seen as an indication that such a painting by his hand might once have existed.[11]

1. Venuti – Amaduzzi, *Vetera Monumenta*, 1774–79, III, pl. 22.1; Van der Meulen, *Antique (CRLB)*, 1994, I, p. 61, n. 85, text ill. 18. See also Kieser, *Antikes*, 1933, pp. 117–118, fig. 6; McGrath, *Rubens's House*, 1978, p. 265, pl. 34d; Büttner, *Allegories (CRLB)*, 2018, I, p. 144, n. 28.

2. Musée du Louvre, Paris, inv. no. MR985; Marble, H. 172 cm; Haskell – Penny, *Antique*, 1982, p. 315, no. 81, fig. 166; Van der Meulen, *Antique (CRLB)*, 1994, III, figs 63 and 276. For an engraving of 1693, with six of the figures, see McGrath, *Rubens's House*, 1978, p. 265, pl. 34b. A dancer seen from behind, inspired by the bacchante with tambourine, can also be found in Rubens's *Feast of Venus* in the Kunsthistorisches Museum in Vienna (Kräftner et al., *Rubens in Wien*, 2004, no. 88).

3. *Drunken Silenus with Faun and Maenad*, Dresden, Staatliche Kunstsammlungen, Kupferstichkabinett, inv. no. C1967–42. Van der Meulen, *Antique (CRLB)*, 1994, II, no. 141; III, fig. 275; Logan – Belkin, *Drawings, I*, 2021, no. 177; II, fig. 231.

4. *A Dancing Faun and Standing Silenus with a Dish*, Copenhagen, Statens Museum for Kunst, Kongelige Kobberstiksammling, inv. no. KKSgb7552 (Rubens Cantoor, III, 41). Van der Meulen, *Antique (CRLB)*, 1994, II, p. 161, under no. 140; III, fig. 62; Logan – Belkin, *Drawings, I*, 2021, under no. 178; II, fig. 232.

5. Oil on panel, 220 × 200 cm; Büttner, *Allegories (CRLB)*, 2018, I, no. 11; II, fig. 61.

6. On this and other occasions when Hercules was drunk, see McGrath, *Rubens's House*, 1978, pp. 264–265; see also Büttner, *ibid*, I, p. 143.

7. Büttner, *Allegories (CRLB)*, 2018, I, no. 12, fig. 66.

8. McGrath, *Rubens's House*, 1978, p. 267; see also Büttner, *ibid.*, I, p. 143.

9. Pliny, *Natural History*, XXXV.69.
10. This was McGrath's 'tentative speculation', *Rubens's House*, 1978, pp. 267–268; accepted as an established fact by, for example, Simson, *Rubens*, 1996, p. 210; but not mentioned, and thus apparently not regarded as possible source, in Büttner's commentary on the Dresden painting (see n. 5).
11. For Parrhasius's character and way of life, see Pliny, *Natural History*, XXXV.69.

No. 16. *Youthful Hero with a Lance and Chariot*: Mural Painting (cf. Figs 18, 106)

Wall painting; approx. 120 × 120 cm.

Formerly on the east façade (facing the courtyard) of the studio wing, lost

c. 1616 (?)

VISUAL SOURCE: Harrewijn print, 1692 (Appendix III.2; Fig. 18; detail: Fig. 106).

LITERATURE: Prims, *Rubenshuis*, 1946, p. 13 (as 'onontcijferd'); McGrath, *Rubens's House*, 1976–78, pp. 143–144; McGrath, *Rubens's House*, 1978, pp. 270–272, pl. 28c.

Facing the courtyard, on the east façade of the studio complex parallel to the street, we see a single painted panel which continues the frieze of monochrome 'reliefs'. Two others, which one might expect alongside it, appear to be covered by a large painting on canvas, representing *Andromeda Liberated by Perseus* (No. 18), but as explained elsewhere,[1] this was part of a single *trompe-l'oeil* and the mythological scene was painted onto a blind wall, with nothing at all hidden 'underneath' (Fig. 107). The scene discussed here is framed differently from the frieze paintings decorating the other two façades: it is contained in a rectangle with volutes either side.

The subject shown in the fictive ancient stone relief has not been identified. We therefore have no idea if Rubens based it on a story known from a literary source, or chose to represent a theme that alluded to one of the paintings praised by classical authors.

The central figure is a young man, shown frontally, wearing only a loincloth and sandals, his head wreathed (?) and with a very long lance in his right hand, an attribute that suggests he might be a huntsman but equally a warrior. He seems to advance towards a chariot. Two of its wheels, which are recognisable by their spokes, can be seen by his left leg. Behind him is a second chariot with rearing horses, restrained by a helmeted figure. To the left stand figures in long robes; they seem to be men, but because of the hatched shadows in this section of the print, this is not clear. Possibly the young man is bidding them farewell and turns to set off in his chariot. Elizabeth McGrath noted that 'the composition is reminiscent in a general way of those departure scenes so common on Roman sarcophagi', but she emphasises that what appears on Rubens's façade does not entirely match any scene found in ancient written or visual sources.[2] Of course, only limited information can be extracted from the small detail in the Harrewijn print, and the possibility that the frieze panel represents quite a different scene cannot be excluded.[3]

1. See Chapter VI, p. 186, n. 48; and Chapter VI, passim.
2. The examples she gives include: Achilles leaving the court of Lycomedes, Bellerophon dismissed by Proetus, Meleager or Hippolytus going off to hunt, and Adonis deserting Venus. For more information about these subjects, and others besides, see McGrath, *Rubens's House*, 1978, pp. 270–271, n. 120. The object shown bottom right is a wheel with spokes (compare with the wheel in No. 8) and certainly not a shield, ruling out some other subjects proposed.
3. McGrath cautiously speculates that it might represent an anecdote recorded by Plutarch: the story of the artist Nealkes who painted over the figure of a tyrant (in a triumphal chariot) in a picture by Melanthius in order to protect the masterpiece from destruction (McGrath, *Rubens's House*, 1978, p. 272, n. 124). However, it seems highly unlikely that the youth is intended as Nealkes in front of the painting. The long lance – certainly not a mahlstick – and the wheels of a chariot beside him argue against this identification.

CATALOGUE No. 17

No. 17. *Loggia with a Figure and Animals*: Mural Painting (cf. Fig. 107)

Mural painting; approx. 300 × 600 cm.

Formerly on the east façade (facing the courtyard) of the studio wing, lost

c. 1616 (?)

VISUAL SOURCE: Harrewijn print, 1692 (Appendix III.2; Figs 18, 30; detail: Fig. 107).

LITERATURE: Baldinucci, *Notizie*, 1702, p. 282 (see Appendix I.32); Rooses, *Maison*, 1888, p. 220 (as 'une galerie ouverte dans laquelle se trouvait le peintre avec sa femme, son lévrier et deux perroquets'); Rooses, *Oeuvre*, 1886–92, V, p. 185; Rooses – Ruelens, *Correspondance*, 1887–1909, II, p. 154; Rooses, *Rubens*, 1904, p. 147 (as 'an Italian gallery with a balustrade with peacocks perched on it'); Muller, *Perseus and Andromeda*, 1981–82, pp. 133–135, 145, fig. 4; Stutz, *Residenz*, 1985, p. 146; Muller, *Rubens's Collection*, 2004, pp. 12, 40; Uppenkamp – Van Beneden, *Architectural Symbolism*, 2011, p. 116; F. Healy, in McGrath et al., *Mythological Subjects I (CRLB)*, 2016, I, p. 210.

In the Harrewijn print of 1692 (Figs 18, 30) a loggia is shown on the east façade of the studio wing, facing the courtyard, level with the first floor; it is open on two sides, to the front and behind, apparently looking onto the street (Fig. 107). Yet this is all an illusion: evidently the loggia is an architectural perspective, painted deceptively onto a blank wall. It is remarkable that the Florentine Filippo Baldinucci (1624–1697) mentions a *trompe-l'oeil* loggia in Rubens's house in his 1681 *Notizia* concerning Rubens, published posthumously in 1702 (Appendix I.32).

A description of the architecture depicted, with columns with Corinthian or composite capitals and a single ceiling coffer with rosette, is provided above.[1] A single figure and some animals give the loggia an exotic character. A black servant (probably a boy rather than a girl), who wears a loose cloak leaving one shoulder bare, stretches over to collar a dog which has got into a precarious position in front of the balustrade; two parrots – probably cockatoos, judging from their crests – are sitting to the right.

With his mural painting with its vista of figures behind a balustrade, Rubens is contributing to a rich tradition. We need only mention three examples. In Antwerp Rubens must certainly have known the house of Quinten Metsys (1466–1530); one of its rooms contained a mural of a gallery with musicians.[2] Also in Antwerp was the 'Staatsiekamer' of the Town Hall, with its vistas of figures behind a balustrade, as is known from nineteenth-century drawings. These lost murals were painted by Hans Vredeman de Vries (1526–1609), and they included images of a woman in a contemporary costume as well as a figure of Mercury.[3]

In his writings on Rubens's house, Rooses drew attention to a mural painting by Paolo Veronese (1528–1588) in the Villa Barbaro in Maser, which shows a woman with her elderly servant behind a balustrade, together with a dog and a parrot (Fig. 108).[4] We have no indication that Rubens saw the beautiful painted vistas in the Villa but other Italian examples doubtless caught his eye.

A decorative scheme with figures behind a balustrade is also found in the work of Jordaens, who was without question directly inspired by the painted loggia in Rubens's courtyard. A loggia open on two sides and seen from the right – that is of the same architectural type and viewed from the same angle as Rubens's *trompe-l'oeil* – can be found in his designs for wall paintings, for example *A Company Making Music in a Loggia* in the Fitzwilliam Museum, Cambridge (Fig. 109).[5]

During the reconstruction of the house a real loggia was built, ignoring the fact that the loggia shown in the Harrewijn print did not actually exist (cf. Figs 11 and 107).

1. See Chapter VI, pp. 183–184.
2. See above, Chapter VI, p. 199, n. 97.
3. The full-size drawings on tracing paper date from c. 1895; see Blockmans, *Krijgstekening*, 1962, pp. 20–21, figs 3, 9–10, 12–13; Borggrefe et al., eds, *Vredeman de Vries*, 2002, p. 303, no. 144, repr. p. 306.
4. Pignatti, *Veronese*, 1968, repr. p. 27.
5. d'Hulst, *Jordaens*, 1974, I, pp. 302–303, no. A219; III, fig. 234; see also *A Company Making Music in a Loggia* (whereabouts unknown), which repeats the motif

of the little dog in front of the balustrade (ibid., I, p. 286, no. A199; III, fig. 214); *Maid Carrying a Dish in a Loggia* (ibid., I, pp. 262–263, no A175; III, fig. 186); and studies for figures on a balcony in *Figures in an Architectural Setting* (ibid., I, pp. 304–305, no. A221; III, fig. 236); also worth noting are the figures behind a balustrade, with a small dog and a parrot, in a tapestry from the *Scenes of Country Life* series (Bauer – Delmarcel, eds, *Tapisseries bruxelloises*, 1977, no. 4). Jordaens's emulation was also noted by Muller, *Perseus and Andromeda*, 1981–82, p. 145, figs 20–21.

no. 18. *Andromeda Liberated by Perseus*: Mural Painting (cf. Figs 107 and 110)

Wall painting; approx. 270 × 390 cm.

Formerly on the east façade (facing the courtyard) of the studio wing, lost

c. 1616 (?) or later

VISUAL SOURCE: Harrewijn print, 1692 (Appendix III.2; Fig. 18; detail: Fig. 110).

COPY. Drawing, partial copy (Fig. 112), by an anonymous artist, Copenhagen, Statens Museum for Kunst, Kongelige Kobberstiksamling, inv. no. KKSgb7905 (Rubens Cantoor, I, 53); black chalk with white highlights on blue paper, 245 × 390 mm. EXH.: Antwerp, 2011, no. 43 (as 'anonymous artist after Rubens'). LIT.: Huvenne, *Tekeningen*, 1993, pp. 157–158, ill. 31bis (as 'anonymous'); Baudouin, *Fresco's*, 1998, p. 22, n. 46; Uppenkamp – Van Beneden, *Architectural Symbolism*, 2011, p. 113, fig. 152; F. Healy in McGrath et al., *Mythological Subjects I (CRLB)*, 2016, I, pp. 228, 230–231, n. 14, fig. 141 (as 'may well be after a lost study by Rubens, perhaps an oil sketch').

LITERATURE: Rooses, *Maison*, 1888, p. 220; Rooses, *Oeuvre*, 1886–92, III, p. 145; V, p. 185; Rooses, *Life*, 1904, p. 154; Sabbe, *Andromeda-sage*, 1927, p. 235; Evers, *Neue Forschungen*, 1943, pp. 267–268, fig. 295; Prims, *Rubenshuis*, 1946, pp. 26–28; Varshavskaya, *Rubens*, 1975, pp. 145–146; McGrath, *Rubens's House*, 1976–78, p. 143, fig. 10; McGrath, *Rubens's House*, 1978, pp. 247–248, 269–270, pl. 28c; Muller, *Perseus and Andromeda*, 1981–82, pp. 131–142, fig. 2; Freedberg, *Fornenbergh and Gerbier*, 1983, p. 250, n. 55, p. 252, n. 101; Tijs, *Rubens en Jordaens*, 1984, p. 158; Stutz, *Residenz*, 1985, p. 146; White, *Rubens*, 1987, pp. 63–65, fig. 85; Scott, *Perseus and Andromeda*, 1988, pp. 250–252, 258–260, pl. 53b; Muller, *Collector*, 1989, p. 26, fig. 6; Von Simson, *Rubens*, 1996, pp. 210–212; Winner, *Rubens' Götterrat*, 1997, pp. 124–126, fig. 7a; Rosenthal, *Occasio*, 2000, pp. 201–202, fig. 14; Heinen, *Gesundheit*, 2004, p. 111; Muller, *Rubens's Collection*, 2004, p. 40, fig. 50; N. Gritsay in Babina – Gritsay, *Cat. St Petersburg, Hermitage (Flemish Painting)*, 2005, p. 339, under no. 328; Rosenthal, *Rubens*, 2005, pp. 187–191, fig. 68; Juntunen, *Mythologische Historien*, 2005, pp. 100 ff., fig. 29a; Sluijter, *Rembrandt / Female Nude*, 2006, pp. 87–89, fig. 24; N. Gritsay in Gritsay – Babina, *Cat. St Petersburg, Hermitage (Flemish Painting)*, 2008, p. 255, under no. 310; Devroe, *Rubens' huis*, 2008, pp. 29–31, fig. 24c; Sluijter, *Andromeda*, 2009, p. 35, fig. 16; Uppenkamp – Van Beneden, *Architectural Symbolism*, 2011, pp. 106, 113–117, fig. 153; Wouk, *Façade of Floris*, 2014, pp. 124–125; F. Healy in McGrath et al., *Mythological Subjects I (CRLB)*, 2016, I, pp. 209, 212, 214, 227–232, 235, fig. 143; Baumstark – Delmarcel, *Decius Mus (CRLB)*, 2019, I, pp. 158–159.

In the Harrewijn print of 1692, a large figurative scene can be seen on the short east façade of the studio wing, which is very different in both format and scale from the frieze panels. The subject represented is clearly legible. It shows an episode from the well-known tale of Andromeda, who was chained to a rock as prey for a terrible sea monster, and rescued by the hero Perseus.

The moment illustrated follows the slaying of the monster by Perseus and we see him stepping towards the chained maiden in order to free her with the help of three putti. To Perseus's right are two further putti who have come to his aid: one of them holds up the Medusa shield and another clasps the reins of the winged horse Pegasus. Victory appears at the top of the scene, holding a palm branch and victor's crown over the hero's head.

CATALOGUE No. 18

Rubens certainly knew the ancient written sources for this tale, mentioned by many authors.[1] In his *Metamorphoses* Ovid gives an extensive account of the story as one of Perseus's heroic deeds. He pays much attention to the battle with the monster, but he also mentions Perseus's love for the beautiful Andromeda, resulting eventually in their marriage (see below).[2]

The story is furthermore the subject of two *ekphrases*. Perseus's heroic deed is the subject of one of the fictitious paintings described in detail in Philostratus's *Imagines*.[3] An Andromeda painting also happens to appear in a novel: *Leucippe and Clitophon* by Achilles Tatius.[4] Tatius describes *Andromada Chained to a Rock*, as part of a diptych by Euanthes, with *Prometheus Bound* as pendant.

There are considerable differences in detail between Ovid's story and Philostratus's *ekphrasis*, and Rubens does not adhere literally to either of them. The moment of the actual rescue by Perseus is not mentioned in these texts, at least not as Rubens shows it, with Perseus approaching the maiden. In the painting described by Philostratus, Perseus lies resting on 'sweet fragrant grass' to recover from the exertions of the fight and it is not he but Cupid – whose help he has called in – that frees Andromeda from her bonds (Fig. 115).[5]

One striking difference, in which Rubens departs from all the ancient written sources mentioned above, is the presence of the horse Pegasus, which plays such an important role in the composition. In Ovid's *Metamorphoses* Perseus certainly flies through the sky and from high up he catches sight of the maiden chained to the rocks, but he is not riding the winged horse. He flies by means of small wings tied to his feet. This motif occurs frequently in the visual arts, including the Ovidian *Andromeda* which Rubens painted in about 1636 for the Torre de la Parada.[6] In the scene on the façade, however, he is following the rich post-classical tradition, in which Perseus is shown more decorously as a knight riding the winged horse which sprang from the blood of Medusa after she was beheaded by the hero.[7]

Both Ovid and Philostratus emphasise Andromeda's exceptional beauty and the instantaneous falling in love of the hero. In Ovid's version Perseus exclaims: 'Oh! Those are not the chains you deserve to wear, but rather those that link fond lovers together!'.[8] Philostratus describes Andromeda's beauty and Perseus's love, and as stated it is Cupid who unfastens the chains. He describes the heroic act as 'the exploit which I think the man undertook voluntarily for love'.[9] In this respect Philostratus's account agrees with that of Ovid, for whom the fable of Perseus and Andromeda is a tale of the triumph of love. In the *Metamorphoses*, Perseus's heroic deed ends in a wedding feast in which the ceremony is led by Cupid and Hymen as torch bearers.[10]

Two different moments of the well-known tale were represented frequently in Rubens's painted oeuvre. Both the painting for the Torre de la Parada mentioned, and another work in Berlin, show Andromeda chained to the rock before the moment of her liberation, with Perseus flying in the background embroiled with the sea monster. Then there are three works, in St Petersburg (Fig. 111), Berlin (Fig. 113) and Madrid, that show Perseus after he has slain the sea monster, and approaching Andromeda to liberate her.[11] The theme as it appears in Rubens's oeuvre, including the wall painting under discussion here, has been treated extensively by Fiona Healy in the first Corpus volume on *Mythological Subjects*.[12]

The scene pictured in the Harrewijn print more or less matches the St Petersburg version, but there are differences. Beginning with the dimensions, the approximate format of the lost wall painting can be deduced from its size relative to the façade (the height and breadth of which are known because they are the same in the present, restored building), and comparison reveals that the paintings in St Petersburg and Berlin are considerably smaller.[13] A second difference is that both were painted on panel, while the Harrewijn print unambiguously shows a work on canvas, tacked to a stretcher.

More striking are the differences in the composition. Strangely, the sea monster which plays an essential role in the tale as well as in both of Rubens's paintings, is absent in the scene represented in the print. Comparison with the St Petersburg version also reveals no trace of the putto carrying Perseus's helmet as he hovers underneath Victory, nor can Victory's wings be made out. These differences could of course be explained by an incorrect reading by the artist who drew the scene as it appeared on Rubens's wall. Indeed, it is hard to explain the omission of Perseus's decorative plumed helmet, which should be present as part of the hero's armour, particularly as he has just returned from a fight.

Other details that differ are certainly reproduced correctly in the print. Unlike the St Petersburg version, Perseus's cloak is now draped over his left shoulder, fastened by the clasp over the right. This variation in his clothing is connected with another difference in the composition. Perseus's long and wide cloak now emerges underneath the Medusa shield, and the boy who is handling the shield holds up a flap of the cloak to cover part of the shield. Is he making a (rather unsuccessful) attempt to conceal the dangerous Gorgon's head, whose gaze could turn any living thing to stone?[14] Perhaps, but we might expect him rather to be helping the love-stricken hero to remove his armour, as the smaller boy does in the painted version; how he might accomplish this, when the shield is snagged in the cloak which is fastened at Perseus's shoulder, remains unclear.

One odd feature in the Harrewijn print is Andromeda's clothing: she is wearing something like a shapeless and short (or pulled up?) shift, which leaves her legs bare. In the St Petersburg version she wears a long, loose yellow-gold cloak which has slipped down from her shoulders, leaving her entirely naked, apart from a very thin piece of white drapery held in the maiden's just freed left hand as a gesture of modesty. Furthermore, the shift does not match the 'modern' pictorial tradition followed by Rubens in all other representations of the theme: Andromeda consistently stands chained to the rock naked, apart from minimal drapery.[15] Her shift is undoubtedly, like the drapery around the hips of the *Hermes Belvedere* on the east or garden façade (No. 5; Fig. 44), a prudish addition. It is difficult to say if this clumsy addition of the shift was simply a detail changed in the print, or was painted onto the wall itself after 1640 by a resident of the house – not necessarily Hendrik Hillewerve, who was a priest, but also an art lover.[16]

Whatever the case, it is clear that very little consideration has been given to the style of this unusual 'clothing' and we can certainly rule out Rubens as its inventor; Andromeda's modest gesture was clumsily retained in the modified composition, but with the presence of the shift it becomes meaningless. It is also worth noting that the three cupids are busy not simply unfastening Andromeda's ropes, but they are also uncovering her beauty to receive the gaze of the hero who has fallen in love with her. This is particularly noticeable in the gesture of the child, who cheekily pulls away a fold of her cloak.[17] With a maiden wearing a shift or *tunica* underneath her cloak, this zealous activity by the cupids is, of course, quite pointless.

As for the composition in general, there is little to observe that differs from the version in St Petersburg (cf. Figs 110 –111). The figures seem to be placed more tightly together, while Andromeda stands on the same level as Perseus, rather than above on a rock. Three of the five children in the scene are represented slightly differently, no longer as chubby toddlers. The figure to the left by Andromeda's shoulder appears upright rather than bending forwards, and has large pointed wings. The main difference to note is in the posture and physiognomy of the two 'helpers' to Perseus's right: both the child bearing the shield, mentioned above, and his companion – boys rather than toddlers – are shown in different postures. The boy who holds Pegasus by the bridle now does so with his other hand (the left) and because he is striding towards the left, his legs are shown differently. With this movement Rubens undoubtedly intended a reference to the ancient statue of *The Horse Tamer* (cf. Figs 122–123) in Rome which he had copied there.[18]

The large mythological scene shown on the courtyard façade in the Harrewijn print has given rise to a great deal of discussion and commentary in the literature. The first question to be asked is what exactly is shown in the print, or rather in what medium the *Andromeda Liberated* was executed. At first sight, one might think that it represents a 'conventional' Rubens painting: not a wall painting applied to the plasterwork but a work on canvas, recognisable by the edges which are fixed to a stretcher with tacks. However, this is a *trompe-l'oeil* which has deceived many authors in the past. It was believed to be a canvas by Rubens (or workshop) that had been left in the courtyard, hanging outside exposed to the weather for more than half a century, which is, on reflection, quite an extraordinary assumption to make. This 'real' painting was thought to be hiding two of the three frieze panels on the façade.[19]

Two suggestions have been put forward to explain the presence of a 'real' painting on canvas in such a strange place in Hillewerve's time. One theory, based on the unfounded assumption that the *Andromeda* had a political meaning (see below), is that it had served as part of city decorations on the occasion of a Joyous Entry, and was subsequently returned to Rubens.[20] The second hypothesis is more interesting but can also be rejected. We know that Rubens would regularly leave paintings outside to dry in the sun in fine weather,[21] and it has been suggested that the *Andromeda Liberated* was an example of this practice, and for some reason the canvas was simply never taken down.

Documentary sources, however, leave no room for doubt that it was a *trompe-l'oeil* representation of an oil painting on canvas. The first indication that such a *trompe-l'oeil* appeared in the courtyard is provided by the anecdote recounted by Filippo Baldinucci, who informs us that when the Infanta Isabella visited Rubens, she asked him to have the painting brought down (Appendix I.32).[22]

Even if one was tempted to ignore this anecdote as no more than an example of the *topos* of the viewer tricked, there is nonetheless another decisive piece of information in the description made by François Mols of the wall paintings (in poor condition) after he saw them on Rubens's house in 1763 when it was up for sale. He mentions several mythological subjects ('plusieurs Sujets de fable') underneath the windows, and in addition, 'l'Andromède peint en couleurs naturelles' (Appendix I.43: I [2]).

We should remember that this illusionistic painting was just one element of a large *trompe-l'oeil* painted onto a section of the wall on the east façade of the block containing the staircase (Fig. 107). We mentioned in the chapter on the wall paintings that with the *Andromeda Liberated* Rubens was employing a principle recommended by Serlio for the painting of façades. A narrative scene should be represented on a fictive support, for example a canvas, so as to avoid the illusion that it was viewed through an opening. An illogical 'aperture' in the wall of this type would be a mistake that interfered with the integrity of the architecture.[23]

While Mols's eighteenth-century eyewitness account confirms that the *Andromeda Liberated* in the courtyard was indeed a fictive painting, his description also provides information that leaves us with unanswered questions and fuelled a whole new discussion. He writes that he noticed – and he says this with some emphasis – that the *Andromeda* which he saw in the courtyard did not have the same composition as the painting reproduced in the Harrewijn print (Appendix I.43: I [3]).[24] Having looked carefully into this matter, he observes that the image of the print corresponds to the Andromeda belonging to the Comte de Bruhl which was engraved by Tardieu and which is now in the Emperor of Russia's cabinet. But the objects are shown the other way around ('l'Andromède du Comte de Bruhl que Tardieu a gravé et qui se trouve actuellement dans le cabinet de l'Imperateur de Russie. Mais, les objets sont du coté opposé') (Appendix I.43: I [Supplementary note]). In other words, he rightly connects it with the print by Pierre François Tardieu (1711–1771), engraved around 1750 (in reverse) after the St Petersburg painting (Fig. 114).[25]

What Mols actually saw when he visited the house, however, was something different. His description indeed closely matches the variant in Berlin (Fig. 113), showing Andromeda to the right but especially also in the distinctive detail of the putti clambering on Pegasus's back ('le pegase vers la gauche etoit retenu par d'autres génies qui badinoient avec lui, en voulant monter sur sa croupe'; Appendix I.43: I [2]). This means that we have the curious situation that in Hillewerve's time the wall was decorated with an image close to the St Petersburg version, while about seventy years later, in 1763, the subject was the same, but with a quite different composition showing Andromeda to the right. Mols is so formal and meticulous that we can be absolutely confident of his record, but there is also no reason to call into question the accuracy of the Harrewijn print.

The only possible explanation for this curious discrepancy is that the original *Andromeda Liberated* was overpainted between 1692 and 1763 with a different composition which corresponded with the Berlin painting. Something that possibly corroborates the hypothesis that it was repainted, is Mols's remark that the *Andromeda* on the façade was in a better state than the frieze panels: 'une entre autres a subsisté le plus longtemps; c'étoit l'Andromède' (one of them had held out the longest; that was Andromeda). This could indicate that the painting was reworked, probably at some time between 1692 and 1763. But no satisfactory explanation can be found to account for the choice of a radically different composition at the moment when restoration was needed.[26] In short: although it cannot be proved, it is safe to assume that it was the St Petersburg composition that appeared on the façade, both in Hillewerve's and in Rubens's lifetimes.

We might ask if there are other sources, besides the print and Mols's description, that might provide a detailed impression of the *Andromeda* composition on the wall. Did any drawn copies survive from the seventeenth century, as with two of the frieze panels in the courtyard (see Nos 11–12)? A number of copies of a similar *Andromeda* composition exist, but these are closer to the St Petersburg version and since it is not easy to establish exactly what was being copied, they add little to what we know about the wall painting.

A drawing of a fragment of an *Andromeda* composition (lacking the uppermost zone showing Victory with a wreath and putto carrying the hero's helmet), attributed to Willem Panneels, survives in the so-called Rubens Cantoor and is included here as a copy (Fig. 112), although it is unlikely that it was directly modelled on the façade painting. In fact, there is nothing that can confirm this, other than to observe that the composition corresponds to the Harrewijn print in the position of the putto restraining the horse (in the posture of the *Horse Tamer*). On the contrary, important details correspond closely with the St Petersburg version: Perseus's cloak fastened on his left shoulder, and nearby the little boy who holds up the shield but without evidence of a fold of Perseus's cloak. Perhaps there is a chance that this sheet gives us an image of a lost preparatory work that was kept in what was known as Rubens's Cantoor.

Another sheet showing a detail of Perseus's cuirass, in the same collection,[27] corresponds with the St Petersburg painting and is not included as a copy of No. 18. The same applies with an anonymous drawing showing another detail: the horse Pegasus, which is in the Albertina in Vienna.[28] Two drawings show a complete composition, one being an exact match with the St Petersburg version, but again these cannot be regarded as copies of the façade.[29]

Before we go on to examine the subject of the wall painting, there is one more question to consider, namely the matter of its possible dating, and in particular the chronological relationship between the wall painting and the similar St Petersburg picture. In her extensive commentary in the *Corpus Rubenianum* on Rubens's Andromeda images, Fiona Healy assumes that the St Petersburg painting must have been made c. 1621–1622.[30] The painted decoration of the studio façades, however, was very likely executed several years earlier, probably c. 1616, since we can be confident that the studio façades were then complete and would not have been left blank for a period of years. As far as the *Andromeda Liberated* is concerned, it indeed seems unlikely that a section of blind wall between the colonnade and the windows would have remained unpainted for as long as four or five years, until into the 1620s. This poses a problem: no obvious explanation can be found for the difference in dating between the two images. Should the St Petersburg painting be dated earlier, or is it the other way around and did Rubens recreate on panel a composition that had been painted on his façade a few years previously? Was there initially a different picture painted on the wall, which was overpainted with an *Andromeda Liberated* around 1621–1622 or later? Neither possibility seems more plausible than the other. If we compare the extant painting with the tiny and casually etched detail in the Harrewijn print we have only the composition to go on, and this offers little conclusive evidence with which to determine a chronological order.

On closer inspection, the dating of the St Petersburg version can perhaps be brought forward by a few years. This is the conclusion of several colleagues who have looked into the problematical question of its dating in connection with this catalogue entry. Arnout Balis believes that certain conclusions can be drawn from the differences between the compositions. He suspects that the St Petersburg panel came first, and that Rubens afterwards created a larger *trompe-l'oeil* version of it, which in his view pays more respect to decorum and aims less at the sense of intimacy which characterises the panel. To Balis, the dating 1621–1622 seems too late for the panel, and he thinks that 1617–1618 is more likely, while the wall painting can be dated somewhat later.[31] Fiona Healy comes to a similar conclusion. She agrees that the St Petersburg *Perseus and Andromeda* is indeed probably earlier than the date she proposed (i.e. 1621–1622), though not necessarily as early as 1616.[32] Corroboration of the earlier dating has also been provided by Brecht Vanoppen, who has drawn attention to comparable motifs in works by Rubens of around 1615–1617. He observed for example that the nimble Andromeda in the *Venus Pudica* pose is conceived in the same spirit as the Pandrosos figure in *The Discovery of Erichthonius by the Daughters of Cecrops* (c. 1616–1617) in the Liechtenstein collection (cf. Figs 116–117),[33] while the Perseus figure can be found, in reverse, in Rubens's *Abraham and Melchizedek* (c. 1616) in Caen (cf. Figs 118–119).[34] The putto standing to Andromeda's left also appears in the *Homage to Ceres* (c. 1612–1615) (Appendix III.13; cf. Figs 120 and 121).[35] Regardless of the dating of these works, Vanoppen is nonetheless also convinced of a dating of c. 1617–1618 for the *Andromeda Liberated by Perseus* in St Petersburg.

Finally on the matter of dating, it can be observed that there is no compelling reason to take the year 1618 as *terminus ante quem* for any of Rubens's *Andromeda* compositions.[36]

Having described the scene and discussed the dating, one important question remains with regard to this striking wall painting. Why did Rubens choose *Andromeda Liberated* as subject for the *trompe-l'oeil* painting in his courtyard? This mythological theme can be interpreted in many different ways depending on the context, and various theories have been put forward to explain its presence in the decoration of Rubens's house.

It was mentioned above that in this composition (as well as in the two paintings now in St Petersburg and Berlin), Rubens emphasised a particular aspect of the Andromeda tale, namely the triumph of love. He does not show the hero fighting with the monster, nor the petrified Andromeda in despair and in chains, as the flying Perseus approaches in the distance (on horseback, or flying using his winged sandals). This is much more of a love scene, in which the little cupids play a part by unfastening the ropes and are literally disarming the hero. In the St Petersburg composition they deal with his helmet and with the dangerous Medusa shield.[37]

The significance of this love theme as a subject for representation on the façade is not immediately obvious,[38] unless Perseus's love for Andromeda is to be interpreted as a metaphor in an art-theoretical sense, a suggestion to which we will return below.

It should be observed that the *Andromeda Liberated* theme was from the middle of the sixteenth, and in the seventeenth century, often given a quite different slant in the Low Countries. It was a popular theme both in the northern and southern regions with which to visualise a particular stance that captured the turbulent political situation. Andromeda is imagined as a city or region which faces a dangerous threat, while Perseus personifies the bold prince or general who ousts the enemy. To people in the north, Perseus represented William of Orange, who freed the Low Countries from tyranny. The vicious monster bringing a threat from overseas was Alva, or Spain in general. For those in the south the hero represented, in contrast, the victor in the battle against heresy and rebellion.[39]

However, it seems rather unlikely, if not out of the question, that Rubens would have intended some political message in the decoration of his courtyard. There seems to be no justification for this, and what argues especially against such a reading is the emphasis on the love aspect of the scene rather than the heroic battle against the monster. Unsurprisingly, this interpretation has been more or less unanimously rejected in the literature.[40]

There is another theory which proposes that the *Andromeda Liberated* should perhaps be interpreted in connection with a key aspect of the painted façade decoration, namely with the subjects represented in the illusionistic ancient reliefs of the frieze, some of which refer to lost paintings made by famous ancient Greek masters.

After all, the Andromeda tale was also among the subjects that appeared in ancient painting. As mentioned above, there were the *ekphrases* of Philostratus and Achilles Tatius, lengthy descriptions of paintings which probably never existed. In addition there is a mention by Pliny, who knew of an 'Andromeda' from the hand of the Greek painter Nicias (Athens, 4th century BC).[41] Pliny gives only the title and no further information, and therefore nothing can be deduced concerning Nicias's composition. However, it is possible that some idea of its image is reflected in works of art from the Roman period depicting the liberation of Andromeda. Certain reliefs have been considered in connection with the lost masterpiece, as well as wall paintings found in Pompeii.[42]

The assumption that in painting the *Andromeda Liberated* on his façade, Rubens principally intended to recreate an ancient masterwork has led some scholars to make further inferences about the picture's meaning. They see the contrast between the monochrome frieze and the colourful scene of the artist's own invention as highly significant. They also give special meaning to the fact that the painting is depicted right next to the frieze panels and apparently actually hanging in front of two of them, hiding them from view. This embodies the idea that 'modern' painting – and especially that of Rubens – has replaced that of the past and even surpassed it. Jeffrey Muller, who has written extensively about the illusionistic painting, regards it not only as a recreation 'of another of the achievements of ancient painting', he was convinced that the contrast between the frieze panels and Rubens's *Andromeda Liberated by Perseus* is an essential element in the façade's decorative programme.[43] Fiona Healy shares this theory about the message which Rubens wanted to convey: Rubens regarded himself as the true heir to the ancient tradition, and demonstrated it 'by hanging his painting over these illustrious masterpieces, now mere shadows since deprived of their once glorious colour'.[44]

Yet it is not easy to judge if it really was Rubens's intention to wrap up this message in the *trompe-l'oeil* painting on his studio façade. The nature of the frieze panels is a somewhat weak point in this interpretation: rather than paintings which have lost their colour, these are stone reliefs that form part of the architecture of Rubens's '*diaeta romana*', true to the pattern employed on Roman *palazzi*. The *Andromeda* is a large canvas which is hanging out on the façade to dry, and so obviously conceals part of the architecture, which happens also to include a loggia.

The interpretation outlined here, however, is not the only one which attributes an art-theoretical meaning to the wall painting showing *Andromeda Liberated*. Several authors have been convinced that Rubens chose this scene to give expression to his views on the art of painting, and they have even regarded it as the key to the house's decorative programme. The most comprehensive accounts which start from that premise are those of Jeffrey Muller, John Beldon Scott, Lisa Rosenthal and Eveliina Juntunen.[45]

These authors focus on various details which they regard as significant. One of these is the motif of Victory crowning the hero, an element that is unusual in the iconography of *Perseus and Andromeda*, but which was woven into the image by Rubens, in the wall painting as well as in the closely related St Petersburg version. In their opinion, the crowning is probably not meant as a reward for the hero who had bravely exerted himself to kill the dangerous monster, and neither is it a reference to the triumph of love. An interpretation of the crowning with laurel along specifically art-theoretical lines links it more closely with works of art in which a 'hero-artist', such as Apelles or Raphael, is honoured.[46] Perseus's victory is thus seen as the triumph of the artist who comes to the support of, and liberates art, beauty or truth. As in the treatment of the subject by Hendrik Goltzius (1558–1617), for example, the scene depicts the triumph of Virtue (Virtus) over the enemies of the arts, including ignorance.[47]

Another interpretation, put forward by John Beldon Scott, argues that Rubens's *Andromeda* concerns the triumph of the art of painting over sculpture. He is convinced that the wall painting alludes to the ancient *paragone*, or debate on the superiority of painting or sculpture. He observes that Rubens does not represent Andromeda as a marble statue, but as a beautiful living woman. This could refer to the idea that a painting is able to render life more convincingly than a sculpture. Hence the conclusion that the art of painting is superior. Scott also comes back to the juxtaposition of the frieze panels and the colourful canvas hanging over them, but with a different emphasis. He is aware that Rubens's canvas is not obscuring ancient painting but sculpture, and he suspects that Rubens intended to suggest that 'painterly naturalism triumphs over ideal sculptural beauty'.[48]

The most substantial commentaries on the meaning of representations of Perseus and Andromeda concentrate on two elements in the Perseus story: the winged horse Pegasus and the Medusa shield, both motifs which feature prominently in the painting. Pegasus occupies an unusually large part of the composition, while the circular Medusa shield is pictured at the very centre of the scene. These two elements play a role not only in the story of Perseus, but they are also important symbols in the iconography of the Arts. When Perseus beheaded Medusa, Pegasus was born from her blood; with a blow of his hooves he struck Mount Helicon, home to Apollo and the Muses, creating Hippocrene, the spring of inspiration; he is thus associated with the Muses and especially with poetry.

In forming their interpretations these authors emphasise the large Medusa shield which they see as the all-important key to the meaning of the illusionistic painting. The shield alludes to the 'act of looking' (the deadly gaze of the Medusa), and the mirrored surface of the shield symbolises the art of painting, which gives a reflection of nature.[49]

There is another aspect of the Perseus tale to which these authors have turned their attention, although it is not something actually represented in the painting. This concerns the gods Mercury and Minerva who played an important part in Perseus's victory over the Medusa, and in the making of the shield. They had armed Perseus, and guided him in battle. According to this line of argument, these gods who were associated with Perseus occupied a pivotal role in the larger iconography of Rubens's house. It is clear that all of these authors are referring to the two statues which – according to the Harrewijn print – stood on top of the portico facing the painting, and which they see as 'presiding deities for the home and for the workshop'.[50] The uncertain status of the statues (Nos R1 and R2; Figs 227–228 and 231), however, means that this interpretation is not as convincing as has been suggested.

1. Apart from the descriptions by Ovid, Philostratus en Achilles Tatius (see below) there is also an account, amounting to only a few lines, in the stories told by Hyginus (Hyginus, *Fabulae*, LXIV). Both Sophocles and Euripides wrote tragedies on this subject, but only fragments survive (Grimal, *Mythologie grecque et romaine*, 1988, p. 36).
2. For the battle, see Ovid, *Metamorphoses*, IV.678–739; for the wedding: IV.758–762; Ovid, *Metamorphoses*, transl. Miller, 1977–84, I, pp. 226–233.
3. Philostratus, *Imagines* I.29; Philostratus, *Imagines*, transl. Fairbanks, 2000, pp. 115–119. Rubens owned a copy of the French translation by Blaise de Vigenère (purchase recorded in the Plantin *Journal* on 25 May 1614; later in the library of Albert Rubens); see Arents, *Bibliotheek*, 2001, p. 141, no. E 21, who identifies the book, possibly correctly, as the unillustrated edition of 1611 (and not that of 1614 as often thought). See also McGrath, *Mythographic Handbooks*, 2009, p. 404, n. 88.
4. Achilles Tatius, *Leucippe and Clitophon*, III.6–7; id., *Leucippe and Clitophon*, transl. S. Gaselee, 1969, pp. 147–151. Tatius explains why these two subjects – Andromeda and Prometheus – were probably associated: both victims were chained to a rock, tortured by a beast (respectively a sea monster and Jupiter's eagle), and both were liberated by a hero ('Argives of the same family': Perseus and Hercules). For Tatius's *Andromeda*, see F. Healy in McGrath et al., *Mythological Subjects I (CRLB)*, 2016, I, pp. 209, 221, 225, n. 41; on the *Prometheus* (Achilles Tatius, *Leucippe and Clitophon*, III.6, 8) and Rubens's painting of the subject in Philadelphia, see Dempsey, *Prometheus Bound*, 1967, passim. A copy of Achilles Tatius's book, in octavo, was in Albert Rubens's

CATALOGUE No. 18

library; see Arents, *Bibliotheek*, 2001, p. 355 (not listed as in Rubens's possession).
5. A rare illustration of a seated Perseus, resting while Cupid unfastens Andromeda's bonds, appears in French editions of the *Imagines* (edition of 1614, p. 254; McAllister Johnson, *Prolegomena*, 1969, fig. 28). It is understandable that painters, not least Rubens, were reluctant to follow Philostratus in this unheroic pose.
6. Alpers, *Torre (CRLB)*, 1971, no. 49a, fig. 161. Ovid explicitly mentions Perseus's manner of flight: 'Then Perseus bound on both his feet the wings he had laid by, […] and soon in swift flight was cleaving the thin air' (Ovid, *Metamorphoses*, IV. 665–667; Ovid, *Metamorphoses*, transl. Miller, 1977–84, I, p. 225). Achilles Tatius also describes Perseus as 'suspended in the air on his wings' (Achilles Tatius, *Leucippe and Clitophon*, transl. S. Gaselee, 1969, p. 147).
7. This idea of Perseus as a knight on horseback is not ancient but developed in the Middle Ages and is possibly a confusion with another heroic figure who rode Pegasus: Bellerophon who killed the Chimera. For full commentary on the iconography of the winged horse, see Brink – Hornbostel, eds, *Pegasus*, 1993. On this matter – the horse Pegasus and/or winglets – see also F. Healy in McGrath et al., *Mythological Subjects I (CRLB)*, 2016, I, pp. 209, 213 (n. 2), 228, 231 (n. 9).
8. Ovid, *Metamorphoses*, IV.678–679; Ovid, *Metamorphoses*, transl. Miller, 1977–84, I, p. 227.
9. Philostratus, *Imagines*, 29.11.
10. Ovid, *Metamorphoses*, IV.758–762.
11. See Rubens's versions of *Andromeda Liberated by Perseus* in the State Hermitage Museum in St Petersburg, inv. no. 461 (F. Healy in McGrath et al., *Mythological Subjects I (CRLB)*, 2016, I, no. 12; II, fig. 138); Gemäldegalerie, Staatliche Museen zu Berlin, Berlin, inv. no. 785 (ibid., I, no. 13; II, fig. 148); Museo Nacional del Prado, Madrid, inv. no. P-1663 (ibid., I, no. 14; II, fig. 154).
12. F. Healy in McGrath et al., *Mythological Subjects I (CRLB)*, 2016, I, pp. 208–247, nos 11–14.
13. If the print can be taken as a reliable indication of the proportions, we arrive at dimensions of approximately 270 × 390 cm. The two extant versions are both much smaller and they have similar dimensions: The St Petersburg painting does not survive in its original form: it was transferred from panel to canvas and reduced from 119 × 147 cm to 99.5 × 139 cm.; the Berlin version is 100 × 138.5 cm.
14. Interpretation proposed by F. Healy in McGrath et al., *Mythological Subjects I (CRLB)*, 2016, I, p. 211.
15. There are indications that in Antiquity the chained Andromeda was not imagined as a nude figure. On this, Ovid and Philostratus leave us in the dark, but Achilles Tatius describes her clothes: she was adorned for a wedding feast, 'as one who was to be the bride of the King of Death. She wore a tunic reaching to her feet', that was white and made of silk (Achilles Tatius, *Leucippe and Clitophon*, III.7). It can also be noted that in ancient painted representations of the subject, in contrast to 'modern', the princess is fully clothed in a long dress that reaches to the ground (see reliefs and wall paintings mentioned in n. 42).
16. His sister Cornelia Hillewerve, who owned the house from 1660 to 1680 (see Chapter II, pp. 72–74; Chapter III, pp. 87–88), is perhaps a more likely candidate for requiring prudish interventions which sanitised the façade decorations.
17. Thus he plays a similar role to the putto who helps disrobe Alexander's bride in Rubens's *Alexander and Roxana* (see below, n. 37).
18. Bober – Rubinstein, *Antique Sculpture*, 2010, no. 125.
19. See Chapter VI, p. 186, n. 48.
20. This was the suggestion of Evers, to which he added 'aber das ist reine Vermutung' (Evers, *Neue Forschungen*, 1943, p. 268); also regarded, with some reservations, as possible, by McGrath, *Rubens's House*, 1978, p. 269; rightly rejected by Muller, *Perseus and Andromeda*, 1981–82, p. 131, n. 1.
21. For more on this practice, see Chapter VI, pp. 187–188.
22. He does not explain why the Infanta makes this request; the suggestion that she did so in order to take a look at the frieze lying underneath (see Chapter VI, p. 187, n. 50) seems without basis.
23. See Chapter VI, pp. 189–190.
24. 'Je puis attester que le sujet gravé par Harrewijn ne se trouvoit nullement sur cette muraille à la vente de cette maison où je l'ai examiné nombre de fois' (I can certify that when the house was sold, the composition engraved by Harrewijn was absolutely not to be found on this wall, which I examined on many occasions); see Rooses, *Oeuvre*, 1886–92, III, p. 145.
25. Evers, *Neue Forschungen*, 1943, p. 272, fig. 296 (incorrectly as engraved by 'Fr. Erlinger'); F. Healy in McGrath et al., *Mythological Subjects I (CRLB)*, 2016, I, p. 226; II, fig. 145, under Prints (1); both publications illustrate the print, omitting its explanatory inscription at the bottom with the arms of Graf Heinrich von Brühl, then owner of the painting.
26. Several explanations were given, including: (1) the Harrewijn print does not show what could actually be seen and the façade was decorated with the composition of the Berlin painting, meaning that the artist of the drawing, Van Croes, inserted an image based for some reason on the composition of the other painting; (2) both sources – the print and Mols's report – are correct, meaning that between 1692 and 1763 the first version was replaced by the second, possibly in the course of a complete restoration of the wall painting which was in poor condition (suggested by Muller, *Perseus and Andromeda*, 1981–82, p. 134). For four possible explanations, see also F. Healy in McGrath et al., *Mythological Subjects I (CRLB)*, 2016, I, p. 214, n. 20; see also ibid., I, pp. 230, 235; according to Healy, Pegasus's colour ('mottled grey') (ibid., p. 212) is one argument in favour of the Berlin version.

27. *Study of a Cuirass*, drawing, by Willem Panneels (?) after Rubens, Copenhagen, Statens Museum for Kunst, Kongelige Kobberstiksamling, inv. no. KKSgb (Rubens Cantoor, no. VI, 73); F. Healy in McGrath et al., *Mythological Subjects I (CRLB)*, 2016, I, p. 230, n. 43; II, fig. 142. The cuirass was copied literally by Willem van Haecht (1593–1637) for the figure of Alexander the Great in his *Art Cabinet of Cornelis van der Geest* (Appendix III. 8).
28. Drawing, by an anonymous artist after Rubens, Vienna, Albertina, inv. no. 8242; pen and ink, wash and watercolour, 27.7 × 21.2 cm, inscribed lower left: *Rubens*. See F. Healy in McGrath et al., *Mythological Subjects I (CRLB)*, 2016, I, pp. 230, 232, n. 44.
29. The two copies referred to are: (1) Drawing, by an anonymous artist, whereabouts unknown; red and black chalk, heightened with white, on pale yellow paper, 362 × 525 mm. PROV.: sale, Monaco (Sotheby's Parke Bennet), 5 March 1984, lot 910 (as 'Héros victorieux'); LIT.: Baudouin, *Fresco's*, 1998, pp. 21–22, n. 46, fig. 15; (2) A drawing which appeared at auction in the 19th century, described as painted by Rubens on his façade, but of which no image is known: drawing, whereabouts unknown; black chalk, Indian ink, red chalk-wash, and bistre, measurements unknown. PROV.: William Young Ottley, London (1771–1836); his sale, London (Phillips), 6 June 1814, lot 1640 (Lugt no. 8533) (The Deliverance of Andromeda by Perseus – painted by Rubens on the outside of his house at Antwerp; – great effect – capital); LIT.: F. Healy in McGrath et al., *Mythological Subjects I (CRLB)*, 2016, I, pp. 230, 233, n. 43 (as a copy or a preparatory design).
30. Ibid., I, p. 226.
31. I am grateful to Arnout Balis for considering this and sharing his views (private correspondence, 2 October 2020).
32. With thanks to Fiona Healy for sharing her opinion (private correspondence, 2 October 2020).
33. F. Healy in McGrath et al., *Mythological Subjects I (CRLB)*, 2016, I, no. 41; II, fig. 333.
34. d'Hulst – Vandenven, *Old Testament (CRLB)*, 1989, no. 17.
35. Büttner, *Allegories (CRLB)*, 2018, I, no. 5; II, fig. 23.
36. In a long poem that Balthasar Gerbier (1592–1663) wrote in 1618 on the death of Hendrik Goltzius (d. 1617), Rubens is mentioned as leading the train of mourners, a cross-section of Northern and Southern Netherlandish artists. Gerbier mentions an Andromeda in chains among paintings by Rubens, which would provide a *terminus ante quem* of 1618 for this subject. But it is more likely that Gerbier is listing fictive paintings, referring to Goltzius's work rather than to extant works by Rubens; for a detailed account, see Freedberg, *Fornenbergh and Gerbier*, 1983, pp. 252–253, nn. 101, 103; see also Muller, *Perseus and Andromeda*, 1981–82, p. 143, n. 45; McGrath et al., *Mythological Subjects I (CRLB)*, 2016, I, pp. 60, 229, 233, n. 34.
37. They play the same role as the putti in Rubens's *Alexander and Roxana* in which Cupid leads Alexander to his beloved, while a putto removes his helmet, and two others help the bride out of her dress and shoes (McGrath, *History (CRLB)*, 1997, I, nos 14–15; II, figs 54–58; on this similarity, see e.g. F. Healy in McGrath et al., *Mythological Subjects I (CRLB)*, 2016, I, p. 209; II, fig. 146.
38. The suggestion that the *Andromeda Liberated* panels can be seen as 'hochzeitliche Bilder', and that they might have something to do with Rubens's wedding or that of his brother Philip, in 1609 (Evers, *Neue Forschungen*, 1943, p. 271), can be rejected simply because of the date; also rejected by F. Healy in McGrath et al., *Mythological Subjects I (CRLB)*, 2016, I, pp. 229, 232, n. 33.
39. In both territories the tale appears in images and in written works, illustrated in pamphlets and also in texts that were declaimed or produced as drama for official occasions, including Joyous Entries; see Sabbe, *Andromeda-sage*, 1927, pp. 235–239; id., *Geestesleven te Antwerpen*, 1927a, p. 47; Sluijter, *Rembrandt / Female Nude*, 2006, pp. 85–86; id., *Andromeda*, 2009, pp. 32–33; esp. for pamphlets with William I of Orange (1533–1584) in the role of Perseus, see Horst, *Metafoor*, 2006, pp. 192–201; see also McGrath et al., *Mythological Subjects I (CRLB)*, 2016, I, pp. 212 (n. 42), 213 (n. 44).
40. Sabbe, *Geestesleven te Antwerpen*, 1927a, p. 47, as doubtful; Muller also points out that 'this interpretation does not make sense in the context of Rubens's courtyard' (Muller, *Perseus and Andromeda*, 1981–82, p. 140); also rejected by F. Healy in McGrath et al., *Mythological Subjects I (CRLB)*, 2016, I, pp. 213, 216, n. 46. There is no ground for suggesting that Rubens executed this scene on his façade only in 1625 as a special token for the Archduchess Isabella (1566–1633), when he welcomed her to his house on the occasion of her visit to Antwerp after the Spanish victory in the siege of Breda.
41. Pliny, *Natural History*, XXXV.132.
42. Unlike the later pictorial tradition, these Roman works have a more static composition. In them Andromeda is represented standing on a rock, not naked but wearing a *peplos*, while Perseus (who is nude apart from his *chlamys*, thrown over his back, and his winged sandals, as is usual for a Greek hero), approaches her with his hand stretched out to help her. For the reliefs, including one that Rubens may have seen, now in the Musei Capitolini, Rome see Muller, *Perseus and Andromeda*, 1981–82, pp. 140–141, n. 37; F. Healy in McGrath et al., *Mythological Subjects I (CRLB)*, 2016, I, pp. 210, 227; II, fig. 144. For two 'Pompeian' painted versions – which Rubens evidently cannot have known – of a different format (one 122 cm high and the other 37 cm high), now in the Museo Archeologico in Naples, see Lippold, *Antike Gemäldekopien*, 1951, pp. 94–96, fig. 76; Ling, *Roman Painting*, 1991, p. 128, ills 134–135. Another composition with the two figures sitting side-by-side appears in an ancient cameo, which probably

came from Rubens's collection, now in the State Hermitage Museum, St Petersburg (F. Healy in McGrath et al., *Mythological Subjects I (CRLB)*, 2016, I, p. 213, n. 10).
43. Muller, *Perseus and Andromeda*, 1981–82, pp. 139–140; followed by Rosenthal, *Rubens*, 2005, p. 189.
44. F. Healy in McGrath et al., ibid., I, p. 210.
45. Muller, *Perseus and Andromeda*, 1981–82, passim; Scott, *Perseus and Andromeda*, 1988, pp. 258–260; Rosenthal, *Rubens*, 2005, pp. 187–190; Juntunen, *Mythologische Historien*, 2005, pp. 100 ff.; see also Winner, *Rubens' Götterrat*, 1997, pp. 124–126. For a brief summary, see F. Healy in McGrath et al., *Mythological Subjects I (CRLB)*, 2016, I, p. 211.
46. Scott, *Perseus and Andromeda*, 1988, p. 259, n. 67.
47. For Perseus as an image of virtue triumphant, see e.g. Muller, *Perseus and Andromeda*, 1981–82, pp. 141–142.
48. Scott, ibid., p. 259; in this connection it is worth mentioning Ovid's description comparing Andromeda's beauty to a 'statue': 'As soon as Perseus saw her there bound by the arms to a rough cliff – save that her hair gently stirred in the breeze, and the warm tears were trickling down her cheeks, he would have thought her a marble statue – he took fire unwitting, and stood dumb. Smitten by the sight of the beauty he sees, he almost forgot to move his wings in the air' (Ovid, *Metamorphoses*, IV. 673–675; Ovid, *Metamorphoses*, transl. Miller, 1977–84, I, p. 227). Scott remarks that Perseus possibly touches Andromeda's arm in order to reassure himself that it is indeed a living woman that stands before him and not a marble statue (Scott, ibid., p. 260), p. 260). But is this not rather a tender, loving gesture?
49. See e.g. Winner, *Rubens's Götterrat*, 1997, pp. 125–126; Scott, *Perseus and Andromeda*, 1988, p. 260; Rosenthal, *Rubens*, 2005, pp. 187–190.
50. Muller, *Perseus and Andromeda*, 1981–1982, p. 141 ff.; Scott, ibid., p. 259; Rosenthal, ibid., pp. 189–190. For a full discussion of the statues on top of the portico, and for the iconography of Mercury and Minerva, see Chapter IX, pp. 278–285, and Nos R1 and R2.

No. 19. *Staircase*: Joinery (cf. Fig. 124)

Wood; measurements unknown.

Probably demolished after 1763, lost

1616–1617

VISUAL SOURCES:
(1) Harrewijn print, 1992 (Appendix III.2; Fig. 18; detail: Fig. 124);
(2) Mols, drawing of the plan, situation of c. 1763 (Appendix III.4; Fig. 3; details: Fig. 125–126).

LITERATURE: Van den Branden, *Schilderschool*, 1883, pp. 509–510; Delen, *Rubens' huis*, 1933, pp. 25–26; Leyssens, *Van Mildert*, 1941, pp. 101–102; Clijmans, *Wederopbouw Rubenshuis*, 1946, p. 36; Muller, *Perseus and Andromeda*, 1981–82, p. 133, fig. 4; Tijs, *Rubens en Jordaens*, 1984, pp. 96, contract ill. pp. 98–99; Muller, *Rubens's Collection*, 2004, p. 12 (as 'an illusionistic fresco'), p. 40; Devroe, *Rubens' huis*, 2008, pp. 53, 138–139; Maclot, *Rubenssite*, 2016, pp. 54–55; Fabri – Lombaerde, *Jesuit Church (CRLB)*, 2018, p. 101; Herremans, *Architectural Sculpture (CRLB)*, 2019, p. 74.

A contract survives for the construction of a wooden staircase for Rubens's house, signed before the notary Jaspar van de Herstraeten on 2 November 1616 (Appendix I.9). The sculptor Jan [Hans] van Mildert (1588–1636), acting on behalf of 'Mr Sr Paulus Rubens', and the 'schrijnwercker' (joiner) Jaspar Bulliau enter into an agreement for 'twee trappen' (two staircases) – a phrase that should probably be interpreted as a pair of flights that were part of one staircase – to be made and installed in Rubens's house on the Wapper.

Some passages in this document are rather muddled and obscure, with corrections and deletions; it provides little detail about the shape of the staircase, and indeed not even its position within the house is clearly described. Broadly speaking, what we learn is that one of the stairs (or flights of stairs) was fitted with banisters and balusters and was to lead up from the ground floor to the 'gaelderye' (gallery), a part of the building that cannot be identified precisely; apparently the other flight – although on this count the text is vague – continued from there to a higher level.

The contract undoubtedly governs the monumental staircase which can be seen in the courtyard in the Harrewijn print of 1692, between the arches of the colonnade on the ground floor (Fig. 124). We know therefore that the staircase was situated on the street side of the courtyard, and led to the upper floor of the studio wing, but no further details are available and nor can anything be deduced from Mols's small drawing (with crossings out) that forms part of his plan of the house 'fait de mémoire' (Fig. 125). It is a problem that we do not know what is meant by

CATALOGUE No. 19

the reference to a gallery (or galleries). And then there is the 'open' character of the staircase which forces us to ask how the adjoining rooms were closed off. During the reconstruction of the house no convincing solution could be found for the lost staircase using available sources, and only the bottom-most part follows (more or less) the image of the print (Fig. 11). For the discussion about its position in the house, see also above.[1]

As mentioned elsewhere, we should observe that the staircase seen on the print is not universally regarded as 'genuine'. Several authors are convinced that what we see at ground level is part of the illusionistic painted decoration of this side of the courtyard.[2] This interpretation, however, contradicts the floor plan drawn by Mols (Fig. 3).

There are some interesting details in the contract of 1616 (Appendix I.9). The work was to be carried out according to Rubens's instructions, adhering to what had been agreed with him in this regard. Moreover, a drawing (or drawings) needed to be followed ('volghens de teeckeninghe[n] daervan synde'); for this, see under No. 19a.

Bulliau would deliver the wood required for the stairs, which had to be of the correct specifications and of sound quality. Rubens himself would arrange to acquire the wood needed for the rails and balusters, and was to pay 175 guilders for having them made. No sum is specified for making the staircase; the contractor will charge for the hours worked, and it is further stipulated that work must not be interrupted, excepting illness or other important unforeseen circumstances.

Mention is also made of a gift, as was customary in transactions of some importance. As with the purchase of his house from Hans Thys, here again Rubens promises to make a gift of something of 'his own' making. If the work is completed to Rubens's satisfaction, he will give Bulliau, in addition to the sum owed, a painting, either on panel or canvas, which is to be a copy rather than an original from his own hand.

The staircase that we see behind the colonnade in the Harrewijn print (Fig. 124) and which, as indicated, we believe to be the staircase referred to in the document, presents a richly decorated face to the side, with mouldings and pilasters. In the panels of the bottom-most section we see a garland and the head of a putto (?), and in the section above, two cartouches and two imaginary half-human creatures, looking somewhat like tritons, but their lower bodies end in acanthus (or vine) scrolls rather than fishtails. The balustrade consists of a broad banister, resting on narrow upward-tapering balusters. As far as we know, no staircase with decorative elements of a comparable form survives in the Netherlands or anywhere else, but it is worth mentioning that there are a few monumental wooden staircases of a somewhat similar type later in the seventeenth century.[3]

The contract does not mention who will be responsible for carving the decorative panels, and it seems unlikely that the joiner Bulliau would have undertaken this task in addition to constructing the actual staircase. It seems eminently reasonable to assume that the sculptor Van Mildert was acting not only as intermediary, but also provided the most important decorative elements. This is suggested, for example, by Isidore Leyssens, who includes the staircase banisters of Rubens's house in the sculptor's oeuvre.[4] On Van Mildert and his work for Rubens's house, see Chapter XI.[5]

1. See Chapter VII, pp. 201–203.
2. For example: Tijs, *Rubens*, 2004, pp. 40–41; Muller, *Rubens's Collection*, 2004, p. 12.
3. To name two examples of staircases (both much grander) which have banisters with arabesque and vine ornaments (but in openwork throughout), and without balusters: the staircase of c. 1677–80, attributed to Edward Pearce (1630–1695), from a House in England, and reconstructed in the Metropolitan Museum of Art in New York (Acc. No. 32.152); a staircase of c. 1700, from a house in The Hague, reconstructed in the Museum Boijmans Van Beuningen, Rotterdam (De Wit, *Grand Staircase*, 2016, pp. 240–251. For 17th-century staircases in the Northern Netherlands with similar balusters, see Janse, *Trap en Trede*, 1995, pp. 72–82.
4. Leyssens, *Van Mildert*, 1941, pp. 101–102.
5. See pp. 327–329.

No. 19a. *Design for the Staircase in Rubens's House*: Drawing(s?) (cf. Figs 124–126)

Technique and measurements unknown; possibly multiple drawings.

Whereabouts unknown, presumably lost

Late 1616

LITERATURE: see under No. 19.

An agreement concerning the construction of a staircase in Rubens's house was made between Hans van Mildert (1588–1638) (for Rubens) and the joiner Jaspar Bulliau, on 2 November 1616, before the notary Jaspar van de Herstraeten (Appendix I.9). It mentions that Rubens had given Bulliau appropriate instructions for the work, and had discussed these with him. The staircase was to be installed in the house as indicated by the said Mr Sgr Paulo and as discussed and agreed between them ('alle tselven by de voorseyde Mr Sgr Paulo gedesigneert ende tussschen hen beijde besproken ende geaccordeert').

Reference is also made to a drawing (or drawings) that needed to be followed, but as this is described simply as the drawing[s] ('de teeckeninghe[n]'), we cannot establish exactly what was represented. Whether this drawing or these drawings were from Rubens's hand also naturally remains in doubt, but the wording of the contract implies that Rubens designed the staircase for his house.

As outlined in No. 19, the contract is certainly for the staircase, part of which can be seen in the Harrewijn print (Fig. 124), and which was drawn by Mols in his plan of the house (Figs 3, 125 and 126).

B. Interior: Nos 20–23

No. 20. *The 'Antiquarium'*: Architecture (cf. Fig. 127)

Technique and measurements unknown.

Demolished after 1763, lost

c. 1618 (?)

VISUAL SOURCES:
(1) Harrewijn print, 1692, transformed into Hillewerve's chapel, in a separate view, bottom left (Appendix III.2; Fig. 18; detail: Fig. 127);
(2) Willem van Haecht, *Apelles Painting Campaspe*, The Hague, c. 1630, in simplified form in the background (Appendix III.8; Text ill. 100; details: Text ill. 103; Fig. 128);
(3) François Mols, drawing of the plan, situation of c. 1763 (Appendix III.4; Fig. 3).

For examples of imaginary 'antiquaria' that are inspired by Rubens (but differ considerably from No. 20), seen in the background of paintings representing a collector's cabinet, see below.

LITERATURE: Bellori, *Vite*, 1672, p. 245 (see Appendix I.28); Sandrart, *Teutsche Academie*, 1675–80, p. 292 (see Appendix I.29); de Piles, *Dissertation*, 1681, pp. 12–14 (see Appendix I.31); Rooses, *Maison*, 1888, pp. 236–237; Rooses, *Rubens*, 1904, pp. 150–152; Van Averbeke, *Rubenshuis, restauratie I*, 1938, p. 27 (p. 30: drawing based on the excavations); Buschmann, *Huis-Rubens*, 1938, repr. p. 57; Van der Meulen – Schregardus, *Rubens*, 1975, p. 15; Muller, *Rubens's Museum*, 1977, pp. 576–581, figs 3–5; Bastet, *Oudheden*, 1980, pp. 76–77, fig. 8; Tijs, *Rubens en Jordaens*, 1984, pp. 143–144, 190, repr. p. 191; Muller, *Collector*, 1989, pp. 40–41; Broos, *Historiestukken*, 1993, p. 144; Von Simson, *Rubens*, 1996, p. 213; Muller, *Rubens's Collection*, 2004, pp. 12, 43, 47–49; Healy, *Vive l'Esprit*, 2006, p. 428; Büttner, *Rubens berühmt*, 2006, pp. 94–95; Muller, *Moribvs Antiqvis*, 2008, p. 23; Devroe, *Rubens's House*, 2008, pp. 75–76, 89, 91; Van Beneden, *Van Haecht*, 2009, p. 81; Van Beneden, *Rubens and Architecture*, 2011, pp. 13,

18–20; Lombaerde, *Rubens*, 2014, pp. 214–217; Jonckheere, *Prototypes (CRLB)*, 2016, pp. 41–46.

One of the parts of Rubens's house that had long since vanished when restoration began was the 'antiquarium', a room intended for the display of ancient sculpture. Chapter VIII above is devoted to this remarkable space[1] and this catalogue entry is confined to a summary, with visual sources, literature and a list of depictions of other 'antiquaria' inspired to a greater or lesser extent by Rubens's room. More detailed information can also be found under the two entries that follow, dealing with two structural components: the cupola (No. 21) and the richly ornamented semicircular wall with its tiers of niches (No. 22).

Rubens's 'antiquarium', a space strongly resembling the famous Roman Pantheon, is mentioned several times in seventeenth-century written sources. The earliest published reference appears in 1672 in Bellori's *Le Vite de' pittori*. Bellori says of Rubens that 'in his house he built a round room with a single *oculus* at the top, similar to the Rotunda of Rome, for the perfection of even lighting'. In this room Rubens placed his 'precious museum, with other rare and sundry curiosities' (Appendix I.28). Roger de Piles, who got his information from Rubens's nephew Philip, wrote in his *Dissertation* of 1681 that this room was located 'between the courtyard and the garden' (Appendix I.31).

The supposed location of the room can be pinpointed on a plan drawn by François Mols, showing the situation of c. 1763 (Fig. 3). Working from memory, he outlined a space on the ground floor that was octagonal in shape, and referred to it as a chapel ('Chapelle, bâtie en octogone'; Appendix I.43: I [6, 8]). This location was confirmed when its foundations were excavated during the restoration campaign of 1939–1947 (Text ill. 99), during which it was established clearly that it was semicircular in shape rather than octagonal, and that it extended further to the north than indicated on Mols's plan.

At the bottom of the 1692 Harrewijn print there is a view of Canon Hillewerve's chapel, semicircular in plan and with an opening at the top of the dome (Fig. 127). The walls were divided into segments by pilasters, between which two tiers of niches can be seen. Although this space was decorated as a chapel, with an altar and reliquaries in the niches, there can be no doubt that it had originally been Rubens's so-called 'antiquarium'. A similar space is also depicted by Willem van Haecht (1593–1637) in the background of his *Apelles Painting Campaspe* (Appendix III.8; Fig. 128). Glimpsed through an archway we see a long barrel-vaulted room that opens into a semicircular chamber, which is lit by natural light via a large round opening, beyond which blue sky can be seen. The space has features similar to the famous Roman Pantheon, which undoubtedly inspired Rubens. Apelles's 'antiquarium' is certainly not a literal representation of Rubens's actual room, but it is evident that Van Haecht incorporated many elements into his imaginary scene that he had seen in the home of the 'Antwerp Apelles'.

The building of the 'antiquarium' is associated with a collection of antique sculptures and objects that Rubens acquired from Sir Dudley Carleton on 20 May 1618. It is believed that this acquisition prompted Rubens to build his 'antiquarium' or pantheon, a very credible hypothesis which allows us to date the room to 'around 1618'.

DEPICTIONS OF *IMAGINARY 'ANTIQUARIA'* INSPIRED BY THE ROOM IN RUBENS'S HOUSE:

1) Hendrik Staben (1578–1658), *Archdukes Albrecht and Isabella Visiting a Picture Gallery*, Brussels, Musées royaux de Beaux-Arts de Belgique, inv. no. 4495, c. 1658; oil on copper, 51 × 65 cm. A second version (oil on panel, 48 × 64 cm) in the Collection of the Château de Beloeil (Belgium). LIT.: Speth-Holterhof, *Cabinets*, 1957, p. 112, fig. 42 (as 'Collection du Prince de Ligne'); Tijs, *Rubens en Jordaens*, 1984, repr. p. 118; Muller, *House of Art*, 2004, p. 49, fig. 64.

(2) Frans Francken II (1581–1642), *Interior of a Picture Gallery*, Salisbury, Wilton House, Collection of the Earl of Pembroke, c. 1625; oil on canvas, 93.3 × 123.2 cm. LIT.: Speth-Holterhoff, *Cabinets*, 1957, pp. 80–81, fig. 20; Tijs, *Rubens en Jordaens*, 1984, repr. p. 111; Muller, *House of Art*, 2004, p. 49, fig. 63.

(3) Frans Francken II, *Encyclopaedic Still Life with a Cabinet*, London, Syon House, Collection

of the Duke of Northumberland, c. 1617; oil on panel, 89 × 120.5 cm. LIT.: Speth-Holterhoff, *Cabinets*, 1957, pp. 90–91, fig. 28; Van Suchtelen – Van Beneden, *Room for Art*, 2009, pp. 27, 29, fig. 9.

(4) Attributed to Cornelis de Baellieur (1607–1671), *Interior of a Picture Gallery*, Florence, Palazzo Pitti, c. 1645–1650; oil on panel, 73 × 185 cm. LIT.: Denucé, *Konstkamers*, 1932, fig. 2; id., *Musson*, 1949, p. XIV; Speth-Holterhoff, *Cabinets*, 1957, pp. 119–121, fig. 49; Tijs, *Rubens en Jordaens*, 1984, p. 106, repr. p. 114, detail p. 11; Muller, *House of Art*, 2004, p. 49, fig. 65 (as 'Willem van Herp'); Koeleman, *Art Gallery of Rubens*, 2015.

1. See pp. 229–248.

No. 21. *The Cupola of the 'Antiquarium'*: Architecture (cf. Fig. 127)

Possibly decorated with *trompe-l'oeil* painting or stucco; measurements unknown.

Demolished after 1763, lost

c. 1618 (?)

VISUAL SOURCES:

(1) Harrewijn print, 1692, with altered decoration as part of Hillewerve's chapel, bottom left inset (Appendix III.2; Fig. 18; detail: Fig. 127);
(2) Van Haecht, *Apelles Painting Campaspe*, The Hague, c. 1630, in simplified form in the background (Appendix III.8; Text ill. 100; detail: Text ill. 103; Fig. 128).

LITERATURE: see under No. 20.

In Hillewerve's time, the semicircular dome of Rubens's 'antiquarium', with light entering from above and modelled on the Pantheon in Rome, remained structurally intact (Fig. 127), but its decoration was very different. To fit with the room's new function of chapel, it was adorned with a view of Heaven, with figures and clouds and the dove of the Holy Spirit in the centre.[1]

Nevertheless we have an approximate idea of the original decoration. The evidence suggests that the sculpture gallery glimpsed in the background of Apelles's studio in the painting by Van Haecht mentioned above (Fig. 128) offers a picture, in slightly simplified form and adapted to an imaginary ancient Greek setting, of what could be seen in the house of the 'Apelles of Antwerp'. That Rubens's 'antiquarium' was used as model is clear from the overall form and especially from details in the decoration of the curved wall beneath the dome (see No. 20).

The 'ancient' cupola as presented in Van Haecht's painting has an *oculus* at the top through which blue sky can be glimpsed, but it is not entirely clear whether the opening there is in direct contact with the open air, as is the case with the Pantheon in Rome. A vertical post can be seen rising above the opening, and this seems to be part of a lantern. The actual cupola in Rubens's house was no doubt crowned by a lantern which protected the interior from the elements. A tiny part of this construction can in fact be glimpsed above the side of the *oculus* in the Harrewijn print (Fig. 127).

The cupola at the back of Apelles's studio is adorned with an intricate pattern of monochrome motifs with stemwork and garlands. The combination is somewhat reminiscent of the playful grotesques known from ancient vaults and cupolas, only in monochrome form. We do not know if these decorations in Rubens's house were painted in *trompe-l'oeil*, or rendered in stucco relief. Rubens was probably aware that the decoration in Roman vaults was not always painted and that some examples were in stucco.[2]

At around the same time another cupola was being constructed with ornamentation that may have been designed by Rubens: the decorated ceiling above the apse in the Antwerp Jesuit Church (Fig. 129).[3] The relief decoration in the church is similarly composed of a lively pattern of curling 'scrolls' and festoons, although it is more substantial and enlivened by cherubs, coats of arms and a wide variety of emblematic elements. One striking similarity between the two half-domes is the motif of continuous scrolls which outline a heart shape as they meander.

CATALOGUE No. 22

1. For a more detailed description of the cupola of Hillewerve's chapel, see Chapter III, pp. 110–112.
2. For surviving monochrome examples in white see, for instance, Ling, *Roman Painting*, 1991, figs 42–43, 46, 48, 62, 201–202.
3. Fabri – Lombaerde, *Jesuit Church (CRLB)*, 2018, pp. 60, 77, fig. 89 (detail). Paintings that show the interiors of the church afford an impression of the cupola before the later alterations, which included replacing the coats of arms; see for example works by Sebastiaan Vrancx (1573–1647) and Wilhelm Schubert van Ehrenberg (1630–1687) (Baisier, ed., *Divine Interiors*, 2016, pp. 138–143, nos 36–37). The decoration has certain curious elements such as bats' wings as well as the fiery vortex that is part of Jupiter's thunderbolt (for this motif, see under No. 25).

No. 22. *The North Wall of the 'Antiquarium'*: Architecture (cf. Fig. 127)

Material and measurements unknown.

Demolished after 1763, lost

c. 1618 (?)

VISUAL SOURCES:
(1) Harrewijn print, 1692, transformed into Hillewerve's chapel, in a separate view, bottom left (Appendix III.2; Fig. 18; detail: Fig. 127);
(2) Van Haecht, *Apelles Painting Campaspe*, The Hague, c. 1630, in simplified form in the background (Appendix III.8; Text ill. 100; details: Text ill. 103 and Fig. 128).

LITERATURE: See under No. 20.

The two seventeenth-century visual sources give an impression of the appearance of the north wall of the room in which Rubens displayed his ancient sculpture and which is known as the 'antiquarium', a part of the house discussed at length in Chapter VIII.[1]

The print by Harrewijn (Fig. 127) shows a semicircular structure, divided into seven bays by pilasters that extend upwards to the cupola. The central bay has a tall, narrow niche, probably crowned by a shell motif. In each of the six remaining bays, that is three on either side of the central one, four niches are shown: two with rounded tops below, and two ovals above. The structure is preceded by a narrow bay with barrel vault; on one side of this bay, towards the garden, is a very tall window, and on the other, a single niche which contains an over life-size statue.

The most striking aspect of Van Haecht's depiction of the 'antiquarium' in Apelles's house (Fig. 128), is the comparable intricate pattern of niches. Indeed, the wall's most characteristic feature is the framework with lines of pale-coloured decoration connecting the niches. However, certain differences can be observed and it is difficult to judge to what extent they are invented. The space in which four visitors can be seen admiring sculptures is much taller than the Antwerp 'antiquarium' would have been. In Hillewerve's chapel there is no sign of the full-length statues stacked in pairs against each pilaster. Nor does the print show anything of the line of stone tables at the bottom on which large busts were displayed.

Busts constituted an important part of the decoration of Rubens's 'antiquarium'. Undoubtedly it housed a group of busts in the round that were part of his ancient sculpture collection.[2] It is possible, however, that as was probably the case with the studio façade, (see Nos 3 and 21) the wall was also decorated with busts painted in *trompe-l'oeil*. In both seventeenth-century images, and so extending into Hillewerve's time, long after Rubens's collections had been sold, a row of almost identical busts on socles appear in the oval niches – and these were probably not real. For further commentary on this, see above.[3]

At the very top of the semicircular wall is a sequence of landscape-shaped panels with figurative scenes. In Hillewerve's chapel (Fig. 127) there are six such panels possibly painted with what appear to be sacred subjects – although if original (i.e. from Rubens's time), their subjects would, of course, not have been religious. The scenes shown in Apelles's 'antiquarium' (Fig. 128) are monochrome and we can assume that the same applied in Rubens's house. In all likelihood the original panels were painted in *grisaille* and featured subjects from classical Antiquity, just like the frieze on the studio façade. By analogy, these panels may also have been fictive antique reliefs. If so, it would mean that the display in Rubens's 'antiquarium' was a combination of real and fictive antique sculpture.

One of the entries in the *Staetmasse*, the final settlement of Rubens's estate, mentions 63 pounds of ivory from the tower ('den thoren'), where the deceased kept his antiquities (Appendix I.23: [1]), which must mean the 'antiquarium'. It is not clear, however, if this precious material was used in the decoration of the room.[4]

1. See pp. 229–248.
2. As explained in Chapter VII (pp. 227–228), it should be remembered that ancient busts were almost certainly also displayed elsewhere in Rubens's house, for example in his study, which in contemporary sources is sometimes confusingly referred to as his 'Museum'.
3. Chapter VIII, pp. 242–243, Text ills. 102, 103.
4. See also Chapter VIII, p. 244, n. 37.

No. 23. *Head of Hercules under a Scallop and Garlands*: Sculpture / Architectural Sculpture (Fig. 131)

(1) Head of Hercules (original or later copy; Fig. 133). Antwerp, Rubenshuis. Inv. no. RH.B.024; plaster, 54 cm.

(2) Scallop (original or later copy Fig. 136); Antwerp, Centraal Depot Musea – Stad Antwerp; plaster, measurements unknown.

(3) Fruit garlands suspended from lion heads (Fig. 131); lost (removed in 1938 or 1939); technique and measurements unknown (wood or plaster?).

LITERATURE: Tijs, *Rubens en Jordaens*, 1984, p. 236, repr.; Muller, *Collector*, 1989, pp. 41–42, fig. 27, p. 153, cat. III, no. 16 (as 'Anonymous Seventeenth-Century Flemish Master' and 'designed by Rubens'); Broos, *Historiestukken*, 1993, p. 144, fig. 8; Muller, *Rubens' Collection*, 2004, pp. 21, 56, fig. 81; Heinen, *Gesundheit*, 2004, pp. 122, 168 (n. 147), 174 (n. 197); Van Beneden, *Van Haecht*, 2009, p. 82, fig. 58; Uppenkamp – Van Beneden, *Architectural Symbolism*, 2011, p. 83, fig. 102; De Clercq, *Moulages*, 2012, p. 15, repr. p. 16; Grimmett, *Drunken Hercules*, 2020, p. 52, fig. 10.

Before a large part of the house was demolished during the restoration in 1938–39, there was a doorway on the ground floor, on the side towards the Wapper, decorated with sculptural elements, possibly original. The only images available are two photographs made in April 1938 (see Fig. 131).[1] This doorway was in the wall separating a room to the right of the main entrance from a large area corresponding to the former studio, or the 'antichambre', between the street and the studio (Fig. 132).[2] It seems unlikely that this was its original location and possibly the door decoration was assembled in the nineteenth century (?), using elements found elsewhere in the house.

As can be seen from the photographs, above the doorway in question, which was set into a recess, there was a head of the *Hercules Farnese* type, resting on a low socle that formed part of the wooden doorframe (not original) (Fig. 131). Over the hero's head was a large scallop shell. Garlands of fruit were attached to volutes either side of this ornament. These hung down, left and right, over the corners of the doorway and they were suspended from rings fixed in the jaws of two lion's heads flanking the doorway, on the curving sides of the recess. During the restoration this door arrangement disappeared, and the elements described were not redeployed in the interior of the house.

The Hercules head has been preserved (Fig. 133) and is now part of the Rubenshuis collection; in the past it was mistakenly regarded simply as a cast of the Hercules statue in the garden pavilion, which is also a variant of the *Hercules Farnese* (No. 40; Fig. 211). However, the detailing of the two heads is different, a discrepancy that has only recently been put right.[3] The large plaster scallop shell is kept in the Antwerp municipal store (Fig. 136),[4] while the garlands and the lion's heads, which may also have been made of plaster, but were possibly carved in wood, have disappeared.

It is possible that elements of this decoration – the head, the scallop and perhaps also the gar-

CATALOGUE No. 23

lands – belonged together originally, but if they did, then it was certainly not in the arrangement in which they survived in 1938. The wooden doorframe to which the head was fixed is of a later date, perhaps early nineteenth-century. The Hercules head may have been part of a bust, including 'shoulders' and a base. But there is no indication that it is in any way connected with the bust – the physiognomy of which is quite different – that appears against the rear wall of the garden pavilion in *The Walk in the Garden* (see No. 39; Fig. 210).

The motif of a bust of Hercules combined with fruit garlands certainly was familiar in Rubens's lifetime, which is an argument for its being an original element of the house. A similar combination – but with garlands hanging underneath rather than alongside the bust – was depicted by Willem van Haecht (1593–1637) in his *Apelles Painting Campaspe* (Appendix III.8; Fig. 135). In that image the sculptural elements crown a doorway with round arch, which leads to a large barrel-vaulted art gallery, at the far end of which we see a variant of Rubens's 'antiquarium'.[5]

It is possible that the large plaster scallop was originally not simply attached to a wall, but was instead set within the rounded top of a niche. The motif of the scallop niche undoubtedly featured in Rubens's house. One example is the decoration above the entrance to the studio, with a bust in a niche and a cornucopia either side (Fig. 36). Furthermore, a niche with a shell is pictured, possibly intended as an element that could be seen in Rubens's house, in the representation of a painter's workshop which has echoes of Rubens's studio (Appendix III.32; Text ill. 88). Jordaens also incorporated the shell motif into his curious amalgam of elements taken from Rubens's house: in the niche that appears over the variant of the garden pavilion in his *Cupid and Psyche* (Appendix III.9; Figs 20, 179).

Moreover, in Rubens's paintings, shells can be found which closely resemble the plaster example under discussion, with large volutes either side: especially similar are his shells in memorial contexts and echoing ancient funerary practice. For example, the rounded niches with shell, containing: the bust of Seneca in *The Four Philosophers* (Florence, Palazzo Pitti) (Fig. 134); the bust of Rubens's deceased brother Philip in an engraving by Cornelis Galle II after Rubens; and the bust of Richardot in the design for his tomb (drawing in the Rijksprentenkabinet, Amsterdam).[6]

There are other, different contexts in which the motif also occurs. A strikingly similar shell, with distinctive volutes, is cut into a niche with round top that forms part of a fountain with the figure of a five-breasted personification of Nature in Rubens's *Discovery of Erichthonius by the Daughters of Cecrops* in the Liechtenstein collection (Fig. 137).[7] This painting is dated 1616–1617, that is to say in the years in which Rubens was occupied with the construction and decoration of his house.

The lost festoons are somewhat reminiscent of those still present in the garden pavilion, carved in wood, either side of the full-length Hercules statue. However, it is difficult to determine if the festoons that followed the curves of the apocryphal recess were original, or from a later period.

To summarise, we can assume that the head and the scallop still in place above the doorway in 1938 may have been original to the house. All the same, we should remain cautious, because these decorative plaster elements are difficult to date, and they may have been later copies, as with the *Bust of a Faun*, described under No. 1 (Fig. 35). But, as explained, there are enough pointers to allow a confident statement that they were Rubens's invention.

1. Photographic prints, showing slightly different views, are kept in the Rubenshuis archive and also in the Antwerp FelixArchief. One of these prints was first reproduced in Tijs, *Rubens en Jordaens*, 1984, p. 236, and subsequently by later authors; see under 'Literature'; there is also a copy in the FelixArchief, inv. no. FOTO-OF#1208. Reproduced here (Fig. 131) is the second photograph (FelixArchief, inv. no. GP#4273; print in reverse, here corrected) which was taken from further away, thus showing more of the surrounding architecture.
2. No location in the house is given anywhere in the literature, but the doorway with rounded niche was identified by Brecht Vanoppen in a plan of the house drawn up in July 1932, at the bottom, on the street side (Fig. 132). This location is confirmed by what can be seen through the door in the 1938 photograph: the torn-up floor and completely dismantled south

wall of the former studio. For comparison, see other photographs of rooms on the ground floor after removal of the plaster and lifting of the floorboards (Tijs, *Rubens en Jordaens*, 1984, pp. 194–195, and esp. p. 194 bottom left).

3. In 2019 the head was carefully examined under the supervision of Lode De Clercq; it was not possible to derive a dating from the composition of the plaster. It was regarded as contemporary, and made to Rubens's design, by Muller, *Collector*, 1989, p. 153, cat. III, no. 16, pl. 137 (as 'Seventeenth-Century Flemish Master'); see also De Clercq, *Moulages*, 2012, p. 15, repr.
4. De Clercq, *Moulages*, 2012, p. 15, repr.
5. See under No. 20.
6. For these three examples, see 1) Vlieghe, *Portraits (CRLB)*, 1987, no. 117, fig. 140; Muller, *Collector*, 1989, pp. 45–46, fig. 28; 2) Judson – Van de Velde, *Title-pages (CRLB)*, 1978, I, no. 29; II, fig. 101; 3) Herremans, *Architectural Sculpture (CRLB)*, 2019, no. 14a, fig. 83.
7. F. Healy in McGrath et al., *Mythological Subjects I (CRLB)*, 2016, I, no. 41; II, figs 333, 343 (detail). For a comprehensive list of Rubensian scallop niches, including seven examples not mentioned here, see Heinen, *Gesundheit*, 2004, p. 174, n. 197.

C. Portico: Nos 24–33

No. 24. *Portico*: Architecture (Fig. 138)

Bluestone, sandstone and brick; 810 × 1213 cm.

c. 1618

Antwerp, Rubenshuis, between the courtyard and garden

TECHNICAL NOTES: the core of the portico consists of red brickwork faced with Belgian bluestone (Arquennes) and Lede stone. The satyr figures in the spandrels are executed in Obernkirchen, and the shell in the central *oculus* in Avesnes stone. In several areas traces of multiple paint layers survive, but these cannot be accurately dated.

From the moment it was constructed by Rubens, the portico has been exposed to the elements and this means that in its current state the structure shows evidence of substantial erosion. Pieces have broken off in various places. Modifications to the portico carried out by later owners of the house and during the restoration campaign of 1939–1947 have also significantly altered its appearance. During that restoration, parts were added and existing elements were remodelled using Massangis stone: the blank left and right sections of the portico; infillings to the niches above the side arches and *oculus*, and the dolphin in the left spandrel of the central arch. During the restoration, the lost rear of the portico was replaced by a neutral design in Belgian bluestone and Massangis stone (Text Ill. 108).

In 1996 a temporary roof was installed to protect the portico against rainwater erosion, an arrangement was replaced in 2019 with a glass butterfly awning.

For a detailed discussion of the chronology of structural interventions in the portico, see De Clercq – Hayen, *Historische schets*, 2019.

VISUAL SOURCES (SEE ALSO COPIES):
(1) Van Dyck, *Portrait of Isabella Brant*, Washington, 1620s, in reverse (Appendix III.5; Fig. 19);
(2) Jordaens, *Cupid and Psyche*, Madrid, 1640–1650, represented twice (Appendix III.9; Fig. 20);

CATALOGUE No. 24

(3) Aylesbury, *Courtyard of Rubens's House*, 1660s (Appendix III.3; Fig. 16; detail: Fig. 141);
(4) Coques, *Portrait of Maria Agnes van Eycke as St Agnes*, London, c. 1675 (Appendix III.11; Text ill. 20);
(5) Harrewijn print, 1684 (Appendix III.1; Fig. 17)
(6) Fierlants, *Rubens's Portico*, photograph, 1860 (Appendix III.52; Text ill. 23).

COPIES:

(1) Anthony van Dyck, *Architectural Study of Rubens's Portico* (Fig. 139), drawing, Paris, Fondation Custodia, inv. no. 2468 (verso), c. 1620; black chalk on paper, 374 × 279 mm. EXH.: Ottawa, 1980, no. 69; Paris, 1981, no. 53 (recto); Antwerp, 2011, no. 45. LIT.: Vey, *Van Dyck*, 1962, no. 50 (verso); Tijs, *Rubens en Jordaens*, 1984, p. 120 (as probably by Rubens); id., *Rubens*, 2004, p. 148 (as probably by Rubens); Van Beneden, *Rubens and Architecture*, 2011, pp. 20 (fig. 15), 165, no. 45; Vergara – Lammertse, *Young Van Dyck*, 2012, p. 83, fig. 27 (recto); White, *Van Dyck*, 2021, pp. 63, 65 (fig. 58).

(2)? Anthony van Dyck, *The Portico of Rubens's House*, whereabouts unknown, probably lost; mentioned in the collection of Alexander Voet I in 1689 (as 'Het portael aende plets van het huys van Rubbens van Van Dijck geschildert'); LIT.: Vey, *Van Dyck*, 1962, p. 120, under no. 50; Duverger, *Kunstinventarissen*, 1984–2009, XI, p. 531; C. Brown in C. Brown, H. Vlieghe, et al., *Van Dyck*, 1999, pp. 154–155 (incorrectly as 'a drawing'); see also Chapter IX, pp. 269–270. EXH.: Antwerp – London, 1999.

(3) Plaster casts of a number of sculpted details (see Chapter IX, p. 251, n. 10, and under Nos 25, 27, 30–33.

LITERATURE: Van den Branden, *Schilderschool*, 1883, pp. 507, 509; Rooses, *Oeuvre*, 1886–92, V, pp. 185–186; Rooses, *Maison*, 1888, pp. 221–222; Rooses – Ruelens, *Correspondance*, 1887–1909, pp. 154–155; Rooses, *Life*, 1904, pp. 147–149, 154; Van de Castyne, *Rubens*, 1931, pp. 116–119; Delen, *Rubens' huis*, 1933, pp. 29–30, 38; Van de Castyne, *Architecture*, 1934, p. 318; Van Averbeke, *Eerste bevindingen*, 1938, p. 32; Delen, *Rubens' huis*, 1940, pp. 31–32, 34, 53–54; Kitlitschka, *Rubens*, 1963, pp. 135–138; Fredlund, *Arkitektur*, 1974, p. 11; Blunt, *Rubens and Architecture*, 1977, pp. 613–614, fig. 16; Baudouin, *Summary Guide*, 1977, pp. 6–8; Van Aerschot, ed., *Bouwen / Antwerpen*, 1979, p. 548; Blommaert, *Woonhuis*, 1980, p. 16; Blommaert, *Barokarchitectuur*, 1982, p. 160; Tijs, *Rubens en Jordaens*, 1984, pp. 120, 122, 125, 132, passim; Forssman, *Säulenordnungen*, 1984, p. 73, fig. 39; Stutz, *Residenz*, 1985, pp. 142, 146; Huvenne, *Rubenshuis*, 1988, pp. 125, 127, 130, 141; Muller, *Collector*, 1989, pp. 26–32, 35–36, 38, 66, figs 13–14; Morford, *Stoics*, 1991, pp. 189–190; Baudouin, *Painter-Architect*, 2002, pp. 15, 32, figs 1, 15; Heinen, *Garten*, 2002, pp. 3–6; Rott, *Palazzi (CRLB)*, 2002, I, pp. 58, 61, 87; Lodewyck et al., *Conservation of the Portico*, 2003, passim; Heinen, *Gesundheit*, 2004, pp. 115–124; Muller, *Rubens's Collection*, 2004, pp. 35, 36, 39; Ottenheym, *Architectural Ornament*, 2007, pp. 125, 128, 130–132; Devroe, *Rubens' huis*, 2008, pp. 23, 67, 104, 112–113; Van Beneden, *Rubens's House Revealed*, 2009, passim; Van Beneden, *Rubens and Architecture*, 2011, pp. 13, 20–25; Uppenkamp – Van Beneden, *Architectural Symbolism*, 2011, passim, and esp. pp. 76–78, 103–104; Uppenkamp – Van Beneden, *Vera simmetria*, 2011, pp. 62–65, 67–68; Lombaerde, *Rubens the Architect*, 2011, pp. 138–140, 150–156; Coekelberghs, *Review Palazzo Rubens*, 2012, [incl. p. 7]; Van Driessche, *Herschepping*, 2013, pp. 26–29; Lombaerde, *Rubens*, 2014, pp. XVII, XVIII; De Staelen, *Rubens*, 2014, p. 257; Boeykens, *Reflections*, 2014, pp. 223–236; Esposito, *Occult Knowlegde*, 2016, pp. 232–233; Büttner, *Allegories (CRLB)*, 2018, I, pp. 108, 110, n. 35; II, fig. 38; Uppenkamp, *Rubens's Palazzetto*, 2018, pp. 224–226, fig. 7 (as 'garden screen'); Van Beneden, *Portiek en tuinpaviljoen*, 2019, pp. 16–19; De Clercq – Hayen, *Historische schets*, 2019, pp. 40–49; Mertens – Stoppie, *Conservatievisie*, 2019, passim; De Clercq, *Conservatie*, 2019, passim; De Clercq et al., *Conservatie–restauratie*, 2020, I–V, passim.

On entering the Rubenshuis courtyard from the Wapper, the visitor is struck by an impressive garden screen, which is referred to in the Rubens literature as the 'portico'. A separate chapter[1] is dedicated to this remarkable structure, undoubtedly designed by Rubens, and this entry is confined to technical information, literature, a list of visual sources and short summary.

Rubens's portico is a triple-arched structure that functions as a bridge between the north and the south wings of the house. The three arches are separated by four heavily rusticated half-columns. Its most distinctive feature is the central archway, which rises slightly above the height of the other two openings. This is a geniculated arch (flat and with angled corners) and it rests on heavy, banded pilasters. The keystone protruding at the centre is decorated with a Medusa's head (No. 25; Fig. 144). The spandrels of the central archway both feature a dolphin in high relief with coiled tail (No. 26; Fig. 150).

The side arches differ markedly from the more robust central archway. Here the openings are crowned by profiled, round arches, which rest on free-standing Doric columns. The columns support not only the arches but also an architrave which connects the archways with the four heavy engaged columns, thus creating a *serliana* motif. In the spandrels of the two side arches are pairs of satyrs, carved in high relief (Nos 30–33; Figs 171, 173, 175–176). They hold up rectangular tablets above the arches, each of which is carved with verses from the Roman poet Juvenal's tenth *Satire*.

The attic storey above the three arches is characterised by a strongly articulated pediment that visually unites the whole. Strikingly, only the central section is complete; to either side, the pediment is interrupted by a panel with a hollow niche, and the two acute angles of the triangle stand in isolation above the outermost, heavily rusticated half-columns. Above each angle is a volute which coils forwards, surmounted by a *bucranium* (No. 29; Figs 165–166). The central section itself contains a circular niche, crowned by a shell-like motif against a profiled rim. On either side, eagles in high relief elegantly frame the niche with outstretched wings (No. 27; Fig. 153). This scene is closed in by sturdy pedestals, on the outer edges of which we see ram's heads carved in high relief and terminating in large volutes (No. 28; Figs 158, 161).

Although the structure follows the Doric order, which is recognisable by its characteristic decorative elements (rosettes, *guttae*, *bucrania*), its general spirit is Tuscan, a confusing matter which is discussed above.[2]

On the basis of the scant archival information and pictorial evidence the portico can be dated c. 1618. Architectural elements similar to those found in the portico appear in drawings and paintings by Rubens and Anthony van Dyck (1599–1641). In any case we can be certain that the portico was finished by the autumn of 1621 at the latest, because Van Dyck must have seen it before his departure to Italy. There are also a number of painted images of the portico, or parts of it, which, although they provide no further information about its dating, are nonetheless interesting because they were produced by artists from Rubens's immediate circle – colleagues who undoubtedly visited the house and thus knew the portico at first-hand (see the list below).

It should be mentioned that in many of these seventeenth-century representations the portico shows elements that were no longer present in the nineteenth century, and were not reconstructed during the restoration campaign of 1939–1947.[3] However, two prominent elements included in the reconstruction are here rejected: the statues of Minerva and the so-called Mercury standing on top of the structure (Nos R.1–R.2; Figs 227–228, 231).

It is important to note that only the front or courtyard face of the portico is preserved. The rear or garden face was radically altered by later owners, in such a way that nothing original remains. As there are no known contemporary pictorial representations of the rear, it was decided during the restoration to reconstruct this side in a neutral form.

As mentioned above, a separate chapter is devoted to Rubens's portico.[4] That chapter also discusses the place occupied by this remarkable piece of architecture in the context of Italian examples as well as architectural theory.

Elements of the portico can be detected in paintings by Rubens, and they were a source of inspiration for Van Dyck and other artists. Parts of the architecture, with its heavy, banded columns can be recognised in the following paintings: see Appendix III.5, 9–11, 14–21, 24, 35, 38–39 and moreover:

(1) A. van Dyck, *St Martin Dividing his Cloak*, in Zaventem, St Martin's Church. LIT.: Barnes et al., *Van Dyck*, 2004, pp. 53, 56, no. I.38.

(2) Rubens, *Abraham and Melchizedek*, Paris, Musée du Louvre (sketch for the lost ceiling painting in the Antwerp Jesuit Church). LIT.: Martin, *Ceiling Paintings (CRLB)*, 1968, no. 7b.

(3) Rubens, *The Birth of Maria de' Medici* (part of the *Medici* series), Paris, Musée du Louvre. LIT.: Thuiller – Foucart, *Galerie Médicis*, 1969, pp. 74, 109, 141, pl. II. For the sketch, see: Held, *Sketches*, 1980, under no. 57.

For variants in the works of other masters, see Chapter IX, passim; Text ills 118–121.

There are also numerous works (paintings and prints in various techniques) from the nineteenth century which show the portico; the artists of these images mostly relied on the Harrewijn print. See for example: Philippe van Brée (1786–1871), *The Farewell of Van Dyck in the Courtyard of Rubens's House*, 1814 (Appendix III.40).

1. Chapter IX, pp. 249–293.
2. Chapter IX, pp. 257–258.
3. See 'Lost Elements', pp. 274–278.
4. Chapter IX, pp. 249–293.

No. 25. *Keystone with the Head of Medusa and a Thunderbolt*: Architectural-Sculptural Element (Fig. 144)

High relief in sandstone, erosion damage, especially at the top; approx. 72 × 52 × 30 cm.

Antwerp, Rubenshuis, central arch of the portico

c. 1618

VISUAL SOURCES: see No. 24.

COPY: Plaster cast, 1942;[1] negative, Antwerp, Centraal Depot Musea – Stad Antwerpen; positive (Fig. 145), Antwerp, Rubenshuis, inv. no. HH.0070; 72 × 52 × 30 cm; LIT.: De Clercq, *Materieel-technisch onderzoek*, 1997, pp. 5–6, fig. 8 (left); Uppenkamp – Van Beneden, *Architectural Symbolism*, 2011, p. 105, fig. 135; De Clercq, *Moulages*, 2012, p. 1, repr. p. 4 (left); Esposito, *Antique Shields*, 2018, p. 261, fig. 7; De Clercq et al., *Conservatie–restauratie*, 2020, I, pp. 109, 125, figs 220–221.

LITERATURE: Uppenkamp – Van Beneden, *Architectural Symbolism*, 2011, pp. 104–106, fig. 135; Uppenkamp, *Rubens's Palazzetto*, 2018, p. 227, fig. 10; Esposito, *Antique Shields*, 2018, pp. 260–262, 266–267, 270; Baumstark – Delmarcel, *Decius Mus (CRLB)*, 2019, II, p. 154.

The keystone above the central archway of the portico has a complicated and unusual structure. It is attached to the projecting architrave that forms the bottom edge of the broken pediment and rests on the heavy half-columns either side of the archway. The profile of this architrave can be seen continuing in the keystone, where it comes forward, and it has *guttae* underneath which characterise it as Doric; above and below this projecting section of moulding are volutes, two smaller ones above, and a single larger one below, which furls inwards, touching the top of the geniculated arch beneath, which is set further back. The original keystone is rather weather-damaged, and some details can be seen more easily in a cast made in 1942 (Fig. 145).

A Medusa's head appears on the projecting moulding with *guttae*: a young woman with mouth open, wings spreading from either side of her head, and with coiled snakes as hair, tangled together underneath her chin. The Gorgon's head cut off by Perseus, which was the apotropaic (averting evil) motif *par excellence*, was a fitting image for this position above the passageway. There are many examples of heads functioning in this way that Rubens may have seen, among them the Medusa's head above the central archway on the garden front of the Villa Medici (Fig. 146).

The winged and round-shaped Gorgon's head with open mouth corresponds to a drawing that Rubens made after an ancient gem which was probably part of his collection (Fig. 147).[2] Rubens's most famous rendering of the monstrous Gorgon is the painting with the horribly 'realistic' disembodied head surrounded by crawling snakes, in the Kunsthistorisches Museum in Vienna, but this is quite different from the stylised Medusa of the keystone.[3]

One aspect to note in the keystone is that the deterrent effect of the truncated head is further strengthened by being combined with a stylised representation of Jupiter's lethal weapon, the thunderbolt. Appearing on coins in Jupiter's hand or as a separate motif, this attribute has since Antiquity taken the form of a bundle of lightning bolts, with two zig-zag shaped arrows emerging either side of the central 'handgrip', and with a wedge-shaped vortex extending in both directions, which can be interpreted as a whirlpool of fire.

Various examples of this type of thunderbolt can be found in representations of ancient shields in Rubens's work: in a title-page and in one of the Decius Mus scenes, *The Death of Decius Mus*.[4] The motif also occurs in the series of Roman imperial portraits: Caligula clasps a thunderbolt in his fist and Trajan has one as a decoration on his helmet.[5] Two predictable settings in which the type appears are in the talons of Jupiter's eagle in *Jupiter and Lycaon* (partly visible), and on Vulcan's anvil in *Vulcan Forging the Thunderbolt for Jupiter*, both paintings of the Torre de la Parada series, now in the Prado, Madrid.[6] More surprising, on the other hand, is the fiery vortex (without lightning bolts) found on the vault of the Antwerp Jesuit Church, where it appears inside the heart shapes formed by scrolls (Fig. 129).[7]

Rubens also used the combination of a thunderbolt with Medusa's head elsewhere – albeit in a different form from the keystone – on a number of shields in historical scenes executed between 1616 and 1618, that is at about the same time as the construction of the portico.[8] This unusual combination can be seen most clearly on a large round shield which sits at the centre of the pile of captured arms in *The Obsequies of Decius Mus* in the Liechtenstein collection (Fig. 148).[9]

Compared to the motif on the shields, the elements of the thunderbolt in the keystone of the portico are joined to the Medusa's head in a more organic manner. The head is not simply placed on top of the thunderbolt. Here we have a single terrifying and deadly creature that both petrifies and strikes its victim with lightning. Like the snakes, the elements of the thunderbolt seem to 'sprout' from the Gorgon's head: to either side of the head is a lightning bolt intertwined with a snake. Part of the monstrous creature, consisting of four lightning bolts and a vortex, projects downwards through a hole at the bottom of the keystone, and is also connected organically to the head. This vortex motif – the fiery whirlpool which narrows to a sharp point – forms a curious extension of the snakes that grow from the Medusa's head. As explained, this detail is a 'whirlpool of fire', which is part of Jupiter's thunderbolt, and not – as some have understandably thought – blood streaming from the Gorgon's severed neck.[10] Thus, there is no direct allusion to Pegasus, the winged horse that was born from the earth soaked by the blood of the murdered Medusa.

Attempts have been made to give special significance to the Medusa's head positioned in the centre of the portico. The authors of *Palazzo Rubens* suggest that, as well as being an *apotropaion* that wards off evil, this motif can be interpreted as a *topos* of stoic reflection, the function of which is to call up and diffuse extreme emotions such as 'bewilderment and fear' but also 'ambivalent feelings such as pity and disgust'. In combination with the texts from Juvenal, its significance is enhanced if understood as an exhortation to 'remain serene and imperturbable'.[11] In addition, they hint at a 'more complex art-theoretical explanation' for the presence of the Medusa's head in the artist's house. Their idea assumes a connection with the mural painting *Andromeda Liberated by Perseus*, which was once visible in the courtyard opposite the portico, in other words facing the Medusa's head (for this, see under No. 18). They conclude that 'the keystone is given a truly key role in the architectural ensemble'.[12]

In a substantial study of Medusa combined with the thunderbolt, Teresa Esposito has looked further into connections with philosophical theory, emphasising some very different aspects. Esposito connects the head with 'Lipsius's natural philosophy, imbued with Platonic and Hermetic ideas', and argues that this background played a crucial role in the complex construction invented for the keystone by Rubens.[13]

In our view there is no need for an esoteric reading of this art-theoretical or philosophical nature. It seems rather far-fetched to give such a complicated (and hidden) meaning to a severed head incorporated in the architecture, in what is after all the appropriate place – above a passageway – for an apotropaic motif.

1. For the plaster casts made from details of the portico, see Chapter IX, p. 251, n. 10.
2. Van der Meulen, *Antique (CRLB)*, 1994, II, no. 175; III, fig. 345; a variant appears in a second drawing, originally on the same sheet (ibid., II, no. 176; III, fig. 346).
3. Kräftner et al., *Rubens in Wien*, 2004, pp. 222–226, no. 50; For a comprehensive discussion of this painting and the theme of the severed Medusa's head, see G. Gruber in Gruber – Tomášek, *Medusa*, 2018, pp. 10–19 and 25–28; on the theme, see also Van Eck, *Medusa*, 2016; for Constantijn Huygens's written comment about the version he saw with a collector in Amsterdam, see for example, Heinen, *Medusa*, 2010, p. 151 ff.
4. For the title-page with shield, see Judson – Van de Velde, *Title-pages (CRLB)*, 1978, I, no. 39; II, fig. 130; in another title-page, Jupiter's weapon is placed in the hand of a putto (ibid., no. 66, fig. 222). For the Decius Mus scenes, with the thunderbolt shield in the hand of the man rushing up from the left, see Baumstark – Delmarcel, *Decius Mus (CRLB)*, 2019, I, fig. 88; II, no. 5a.
5. Jonckheere, *Prototypes (CRLB)*, 2016, no. 24, fig. 88; no. 34, fig. 135.
6. Alpers, *Torre (CRLB)*, 1971, no. 35, fig. 132 and no. 60, fig. 193.
7. See above, under No. 21, p. 392, n. 3.
8. In her extensive study of the theme, Teresa Esposito draws attention to a similar combination in a number of classical images, as well as to a drawing retouched by Rubens (Esposito, *Antique Shields*, pp. 249–252, figs 1–2).
9. Baumstark – Delmarcel, *Decius Mus (CRLB)*, 2019, I, fig. 120; II, no. 6a; on the motif, see ibid., II, p. 17, n. 42. A similar shield, though less clearly visible, lies in the foreground of *Achilles Discovered among the Daughters of Lycomedes* in the Prado, Madrid, apparently showing the head of a bearded man (Jupiter?) between the lightning bolts (G. Martin in McGrath et al., *Mythological Subjects I (CRLB)*, 2016, I, no. 1; for a detail, see Padrón, *Cat. Madrid, Prado (Pintura flamenca)*, 1995, II, p. 1089, under no. 1661). Comparable shields in Rubens's oeuvre sometimes feature the Medusa's head on its own (see for instance No. 18), or just the thunderbolt (see under n. 4).
10. Uppenkamp, *Rubens's Palazzetto*, 2018, p. 227.
11. Uppenkamp – Van Beneden, *Architectural Symbolism*, 2011, p. 105; for detailed and like-minded commentary, not on the keystone but about the painting in Vienna mentioned under n. 3, see Heinen, *Medusa*, 2010, passim.
12. Uppenkamp – Van Beneden, *Architectural Symbolism*. pp. 106, 113.
13. She understands it as 'the embodiment of the laws of nature and God, bringing to mind the theological and philosophical discussions circulating among intellectuals in the beginning of the seventeenth century' (Esposito, *Antique Shields*, 2018, p. 244).

No. 26. *Dolphins*: Relief (Figs 149–150)

(1) left dolphin; lost, replaced by a copy (Fig. 149); approx. 72 cm.

(2) right dolphin (Fig. 150); sandstone; damaged beyond recognition, approx. 72 cm.

Antwerp, Rubenshuis, portico

c. 1618

VISUAL SOURCES: see No. 24.

LITERATURE: Uppenkamp – Van Beneden, *Architectural Symbolism*, 2011, p. 91; Fabri – Lombaerde, *Jesuit Church (CRLB)*, 2018, p. 208; Van Beneden, *Portiek en tuinpaviljoen*, 2019, p. 19.

In each spandrel of the central archway of the portico is a high relief carving of a writhing dolphin, its body entirely filling the triangle. To the right we can still see the original sculpture, albeit severely damaged by erosion and barely recognisable, while the one to the left is a modern copy. As with the satyrs and other sculptures of the portico, it can reasonably be assumed that the dolphins were executed by Hans van Mildert (1588–1638).

It is not obvious if anything more than a decorative function can be found in this motif. The playful animals enliven the rather austere Doric architecture of the portico. Undoubtedly they allude, like the satyrs, to nature which lies beyond the portico, and they also have an erotic connotation, but in our opinion there is no reason to look for a more sophisticated interpretation.[1]

It is worth noting that dolphins also appeared elsewhere in the decoration of Rubens's house. Writhing dolphins – in a different position, with beaks pointing down and perhaps painted rather than sculpted – decorated the spandrels of the five windows of the studio's north façade (Fig. 151). Here again there is no reason to assume that the maritime motif had anything more than a decorative function. For a Rubensian fountain with Cupid and a dolphin, which provides an unambiguous allusion to Venus who was born from the sea, and can therefore be understood as an erotic symbol, see No. 40.

A related motif – less a dolphin and more a sea monster making a frightening grimace, diving head first – appears in a completely different context, namely in the spandrels of one of the *serlianas* of the bell tower of the Church of St Carolus Borromeus, the design of which is attributed to Rubens (Fig. 152).[2]

1. See the rather far-fetched suggestion that the dolphins provide not only 'a mental link' with the garden but also between the portico and the studio, or that they can be connected with the figure of Apollo in one of the frieze paintings (No. 9); see Uppenkamp – Van Beneden, *Architectural Symbolism*, 2011, p. 91. For a reference to the story of Arion, see ibid., p. 91.
2. There are also sea creatures (tritons and sirens) visible in the other *serlianas* of the bell tower, and these maritime motifs have sometimes been linked with the Scheldt; see Fabri – Lombaerde, *Jesuit Church (CRLB)*, 2018, pp. 207–208, fig. 142.

No. 27. *Pediment with a Niche, Flanked by Two Eagles Holding a Fruit Garland:* Relief (Fig. 153)

Sandstone, erosion damage (e.g. parts of the talons have disappeared); approx. 200 × 310 cm.

Antwerp, Rubenshuis, above the central arch of the portico

c. 1618

VISUAL SOURCES: see No. 24.

COPY: Plaster cast, 1942;[1] negative and fragment of positive, Antwerp, Centraal Depot Musea – Stad Antwerpen. Positive (fragment of left eagle and garland): LIT.: De Clercq, *Materieel-technisch onderzoek*, 1997, pp. 5–6, fig. 7; De Clercq, *Moulages*, 2012, p. 1, repr. p. 3 (bottom); Mertens – Stoppie, *Conservatievisie*, 2019, p. 64, repr.; De Clercq et al., *Conservatie–restauratie*, 2020, I, pp. 109, 122, fig. 211.

LITERATURE: Prims, *Rubenshuis*, 1946, p. 32; Heinen, *Garten*, 2002, p. 3; Heinen, *Gesundheit*, 2004, pp. 118, 120–122, fig. 62; Uppenkamp – Van Beneden, *Architectural Symbolism*, 2011, pp. 93, 95, fig. 116; Van Beneden, *Portiek en tuinpaviljoen*, 2019, p. 19.

The central section of the portico's tympanum consists of a round niche flanked by two eagles which frame the circular opening with their outspread wings. In their beaks they clutch a ribbon from which a fruit garland hangs down, encircling the bottom half of the niche.

Examples of this motif can be found in Italian sculpture. Eagles, similar in form and performing the same function, appear on the attic of a portal leading to the garden at the villa of Cardinal Rodolfo Pio da Carpi (the Villa Carpi) in Rome, built between 1560 and 1564. Rubens is very likely to have known this gateway. He could have seen it in Rome, besides which it is illustrated, like the Porta Pia, in a supplement to Vignola's *Regola delli cinque ordini d'architettura*, a book that Rubens probably owned (Fig. 154).[2] It was one of the innovative designs for portals built as entrances to gardens on the edge of Rome, and which displayed their owners' names above the gateway.

A second Italian example that has been connected with the eagles on the portico is a relief carved in marble by Antonio Lombardo (c. 1458–1615) in the Liechtenstein collection. It shows a remarkably similar scheme: the eagles are in the same position, each with one wing spread open, but holding a fruit garland aloft using their wings rather than their beaks; between them is again a round shape, here not a niche, but two wreaths which encircle a tablet inscribed with a line of Seneca (Fig. 155).[3]

Undoubtedly Rubens had the gateway of the Villa Carpi in mind when he placed decorative

CATALOGUE No. 28

elements onto the pediment of his portico, hence the echoes it contains of Roman gardens. It is difficult to be sure if the eagles with their rich visual associations carry a specific additional meaning that would explain their presence on the portico. It would be helpful to have more information about one important contextual element which remains unknown: the contents – if any – of the round niche flanked by the eagles offering up their garlands. Was it meant to house of bust? Ulrich Heinen is convinced that the niche was left empty on purpose and sees the birds in the Italian examples mentioned as a combination of the 'imperial eagle motif' and the stoic concept of leisure, which is articulated – on the relief by Lombardo – by the inscription from Seneca. The *Palazzo* authors, who tend to regard the iconography of the portico as linked to Rubens's profession, cautiously suggest, as one of several possible explanations, that the eagles may have been introduced to symbolise sharp vision and to embody the idea of the virtuoso artist.[4]

The pose and completely symmetrical placing of the eagles corresponds more or less literally, as stated, with the relief by Lombardo, and was certainly based on an Italian example. For the details of the birds Rubens would have been able to use drawings in his possession. The rather 'flaky' rendering of their feathered breasts and legs suggests ancient sculptures of eagles which he had drawn while in Rome, for example the 'Mattei' eagle.[5]

One final observation to be made is that the birds on the portico have raised feathers underneath their beaks, resembling a 'goatee', a detail that is not present in the sculptural examples mentioned (still less in real eagles) (Fig. 157). But this unusual detail had been used by Rubens before, around 1612, on the eagle which carries Ganymede to Olympus (Fig. 156).[6]

As with the other sculptures of the portico, it can reasonably be assumed that the eagles were executed by Hans van Mildert to Rubens's design.

1. For the plaster casts made from details of the portico, see Chapter IX, p. 251, n. 10.
2. For this book and the Porta Pia, see above, Chapter IX, n. 107; for the gateway in the Villa Carpi, see Montano, *Aggiunta delle Porte*, 1610, pl. XXXXV (with sincere thanks to Piet Lombaerde, who provided information about this book). It was Heinen who made the connection between this gateway and Rubens's portico, see Heinen, *Gesundheit*, 2004, pp. 118, 120, 122, fig. 63; Uppenkamp – Van Beneden, *Architectural Symbolism*, 2011, p. 93, fig. 118.
3. Vaduz – Vienna, Liechtenstein, The Princely Collections, inv. no. 146; it came from the *studio di marmo* of the Palazzo d'Este in Ferrara; Seneca's text on the tablet reads: 'et quiescenti agendum est et agenti quiescendum' (he who rests must also act, and he who acts must rest). The connection between the relief and the portico was made by Heinen, *Gesundheit*, 2004, p. 121, fig. 67; Uppenkamp – Van Beneden, *Architectural Symbolism*, 2011, p. 93, fig. 117, p. 161, no. 21.
4. See their comments about the iconography of the eagle, which includes reference to a similar eagle on the title-page of Aguilón's *Opticorum*, etc. (Uppenkamp – Van Beneden, *Architectural Symbolism*, 2011, pp. 93–95, fig. 119). They concede that 'the eagle's multi-layered symbolism makes it difficult to offer an unambiguous interpretation' (ibid., p. 95).
5. Rubens drew this *Eagle with Spread Wings* (Rome, Musei Vaticani) from a number of viewpoints (known from copies preserved in the 'Rubens Cantoor'), see Van der Meulen, *Antique (CRLB)*, 1994, I, p. 77; II, pp. 112–114, nos 103–104; III, figs 182–183. For a second ancient eagle (known as 'Capitoline'), see Jaffé, *Rubens and Italy*, 1977, pp. 81, 116 (n. 33), fig. 267; Heinen made the connection between this eagle and portico, *Gesundheit*, 2004, p. 121, fig. 65. For the eagles copied by Rubens, see also A. Balis in Herremans, *Architectural Sculpture (CRLB)*, 2019, pp. 185, 192 (n. 13, under no. 15).
6. See E. McGrath in McGrath et al., *Mythological Subjects I (CRLB)*, 2016, I, no. 43; II, fig. 378 (esp. I, p. 444, n. 48; II, detail fig. 386).

No. 28. *Ram's Heads Ending in a Volute and a Snake's Head*: Relief (Figs 158, 161)

1) left ram's head and volute (Fig. 158); sandstone, 121 cm.

2) right ram's head and volute (Fig. 161); sandstone, 121 cm.

Antwerp, Rubenshuis, portico

c. 1618

VISUAL SOURCES: see No. 24.

LITERATURE: Uppenkamp – Van Beneden, *Architectural Symbolism*, 2011, pp. 107–110; Fabri – Lombaerde, *Jesuit Church (CRLB)*, 2018, p. 163; Van Beneden, *Portiek en tuinpaviljoen*, 2019, p. 19; Baumstark – Delmarcel, *Decius Mus (CRLB)*, 2019, II, p. 157, n. 21.

Ram's heads, carved in profile, and with long curly hair flowing down from their chests, can be found on the sides of the two pedestals supporting the central pediment of the portico. Their necks merge into large volutes that are severely damaged by erosion. A curious detail needs mentioning, which has in fact disappeared but is clearly visible in seventeenth-century images of the portico as well as on old photographs: the volutes spiral inwards and then curl out again underneath to end in a snake's head with open mouth (Fig. 159). A variant of this unusual motif can be found in the cupola of the Antwerp Jesuit Church, where one of the ornamental banderoles also ends in a snake's head (Fig. 162)].[1]

From the long *vittae* (attached to the *infula*) which hang down from their horns, these rams can be identified as sacrificial animals. Similar ram's heads frequently occur on the corners of sacrificial altars as well as on the stelae that marked Roman tombs. Rubens undoubtedly knew examples of this motif in ancient sculpture and he employed it more than once in his work, naturally in the depiction of ancient altars in paintings of Roman history scenes,[2] but also in designs for title-pages.[3] An altar with ram's heads also appeared in one of the scenes of the painted frieze on the studio façade, *The Sacrifice of Iphigenia* (No. 11; Figs 69 and 71).

There are a number of other occasions on which Rubens included ram's heads in profile in his architectural decorations: for example, on the sides of a base supporting a Madonna statue in a design for an altarpiece (Fig. 163),[4] and on two pedestals crowning the *Stage of Welcome* in the *Pompa Introitus Ferdinandi* (Fig. 164).[5]

Thus, apart from alluding to ancient sacrificial rituals, the meaning of ram's heads seems elusive, and it is doubtful that they represent more than a striking decorative element of a classicising kind on the portico. In any case it is not obvious that they have special significance. One explanation offered is that the ram is an attribute of the god Mercury and can therefore be linked to his statue standing above the portico.[6] This idea is far-fetched in itself, and can clearly be rejected if we agree that in Rubens's day the portico was not topped by a figure of this deity.[7]

The ram's head motif, viewed from the front, and in the form of a skull (*aegicranium*), could be found elsewhere in Rubens's house. As can been deduced from a number of visual sources, including the Berlin double portrait (Fig. 22) and the Harrewijn print of 1692 (Fig. 183), such a skull featured above the keystone of the central archway in the Doric frieze of the garden pavilion. By the nineteenth century it had disappeared. This *aegicranium* can be seen as a variant of the ox skull or *bucranium*, a motif belonging to the Doric order. It is worth noting that a similar motif also appears in a Doric frieze decorating the first storey of the bell tower of the Antwerp Jesuit Church.[8]

1. For this cupola that may have been designed by Rubens, see under No. 21, p. 392, n. 3.
2. For a discussion of this motif, see Uppenkamp – Van Beneden, *Architectural Symbolism*, 2011, pp. 107–110, with reference to an ancient altar which Rubens had probably seen in the Palazzo Mattei di Giove (ibid., p. 109, fig. 142). Altars with ram's heads occur, for example, in *The Fortitude of Scaevola* (Budapest, Szépművészeti Muzeum; McGrath, *History (CRLB)*, 1997, no. 163) and in *The Interpretation of the Victim* (Liechtenstein collection), a scene from the *Decius Mus* series (Baumstark – Delmarcel, *Decius Mus (CRLB)*, 2019, I, fig. 42; II, no. 2a).
3. Judson – Van de Velde, *Title-pages (CRLB)*, 1978, I, nos 40, 43, 52, 62.
4. There is no agreement about the intended location for this altar, making it difficult to settle on a title for the sketch in the collection of the Rubenshuis, inv. no. RH.S.194. It is thought to be a design for the crowning of the high altar of the Antwerp Jesuit Church (Fabri – Lombaerde, *Jesuit Church (CRLB)*, 2018, no. 9a, fig. 101), a view contested for example by Herremans, *Architectural Sculpture (CRLB)*, 2019, p. 175, no. 13b, fig. 80, Appendix I, pp. 221–225.
5. Martin, *Pompa (CRLB)*, 1972, no. 1, fig. 2. A ram's head can also be seen at the foot of the bier on which Decius Mus is laid out in *The Obsequies of Decius Mus* (Liechtenstein collection) (Baumstark – Delmarcel, *Decius Mus (CRLB)*, 2019, I, fig. 120; II, no. 6a).
6. Uppenkamp – Van Beneden, *Architectural Symbolism*, 2011, p. 109. Indeed, the ram frequently appears as an attribute of Mercury; see the façade of Giulio Romano's house in Mantua (Text ill. 70), where the animal appears standing by the deity's feet; the

same façade also includes ram's heads in frontal view in the frieze below the cornice, but these, in our opinion, bear no direct relation to the god (Uppenkamp – Van Beneden, *Architectural Symbolism*, 2011, figs 144–146); See also Quellinus's *Mercury*, flanked by a cockerel and a goat instead of a ram, in the Royal Palace Amsterdam (Text ill. 153).
7. For this problematic matter, see Chapter IX, pp. 278–285 and No. R1.
8. Uppenkamp – Van Beneden, *Architectural Symbolism*, 2011, fig. 143; Fabri – Lombaerde, *Jesuit Church (CRLB)*, 2018, p. 205, fig. 133.

No. 29. *Bucrania*: Sculpture / High Relief (Figs 165–166)

1) left *bucranium* (Fig. 165); sandstone, 63 cm.
2) right *bucranium* (Fig. 166); sandstone, 63 cm.

Antwerp, Rubenshuis, portico

c. 1618

VISUAL SOURCES: see No. 24.

LITERATURE: Devroe, *Rubens' huis*, 2008, pp. 25, 76; Uppenkamp – Van Beneden, *Architectural Symbolism*, 2011, pp. 106–107, fig. 137; Van Beneden, *Portiek en tuinpaviljoen*, 2019, p. 19.

A *bucranium*, or ox skull, appears on either side of the portico, at the far left and right, underneath the balustrade, above the volutes which continue upwards the line of the heavy columns at the ends of the portico. As usual it appears with the *infula* and trailing *vittae*, with which the Romans used to dress their sacrificial animals. Authors of architectural treatises categorised this motif among the decorations that belonged in the metopes of the Doric frieze, along with other ritual objects (Figs 169 and 170).[1] As with the other plainly decorative Doric motifs, the rosettes and *guttae*, it makes little sense to search for a specific symbolic meaning for this motif in Rubens's portico.[2]

It has often been mentioned that a very similar *bucranium*, its horns bound with *vittae*, can be seen, together with an array of sacrificial paraphernalia, in the architrave of the Temple of Vespasian, which Rubens had drawn in Rome.[3]

Rubens later used this motif in a quite different context, in a pen drawing with a design for the Plantin printer's mark.[4] In this emblematic composition the *bucranium* certainly does have a meaning; here the ox, the patient beast of burden, can be connected with '*labor*' or '*patientia*', thus alluding to the motto of the Plantin printing house ('Labore et Constantia') and to the figure of Hercules in the printer's mark.[5]

The sacrificial animal motif also appears elsewhere in the classically inspired decoration of Rubens's house. *Bucrania* can be seen in several of the panels underneath the studio's wide cornice (Fig. 168). The decoration also included the other ancient sacrificial animal, the ram, both in the form of a ram's head with *vittae*, and as a ram's skull (*aegicranium*).[6]

The two *bucrania* which are original to the portico have not always remained in their proper places. When the portico was drastically altered and extended at the top in the eighteenth century, they were moved and placed much higher up, underneath the raised balustrade. They were then joined by two additional examples, forming a row of four *bucrania*, one above each of the heavy columns (see photographs of the raised-up portico: Fig. 143; Text ill. 104). During the twentieth-century restoration the two originals were returned to their old positions; the two eighteenth-century copies have been preserved in the Antwerp municipal museums store.[7]

1. Including texts by Vignola, Serlio, Scamozzi and Palladio; for this, and other aspects of the bucrania, see Uppenkamp – Van Beneden, *Architectural Symbolism*, 2011, pp. 106–107; see also Lemerle, *Le bucrane*, 1996, pp. 85–62.
2. For the suggestion – in our opinion to be rejected – that the *bucranium* should perhaps be connected with the scene of *The Sacrifice of an Ox* in the frieze of the studio façade (No. 10), see Uppenkamp – Van Beneden, *Architectural Symbolism*, 2011, p. 106.
3. This drawing was engraved as illustration to Philip Rubens's *Electorum Libri II* of 1608 (Rubens, *Electorum Libri*, 1608, between p. 74 and p. 75; Judson – Van de Velde, *Title-pages (CRLB)*, 1978, I, no. 5; II, fig. 46; Uppenkamp – Van Beneden, *Vera simmetria*, 2011, p. 64, fig. 80.
4. Judson – Van de Velde, *ibid.*, no. 74a, fig. 255.
5. For this, and for the *bucranium* motif used in emblems by Achille Bocchi (1488–1562), see Uppenkamp – Van Beneden, *Architectural Symbolism*, 2011, pp. 106–107.

6. For the motifs of the ram and the *aegicranium*, see under No. 28.
7. De Clercq, *Materieel-technisch onderzoek*, 1997, p. 7, figs 11–12, 14; Maclot, *Rubenssite*, 2016, pp. 96–97, repr. p. 96; De Clercq – Hayen, *Historische schets*, 2019, repr. p. 43 (incorrectly as 'moulages').

No. 30. *Male Satyr Facing Right*: Relief (Fig. 171)

High relief in sandstone; erosion damage; right hand missing (Fig. 172); approx. 150 × 100 cm.

Antwerp, Rubenshuis, left spandrel of the left arch of the portico

c. 1618

VISUAL SOURCES: see No. 24.

COPY: Plaster cast, 1942;[1] negative, Antwerp, Centraal Depot Musea – Stad Antwerpen; LIT.: De Clercq et al., *Conservatie–restauratie*, 2020, I, pp. 109, 118, fig. 203. The positive is lost.

LITERATURE: Prims, *Rubenshuis*, 1946, p. 32; Kitlitschka, *Van Mildert*, 1972, p. 224; Baudouin, *Cat. Antwerp, Rubenshuis*, 1974, no. 18 [left] (as attributed to Hans van Mildert); Baudouin, *Toren*, 1983, p. 39; Tijs, *Rubens en Jordaens*, 1984, p. 136; Muller, *Collector*, 1989, p. 29; McGrath, *History (CRLB)*, 1997, p. 80; De Koomen, *Monsters*, 2003, pp. 73–74; Muller, *Rubens's Collection*, 2004, pp. 35–36, figs 37–38; Heinen, *Gesundheit*, 2004, pp. 129–130; Uppenkamp – Van Beneden, *Architectural Symbolism*, 2011, pp. 86–89.

The two pairs of satyrs in high relief in the spandrels of the two side arches are certainly the most remarkable elements of the portico. They should be seen as representatives of the (positive) force of nature, and they underline the rustic character of the architecture. Yet they are not simply half-bestial creatures or wild men who are driven purely by their instincts. By the act of holding up tablets with verses from Juvenal's *Satyrae* they demonstrate wisdom, which they impress upon all who enter Rubens's courtyard or pass through the arches of the portico into the garden.

The four satyrs are carved to fill the triangular spaces of the spandrels and their small goat's hooves fit into a narrow slot at the bottom. All four woodland creatures are draped with short and loose cloaks which barely cover their naked bodies; the billowing ends of fabric help to fill out the upper corners of the spandrels. The satyr under discussion, who has a goatlike profile and distinctly long and pointed ears, is the most 'dressed' of the four. Drapery hangs loosely around his hips and over his shoulder.

That Rubens was the inventor of these dynamic figures is beyond doubt; they are related to satyr figures in the master's painted work, as is clear from examples given under No. 31.

The satyr reliefs as well as the portico's other sculptural elements are traditionally assigned to Hans van Mildert (1588–1638) and there is no reason to doubt this attribution. There is no direct evidence, but we know that Van Mildert was closely involved in the construction of Rubens's house, a fact that emerges from the agreement for making a staircase, which he signed on behalf of Rubens before a notary in November 1616. Furthermore, it is well known that Rubens and the sculptor enjoyed a good relationship and had frequent contact.[2]

For further commentary on the four satyrs, see also under Chapter IX.[3]

1. For the plaster casts made from details of the portico, see Chapter IX, p. 251, n. 10.
2. For Rubens and Van Mildert, see Chapter XI, pp. 327–329; for the staircase, see No. 19 and Appendix I.9.
3. See pp. 261–262.

No. 31. *Female Satyr Seen from Behind, Facing Left*: Relief (Fig. 173)

High relief in sandstone; erosion damage; approx. 150 × 100 cm.

Antwerp, Rubenshuis, right spandrel of the left arch of the portico

c. 1618

VISUAL SOURCES: see No. 24.

CATALOGUE No. 31

COPIES: (1) Drawing (Fig. 174), by Willem Panneels; black chalk, pen, brown ink on grey paper, 285 × 141 mm. Inscribed in code: *dit rugesken hebbe ick geteekent naer een gesneden dat opde pledts tot rubbens staet* (I copied this back after a carved [one] that stands in Rubens's courtyard). Copenhagen, Statens Museum for Kunst, Kongelige Kobberstiksamling, inv. no. KKSgb9686 (Rubens Cantoor, V.51). EXH.: Antwerp, 1993a, no. 63; Antwerp, 2011, no. 44. LIT.: Garff – de la Fuente Pedersen, *Panneels*, 1988, no. 60; Held, *Review Garff – de la Fuente Pedersen*, 1991, p. 426, no. 60, fig. 9; Huvenne, *Tekeningen*, 1993, pp. 156, 162, no. 63, repr. p. 161; Uppenkamp – Van Beneden, *Architectural Symbolism*, 2011, p. 87, fig. 109.

(2) Plaster cast, 1942;[1] negative, Antwerp, Centraal Depot Musea – Stad Antwerpen; LIT.: De Clercq et al., *Conservatie–restauratie*, 2020, I, pp. 109, 121, fig. 209. The positive is now lost (after 1997); EXH.: Antwerp, 1993a, no. 64; LIT.: De Clercq, *Moulages*, 2012, repr. p. 3 (photograph of 1997).

LITERATURE: Konrad, *Meisterwerke*, 1928–34, I, pl. 79; Prims, *Rubenshuis*, 1946, p. 32; Kitlitschka, *Van Mildert*, 1972, p. 224; Baudouin, *Cat. Antwerp, Rubenshuis*, 1974, no. 18 [right] (as attributed to Hans van Mildert); Tijs, *Rubens en Jordaens*, 1984, p. 136; Muller, *Collector*, 1989, p. 29; Held, *Review Garff – de la Fuente Pedersen*, 1991, p. 426, fig. 8; Huvenne, *Tekeningen*, 1993, pp. 156, 159, fig. ill. 31; De Koomen, *Monsters*, 2003, pp. 73–74; Uppenkamp – Van Beneden, *Architectural Symbolism*, 2011, p. 87, fig. 109.

This satyress, with rounded buttocks and a curly tail, is certainly an eye-catching element of the portico. She is seen from behind, her torso twisted to the left, and with both hands she holds up a tablet with verses from Juvenal. In comparison with her rough, goat-like counterpart on the other side of the archway, she is – from the waist up, at least – more human in appearance, with a beautiful face and hair artfully arranged in plaits. Nonetheless her long and pointed ears betray her true nature.

The satyrs in the spandrels of the side arches resemble figures in some of Rubens's mythological paintings. This satyress shows a certain similarity to the blonde sylvan creature with hoof raised who, together with a satyr, supports Hercules in Rubens's *Hercules Drunk* in the Gemäldegalerie Alte Meister in Dresden, a painting of around 1613–1614 (Fig. 105).[2] In the sculpted version she is in mirror-image and her goat's ears and short tail give her a more 'animal-like' appearance. The pose is somewhat similar to that of the male satyr (bottom right, seen from behind) in *Nature Adorned by the Graces* in Kelvingrove Art Gallery and Museum, Glasgow.[3] It is evident from this example that the satyrs of the portico are 'Rubensian' figures which can only have been designed by the master himself.

Willem Panneels found the figure in the spandrel sufficiently interesting to draw a copy of it (Copy, 1; Fig. 174). The inscription on the sheet, written in his secret code, reveals that he made his copy from the sculpted ('gesneden') figure that was visible in the courtyard ('de pledts tot Rubbens') The angle from which it is viewed makes clear that he did indeed make his drawing from the portico and not from a (lost) preparatory drawing by Rubens. Panneels drew the high relief from below and, as can be established on the spot, exactly matching the viewpoint of somebody standing a few metres from the portico. As he wrote on the sheet, it was the striking back ('het rugesken') that particularly interested him: he concentrated on this part of the sculpture and showed the head, arms and hooves of the satyress only summarily.

For further commentary on the four satyrs, see also No. 30 and Chapter IX.[4]

1. For the plaster casts made from details of the portico, see Chapter IX, p. 251, n. 10.
2. The similarity was first noticed by Konrad, *Meisterwerke*, 1928–34, I, pl. 79; for the painting, see also Muller, *Rubens's Collection*, 2004, p. 122, no. 157, pl. 74; Rosenthal, *Rubens*, 2005, pp. 64–70, pl. V (with earlier date: c. 1612).
3. Van Mulders, *Collaborations Brueghel (CRLB)*, 2016, no. 5, fig. 18.
4. See pp. 261–262.

No. 32. *Male Satyr Facing Left*: Relief (Fig. 175)

High relief in sandstone; erosion damage; approx. 150 × 100 cm.

Antwerp, Rubenshuis, left spandrel of the right arch of the portico

c. 1618

VISUAL SOURCES: see No. 24.

COPY: Plaster cast, 1942;[1] negative and positive, Antwerp, Centraal Depot Musea – Stad Antwerpen. Positive: LIT.: De Clercq, *Materieel-technisch onderzoek*, 1997, pp. 5–9, fig. 1, left; De Clercq, *Moulages*, 2012, p. 1, repr. p. 2 (bottom left); De Clercq et al., *Conservatie–restauratie*, 2020, I, pp. 109, 117, fig. 201.

LITERATURE: Prims, *Rubenshuis*, 1946, p. 32; Kitlitschka, *Van Mildert*, 1972, p. 224; Baudouin, *Cat. Antwerp, Rubenshuis*, 1974, no. 19 [left] (as attributed to Hans van Mildert); Tijs, *Rubens en Jordaens*, 1984, p. 137; Muller, *Collector*, 1989, p. 29; De Koomen, *Monsters*, 2003, pp. 73–74; Uppenkamp – Van Beneden, *Architectural Symbolism*, 2011, p. 87, fig. 109.

The Satyr in the spandrel of the right-hand archway has a long beard and his little horns are more pronounced than those of his companion on the other side. He turns his back to the arch, against which he leans his hip and the fist of his left hand. He is the only one who is not supporting an inscribed tablet. Rather he seems to be using his right hand to hold up the entablature above his head. It has sometimes been thought that this satyr was shown as a sleeping figure, but it is not clear if this was Rubens's intention (see under No. 33).

For further commentary on the four satyrs, see also No. 30 and Chapter IX.[2]

1. For the plaster casts made from details of the portico, see Chapter IX, p. 251, n. 10.
2. See pp. 261–262.

No. 33. *Female Satyr Facing Left*: Relief (Fig. 176)

High relief in sandstone; erosion damage; approx. 150 × 100 cm.

Antwerp, Rubenshuis, right spandrel of the right archway of the portico

c. 1618

VISUAL SOURCES: see No. 24.

COPY: Plaster cast, 1942;[1] negative and positive, Antwerp, Centraal Depot Musea – Stad Antwerpen; 1942. Positive: LIT.: De Clercq, *Materieel-technisch onderzoek*, 1997, pp. 5–6, fig. 1, right; De Clercq, *Moulages*, 2012, p. 1, repr. p. 2 (bottom); De Clercq et al., *Conservatie–restauratie*, 2020, I, pp. 109, 120, fig. 207.

LITERATURE: Prims, *Rubenshuis*, 1946, p. 32; Kitlitschka, *Van Mildert*, 1972, p. 224; Baudouin, *Cat. Antwerp, Rubenshuis*, 1974, no. 18 [right] (as attributed to Hans van Mildert); Tijs, *Rubens en Jordaens*, 1984, p. 137; Muller, *Collector*, 1989, p. 29; Huvenne, *Tekeningen*, 1993, p. 159, De Koomen, *Monsters*, 2003, pp. 73–74; Muller, *Rubens's Collection*, 2004, p. 35; Uppenkamp – Van Beneden, *Architectural Symbolism*, 2011, p. 87, fig. 109.

The satyress in the right-hand spandrel of the right archway is shown frontally. She leans backwards as if resting on the curvature of the arch. She has a rounded face framed by long curly hair and her slanting eyes are half closed. As with her companion on the other side of the archway, we cannot make out – due to the rather weather-beaten state of the sculptures – if this satyress has her eyes closed and was intended as sleeping. This supposition has given rise to a notion, which is difficult to support and may be incorrect, that the satyrs above the left-hand archway of the portico represent 'diurnal spirits' and those to the right 'nocturnal'.[2]

For further commentary on the satyrs, see also No. 30 and Chapter IX.[3]

1. For the plaster casts made from details of the portico, see Chapter IX, p. 251, n. 10.
2. See, for example, Prims and Huvenne (references above); Muller also sees the satyrs above the left arch as 'awake' and those to the right as 'asleep' (Muller, *Rubens's Collection*, 2004, p. 35).
3. See pp. 261–262.

D. Garden Pavilion and Garden: Nos 34–41

No. 34. *Garden Pavilion*: Architecture (Figs 177–178)

Brick and blue stone, slate roof; 454 × 667 cm

c. 1618

Antwerp, Rubenshuis, garden

VISUAL SOURCES:
(1)? Rubens and studio, *The Walk in the Garden*, Munich, 1630s (Appendix III.6; Fig. 25; detail: Fig. 182);
(2) Anonymous, *Portrait of a Couple in a Garden*, Berlin, c. 1655 (Appendix III.10; Fig. 22; detail Fig. 181);
(3) Harrewijn print, 1684; shown very small in the background (Appendix III.1; Fig. 17; detail: Fig. 180);
(4) Harrewijn print, 1692 (Appendix III.2; Fig. 18; detail: Fig. 183).
(5) Louis Schweig, stereoscopic photograph, 1856–1857 (Appendix III.50);
(6) Edmond Fierlants, two photographs, 1860 (Appendix III.51; Text ill. 22);
(7) Adolphe Braun, photograph, 1864 (Appendix III.53).
For variants, see below.

LITERATURE: Van Grimbergen, *Rubens*, 1840, p. 387; Van Vyve, *Guide*, 1854, pp. 114–115; Van den Branden, *Schilderschool*, 1883, p. 509; Rooses, *Oeuvre*, 1886–92, V, p. 186; Rooses, *Maison*, 1888, p. 229; Rooses – Ruelens, *Correspondance*, 1887–1909, II, pp. 154–155; Rooses, *Life*, 1904, pp. 148–149, 154; Van de Castyne, *Rubens*, 1931, pp. 110–111, 116–118; Delen, Rubens' huis, 1933, p. 31; Van de Castyne, *Architecture*, 1934, p. 318; Delen, *Rubens' huis*, 1940, p. 36; Evers, *Neue Forschungen*, 1943, p. 337; Fredlund, *Arkitektur*, 1974, p. 11; Blunt, *Rubens and Architecture*, 1977, p. 613; Baudouin, *Summary Guide*, 1977, p. 28; Van Aerschot, ed., *Bouwen / Antwerpen*, 1979, p. 548; Tijs, *Rubens en Jordaens*, 1984, passim; Huvenne, *Rubenshuis*,

1988, pp. 125, 127, 129, 142; Muller, *Collector*, 1989, pp. 33, 35–36, 38; Heinen, *Gesundheit*, 2004, pp. 80–85; Devroe, *Rubens' huis*, 2008, pp. 23, 67, 104, 113; Lombaerde, *Rubens the Architect*, 2011, pp. 124, 139, 150–152, 156; Uppenkamp – Van Beneden, *Vera simmetria*, 2011, pp. 65 ff., figs 88, 91; Uppenkamp – Van Beneden, *Architectural Symbolism*, 2011, p. 85; Coekelberghs, *Review Palazzo Rubens*, 2012, passim; Van Driessche, *Herschepping*, 2013, pp. 29–30; Lombaerde, *Rubens*, 2014, p. XVII; De Staelen, *Rubens*, 2014, p. 245; Boeykens, *Reflections*, 2014, pp. 223–236; Uppenkamp, *Rubens's Palazzetto*, 2018, p. 226, fig. 8; Van Beneden, *Portiek en tuinpaviljoen*, 2019, pp. 18–19; De Clercq – Hayen, *Historische schets*, 2019, pp. 49–51; Mertens – Stoppie, *Conservatievisie*, 2019, passim; De Clercq, *Conservatie*, 2019, passim; De Clercq et al., *Conservatie–restauratie*, 2020, I–V, passim.

Looking inwards from the entrance gate on the Wapper, the visitor can see a pavilion in the distance at the end of the garden: this small and elegant building is, besides the portico, the only original part of Rubens's house that survives. A whole chapter (Chapter X) is dedicated to this pavilion, which was undoubtedly designed by Rubens, and this catalogue entry is confined to technical information, literature, a list of visual sources and short summary.

The main feature of the front of the pavilion is the central round arch, flanked either side by a horizontal lintel or architrave resting on Doric columns. This combination is known as a *serliana* motif and is repeated, in simplified form, on the two sides of the pavilion. In each spandrel of the central arch is a circular niche crowned by a curved, eyebrow-like hood moulding. The building has a hipped (slate) roof fronted by a dormer with niche, which is crowned by a broken pediment. The pediment rests on two posts embellished with sphinx-like caryatids with Ionic capitals (No. 35).

Three statues of ancient gods are sited in the pavilion. In front of a shallow niche in the centre of the rear wall, stands an impressive over-lifesize statue of Hercules (No. 40). To the right, between the columns, is a youthful figure of Bacchus (No. 38). He is balanced on the left by a modern Venus, which was introduced during the restoration to replace a figure of Ceres. The Ceres (R4) was not original, but replaced a lost Venus (No. 37) that had in all probability been present in Rubens's lifetime. A fourth statue, a youth with cornucopia, appears in the niche of the roof dormer (No. 36).

Variants of the pavilion, shown either complete or in part, appear in a number of seventeenth-century paintings by Rubens and other Antwerp masters:

(1) Rubens, *Henri IV Consigns the Regency to Maria de' Medici*, 1622–1625 (Appendix III.18–19);

(2) Rubens, *The Supper at Emmaus*, Madrid, c. 1638 (Appendix III.25);

(3) Philip Fruytiers, *Four Children of Peter Paul Rubens with a Maid and Helena Fourment (?)*, c. 1638–1639 (Appendix III.26);

(4) Jacques Jordaens, *Cupid and Psyche*, Madrid, c. 1640–1650 (Appendix III.9; Fig. 20; detail: Fig. 179);

(5) David Teniers II, *Elegant Company in a Garden*, c. 1651. Antwerp, The Phoebus Foundation (Appendix III.34);

(6) Anonymous, *Elegant Company in a Garden*, whereabouts unknown, c. 1640 (Appendix III.36a-b);

(7) Anonymous, *Elegant Company in a Garden*, whereabouts unknown, c. 1640 (Appendix III.37).

No. 35. *Caryatids Left and Right (Sphinxes?)*: Sculptures (Cf. Figs 184–185)

Stone. Replaced by modern copies during the restoration, c. 1939 (see Copy 1).

Antwerp, Rubenshuis, garden pavilion, lost

c. 1618

VISUAL SOURCES: see No. 34.

COPIES: (1) Sculptures (Figs 184–185), by Frans Claessens after ? Hans van Mildert,[1] late 1930's;

CATALOGUE No. 36

with Vaurion stone (Massangis). LIT.: De Clercq et al., Conservatie-restauratie, 2020, I, p. 31.

(2) Plaster cast (of one caryatid), postive, 1939 (?), Antwerp, Centraal Depot Musea – Stad Antwerpen. LIT.: De Clercq et al., *Conservatie–restauratie*, 2020, I, p. 21, fig. 31.

LITERATURE: Van Driessche, *Herschepping*, 2013, p. 29; Fabri – Lombaerde, *Jesuit Church (CRLB)*, 2018, p. 162; Lombaerde, *Rubens / Vredeman de Vries*, 2018, p. 125, fig. 13; Mertens – Stoppie, *Conservatievisie*, 2019, repr. p. 58; De Clercq et al., *Conservatie–restauratie*, 2020, I, p. 21.

The pediment of the garden pavilion is supported by two identical caryatids, female heads crowned by Ionic capitals. Their braided hair is tied in a bow, which hangs over a projecting trapezoid pedestal (rather like a 'breastplate') that stands on two small volutes. From a distance these volutes have the appearance of small stylised 'feet', which make the caryatids seem rather sphinx-like, and perhaps that is how they were intended.

As has been observed by Ria Fabri and Piet Lombaerde, the caryatids of the garden pavilion are somewhat like the sphinx-angels with a similar headdress – a hat or a helmet? – which can be seen supporting an Ionic capital on the façade of the Antwerp Jesuit Church, which was built at about the same time. In Rubens's drawing related to one of these hybrid caryatids, there are also long plaits tied together over the bust (Fig. 186).[2]

As with the sculptural elements of the portico and the statue in the roof niche of the pavilion, the original caryatids (replaced c. 1939 during the restoration) can be attributed to Hans van Mildert (1588–1638).[3]

1. According to Thomas Van Driessche they were carved by Claessens (together with two capitals, two volutes and the bottom part of the statue in the niche) by the Antwerp sculptor Frans Claessens (Van Driessche, *Herschepping*, 2013, pp. 29, 41, n. 124).
2. These Jesuit Church caryatids differ in that they are angels with large wings either side of the head; for the two carved heads decorating the church façade, see Fabri – Lombaerde, *Jesuit Church (CRLB)*, 2018, no. 7, figs 62, 64; for the drawing (by Rubens or retouched by him) (Fig. 186), of a head of a Sphinx-Angel in profile, see ibid., no. 7a, fig. 63.
3. See above, Chapter XI, p. 328.

No. 36. *Youth with a Cornucopia (Genius Loci?)*: Statue (Fig. 187)

Avesnes stone; erosion damage; the right arm and both legs were replaced in Savonnières stone during the restoration campaign of 1939–1947;[1] approx. 178 × 75 cm.

Antwerp, Rubenshuis, garden pavilion. Inv. no. RH. PR2.1

? c. 1618.

VISUAL SOURCES:
(1) Rubens and studio, *The Walk in the Garden*, Munich, 1630s; partly visible (Appendix III.6; Fig. 25; detail: Fig. 182);
(2) Harrewijn print, 1684; minuscule, in the background (Appendix III.1; Fig. 17; detail Fig. 180);
(3) Harrewijn print, 1692; with alterations and in reverse: (Appendix III.2; Fig. 18; details: Figs 183, 188);
(4) David Teniers II, *An Elegant Company in a Garden*, 1651; variant (Appendix III.34; detail: Fig. 190).
(5) Anonymous, *Portrait of a Couple in a Garden*, Berlin, c. 1655; partly visible (Appendix III.10; Fig. 22; detail: Fig. 181);
See also the early photographs under No. 35, Visual Sources (5) – (7).

LITERATURE: Van den Branden, *Schilderschool*, 1883, p. 508 (as 'halfnaakte maagd met den overvloedshoorn in den arm'); Rooses, *Oeuvre*, 1886–92, V, p. 186 (as 'Abondance'); Delen, *Rubens' huis*, 1933, pp. 31, 54 (as 'overvloed', and replaced); Delen, *Rubens' huis*, 1940, p. 36 (as 'overvloed', not original/replaced); Prims, *Rubenshuis*, 1946, p. 36 (as 'Ops'); Prims, *Prieel van Rubens*, 1948, pp. 140–141(as 'Ops'); Kitlitschka, *Rubens*, 1963, p. 139 (as 'Überfluss, Original oder Kopie?'); Baudouin, *Rubens en zijn tijd*, 1971, p. 83; Baudouin, *Cat. Antwerp, Rubenshuis*, 1974, under no. 23 (as 'Honos'); Baudouin, *Summary Guide*, 1977, p. 29 (as 'Honour'); Baudouin, *Rubens House*, 1977, p. 183 (as 'Honour'); Stutz, *Residenz*, 1985, p. 142 (as 'Honor'); Muller, *Collector*, 1989, pp. 33, 154, cat. III, no. 20, pl. 138 (as *'Genius Loci'*, by an Anonymous Seventeenth-Century Flemish Master); Baudouin, *Rubens House*, 2005, p. 177 (as Honour); De Clercq – Hayen, *Historische Schets*, 2019, pp. 49–50; Mertens – Stoppie, *Conservatievisie*, 2019, p. 56, repr. p. 55.

A life-size statue in the round of a youth, with a cloak draped loosely over his shoulders and hips, stands in the roof niche of the garden pavilion; he stretches his right hand out in front, and in his left he holds a cornucopia which he supports on his arm. A statue such as this undoubtedly stood in the pavilion in Rubens's lifetime. It can be partially seen, with enough detail to identify it – although with some variations – in *The Walk in the Garden* (Appendix III.6; Figs 25 and 182), and in the Berlin *Portrait of a Couple in a Garden* (Appendix III.10; Figs 22 and 181). It also features in the Harrewijn print of 1692 with certain differences from its present appearance: it is reversed, that is with the right leg to the fore and the cornucopia to the left; the drapery is shorter, leaving both knees uncovered; the left hand is placed on the youth's chest (Fig. 188). A variant of the sculpture can also be seen in the free interpretation of Rubens's garden pavilion that appears in Teniers's *Elegant Company in a Garden*, dated 1651 (Appendix III.34; Fig. 190).

The earliest 'realistic' record of the current statue can be obtained from photographs from around 1860, including the one by Edmond Fierlants (Appendix III.51; Fig. 189). From the visual sources listed we can deduce that from before 1630 to the present day, that is for nearly four centuries, it was probably one and the same statue. At least there is no reason to think that it was replaced by an exact copy or variant, although naturally this cannot be ruled out.[2] That said, the statue that remains in place today, in the open, and facing west, where it is very much exposed to wind and rain, has not come down to us unscathed. During – and possibly even long before – the restoration of the site, badly damaged parts were replaced: the lower half of the legs and the outstretched right arm have been completely renewed.

Therefore it is difficult to judge if an important detail such as the right hand of the youth, as it appears today, outstretched in a welcoming gesture and without attribute, matches the original. In the seventeenth-century images mentioned, the youth's hand is not in view, except in the Harrewijn print where it is not stretched out, but touching or close to the chest (Fig. 188). In the variant that appears in the Teniers painting, the youth makes a different gesture: in his raised hand he seems to be holding a fruit (or a drinking cup?) (Fig. 190). The visual evidence from the nineteenth century and later provides no clarity about this.[3]

This uncertainty surrounding the position of the right arm and the possible presence of an attribute in the hand makes identification of the youth difficult. There is no general agreement in the literature about his identity or about his significance in Rubens's garden pavilion. We can ignore the opinions of earlier authors, including Rooses and Delen and even Kitlitschka, who saw the youthful figure with curly hair as a woman, whom they tended to identify as Abundantia because of the cornucopia.[4]

It has been remarked, correctly, that the youth in the roof niche shows a striking resemblance to representations of Honos (Honour), who is always accompanied by Virtus (Virtue, more specifically 'Virility'), two personifications elevated to divinities by the ancient Romans and worshipped in the same temple.[5] These divinities appear frequently in Rubens's inventions, based on the images of ancient coins and Cartari's *Imagini* (Fig. 194).[6]

The youth of the garden pavilion is very close to the image of Honos in Rubens's drawing in the Museum Plantin-Moretus in Antwerp (Fig. 191),[7] which may have been a design for two statues. It is particularly interesting that the figures on this sheet are identified by accompanying autograph inscriptions by Rubens. In the drawing, the youth with laurel wreath, staff and cornucopia is described as 'Honos', while a second figure, a woman dressed for battle, with helmet, spear and *parazonium* (a short sword or dagger) is labelled 'Virtus'. The sheet has been connected with two limewood statues also in the Museum Plantin-Moretus, *Honos* and *Virtus*, which follow Rubens's drawing in every detail, although their forms are

CATALOGUE No. 36

more elongated (Text ill. 152). These statues are problematical, however, both in terms of their dating and maker[8] and we will not discuss them further here.

Virtue and Honour are almost obligatory personifications in the elaborate programmes that paid tribute to rulers. Statues representing them had appeared in public street decorations in Antwerp as early as 1599, set on inscribed bases for the Joyous Entry of Albrecht and Isabella.[9] So it is no surprise that the pair can be found in Rubens's work in a similar thematic context. Thus they appear in the *Henri IV* series, in the Whitehall ceiling,[10] and also of course in one of the arches of the *Pompa Introitus Ferdinandi* – on the verso of *The Arch of Ferdinand*, either side of the central image showing the *Triumph of Prince Ferdinand*. There too they are identified unambiguously by an inscription.[11]

From the foregoing – and especially from Rubens's inscription on the Plantin-Moretus drawing with virtually the same figure – one might conclude that this statue on the garden pavilion also represents Honos (Honour) and many authors have identified it as such. Yet this may be too hasty. Unlike Honos in the Rubens images mentioned, the youth in the roof niche holds neither a staff nor a spear in his hand; nor is his head crowned with a laurel wreath. First and foremost it is difficult to see why Honour would be placed in such a prominent position, immediately visible on entering the house, beyond the courtyard. In attempting to explain the relationship of the four statues of the pavilion (including the apocryphal statue of Ceres), some have constructed rather complicated, and implausible, 'rebus-like' hypotheses. Thus it has been proposed, for example, that Rubens used the four statues to express the idea that Labour (Hercules) leads to Fertility (Bacchus and Ceres) and Honour (the youth), an idea seen as 'highly appropriate to Rubens's industrious and successful career'.[12]

Jeffrey Muller preferred a very different and more meaningful identification, seeing the youth as an embodiment of *Genius Loci* (genius of the place) who presides over the founding and prosperity of the house.[13]

This identification may well be correct. Muller based it on the texts and images in Cartari's *Imagini delli dei*. In the 1608 edition Cartari gives an image with three personifications of the good genius ('Genio buono'), who protects mortals and their homes (Fig. 194). In the middle is a boy with a laurel wreath and cornucopia in his left hand; to the left is a bearded man, also with laurel wreath and cornucopia and holding a *patera* in his outstretched right hand. The commentary speaks of 'il Dio della hospitalità, del piacere, e buon tempo e della natura' (the god of hospitality, pleasure, a good time, and nature). 'Nature' is explained further: 'for it is said that anyone who gives himself a good time and takes advantage of everything that Nature offers is in harmony with Genius'.[14] This description seems highly appropriate for a statue displayed in such a prominent position in Rubens's garden.

To this we can add that original sculptures survive that show these tutelary Roman divinities known as 'Genii' as well as 'Lares', varying considerably in size and with small variations in appearance. The Genius, or Lar, is consistently represented as a youth with a short tunic, and making the pouring gesture with the *patera* (Fig. 193).[15]

Rubens was certainly familiar with this Genius figure who brings good fortune, as is clear from a variant image that occurs in his work. A similar youth with cornucopia can be identified among the many gods and personifications decorating the *Pompa Introitus* as part of the *Stage of Welcome*. He stretches a *patera* forwards in his right hand and, according to the inscription on the arch, he is the 'Genius urbis antverpiensis' (Fig. 192). Gevartius's commentary explains that the figure ('iuvenili formâ') with cornucopia and *patera* goes back to Roman coins, but that he is here given a crown of white and red roses that symbolise the City of Antwerp.[16] Mainly because of the statue's eroded state, it is difficult to say if the youth in the roof niche is also wearing roses or other flowers in his hair. He is certainly not wearing a laurel wreath, which is part of the iconography of 'Honos'. The pronounced 'relief' of his hair, with swelling locks over his forehead and either side, certainly suggests that he was represented with some kind of head decoration. Indeed, perhaps he was also crowned with roses, although these flowers are a specific feature of Antwerp heraldry, and therefore less pertinent to a figure in Rubens's garden.

If the identification as a *Genius*, bringer of prosperity, is sound, and there are strong arguments in its favour, then perhaps the hand has been restored incorrectly. It is possible that the youth originally held a *patera* in his right hand, as in the *Stage of Welcome*.[17]

It seems extremely unlikely that Rubens's drawing of Honos and Virtus, mentioned above, and preserved in the Museum Plantin-Moretus, originated as a design for the statue in the roof niche. This sheet has not one but two figures and, as explained, the youth represents a different personification. It can be assumed, however, that the drawing was retained after its first usage, and then served as model, with slight alterations, for the statue in the niche. There has been no agreement about the dating of the drawing and so it cannot provide a possible *terminus post quem* for the stone statue. This was probably made at the time of the construction of the pavilion (so possibly around 1618). Equally it is possible – although given the prominent position, this is unlikely – that the niche remained empty for a while and a statue was only placed there later.

As for the sculptor, it is reasonable to consider an attribution – although there is no conclusive evidence – to Hans van Mildert (1588–1636), whose name has been mentioned in connection with the limewood sculptures. This is certainly possible given his involvement in the construction of Rubens's house.[18]

In any case it is clear from the drawing that the youth with Cornucopia corresponds almost exactly to a design by Rubens, which means that it is certainly based on his invention, something which cannot be established with certainty for any of the other statues in the garden pavilion.

1. De Clercq – Hayen, *Historische Schets*, 2019, p. 50.
2. A number of nineteenth-century authors believed that all of the statues of the pavilion had been replaced over time; for this discussion, see above Chapter X, pp. 310–311; similarly, Kitlitschka was unsure if the statue was an original from the seventeenth century, or a later copy (Kitlitschka, *Rubens*, 1963, p. 139).
3. The youth's hand seems to be missing in the two Fierlants photographs of 1860 (Appendix III.51; Fig. 189), but, surprisingly, it is present in the engraving made by Erin Corr twenty years earlier (Appendix III.46), as well as in the photograph by Adolphe Braun of 1914 (Appendix III.53).
4. Floris Prims also saw the figure as female; he regarded the pavilion as a 'rustic temple' ('landtempeltje'), a suggestion that can be rejected (see above, Chapter X, p. 314). He thought that the niche figure represented Ops, the Roman goddess of Abundance, responsible for the fertility of the earth (Prims, *Prieel van Rubens*, p. 141).
5. Simon, *Götter*, 1990, pp. 213, 240.
6. The couple appear in both text and images of the *Imagini* of Cartari, whose information came from ancient coins (Cartari, *Imagini*, 1963, p. 196) (Fig. 194). As the accompanying text shows, his Honos figure, seen and described as a female, is derived from 'una medaglia di Vitellio'. For the coin of Vitellius, see reproduction by Du Choul (Baumstark – Delmarcel, *Decius Mus (CRLB)*, 2019, I, fig. 153). There are many earlier images of these two personifications: Honos as a young man (or sometimes a woman) with cornucopia and staff, accompanied by Virtus, with helmet and *parazonium*. Examples include the statues mentioned above, which were installed in 1599 in Antwerp (see n. 8) and the figures incorporated in a medallion in the title-pages of Lipsius's *Seneca* editions of 1605 and 1615 (Judson – Van de Velde, *Title-pages (CRLB)*, 1978, II, figs 102–103). On this pair of deities, see also McGrath, *Pompa*, 1971, I, pp. 240–250, II, figs 155–159; Büttner, *Allegories (CRLB)*, 2018, I, pp. 339, 342, nn. 55–59.
7. *Design for two Statues Representing 'Virtus' and 'Honos'*, Museum Plantin-Moretus, Antwerp, inv. no. MPM. TEK 152; Held, *Drawings*, 1959, I, p. 147, no. 138; II, pl. 148, dated 1612–1615; id., *Drawings*, 1986, pp. 120–121, no. 133, fig. 104 (p. 214), commenting that they 'could have been done several years later [than 1612–1615]'; Baudouin, *Rubens en zijn tijd*, 1971, pp. 81–84, no. 62, fig. 6.
8. For the statue of Honos (limewood, H.120 cm; inv. no. MPM.V.III.01.007) see Kitlitschka, *Van Mildert*, 1972, pp. 222–224, fig. 145, as Hans van Mildert. The Plantin printing house paid Van Mildert in 1622 for various tasks (Leyssens, *Van Mildert*, 1941, p. 105), but it is not possible to tell if these included carving the figures of *Honos* and *Virtus*. The statues have been regarded as originals by Van Mildert, but also as work of a much later date (Held, *Drawings*, 1986, under no. 133; L. van Liebergen, in Stiegemann, ed., *Rubens*, 2020, pp. 437–438, no. 93 (as 'unbekannter Künstler, Ende 18. Jahrhundert').
9. Bochius, *Historica narratio*, 1602, p. 234, repr. p. 235.
10. Sitting opposite one another in the *Henri IV* series (Merle du Bourg, *Henri IV Series (CRLB)*, 2017, pp. 190–196, and esp. p. 192, nos 2a–2b, figs 9–10); in the ceiling, standing at the entrance to the temple of Virtue and Honour (Martin, *Banqueting Hall (CRLB)*,

CATALOGUE No. 37

11. 2005, I, p. 243, n. 8, and passim; II, fig. 19; Büttner, *Allegories (CRLB)*, 2018, I, pp. 334–343, no. 44; II, fig. 199).
11. Gevartius, *Pompa Introitus*, 1642, pl. 108a; Martin, *Pompa (CRLB)*, 1972, p. 155, figs 73–74. There, Honos is shown with a cornucopia, a short staff in his hand, and with laurel wreath; the helmeted Virtus with *parazonium* and with the club and lion skin of Hercules. The heads of Honos and Virtus appear on the 'good' (i.e. right) side of the *Temple of Janus*, in a medallion, surrounded by attributes of the fine arts: a palette, brushes, lyre and compass (ibid., p. 165, fig. 85).
12. See under Chapter X, p. 315, n. 44.
13. Muller, *Collector*, 1989, pp. 33, 154, cat. III, no. 20.
14. Cartari, *Imagini*, 1963, p. 234; it is not clear from Cartari's text if this sentence refers specifically to one of the three figures reproduced on that page. For the English translation quoted here, see id., *Images*, transl. Mulryan, 2012, p. 351.
15. The most famous was a colossal Genius, more than four metres high, formerly in the Villa Madama in Rome, now in the Museo Archeologico Nazionale, Naples (Bober – Rubinstein, *Antique Sculpture*, no. 188). For a full discussion of the meaning and iconography of the Lares, see Simon, *Götter*, 1990, pp. 119–125, figs 146–153; see esp. the bronze statuette with *patera* and double cornucopia (ibid., fig. 153).
16. Gevartius, *Pompa Introitus*, 1642, p. 14, pl. 11a; Martin, *Pompa (CRLB)*, 1972, p. 39, figs 2–3.
17. *Genius Loci* was not the only figure shown with a *patera*; the object also appears in the hand of personifications of related 'propitious' concepts; see also *Bonus Eventus* (Good Outcome or Success), with a *patera* in the right hand and a corn ear and poppies in the left, in a painting installed on the rear of the *Arch of the Portuguese*. Jan Gaspar Gevartius (1593–1666) describes it as 'cum paterâ, Spicis & Papavere' and refers to ancient coins (Gevartius, *Pompa*, 1942, pp. 22–23, ill. opp. p. 22); the arch was not designed by Rubens and so is not reproduced in Martin, *Pompa (CRLB)*, 1972.
18. See Chapter XI, pp. 327–329.

No. 37. *Venus (and Cupid)*: Statue (cf. Figs 195–197)

Stone, approx. 200 × 64 cm.

Lost; replaced at unknown date (between 1692 and c. 1830) by a statue of Ceres (No. R4)[1]

Date unknown

VISUAL SOURCES:
(1) Rubens and studio, *The Walk in the Garden*, Munich, 1630s (Appendix III.6; Fig. 25; details: Figs 182, 196;
(2) Harrewijn print, 1684; minuscule, in the background (Appendix III.1; Fig. 17);
(3) Harrewijn print, 1692 (Appendix III.2; Fig18; details (Fig. 183; Fig. 195).

LITERATURE: Prims, *Prieel van Rubens*, 1948, pp. 141–142; Muller, *Collector*, 1989, pp. 33–34, 155, cat. III, no. 25, fig. 21 (detail from the Harrewijn print; as 'Venus and Cupid' and as 'Anonymous Early Modern Master?'); Heinen, *Gesundheit*, 2004, p. 85.

Two seventeenth-century images show a statue certainly representing Venus, between the columns on the left-hand side of the garden pavilion (Figs 195–196). However, these two Venus statues, partly hidden by a column, are not completely identical. In the Harrewijn print of 1692 (Fig. 195) the goddess is accompanied by Cupid, who raises his hand to offer an arrow with its point upwards. The curls of Venus's hair are tied in a bun, and drapery hangs over her right arm, also concealing her right hip. Part of her left arm and hand can be seen (above Cupid's head) to the right of the column which partly conceals her.

The painting *The Walk in the Garden* in the Alte Pinakothek in Munich (Fig. 196) provides an image of the garden pavilion in about 1630 and it shows a Venus without Cupid, but again with drapery over her arm in the same place, and likewise with the bent knee of her left leg in front of the other. She holds a part of the drapery over her hips, and her left hand is out of sight.

The differences between the two statues of Venus cannot be explained. Perhaps there were two different statues, but equally it is possible that what we see in the '*The Walk*' deviates somewhat from the actual situation. It should be noted that unfortunately the frontal view of the garden pavilion in the Berlin double portrait of c. 1655 (Appendix III.10; Fig. 181) is no help in this matter: the edge of the painting truncates the little building so that the left end, where the statue stood, is not in view.

The appearance of a Venus in the two images mentioned has not always been regarded as valid evidence that Rubens at some point installed a statue of this goddess in his garden pavilion. Several authors have firmly believed that the figure present in Rubens's lifetime was a Ceres, the statue that stood there throughout the nineteenth century and right up until the restoration of the house, when it was removed and disappeared without trace (No. R4; Fig. 235).[2]

As far as the statue in 'The Walk' is concerned, two arguments for rejecting a Venus in Rubens's garden pavilion around 1630 have been put forward. The first is a belief that the statue shown in 'The Walk' is not Venus but a nude Ceres, a groundless misapprehension, in our view.[3] Secondly, it is said that the painting indeed shows a Venus, but does not provide a reliable documentary source as it does not reflect the true situation.[4]

It is certainly a valid approach to say that the painting with its idyllic image of Rubens walking with his young bride should not be regarded as 'realistic'. It would be reasonable to think that in this painting the artist chose to introduce an imaginary statue of Venus in order to set the scene within a garden of love, just as the argument can be made that the peacock and little dog are allegorical symbols.[5] However, this critical questioning of the imagery of 'The Walk' has no bearing on the statue in the pavilion. As already stated, the Harrewijn print of 1692 confirms that there was a Venus in exactly the same spot, although of a different type. The documentary accuracy of the Harrewijn prints is beyond doubt, and even if it were not, since the pavilion was the property of a clergyman, it cannot be so that in the print a Ceres would have been replaced by a Venus in order to allude to the garden of love.

Ceres's supporters, however, did not give up easily. Floris Prims, who was absolutely determined to see a Ceres in the pavilion, not Venus, described Hillewerve's statue as 'a draped figure' which had to be Ceres.[6] It must be said that he mis-read the print: the 'drapery' that he interpreted as belonging to the statue is in reality part of the long cloak of the priest shown sitting behind at a table (Fig. 195). Moreover he produces no explanation for the presence of a child holding an arrow. Authors who followed Prims tried to clarify the matter: without any justification they saw the child as 'a putto' accompanying Ceres, erroneously relating the figure to the putti in Rubens's *Homage to Ceres* in the State Hermitage Museum in St Petersburg (Appendix III.13; Figs 23, 121).[7]

Once again, it should be stressed that there can be no doubt about the identification of Hillewerve's statue. It is a Venus with the infant Cupid by her side holding up an arrow. Jeffrey Muller also correctly saw it as the goddess of love with Cupid by her side, and included the statue in his catalogue of works of art in Rubens's collection.[8]

An interesting observation, and one not so far made, is that the statue that stood in the pavilion in Hillewerve's time corresponds closely with a Venus type that we know from the celebrated statuette of about 40 cm high, by Georg Petel, in the Ashmolean Museum in Oxford (Figs 197–198).[9] The general bearing of the goddess, her coiffure and the drapery over her right arm, Cupid's crossed legs (with the right in front of the left) and upstretched arm, all match the statuette by Petel. There is a small difference to be observed in the drapery over her arm (for which see below); furthermore, in the statuette Cupid is not holding an arrow, but he seems to reach for the drapery which Venus holds in her left hand, probably to undress her.

However, this observation about the related statuette, signed by Petel, can bring us little clarity about the statue in the pavilion, at least not concerning its dating, maker or designer. It is generally assumed that the precious object in Oxford, was in Rubens's collection and that Rubens sold it in 1626 to the Duke of Buckingham. If Rubens indeed owned it, he might have acquired it during Petel's visit to Antwerp in 1624.[10]

The important question in the present context is the identity of the statuette's designer. It is often thought that Petel carved it (in 1624) from a design by Rubens, an attribution that is principally based on the assumption that it was in his possession, but there is no evidence to support this attribution. As Nicholas Penny rightly observed: even if it came from Rubens's collection, 'it would not follow that it was made for Rubens, or to his designs: it might simply have been acquired by him or presented to him'.[11]

From a stylistic point of view a design by Rubens seems rather unlikely. The type of woman and her proportions are not consistent with Rubens's figures. The perfectly balanced, idealised beauty of the goddess seems somewhat archaic in comparison with other female nudes by Rubens of the 1620s.[12] Petel's infant Cupid, crossing his legs and with upraised arm, somewhat resembles Cupid in Rubens's *Youthful and Fertile Love (Venus Frigida)* in the Musées royaux des Beaux-Arts de Belgique, Brussels, dated c. 1625–1632,[13] but the similarity is too faint for it to be described as a Rubensian motif.

The connection between the ivory statuette and Hillewerve's life-size Venus remains unclear. It seems unlikely that the statue in the pavilion was made by Petel; indeed, what we know of his oeuvre does not suggest that he was a maker of life-size stone statues. That said, there is another matter which makes this question even more complicated: no life-size version corresponding to the Oxford *Venus and Cupid* survives, although a large statue (in stone or plaster) is shown in Van Haecht's *Art Gallery of Cornelis van der Geest* (Fig. 199).[14] That statue matches the Oxford statuette in every detail except its proportions: the figure is elongated and the head is smaller in relation to the body (about 1/7 instead of 1/6.5).

The *Venus and Cupid* shown in Van der Geest's *Art Gallery* is one of a series of six over-lifesize statues on bases, shown standing together, three of them 'modern' and three ancient, including the famous *Apollo Belvedere* and *Hercules Farnese*. One of the visitors to the gallery, the man standing close-by and gesturing towards one of the statues, has often been seen as Georg Petel. We should add that there is no agreement about how we should interpret the statues shown in the gallery: are they casts or were they carved in stone? It has even been suggested that, in contrast to the paintings in the gallery, they did not exist at all and that Van Haecht simply modelled the three modern statues on statuettes, which is of course possible.[15] Hence, the existence of a life-size statue in Rubens's house in Hillewerve's time adds a new dimension to the discussion.

In the context of the above, we should also mention two drawings in red chalk by Willem Panneels in the collection known as the Rubens Cantoor. They illustrate Petel's Venus type from two different angles, frontally and viewed slightly from the left (Figs 197–198).[16] Exactly what object in Rubens's house was copied in these sheets is difficult to assess. Did Panneels copy drawings by Rubens that he found in Rubens's Cantoor, as with many other sheets in Copenhagen? If so, we can only conclude from this that Rubens had copied a Venus of the Petel type, but not that he had designed the statuette or the life-size statue. Or did Panneels simply copy the Oxford statuette, to which his drawings closely correspond? It is worth noting that, if the provenance of the statuette given above is correct, it was no longer present in Rubens's house during his period abroad when Panneels probably made most (or all) of his 'Cantoor' drawings. Did Rubens perhaps have another example of the Petel Venus, in ivory or another material? There is in any case a second version of the statuette, a bronze cast, in the Victoria and Albert Museum in London.[17] As Fiona Healy has noticed, this bronze version as well as the two Rubens Cantoor drawings and Van der Geest's large statue all lack one detail present in the Oxford statuette: the wad of cloth between the goddess's elbow and waist.[18]

Whatever the truth, it seems most unlikely that the two Cantoor drawings were made as copies of the life-size statue, which was possibly then standing in the garden pavilion. They differ in several details, for example Cupid's hand which matches that of the statuette.

Summarising the above facts, we can deduce that at a certain moment (after 1624?) Rubens had set up a Venus in his garden pavilion which was very much of the same type as Petel's statuette. This does not answer the important question: who designed the life-size statue? If Petel carved the well-known statuette to his own design and not Rubens's – which seems entirely possible – it follows that the attribution of the design of Hillewerve's statue remains uncertain. Did Rubens make a design largely inspired by Petel's work, with some minor alterations? Because of the numerous unanswered questions, the Venus in the pavilion is included in the catalogue of Rubens's oeuvre, with reservations. As to the identity of the maker of the stone statue, which was removed from the pavilion (probably in the eigthenth century), and has disappeared without trace, we naturally remain completely in the dark.

In summary:

1) It was a statue of Venus and not Ceres that stood in the pavilion.

2) Assuming that it existed, there was at first perhaps a *Venus* of the type that appears in *The Walk in the Garden*; but this was later replaced by a *Venus and Cupid* of the Petel type. Both are lost.

3) There is no evidence that Rubens designed either statue, despite the fact that the Petel statuette has been thought to be designed by Rubens.

1. See also Chapter X, pp. 311–312.
2. For discussion of these statues (Ceres or Venus), see also Chapter X, pp. 311–312 and No. R4.
3. For the statue as a nude Ceres figure, see for example, De Clercq, *Tuinpaviljoen*, 2012, p. 10; the identification can be disregarded because Ceres's attributes, a sickle or a corn wreath, are missing.
4. Prims, *Prieel van Rubens*, 1948, p. 142.
5. The peacock ('sacred to Juno, the patroness of wedlock') at the feet of Helena Fourment can be seen as a symbol of marriage, and the little dog to its right as an allusion to marital fidelity. For discussion of the painting's reliability as a historical document, see Chapter X, pp. 301–302, n. 19.
6. Prims, *Prieel van Rubens*, 1948, p. 141.
7. Uppenkamp – Van Beneden, *Architectural Symbolism*, 2011, p. 121.
8. Muller, *Collector*, 1989, p. 155, cat. III, no. 25 (as 'Anonymous Early Modern Master?').
9. Oxford, Ashmolean Museum, inv. no. WA1932.194; Muller, *Collector*, 1989, p. 153, cat. III, no. 13, pl. 135 (as 'probably after a design by Rubens'); id., *Rubens's Collection*, p. 56, fig. 80; see also Feuchtmayr – Schädler, *Petel*, 1973, pp. 85–87, no. 4, figs 11, 13–14; Rowlands, *Rubens Drawings*, 1977, p. 131, no. 176; Penny, *Cat. Ashmolean Museum*, 1992, II, pp. 145–148, no. 361; Krempel, *Petel*, 2007, pp. 149–150, no. 4.
10. Most authors assume that Rubens acquired the statuette in 1624 and sold it to Buckingham in 1626 (see e.g. Feuchtmayr – Schädler, *Petel*, 1973, p. 86). According to Nicholas Penny, however, this provenance is not certain ('although surely likely') (Penny, *Cat. Ashmolean Museum*, 1992., II, pp. 145–146).
11. Penny, *Cat. Ashmolean Museum*, 1992, II, p. 145.
12. Useful for comparison are the ivory nude figures, also carved by Petel, on the salt cellar with *The Triumph (or Birth) of Venus* in Stockholm (Royal Collections Sweden, inv. no. S.S. 143; Feuchtmayr – Schädler, *Petel*, 1973, pp. 98–102, no. 14, figs 51–56;

Cavalli-Björkman, ed., *Rubens i Sverige*, 1977a, pp. 133–139, figs 107, 110; Lammertse – Vergara, *Rubens Sketches*, 2018, pp. 49–50, fig. 27). Scholten likewise remarks that the Venus statuette is 'fairly classical and restrained' and bears little resemblance to drawn or painted nudes by Rubens (Scholten, *Werkplaats-academie*, 2004, p. 37). Moreover, it is reasonable to ask if Petel's signature (on the base behind the goddess's feet) implies that he was both maker and designer of the statuette.
13. Musées royaux des Beaux-Arts de Belgique, inv. no. 1372. See Büttner, *Allegories (CRLB)*, 2018, no. 50, fig. 253.
14. Van Beneden, *Van Haecht*, 2009, p. 69; the same statue can be seen in the background of another *Art Gallery* by the same master, of about 1630 in Mount Stuart, The Bute Collection (see Appendix III.31).
15. Concerning the ancient sculptures in Van der Geest's *Art Gallery*, it has been regarded as distinctly unlikely that life-size sculptures such as these (whether in stone or plaster) could be seen in Antwerp at that time (Haskell – Penny, *Antique*, 1982, p. 35, fig. 18). Fiona Healy, who devoted a detailed study to the six statues, also assumed that in all likelihood they did not exist, but were added to the gallery by Van Haecht as a tribute to his patron Van der Geest (Healy, *Vive l'Esprit*, 2006, pp. 429–430). In the gallery two further, 'modern' statues also appear, which may be based on works by Petel, a *Ceres* and a *Bacchus on a Barrel*; of these, no statuettes or other versions are known. Scholten also regards the large Venus in the *'kunstkamer'* as fictitious (Scholten, *Werkplaats-academie*, 2004, p. 37).
16. Copenhagen, Statens Museum for Kunst, Kongelige Kobberstiksamling, inv. nos KKSgb6247 (frontal; Rubens Cantoor, III.85) and KKSgb6246 (from the left; Rubens Cantoor, III.86). Garff – de la Fuente Pedersen, *Panneels*, 1988, respectively nos 191 and 190. See also Huvenne, *Cantoor*, 1993, p. 18, fig. 2; F. Healy in Belkin – Healy, *House of Art*, 2004, pp. 304–306, nos 82–83.
17. Inv. no. A.27–1956. See Feuchtmayr – Schädler, *Petel*, 1973, p. 146, no. 69, fig. 9.
18. F. Healy in Belkin – Healy, *House of Art*, 2004, p. 304. However, it is possible that this detail was also originally present in the Oxford statuette; the discussion is on-going.

No. 38. *Bacchus*: Statue (Figs 201–203)

Oldest part: Avesnes stone.[1] Substantially restored (see below); approx. 203 × 83 cm.

Antwerp, Rubenshuis, garden pavilion. Inv. no. RH.PR1.3. *Original possibly lost and replaced (see below)*

Date unknown

CATALOGUE No. 38

VISUAL SOURCES:
(1) Rubens and studio, *The Walk in the Garden*, Munich, 1630s (Appendix III.6; Fig. 25; details: Figs 182 and 205);
(2) Anonymous 17th-century artist, *Portrait of a Couple in a Garden*, Berlin, c. 1655 (Appendix III.10; Fig. 22; details: Fig. 181 and 208);
(3) Harrewijn print, 1684, minuscule, in the background (Appendix III.1; Fig. 17);
(4) Harrewijn print, 1692 (Appendix III.2; Fig. 18; details: Figs 183, 206);
(5) Philippe van Brée, *Rubens Painting in his Garden*, Brussels, 1833 (Appendix III.42).
See also the early photographs under No. 35, Visual Sources (5) – (7).

LITERATURE: Van Grimbergen, *Rubens*, 1840, p. 387, n. 10 (as not original); Thys, *Historiek der straten*, 1893, p. 429 (as not original); Van den Branden, *Schilderschool*, 1883, p. 508; Delen, *Rubens' huis*, 1933, pp. 31, 54 (as replaced); Delen, *Rubens' huis*, 1940, p. 36 (as replaced); Prims, *Rubenshuis*, 1946, p. 36; Prims, *Prieel van Rubens*, 1948, pp. 141–142; Kitlitschka, *Rubens*, 1963, p. 139 (as 'stammt aus neuerer Zeit'); Baudouin, *Cat. Antwerp, Rubenshuis*, 1974, under no. 23; Baudouin, *Rubens House*, 1977, p. 183; Tijs, *Rubens en Jordaens*, 1984, p. 234, repr. p. 235; Stutz, *Residenz*, 1985, p. 142; Muller, *Collector*, 1989, p. 31, n. 32 (surviving statue, as 'not contemporary'), p. 155, cat. III, no. 26 (statue in Harrewijn print, as 'Women holding a patera'); Baudouin, *Rubens House*, 2005, p. 177; Uppenkamp – Van Beneden, *Architectural Symbolism*, 2011, pp. 118, 121; Coekelberghs, *Review Palazzo Rubens*, 2012, pp. 5, 16, n. 17 (as probably not by Faydherbe, but perhaps more likely by Van Mildert); De Clercq, *Moulages*, 2012, p. 6; Mertens – Stoppie, *Conservatievisie*, 2019, p. 62.

In its present arrangement the garden pavilion includes a statue of the youthful Bacchus (Figs 201–203) between the columns on the right-hand side. He is represented as a slender youth, nonchalantly leaning against a tree stump, his right leg crossed over the left. There is no doubt that he is Bacchus, the god of harvests, especially the vintage, as is clear from the bunches of grapes which he holds in each hand. His right arm rests on top of the tree stump. An animal skin, probably that of a panther, is tied around his hips by the animal's long tail. His head with an abundance of shoulder-length curls is crowned with vine tendrils.

The present statue was certainly standing in the same position in the first half of the nineteenth century, as can be deduced from images of the garden pavilion; see for instance the earliest known nineteenth-century image of the Bacchus in Philippe van Brée's *Rubens Painting in his Garden*, dated 1833 (Appendix III.42) and also the photographs made by Edmond Fierlants in 1860 (Appendix III.51; Text ill. 22). A major question that remains unanswered is if the present, substantially restored, statue is the same as the Bacchus that can be made out in the seventeenth-century illustrations, mentioned above under 'Visual Sources'. According to Victor Van Grimbergen, followed by Augustin Thys, neither the Bacchus nor a number of the other statues then in the pavilion were original, but it is not known on what information his statement was based. It is certainly the case that discrepancies with the seventeenth-century visual documents can be detected.

A statue of a nude youth on a pedestal (Fig. 205) can be seen in *The Walk in the Garden*, which provides an image of the pavilion around 1630. He stands half-hidden by the columns: his most striking feature is the leg pushed forward diagonally with the knee sticking out, as in the surviving statue. No animal skin can be detected around his waist.

A clearer picture is provided by the Berlin double portrait of around 1655, which shows the Bacchus in its entirety and from the front: a youthful figure by and large matching the surviving statue, although in reverse (Fig. 208). It has the crossed legs, the animal skin draped in the same way, and one arm resting on a tree stump. Yet, differences can be observed: for example, the youth's head with short hair rather than curls falling to the shoulders. The most striking variation is that in the painting he is shown clutching a bunch of grapes in only one hand. On the side by the tree stump he holds up a drinking cup (a *patera*), another of the wine god's attributes.

In the Harrewijn print of 1692, as in *The Walk in the Garden*, the statue is mostly hidden by the columns, and the figure cannot be made out properly (cf. Figs 205 and 206). Its pose agrees with both the surviving statue and the Berlin version: Bacchus leans on his right arm, with right leg pushed forward, and he is draped with an animal skin. The figure in the print differs from the surviving statue, but agrees with the Berlin version in having shorter hair as well as a drinking cup in his right hand, which is clearly visible in the bright space between the two columns.

Jeffrey Muller correctly identified the object in the statue's right hand seen in the print, describing it as a *patera*. But, probably confused by the bulge of hair at the back of the head which looks like a bun, he wrongly assumed the figure to be female and listed the statue in his catalogue of sculpture in Rubens's collection as a lost 'Woman Holding a Patera'.[2]

The drinking cup in Bacchus's hand in the two seventeenth-century images thus constitutes an important difference with the extant statue. It is not clear what can be concluded from this. Is the surviving statue not the original but a variant with longer, curly hair down to the shoulders and with a bunch of grapes in either hand? Perhaps; but it also seems possible that the 'core' of the statue is indeed original, and that the differences can be explained by a major restoration which altered certain elements and took place sometime between 1692 (the date of the second Harrewijn print) and 1833, when the Bacchus was depicted in his current form in *Rubens Painting in his Garden* by Philippe van Brée (Appendix III.42).

The right forearm and hand are certainly a restoration. It is therefore possible that the original hand holding up a drinking cup was badly damaged or even lost, and this deficiency was made good by replacing the statue's right hand with one of the restorer's invention. One element that argues in favour of this hypothesis is that in the surviving statue the right hand, with a bunch of grapes, seems to be more or less copied from the left, which was thus rather unimaginatively replicated. It is more difficult to know what to make of the head, which looks different from the one in the seventeenth-century images. Although not carved from the same block, it is of the same stone type as the torso. Thus it is impossible to judge whether or not this is original.[3]

In summary: we can safely assume that it was a Bacchus with drinking cup that Rubens placed in his pavilion, but we cannot confirm that the statue standing there now is the same (partly altered by restoration).

From the above it will be clear that a discussion about the maker of the Bacchus (or possibly of different versions of the statue) in Rubens's pavilion has little point. Two names have nonetheless been put forward. Lucas Faydherbe (1617–1697) has often been suggested as the maker of all of the pavilion statues, but without evidence; and for the Bacchus, Artus Quellinus I (1609–1668) has also sometimes been proposed.[4] Both, however, can be ruled out as makers of the original Bacchus, for we know from *The Walk in the Garden* that there already was a Bacchus in the pavilion around 1630 (Fig. 205), and neither artist can be considered for the carving of statues before the end of that decade.[5]

It is equally difficult to determine if the original statue derived from an invention of Rubens and it is therefore with some reservation that we have included the statue in the catalogue.

One argument in favour of an attribution to Rubens is that the figure of the slender young man leaning to one side has parallels in ancient sculptures that Rubens may have seen. Several statues are known that show a young man in a similar nonchalant pose. Examples include a *Faun with Pipes* in the Musée du Louvre[6] and a *Resting Faun* (with right arm resting on a tree trunk and panther skin draped diagonally over his chest) in the Fondazione Torlonia in Rome (Fig. 207), of which Rubens made a drawing.[7] The closest parallel for the crossed legs can be found in a *Mercury* in the Galleria degli Uffizi in Florence, which is sometimes attributed to Praxiteles, but is now usually placed in the period just after him.[8] There are indications that Rubens knew this statue and may also have drawn it. There is no known drawing by him after the statue in Florence, but an echo of it can be found in Rubens's early, or 'small' *Judgement of Paris* in the Prado, Madrid, where Mercury appears in a comparable nonchalant pose with legs crossed.[9]

CATALOGUE No. 39

In a note preserved in the Rubens documentation at the Rubenianum, Antwerp, Ludwig Burchard recorded that the surviving Bacchus in the garden pavilion is distinctly Rubensian. In his opinion, it is possible that both its dependency on classical examples as well as its reflection of Rubens's style signal an 'invention of the master himself'.

1. Avesnes stone, and not Pierre de Caen, used in the nineteenth century, as stated by Tijs, *Rubens en Jordaens*, 1984, p. 257; see De Clercq, *Moulages*, 2012, p. 6.
2. Muller, *Collector*, 1989, p. 155, cat. III, no. 26 (as 'Anonymous Early Modern Master?'); consequently he makes no mention of a Bacchus statue.
3. Both torso and head are of Avesnes stone. The head and part of the shoulders are carved from separate blocks of stone – a horizontal 'seam' can be seen underneath the throat – but it was customary, because of the limited height of blocks of this type of stone, to piece several blocks together (information provided by Lode de Clercq).
4. Frans Baudouin was convinced that both the Hercules and the Bacchus have stylistic features that justify an attribution to Artus Quellinus I. For this, see also No. 40. For the Bacchus he saw a similarity in facial type with the youthful gods Apollo (1650; Goossens, *Amsterdamse stadhuis*, 1996, p. 34, fig. V, p. 52, fig. 43) and Mercury (between 1650 and 1664; ibid., p. 58, fig. 49) in the panels in the galleries of the Amsterdam Town Hall (now the Royal Palace).
5. For the work of these sculptors and on their dating, see Chapter XI, pp. 330–335.
6. Haskell – Penny, *Antique*, 1991, pp. 212–213, no. 38, fig. 110.
7. For this statue, attributed to Praxiteles, and a copy of a drawing by Rubens in the 'Rubens Cantoor' in Copenhagen, see Van der Meulen, *Antique (CRLB)*, 1994, II, pp. 32–33, no. 5; III, figs 15–16; Rubens mentions it in his *Theoretical Notebook* (ibid., p. 33); better known is the version in the Musei Capitolini, Rome (Haskell – Penny, ibid., pp. 209–210, no. 36, fig. 108). For a full discussion of this sculpture type, and the many variants, see Pasquier – Martinez, eds, *Praxitèle*, 2007, pp. 236–267.
8. Marble, H. 155 (Haskell – Penny, ibid., pp. 266–267, no. 61, fig. 138). This sculpture was first mentioned in 1536, when it was in the statue court of the Belvedere in the Vatican. Shortly after 1550 it was removed to Florence.
9. Madrid, Museo Nacional del Prado, inv. no. 1731; Díaz Padrón, *Cat. Madrid, Prado (Pintura flamenca)*, 1995, II, p. 1024, no. 1731, repr. p. 1025; Healy, *Judgement of Paris*, 1997, pp. 73 ff., pl. 3.

No. 39. *Bust of Hercules*: sculpture (Fig. 210)

Stone or stucco (?), measurements unknown.

If it ever existed: formerly above a blind door against the rear wall of the garden pavilion, lost

c. 1618 (?)

VISUAL SOURCE: Rubens and studio, *The Walk in the Garden*, Munich, 1630s (Appendix III.6; Fig. 182; detail: Fig. 210).

LITERATURE: Held, *Sketches*, 1980, I, p. 332; Muller, *Collector*, 1989, p. 31, fig. 18.

In *The Walk in the Garden* a bust can be seen placed above a blind door, against the rear wall of the garden pavilion. Although situated in a rather dark area, and sketchily painted, it is assumed that it represents a bust of Hercules. As suggested by Julius S. Held, we seem to be looking at the image of an arrangement in the pavilion that existed before the current situation with the over-lifesize statue of Hercules in a niche and garlands draped above and around (No. 40).

Probably the image in *The Walk in the Garden* is indeed that of the ancient hero. This is suggested not only by the presence of the large statue seen there today, which can be dated to the later 1630s. There is one further detail that points in this direction. Arnout Balis was convinced that the bust with its peculiar profile showed Hercules, but with a physiognomic quirk: a snub nose. The same type appears in a small pen drawing, attributed to Rubens, after an unidentified (sixteenth-century?) model, in the British Museum, London (Fig. 209).[1]

We should, however, remain cautious. As stated, the image in the painting is difficult to read. Furthermore, since not every detail in *The Walk in the Garden* corresponds to reality[2] there is no certainty that this bust – a snub-nosed Hercules or another bearded man – ever existed.

1. Rowlands, *Rubens Drawings*, 1977, p. 91, no. 105, fig. 105. With thanks to Arnout Balis for this information.
2. See Chapter X, pp. 301–302.

No. 40. *Hercules*: Statue (Fig. 211)

Avesnes stone (Hercules) and oak wood (garlands and club); approx. 203 × 112 cm.

Antwerp, Rubenshuis, garden pavilion. Inv. no. RH. PR1.2.

Fragment: Hercules's right hand with an apple (Fig. 215); Avesnes stone, 18 × 28 cm; Antwerp, Rubenshuis. Inv. no. RH.B.055. The original hand has been replaced.

Late 1630s?

VISUAL SOURCES:
(1) Anonymous, *Portrait of a Couple in a Garden*, Berlin, c. 1655 (Appendix III.10; Fig. 22; detail: Fig. 212);
(2) Harrewijn print, 1684, minuscule, in the background (Appendix III.1; Figs 17, 180);
(3) Mathieu Ignace van Bree, *Rubens Surrounded by his Colleagues in the Garden Pavilion*, Weimar, Klassik Stiftung, 1825 (Appendix III.41).
See also the early photographs under No. 35, Visual Sources (5) – (7).

COPY: Modern plaster cast after ? Hans van Mildert after Rubens (Fig. 214), after 1947; Antwerp, Rubenshuis, inv. no. RH.B.053; H. 237 cm. The commission for the plaster mold was given to the sculptor Frans Claessens (1885–1968) in December 1947; the cast was made later;
LIT.: Uppenkamp – Van Beneden, *Architectural Symbolism*, 2011, p. 81, fig. 100; De Clercq, *Moulages*, 2012, p. 14; Grimmett, *Drunken Hercules*, 2020, p. 52, fig. 12.

LITERATURE: Van Grimbergen, *Rubens*, 1840, p. 387, n. 10 (as by Faydherbe); Thys, *Historiek der straten*, 1893, p. 429 (as by Faydherbe); Van den Branden, *Schilderschool*, 1883, p. 508; Rooses, *Oeuvre*, 1886–92, V, p. 186; Delen, *Rubens' huis*, 1933, pp. 31, 54 (as 'vervangen'); Delen, *Rubens' huis*, 1940, p. 36 (as 'vervangen'); Prims, *Prieel van Rubens*, 1948, pp. 141–142; Baudouin, *Rubens's House*, 1955, p. 31 (as probably by Faydherbe); Kitlitschka, *Rubens*, 1963, pp. 139–141 (as probably not by Fayderbe); Baudouin, *Cat. Antwerp, Rubenshuis*, 1974, no. 23 (as Faydherbe); Baudouin, *Rubenshuis*, 1977, p. 29 (as probably by Faydherbe); Baudouin, *Summary Guide*, 1977, p. 28 (as probably by Faydherbe); Baudouin, *Rubens House*, 1977, p. 183; Held, *Sketches*, 1980, I, p. 332 (as 'placed in the pavilion in modern times'); Tijs, *Rubens en Jordaens*, 1984, p. 234, repr. pp. 125, 235, 255–256 (as 'mogelijk het werk van Faydherbe'); Muller, *Collector*, 1989, pp. 31–33, 155, no. III.17 (as 'Anonymous Seventeenth Century Flemish Master? [lost and replaced?]'); Van Riet – Kockelbergh, *Faydherbe*, 1997, p. 51 (as probably not by Faydherbe); Härting, *Rubens' Garten*, 2000, pp. 62, 65, n. 16 (as Faydherbe); Muller, *Rubens' Collection*, 2004, pp. 21, 32, 75, fig. 14 (as 'probably carved during the late 1630s by Lucas Fayd'herbe after Rubens's design'); Heinen, *Gesundheit*, 2004, pp. 103–106, 126, fig. 33 (as 'Faydherbe?'); Baudouin, *Rubens House*, 2005, p. 177; Uppenkamp – Van Beneden, *Architectural Symbolism*, 2011, pp. 80 (n. 19), 118, 121 (as 'anonymous' and 'possibly designed by Rubens'); Coekelberghs, *Review Palazzo Rubens*, 2012, pp. 5, 16, n. 17 (as probably not by Faydherbe, but more likely by Van Mildert); Büttner, *Allegories (CRLB)*, 2018, I, p. 136 (as ascribed with good reason to 'Faydherbe'); Mertens – Stoppie, *Conservatievisie*, 2019, pp. 62, 68, nn. 16–18 (as undatable); Grimmett, *Drunken Hercules*, 2020, pp. 52–53 (as 'in all likehood Lucas Faidherbe').

From its central position in the garden pavilion, standing on a socle in a shallow niche against the wall that backs onto the Kolveniershof, the larger than life-size statue of Hercules dominates the space. The hero leans on a gnarled club (of wood, imitating stone) that rests under his left shoulder. He has an unusually muscular and powerful torso. Decorative garlands are fixed to the wall above and either side of the statue.[1]

Hercules is just about covered by the skin of the Nemean lion slain by him. The head of the terrifying beast with wide-open jaws and shaggy mane is slung over his left shoulder; the skin hangs around the hero's back, and its lower ends are fastened at his waist with one of the paws hanging down over his thigh. The lion's long tail curls down to the ground and the tuft at the end appears between the hero's feet. In each hand Hercules holds one of the apples taken from the garden of the Hesperides: one is held against his thigh and the other – more difficult to see – is clutched by the hand resting against his hip.

There can be no doubt that this impressive piece of seventeenth-century sculpture was already in place in the pavilion at the time of Rubens's death. For it can be seen clearly in the image of the garden pavilion in the background of the Berlin double portrait of about 1655 (Appendix III.10; Figs 181 and 212). We can make out the giant club and the lion skin over the shoulder, the raised left elbow as well as part of the surrounding garlands on the rear wall. Its appearance in about 1655 means that the statue was already standing there in 1640. Indeed, it is extremely unlikely that this important sculpture would have been installed in the pavilion between 1640 and 1655, when the house was in the ownership of Rubens's heirs who were planning to sell, and who let it, from 1648 onwards, to the Cavendishes.[2]

The Harrewijn prints are less informative about the sculpture. The statue cannot be seen in the second print, of 1692, in which we see a side view of the garden pavilion; the rear wall is largely hidden by the columns and by the figures of the two clergymen sitting at a table (Fig. 183). The garlands are only partially visible. However, from the first (1684) Harrewijn print we know that the statue was indeed there: the full-length Hercules can be made out, on a miniature scale, in the pavilion in the distance (Fig. 180).

The statue, however, has not always been accepted as original, that is as dating from Rubens's lifetime. Victor Van Grimbergen (in 1840), followed by Augustin Thys and others, claimed that the original statues of the pavilion had long since disappeared and been replaced.[3] Further recent authors, who were unaware of the detail in the background of the Berlin portrait, have sometimes mistakenly assumed that the Hercules could not be contemporary. This view was put forward for example by Julius Held, who assumed that the statue had been installed in the pavilion in 'modern times', and implicitly by Jeffrey Muller, who agreed that Rubens probably placed a full-length Hercules in his pavilion, but believed that it did not correspond to the one that survives.[4]

The fact that the Hercules was undoubtedly in place around 1655, and therefore must have been there already in 1640, does not mean that the sculptural decoration of the pavilion remained the same from the moment of its construction (around 1618) and for the whole of Rubens's lifetime. As explained elsewhere, it is possible that around 1630 the pavilion's rear wall looked quite different. *The Walk in the Garden* (Appendix III.6, Fig. 25) may provide a picture of an earlier arrangement, in which there was no full-length Hercules, but rather a bust, representing the ancient hero (No. 39; Fig. 210).

The fine full-length statue of Hercules which, according to the evidence given above, was placed in the pavilion by Rubens himself, has received little attention in the literature. Authors who have written about Rubens's house, including Max Rooses, ignored it completely. It was apparently not deemed worthy of more than a passing mention. None of the earlier authors who produced surveys of Flemish Baroque sculpture or wrote about Rubens's influence on contemporary sculpture, gave it any attention, with the exception of Werner Kitlitschka who underlined its artistic importance.[5]

The figure has echoes of two well-known ancient statues of Hercules. The obvious comparison, of course, is with one of the most celebrated sculptures from Antiquity, the *Hercules Farnese*, now in Naples, of which Rubens made several drawings (Fig. 216).[6] As with the statue in the pavilion, the formidable hero leans on his club and holds the apples picked in the garden of the Hesperides behind his back, in his right hand. But as Ludwig Burchard remarked in a note preserved in his Rubens documentation, there is a second statue that deserves to be mentioned. The pose of the Hercules in Rubens's garden pavilion in some respects matches the marble statue of Hercules with his son Telephus on his arm (also known as the Emperor Commodus as Hercules), which was found in 1507 and installed in Pope Julius II's new Belvedere statue court (Fig. 217).[7] It can be assumed that Rubens also knew that statue and possibly made drawings of it.[8]

The similarities between this Hercules 'Commodus' and the statue in the garden pavilion are as follows: the general position of the torso and legs; the right arm hanging down alongside the body; the hand in line with the thigh, and with the lion's head shown in the same place, hanging over the left shoulder. There are also differences: the Hercules 'Commodus' is shown more or less nude and he is not holding apples. Other elements of the Antwerp statue are more reminiscent of the *Hercules Farnese* than the 'Commodus', in particular the hero's more athletic torso and, more generally, the very detailed and exaggerated musculature. The masterful way in which the two ancient examples have been combined into a new figure may imply that the statue was designed by Rubens. But it is important to keep an open mind. It is therefore with a certain caution that, following the opinion of Ludwig Burchard (and Frans Baudouin), it is included in the catalogue.[9]

As will be clear from the literature cited above, it was often taken for granted by authors who regarded the Hercules statue as contemporary that it was the work of Lucas Faydherbe. However, opinions have varied. Frans Baudouin, who initially named Faydherbe in several publications, later changed his mind. Eventually he was convinced that both this Hercules and the Bacchus in the garden pavilion (No. 38) could be the work of Artus Quellinus I (1609–1668) after lost designs by Rubens. His research into possible artists among sculptors contemporary with the master led him to conclude that only Quellinus was in a position to turn Rubens's design into stone in such an accomplished manner.[10] He pointed to the handling of textures which he saw as characteristic, for example in the elegant curls of Bacchus's hair and the mane of the lion skin over Hercules's shoulders.[11]

In connection with the statue in the garden pavilion, we should mention another more than life-size Hercules statue in Mechelen, which stood in a niche at the end of the garden of the house of Jan Lucas Faydherbe (1654–1704), who was the son of the sculptor Lucas Faydherbe (Fig. 213). It was still there in 1948 in a very battered state (caused by fire in 1905), headless and missing its right arm. The 'remains' have now been 'removed' (leaving no trace) and only the empty niche is left. A nineteenth-century description mentions its attributes as 'le serpent dans la main, et le dragon terrassé'.[12] We cannot determine exactly when this statue was produced, but archival documents reveal that it was made by Lucas Faydherbe and that it was in position by 1657.

This lost Hercules needs to be mentioned here because it has been linked to the statue in the garden pavilion, and not simply because it represents the same hero and has a similar function, standing at the end of a garden. There is also undoubtedly a relationship with Rubens. Julius Held pointed out that the pose of the Hercules in Mechelen is the same as that in Rubens's oil sketch *Hercules Overcoming Discord* in the Museum Boijmans Van Beuningen in Rotterdam.[13] He presumed that Rubens originally made this sketch as model for a statue in his garden pavilion, but which was never completed. In his view, Rubens must have altered his plans and instead of a full-length Hercules, placed only a bust against the rear wall, thus matching the arrangement seen in *The Walk in the Garden* (Appendix III.6; Fig. 210). As mentioned above, he was unaware of the image in the Berlin double portrait, and wrongly concluded that the present statue was only placed in the pavilion later ('in modern times').

Various hypotheses have been put forward to explain the meaning of the Hercules in the garden pavilion. Showing Hercules here with an apple from the garden of the Hesperides in each hand is a reference to the successful accomplishment of one of his labours. Clearly Rubens here intended to represent Hercules at the moment when his hard labour had earned him a virtuous and peaceful life (see also below). The golden apples from the garden of the Hesperides show that he has achieved his goal.

The question remains if the Hercules, in combination with the other statues in the pavilion (Nos 36–38; Figs 187, 195, 202), forms part of a well thought-out programme, and what this might be. The idea that the garden pavilion should be seen as a 'rural temple' in which Hercules features – accompanied by Ops, Bacchus and Ceres – as protector of agriculture and the fertility of the earth was dismissed above.[14]

Other interpretations assume that the Hercules, which is visible from the entrance to the house through the central arch of the portico, can be connected with the iconography of the portico. An interesting link between the Hercules in the garden pavilion and the portico, a gateway to the garden, was proposed by Jeffrey Muller. He sees a connection with the verses of Juvenal inscribed on the rectangular tablet above the right arch of the portico: 'One must pray for a healthy mind in a healthy body, for a courageous soul which is not afraid of death and free of wrath and desires nothing'. The quotation on the portico ends here, but Juvenal's text continues thus: 'and think that the woes and hard labours of Hercules are better than the loves and the banquets and downy cushions of Sardanapalus. What I commend to you, you can give to yourself; for it is assuredly through virtue that lies the one and only path to a life of peace.'[15] Thus, Muller concludes, 'Hercules at rest after his labours would have been an appropriate symbol of virtuous peace at the center of Rubens's garden'. It seems indeed plausible that the presence of the resting hero was a key element of the Lipsian or Neo-Stoic concept that underlies the programme for Rubens's garden, as shown in detail by Ulrich Heinen.[16] Venus and Bacchus, who are installed on either side of the hero, fit logically into this iconography of a garden in which one can rest once the day's work is done. Seen in this light they represent the delights that the garden can offer and which can be enjoyed legitimately (though in moderation).

Another hypothesis links the statue with the portico, or rather with the two statues which crowned the portico in Hillewerve's time. The Hercules in the pavilion has been thought to be linked, in his role as protector of the arts, to Mercury and Minerva. Indeed, as a personification of virtue, the hero has been related to the idea expressed by Karel van Mander and others, that a focus on virtue ('een eerlyck gemoet') is the only route to progress in the arts.[17] It is certainly intriguing that the hero and the two Olympian gods – including Mercury with painting equipment in his hand – do indeed play this role as protectors of the art of painting in a trio of canvases by Hendrik Goltzius (1558–1617).[18] However, this hypothesis is difficult to defend in relation to the Hercules in Rubens's house, given that the portico statues very probably do not go back to Rubens's lifetime, and moreover we cannot be certain that the statue to the left is Mercury (see above and Nos R1– R2).[19] In other words: given the highly problematic status of the two portico statues, there is no convincing evidence that Rubens intended to assign the same meaning to his Hercules as Goltzius. There is certainly more evidence for the Neo-Stoic interpretation, relating the statue not to Rubens's profession, but to the garden, a place of leisure and delight (as mentioned above).

1. For these garlands, carved in a combination of Avesnes stone and oak, see Van Bos – Hayen, *Verborgen polychromie*, 2019, pp. 78–79. For many years they were gilded, but recently they were returned to the red-brown colour which the conservators regard as original. However, it is doubtful if this colour is indeed original: in the Berlin double portrait (Fig. 212) the garland as well as the (wooden?) club appear in the same greyish colour as the statue itself, imitating stone. Concerning the garlands, see also No. 23.
2. See above, Chapter II, p. 66 ff.
3. See under Literature.
4. Held, *Sketches*, 1980, I, p. 332; Muller, *Collector*, 1989, p. 155, no. 27.
5. Kitlitschka, *Rubens*, 1963, pp. 139–141.
6. Naples, Museo Archeologico Nazionale di Napoli, inv. no. 6001; Haskell – Penny, *Antique*, 1982, pp. 229–232, no. 46. In Rubens's lifetime the statue was installed in one of the courtyards of the Palazzo Farnese in Rome; for Rubens's drawings of the statue, in its entirety as well as details, see Van der Meulen, *Antique (CRLB)*, 1994, II, pp. 40–48, nos 14–24; III, fig. 31 ff.
7. Rome, Musei Vaticani, Chiaramonti Museum, inv. no. Cat.1314. The statue, which is also mistakenly regarded as Commodus in the guise of Hercules, is a Roman copy of a Greek statue of the 4th century BC (Haskell – Penny, *Antique*, 1982, pp. 188–189, no. 25, fig. 97 (as 'Commodus as Hercules'); Bober – Rubinstein, *Antique Sculpture*, 2010, pp. 180–181, no. 131).
8. There is no known surviving drawing of it from Rubens's hand. A drawing of this statue in the 'Rubens Cantoor' in Copenhagen (Statens Museum for Kunst, Kongelige Kobberstiksamling, inv. no. III, 21; black chalk, 320 × 170 mm; not in Garff – de la Fuente Pedersen, *Panneels*, 1988) is sometimes attributed to Rubens, but opinions differ. Jaffé saw

it as autograph (Jaffé, *Antwerp Sketchbook*, 1966, I, p. 118, pl. XLVII (as Rubens)), but most regard the sheet as by another hand; for some it is not even copied after a drawing by Rubens; see Van der Meulen, *Antique (CRLB)*, 1994, I, p. 258, n. 2; II, p. 9. There is evidence, however, that Rubens must have known the ancient statue and made a drawing of it. It is named among the most important statues which an artist visiting Rome could take as examples, in a passage in the manuscript *De Figuris Humanis*, better known as Ms. De Ganay, derived from Rubens's so-called lost *Notebook* (Van der Meulen, *Antique (CRLB)*, 1994, I, pp. 255, 257). A small drawing of the Hercules 'Commodus' appeared on two sheets in the section about the prime ancient examples of a strong man (Jaffé, *Antwerp Sketchbook*, 1966, I, pl. LXXIX; Chatsworth Sketchbook, 48r [at bottom]; ibid., II, p. 235, fig. 48r).

9. Rubens's authorship was doubted by Werner Kitlitschka, who saw in it an un-Rubensian and 'rigid frontality' (Kitlitschka, *Rubens*, 1963, p. 141).
10. In his view, none of Quellinus's colleagues could have produced such a solid, balanced pose, with pronounced frontality, which is the distinguishing feature of his later statues; see for example *Jupiter* and *Mars* in the galleries of the Amsterdam Town Hall (Goossens, *Amsterdamse stadhuis*, 1996, pp. 53 (fig. 44), 59 (fig. 50)).
11. According to him, there is a striking similarity with the coiffure of Helena de Montmorency in her reclining statue on the tomb of Engelbert van Immerzeel and his wife in the Church of St Anthony Abbot in Bokhoven near 's-Hertogenbosch (On 20 June 1649, Quellinus signed a contract for this in Antwerp, and it was installed in the church in 1651; Gabriëls, *Quellien*, 1930, pp. 219 (pl. LXII), 221–222; Scholten, *Quellinus*, 2010, p. 10, fig. 7).
12. Libertus, *Faydherbe*, 1938, p. 42 [without repr.]; Leyssens, *Hercules*, 1948, pp. 211–215, repr. p. 212; Baudouin, *Nota's*, 1953, p. 51, fig. 1; Bussers, *Faydherbe*, 1986, pp. 82–84, 87, 94, 97–98, fig. 9; Van Riet – Kockelbergh, *Faydherbe*, 1997, p. 51. The empty niche can be seen in a carpark (accessible from Leermarkt 62) behind the buildings on the Bruul (Mechelen's main street).
13. Held, *Sketches*, 1980, I, p. 332.
14. See the discussion in Chapter X, pp. 314–315.
15. Juvenal, *Satyrae*, X, 356–366. Muller, *Rubens' Collection*, 2004, p. 32, citing translation given in Juvenal–Persius, *Juvenal – Persius*, ed. and trans. Ramsay, 1979. For a more recent rendering, see Juvenal–Persius, *Juvenal – Persius*, ed. and trans. Mourton Braund, 2004. See also Heinen, *Gesundheit*, 2004, p. 126.
16. Heinen, *Garten*, 2002, pp. 1–8; id., *Gesundheit*, 2004, pp. 72–182. On the Hercules, see ibid., pp. 103–106. Part of his interpretation seems to us completely without foundation: he suggests that there is significance in the hero turning his back towards the *kolveniers* (an arm-bearing guild), thus showing that the peaceful garden is protected from the violence of war as well as other threats and worries (ibid., pp. 105–106).
17. De Jongh, *Realisme en schijnrealisme*, 1971, p. 54, nos 37–38, repr. pp. 52–53, 163.
18. *Mercury as Painter*, dated 1611, Haarlem, Frans Hals Museum (Leeflang – Luijten, eds, *Goltzius*, 2003, pp. 290–293, nos 106.1–106.3; Nichols, *Goltzius*, 2013, pp. 149–153, nos A-39, A-40).
19. Chapter IX, p. 282.

No. 41. *Fountain with a Putto (Cupid) on a Dolphin*: Sculpture (cf. Fig. 218)

Possibly made of stone; measurements unknown.

Lost, if it ever existed

Date unknown

VISUAL SOURCE: Rubens and studio, *The Walk in the Garden*, Munich, 1630s (Appendix III.6; Fig. 25; detail: Fig. 218).

See also the list of variants below.

LITERATURE: Held, *Sketches*, 1980, I, pp. 321–322, under no. 233; Held, *Rubens*, 1982, p. 164; Muller, *Collector*, 1989, p. 35; Fuhring, *Rubens' zilveren sierstel*, 2001, pp. 30–31; Heinen, *Garten*, 2002, p. 2; Heinen, *Gesundheit*, 2004, pp. 82–85, 156, n. 31; Uppenkamp – Van Beneden, *Architectural Symbolism*, 2011, p. 91; G. Martin in McGrath et al., *Mythological Subjects I (CRLB)*, 2016, I, pp. 366–367, n. 57.

A fountain appears in the background of *The Walk in the Garden* (Appendix III.6; Fig. 218): a writhing dolphin can be seen on top of a wide basin on a raised foot, its tail pointing upwards, and with water spouting from its gaping mouth; a child, upside-down with legs in the air, is gripping the dolphin tightly with its arms. The entangled beings seem to be diving into the water together.

No trace of this fountain is to be found in the prints made in Hillewerve's time and it makes sense to ask if it ever existed, even if not in exactly the same position shown in *The Walk in the Garden*. There is, however, a convincing argument in favour of the existence of a fountain of this type.

CATALOGUE No. 41

For a variant of it appears in Jordaens's *Cupid and Psyche* in Madrid (Appendix III.9; Figs 20 and 220), a scene that is set in a palace garden with architectural elements taken from Rubens's house and garden. At the right of Jordaens's painting appears a monumental fountain, of a more complex structure than the one in *The Walk in the Garden*, but topped by a similar combination of dolphin and winged putto. The fountain in Cupid's fairy-tale palace, which is encircled by a balustrade, is built from more precious materials: parts of it are yellowish and shiny to suggest copper or gold.

Moreover, there are countless other variants in Rubens's work (see the list below).

The dolphin, treated as a decorative 'sea creature' with a large expressive head, was an almost standard motif for fountain decoration, and turns up in countless examples.[1] Often, however, the animal had a more complex significance, referring not just to water or the sea in general. In Antiquity the dolphin was associated with Venus, who was born from the sea, as well as with her son Cupid. Combined with Cupid or a putto, this playful and fast-moving creature functions predictably as an unambiguous symbol of love. There are numerous images, beginning in Antiquity, of Cupid, as young boy or a child sitting astride a dolphin as though riding a horse – sometimes even holding a bridle and reins.[2] It is worth remembering that Rubens represented this motif, symbolising the impatience of love, in one of the panels for the Torre de la Parada.[3]

In Rubens's garden we see a more dynamic variant of the fountain: the child is not sitting upright on the dolphin, but hugs it head-down, with his legs in the air, as if they are diving into the water together – a form also found in Antiquity. A dolphin with a small upside-down Cupid accompanies the *Gatchina Venus* in the State Hermitage Museum, St Petersburg (Fig. 219).[4] Particularly striking is a statue that Rubens may have seen in Rome, or possibly knew from an engraving. In the Palazzo Farnese, in Rubens's time, there was an ancient marble group with Cupid and a dolphin, locked together in a downward spiral (Fig. 221).[5] In it Cupid is a winged boy rather than an infant; he is held tightly by the coils of the tail, and holds the animal with both arms, with his legs sticking up into the air.

It has been pointed out more than once that variants of the 'Cupid and Dolphin' fountain occur frequently in works by Rubens and his contemporaries.[6] Intriguingly, the earliest example of a variant appears in a painting that Rubens made several years before work on his house began: *Susanna and the Elders* in Madrid (Appendix III.12; Fig. 222), which is dated on stylistic grounds to around 1610. The motif appears, about six years later, in *Cimon and Iphigenia*, of about 1617 (Fig. 223), and also in the 1620s en 1630s in other versions of *Susanna and the Elders* (Appendix III.22; Fig. 225) and in *The Discovery of Erichthonius by the Daughters of Cecrops* (Appendix III.23; Fig. 226). For these examples, and further works by Rubens with variants of the fountain, see the list below.

Jordaens included a similar fountain in other works besides the *Cupid and Psyche* (Fig. 220) mentioned. A variant appears in his *Discovery of Erichthonius by the Daughters of Cecrops* in the Kunsthistorisches Museum in Vienna: a fountain with a winged Cupid clinging to a dolphin's head, with his feet in the air (see below (8)). Yet another variant, with Cupid sitting upright, astride a dolphin and held in the coils of its tail, can be seen in the background of Jordaens's *Self-portrait with Family* in the Prado, Madrid (see below (7)). A fountain with a Cupid sitting upright on a dolphin, which may be Van Haecht's invention rather than one that actually existed, can be glimpsed through an open door, in the courtyard adjoining Cornelis van der Geest's *Art Gallery* (Appendix III.30; Fig. 224).[7]

Finally mention should be made of another variant of the fountain which also derives from an ancient motif: that of a putto, or Cupid, with a swan or goose, which is inspired by the well-known statue of a *Child Embracing a Goose*.[8] This type is relevant because there are two paintings in which an example is depicted in combination with variants of other elements present in Rubens's garden or courtyard. A fountain of this type appears in Teniers's *Elegant Company in a Garden*, with a variant of Rubens's garden pavilion in the background (Appendix III.34). There is also an anonymous painting of *Bathsheba Bathing*, in which an example appears in front of a variant of the portico (Appendix III.38).[9]

In the collection of ancient sculpture which Rubens bought in May-June 1618 from Dudley Carleton, and later sold to Buckingham, there was 'a boy ryding vpon a dolphin',[10] which can no longer be located. We can reject the idea, proposed by some, that the fountain known from *The Walk in the Garden* was somehow related to this ancient sculpture.[11] The term 'riding upon' clearly describes the variant mentioned above, with Cupid sitting upright and astride. Furthermore, Rubens had already incorporated the motif of the child with dolphin into paintings made before the acquisition of the collection (see above).

The dolphin fountain had almost certainly disappeared by Hillewerve's time. In any case, as said, it does not appear in the Harrewijn prints, and there is no other fountain visible in the garden. However, we are shown a quite different fountain in the courtyard, with a shepherd playing the bagpipes (Text ill. 50).[12]

Several dolphins are in evidence in the Harrewijn prints: not only as Rubens's decorations of the portico and the studio façade, but also as the main motif in Hendrick Hillewerve's coat of arms: a swimming dolphin alluding to his motto 'tranquilis in undis' (Text ill. 29).[13] Furthermore, two vertical twisting dolphins, sitting on a base and supporting a console, intriguingly appear left and right in the bottom corners of the print of 1692 (Text ill. 33). Is this a section of decorative 'filler' invented by Van Croes or Harrewijn, or does it show an extant sculpture (or pair of symmetrical sculptures) in Hillewerve's possession? Either way, the motif may be connected with the Canon's coat of arms. Although a dolphin with its head pointing down is somewhat reminiscent of fountains depicted by Rubens, there is insufficient evidence to suggest that these two narrow strips show a sculpture created in Rubens's lifetime.[14]

In the two painted records – *The Walk in the Garden* (Fig. 218) and Jordaens's *Cupid and Psyche* (Fig. 220) – the *Cupid and Dolphin* sculpture is presented as a fountain, with water streaming out of the animal's wide mouth. It is not clear if this hydraulic effect would have been possible in Rubens's time. We would need to explain how sufficient water pressure could have been generated. The same applies, incidentally, to Hillewerve's bagpiper fountain, from which a water jet is shown shooting several metres into the air. Was there perhaps a water tank somewhere high up in the studio wing?

LIST OF VARIANTS OF A FOUNTAIN WITH PUTTO:

(1) Rubens, *Susanna and the Elders*, Madrid, Academia de Bellas Artes de San Fernando, c. 1610 (Appendix III.12;detail: Fig. 222);

(2) Rubens, *Cimon and Iphigenia*, c. 1616–1617: versions in Longniddry (Scotland), Gosford House, The Earl of Wemyss and March (Fig. 223) (see Held, *Sketches*, 1980, I, no. 233; Büttner, *Allegories (CRLB)*, 2018, I, no. 59a; II, fig. 300) and Vienna, Kunsthistorisches Museum (Vienna, 2004b, no. 43; Büttner, ibid., I, no. 59; II, fig. 290);

(3) Rubens, various versions of *The Discovery of Erichthonius by the Daughters of Cecrops*, including a composition of c. 1631–1632, with a sketch in Stockholm, Nationalmuseum (Appendix III.23; Text ill. 138; detail: Fig. 226); see Held, *Sketches*, 1980, I, no. 232; F. Healy in McGrath et al., *Mythological Subjects I (CRLB)*, 2016, I, no. 42a; II, figs 370, 373;

(4) Rubens, *Bathsheba Receiving David's Letter*, Dresden, Gemäldegalerie Alte Meister, c. 1635 (d'Hulst – Vandenven, *Old Testament (CRLB)*, 1989, no. 44, fig. 98);

(5) Studio of Rubens, *The Bath of Diana*, fragment of a *Diana and Actaeon*, Rotterdam, Museum Boijmans Van Beuningen (G. Martin in McGrath et al., *Mythological Subjects I (CRLB)*, 2016, I, no. 32; II, fig. 286, as after 1635 (?); the fountain was copied by Frans Wouters (see below);

(6) Anthony van Dyck, *Portrait of Caterina Balbi (?)*, Genoa, Palazzo Reale (Barnes et al., *Van Dyck*, 2004, pp. 173–174, no. II. 29; see URL: https://www.museidigenova.it/en/anton-van-dyck-portrait-caterina-balbi-durazzo).

(7) Jacques Jordaens, *Self-portrait with Family*, Madrid, Museo Nacional del Prado, 1621–1622 (Devisscher – De Poorter, eds, *Jordaens*, 1993, no. A30; Merle du Bourg, ed., *Jordaens*, 2013, pp. 70–71, no. I-03);

(8) Jacques Jordaens, *The Discovery of Erichthonius by the Daughters of Cecrops*, Vienna,

CATALOGUE No. R1

Kunsthistorisches Museum, c. 1640 (Van der Auwera et al., eds, *Jordaens*, 2012, no. 51);

(9) Jacques Jordaens, *Cupid and Psyche*, Madrid, Museo Nacional del Prado, c. 1640–1650 (Appendix III.9; Fig. 20 and Fig. 220);

(10) Frans Wouters, *The Discovery of Callisto's Pregnancy*, Kroměříž, Archbishop's Palace, c. 1641–1644 (Appendix III.39);

(11) Theodoor Rogiers I (1602–1645?), *Susanna and the Elders*, embossed silver (decoration of a basin), 1635–1636. Antwerp, Rubenshuis (Fuhring, *Rubens' zilveren sierstel*, 2001, passim).

1. See for example Stokroos, *Fonteinen*, 2005, repr. pp. 46, 49, 55, 58, 61; Avery, *Dolphins*, 2009, passim.
2. On this theme, see Held, *Sketches*, 1980, I, pp. 266–267, under no. 179; Avery, ibid., pp. 40–55.
3. Held, *Sketches*, 1980, I, no. 179; Alpers, *Torre (CRLB)*, 1971, nos 12 and 12a, figs 86–87. A winged child on a swimming dolphin also appears in the foreground of Titian's *Rape of Europa*, which Rubens copied (Wood, *Copies, Titian (CRLB)*, 2010, I, no. 122; II, fig. 65; Büttner, *Allegories (CRLB)*, 2018, I, p. 338, under no. 44; II, fig. 201).
4. Roman copy after a Greek original, one of the many versions of the *Capitoline Venus* (also called the *Medici Venus*); see Boele et al., eds, *Liefde*, 2002, p. 72, no. 132, repr.
5. Now in Naples, Museo Archeologico di Napoli; white marble, H. 164 cm; Avery, *Dolphins*, 2009, p. 58, repr.; Fuhring, *Rubens' zilveren sierstel*, 2001, pp. 23, 29, repr.); for a bronze statuette in an Antwerp private collection (H. 25 cm), see ibid., p. 30, repr.; Rubens might have known the engraving by Giovanni Battista Cavalieri (1526–1597), in the print series *Antiquarum Statuarum urbis Romae*, Liber II, Rome, 1584, no. 63 (ibid., p. 23, repr.); a copy of this publication was in the library of Albert Rubens (Arents, *Bibliotheek*, 2001, p. 349).
6. Examples are listed by Held, *Sketches*, 1980, I, p. 321, under no. 233; id., *Rubens*, 1982, pp. 163–164; d'Hulst–Vandenven, *Old Testament (CRLB)*, 1989, p. 204, under no. 59; Büttner, *Allegories (CRLB)*, 2018, I, pp. 441–442, n. 24.
7. Van Suchtelen – Van Beneden, *Room for Art*, 2009, no. 10, detail repr. p. 63.
8. Rome, Museo Nazionale delle Terme (Van der Meulen, *Antique (CRLB)*, 1994, III, fig. 133); for studies by Rubens after this statue, known from a copy by Panneels, see ibid. II, no. 70; III, fig. 134.
9. For one of the few surviving examples of this type, see the fountain in the garden of Gaasbeek Castle (Klinge – Lüdke, eds, *Teniers*, 2005, p. 274, fig. 85/c).
10. Muller, *Collector*, 1989, p. 84; in 1635 the work was listed in the inventory of Buckingham's widow (ibid., p. 84; Van der Meulen, *Antique (CRLB)*, 1994, I,

p. 222). For Rubens's acquisition of the collection of ancient sculpture, see above, Chapter VIII, pp. 237–238, n. 21 .

11. It has even been suggested, quite wrongly, that Rubens used this ancient statue for a fountain in his garden (although in 1635 it appears in the inventory of Buckingham's widow; see previous note); see Muller, *Collector*, 1989, p. 35 ('Perhaps Rubens incorporated this piece into the decoration of his garden'); also regarded as possible by Heinen, *Gesundheit*, 2004, pp. 82, 156, n. 31; Uppenkamp – Van Beneden, *Architectural Symbolism*, 2011, p. 91.
12. See Chapter III, pp. 114–115.
13. The coat of arms appears once in the print of 1684 (in a medallion at the foot), and twice in that of 1692 (underneath the image of the Canon's bedchamber and above the entrance to his garden pavilion in the distance). For Hillewerve's coat of arms, see also above: Chapter III, pp. 94, 97, Text ill. 29.
14. The only author to notice the two dolphins at the bottom of the print was Julius Held, who remarked that they reminded him of certain bases of Roman copies after Greek sculpture (Held, *Sketches*, 1980, I, p. 322).

E. Rejected Attributions: Nos R1–R4

No. R1. ? *Pictura*: Statue Known as Mercury (cf. Figs 227–228)

Technique unknown; approx. 230 cm.

Formerly on top of the portico, lost

Before 1684

VISUAL SOURCE: Harrewijn print, 1684 (Appendix III.1; Fig. 18; details: Figs 227–228).

LITERATURE: Van den Branden, *Schilderschool*, 1883, p. 507 (as Pictura); Rooses, *Oeuvre*, 1886–92, p. 186 (as Mercury); Rooses, *Huis van Rubens*, 1910, p. 197 [p. 8] (as Mercury); Delen, *Rubens' huis*, 1933, p. 29 (as Pictura); Van Averbeke, *Rubenshuis, restauratie II*, 1938, p. 16 (as not original); Delen, *Rubens' huis*, 1940, pp. 32–34 (as Pictura); Gordon, *Whitehall*, 1975, pp. 45–49; McGrath, *Rubens's House*, 1978, p. 251 (as Mercury); Muller, *Perseus and Andromeda*, 1981–

82, pp. 141–143, figs 12–13; Tijs, *Rubens en Jordaens*, 1984, p. 201; McGrath, *Musathena*, 1987, p. 240, n. 52; Muller, *Collector*, 1989, pp. 26–29, figs 7, 154, cat. III, no. 17 (as 'Mercury, by an Anonymous Seventeenth-Flemish Master', and 'after Rubens's design'); Rosenthal, *Occasio*, 2000, pp. 202–203 (as Mercury); Muller, *Rubens's Collection*, 2004, pp. 38–39, fig. 39 (as Mercury); Heinen, *Gesundheit*, 2004, pp. 113–115, 172, n. 179 (as not original); Rosenthal, *Rubens*, 2005, pp. 189–190 (as Mercury); Sluijter, *Rembrandt / Female Nude*, 2006, p. 88 (as Mercury); Devroe, Rubens' huis, 2008, I, p. 123; Heinen, *Text- und Bild-Formen*, 2008, p. 211 (as not original); Heinen, *Auctores*, 2009, p. 59 (as not original); Sluijter, *Andromeda*, 2009, pp. 35–36, fig. 18 (as Mercury); Uppenkamp – Van Beneden, *Architectural Symbolism*, 2011, pp. 76–80, 100, 109, 112–113, fig. 94 (as Mercury); F. Healy, in McGrath et al., *Mythological Subjects I (CRLB)*, 2016, I, p. 215, n. 40; Van Beneden, *Portiek en tuinpaviljoen*, 2019, p. 19 (as Mercury); Van Driessche, *Herschepping*, 2019, pp. 36–37.

As explained briefly in No. R2, and at more length in Chapter IX,[1] the two statues that appear on top of the portico (Fig. 227) in the Harrewijn print are problematical in many ways. It is doubtful if either statue was part of the decoration of Rubens's house in his lifetime. Furthermore, we can on stylistic grounds reject the idea that they were designed by Rubens. Nor are there any indications of a date, except that 1684 (the date of the Harrewijn print) can be taken as a *terminus ante quem*.

For the statue that stands to the left (Fig. 228) there is another issue that is yet to be fully resolved: there is no agreement about what figure it represents, or even whether it shows a male or a female figure. At first sight one might think that the figure is Mercury because of the wings on top of his head, and – characteristic of the agile god – his nonchalant pose with hand on hip, and legs crossed. However, there are details that contradict this identification. The attributes in the right hand, clearly recognisable as a palette, brushes and a mahlstick, could just about be construed as replacing the god's caduceus. Yet, we should note that the wings are not part of Mercury's sun hat, the *petasus*, but are attached to the actual head of the figure. The long drapery, reaching down over his (or her) feet, is particularly odd, and certainly not part of Mercury's iconography.

From this we can conclude that it is very likely a personification of Pictura ('Painting'), and therefore a female figure. From this it follows that there is no justification for elaborate arguments which attribute a significant meaning to the pair of statues, interpreted as Minerva accompanied by Mercury.

We will now look in more detail than in Chapter IX at the puzzling figure with winged head who, given the presence of painter's equipment, should probably be interpreted as Pictura.

In his *Iconologia* Cesare Ripa describes (and also sometimes illustrates) several personifications with a winged head. These include concepts in which inspiration plays a role, such as *Furor Poetico* and *Imaginatione*.[2] An interesting example can also be found in the title-page of the Dutch language edition of Ripa of 1644, which was designed by Adriaen van Nieulandt (1586/87–1658) and shows *Poëzie* as a woman with a winged head.[3]

We have succeeded in tracing a number of instances which are related to these Ripa images, although not in the work of seventeenth-century Flemish masters.[4] There is an 'Imagination' which is directly inspired by Ripa's *Imaginatione*, in an allegory by Adriaen van der Werff (1659–1722). A female figure, with a winged head and painter's equipment in her hand (undoubtedly Pictura), appears seated at an easel, painting, in a print made as frontispiece for the *Schouburgh der Nederlandse veranderingen* (1674) by Romeyn de Hooghe (1645–1708). And finally, a Pictura with winged head is the main figure in a frontispiece to *El Museo Pictórico* by Antonio Palomino (1653–1726) (Fig. 229).[5] What connection, however, these later Northern-Netherlandish and Spanish examples might have with Hillewerve's statue, remains a complete mystery.

Also worth mentioning is a rare illustration by Rubens of a figure with winged head, which has some iconographic relationship with Ripa's imagery. In Rubens's design for the title-page of S. Pietrasanta's *De Symbolis Heroicis Libri IX*, of

CATALOGUE No. R2

1634, 'Talent' (*Ingenium*) is shown as a young man with two wings on the crown of his head.[6]

1. Chapter IX, pp. 278–285
2. For *Furor poetico*, described as 'Giovane vivace, [...] con l'ali alla testa', see Ripa, *Iconologia*, 1603, p. 178, repr.; for *Imaginatione* or *Inbeeldinge* (with 'wiekxkens aen beide hoofdslapen'), see id., *Iconologia*, ed. Pers, 1644, p. 216, repr. For a detailed discussion of the iconography of Imagination and the related concept of *Fantasia*, both with winged heads, see Warnke, *Chimären*, 1993, pp. 61–69 (with ill. of *Imaginatione* in the 1618 edition of Ripa: ibid., fig. 2).
3. Engraved by Reinier van Persijn (1615–1668) (Ripa, *Iconologia*, ed. Pers, 1644, title-page).
4. In Flemish painting from the first half of the 17th century, Pictura is simply a woman with mahlstick, palette and brushes, without any further attributes or particular costume. See, for instance the *kunstkamers* with Pictura at work (Appendix III.32–33). For a Pictura seated on top of a stage (not invented by Rubens), see Gevartius, *Pompa Introitus*, 1642, p. 195.
5. In his allegory *The Introduction to the Temple of Fine Arts*, of c. 1693–1694, Adriaen Van der Werff shows Fantasy (*Imaginatione*) leading a youth towards a temple with statue of Pictura (Mai – Wettengl, eds, *Wettstreit*, 2002, pp. 272–273, no. 71). For the print by De Hooghe, see Van Nierop et al., eds, *Romeyn de Hooghe*, 2008, p. 97, fig. 18, and p. 133, fig. 5 (wrongly as 'the art of drawing'); Van Nierop, *Romeyn de Hooghe*, 2018, p. 130, fig. 3.24. For the Spanish frontispiece, see Palomino, *Museo Pictórico*, 1715–24, II.
6. The text explains: 'Talent (*Ingenium*) is receiving material from Nature and from Art in order to write about Heroic Devices'. The original drawing is lost, but known from a copy; see Judson – Van de Velde, *Title-pages (CRLB)*, 1978, I, pp. 287–291, and esp. p. 288, no. 69a; II, fig. 235; interestingly, in the final title-page, engraved by C. Galle I, the wings on the head have been omitted (ibid., no. 69, fig. 234).

No. R2. *Minerva*: Statue (cf. Figs 227, 231)

Technique unknown; approx. 230 cm (without the lance).

Formerly on top of the portico, lost

Before 1684

VISUAL SOURCE: Harrewijn print, 1684 (Appendix III.1; Fig. 17; details: cf. Figs 227, 231).

LITERATURE: Van den Branden, *Schilderschool*, 1883, p. 507; Rooses, *Oeuvre*, 1886–92, p. 186; Rooses, *Huis van Rubens*, 1910, p. 197 [p. 8]; Delen, *Rubens' huis*, 1933, p. 29; Van Averbeke, *Rubenshuis, restauratie II*, 1938, p. 16 (as not original); Delen, *Rubens' huis*, 1940, pp. 32–34; Gordon, *Whitehall*, 1975, pp. 45–49; McGrath, *Rubens's House*, 1978, p. 251; Muller, *Perseus and Andromeda*, 1981–82, pp. 141–143, figs 12–13; Tijs, *Rubens en Jordaens*, 1984, p. 201; McGrath, *Musathena*, 1987, p. 240, n. 52; Muller, *Collector*, 1989, pp. 26, 154, cat. III, no. 18 (as 'by an Anonymous Seventeenth-Flemish Master', and 'after Rubens's design'); Rosenthal, *Occasio*, 2000, pp. 202–203; Muller, *Rubens's Collection*, 2004, p. 38, fig. 39; Heinen, *Gesundheit*, 2004, pp. 113–115, p. 172, n. 179 (as not original); Rosenthal, *Rubens*, 2005, pp. 189–190; Sluijter, *Rembrandt / Female Nude*, 2006, p. 88; Devroe, Rubens' huis, 2008, I, p. 123; Heinen, *Text- und Bild-Formen*, 2008, p. 211 (as not original); Heinen, *Auctores*, 2009, p. 59 (as not original); Sluijter, *Andromeda*, 2009, pp. 35–36, fig. 18; Uppenkamp – Van Beneden, *Architectural Symbolism*, 2011, pp. 76–80, 100, 109, 112–113; F. Healy, in McGrath et al., *Mythological Subjects I (CRLB)*, 2016, I, p. 215, n. 40; Van Beneden, *Portiek en tuinpaviljoen*, 2019, p. 19; Van Driessche, *Herschepping*, 2019, pp. 36–37.

In the Harrewijn print of 1684 two over life-size statues are shown on top of the portico, including a Minerva holding a shield with the head of Medusa, and a long lance (Fig. 227). This pair of statues is undoubtedly the most problematical element of the print's image. In our view, there can be no doubt that they were actually in position in Hillewerve's time; some, however, have called even this assumption into question. Van Averbeke was convinced that the top of the portico was too narrow to support the bases of the statues.[1] He suspected that they were invented to give greater allure to the image of the house, an idea which can be dismissed.

Naturally the question remains: were the two statues already present in Rubens's lifetime? No other image of them is known, not even a variant. The statue visible on the balustrade in the background of Van Dyck's *Portrait of Isabella Brant* (Appendix III.5; Fig. 232) has sometimes been seen as the Minerva of the portico, but this is a misconception: the figure (possibly a youth) does have a lance, but besides this none of the goddess's usual attire or attributes are visible.

The question of authenticity is not just a matter of deciding which interesting decorative and architectural elements were visible during Rubens's lifetime. Assuming that the statues on top of the portico were placed there by Rubens, several authors who see the statues as Minerva accompanied by Mercury believe that – as often paired protectors of the fine arts – these two bear a significant or even essential meaning in the iconography of the house. Once we reject the interpretation of the left-hand statue as Mercury, this often-repeated hypothesis evidently becomes groundless.

Aside from this discussion about their iconographic meaning, it should be added that we can rule out Rubens's authorship on stylistic grounds. The rather slight Minerva figure bears no relation to the many images of the goddess that appear in Rubens's oeuvre. We have no alternative attribution to offer, and there is no evidence to put forward in support of a dating, even an approximate one. Possibly they were placed on top of the portico between 1660 and 1684, that is when the Van Eycke family, and subsequently Hillewerve, were living in the house. For the statues and the questions that they raise, see the detailed discussion in Chapter IX.[2]

1. Van Averbeke, *Rubenshuis, restauratie II*, 1938, p. 16; see also Van Driessche, *Herschepping*, 2019, p. 36. Assuming that there is something in Van Averbeke's belief that the portico could not support the statues, then one might wonder if Hillewerve's statues were possibly made of a lighter material such as plaster; it could even be argued that they were not statues in the round, but flat two-dimensional 'cut-outs' painted on panels, like those made for temporary city decorations (see Martin, *Pompa (CRLB)*, 1972, p. 69, under no. 5, fig. 19; see also Chapter IX, p. 283, n. 95). It is also possible that Van Averbeke was wrong, and had simply formed a false impression of the portico's construction in its original form.
2. See pp. 278–285.

No. R3. *Bundle of Attributes*: Painted or Relief (cf. Fig. 233)

Painted or in relief.

Formerly in the spandrel on the side of the garden pavilion, lost

Before 1692

VISUAL SOURCE: Harrewijn print, 1692 (Appendix III.2; Fig. 18; detail: Fig. 233.

LITERATURE: Muller, *Rubens's Emblem*, 1981, pp. 221–222; Muller, *Collector*, 1989, p. 9, fig. 1.

In the Harrewijn print of 1692 an intricate decorative motif can be seen in the spandrel on the side of the garden pavilion (Fig. 233), in the place where a round niche appears in *The Walk in the Garden* (Appendix III.6; Figs 25 and 182). It is impossible to make out if this was painted or a relief made in stucco or some other material. It is not clear if it was already present during Rubens's lifetime, and therefore to be considered as something of his design. A bundle of three attributes is attached to a peg. A ribbon is tied in a large bow at the top, and it is weighed down at the bottom by a tassel. A festoon of attributes assembled in this way strikes us as odd for Rubens; at least, there are no other examples in his work. On the other hand, it does match decorative elements frequently used by Artus Quellinus I (1609–1668) (Fig. 234).[1]

The decorative attributes assembled in the garden pavilion motif can be identified as: Mercury's caduceus, Apollo's lyre, and a mirror with what looks like Prudentia's snake, but possibly rather to be seen as an attribute of Venus. Believing that the motif was original and designed by Rubens, Jeffrey Muller described it in some detail. He misread elements, however, seeing the peg and bow as 'a winged [female] figure in a glory of light', and came to a conclusion which can no longer be upheld. He saw the 'female figure' as 'the *ingenium* of the painter', and this led him, wrongly, to decode the motif as an emblem of the art of painting, conceived by Rubens.[2]

CATALOGUE No. R4

1. Bundles of attributes, hanging by a ribbon from a peg as festoons, sometimes with a similar tassel at the bottom, play an important role in the decoration of the Amsterdam Town Hall (see Fremantle – Halsema-Kubes, *Beelden kijken*, 1977, figs 36, 41, 48, 80–81). Curiously, an earlier example of pegs with bows and tassels (fastening garlands) can be seen in the decoration of the façade of the Antwerp Jesuit Church (Fabri – Lombaerde, *Jesuit Church (CRLB)*, 2018, figs 14–16).
2. Muller, *Rubens's Emblem*, 1981, pp. 221–222. He concludes: 'Rubens's emblem thus sums up the essentials of the Renaissance comparison of the learned poet and painter: that mastery of the art comes from the synthesis of practical skill, theoretical knowledge, prudence and the inspiration of *ingenium*'.

No. R4. *Ceres*: Statue (Fig. 235)

Stone, measurements unkown.

Formerly (until c. 1938) Antwerp, Rubenshuis, garden pavilion; whereabouts unknown

Date unknown.

VISUAL SOURCES:
(1) Philippe van Brée, *Rubens Painting in his Garden*, painting, Brussels, 1833, partly hidden by a figure in the foreground (Appendix III.42; Fig. 236);
(2) Photographs of the garden pavilion before c. 1938, the earliest of which are by Louis Schweig (1856–57) and Edmond Fierlants (1860) (Appendix III.50–51 and Text ill. 22; see n. 2).

LITERATURE: Van Grimbergen, *Rubens*, 1840, p. 387, n. 10 (as not original figure); Thys, *Historiek der straten*, 1893, p. 429 (as not original figure); Van den Branden, *Schilderschool*, 1883, p. 508; Delen, *Rubens' huis*, 1933, pp. 31, 54 (as 'vervangen'); Delen, *Rubens' huis*, 1940, p. 36 (as 'vervangen'); Prims, *Rubenshuis*, 1946, p. 36 (as original design); Prims, *Prieel van Rubens*, 1948, pp. 141–142 (as original design); Kitlitschka, *Rubens*, 1963, p. 139 (as 'stammt aus neuerer Zeit'); Baudouin, *Cat. Antwerp, Rubenshuis*, 1974, under no. 23 (as original design); Tijs, *Rubens en Jordaens*, 1984, repr. p. 234; Muller, *Collector*, 1989, p. 31, n. 32 (as not contemporary); Baudouin, *Rubens House*, 2005, p. 177 (as original design); Uppenkamp – Van Beneden, *Architectural Symbolism*, 2011, p. 121 (as original design); De Clercq, *Moulages*, 2012, pp. 7–9.

There used to be a stone, life-size statue of the goddess Ceres standing between the columns at the front on the left-hand side of the garden pavilion. It was present in the nineteenth century and remained there until the restoration of the house. At that point it was removed and there has been no sign of it since.[1] Although it has vanished, there is plenty of visual documentation for it. It was depicted by a number of romantic painters, who used the garden pavilion as backdrop for scenes from Rubens's daily life; the earliest – *Rubens Painting in his Garden* by Philippe van Brée – dates from 1833 (Fig. 236). Furthermore, the statue appears in photographs of the garden pavilion made in the nineteenth century and later (Fig. 235 and Appendix III.50–51, 53).[2]

The goddess is wrapped in a dress with a complicated pattern of folded drapery. Her attributes comprise: sheafs of corn standing upright beside her, a sickle in her left hand, and a blazing torch underneath her foot.

On stylistic grounds we can exclude the possibility that the lost Ceres statue originated in Rubens's lifetime, and Jeffrey Muller excluded it, rightly so in our opinion, from his catalogue of Rubens's sculpture collection.[3] Even if we were to consider the work as contemporary, we can in any case dismiss the idea that it goes back to a design by Rubens. It is distinctly un-Rubensian in style and unlike the Ceres types that occur in Rubens's work. The difference is illustrated by various nude or semi-nude figures of the goddess, her head crowned with ears of corn, as for example in the *Venus with Ceres and Bacchus* in the Gemäldegalerie Alte Meister in Kassel, as well as the buxom herm that features on the *Portico of the Emperors* constructed for the *Pompa Introitus Ferdinandi* (Text ill. 62).[4]

Yet, several authors have endorsed the statue as authentically Rubensian, convinced that this Ceres, rather than Venus, did indeed originally belong among the gods standing in the garden pavilion. In the chapter about the garden pavilion we give a detailed account of the heated discussion that arose during the restoration, which eventually led to Ceres losing the battle and to her disappearance.[5]

1. As with the lost busts of Minerva and a Bacchante, which were displaced from the niches of the portico, the removed statue has probably somehow ended up in private ownership. In any case, searches for the *Ceres* in the Antwerp municipal collections have produced nothing (see for example De Clercq, *Moulages*, 2012, p. 7).
2. Fig. 235 shows an anonymous and undated photograph in the Rubenshuis archive of *Ceres between the Columns of the Pavilion* (Devroe, *Rubens' huis*, 2008, II, p. 109); also in the same archive is a photograph of 1938, taken more or less from the same spot, and signed 'Foto Jozef, Antwerpen' (Tijs, *Rubens en Jordaens*, 1984, repr. p. 234). The Ceres is clearly visible, although with her head in shadow, in the earliest photographs of the garden pavilion as a whole, by Louis Schweig (1856–57), Edmond Fierlants (1860) and Adolphe Braun (1864) (see Appendix III.50–51, 53).
3. For his catalogue, see Muller, *Collector*, 1989, Cat. III (pp. 150–155).
4. For the painting in Kassel, see Büttner, *Allegories (CRLB)*, 2018, no. 53, fig. 271; for the herm, see Martin, *Pompa (CRLB)*, 1972, fig. 39. In the *Homage to Ceres* in St Petersburg (see Appendix III.13), her appearance is quite different, but strictly speaking this Ceres is not an invention by Rubens as it represents an ancient white marble statue of a veiled Ceres draped in a *himation*, the so-called *Palliata as Ceres* or *Ceres Palliata*, now in the Villa Borghese, Rome (see Van der Meulen, *Antique (CRLB)*, 1994, II, under no. 61; III, figs 114–115; Büttner, ibid., I, no. 5; II, figs 23, 28–29.
5. See Chapter X, pp. 311–312.

CORPUS RUBENIANUM LUDWIG BURCHARD

PATRON
HSH Prince Hans-Adam II von und zu Liechtenstein

Rubenianum Fund

BOARD
Thomas Leysen (Chairman)
Jérémie Leroy, Nils Büttner, Michel Ceuterick, Gregory Martin, Ben van Beneden

BENEFACTORS
Fonds Baillet Latour
The Colnaghi Foundation
Fonds Léon Courtin-Marcelle Bouché, managed by the King Baudouin Foundation
The Klesch Collection
Catherine Lewis Foundation / Schorr Collection
The Samuel H. Kress Foundation
The Michael Marks Charitable Trust
vzw Natuurbehoud Pater David
Broere Charitable Foundation
The Hans K. Rausing Trust

Allaert-d'Hulst family
Arnout Balis
Joris Brantegem
Annette Bühler
Michel Ceuterick
Herman De Bode
Georges De Jonckheere
Eijk and Rose-Marie de Mol van Otterloo
Dr Willem Dreesmann
Antoine Friling
Bob Haboldt
Gaëtan and Bénédicte Hannecart
Jules-André Hayen

Fiona Healy
Steven Heinz
Willem Jan and Karin Hoogsteder
Baroness Paul Janssen
David Koetser
David Kowitz
Eric Le Jeune
Bettina Leysen
Thomas and Nancy Leysen
Stichting Liedts-Meessen
Elizabeth McGrath
Pierre Macharis
Patrick Maselis

Otto Naumann
Natan Saban
Cliff Schorer
Léon Seynaeve
Vic and Lea Swerts
Daniel Thierry
Michel Thoulouze
Tomasso, UK
Johnny Van Haeften
Eric Verbeeck
Juan Miguel Villar Mir
Matthew and Susan Weatherbie
Mark Weiss

DONORS
Patricia Annicq
Bijl-Van Urk Master Paintings
Ingrid Ceusters
Manny and Brigitta Davidson
Jean-Marie De Coster
Baron Bertrand de Giey
Koen De Groeve
Joseph de Gruyter
Philip de Haseth-Möller
Ann Dejonckheere
Jan De Maere
Michel Demoortel
Elisabeth de Rothschild
Bernard Descheemaeker
François de Visscher
Eric Dorhout Mees
Count Ghislain d'Ursel
Jacqueline Gillion
Alice Goldet

Dov Gottesman
Fergus and Olivia Hall
Stéphane Holvoet
Horsch and Huebscher
Christophe Janet
Baron Daniel Janssen
Baron Paul-Emmanuel Janssen
Jean-Louis and Martine Juliard-Reynaers
Gijs Keij
Cécile Kruyfhooft
Christian Levett
Christian and Brigitte Leysen
Sabina Leysen
Anne Leysen-Ahlers
Sergey Litvin
Anne-Marie Logan
Gregory Martin
Filip Moerman
Baron Jean-Albert Moorkens

Philip Mould
Jan Muller
Klaas Muller
Simon and Elena Mumford
Marnix Neerman
Paulson Family Foundation
Joseph and Jane Roussel
Eric Speeckaert
Alexander Thijs and Joop Scheffers
Eric Turquin
Rafael Valls
Lieve Vandeputte
Philippe Van de Vyvere
Guido Vanherpe
Jeannot Van Hool
Tijo and Christine van Marle
Rijnhard and Elsbeth van Tets
Axel Vervoordt
Morris Zukerman

CORPORATE BENEFACTORS
Thomas Agnew's & Co.
BASF Antwerpen NV
Belfius Bank
Bernaerts NV
Biront NV
Christie's

Crop's NV
Dorotheum
Groupe Bruxelles Lambert SA
KBC Group NV
Koller Auctions Ltd
Lazard Frères
Lhoist SA

Matthiesen Ltd
Noortman Master Paintings
Rosy Blue NV
Sibelco – SCR NV
Sotheby's
Telenet NV

and a number of donors and benefactors who wish to remain anonymous